UNDERSTANDING AND USING

ENGLISH GRAMMAR

Third Edition

with Answer Key

Longman

Betty Schrampfer Azar

**Understanding and Using English Grammar, Third Edition
with Answer Key**

Pearson Education, 10 Bank Street, White Plains, NY 10606

Vice president, director of publishing: Allen Ascher
Editorial manager: Pam Fishman
Project manager: Margo Grant
Development editor: Janet Johnston
Vice president, director of design and production: Rhea Banker
Director of electronic production: Aliza Greenblatt
Executive managing editor: Linda Moser
Production manager: Ray Keating
Production editor: Robert Ruvo
Director of manufacturing: Patrice Fraccio
Senior manufacturing buyer: Dave Dickey
Cover design: Monika Popowitz

The Library of Congress has cataloged the book as follows:

Azar, Betty Schrampfer
    Understanding and using English grammar / Betty Schrampfer Azar
    - - 3rd ed.
          p.   cm.
    Includes index.
    ISBN 0-13-097605-9
    1. English language– –Textbooks for foreign speakers.   2. English
    language– –Grammar– –Problems, exercises, etc.   I. Title.
    PE1128.A97   1998   97-47425
    428.2'4– –dc21   CIP

ISBN 0-13-097605-9 (Regular Edition)   6 7 8 9 10–CRK–05

ISBN 0-13-193305-1 (International Edition)   2 3 4 5 6 7 8 9 10–CRK–07 06 05

In memoriam

To my wonderful parents,

Frances Nies Schrampfer

and

William H. Schrampfer,

who set me on my path.

CONTENTS

Preface to the Third Edition

Understanding and Using English Grammar is a developmental skills text for intermediate to advanced students of English as a second or foreign language. While focusing on grammar, it promotes the development of all language skills in a variety of ways. It functions principally as a classroom teaching text but also serves as a comprehensive reference text for students.

The eclectic approach and abundant variety of exercise material remain the same as in the earlier editions, but each new edition incorporates new ways and means. In particular:

- The communicative aspects of *Understanding and Using English Grammar* are more fully developed and explicit in the third edition. There are numerous "real communication" opportunities for the teacher to exploit. The text often uses the students' own life experiences as context and regularly introduces topics of interest to stimulate the free expression of ideas in structured as well as open discussions. The text supports the view of many experienced teachers that grammar-based and communicative approaches are not mutually exclusive, but rather mutually supportive, and can advantageously co-exist in the same language program, even in the same class, even in the same lesson.

- Similarly, the interactive aspects of the text receive greater emphasis in the third edition. Many of the exercises formerly designated ORAL or ORAL (BOOKS CLOSED) are now reformatted to be more clearly available for pair work or group work, in addition to still being viable as class work led by a teacher. This edition encourages interactivity but leaves it open for the users to decide what degree of interactivity best suits their needs.

- There is now an even wider variety of exercise types. This edition has a larger number of free-response exercises and open-ended communicative tasks, while still providing ample controlled-response exercises to aid initial understanding of the form, meaning, and usage of the target structures. It also includes more writing topics, more speaking activities, expanded error analysis exercises, and additional extended-context exercises.

- Long chapters have been broken into shorter units, and certain grammar units have been reorganized.

The bird soaring upward and forward on the cover of this new edition is a swallow. Found throughout the world, swallows are joyful, playful, energetic birds whose comings and goings announce changes in the seasons. Like the butterfly on the second edition, the swallow on this edition signals new beginnings—as student, teacher, and text writer come together in our shared journey toward the learning of a new language.

Understanding and Using English Grammar is accompanied by

- a *Workbook,* consisting principally of selfstudy exercises for independent work.
- a *Chartbook,* a reference book consisting of only the grammar charts.
- an *Answer Key,* with the answers to the exercises.
- a *Teacher's Guide,* with teaching suggestions and additional notes on grammar, as well as the answers to the exercises.

The ***Azar Grammar Series*** consists of

- *Understanding and Using English Grammar* (blue cover) for upper-level students.
- *Fundamentals of English Grammar* (black) for mid-level students.
- *Basic English Grammar* (red) for lower or beginning levels.

Supplementary works by other authors

- *Fun with Grammar,* a teacher resource text by Suzanne Woodward
- *Azar Interactive,* a CD-ROM program by Howard Beckerman

Acknowledgments

The second edition of *UUEG* was thoroughly reviewed by twenty-five ESL/EFL professionals. Their reviews were outstandingly helpful in their insights and suggestions. I studied the reviews with great care, and they greatly influenced the revision in matters large and small. I could not, unfortunately, make every change and addition that every reviewer sought (not without writing a 1000-page book—which my publisher would definitely frown upon!). I wish to express my heartfelt thanks for the care and thought these colleagues put into their reviews. They are Catherine Sajna, Hawaii Pacific University, English Foundations Program; Brian White, Lakeview Learning Center/ALSP; Anne Albarelli-Siegfried, North Harris Community College; Akabi Danielan, Glendale Career College; M. Cristina Parsons, Pueblo High School; Peter Jarvis, Pace University; Cheri Boyer, University of Arizona, CESL; Molly Burns, Wisconsin ESL Language Institute; Molly McGrath, Hunter College, IELI; James Burke, El Paso Community College; Deborah Healey, Oregon State University, ELI; Dan Manolescu, Adelphi University, Berlitz on Campus Language Institute for English; Gerald Lee Boyd, Northern Virginia Community College; Karen Richelli-Kolbert, Manhattanville College, School of Education; Marjorie Friedman, Eckerd College, ELS Language Center; Natalie Gast, Customized Language Skills Training; Anna Krauthammer, Touro College; Russell Hirsch, Touro College; Stacy Hagen, Edmonds Community College, Intensive ESL; Lida Baker, University of California, Los-Angeles; Susan Kash-Brown, Southeast Community College.

I have a topnotch professional support team. They allow me to do what I do with enjoyment and ease. Chief among them are Shelley Hartle, my managing editor, whose wide-ranging skills make her my indispensable right hand in all matters; Janet Johnston, publishing and wordsmithery expert par excellence, who cheerfully holds me to account for every dot and letter; Barbara Matthies, the teacher's guide co-author, who is my most splendid (i.e., toughest) critic; and our publisher, Mary Jane Peluso, who smooths our paths in myriad, much appreciated ways. In addition I wish to thank Robin Baliszewski, who as the new president of Prentice Hall Regents has brought a breath of fresh air and renewed dedication to quality in ESL/EFL publication; Stella Reilly, especially for the superb job she did in collating the reviews; Christine Mann, who transformed our disk into a beautifully and precisely formatted text; her colleague, Rachel Baumann; and also Julie Alexander, Aliza Greenblatt, Dom Mosco, Merle Krumper, and Eric Dawson.

I also once again thank Don Martinetti, the illustrator, whose touches of whimsy are so delightful. My appreciation also goes to graphic designer Christine Shrader, creator of the swallow that heralds this third edition.

I wish to express special acknowledgment of the contributing writers for the *Understanding and Using English Grammar Workbook*, Second Edition: Rachel Spack Koch, Susan Jamieson, Barbara Andrews, and Jeanie Francis. Some of the exercise material originally created for the workbook has been woven into this third edition of the student book, and I thank them for the ways in which this material has enriched the text.

In addition, my thanks go to Tina Carver, Stacy Hagen, Mary Barratt, Ayse Stromsdorfer, Bonnie Arndt, Chelsea Azar, Rachel Flaherty, Nick Harris, Joy Edwards, Carolyn Cliff, Sue Van Etten, Patti Gulledge-White, R.T. Steltz, Buffy Cribbs, Bruce Morrow, and in loving memory, Holly Turner. And finally, very special thanks to Larry Harris for his support, his strength, his *joie de vivre* — and for opening doors.

UNDERSTANDING AND USING

ENGLISH GRAMMAR

Third Edition

with Answer Key

CHAPTER 1
Overview of Verb Tenses

CONTENTS

Note: Chapter 1 presents an overview of English verb tenses. The tenses will be studied in more detail in Chapters 2, 3, 4, and 5.

☐ **EXERCISE 1. Introductions and interviews.**

Directions: Do one or more of the following activities.

ACTIVITY A. Interview another student in your class. Take notes during the interview, and then introduce this student to the rest of the class or to a small group of classmates. Possible topics for the interview follow. What questions might you ask to elicit this information?

1. name
2. spelling of name
3. country of origin
4. present residence
5. length of time in *(this city or country)*, both past and future
6. reason for coming here
7. field of study or work
8. activities in free time
9. general well-being and adjustment to living here
10. comments on living here

ACTIVITY B. Write a brief autobiographical paragraph telling who you are, what you have done in the past two years, and what your plans are for the next two years. Then exchange your paper with a classmate. Ask each other questions to clarify your understanding and elicit further information.

   Next, join two other students to form a group of four. Tell the others in the group about the classmate whose paragraph you read.

ACTIVITY C. Interview a classmate outside of class and write a biography of his/her life.

ACTIVITY D. Interview a native speaker of English and write a biography of his/her life.

ACTIVITY E. With a classmate, take a trip to a particular place, such as a museum, a theater, or a restaurant. Write a report of your excursion, or give an oral report to your classmates.

☐ EXERCISE 2. Overview of verb tenses. (Chapters 1 → 5)

Directions: Pair up with a classmate.

Speaker A: Your book is open. Ask a classmate a question using **what** + *a form of* **do** (e.g., *What are you doing? What did you do? What have you done?*). Use the given time expressions.

Speaker B: Your book is closed. Answer Speaker A's questions in complete sentences.

Example: every morning

SPEAKER A *(book open):*   What do you do every morning?

SPEAKER B *(book closed):* I (go to classes / eat breakfast / etc.) every morning.

Switch roles.

1. every day before you leave home
2. last night
3. at (this exact time) yesterday
4. right now
5. since you got up this morning

6. for the past five minutes
7. tomorrow
8. at (this exact time) tomorrow
9. by the time you got here today
10. by the time you go to bed tonight

The diagram shown below will be used in the tense descriptions:

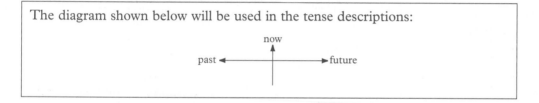

1-1 THE SIMPLE TENSES

TENSE	EXAMPLES	MEANING
SIMPLE PRESENT	(a) It *snows* in Alaska. (b) Tom *watches* television every day.	In general, the simple present expresses events or situations that exist *always, usually, habitually;* they exist now, have existed in the past, and probably will exist in the future.
SIMPLE PAST	(c) It *snowed* yesterday. (d) Tom *watched* television last night.	*At one particular time in the past,* this happened. It began and ended in the past.
SIMPLE FUTURE	(e) It *will snow* tomorrow. It *is going to snow* tomorrow. (f) Tom *will watch* television tonight. Tom *is going to watch* television tonight.	*At one particular time in the future,* this will happen.

☐ EXERCISE 3. The simple tenses. (Chart 1-1)
> *Directions:* Answer the questions.

1. Can you think of a "general truth"? What are some other general truths?
2. What are some of the things you do every day or almost every day? Name three activities.
3. What did you do yesterday? Name three separate activities.
4. What are you going to do tomorrow?

1-2 THE PROGRESSIVE TENSES

Form: **be** + **-ing** (*present participle*)
Meaning: The progressive tenses★ give the idea that an action is in progress during a particular time. The tenses say that an action *begins before*, *is in progress during*, and *continues after* another time or action.

PRESENT PROGRESSIVE	(a) Tom *is sleeping* right now.	It is now 11:00. Tom went to sleep at 10:00 tonight, and he is still asleep. His sleep began in the past, *is in progress at the present time*, and probably will continue.
PAST PROGRESSIVE	(b) Tom *was sleeping* when I arrived.	Tom went to sleep at 10:00 last night. I arrived at 11:00. He was still asleep. His sleep began before and *was in progress at a particular time in the past*. It continued after I arrived.
FUTURE PROGRESSIVE	(c) Tom *will be sleeping* when we arrive.	Tom will go to sleep at 10:00 tomorrow night. We will arrive at 11:00. The action of sleeping will begin before we arrive, and it *will be in progress at a particular time in the future*. Probably his sleep will continue.

★The progressive tenses are also called the "continuous" tenses: present continuous, past continuous, and future continuous.

☐ EXERCISE 4. The progressive tenses. (Chart 1-2)
> *Directions:* Answer the questions.

1. What are you doing right now? What are your classmates doing right now? What is happening outside the classroom right now?
2. Where were you at two o'clock this morning? What were you doing?
3. Where will you be at two o'clock tomorrow morning? What will you be doing?

1-3 THE PERFECT TENSES

Form: **have** + *past participle*
Meaning: The perfect tenses all give the idea that one thing *happens before* another time or event.

PRESENT PERFECT	(a) Tom **has** already *eaten*.	Tom *finished* eating *sometime before now*. The exact time is not important.
PAST PERFECT	(b) Tom **had** already *eaten* when his friend arrived.	First Tom finished eating. Later his friend arrived. Tom's eating was completely *finished before another time in the past*.
FUTURE PERFECT	(c) Tom **will** already **have eaten** when his friend arrives.	First Tom will finish eating. Later his friend will arrive. Tom's eating will be completely *finished before another time in the future*.

Tom has already eaten.

☐ EXERCISE 5. The perfect tenses. (Chart 1-3)
   Directions: Answer the questions.

   1. Have you eaten today? When did you eat?
   2. Had you eaten before you went to bed last night?
   3. Will you have eaten by the time you go to bed tonight?

1-4 THE PERFECT PROGRESSIVE TENSES

Form: ***have + been + -ing*** (*present participle*)
Meaning: The perfect progressive tenses give the idea that one event is *in progress immediately before, up to, until another time or event.* The tenses are used to express the *duration* of the first event.

PRESENT PERFECT PROGRESSIVE	(a) Tom ***has been studying*** for two hours.	Event in progress: studying. When? *Before now, up to now.* How long? For two hours.
PAST PERFECT PROGRESSIVE	(b) Tom ***had been studying*** for two hours before his friend came.	Event in progress: studying. When? *Before another event in the past.* How long? For two hours.
FUTURE PERFECT PROGRESSIVE	(c) Tom ***will have been studying*** for two hours by the time his friend arrives.	Event in progress: studying. When? *Before another event in the future.* How long? For two hours.

☐ EXERCISE 6. The perfect progressive tenses. (Chart 1-4)
Directions: Answer the questions.

1. What are you doing right now? How long have you been *(doing that)*?

2. What were you doing last night at nine o'clock? What time did you stop *(doing that)*? Why did you stop *(doing that)*? How long had you been *(doing that)* before you stopped?

3. What are you going to be doing at nine o'clock tomorrow night? What time are you going to stop *(doing that)*? Why? How long will you have been *(doing that)* before you stop?

1-5 SUMMARY CHART OF VERB TENSES

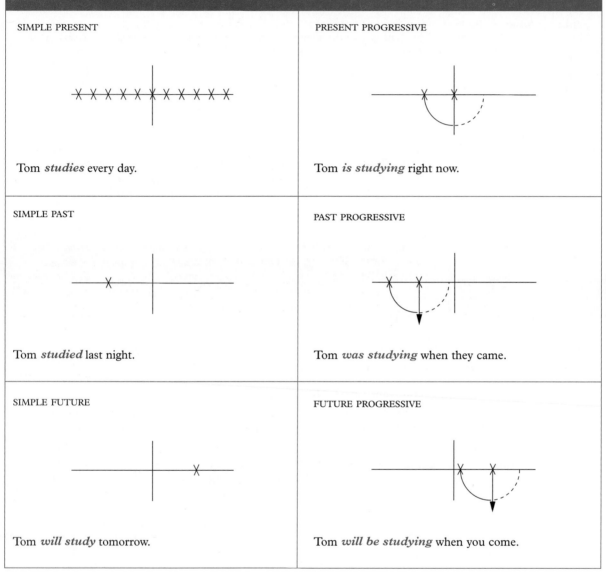

SIMPLE PRESENT

Tom *studies* every day.

PRESENT PROGRESSIVE

Tom *is studying* right now.

SIMPLE PAST

Tom *studied* last night.

PAST PROGRESSIVE

Tom *was studying* when they came.

SIMPLE FUTURE

Tom *will study* tomorrow.

FUTURE PROGRESSIVE

Tom *will be studying* when you come.

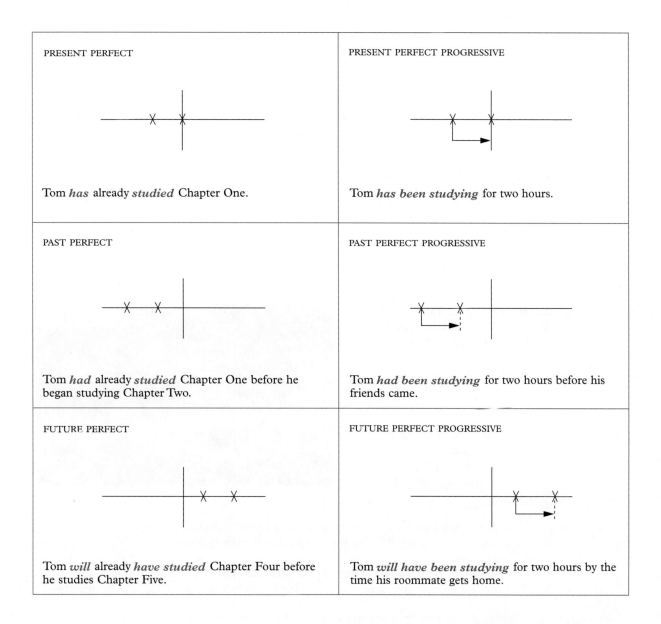

PRESENT PERFECT

Tom *has* already *studied* Chapter One.

PRESENT PERFECT PROGRESSIVE

Tom *has been studying* for two hours.

PAST PERFECT

Tom *had* already *studied* Chapter One before he began studying Chapter Two.

PAST PERFECT PROGRESSIVE

Tom *had been studying* for two hours before his friends came.

FUTURE PERFECT

Tom *will* already *have studied* Chapter Four before he studies Chapter Five.

FUTURE PERFECT PROGRESSIVE

Tom *will have been studying* for two hours by the time his roommate gets home.

□ **EXERCISE 7. Overview of verb tenses. (Charts 1-1 → 1-5)**

Directions: In the following dialogues, many of the verbs are in *italics.** In pairs, in small groups, or as a class, discuss the meanings of the *italicized* verbs. Name the tenses of these verbs. If you wish, draw diagrams like the ones in Chart 1-5.

1. A: What *do* you *do* every morning?
   B: I *take* a bus to school.

   → *The speakers are talking about habitual activities. The name of the tense is the simple present.*

2. A: What *did* you *do* last night?
   B: I *watched* a movie on television.

3. A: What *are* you *doing* right now?
   B: I *am working* on English grammar.

4. A: What *were* you *doing* at this time yesterday?
   B: At this exact time yesterday, I *was walking* from the bookstore to the classroom building.

5. A: *Have* you ever *seen* a comet?
   B: I*'ve seen* shooting stars, but I*'ve* never *seen* a comet.

6. A: What *will* you *do* if you miss the bus tomorrow morning?
   B: I *will walk* to school.

7. A: What *will* you *be doing* at this exact moment tomorrow?
   B: At this exact time tomorrow, I *will be attending* my English class.

8. A: How long *have* you *been working* on this grammar exercise?
   B: I *have been working* on this grammar exercise for ten minutes.

9. A: How long *will* you *have been working* on this exercise by the time you finish it?
   B: By the time I finish this exercise, I *will have been working* on it for fifteen minutes.

10. A: What *had* you *done* by the time you got to class today?
    B: I *had eaten* lunch.

11. A: What *will* you *have done* by the time you go to bed tonight?
    B: I *will have finished* my homework.

12. A: Were you asleep when your friend called last night?
    B: Yes. I was sleeping when he called. I *had been sleeping* for almost an hour when the phone rang.

---

*Words that are "italicized" or "in italics" have a slanted print. Regular print looks like this. *Italic print looks like this.*

☐ **EXERCISE 8. Overview of verb tenses. (Charts 1-1 → 1-5)**

Directions: Practice using tenses by answering the questions in complete sentences, either orally (in pairs, in groups, or as a class) or in writing.

1. What do you do every day?
2. What did you do yesterday?
3. What will you do tomorrow?
4. What are you doing right now?
5. What were you doing at this time yesterday?
6. What will you be doing at this time tomorrow?
7. What have you done since you got up this morning?
8. What had you done before you went to bed last night?
9. What will you have done by the time you go to bed tonight?
10. What are you doing? How long have you been doing that?
11. What were you doing before (*name of the teacher*) walked into the classroom today? How long had you been doing that?
12. What will you be doing before (*name of the teacher*) walks into the classroom tomorrow? How long will you have been doing that?

☐ **EXERCISE 9. Error analysis: questions and negative verb forms.**
        (Appendix Charts B-1, B-2, and D-1)

Directions: This exercise covers question and negative verb forms you will be using in the following chapters. Check your understanding of these forms by finding and correcting the errors in the sentences below.★

1. Does Pedro walks to work every morning?

2. What you are talking about? I'm not understand you.

3. Did you finished your work?

4. My friend doesn't liking her apartment.

5. Do you are working for this company?

6. What time your plane did it arrive?

7. How long have you are living in this city?

8. My brother don't have no job right now.

9. Ali wont to be in class tomorrow.

10. I hadn't never saw snow before I moved to Canada last year.

★For information about forming questions and negatives, see the Appendix, Units B-1 (Forms of Yes/No and Information Questions), B-2 (Question Words), and D-1 (Using *Not* and Other Negative Words).

□ EXERCISE 10. Spelling pretest. (Chart 1-6)

Directions: You will be using many verbs in their **-ing** and **-ed** forms in the following chapters. Use this pretest to check yourself on spelling rules. Close your book. On another piece of paper, write the words that your teacher says.

Example: (cry + −*ed*)

TEACHER: Cried. I cried because I was sad. Cried.

WRITTEN RESPONSE: cried

1. (hope + -*ed*)	7. (listen + -*ing*)	13. (enjoy + -*ed*)
2. (dine + -*ing*)	8. (happen + -*ed*)	14. (play + -*ing*)
3. (stop + -*ed*)	9. (begin + -*ing*)	15. (study + -*ing*)
4. (plan + -*ing*)	10. (occur + -*ed*)	16. (worry + -*ed*)
5. (rain + -*ed*)	11. (start + -*ing*)	17. (die + -*ed*)
6. (wait + -*ing*)	12. (warn + -*ed*)	18. (lie + -*ing*)

1-6 SPELLING OF -*ING* AND -*ED* FORMS

(1) VERBS THAT END IN A CONSONANT AND *-E*	(a) hope date injure	hoping dating injuring	hoped dated injured	*-ING* FORM: If the word ends in *-e*, drop the *-e* and add *-ing*.* *-ED* FORM: If the word ends in a consonant and *-e*, just add *-d*.
(2) VERBS THAT END IN A VOWEL AND A CONSONANT	**ONE-SYLLABLE VERBS** (b) stop rob beg	stopping robbing begging	stopped robbed begged	*1 vowel → 2 consonants***
	(c) rain fool dream	raining fooling dreaming	rained fooled dreamed	*2 vowels → 1 consonant*
	TWO-SYLLABLE VERBS (d) lísten óffer ópen	listening offering opening	listened offered opened	*1st syllable stressed → 1 consonant*
	(e) begín prefér contról	beginning preferring controlling	(began) preferred controlled	*2nd syllable stressed → 2 consonants*
(3) VERBS THAT END IN TWO CONSONANTS	(f) start fold demand	starting folding demanding	started folded demanded	If the word ends in two consonants, just add the ending.
(4) VERBS THAT END IN *-Y*	(g) enjoy pray buy	enjoying praying buying	enjoyed prayed (bought)	If *-y* is preceded by a vowel, keep the *-y*.
	(h) study try reply	studying trying replying	studied tried replied	If *-y* is preceded by a consonant: *-ING* FORM: keep the *-y*, add *-ing*. *-ED* FORM: change *-y* to *-i*, add *-ed*.
(5) VERBS THAT END IN *-IE*	(i) die lie	dying lying	died lied	*-ING* FORM: Change *-ie* to *-y*, add *-ing*. *-ED* FORM: Add *-d*.

*Exception: If a verb ends in *-ee*, the final *-e* is not dropped: *seeing, agreeing, freeing*.

**Exception: *-w* and *-x* are not doubled: *plow → plowed; fix → fixed*.

☐ **EXERCISE 11. Spelling of -ING and -ED forms. (Chart 1-6)**

PART I. Write the correct *-ing* form for the following.

1. hold → ___holding___
2. hide _____
3. run _____
4. ruin _____
5. come _____
6. write _____
7. eat _____
8. sit _____

9. act _____
10. pat _____
11. open _____
12. begin _____
13. earn _____
14. fry _____
15. die _____
16. employ _____

PART II. Write the correct *-ing* and *-ed* forms for the following.

1. boil → ___boiling, boiled___
2. try _____
3. stay _____
4. tape _____
5. tap _____
6. offer _____
7. prefer _____
8. gain _____

9. plan _____
10. tie _____
11. help _____
12. study _____
13. admit _____
14. visit _____
15. hug _____
16. rage _____

☐ **EXERCISE 12. Spelling of -ING and -ED forms. (Chart 1-6)**

PART I. Write the correct *-ed* form.

1. dare → ___dared___
2. jar _____
3. jeer _____
4. dot _____
5. loot _____
6. point _____

7. exit _____
8. permit _____
9. intensify _____
10. destroy _____
11. suffer _____
12. occur _____

PART II. Write the correct *-ing* form.

13. raid → ___raiding___
14. ride _____
15. bid _____
16. bury _____
17. decay _____
18. tie _____

19. tame _____
20. teem _____
21. trim _____
22. harm _____
23. ripen _____
24. regret _____

CHAPTER 2
Present and Past, Simple and Progressive

☐ EXERCISE 1. Preview: present and past verbs. (Chapter 2; Appendix Charts B-1, B-2, and D-1)

Directions: Correct the errors.

do
1. I ~~am~~ not agree with your opinion.

2. I'm not knowing Sam's wife.

3. A: What you are talking about?

   B: I talking about the political situation in my country.

4. My roommate usually watch television, listen to music, or going out in the evening.

5. When I turned the ignition key, the car was starting.

6. This class is consisting of students who are wanting to learn English.

7. The children drawed some pictures in school this morning.

8. While Tom's reading in bed last night, his phone ring. When he was answering it,

   the caller hanged up.

9. Right now Sally in the kitchen eating breakfast.

10. When the sun raises, it is appearing from below the horizon.

2-1 SIMPLE PRESENT

	(a) Water *consists* of hydrogen and oxygen. (b) The average person *breathes* 21,600 times a day. (c) The world *is* round.	The simple present says that something was true in the past, is true in the present, and will be true in the future. It expresses *general statements of fact and timeless truths.*
	(d) I *study* for two hours *every night.* (e) I *get* up at seven *every morning.* (f) He *always eats* a sandwich for lunch.	The simple present is used to express *habitual or everyday activities.*

2-2 PRESENT PROGRESSIVE

	(g) John *is sleeping* right now. (h) I need an umbrella because it *is raining*. (i) The students *are sitting* at their desks right now.	The present progressive expresses an activity that is *in progress at the moment of speaking*. It is a temporary activity that began in the past, is continuing at present, and will probably end at some point in the future.
	(j) I *am taking* five courses this semester. (k) John *is trying* to improve his work habits. (l) Susan *is writing* another book this year.	Often the activity is of a general nature: something generally in progress this week, this month, this year. Note (l): The sentence means that writing a book is a general activity Susan is engaged in at present, but it does not mean that at the moment of speaking she is sitting at her desk with pen in hand.

☐ EXERCISE 2. Simple present vs. present progressive. (Charts 2-1 and 2-2)
   Directions: Practice using present verbs.

   1. Give some examples of your daily habits. Use the simple present.
   2. Give some examples of "general statements of fact or timeless truths."
   3. Describe activities that are in progress in this classroom right now.
   4. Describe activities that are in progress in the world right now.
   5. Thumb through this text. Stop when you see an illustration. Are there any activities in progress in the illustration? Describe them.

☐ EXERCISE 3. Activity: using the present progressive. (Chart 2-2)
   Directions: On a piece of paper, write an action that a classmate can demonstrate (e.g., *stand up, smile, open the door, sneeze, write on the chalkboard*). Give your paper to the teacher, who will redistribute the papers at random to the class. Then everyone will take turns performing these actions for the entire class to guess and describe, using the present progressive.

☐ EXERCISE 4. Simple present vs. present progressive. (Charts 2-1 and 2-2)
   Directions: Use either the simple present or the present progressive of the verbs in parentheses.

1. Diane can't come to the phone because she *(wash)* _____is washing_____ her hair.

2. Diane *(wash)* _____ her hair every other day or so.

3. Kathy *(sit, usually)* _____ in the front row during class,
   but today she *(sit)* _____ in the last row.

4. Please be quiet. I *(try)* _____ to concentrate.

5. *(you, lock, always)* _____ the door to your apartment
   when you leave?

6. I wrote to my friend last week. She hasn't answered my letter yet. I *(wait, still)*
   _____ for a reply.

7. After six days of rain, I'm glad that the sun *(shine)* _____
   again today.

8. Every morning, the sun *(shine)* _____ in my bedroom window and
   (wake) _____ me up.

9. A: Look! It *(snow)* _____ .
   B: It's beautiful! This is the first time I've ever seen snow. It *(snow, not)*
   _____ in my country.

10. A: Close your eyes. Now listen carefully. What *(I, do)* _____ ?
    B: You *(rub)* _____ the top of your desk with your hand.
    A: Close, but not exactly right. Try again.

    B: Aha! You *(rub)* _____ your hands together.
    A: Right!

☐ EXERCISE 5. Activity: using present verbs. (Charts 2-1 and 2-2)
   Directions: Work in pairs. Follow the directions in each item. Switch roles in each item.

1. Speaker A: Close your eyes.
   Speaker B: Make a sound.
   Speaker A: Describe what your partner is doing without opening your eyes. Use the
              present progressive.

2. Speaker A: Watch Speaker B carefully.
   Speaker B: Make a subtle movement, that is, a very small, slight, barely noticeable
              movement (e.g., blink faster, move your little finger).
   Speaker A: Describe what your partner is doing. Use the present progressive.

3. Speaker A: Describe a classmate, but do not name him or her.
   Speaker B: Identify who Speaker A is describing.
   Speaker A: Describe several other classmates for Speaker B to identify.

2-3 STATIVE VERBS

(a) Yum! This food *tastes* good.
    I *like* it very much.
(b) *INCORRECT:* This food *is tasting* good.
    I *am liking* it very much.
	Some English verbs have *stative* meanings. They describe states: conditions or situations that exist. When verbs have stative meanings, they are usually not used in progressive tenses.
	In (a): *tastes* and *like* have stative meanings. Each describes a state that exists.

(c) The chef is in his kitchen. He *is tasting* the sauce. (d) It *tastes* too salty. (e) He *doesn't like* it. The chef is tasting the sauce. It tastes too salty. He doesn't like it.	A verb such as *taste* has a *stative* meaning, but also a *progressive* meaning. In (c): *tasting* describes the action of the chef putting something in his mouth and actively testing its flavor (progressive). In (d): *tastes* describes the person's awareness of the quality of the food (stative). A verb such as *like* has a stative meaning. It is rarely, if ever, used in progressive tenses. In (e): It is incorrect to say *He isn't liking it.*

COMMON VERBS THAT HAVE STATIVE MEANINGS

Note: Verbs with an asterisk (★) are like the verb *taste*: they can have both stative and progressive meanings and uses.

(1) MENTAL STATE	know realize understand recognize	believe feel suppose think★	imagine★ doubt★ remember★ forget★	want★ need desire mean★
(2) EMOTIONAL STATE	love like appreciate please prefer	hate dislike fear envy	mind care	astonish amaze surprise
(3) POSSESSION	possess	have★	own	belong
(4) SENSE PERCEPTIONS	taste★ smell★	hear feel★	see★	
(5) OTHER EXISTING STATES	seem look★ appear★ sound resemble look like	cost★ owe weigh★ equal	be★ exist matter	consist of contain include★

□ **EXERCISE 6. Verbs that have both stative and progressive meanings. (Chart 2-3)**

Directions: Discuss the differences in meaning of the *italicized* verbs in each group of sentences.

1. a. These flowers *smell* good.
   b. Hiroki *is smelling* the flowers.

2. a. I *think* Roberto is a kind man.
   b. I *am thinking* about this grammar.

3. a. I *see* a butterfly. Do you *see* it too?
   b. Jane *is seeing* a doctor about her headaches.
   c. Jack and Ann *are seeing* each other. They go out together every weekend.

4. a. Kathy *looks* cold. I'll lend her my coat.
   b. Tina *is looking* out the window. She sees a butterfly.

5. a. Sam *appears* to be asleep. Let's not disturb him.
   b. My favorite actor *is* currently *appearing* at the Paramount.

6. a. Sue *is feeling* the cat's fur.
   b. The cat's fur *feels* soft.
   c. I'*m not feeling* well today.
   d. I *feel* that it is important to respect other people's opinions.

7. a. Ann *has* a car.
   b. I *am having* a hard time, but Olga *is having* a good time.

8. a. I *remember* my first teacher. *Do* you *remember* yours?
   b. Aunt Sara is looking through an old picture album. She *is remembering* the wonderful days of her childhood.

9. a. This piano is too heavy for me to lift. It *weighs* too much.
   b. The grocer *is weighing* the bananas.

2-4 AM / IS / ARE BEING + ADJECTIVE

(a) Ann *is sick* today. Alex *is nervous* about the exam. Tom *is tall* and *handsome*.	*Be* + *an adjective* usually expresses a stative meaning, as in the examples in (a). (See Appendix Chart A-3, p. A4, for information about adjectives.)
(b) Jack doesn't feel well, but he refuses to see a doctor. He *is being foolish*. (c) Sue *is being* very *quiet* today. I wonder if anything is wrong.	Sometimes main verb *be* + *an adjective* is used in the progressive. It is used in the progressive when it describes temporary, in-progress *behavior*. In (b): Jack's foolishness is temporary and probably uncharacteristic of him.
(d) *INCORRECT:* Mr. Smith *is being* old. *CORRECT:* Mr. Smith *is old*.	In (d): Age does not describe a temporary behavior. *Be* + *old* cannot be used in the progressive. Examples of other adjectives that cannot be used with *am/is/are being:* angry, beautiful, handsome, happy, healthy, hungry, lucky, nervous, sick, tall, thirsty, young.

ADJECTIVES THAT CAN BE USED WITH *AM/IS/ARE BEING*

bad (ill-behaved)	good (well-behaved)	loud	responsible
careful	illogical	nice	rude
cruel	impolite	noisy	serious
fair	irresponsible	patient	silly
foolish	kind	pleasant	unfair
funny	lazy	polite	unkind
generous	logical	quiet	unpleasant

☐ EXERCISE 7. AM / IS / ARE BEING + adjective. (Chart 2-4)

Directions: Mark the adjectives that can be used to complete each sentence.

1. Don't pay any attention to Johnny. He's just being _____ .

    ~~tired~~   ✔ funny

    ✔ foolish   ✔ silly

2. A: You shouldn't act like that, Tommy. You're not being _____ .
   B: Okay, Dad. I'm sorry.

    careful   kind

    healthy   responsible

3. A: There's something different about Tom today.
   B: What do you mean?
   A: He's being so _____ today.

    handsome   quiet

    polite   tall

4. I don't approve of Ann's behavior. She is being _____ .

    angry   unfair

    cruel   unpleasant

5. The children are being awfully _____ today.

    good   noisy

    hungry   sick

□ **EXERCISE 8. Simple present vs. present progressive. (Charts 2-1 → 2-4)**

Directions: Use either the simple present or the present progressive of the verbs in parentheses.

1. I can't afford that ring. It *(cost)* _____costs_____ too much.

2. Look. It *(begin)* _____ to rain. Unfortunately, I *(have, not*)* _____ my umbrella with me. Tom is lucky. He *(wear)* _____ a raincoat.

3. I *(own, not)* _____ an umbrella. I *(wear)* _____ a waterproof hat on rainy days.

4. As a rule, I *(sleep)* _____ until 6 o'clock in the morning, and then I *(get)* _____ up and *(study)* _____ for my classes.

5. Shhh. Grandpa *(take)* _____ a nap in the living room. We *(want, not)* _____ to wake him up. He *(need)* _____ his rest.

6. Right now I *(look)* _____ at Janet. She *(look)* _____ angry. I wonder what's the matter. She *(have)* _____ a frown on her face. She certainly *(have, not)* _____ any fun right now.

7. Right now I *(look)* _____ around the classroom. Yoko *(write)* _____ in her book. Carlos *(bite)* _____ his pencil. Wan-Ning *(scratch)* _____ his head. Ahmed *(stare)* _____ out the window. He *(seem)* _____ to be daydreaming, but perhaps he *(think)* _____ hard about verb tenses. What *(you, think)* _____ Ahmed *(do)* _____ _____ ?

---

*A form of **do** is usually used in the negative when the main verb is **have** (especially in American English but also commonly in British English): *I don't have a car.* Using **have** without a form of **do** is also possible but less common: *I haven't a car.*

8. I (*want*) _____ to figure out the meaning of this saying: "The pen is mightier than the sword." I (*know*) _____ that "mightier" (*mean*) _____ "more powerful," but what's a "sword"? What (*"sword," mean*) _____ ?

9. Right now Martha is in the science building. The chemistry experiment she (*do*) _____ is dangerous, so she (*be*) _____ very careful. She (*want, not*) _____ to spill any of the acid. She (*be, always*) _____ careful when she does a chemistry experiment.

☐ **EXERCISE 9. Activity: using present verbs in writing. (Charts 2-1 → 2-4)**
Directions: Go to a place where there are many people (such as a zoo, a hotel lobby, a street corner) or imagine yourself to be there. Describe what you see. Let your reader "see" what you see by drawing a picture in words. Use present tenses. Begin with a description of what you are doing: *I am sitting on a bench at the zoo.*

2-5 REGULAR AND IRREGULAR VERBS

REGULAR VERBS: The simple past and past participle end in -ed.				English verbs have four principal parts:
SIMPLE FORM	SIMPLE PAST	PAST PARTICIPLE	PRESENT PARTICIPLE	(1) simple form
hope	*hoped*	*hoped*	*hoping*	(2) simple past
stop	*stopped*	*stopped*	*stopping*	(3) past participle
listen	*listened*	*listened*	*listening*	(4) present participle
study	*studied*	*studied*	*studying*	
start	*started*	*started*	*starting*	

IRREGULAR VERBS: The simple past and past participle do not end in -ed.				Some verbs have irregular past forms.
SIMPLE FORM	SIMPLE PAST	PAST PARTICIPLE	PRESENT PARTICIPLE	Most of the irregular verbs in English are given in the alphabetical list in Chart 2-7, p. 22.
break	**broke**	**broken**	*breaking*	
come	**came**	**come**	*coming*	
find	**found**	**found**	*finding*	
hit	**hit**	**hit**	*hitting*	
swim	**swam**	**swum**	*swimming*	

2-6 REGULAR VERBS: PRONUNCIATION OF -ED ENDINGS

Final **-ed** has three different pronunciations: /t/, /d/, and /əd/.

(a) *looked* → *look*/t/ *clapped* → *clap*/t/ *missed* → *miss*/t/ *watched* → *watch*/t/ *finished* → *finish*/t/ *laughed* → *laugh*/t/	Final **-ed** is pronounced /t/ after voiceless sounds. Voiceless sounds are made by pushing air through your mouth; no sound comes from your throat. Examples of voiceless sounds: "k," "p," "s," "ch," "sh," "f."
(b) *smell* → *smell*/d/ *saved* → *save*/d/ *cleaned* → *clean*/d/ *robbed* → *rob*/d/ *played* → *play*/d/	Final **-ed** is pronounced /d/ after voiced sounds. Voiced sounds come from your throat. If you touch your neck when you make a voiced sound, you can feel your voice box vibrate. Examples of voiced sounds: "l," "v," "n," "b," and all vowel sounds.
(c) *decided* → *decide*/əd/ *needed* → *need*/əd/ *wanted* → *want*/əd/ *invited* → *invite*/əd/	Final **-ed** is pronounced /əd/ after "t" and "d" sounds. The sound /əd/ adds a whole syllable to a word. COMPARE: *looked* = one syllable → look/t/ *smelled* = one syllable → smell/d/ *needed* = two syllables → need/əd/ *wanted* = two syllables → want/əd/

☐ EXERCISE 10. Pronunciation of -ED endings. (Chart 2-6)
Directions: Practice pronouncing the words. Write the pronunciation of the **-ed** ending after each word.

1. talked   _____talk/t/_____
2. sobbed   _____
3. graded   _____
4. asked   _____
5. helped   _____
6. watched   _____
7. filled   _____
8. defended   _____
9. poured   _____
10. waited   _____
11. enjoyed   _____
12. loaded   _____

13. roamed   _____
14. kissed   _____
15. halted   _____
16. laughed   _____
17. dried   _____
18. believed   _____
19. judged   _____
20. counted   _____
21. added   _____
22. boxed   _____
23. rested   _____
24. pushed   _____

☐ EXERCISE 11. Pronunciation of -ED endings. (Chart 2-6)
Directions: Practice the sentences aloud. Write the pronunciation of the **-ed** endings.

                        /t/   /d/
1. Jane blinked and yawned.

2. We hoped for the best.

3. She mopped the kitchen floor, vacuumed the carpet, and dusted the furniture.

4. The concert lasted for two hours.

5. She tapped the top of her desk.

6. He described his house.

7. They demanded to know the answer.

8. Alice pushed and I pulled.

9. He handed me his dictionary.

10. Jack tooted his horn.

11. They asked us to help them.

12. With the coming of spring, the river flooded.

13. The airplane departed at six and landed at eight.

14. My friend jumped up and down and shouted when she got the news.

☐ EXERCISE 12. Activity: pronunciation of -ED endings. (Chart 2-6)
Directions: On a separate sheet of paper draw three vertical columns. At the top of the columns, write /t/, /d/, and /əd/. Using words of their own choosing, your classmates in turn will say a word that has a final **-ed**. Write that word in the appropriate column according to how the ending is pronounced.

Example:

SPEAKER A: Number one. *wanted*
SPEAKER B: Number two. *reached*
SPEAKER C: Number three. *licked*
SPEAKER D: Number four. *spilled*
Etc.

	/t/	/d/	/əd/
1.			wanted
2.	reached		
3.	licked		
4.		spilled	
5.			
Etc.			

2-7 IRREGULAR VERBS: AN ALPHABETICAL LIST

Note: Verbs followed by a bullet (•) are defined at the end of the list.

SIMPLE FORM	SIMPLE PAST	PAST PARTICIPLE	SIMPLE FORM	SIMPLE PAST	PAST PARTICIPLE
arise	arose	arisen	forbid	forbade	forbidden
be	was,were	been	forecast•	forecast	forecast
bear	bore	borne/born	forget	forgot	forgotten
beat	beat	beaten/beat	forgive	forgave	forgiven
become	became	become	forsake•	forsook	forsaken
begin	began	begun	freeze	froze	frozen
bend	bent	bent	get	got	gotten/got★
bet•	bet	bet	give	gave	given
bid•	bid	bid	go	went	gone
bind•	bound	bound	grind•	ground	ground
bite	bit	bitten	grow	grew	grown
bleed	bled	bled	hang★★	hung	hung
blow	blew	blown	have	had	had
break	broke	broken	hear	heard	heard
breed•	bred	bred	hide	hid	hidden
bring	brought	brought	hit	hit	hit
broadcast•	broadcast	broadcast	hold	held	held
build	built	built	hurt	hurt	hurt
burn	burned/burnt	burned/burnt	keep	kept	kept
burst•	burst	burst	kneel	kneeled/knelt	kneeled/knelt
buy	bought	bought	know	knew	known
cast•	cast	cast	lay	laid	laid
catch	caught	caught	lead	led	led
choose	chose	chosen	lean	leaned/leant	leaned/leant
cling•	clung	clung	leap	leaped/leapt	leaped/leapt
come	came	come	learn	learned/learnt	learned/learnt
cost	cost	cost	leave	left	left
creep•	crept	crept	lend	lent	lent
cut	cut	cut	let	let	let
deal•	dealt	dealt	lie	lay	lain
dig	dug	dug	light	lighted/lit	lighted/lit
do	did	done	lose	lost	lost
draw	drew	drawn	make	made	made
dream	dreamed/dreamt	dreamed/dreamt	mean	meant	meant
eat	ate	eaten	meet	met	met
fall	fell	fallen	mislay	mislaid	mislaid
feed	fed	fed	mistake	mistook	mistaken
feel	felt	felt	pay	paid	paid
fight	fought	fought	put•	put	put
find	found	found	quit★★★	quit	quit
fit	fit/fitted	fit/fitted	read	read	read
flee•	fled	fled	rid	rid	rid
fling•	flung	flung	ride	rode	ridden
fly	flew	flown	ring	rang	rung

★In British English: *get–got–got.* In American English: *get–got–gotten/got.*

★★*Hang* is a regular verb when it means to kill someone with a rope around his/her neck. COMPARE: *I **hung** my clothes in the closet. They **hanged** the murderer by the neck until he was dead.*

★★★Also possible in British English: *quit–quitted–quitted.*

SIMPLE FORM	SIMPLE PAST	PAST PARTICIPLE	SIMPLE FORM	SIMPLE PAST	PAST PARTICIPLE
rise	rose	risen	spring•	sprang/sprung	sprung
run	ran	run	stand	stood	stood
say	said	said	steal	stole	stolen
see	saw	seen	stick	stuck	stuck
seek•	sought	sought	sting•	stung	stung
sell	sold	sold	stink•	stank/stunk	stunk
send	sent	sent	strike•	struck	struck/stricken
set	set	set	strive•	strove/strived	striven/strived
shake	shook	shaken	string	strung	strung
shed•	shed	shed	swear	swore	sworn
shine	shone/shined	shone/shined	sweep	swept	swept
shoot	shot	shot	swim	swam	swum
show	showed	shown/showed	swing•	swung	swung
shrink•	shrank/shrunk	shrunk	take	took	taken
shut	shut	shut	teach	taught	taught
sing	sang	sung	tear	tore	torn
sink•	sank	sunk	tell	told	told
sit	sat	sat	think	thought	thought
sleep	slept	slept	throw	threw	thrown
slide•	slid	slid	thrust•	thrust	thrust
slit•	slit	slit	understand	understood	understood
smell	smelled/smelt	smelled/smelt	undertake	undertook	undertaken
speak	spoke	spoken	upset	upset	upset
speed	sped/speeded	sped/speeded	wake	woke/waked	woken/waked
spell	spelled/spelt	spelled/spelt	wear	wore	worn
spend	spent	spent	weave•	wove	woven
spill	spilled/spilt	spilled/spilt	weep•	wept	wept
spin•	spun	spun	win	won	won
spit	spit/spat	spit/spat	wind•	wound	wound
split•	split	split	withdraw	withdrew	withdrawn
spoil	spoiled/spoilt	spoiled/spoilt	write	wrote	written
spread•	spread	spread			

•Definitions of some of the less frequently used irregular verbs:

bet . . . . . . wager; offer to pay money if one loses

bid . . . . . . make an offer of money, usually at a public sale

bind . . . . . fasten or secure

breed . . . . . bring animals together to produce young

broadcast . . send information by radio waves; announce

burst . . . . . explode; break suddenly

cast . . . . . . throw

cling . . . . . hold on tightly

creep . . . . . crawl close to the ground; move slowly and quietly

deal . . . . . . distribute playing cards to each person; give attention to (deal with)

flee . . . . . . escape; run away

fling . . . . . throw with force

forecast . . . predict a future occurrence

forsake . . . abandon or desert

grind . . . . crush, reduce to small pieces

seek . . . . . look for

shed . . . . . drop off or get rid of

shrink . . . . become smaller

sink . . . . . move downward, often under water

slide . . . . . glide smoothly; slip or skid

slit . . . . . . cut a narrow opening

spin . . . . . turn rapidly around a central point

split . . . . . divide into two or more parts

spread . . . push out in all directions (e.g., butter on bread, news)

spring . . jump or rise suddenly from a still position

sting . . . cause pain with a sharp object (e.g., pin) or bite (e.g., by an insect)

stink . . . have a bad or foul smell

strike . . hit something with force

strive . . try hard to achieve a goal

swing . . move back and forth

thrust . . push forcibly; shove

weave . . form by passing pieces of material over and under each other (as in making baskets, cloth)

weep . . . cry

wind . . . (sounds like *find*) turn around and around

☐ EXERCISE 13. Oral review of irregular verbs. (Chart 2-7)
NOTE: Exercises 13 through 16 are quick oral reviews of the simple past of irregular verbs. Although a short answer is usually given to a yes/no question *(Did you sit down? Yes, I did.)*, in this exercise, answer with "yes" and a complete sentence. Which irregular verbs come easily for you? Which ones are a little more troublesome? Which ones don't you know?

Directions: Work in pairs.
Speaker A: Your book is open. Ask the questions in the text.
Speaker B: Your book is closed. Begin each answer with "Yes . . . ."

Example:
SPEAKER A *(book open):* Did you sit down?
SPEAKER B *(book closed):* Yes, I sat down. OR Yes, I did. I sat down.

Switch roles.

1. Did you drink some coffee before class?
2. Did you bring your books to class?
3. Did you forget your briefcase?
4. Did you shake your head?
5. Did you catch the bus this morning?
6. Did you drive to school?
7. Did you lose your book?
8. Did you mislay your book?
9. Did you find your book?
10. Did you understand what I said?
11. Did you tell your friend the news?
12. Did you spread the news?
13. Did you fall on the ice?
14. Did you hurt yourself when you fell?
15. Did you fly to (this city)?
16. Did you wear a coat to class?
17. Did you hang your bookbag on a hook?
18. Did you eat lunch?
19. Did you take chemistry in high school?
20. Did you ride the bus to school?
21. Did you swear to tell the truth?
22. I made a mistake. Did you forgive me?
23. Did you write a letter to your family?
24. Did you bite the dog???

☐ EXERCISE 14. Oral review of irregular verbs. (Chart 2-7)
Directions: Work in pairs.
Speaker A: Your book is open. Ask the questions in the text.
Speaker B: Your book is closed. Begin each answer with "No, someone else . . . ."

Example:
SPEAKER A *(book open):* Did you shut the door?
SPEAKER B *(book closed):* No, someone else shut it.

Switch roles.

1. Did you make that cake?
2. Did you break that window?
3. Did you steal my wallet?
4. Did you take my piece of paper?
5. Did you draw that picture?
6. Did you sweep the floor this morning?
7. Did you teach class yesterday?
8. Did you dig that hole in the garden?
9. Did you feed the cat?
10. Did you hide my book from me?
11. Did you blow that whistle?
12. Did you throw a piece of chalk out the window?
13. Did you tear that piece of paper?
14. Did you build that house?
15. Did you speak to (. . .)?
16. Did you weave that cloth?

☐ EXERCISE 15. Oral review of irregular verbs. (Chart 2-7)
Directions: Work in pairs.
Speaker A: Your book is open. Ask the questions in the text.
Speaker B: Your book is closed. Begin your answer with "yes."

Example:
SPEAKER A *(book open):*   Did you sit down?
SPEAKER B *(book closed):*   Yes, I sat down.

Switch roles.

1. Did you give me some money?
2. Did you stand at the bus stop?
3. Did you choose the blue pen?
4. Did you run to class this *(morning)?*
5. Did you sleep well last night?
6. Did you hear that noise outside the window?
7. Did you withdraw some money from the bank?
8. Did you wake up at seven this morning?
9. Did you swim in the ocean?
10. Did you go home after class yesterday?
11. Did you bend over to pick up a pencil?
12. Did you send a letter?
13. Did you sing a song?
14. Did you stick your hand in your pocket?
15. Did you grind the pepper?
16. Did you strike the desk with your hand?
17. Did you light a match?
18. Did you mean what you said?
19. Did you hold your hand up?
20. Did you speak to (. . .)?

☐ EXERCISE 16. Oral review of Irregular verbs. (Chart 2-7)
Directions: Work in pairs.
Speaker A: Your book is open. Ask the questions in the text.
Speaker B: Your book is closed. Begin your answer with "yes."

Example:
SPEAKER A *(book open):*   Did the students come to class?
SPEAKER B *(book closed):*   Yes, they came to class.

Switch roles.

1. Did class begin at (nine)?
2. Did the sun rise at six this morning?
3. Did you cut your finger?
4. Did it bleed when you cut it?
5. Did the grass grow after the rain?
6. Did a bee sting you?
7. Did the telephone ring?
8. Did the water freeze?
9. Did your friend quit school?
10. Did the soldiers fight?
11. Did the thief creep into the room?
12. Did the policeman shoot at the thief?
13. Did the thief flee?
14. Did your team win the game yesterday?
15. Did your car slide on the ice?
16. Did the door swing open?
17. Did the children blow up some balloons?
18. Did the balloons burst?
19. Did the radio station broadcast the news?
20. Did you know all of the irregular verbs?

2-8 TROUBLESOME VERBS: *RAISE / RISE, SET / SIT, LAY / LIE*

	TRANSITIVE		INTRANSITIVE	*Raise, set,* and *lay* are *transitive* verbs; they are followed by an object. *Rise, sit,* and *lie* are *intransitive;* i.e., they are NOT followed by an object.*
(a)	*raise, raised, raised* Tom **raised** his hand.	(b)	*rise, rose, risen* The sun **rises** in the east.	In (a): **raised** is followed by the object **hand**.
(c)	*set, set, set* I **will set** the book on the desk.	(d)	*sit, sat, sat* I **sit** in the front row.	In (b): **rises** is not followed by an object.
(e)	*lay, laid, laid* I **am laying** the book on the desk.	(f)	*lie,** lay, lain* He **is lying** on his bed.	Note: **Lay** and **lie** are troublesome for native speakers too and are frequently misused.

*See Appendix Chart A-1, p. A1, for information about transitive and intransitive verbs.

Lie is a regular verb *(lie, lied)* when it means "not tell the truth": *He lied to me about his age.*

☐ **EXERCISE 17. Troublesome verbs. (Chart 2-8)**
Directions: Choose the correct word in parentheses.

1. The student *(raised, rose)* his hand in class.

2. Hot air *(raises, rises)*.

3. Ann *(set, sat)* in a chair because she was tired.

4. I *(set, sat)* your dictionary on the table a few minutes ago.

5. Hens *(lay, lie)* eggs.

6. Sara is *(laying, lying)* on the grass in the park right now.

7. Jan *(laid, lay)* the comb on top of the dresser a few minutes ago.

8. If you are tired, you should *(lay, lie)* down and take a nap.

9. San Francisco *(lay, lies)* to the north of Los Angeles.

10. Mr. Faust *(raises, rises)* many different kinds of flowers in his garden.

11. The student *(raised, rose)* from her seat and walked to the front of the auditorium to receive her diploma.

12. Hiroki is a very methodical person. Every night before going to bed, he *(lays, lies)* his clothes for the next day on his chair.

13. Where are my keys? I *(lay, laid)* them here on the desk five minutes ago.

14. Fred *(set, sat)* the table for dinner.

15. Fred *(set, sat)* at the table for dinner.

16. The fulfillment of all your dreams *(lies, lays)* within you—if you just believe in yourself.

☐ **EXERCISE 18. Troublesome verbs. (Chart 2-8)**
    Directions: Follow the directions.

1. Name things that rise.
2. Lift something above your head. Use *raised* or *rose* in a sentence to describe that action.
3. Put something on your desktop. Use *set* or *sat* in a sentence to describe this action. Then use *laid* or *lay* to describe this action.
4. Look at the object on your desktop. What is it doing? Describe its "activity in progress" by using *setting* or *sitting* in a sentence. Then use *laying* or *lying* in a similar sentence to describe this object.
5. Describe the geographical location of your country by naming at least two countries or bodies of water that border it on the north, south, east, or west. Use *lies* or *lays*. For example, *Canada (lies/lays?) to the north of the United States.*

2-9 SIMPLE PAST

	(a) I **walked** to school yesterday. (b) John **lived** in Paris for ten years, but now he lives in Rome. (c) I **bought** a new car three days ago.	The simple past indicates that an activity or situation *began and ended at a particular time in the past.*
	(d) Rita **stood** under a tree *when it began to rain.* (e) *When Mrs. Chu heard a strange noise,* she **got** up to investigate. (f) *When I dropped my cup,* the coffee **spilled** on my lap.	If a sentence contains **when** and has the simple past in both clauses, the action in the *when* clause happens first. In (d): 1st: The rain began. 2nd: She stood under a tree.

1st: It began to rain.   2nd: Rita stood under a tree.

Rita **stood** under a tree when it **began** to rain.

2-10 PAST PROGRESSIVE

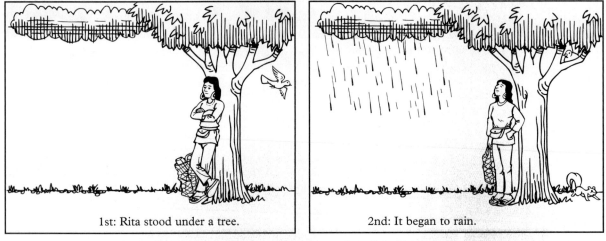

	(g) I *was walking* down the street when it began to rain. (h) While I *was walking* down the street, it began to rain. (i) Rita *was standing* under a tree when it began to rain. (j) At eight o'clock last night, I *was studying*. (k) Last year at this time, I *was attending* school.	In (g):1st: I was walking down the street. 2nd: It began to rain. Both actions occurred at the same time, but *one action began earlier and was in progress when the other action occurred.* In (j): My studying began before 8:00, was in progress at that time, and probably continued.
	(l) While I *was studying* in one room of our apartment, my roommate *was having* a party in the other room.	Sometimes the past progressive is used in both parts of a sentence when two actions are in progress simultaneously.

1st: Rita stood under a tree.

2nd: It began to rain.

Rita **was standing** under a tree when it **began** to rain.

☐ **EXERCISE 19. Simple past vs. past progressive. (Charts 2-9 and 2-10)**
Directions: Use the simple past or the past progressive of the verbs in parentheses.

1. I am sitting in class right now. I (sit) _____ was sitting _____ in class at this exact same time yesterday.

2. I don't want to go to the zoo today because it is raining. The same thing happened yesterday. I (want, not) _____ to go to the zoo because it (rain) _____ .

3. I (call) _____ Roger at nine last night, but he (be, not) _____ at home. He (study) _____ at the library.

4. I (hear, not) _____ the thunder during the storm last night because I (sleep) _____ .

5. It was beautiful yesterday when we went for a walk in the park. The sun *(shine)*
_____ . A cool breeze *(blow)* _____ .
The birds *(sing)* _____ .

6. My brother and sister *(argue)* _____ about something when I
(walk) _____ into the room.

7. I got a package in the mail. When I *(open)* _____ it, I *(find)*
_____ a surprise.

8. While Mrs. Emerson *(read)* _____ the little boy a story, he
(fall) _____ asleep, so she *(close)* _____ the book and quietly
(tiptoe) _____ out of the room.

9. A: Why weren't you at the meeting?
   B: I *(wait)* _____ for an overseas call from my family.

10. A: *(you, hear)* _____ what she just said?
    B: No, I *(listen, not)* _____ . I *(think)* _____
    about something else.

11. A: How *(you, break)* _____
    your arm?
    B: I *(slip)* _____ on the ice
    while I *(cross)* _____
    the street in front of the dorm.

12. A: I'm sure you met Carol Jones at the party last night.
    B: I don't remember her. What *(she, wear)* _____
    _____ ?

13. It was my first day of class. I *(find, finally)* _____ the right
room. The room *(be, already)* _____ full of students. On one
side of the room, students *(talk, busily)* _____ to each other
in Spanish. Other students *(speak)* _____ Japanese, and
some *(converse)* _____ in Arabic. It sounded like the United
Nations. Some of the students, however, *(sit, just)* _____
quietly by themselves. I *(choose)* _____ an empty seat in the last row
and *(sit)* _____ down. In a few minutes, the teacher *(walk)*
_____ into the room and all the multilingual conversation
(stop) _____ .

14. I really enjoyed my vacation last January. While it *(snow)* _____ in Toronto, the sun *(shine)* _____ in Florida. While you *(shovel)* _____ snow in Iowa, I *(lie)* _____ on the beach in Florida.

☐ EXERCISE 20. Activity: using past verbs in speaking. (Charts 2-9 and 2-10)
Directions: Come to class prepared to do a pantomime. While you are doing your pantomime, your classmates will try to determine what you are doing and then, when you are finished, will describe what you did, step by step.

Examples of subjects for a pantomime:
1. threading a needle and sewing on a button
2. washing dishes, and perhaps breaking one
3. bowling
4. reading a newspaper while eating breakfast

☐ EXERCISE 21. Activity: using past verbs in writing. (Charts 2-9 and 2-10)
Directions: In writing, describe one or more of the pantomimes that were performed by your classmates. Give a title to the pantomime and identify the pantomimist. Use a few "time words" to show the order in which the actions were performed: *first, next, then, after that, before, when, while, etc.*

☐ EXERCISE 22. Activity: using present and past verbs in writing. (Chapter 2)
Directions: Describe your first day or two in this country or city. What did you do? What did you think? What did you see? Who did you meet? Did you have any interesting experiences? How did you feel about this place?

Then write about how you feel about this place now. In what ways are your present experiences here different from your earlier experiences?

2-11 USING PROGRESSIVE VERBS WITH *ALWAYS* TO COMPLAIN

(a) Mary *always leaves* for school at 7:45.	In sentences referring to present time, usually the simple present is used with *always* to describe habitual or everyday activities, as in (a).
(b) Mary *is always leaving* her dirty socks on the floor for me to pick up! Who does she think I am? Her maid?	In special circumstances, a speaker may use the present progressive with *always* to complain, i.e., to express annoyance or anger, as in (b).★
(c) I *am always/forever/constantly picking* up Mary's dirty socks!	In addition to *always,* the words *forever* and *constantly* are also used with the present progressive to express annoyance.
(d) I didn't like having Sam for my roommate last year. He *was always leaving* his dirty clothes on the floor.	*Always, forever,* and *constantly* can also be used with the past progressive to express annoyance or anger.

★COMPARE:
(1) *"Mary is always leaving her dirty socks on the floor"* expresses annoyance.
(2) *"Mary always leaves her dirty socks on the floor"* is a statement of fact in which the speaker is not necessarily expressing an attitude of annoyance. Annoyance may, however, be shown by the speaker's tone of voice.

□ EXERCISE 23. Using progressive verbs with ALWAYS. (Chart 2-11)

Directions: Your roommate, Jack, has many bad habits. These bad habits annoy you! Pretend you are speaking to a friend and complaining about Jack. Use the present progressive of a verb in Column A and complete the sentence with a phrase from Column B. Use **always, constantly,** or **forever** in each sentence. Say your sentence aloud with annoyance, impatience, or anger in your voice.

Example: He's always messing up the kitchen!

COLUMN A	COLUMN B
1. mess up	a. about himself
2. leave	✔ b. the kitchen
3. borrow	c. my clothes without asking me
4. brag	d. to give me my phone messages
5. try	e. his dirty dishes on the table
6. crack	f. to show me he's smarter than me*
7. forget	g. his knuckles while I'm trying to study

8. *Complete the following with your own words.*

A: I really don't know if I can stand to have Sue for a roommate one more day. She's driving me crazy.

B: Oh? What's wrong?

A: Well, for one thing she's always _____!

B: Really?

A: And not only that. She's forever _____!

B: That must be very inconvenient for you.

A: It is. And what's more, she's constantly _____!

Can you believe that? And she's always _____!

B: I think you're right. You need to find a new roommate.

2-12 USING EXPRESSIONS OF PLACE WITH PROGRESSIVE VERBS

(a) —What is Kay doing? — She's *studying* **in her room.** (b) —Where's Kay? — She's **in her room** *studying.*	An expression of place can sometimes come between the auxiliary **be** and the **-ing** verb in a progressive tense, as in (b) and (d): *is + in her room + studying* *was + in bed + reading*
(c) —What was Jack doing when you arrived? — He *was reading* a book **in bed.** (d) —Where was Jack when you arrived? — He *was* **in bed** *reading* a book.	In (a): The focus of both the question and the answer is on Kay's activity in progress, i.e., on what she is doing. In (b): The focus of both the question and the answer is on Kay's location, i.e., on where Kay is.

---

*In formal English, a subject pronoun follows **than:** *He's older than I (am).* In everyday informal English, an object pronoun is frequently used after **than:** *He's older than me.*

□ EXERCISE 24. Using expressions of place with progressive verbs. (Chart 2-12)

PART I. Use the given verbs and expressions of place to complete the dialogues. Use usual word order if the focus is on an activity in progress. Use inverted word order if the focus is on the person's location.

1. *listen to music \ in her room*

   A: Where's Sally?

   B: She's ___in her room listening to music.___

2. *listen to music \ in the living room*

   A: What's Surasuk doing?

   B: He's ___listening to music in the living room.___

3. *watch TV \ in his bedroom*

   A: Where was Jack when you got home?

   B: He was _____

4. *watch TV \ in his bedroom*

   A: What was Jack doing when you got home?

   B: He was _____

5. *take a nap \ on the couch in the living room*

   A: What's Roy doing?

   B: He's _____

6. *take a nap \ on the couch in the living room*

   A: Where's Roy?

   B: He's _____

7. *attend a conference \ in Singapore*

   A: Where's Ms. Chang this week?

   B: She's _____

PART II. Answer the questions, using the present progressive or the past progressive. Use the expression of place in parentheses and add your own words.

8. A: Where's Joan? *(at the library)*

   B: ___She's at the library studying for a test.___

9. A: Is Mark here? *(upstairs)*

   B: Yes. _____

10. A: Have you seen Professor Marx? *(in her office)*

    B: Yes. _____

11. A: Where's your mother, Jimmy? *(in the kitchen)*

    B: _____

12. A: Ahmed was absent yesterday. Where was he? *(at home)*

    B: _____

13. A: Was Mr. Rivera out of town last week? *(in New York)*

    B: Yes. _____

PART III. Add expressions of place between **be** and the **-ing** verb.

14. My sister is visiting some relatives.
    → *My sister is in Chicago visiting some relatives.*

15. I'm back to work now, but a month ago I was lying in the sun.

16. We are studying English grammar.

17. No one could see the thief because he was hiding from the police.

18. When I saw Diana, she was trying to find out what she was supposed to do.

☐ EXERCISE 25. Error analysis: present and past verbs. (Chapter 2)
Directions: Correct the errors.

1. Breakfast is an important meal. I'm always eating breakfast.

2. During I was working in my office yesterday, my cousin stops by to visit me.

3. Portugal lays to the west of Spain.

4. Yuki staied home because she catched a bad cold.

5. My brother is looking like our father, but I am resembling my mother.

6. As a verb, "sink" is meaning "move downward." What it means as a noun?

7. Sang-Joon, are you listen to me? I am talk to you!

8. I rewinded the rented video before I return it to the store yesterday.

9. Abdallah is want a snack. He's being hungry.

10. Anna rose her eyebrows in surprise.

11. Yesterday I was working at my computer when Shelley was coming to the door of my office. I wasn't knowing she was there. I was concentrate hard on my work. When she suddenly speak, I am jump. She startle me.

12. While I was surfing the net yesterday, I was finding a really interesting Web site.

CHAPTER 3

Perfect and Perfect Progressive Tenses

☐ EXERCISE 1. Review of irregular past participles. (Charts 2-5 and 2-7)
Directions: Work in pairs.
Speaker A: Your book is open. Ask a question that begins with "Have you ever . . ."
Speaker B: Your book is closed. Answer the question, beginning with "No, I haven't. I've
never . . . ."

Example: see that movie
SPEAKER A *(book open):*   Have you ever seen that movie?
SPEAKER B *(book closed):* No, I haven't. I've never seen that movie.

1. buy an airplane
2. break a window
3. hide from the police
4. teach English
5. make an apple pie
6. win a lottery
7. fly an airplane
8. speak to *(name of a local person)*

Switch roles.

9. steal anything
10. fall off a mountain
11. hold a snake

12. feed a lion
13. build a house
14. forget your name
15. understand quantum physics
16. eat an ostrich egg

☐ EXERCISE 2. Review: regular and irregular past participles. (Charts 2-5 and 2-7)

Directions: Work in pairs.

Speaker A: Your book is open. Ask a question that begins with "Have you ever . . . ?"

Speaker B: Your book is closed. Answer the question.

Example: break your arm

SPEAKER A *(book open):* Have you ever broken your arm?

SPEAKER B *(book closed):* Yes, I have. OR No, I haven't.

1. climb a mountain
2. write a book
3. be to *(a particular country)*★
4. tell a lie
5. smoke a cigar
6. ride a motorcycle
7. teach *(a particular subject)*
8. see *(title of a movie)*
9. meet (. . .)'s★★ parents
10. give a speech in English
11. eat *(Thai)* food
12. study biology
13. play a violin

14. go to *(a particular place in this city)*
15. walk on the moon
16. watch *(a particular TV show)*
17. take a course in chemistry
18. drive *(a particular kind of car)*

Switch roles.

19. fall asleep during class
20. have *(a particular kind of food)*
21. drive a truck
22. read *(name of a book)*
23. draw a picture of yourself
24. ride a horse
25. catch a butterfly
26. sleep in a tent
27. write a letter to *(a famous person)*
28. lose your wallet
29. have a car accident
30. bring a friend to class
31. wear a kimono
32. drink Turkish coffee
33. leave your umbrella at a restaurant
34. dig a hole to plant a tree
35. shake (. . .)'s hand
36. sing in public

_____

★Supply your own words for the expressions in parentheses.

★★Supply the name of a classmate.

3-1 PRESENT PERFECT

(time?)	(a) They *have moved* into a new apartment. (b) *Have you* ever *visited* Mexico? (c) I *have* never *seen* snow. (d) I *have* already *seen* that movie. (e) Jack *hasn't seen* it *yet*. (f) Ann started a letter to her parents last week, but she *still hasn't finished* it. (g) Alex feels bad. He *has just heard* some bad news.	The present perfect expresses the idea that something happened (or never happened) *before now, at an unspecified time in the past.* The exact time it happened is not important. If there is a specific mention of time, the simple past is used: *They moved into a new apartment last month.* Notice in the examples: the adverbs ***ever, never, already, yet, still,*** and ***just*** are frequently used with the present perfect.
	(h) We *have had* four tests *so far* this semester. (i) I *have written* my wife a letter every other day *for* the last two weeks. (j) I *have met* many people *since* I came here in June. (k) I *have flown* on an airplane *many times*.	The present perfect also expresses the *repetition of an activity before now.* The exact time of each repetition is not important. Notice in (h): ***so far*** is frequently used with the present perfect.

	(l) I *have been* here *since seven o'clock.*
	(m) We *have been* here *for two weeks.*
	(n) I *have had* this same pair of shoes *for three years.*
	(o) I *have liked* cowboy movies ever *since I was a child.*
	(p) I *have known* him *for many years.*
		The present perfect, when used with ***for*** or ***since***, also expresses a situation that *began in the past and continues to the present.**
		In the examples, notice the difference between ***since*** and ***for***:
		   since + a particular time
		   for + a duration of time

*The verbs used in the present perfect to express a *situation* that began in the past and still exists are typically verbs with a stative meaning (see Chart 2-3, p. 15).
   The present perfect progressive, rather than the present perfect, is used with action verbs to express an *activity* that began in the past and continues to the present (see Chart 3-2, p. 42):
   I've been sitting at my desk for an hour. Jack has been watching TV since seven o'clock.

☐ EXERCISE 3. Present perfect vs. simple past. (Charts 2-9 and 3-1)
   Directions: Use the simple past or the present perfect. In some sentences, either tense is possible but the meaning is different.

1. I *(attend, not)* __haven't attended__ any parties since I came here.

2. Al *(go)* _____ to a party at Sally's apartment last Saturday night.

3. Bill *(arrive)* _____ here three days ago.

4. Bill *(be)* _____ here since the 22nd.

5. Try not to be absent from class again for the rest of the term. You *(miss, already)*

   _____ too many classes. You *(miss)* _____

   two classes just last week.

6. So far this week, I *(have)* _____ two tests and a quiz.

7. Alex is an artist. He *(draw)* _____ many beautiful pictures in his lifetime. Last week he *(draw)* _____ a beautiful mountain scene.

8. Jack really needs to get in touch with you. Since this morning, he *(call)* _____ _____ here four times trying to reach you. He *(call)* _____ at 9:10, 10:25, 12:15, and 1:45.

9. Janet *(wear)* _____ her new blue dress only once since she bought it. She *(wear)* _____ it to her brother's wedding last month.

10. The night has ended, and it's daylight now. The sun *(rise)* _____ . It *(rise)* _____ at 6:08.

11. Last January, I *(see)* _____ snow for the first time in my life.

12. Fatima *(see, never)* _____ snow in her entire lifetime.

13. I *(know)* _____ Greg Adams for ten years.

14. A: Is Ahmed here yet?

    B: Yes. He *(arrive, just*)* _____ .

15. A: I *(be, not)* _____ able to reach Mr. Chang yet. So far he *(respond, not)* _____ to any of my attempts to reach him.

    B: Oh?

    A: I *(start)* _____ trying to reach him three days ago. Since then, I *(fax)* _____ him twice. I *(phone)* _____ him four times. And I *(send)* _____ at least six e-mails.

    B: I guess modern communications don't mean much if there's no one at the other end.

☐ **EXERCISE 4. Present perfect.** (Chart 3-1)

Directions: Work in pairs, in groups, or as a class.
Speaker A: Your book is open. Ask the questions.
Speaker B: Your book is closed. Answer in complete sentences.

Example:

SPEAKER A *(book open):* How many tests have you taken since you started coming to this class?

SPEAKER B *(book closed):* I have taken *(three, several, many)* tests since I started coming to this class. OR I haven't taken any tests since I started coming to this class.

---

*Just can indicate that something happened a very short time ago, very close in time to the present moment, but still in the past. When *just* expresses this meaning, it is frequently used with the present perfect. However, in informal English the simple past is also often used. Both (a) and (b) are correct:

    (a) *I've just finished a letter to my parents.*
    (b) *I just finished a letter to my parents.*

1. How many books have you bought since the beginning of the year / this term?
2. How many letters / e-mails have you gotten so far this month / week?
3. How many letters / e-mails have you written since the beginning of the month / week?
4. How many questions have I asked so far?
5. How many times have you flown in an airplane?
6. How many times have you . . . ?

(Switch roles if working in pairs.)

7. How many people have you met since you came here?
8. How many classes have you missed since the beginning of the *(semester)*?
9. How many cups of coffee have you had since you got up this morning?
10. How many classes have you had so far today?
11. How many times have you eaten *(your native)* food / eaten at a restaurant since you came here?
12. How many times have you . . . ?

☐ EXERCISE 5. Present perfect. (Chart 3-1)
   Directions: Complete the sentences with any appropriate time expressions.

1. Today is ___the 14th of June___ . I bought this book ___two weeks___ ago.

   I have had this book since ___the first of June___ .

   I have had this book for ___two weeks___ .

2. I have a pen. I bought it _____ ago.

   I have had this pen for _____ .

   I have had this pen since _____ .

3. Today is _____ .

   I moved to this city _____ .

   I have been in this city since _____ .

   I have been here for _____ .

4. It is the year _____ .

   I started going to school in the year _____ .

   I have been a student for _____ .

   I have been a student since _____ .

5. I first met our teacher _____ .

   I have known her/him for _____ .

   I have known her/him since _____ .

□ EXERCISE 6. Present perfect. (Chart 3-1)
> *Directions:* The person who gives the cues has an open book. (This person can be the teacher or the leader of a small group.) Everyone else's books are closed.
> Answer the questions in complete sentences, first using *for* and then using *since*.
>
> *Example:*
> To SPEAKER A: When did you come to *(this city / country)?*
> —I came here on June 2nd.
> To SPEAKER B: How long has (Speaker A) been here?
> —He/She has been here for two weeks.
> Or, using *since?*
> —He/She has been here since June 2nd.

1. To A: When did you arrive *(in this city /country)?*
   To B: How long has (. . .) been here?
2. To A: When did you get to class today?
   To B: How long has (. . .) been in class?
3. To A: What time did you get up this morning?
   To B: How long has (. . .) been up?
4. To A: Who in this class owns a car /bicycle? When did you buy it?
   To B: How long has (. . .) had a car /bicycle?
5. To A: Who is wearing a watch? When did you get it?
   To B: How long has (. . .) had his /her watch?
6. To A: Who is married? When did you get married?
   To B: How long has (. . .) been married?
7. To A: Do you know (. . .)? When did you meet him /her?
   To B: How long has (. . .) known (. . .)?
8. To A: Is that your pen /notebook /pencil sharpener? When did you buy it?
   To B: How long has (. . .) had his /her pen /notebook /pencil sharpener?
9. To A: Is that your . . . ? When did you get it?
   To B: How long has (. . .) had . . . ?

□ EXERCISE 7. Present perfect. (Chart 3-1)
> *Directions:* **Have** and **has** (when used as auxiliary verbs, not as main verbs) are usually contracted with personal pronouns in both speaking and informal writing. **Have** and **has** are often contracted with nouns and other words in informal speaking, but not usually in writing. (See Appendix Chart C, p. A17.) Practice pronouncing contracted **have** and **has** in the sentences.

1. You've been there. They've been there. She's been there. We've all been there.
2. Mary has never been there. → *"Mary's" never been there.*
3. The weather has been nice lately.
4. My neighbors have asked me over for dinner.
5. The teacher has never eaten hot Vietnamese food.
6. The teacher has a red dog. *(No contraction; **has** is the main verb.)*
7. My parents have lived in the same house for over thirty years.
8. My parents have a house.
9. Where have you been?
10. What have you done with my books?

☐ EXERCISE 8. Present perfect vs. simple past. (Charts 2-9 and 3-1)
   Directions: Use the simple past or the present perfect.

1. What *(you, learn)* __have you learned__ since you *(come)* _____ here?
   And how many new friends *(you, make)* _____ ?

2. Since classes began, I *(have, not)* _____ much free time. I *(have)*
   _____ several big tests to study for.

3. Last night my friend and I *(have)* _____ some free time, so we *(go)*
   _____ to a show.

4. I admit that I *(get★)* _____ older since I last *(see)* _____
   you, but with any luck at all, I *(get, also)* _____ wiser.

5. The science of medicine *(advance)* _____ a great deal in the
   19th century.

6. In the last fifty years, medical scientists *(make)* _____ many important
   discoveries.

7. Libraries today are different from those in the 1800s. For example, the contents of
   libraries *(change)* _____ greatly through the years. In the 1800s,
   libraries *(be)* _____ simply collections of books. However, today most libraries
   (become) _____ multimedia centers that contain tapes, computers,
   disks, films, magazines, music, and paintings. The role of the library in society
   (change, also) _____ . In the 1800s, libraries *(be)* _____
   open only to certain people, such as scholars or the wealthy. Today libraries serve
   everyone.

8. A: Are you taking Chemistry 101 this semester?
   B: No, I *(take, already★★)* _____ it. I *(take)* _____
   it last semester. This semester I'm in 102.

★COMPARE:

(a) *I **have gotten** OR **have got** four letters so far this week.* In this sentence, *have gotten / have got* is present perfect.
   (NOTE: *Got* is used as the past participle of *get* in both American English and British English. *Gotten* occurs only
   in American English.)

(b) *I **have got** a problem.* In this sentence, *have got* is NOT present perfect. *I've got a problem = I have a problem.* The
   expression *have got* means "have" and is common in informal spoken English. Its meaning is present; it has no
   past form.

★★Typically, the present perfect is used in sentences with *already, yet,* and *just,* but in some situations the simple past
   is also commonly used with these adverbs in informal English, with no difference in meaning.

9. A: Hi, Judy. Welcome to the party. *(you, meet, ever)* _____ my
cousin?

B: No, I _____ .

10. A: Do you like lobster?

B: I don't know. I *(eat, never)* _____ it.

11. A: *(you, eat)* _____ yet?

B: No. You?

A: Yeah. I *(eat, already)* _____ . I *(finish, just)* _____ .

12. A: Do you do much traveling?

B: Yes. I like to travel.

A: What countries *(you, visit)* _____ ?

B: Well, I *(be)* _____ to India, Turkey, Afghanistan, and Nepal,
among others.

A: I *(be, never)* _____ to any of those countries. When *(you, be)*
_____ in India?

B: Two years ago. I *(visit, also)* _____ many of the countries in
Central America. I *(take)* _____ a tour of Central America
about six years ago.

A: Which countries *(you, visit)* _____ ?

B: Guatemala, El Salvador, Honduras, and Nicaragua.

A: I *(want, always)* _____ to travel to other countries, but I
(have, not) _____ the opportunity to travel extensively. I
(go) _____ to England six years ago, but I *(go, not)* _____
_____ anywhere since then.

☐ EXERCISE 9. Activity: using the present perfect. (Chart 3-1)
Directions: Discuss and/or write answers to some or all of the following questions.

1. What significant changes have taken place in your life since you were thirteen years old?
2. What are some interesting experiences you have had in your lifetime?
3. What are some things you have not yet done in your lifetime but would like to do?
4. Who are some of the people you have met, and what are some of the things you have
done in the past couple of months?
5. What are some of the places you have visited in the world or in your country, and
when did you visit them?

3-2 PRESENT PERFECT PROGRESSIVE

	Right now I am sitting at my desk. (a) I *have been sitting* here *since* seven o'clock. (b) I *have been sitting* here *for* two hours. (c) You *have been studying* *for* five straight hours. Why don't you take a break? (d) It *has been raining* *all day*. It is still raining right now.	This tense is used to indicate the *duration* of an activity that *began in the past and continues to the present*. When the tense has this meaning, it is used with time words, such as *for, since, all morning, all day, all week*.
	(e) I *have known* Alex since he was a child. (f) INCORRECT: I *have been knowing* Alex since he was a child.	Reminder: verbs with stative meanings are not used in the progressive. (See Chart 2-3, p. 15.) The present perfect, NOT the present perfect progressive, is used with stative verbs to describe the duration of a *state* (rather than an activity) that began in the past and continues to the present.
(recently)	(g) I *have been thinking* about changing my major. (h) All of the students *have been studying* hard. Final exams start next week. (i) My back hurts, so I *have been sleeping* on the floor lately. The bed is too soft.	When the tense is used without any specific mention of time, it expresses *a general activity in progress recently, lately*.
	(j) I *have lived* here since 1995. I *have been living* here since 1995. (k) He *has worked* at the same store for ten years. He *has been working* at the same store for ten years.	With certain verbs (most notably *live, work, teach*), there is little or no difference in meaning between the two tenses when *since* or *for* is used.

☐ EXERCISE 10. Error analysis: present perfect progressive. (Chart 3-2)
Directions: Which verbs in these sentences should be present perfect progressive? Correct the errors in verb tense usage.

1. The boys are playing soccer right now. They are playing for almost two hours. They must be getting tired.

2. Alex is talking on the phone. He talked on the phone for more than half an hour. He should hang up soon. Long distance is expensive.

3. I'm trying to study. I try to study for the last hour, but something always seems to interrupt me. I think I'd better go to the library.

4. Mr. Ford is waiting in the dentist's office. He was waiting there for the last twenty minutes. He hopes the dentist can see him soon because he has a bad toothache.

☐ EXERCISE 11. Present perfect vs. present perfect progressive. (Charts 3-1 and 3-2)
   Directions: Use the present perfect or the present perfect progressive. In some sentences, either tense may be used with little or no change in meaning.

   1. It *(snow)* _____ all day. I wonder when it will stop.

   2. We *(have)* _____ three major snowstorms so far this winter. I wonder how many more we will have.

   3. It's ten P.M. I *(study)* _____ for two hours and probably won't finish until midnight.

   4. I *(write)* _____ them three times, but I still haven't received a reply.

   5. The telephone *(ring)* _____ four times in the last hour, and each time it has been for my office mate.

   6. The telephone *(ring)* _____ for almost a minute. Why doesn't someone answer it?

   7. A: *(you, be)* _____ able to reach Bob on the phone yet?
      B: Not yet. I *(try)* _____ for the last twenty minutes, but all I get is a busy signal.

   8. A: Hi, Jenny. I *(see, not)* _____ you for weeks. What *(you, do)* _____ lately?
      B: Studying.

9. A: What are you going to order for dinner?

 B: Well, I *(have, never)* _____ vegetarian pizza, so I think I'll order that.

10. A: What's the matter? Your eyes are red and puffy. *(you, cry)* _____ _____ ?

 B: No. I just finished peeling some onions.

11. A: Dr. Jones is a good teacher. How long *(he, be)* _____ at the university?

 B: He *(teach)* _____ here for twenty-five years.

12. The little girl is dirty from head to foot because she *(play)* _____ in the mud.

□ **EXERCISE 12. Present perfect and present perfect progressive with SINCE and FOR.**
      (Charts 3-1 and 3-2)
Directions: Complete the sentences with your own words.

1. . . . since eight o'clock this morning.
    → *I have been sitting in class since eight o'clock this morning.*
    → *I have had three classes since eight o'clock this morning.*
2. . . . since I came to . . . .
3. . . . since *(year)*.
4. . . . since *(month)*.
5. . . . since *(day)*.
6. . . . since . . . o'clock this morning / afternoon / evening.
7. . . . since the beginning of this century.
8. . . . since . . . .
9. . . . for *(number of years)*.
10. . . . for a long time.
11. . . . for several months.
12. . . . for the last ten minutes.

☐ EXERCISE 13. Activity: using the present perfect and present perfect progressive in writing. (Charts 3-1 and 3-2)

Directions: Choose one to write about.

1. Write about your first day in this class. What did you see, hear, feel, think? Then write about what you have done and have been doing in this class since the first day.

2. Describe your last week at home before you came to this city/country. Then describe what you have done and have been doing since you arrived here.

3-3 PAST PERFECT

	(a) Sam *had* already *left* by the time Ann got there. (b) The thief simply walked in. Someone *had forgotten* to lock the door.	The past perfect expresses an activity that was *completed before another activity or time in the past.*
× ×	(c) Sam *had* already *left* when Ann got there.	In (c): *First:* Sam left. *Second:* Ann got there.★
	(d) Sam *had left* before Ann got there. (e) Sam *left* before Ann got there. (f) *After* the guests *had left*, I went to bed. (g) *After* the guests *left*, I went to bed.	If either *before* or *after* is used in the sentence, the past perfect is often not necessary because the time relationship is already clear. The simple past may be used, as in (e) and (g). Note: (d) and (e) have the same meaning; (f) and (g) have the same meaning.

★COMPARE: *Sam **left** when Ann got there.* = First: *Ann got there.*
Second: *Sam left.*

Sam *had* already *left* when Ann got to the cafeteria.

□ EXERCISE 14. Contracting HAD. (Appendix Chart C)
Directions: The auxiliary verb **had** (but not the main verb **had**) is usually contracted with personal pronouns in both speaking and informal writing. **Had** is also often contracted with nouns and other words in informal speaking, but not in writing. (See Appendix Chart C, p. A17.) Practice pronouncing contracted **had** in these sentences.

1. We'd never seen it before. He'd never seen it. They'd never seen it.
2. I'd never seen it before. I'd like to see it again.*
3. We got home late. The children had already fallen asleep.
4. My roommates had finished dinner by the time I got home.
5. My roommates had dinner early.
6. We couldn't cross the river. The flood had washed away the bridge.
7. You were at Jim's at eight. Where had you been before that?
8. Who had been there before you?

□ EXERCISE 15. Simple past vs. past perfect. (Charts 2-9 and 3-3)
Directions: Use the simple past or the past perfect to complete the sentences. Are there some blanks where either tense is possible?

1. Sam *(be)* _____ a newspaper reporter before he *(become)*

   _____ a businessman.

2. I *(feel)* _____ a little better after I *(take)* _____ the

   medicine.

3. I was late. The teacher *(give, already)* _____ a quiz when I

   (get) _____ to class.

4. It was raining hard, but by the time class *(be)* _____ over, the rain

   (stop) _____ .

5. Millions of years ago, dinosaurs *(roam)* _____ the earth, but they

   (become) _____ extinct by the time humankind first *(appear)*

   _____ .

_____
*COMPARE: **I'd seen** = **I had seen** ('d + past participle = past perfect)
I'd like = **I would like** ('d + simple form = **would**)

6. I *(see, never)* _____ any of Picasso's paintings before I *(visit)* _____ the art museum.

7. Yesterday at a restaurant, I *(see)* _____ Pam Donnelly, an old friend of mine. I *(see, not)* _____ her in years. At first, I *(recognize, not)* _____ her because she *(lose)* _____ a great deal of weight.

8. In 1980, my parents *(emigrate)* _____ to the United States from China. They *(travel, never)* _____ outside of China and were, of course, excited by the challenge of relocating in a foreign country. Eventually, they *(settle)* _____ in California. My sister and I were born there and *(grow)* _____ up there. Last year, I *(go)* _____ to China for the first time to study at Beijing University. I *(want, always)* _____ _____ to visit China and learn more about my own family background. My dream was finally realized.

☐ **EXERCISE 16. Past perfect. (Chart 3-3)**
Directions: Complete the sentences with your own words.

1. I had never . . . before I . . . .
2. By the time . . . , he had already . . . .
3. I had never . . . until I . . . .
4. My . . . after I had already . . . .
5. The movie had . . . by the time we . . . .
6. In *(year)*, I . . . . Prior to that time, I had . . . .
7. When I . . . , someone else had already . . . .
8. Last *(month)*, I . . . . Before that, I had never . . . .

3-4 PAST PERFECT PROGRESSIVE

(a) The police **had been looking** for the criminal *for* two years before they caught him. (b) Eric finally came at six o'clock. I **had been waiting** for him *since* four-thirty.	The past perfect progressive emphasizes the *duration* of an activity that was *in progress before another activity or time in the past.*
(c) When Judy got home, her hair was still wet because she **had been swimming**. (d) I went to Jane's house after the the funeral. Her eyes were red because she **had been crying**.	This tense also may express an activity *in progress close in time to another activity or time in the past.*

□ EXERCISE 17. Present perfect progressive and past perfect progressive. (Charts 3-2 and 3-4)

Directions: Use the present perfect progressive or the past perfect progressive to complete the sentences.

1. We *(wait)* _____*have been waiting*_____ for Nancy for the last two hours, but she still hasn't arrived.

2. We *(wait)* _____*had been waiting*_____ for Nancy for over three hours before she finally arrived yesterday.

3. It is midnight. I *(study)* _____ for five straight hours. No wonder I'm getting tired.

4. It was midnight. I *(study)* _____ for five straight hours. No wonder I was getting tired.

5. Jack suddenly realized that the teacher was asking him a question. He couldn't answer because he *(daydream)* _____ for the last ten minutes.

6. Wake up! You *(sleep)* _____ long enough. It's time to get up.

□ EXERCISE 18. Review of verb tenses. (Chapters 1 → 3)

Directions: In pairs or groups, discuss the meaning of the verb forms and answer the questions about the pairs of sentences.

1. a. Dan was leaving the room when I walked in.
   b. Sam had left the room when I walked in.
   QUESTION: *Who did I run into when I walked into the room?*
   ANSWER: Dan.

2. a. When the rain stopped, Gloria was riding her bicycle to work.
   b. When the rain stopped, Paul rode his bicycle to work.
   QUESTION: *Who got wet on the way to work?*

3. a. Ken went to the store because he was running out of food.
   b. Ann went to the store because she had run out of food.
   QUESTION: *Who is better at planning ahead?*

4. a. Ms. Lincoln taught at this school for nine years.
   b. Mr. Sanchez has taught at this school for nine years.
   QUESTION: *Who is teaching at this school now?*

5. a. Alice was walking to the door when the doorbell rang.
   b. George walked to the door when the doorbell rang.
   QUESTION: *Who had been expecting the doorbell to ring?*

6. a. When I got there, Marie had eaten.
   b. When I got there, Joe ate.
   QUESTION: *Who was still hungry when I got there?*

7. a. Donna lived in Chicago for five years.
   b. Carlos has been living in Chicago for five years.
   QUESTION: *Who still lives in Chicago?*

8. a. Jane put some lotion on her face because she had been lying in the sun.
   b. Sue put some lotion on her face because she was lying in the sun.
      QUESTION: *Who put lotion on her face after she finished sunbathing?*

9. a. I looked across the street. Mr. Fox was waving at me.
   b. I looked across the street. Mrs. Cook waved at me.
      QUESTION: *Who began to wave at me before I looked across the street?*

☐ EXERCISE 19. Error analysis: present and past verbs. (Chapters 1 → 3)
Directions: Correct the errors.

1. Since I came to this country, I am learning a lot about the way of life here.

2. Before I come here, I never was buying anything from a vending machine.

3. I arrive here only a short time ago. I am here only since last Friday.

4. When I arrived here, I hadn't known much about the United States. I saw many movies about America, but that wasn't enough.

5. My understanding of this country changed a lot since I arrived.

6. When I was in my country, I had coached a children's soccer team. When I came here, I had wanted to do the same thing. Now I am coaching a soccer team at a local elementary school. I am coaching this team for the last two months.

7. My grandfather had lived in a small village in Italy when he was a child. At nineteen, he had moved to Rome, where he had met and had married my grandmother in 1947. My father had been born in Rome in 1950. I am born in Rome in 1979.

8. I'm living in my cousin's apartment since I have arrived here. I'm not able to find my own apartment yet. I look at several places for rent, but I don't find one that I can afford.

9. How long you been living here? I been here for almost two year.

10. Why you no have been in class the last couple of days?

☐ EXERCISE 20. Activity: using verb tenses. (Chapters 1 → 3)
Directions: From the given situation, make up a "chain story." One person begins the story; then others continue the story in turn, using the cue words in the given list. Work in groups or as a class.

Example: (Pierre) had a terrible day yesterday. The trouble began early in the morning. His alarm clock rang at 7:00.
CUE: *when*
SPEAKER A: When his alarm clock rang, he got out of bed and stepped on a snake. He was nearly frightened to death, but the snake slithered away without biting him.

CUE: *after*
SPEAKER B: After the snake left, Pierre got dressed in a hurry and ran downstairs to have
            breakfast.
CUE: *while*
SPEAKER C: While he was running downstairs, he fell and broke his arm.
Etc.

Possible situations to begin chain stories:
>   1. (. . .) had a terrible day yesterday.
>   2. (. . .) had a great vacation last summer.
>   3. (. . .) got into a lot of trouble a couple of days ago.
>   4. (. . .) had an interesting experience last week.
>   5. *(Make up the beginning of a story.)*

Cue words (may be used in any order):

1. when	6. as soon as	11. after that
2. after	7. already	12. later
3. before	8. never	13. for *(a length of time)*
4. while	9. then	14. since
5. by the time	10. next	15. because

☐ **EXERCISE 21. Activity: using verb tenses. (Chapters 1 → 3)**

Directions: Form a group and sit in a circle. Take out a piece of paper and write the
following sentence, using the name of the person sitting to your right.

>   (. . .) *had a strange experience yesterday.*

Then write two or three additional sentences, and pass your paper to the person sitting
to your left, who will continue the story. Continue to pass the papers to the left until
everyone in the group has had a chance to write part of the story.

Then decide which story in your group is the most entertaining or the most interesting.
As a group, make any necessary corrections in grammar or spelling. Read the story aloud
to the rest of the class.

NOTE: You may wish to establish a time limit for each contribution to the story. When the
time limit is up, each person must pass on his/her paper even if it contains an unfinished
sentence. The next person will then have to finish the sentence and continue writing the
story.

☐ **EXERCISE 22. Using verb tenses in writing. (Chapters 1 → 3)**

Directions: Choose one to write about.

>   1. Describe the state of the world in the year of your birth. What significant or historical
>   events occurred or were occurring at that time? Who were the leaders of your country?
>   Then describe the changes that have occurred since that time and discuss the state of
>   the world today.

>   2. Describe your family in the year you were born. Where were they living and working?
>   Were they in a good situation? Who did your family consist of? Who in your family
>   hadn't been born yet? Then describe the changes in your family that have occurred
>   since the year of your birth and your family's current situation.

CHAPTER 4
Future Time

CONTENTS	

4-1 SIMPLE FUTURE: *WILL* AND *BE GOING TO*

(a) Jack *will finish* his work tomorrow. (b) Jack *is going to finish* his work tomorrow. (c) Anna *will not be* here tomorrow. (d) Anna *won't be* here tomorrow.	*Will* or *be going to* is used to express future time.* In speech, *going to* is often pronounced "gonna." In (d): The contracted form of *will* + *not* is *won't*.

*The use of *shall* with *I* or *we* to express future time is possible but uncommon in American English. *Shall* is used more frequently in British English than in American English.

☐ EXERCISE 1. Simple future. (Chart 4-1)
Directions: *Will* is usually contracted with personal pronouns in both speaking and informal writing. *Will* is often contracted with nouns and with other words in speaking, but not in writing. Practice pronouncing contracted *will* in these sentences.

1. I'll come. He'll come. You'll come.
2. She'll help us. They'll help us too.
3. I'm sure we'll do well on the test.
4. It'll probably rain tomorrow.
5. Bob will ("Bob'll") be here soon.
6. The weather will be hot in August.
7. Mary will come tomorrow.
8. Bill will be here too.
9. The children will be home at 3:00.
10. Who will be at the meeting?
11. Where will you be around five?
12. How long will Tom be here?
13. Nobody will recognize you in that wig.
14. That will be a lot of fun.
15. What will you do?

4-2 WILL vs. BE GOING TO

To express a PREDICTION: Use either WILL or BE GOING TO.

(a) According to the weather report, it *will be* cloudy tomorrow. (b) According to the weather report, it *is going to be* cloudy tomorrow. (c) Be careful! You*'ll hurt* yourself! (d) Watch out! You*'re going to hurt* yourself!	When the speaker is making a prediction (a statement about something s/he thinks will be true or will occur in the future), either *will* or *be going to* is possible. There is no difference in meaning between (a) and (b). There is no difference in meaning between (c) and (d).

To express a PRIOR PLAN: Use only BE GOING TO.

(e) A: Why did you buy this paint? B: I*'m going to paint* my bedroom tomorrow. (f) I talked to Bob yesterday. He is tired of taking the bus to work. He*'s going to buy* a car. That's what he told me.	When the speaker is expressing a prior plan (something the speaker intends to do in the future because in the past s/he has made a plan or decision to do it), only *be going to* is used.* In (e): Speaker B has made a prior plan. Last week she decided to paint her bedroom. She intends to paint it tomorrow. In (f): The speaker knows Bob intends to buy a car. Bob made the decision in the past, and he plans to act on this decision in the future. *Will* is not appropriate in (e) and (f).

To express WILLINGNESS: Use only WILL.

(g) A: The phone's ringing.
   B: I*'ll get* it.
 (h) A: I don't understand this problem.
   B: Ask your teacher about it. She*'ll help* you.
	In (g): Speaker B is saying "I am willing; I am happy to get the phone." He is not making a prediction. He has made no prior plan to answer the phone. He is, instead, volunteering to answer the phone and uses *will* to show his willingness.
	 In (h): Speaker B feels sure about the teacher's willingness to help. *Be going to* is not appropriate in (g) and (h).

*COMPARE:

Situation 1: A: *Are you busy this evening?*

B: *Yes. I'm going to meet Jack at the library at seven. We're going to study together.*

In Situation 1, only *be going to* is possible. The speaker has a prior plan, so he uses *be going to.*

Situation 2: A: *Are you busy this evening?*

B: *Well, I really haven't made any plans. I'll eat* OR *I'm going to eat dinner, of course. And then I'll probably watch* OR *I'm probably going to watch TV for a little while.*

In Situation 2, either *will* or *be going to* is possible. Speaker B has not planned his evening. He is "predicting" his evening (rather than stating any prior plans), so he may use either *will* or *be going to.*

☐ EXERCISE 2. WILL vs. BE GOING TO. (Chart 4-2)

PART I. EXPRESSING PREDICTIONS

Use *will* and/or *be going to* with the verb in parentheses.

1. Sue *(graduate)* __will graduate/ is going to graduate__ in June. After that, she

   (begin) ___will begin / is going to begin___ work at an electronics firm.

2. Fred *(be)* _____ at the meeting tomorrow. I think Jane *(come)*

   _____ too.

3. A: Can you give Ed a message for me?

   B: Sure. I *(see, probably)* _____ him at the meeting this evening.

4. A: Mr. Swan *(be, not)* _____ here next term. He has resigned. Who *(be)* _____ the new teacher? Do you know?

   B: Yes. Ms. Mary Jefferson. Ms. Jefferson *(teach)* _____ the same courses Mr. Swan taught: English, algebra, and geometry. I *(be)* _____ _____ in her algebra class.

5. In what ways *(the damage we do to our environment today, affect)* _____ _____ the quality of life for future generations?

PART II. EXPRESSING PRIOR PLAN VS. WILLINGNESS
Use **be going to** if you think the speaker is expressing a prior plan. If you think she/he has no prior plan, use **will.**

6. A: This letter is in French, and I don't speak French. Can you help me?

   B: Sure. I *(translate)* ____will translate____ it for you.

7. A: Do you want to go shopping with me? I *(go)* ____am going to go____ to the shopping mall downtown.

   B: Sure. What time do you want to leave?

8. A: Who wants to erase the board? Are there any volunteers?

   B: I *(do)* _____ it!

   C: I *(do)* _____ it!

9. A: Why does he have an eraser in his hand?

   B: He *(erase)* _____ _____ the board.

10. A: How about getting together for dinner after work?

B: Sounds good. Where?

A: How about Alice's Restaurant or the Gateway Cafe? You decide.

B: Alice's Restaurant. I *(meet)* _____ you there around six.

A: Great.

11. A: Do you have plans for dinner?

B: Yes. I *(meet*)* _____ a co-worker for dinner at Alice's Restaurant. Want to join us?

12. A: This light doesn't work. The bulb is probably burned out. Do we have any new light bulbs?

B: I *(get)* _____ one for you.

A: Thanks.

13. A: I *(enroll)* _____ in the community college next spring.

B: Oh? I didn't know you wanted to go back to school.

A: I need to sharpen my skills so I can get a better job. I *(take)* _____ a course in word processing.

14. A: Uh, oh! I've spilled coffee on my shirt!

B: Just a minute. I *(get)* _____ a damp cloth for you.

15. A: Janice, do you want to come with us?

B: I can't. I have to study.

A: Oh, c'mon! You can't study all day <u>and</u> all night.

B: All right, I *(go)* _____ with you. I guess I can finish this stuff tomorrow.

16. A: I *(sell)* _____ my bicycle. I have to.

B: What? Why? You need your bicycle to get to work.

A: I know. But I need money right now to pay for my baby's doctor and medicine. I can walk to work.

17. A: How do you spell "accustomed"?

B: I'm not sure. I *(look)* _____ it up for you.

A: Thanks.

B: Here it is. It has two "c"s but only one "m."

---

*When *be going to* expresses a prior plan, it is often also possible to use the present progressive with no change in meaning. See Chart 4-4, p. 57. There is no difference in meaning between these sentences:

I **am going to meet** Larry at Alice's Restaurant at six.

I **am meeting** Larry at Alice's Restaurant at six.

4-3 EXPRESSING THE FUTURE IN TIME CLAUSES

(a) Bob will come soon. *When Bob comes,* we will see him. (b) Linda is going to leave soon. *Before she leaves,* she is going to finish her work. (c) I will get home at 5:30. *After I get home,* I will eat dinner. (d) The taxi will arrive soon. *As soon as it arrives,* we'll be able to leave for the airport. (e) They are going to come soon. I'll wait here *until they come.*	In (a): *When Bob comes* is a time clause.* *when* + *subject* + *verb* = *a time clause* **Will** or **be going to** is NOT used in a time clause. The meaning of the clause is future, but the **simple present** tense is used.
	A time clause begins with such words as **when, before, after, as soon as, until, while** and includes a subject and a verb. The time clause can come either at the beginning of the sentence or in the second part of the sentence: *When he comes,* we'll see him. OR We'll see him *when he comes.*
(f) *While I am traveling in Europe next year,* I'm going to save money by staying in youth hostels.	Sometimes the present progressive is used in a time clause to express an activity that will be in progress in the future, as in (f).
(g) I will go to bed *after I finish my work.* (h) I will go to bed *after I have finished my work.*	Occasionally, the present perfect is used in a time clause, as in (h). Examples (g) and (h) have the same meaning. The present perfect in the time clause emphasizes the completion of the act before the other act occurs in the future.

*A "time clause" is an adverb clause. See Charts 5-1 (p. 70), 5-2 (p. 72), and 17-1 (p. 359) for more information.

☐ EXERCISE 3. Expressing the future in time clauses. (Chart 4-3)
Directions: Find the time clause in each sentence. Draw brackets [. . .] around it and underline the verb in the time clause. Identify and discuss the use of verb tenses.

1. We'll be here [when you <u>arrive</u> tomorrow.]

2. After the rain stops, I'm going to sweep the front porch.

3. I'm going to start making dinner before my wife gets home from work today.

4. I'm going to wait right here until Jessica comes.

5. As soon as the war is over, there will be great joy throughout the land.

6. Right now the tide is low, but when the tide comes in, the ship will leave the harbor.

7. While I'm driving to work tomorrow, I'm going to listen to my Greek language tapes.

☐ EXERCISE 4. Expressing the future in time clauses. (Chart 4-3)
Directions: Use **will** / **be going to** or the simple present. (In this exercise, both **will** and **be going to** are possible when a future tense is necessary, with little or no difference in meaning.)

1. Peter is going to leave in half an hour. He *(finish)* <u>will finish / is going to finish</u>

    all of his work before he *(leave)* <u>leaves</u> .

2. I'm going to eat lunch at 12:30. After I *(eat)* _____ , I *(take, probably)*

    _____ a nap.

3. I'll get home around six. When I *(get)* _____ home, I *(call)* _____ Sharon.

4. I'm going to watch a TV program at nine, but before I *(watch)* _____ the program, I *(write)* _____ a letter to my parents.

5. Gary will come soon. I *(wait)* _____ here until he *(come)* _____ .

6. I'm sure it will stop raining soon. As soon as the rain *(stop)* _____ , I *(walk)* _____ to the store to get some film.

7. I'm a junior in college this year. After I *(graduate)* _____ with a B.A. next year, I *(intend)* _____ to enter graduate school and work for an M.A. Perhaps I *(go)* _____ on for a Ph.D. after I *(get)* _____ my Master's degree.

8. I *(listen)* _____ to English language tapes while I *(sleep)* _____ tonight. Do you think it will help me learn English faster?

9. A: How long *(you, stay)* _____ _____ in this country?

   B: I *(plan)* _____ to be here for about one more year. I *(hope)* _____ to graduate a year from this June.

   A: What *(you, do)* _____ after you *(leave)* _____ ?

   B: I *(return)* _____ home and *(get)* _____ a job. How about you?

   A: I *(be)* _____ here for at least two more years before I *(return)* _____ home and *(get)* _____ a job.

□ EXERCISE 5. Expressing the future in time clauses. (Chart 4-3)
   Directions: Complete the sentences with your own words.

1. When I . . . later this afternoon, I . . . .

   → *When I go downtown later this afternoon, I'm going to go to the bank and the post office.*

2. After I . . . tomorrow morning, I . . . .
3. Tomorrow, I . . . before I . . . .
4. I . . . when . . . next year.
5. As soon as class . . . , I'm going to . . . .
6. I'm not going to . . . until my friend . . . .
7. When I . . . tomorrow, I . . . .
8. While I'm visiting . . . next week, I . . . .

4-4 USING THE PRESENT PROGRESSIVE AND THE SIMPLE PRESENT TO EXPRESS FUTURE TIME

PRESENT PROGRESSIVE	
(a) My wife has an appointment with a doctor. She *is seeing* Dr. North *next Tuesday.* (b) Sam has already made his plans. He *is leaving at noon tomorrow.* (c) A: What are you going to do this afternoon? 　　B: *After lunch* I *am meeting* a friend of mine. We *are going* shopping. Would you like to come along?	The present progressive may be used to express future time when the idea of the sentence concerns a planned event or definite intention. (COMPARE: A verb such as *rain* is not used in the present progressive to indicate future time because rain is not a planned event.) A future meaning for the present progressive tense is indicated either by future time words in the sentence or by the context.
SIMPLE PRESENT	
(d) The museum *opens* at ten tomorrow morning. (e) Classes *begin next week.* (f) John's plane *arrives at 6:05 P.M. next Monday.*	The simple present can also be used to express future time in a sentence concerning events that are on a definite schedule or timetable. These sentences usually contain future time words. Only a few verbs are used in this way: e.g., *open, close, begin, end, start, finish, arrive, leave, come, return.*

□ EXERCISE 6. Using the present progressive and the simple present to express future time. (Chart 4-4)
   Directions: Indicate the meaning expressed by the *italicized* verbs by writing **in the future**, **now**, or **habitually** in the blanks.

1. I *am taking* four courses next semester.   <u>in the future</u>

2. I *am taking* four courses this semester.   <u>now</u>

3. Students usually *take* four courses every semester.   <u>habitually</u>

4. I'll mail this letter at the corner when I *take* Susan home.   _____

5. My brother's birthday is next week. I *am giving* him a sweater.   _____

6. Shhh. The broadcaster *is giving* the latest news about the crisis in England. I want to hear what she's saying.   _____

7. When I *graduate,* I'm going to return home. _____

8. When students *graduate,* they receive diplomas. _____

9. I'm tired. I *am going* to bed early tonight. _____

10. When I *am* in New York, I'm going to visit the Museum of Modern Art. _____

11. When I *am* home alone in the evening, I like to read or watch television. _____

12. A: Are you busy? _____
    B: Not really.
    A: What *are you doing?* A: _____

    B: I'*m writing* a letter to my folks. B: _____

    A: When you *finish* your letter, do you want to play a game of chess? A: _____

13. A: What *are you doing* after work today? A: _____

    B: I'*m playing* tennis with Brown at the health club. And you? B: _____
    A: I'*m meeting* Smith for a round of golf. A: _____

14. Tony *will arrive* at eight tomorrow evening. _____

15. Tony *is going to arrive* at eight tomorrow night. _____

16. Tony *is arriving* at eight tomorrow evening. _____

17. Tony *arrives* at eight tomorrow evening. _____

18. When Tony *arrives,* we'll have a party. _____

□ EXERCISE 7. Using the present progressive to express future time. (Chart 4-4)
Directions: Use the present progressive to complete the sentences. Use any verb that makes sense.

1. A: How about going across the street for a cup of coffee?

   B: I can't. I _____ *am meeting* _____ Jennifer at the library at 5:00.

2. A: Why are you in such a hurry?

   B: I have to be at the airport in an hour. I _____ the 4 o'clock plane to New York. I have an important meeting there tomorrow.

3. A: We got an invitation in the mail from Ron and Maureen. They _____ a dinner party next Saturday evening. Do you want to go? I'd like to.

   B: Sure. I always enjoy spending time with them. Let's call and tell them we _____ .

4. A: Your cough sounds terrible! You should see a doctor.

   B: I know. It just won't go away. I _____ Dr. Murray later this afternoon.

5. A: Have you seen Jackie?

   B: She just left. She has some shopping to do, and then she _____ to the health club for her yoga class. She should be back around 4:30.

6. A: Where are you and your family going for your vacation this summer?

   B: Ontario.

   A: Are you planning to fly?

   B: No, we _____ so we can take our time and enjoy the scenery.

7. A: We're going to a soccer match next week.

   B: Who _____ ?*

   A: A team from Brazil and a team from Argentina. It ought to be a really exciting game.

8. A: I see you're smoking. I thought you stopped last month.

   B: I did. I don't know why I started again. I _____ again tomorrow, and this time I mean it.

_____
*When *who* is used as the subject of a question, the verb is singular. See Appendix Chart B-2, p. A9.

☐ EXERCISE 8. Using the present progressive to express future time. (Chart 4-4)
Directions: Answer the questions. Practice using the present progressive to express future time.

1. What are your plans for the rest of today?
2. What are your plans for tomorrow?
3. Do you have any travel plans? What are they?
4. Think of someone you know. Does this person have any plans that you are aware of?

☐ EXERCISE 9. Using the present progressive and the simple present to express future time. (Chart 4-4)
Directions: Pretend that you are going to take your ideal vacation next week. All of your plans are made, and your itinerary is in front of you. Write your travel plans. Use present tenses where appropriate.

Example: This coming Saturday I am beginning my "vacation of a lifetime." The first place I'm going to is Bali. My plane leaves at six-thirty Saturday morning. I arrive in Bali late that afternoon. I'm staying at the Nusa Dua Beach Hotel. I leave Bali on the fifteenth and travel to the Philippines. While I'm there, I'm staying with some friends. Etc.

4-5 FUTURE PROGRESSIVE

	(a) I will begin to study at seven. You will come at eight. I *will be studying* when you come. (b) Right now I am sitting in class. At this same time tomorrow, I *will be sitting* in class.	The future progressive expresses an activity that will *be in progress at a time in the future.*
	(c) Don't call me at nine because I won't be home. I *am going to be studying* at the library.	The progressive form of *be going to:* *be going to + be + -ing*
	(d) Don't get impatient. She *will be coming* soon. (e) Don't get impatient. She *will come* soon.	Sometimes there is little or no difference between the future progressive and the simple future, especially when the future event will occur at an indefinite time in the future, as in (d) and (e).

☐ EXERCISE 10. Using the future progressive. (Chart 4-5)
Directions: Use the future progressive or the simple present.

1. Right now I am attending class. Yesterday at this time, I was attending class.

   Tomorrow at this time, I *(attend)* _____ class.

2. Tomorrow I'm going to leave for home. When I *(arrive)* _____

   at the airport, my whole family *(wait)* _____ for me.

3. When I *(get)* _____ up tomorrow morning, the sun *(shine)* _____ , the birds *(sing)* _____ , and my roommate *(lie, still)* _____ in bed fast asleep.

4. A: When do you leave for Florida?

   B: Tomorrow. Just think! Two days from now I *(lie)* _____ on the beach in the sun.

   A: Sounds great! I *(think)* _____ _____ about you.

5. A: How can I get in touch with you while you're out of town?

   B: I *(stay)* _____ at the Pilgrim Hotel. You can reach me there.

6. Next year at this time, I *(do)* _____ exactly what I am doing now. I *(attend)* _____ school and *(study)* _____ hard next year.

7. Look at those dark clouds. When class *(be)* _____ over, it *(rain, probably)* _____ .

8. A: Are you going to be in town next Saturday?

   B: No. I *(visit, in Chicago)** _____ my aunt.

9. A: Where are you going to be this evening?

   B: I *(work, at the library)* _____ on my research paper.

10. A: Do you think life will be very different 100 years from now?

    B: Of course. I can picture it in my mind. People *(live)* _____ in modular mobile residential units that they can take with them if they have to move, and they *(drive)* _____ air cars that can go at tremendous speeds.

    A: That sounds pretty far-fetched to me. Why would people want to take their houses with them when they move?

---

*Expressions of place can often be used between the helping verb and the main verb in progressive tenses. See Chart 2-12, p. 31.

4-6 FUTURE PERFECT

(a) I will graduate in June. I will see you in July. By the time I see you, I *will have graduated*. (b) I *will have finished* my homework by the time I go out on a date tonight.	The future perfect expresses an activity that will be *completed before another time or event in the future*. (Note: *by the time* introduces a time clause; the simple present is used in a time clause.)

4-7 FUTURE PERFECT PROGRESSIVE

(c) I will go to bed at ten P.M. Ed will get home at midnight. At midnight I will be sleeping. I *will have been sleeping* for two hours by the time Ed gets home.	The future perfect progressive emphasizes the *duration* of an activity that will be *in progress before another time or event in the future*.
(d) When Professor Jones retires next month, he *will have taught* for 45 years. (e) When Professor Jones retires next month, he *will have been teaching* for 45 years.	Sometimes the future perfect and the future perfect progressive have the same meaning, as in (d) and (e). Also, notice that the activity expressed by either of these two tenses may begin in the past.

☐ EXERCISE 11. Perfect and perfect progressive tenses. (Chapter 3; Charts 4-6 and 4-7)
Directions: Use any appropriate tense.

1. Ann and Andy got married on June 1st.

   Today is June 14th. They *(be)* _____ married for two weeks.

   By June 7th, they *(be)* _____ married for one week.

   By June 28th, they *(be)* _____ married for four weeks.

2. This traffic is terrible. We're going to be late. By the time we *(get)* _____ to the airport, Bob's plane *(arrive, already*)* _____, and he'll be wondering where we are.

3. The traffic was very heavy. By the time we *(get)* _____ to the airport, Bob's plane *(arrive, already)* _____ .

_____

*With the future perfect, *already* has two possible midsentence positions:
   I *will already have* finished.
   I *will have already* finished.

4. This morning I came to class at 9:00. Right now it is 10:00, and I am still in class. I *(sit)* _____ at this desk for an hour. By 9:30, I *(sit)* _____ here for a half an hour. By 11:00, I *(sit)* _____ here for two hours.

5. I'm getting tired of sitting in the car. Do you realize that by the time we arrive in Phoenix, we *(drive)* _____ for twenty straight hours?

6. Margaret was born in 1975. By 1995, she *(live)* _____ on this earth for 20 years. By the year 2025, she *(live)* _____ on this earth for 50 years.

7. Go ahead and leave on your vacation. Don't worry about this work. By the time you *(get)* _____ back, we *(take)* _____ care of everything.

8. I don't understand how those marathon runners do it! The race began more than an hour ago. By the time they reach the finish line, they *(run)* _____ steadily for more than two hours. I don't think I can run more than two minutes!

9. What? He got married again? At this rate, he *(have)* _____ a dozen wives by the time he *(die)* _____ .

10. We have been married for a long time. By our next anniversary, we *(be)* _____ married for 43 years.

☐ **EXERCISE 12. Review: future time. (Charts 4-1 → 4-7)**
Directions: These sentences describe typical events in a day in the life of a man named Bill. The sentences are in the past, but all of these things will happen in Bill's life tomorrow. Change all of the sentences to the future.

1. When Bill got up yesterday morning, the sun was shining. And tomorrow?
   → *When Bill gets up tomorrow morning, the sun will be shining.*
2. He shaved and showered, and then made a light breakfast. And tomorrow?
3. After he ate breakfast yesterday, he got ready to go to work. And tomorrow?
4. By the time he got to work yesterday, he had drunk three cups of coffee. And tomorrow?
5. Between 8:00 and 9:00, Bill answered his e-mail and planned his day. And tomorrow?
6. By 10:00 yesterday, he had called new clients. And tomorrow?
7. At 11:00 yesterday, he was attending a staff meeting. And tomorrow?
8. He went to lunch at noon and had a sandwich and a bowl of soup. And tomorrow?
9. After he finished eating, he took a short walk in the park before he returned to the office. And tomorrow?

10. He worked at his desk until he went to another meeting in the middle of the afternoon. And tomorrow?

11. By the time he left the office, he had attended three meetings. And tomorrow?

12. When Bill got home, his children were playing in the yard. And tomorrow?

13. They had been playing since 3:00 in the afternoon. And tomorrow?

14. As soon as he finished dinner, he took the children for a walk to a nearby playground. And tomorrow?

15. Afterward, the whole family sat in the living room and discussed their day. And tomorrow?

16. They watched television for a while, and then he and his wife put the kids to bed. And tomorrow?

17. By the time Bill went to bed yesterday, he had had a full day and was ready for sleep. And tomorrow?

☐ EXERCISE 13. Review: future time. (Chapter 4)

Directions: What do you think the world will be like a hundred years from now? What changes will have occurred between then and now? Use your imagination and make some predictions.

Possible topics:

1. means of transportation
2. sources of energy
3. population growth
4. food sources
5. extinction of animal species
6. architecture
7. clothing styles
8. exploration of the oceans; of the earth's interior
9. space exploration; contact with beings from outer space
10. weapon technology
11. role of computers in daily life
12. long-term solutions to today's political crises
13. international language
14. international world government

NOTE: You may wish to make comparisons among the past, the present, and the future. For example:

A hundred years ago, the automobile hadn't been invented. Today it is one of the most common means of transportation and has greatly changed the way people lead their lives. By the year ———, the automobile will have become obsolete. A hundred years from now, people will use small, jet-propelled, wingless flying machines in place of cars.

CHAPTER 5

Adverb Clauses of Time and Review of Verb Tenses

CONTENTS	
5-1	Adverb clauses of time: form
5-2	Using adverb clauses to show time relationships

☐ **EXERCISE 1. Error analysis: review of verb tenses. (Chapters 1 → 4)**
   Directions: Correct the errors.

        have been

1. I ~~am~~ studying here since last January.

2. By the time I return to my country, I am away from home for more than three years.

3. As soon as I will graduate, I going to return to my hometown.

4. By the end of the 21st century, scientists will had discovered the cure for the common cold.

5. I want to get married, but I don't meet the right person yet.

6. I have been seeing that movie three times, and now I am wanting to see it again.

7. Last night, I have had dinner with two friend. I knew both of them for a long time.

8. I am not like my job at the restaurant. My brother wants me to change it. I am thinking he is right.

9. So far this week, the teachers are giving us a lot of homework every day.

10. There are more than forty presidents of the United States since it became a country. George Washington had been the first president. He was become the president in 1789.

11. While I will be studying tonight, I'm going to listen to Beethoven's Seventh Symphony.

12. We washed the dishes and clean up the kitchen after our dinner guests were leaving.

13. My neighbors are Mr. and Mrs. Jones. I know them ever since I am a child.

14. It's raining tomorrow morning.

15. Many scientists believe there is a major earthquake in California in the next few years.

16. When I got home to my apartment last night,

I use my key to open the door as usual. But the

door didn't open. I trying my key again and again

with no luck. So I am knocking on the door for my

wife to let me in. Finally the door opens, but I don't

saw my wife on the other side. I saw a stranger. I had

been try to get into the wrong apartment! I quickly

apologizing and am went to my own apartment.

☐ EXERCISE 2. Review of verb tenses. (Chapters 1 → 4)
> *Directions:* Discuss the differences (if any) in meaning in these groups of sentences. Some of the sentences need to be completed to make their meanings clear.

1. a. He watches television.
   b. He is watching television.

2. a. I am sitting in class . . . .
   b. I was sitting in class . . . .

3. a. I have finished my homework.
   b. I had finished my homework . . . .
   c. I will have finished my homework . . . .

4. a. The students had left before the teacher arrived.
   b. The students left before the teacher arrived.
   c. The students had left when the teacher arrived.
   d. The students left when the teacher arrived.
   e. The students were leaving when the teacher arrived.

5. a. I have been waiting for her for two hours.
   b. I had been waiting for her for two hours . . . .
   c. I will have been waiting for her for two hours . . . .

6. a. Ali has been studying Chapter Five.
   b. He has studied Chapter Two.
   c. He studied Chapter Two . . . .

7. a. She has been doing a lot of research on that project.
   b. She has done a lot of research on that project.

8. a. I will study when you come.
   b. I am going to study when you come.
   c. I will be studying when you come.
   d. I am going to be studying when you come.
   e. I will have studied by the time you come.
   f. I will have been studying for two hours by the time you come.

9. a. He worked for that company for two years.
   b. He has been working for that company for two years.

10. a. The train will leave at 10:00 tomorrow morning.
    b. The train is going to leave at 10:00 tomorrow morning.
    c. The train leaves at 10:00 tomorrow morning.
    d. The train is leaving at 10:00 tomorrow morning.

☐ EXERCISE 3. Review of verb tenses. (Chapters 1 → 4)
Directions: In order to practice verb tenses, answer the questions in complete sentences. The questioner's book is open. The answerer's book is closed. Work in pairs, in groups, or as a class. If you use this exercise in pairwork, switch roles after Item 9.

1. What have we been studying? What is one tense we have studied since the beginning of the term? When, to the best of your recollection, did we study it?
2. What else will we have studied in this class by the time the term ends?
3. This class began on *(date)*. Had you studied verb tenses before that?
4. We're going to finish studying Chapter 5 on *(day or date)*. How long will we have been studying Chapter 5 by that time?
5. What were you doing at this time yesterday? What did you do after that?
6. What are you doing right now? How long have you been doing that?
7. What are you going to be doing at this time tomorrow?
8. What will you be doing tonight at midnight? What were you doing last night at midnight?
9. Where will you be living three years from now? Where were you living three years ago? Can you name one specific thing you did three years ago? Can you name one specific thing you will do three years from now?
10. What places have you been to since you came to *(this city)?*
11. Make some generalizations about things you do.
12. What are some things you have done many times since you came to *(this city)?*
13. What are some of the things you have done in your lifetime? When did you do them?
14. What have you done that no one else in this class (or in the world) has ever done?
15. What is the exact place you are sitting right now?
    How long have you been sitting there today?
    How long will you have been sitting there by the time class is over?
    How often do you sit there during class?
    How many times have you sat there?
    Before today, when did you last sit there?
    Had you sat there before that?
    Where were you sitting at this time yesterday?
    Where are you going to be sitting at this time tomorrow?

☐ **EXERCISE 4. Review of verb tenses. (Chapters 1 → 4)**

Directions: Use any appropriate tense of the verbs in parentheses.

1. John is in my English class. He *(study)* _____ English this semester. He *(take, also)* _____ some other classes. His classes *(begin)* _____ at 9:00 every day.

2. Yesterday John ate breakfast at 8:00. He *(eat, already)* _____ breakfast when he *(leave)* _____ for class at 8:45. He *(eat, always)* _____ breakfast before he *(go)* _____ to class. Tomorrow before he *(go)* _____ to class, he *(eat)* _____ breakfast.

3. John is in class every morning from 9:00 to 12:00. Two days ago, I *(call)* _____ him at 11:30, but I could not reach him because he *(attend)* _____ class at that time.

4. Don't try to call John at 11:30 tomorrow morning because he *(attend)* _____ _____ class at that time.

5. Yesterday John took a nap from 1:00 to 2:00. I arrived at 1:45. When I *(get)* _____ there, John *(sleep)* _____. He *(sleep)* _____ for 45 minutes by the time I got there.

6. Right now John *(take)* _____ a nap. He *(fall)* _____ asleep an hour ago. He *(sleep)* _____ for an hour.

7. Three days ago, John *(start)* _____ to read *A Farewell to Arms*, a novel by Ernest Hemingway. It is a long novel. He *(finish, not)* _____ reading it yet. He *(read)* _____ it because his English teacher assigned it.

8. Since the beginning of the semester, John *(read)* _____ three novels. Right now he *(read)* _____ *A Farewell to Arms*. He *(read)* _____ that novel for the past three days. He *(intend)* _____ to finish it next week. In his lifetime, he *(read)* _____ many novels, but this is the first Hemingway novel he *(read, ever)* _____.

9. Tomorrow, after he *(eat)* _____ dinner, John *(go)* _____ to a movie. In other words, he *(eat)* _____ dinner by the time he *(go)* _____ to the movie.

□ **EXERCISE 5. Review of verb tenses. (Chapters 1 → 4)**
      Directions: Work in pairs.
    SPEAKER A:
- Use the questions in this exercise to initiate conversation with Speaker B.
- Do not simply read the questions. Look at the text briefly, then look directly at Speaker B each time you ask a question.
- If Speaker B does not answer fully or if you would like more information, ask your own questions in addition to those suggested.
- Pay special attention to verb tense usage in both the questions and the responses.

    SPEAKER B:
- Your book is closed.
- Answer the questions fully. Often your response will consist of more than one sentence.
- Answer in complete sentences in order to practice using verb tenses.

PART I.
1. What is happening in this room?
   What else is happening?
2. What was happening in this room when you walked in today?
   What else was happening?
3. What did you do yesterday? *(Speaker A: Listen carefully for past tense verbs*
   What else did you do?   *in the responses.)*
   And what else did you do?
4. How long have you been living in *(this city)?*
   How long will you have been living here by the end of *(the semester/term, etc.)?*
5. Where did you eat dinner last night?
   What did you have?
   How was it?
   What did you do after you had eaten?
6. What were you doing at 8 o'clock last night?
   What will you be doing at 8 o'clock tomorrow night?
7. Are you taking any courses besides English?
   How is everything going?
   What are you doing in one of your *(other courses/other English classes)?*
8. How long have we been talking to each other?
   What have we been talking about?
9. How do you like living here?
   Have you had any interesting experiences since you came here?
   Have you met any interesting people?
10. What do you think the world will be like when you are seventy years old?

PART II. Switch roles.
11. What are you doing right now?
    What are you going to be doing for the next ten minutes or so?
12. What did you do last weekend? *(Speaker A: Listen carefully for past tense*
    What else did you do?   *verbs in the responses.)*
    And what else did you do?
13. What is the teacher doing?
    How long has he/she been *(doing that)?*
14. What are you going to do for the rest of today?
    What will you be doing at midnight?

15. What will you have done by the time you go to bed tonight?
16. How long have you been studying English since you came here?
    How long had you studied English before you came here?
    What have you been doing outside of class to improve your English?
17. What have we been doing for the past ten minutes or so?
    Why have we been *(doing that)?*
18. What are some of the things you have done since you came to *(this city)?*
19. Have you read a newspaper lately?
    What is happening in the world?
20. What countries have you visited?
    When did you visit *(a particular country)?* Why did you go there?
    What did you like about that country? What did you dislike about that country?
    Are you planning to go there again someday?

5-1 ADVERB CLAUSES OF TIME: FORM

adverb clause main clause (a) **When the phone rang,** the baby woke up.	In (a): **When the phone rang** is an adverb clause of time. An adverb clause is one kind of dependent clause. A dependent clause must be attached to an independent, or main, clause. In (a): **the baby woke up** is the main clause.
(b) *INCORRECT:* When the phone rang. The baby woke up. (c) The phone rang. The baby woke up.	Example (b) is incorrect because the adverb clause is not connected to the main clause. Example (c) is correct because there is no adverb clause. The two main clauses are both independent sentences.
(d) **When the phone rang,** the baby woke up. (e) The baby woke up **when the phone rang.**	Examples (d) and (e) have the same meaning. An adverb clause can come in front of a main clause, as in (d), or follow the main clause, as in (e). Notice that a comma is used to separate the two clauses when the adverb clause comes first.

☐ **EXERCISE 6. Adverb clauses of time. (Chart 5-1)**
    Directions: Add necessary punctuation and capitalization. Identify adverb clauses and main clauses. Do not add or delete any words.

    Example: when Sam was in New York he stayed with his cousins
        → **W**hen Sam was in New York**,** he stayed with his cousins.

    1. we went inside when it began to rain

    2. it began to rain we went inside

    3. when it began to rain we went inside

    4. when the mail comes my assistant opens it

    5. my assistant opens the mail when it comes

    6. the mail comes around ten o'clock every morning my assistant opens it

☐ **EXERCISE 7. Preview of Chart 5-2.**

Directions: Complete the sentences with your own words. Then, put brackets around the adverb clause in each sentence.

1. I will call you [before I ___come over___.]

2. Last night I went to bed after I _____ my homework.

3. Tonight I will go to bed after I _____ my homework.

4. Ever since I was a child, I _____ afraid of dogs.

5. Jane's contact lens popped out while she _____ basketball.

6. Be sure to reread your composition for errors before you _____ it in to the teacher tomorrow.

7. By the time I left my apartment this morning, the mail carrier _____ the mail.

8. I have known Jim Bates since he _____ ten years old.

9. A black cat ran across the road as I _____ my car to work this morning.

10. By the time I leave this city, I _____ here for four months.

11. Whenever Mark _____ angry, his nose gets red.

12. I _____ to the beach whenever the weather was nice, but now I don't have time to do that because I have to study.

13. We will have a big party when _____.

14. The next time I _____ to Hawaii, I'm going to visit Mauna Loa, the world's largest active volcano.

15. I had fried chicken the last time I _____ at that restaurant.

5-2 USING ADVERB CLAUSES TO SHOW TIME RELATIONSHIPS

*after**	(a) **After** *she graduates*, she will get a job. (b) **After** *she (had) graduated*, she got a job.	A present tense, NOT a future tense, is used in an adverb clause of time, as in examples (a) and (c). (See Chart 4-3, p. 55, for tense usage in future time clauses.)
*before**	(c) I will leave **before** *he comes*. (d) I (had) left **before** *he came*.	
when	(e) **When** *I arrived*, he *was talking* on the phone. (f) **When** *I got there*, he *had* already *left*. (g) **When** *it began to rain*, I *stood* under a tree. (h) **When** *I was in Chicago*, I *visited* the museums. (i) **When** *I see him tomorrow*, I *will ask* him.	**when** = *at that time* Notice the different time relationships expressed by the tenses.
while *as*	(j) **While** *I was walking home*, it began to rain. (k) **As** *I was walking home*, it began to rain.	**while, as** = *during that time*
by the time	(l) **By the time** *he arrived*, we *had* already *left*. (m) **By the time** *he comes*, we *will have* already *left*.	**by the time** = *one event is completed before another event* Notice the use of the past perfect and future perfect in the main clause.
since	(n) I *haven't seen* him **since** *he left this morning*. (o) I*'ve known* her **ever since** *I was a child*.	**since** = *from that time to the present* In (o): **ever** adds emphasis. Note: The present perfect is used in the main clause.
until *till*	(p) We stayed there **until** *we finished our work*. (q) We stayed there **till** *we finished our work*.	**until, till** = *to that time and then no longer* (**Till** *is used more in speaking than in writing; it is generally not used in formal English.*)
as soon as *once*	(r) **As soon as** *it stops raining*, we will leave. (s) **Once** *it stops raining*, we will leave.	**as soon as, once** = *when one event happens, another event happens soon afterward*
as long as *so long as*	(t) I will never speak to him again **as long as** *I live*. (u) I will never speak to him again **so long as** *I live*.	**as long as, so long as** = *during all that time, from beginning to end*
whenever *every time*	(v) **Whenever** *I see her*, I say hello. (w) **Every time** *I see her*, I say hello.	**whenever** = *every time*
the first time *the last time* *the next time*	(x) **The first time** *(that) I went to New York*, I went to an opera. (y) I saw two plays **the last time** *(that) I went to New York*. (z) **The next time** *(that) I go to New York*, I'm going to see a ballet.	Adverb clauses can be introduced by the following: **the** $\left\{\begin{array}{l}\textbf{\textit{first}}\\\textbf{\textit{second}}\\\textbf{\textit{third, etc.}}\\\textbf{\textit{last}}\\\textbf{\textit{next}}\\\textbf{\textit{etc.}}\end{array}\right\}$ **time (that)**

*After and *before* are commonly used in the following expressions:

shortly *after*	**shortly** *before*
a short time *after*	**a short time** *before*
a little while *after*	**a little while** *before*
not long *after*	**not long** *before*
soon *after*	

□ EXERCISE 8. Using adverb clauses to show time relationships.
(Chapters 1 → 4; Charts 5-1 and 5-2)
Directions: Combine each pair of sentences. Use the given time words if they are possible and appropriate to the meaning. Cross out inappropriate ones.
In the new sentences, omit unnecessary words, make any necessary changes (paying special attention to verb forms), and punctuate carefully.

1. The other passengers will get on the bus soon. Then we'll leave.
   a. while   b. as soon as   c. the last time

   → *As soon as the other passengers get on the bus, we'll leave.*

2. I turned off the lights. After that, I left the room.
   a. before   b. by the time   c. after

   → *I turned off the lights before I left the room.*
   → *By the time I left the room, I had turned off the lights.*
   → *After I turned off the lights, I left the room.*

3. Susan sometimes feels nervous. Then she chews her nails.
   a. whenever   b. before   c. every time

4. The frying pan caught on fire. I was making dinner at that time.
   a. by the time   b. while   c. as soon as

5. We were sitting down to eat. Someone knocked on the door at that moment.
   a. just as*   b. just after*   c. just before*

6. The singer finished her song. The audience immediately burst into applause.
   a. as long as   b. as soon as   c. immediately after

7. We have to wait here. Nancy will come.
   a. as soon as   b. after   c. until

8. Nancy will come. We can leave for the theater.
   a. after   b. as soon as   c. when

9. My roommate walked into the room yesterday. I immediately knew that something was wrong.
   a. just as soon as   b. when   c. whenever

10. I stood up to give my speech. Immediately before that, I got butterflies in my stomach.
    a. until   b. while   c. just before

11. I saw the great pyramids of Egypt in the moonlight. I was speechless.
    a. until   b. the first time   c. before

12. Jane has gotten three promotions in the last six months. She started working at this company six months ago.
    a. before   b. since   c. when

13. I had gone to bed. The phone rang.
    a. shortly after   b. not long after   c. a short time after

---

*Just adds the idea of "immediately":
    just as = at that immediate or same moment
    just before = immediately before
    just after = immediately after

14. The weather will get warmer soon. Then we can start playing tennis again.
    a. while   b. when   c. once

15. Shakespeare died in 1616. He had written more than 37 plays before then.
    a. while   b. once   c. by the time

16. Sam will go to the movies again. He'll remember to take his glasses then.
    a. the next time   b. as long as   c. by the time

17. I will not forget Mr. Tanaka. I will live for a long time.
    a. as   b. as long as   c. so long as

18. Mohammad had never heard about Halloween.*
    Then he came to the U.S.
    a. before
    b. until
    c. since

□ **EXERCISE 9. Verb tenses in adverb clauses of time. (Chart 5-2)**
    Directions: Choose the best completion. Give yourself seven minutes to complete this exercise.

1. As soon as Martina saw the fire, she _____ the fire department.
      A. was telephoning   B. telephoned   C. had telephoned   D. has telephoned

2. Before Jennifer won the lottery, she _____ any kind of contest.
      A. hasn't entered   B. doesn't enter   C. wasn't entering   D. hadn't entered

3. Every time Prakash sees a movie made in India, he _____ homesick.
      A. will have felt   B. felt   C. feels   D. is feeling

4. Since I left Venezuela six years ago, I _____ to visit friends and family several times.
      A. return   B. will have returned C. am returning   D. have returned

5. While he was washing his new car, Mr. De Rosa _____ a small dent in the rear fender.
      A. has discovered   B. was discovering   C. is discovering   D. discovered

6. Yesterday while I was attending a sales meeting, Matthew _____ on the company's annual report.
      A. was working   B. had been working C. has worked   D. works

7. Tony _____ to have children until his little daughter was born. After she won his heart, he decided he wanted a big family.
      A. doesn't want   B. hadn't wanted   C. wasn't wanting   D. hasn't wanted

---

*Halloween (which occurs every year on October 31) is a holiday celebrated in the U.S., Canada, Great Britain, and Ireland. Children dress up in costumes and go from house to house, asking for a "treat" such as candy or fruit.

8. After the horse threw her to the ground for the third time, Jennifer picked herself up and said, "I _____ on another horse as long as I live."
   A. never ride
   B. have never ridden
   C. will never ride
   D. do not ride

9. The next time Paul _____ to New York, he will visit the Metropolitan Museum's famous collection of international musical instruments.
   A. will fly   B. flies   C. has flown   D. will have flown

10. Ever since Maurice arrived, he _____ quietly in the corner. Is something wrong?
    A. sat   B. has been sitting   C. had been sitting   D. will have sat

11. After Nancy _____ for twenty minutes, she began to feel tired.
    A. jogging   B. had been jogging   C. has been jogging   D. has jogged

12. Peter, _____ since you got home from football practice?
    A. have you eaten   B. will you eat   C. are you eating   D. do you eat

13. By the time the young birds _____ the nest for good, they will have learned how to fly.
    A. will leave   B. will have left   C. are leaving   D. leave

14. The last time I _____ in Athens, the weather was hot and humid.
    A. had been   B. was   C. am   D. will have been

☐ EXERCISE 10. Using adverb clauses to show time relationships. (Chart 5-2)
   Directions: Create a sentence from the given words. Do not change the order of the words. Use any appropriate verb forms and punctuate correctly.

   Examples: as soon as + I + finish + I
                → ***As soon as I finish*** my report, ***I***'ll call you and we'll go out to dinner.
                I + after + I + climb
                → *I was exhausted **after I climbed** the stairs to the eighth floor.*

   1. whenever + I + go + I
   2. by the time + I + get + I
   3. I + since + I + leave
   4. just as + I + open + I
   5. I + as soon as + I + eat
   6. I + when + I + be
   7. the first time + I + see + I
   8. I + until + I + be
   9. while + I + look + I
   10. I + before + I + drive

☐ EXERCISE 11. Review of verb tenses. (Chapters 1 → 5)

Directions: Use any appropriate tense for the verbs in parentheses. In some instances, more than one tense is possible.*

1. A: There is something I have to tell you.

   B: Go ahead. I *(listen)* _____ .

2. A: Hi, Ann. *(you, meet)* _____ my friend George Smith?

   B: No, I *(have, never)* _____ the pleasure.

   A: Then let me introduce you.

3. A: Stop! What *(you, do)* _____ ?

   B: I *(try)* _____ to get this piece
   of toast out of the toaster. It's stuck.

   A: Well, don't use a knife. You *(electrocute)*
   _____ yourself!

   B: What do you suggest I do?

   A: Unplug it first.

4. A: There's Jack.

   B: Where?

   A: He *(lie)* _____ on the grass under that tree over there.

   B: Oh, yes. I *(see)* _____ him. He *(look, certainly)* _____
   _____ comfortable. Let's go talk to him.

5. A: I *(go)* _____ to a play last night.

   B: *(it, be)* _____ any good?

   A: I thought so. I *(enjoy)* _____ it a lot.

   B: What *(you, see)* _____ ?

   A: *Arsenic and Old Lace.* I *(see, never)* _____ it before.

   B: Oh, I *(see)* _____ that play too. I *(see)* _____ it a
   couple of years ago. It *(be)* _____ good, *(be, not)* _____ it?

6. A: I was in your hometown last month. It looked like a nice town. I *(be, never)*
   _____ there before.

   B: What *(you, do)* _____ in that part of the country?

   A: My wife and I *(drive)* _____ to Washington, D.C., to
   visit her family.

_____

*Your teacher can tell you if one tense is more idiomatic, i.e., more likely to be used by a native speaker.

7. A: *(you, take)* _____ Econ 120 this semester?

B: No, I _____ .

A: *(you, take, ever)* _____ it?

B: Yes, I _____ .

A: When *(you, take)* _____ it?

B: Last semester.

A: Who *(be)* _____ your professor?

B: Dr. Lee.

A: Oh, I have the same professor. What *(he, be)* _____ like?

B: He *(be)* _____ very good.

8. A: May I borrow some money? My check *(be)* _____ supposed to arrive yesterday, but I still *(receive, not)* _____ it. I need to buy a book for one of my classes, but I *(have, not)* _____ any money.

B: Sure. I'd be happy to lend you some. How much *(you, need)* _____ ?

A: How about five dollars? Thanks. I *(pay)* _____ you back as soon as I *(get)* _____ my check.

9. A: Hello?

B: Hello. May I speak to Sue?

A: She *(be, not)* _____ in right now. May I take a message?

B: Yes. This is Art O'Brien. Would you please ask her to meet me at the library this afternoon? I *(sit)* _____ at one of the study booths on the second floor.

10. A: Alex, *(you, know)* _____ where Ms. Rodriguez is? I *(look)* _____ for her for the past hour.

B: She *(see)* _____ Mr. Frost at the moment about the shipment of parts which we *(receive)* _____ earlier today. Some of the parts are missing.

A: Uh, oh. That *(sound)* _____ like trouble. Please tell Ms. Rodriguez to phone me when she *(have)* _____ some free time. I *(work)* _____ in my office all afternoon.

☐ EXERCISE 12. Review of verb tenses. (Chapters 1 → 5)

Directions: Use any appropriate tense.

JOSE: Hi, my name is Jose.

ALI: Hi, my name is Ali.

(1) JOSE: *(you, study)* ———————————— at this university?

(2) ALI: Yes, I *(be)* —————————— . And you?

(3) JOSE: Yes, I *(be)* ———————————— here since last September. Before that I

(study) ———————————— English at another school.

(4) ALI: What *(you, take)* ———————————— this term?

(5) JOSE: I *(take)* ———————————— chemistry, math, psychology, and American

history. What *(you, take)* ————————————?

(6) ALI: I *(study)* ———————————— English. I *(need)* —————————— to improve

my English before I *(take)* —————————— regular academic courses next semester.

(7) JOSE: How long *(you, be)* ———————————— here?

(8) ALI: I *(be)* ———————————— here since the beginning of this semester.

Actually, I *(arrive)* ———————————— in the United States six months ago, but I

(study) ———————————— English at this university only since

January. Before that I *(live)* —————————— with my brother in Washington, D.C.

(9) JOSE: You *(speak)* —————————— English very well. *(you, study)* ————————————

———————————— a lot of English before you *(come)* —————————— to the

United States?

(10) ALI: Yes. I *(study)* —————————— English for ten years in my own country. And

also, I *(spend)* —————————— some time in Canada a couple of years ago. I

(pick) —————————— up a lot of English while I *(live)* —————————— there.

(11) JOSE: You *(be)* —————————— lucky. When I *(come)* —————————— to the United

States, I *(study, never)* ———————————————— any English at all. So I

had to spend a whole year studying nothing but English before I *(start)*

———————————— school.

(12) ALI: How long *(you, plan)* ———————————————— to be in the United States?

(13) JOSE: I *(be, not)* —————————— sure. Probably by the time I *(return)*

———————————— home, I *(be)* ———————————— here for at least

five years. How about you?

(14) ALI: I *(hope)* —————————— to be finished with all my work in two and a half years.

☐ EXERCISE 13. Review of verb tenses. (Chapters 1 → 5)

Directions: Use any appropriate tense.

Dear Ann,

(1)   I *(receive)* _____ your letter about two weeks ago and *(try)*

(2)   _____ to find time to write you back ever since. I *(be)* _____

(3)   very busy lately. In the past two weeks, I *(have)* _____ four tests, and I

(4)   have another one next week. In addition, a friend *(stay)* _____

(5)   with me since last Thursday. She wanted to see the city, so we *(spend)* _____

(6)   _____ a lot of time visiting some of the interesting places here. We *(be)*

(7)   _____ to the zoo, the art museum, and the botanical gardens. Yesterday

(8)   we *(go)* _____ to the park and *(watch)* _____ a

balloon race. Between showing her the city and studying for my exams, I *(have, barely)*

(9)   _____ enough time to breathe.

(10)   Right now it *(be)* _____ 3:00 A.M. and I *(sit)* _____

(11)   at my desk. I *(sit)* _____ here five hours doing my studying. My

(12)   friend's plane *(leave)* _____ at 6:05, so I *(decide)* _____ _____

(13)   not to go to bed. That's why I *(write)* _____ _____ to you at such an early hour

(14)   in the day. I *(get)* _____ a little sleepy, but I would rather stay up.

(15)   I *(take)* _____ a nap after I *(get)* _____ back

from taking her to the airport.

(16)   How *(you, get)* _____ along? How *(your classes, go)*

(17)   _____? Please write soon.

Yours,

Janet

☐ EXERCISE 14. Writing. (Chapters 1 → 5)

Directions: Write a letter to a friend or family member. Discuss your activities, thoughts, feelings, and adventures in the present, past, and future. The purpose of this exercise is for you to use every possible tense.

Write about what you *do, are doing, have done, have been doing, did, were doing, had done, had been doing, will do, are going to do, will be doing, will have done,* and *will have been doing.* Include appropriate time expressions: *today, every day, right now, already, so far, since, next week, etc.*

Use the verb tenses in any order you wish and as many times as necessary. Try to write a natural-sounding letter.

□ **EXERCISE 15. Review of verb tenses. (Chapters 1 → 5)**

Directions: Complete the sentences with the words in parentheses. Use any appropriate tense.

(1)   Almost every part of the world *(experience)* ———————————— an earthquake

(2)   in recent years, and almost every part of the world *(experience)* ————————————

(3)   earthquakes in the years to come. Since the ancient Chinese *(begin)* ——————— to keep

(4)   records several thousand years ago, more than 13 million earthquakes *(occur)* ———————

(5)   ——————— worldwide by some estimates. What *(cause)* ————————————

(6)   earthquakes? Throughout time, different cultures *(develop)* ————————————

myths to explain these violent earth movements.

According to a Japanese myth, a playful catfish lives in the mud under the earth. Whenever it

(7)   feels like playing, it *(wave)* ——————— its fat tail around in the mud. The result?

(8)   Earthquakes. From India comes the story of six strong elephants who *(hold)* ——————— up

(9)   the earth on their heads. Whenever one elephant *(move)* ——————— its head, the earth

trembles.

(10)   Nowadays, although scientists *(know)* ——————— more about the causes of

earthquakes, they still cannot prevent the terrible damage. One of the strongest quakes in the

(11)   20th century *(happen)* ——————— in Anchorage, Alaska, on March 24, 1964, at

(12)   about six o'clock in the evening. When the earthquake *(strike)* ——————— that

(13)   evening, many families *(sit)* ——————— down to eat dinner. People in the city

(14)   *(find, suddenly)* ——————— themselves in the dark because most of

the lights in the city went out when the earthquake occurred. Many people *(die)*

(15)   ——————— instantly when tall buildings *(collapse)* ——————— and *(send)*

(16)   ——————— tons of brick and concrete crashing into the streets.

(17)   When *(the next earthquake, occur)* ———————————————? No

one really knows for sure.

(18)   Interestingly enough, throughout history animals *(help, often)* ————————————

people predict earthquakes shortly before they happen. At present, some scientists *(study)*

(19)   ——————— catfish because catfish swim excitedly just before an earthquake.

(20)   According to some studies, snakes, monkeys, and rodents *(appear, also)* ———————

(21)   ——————— to be sensitive to the approach of violent movement in the earth's

(22)   surface. Some animals *(seem)* ——————— to know a great deal more than humans

about when an earthquake will occur.*

———————

*NOTE: *When an earthquake will occur* is a noun clause, not an adverb clause of time. See Chapter 12 for information about noun clauses.

(23)   In recent years, scientists (*develop*) _____ many extremely

(24)   sensitive instruments. Perhaps someday the instruments (*be*) _____ able to

give us a sufficiently early warning so that we can be waiting calmly in a safe place when the

(25)   next earthquake (*strike*) _____ .

☐ EXERCISE 16. Activity: review of verb tenses. (Chapters 1 → 5)
     Directions: Before you come to class, think of an interesting, dangerous, or amusing experience you have had. You will then tell the story to a classmate, who will report that experience in a composition.

☐ EXERCISE 17. Activity: review of verb tenses. (Chapters 1 → 5)
     Directions: In a short speech (two or three minutes), summarize an article in a recent newspaper. You may speak from notes if necessary, but your notes should contain no more than fifteen words. Use your notes only for a very brief outline of important information.
          Present your speech to a small group or to the class. Listeners can write one- or two-sentence summaries of each speech.

☐ EXERCISE 18. Activity: review of verb tenses. (Chapters 1 → 5)
     Directions: Form a small group. Discuss the past, present, and future of one (or more) of the topics. As a group, write a summary of the discussion.

     Topics:
          1. means of transportation
          2. clothes
          3. agriculture
          4. medical science
          5. means of communication

☐ EXERCISE 19. Error analysis: general review. (Chapters 1 → 5)
     Directions: The following sentences are adapted from student writing and contain typical errors of different kinds. See how many of these errors you can find and correct.

     1. I am living at 3371 grand avenue since last September.

     2. I have been in New York city two week ago.

     3. My country have change its capital city five time.

     4. Dormitory life is not quiet. Everyone shouted and make a lot of noise in the halls.

     5. My friends will meet me when I will arrive at the airport.

     6. Hasn't anyone ever tell you to knock on the door before you enter someone else's

          room? Didn't your parents taught you that?

7. When I was a child, I viewed thing from a much lower height. Many physical objects around me appear very large. When I want to move something such as a chair, I need help.

8. I will intend to go back home when I will finish my education.

9. The phone rung while I doing the dishes. I dry my hands and answer it. When I am hear my husband voice, I very happy.

10. I am in the United States for the last four months. During this time, I had done many thing and saw many place.

11. When the old man started to walk back to his cave, the sun has already hided itself behind the mountain.

12. While I am writing my composition last night, someone knocks on the door.

13. I'm studing English at an English conversation school two time a week.

14. Getting accustomed to a different cultures are not easy.

15. I'm really glad you to visit my hometown this year.

16. While I was visitting my cousin in Los Angeles. We went to a restaurant and eat Thai food.

17. We ate dinner. We watched TV after.

18. When I was in my country, I am afraid to come to the United States. I thought I couldn't walk outside at night because of the terrible crime. But now I am having a different opinion. I live in this small town for three month and learn that there is very little crime here.

19. Before I came to the United State. I pictured the U.S. as an exciting place with honesty, hard-working, well-mannered peoples. After I came to United State since four month ago this picture had changed. The manners of the students while they are in the cafeteria. They are really bad. I am also thinking that office workers here lazy. People in my country works a lot harder.

CHAPTER 6
Subject–Verb Agreement

CONTENTS

☐ EXERCISE 1. Preview: using -S/-ES. (Charts 2-1, 6-1, 6-2, and 7-4)

Directions: In the following sentences, add final *-s/-es.* Do not change or omit any other words. Discuss spelling and pronunciation. Discuss why you need to add *-s/-es.* All of the sentences are simple present.

1. I have two ~~pen~~. (pens = a plural noun) *(pens)*

2. Tom work hard every day.

3. Our solar system consist of nine planet.

4. The earth rotate around the sun.

5. All animal need water.

6. A dog need fresh water every day.

7. Student take test.

8. A swallow is a small, graceful bird with a long tail and powerful wing.

9. Swallow are joyful creature.

10. Butterfly are beautiful.

11. Hawaii has beautiful sunset.

12. A library contain a lot of book.

13. Encyclopedia contain information about many thing.

14. Martha watch TV every evening.

15. Alex almost never change his mind.

6-1 FINAL -S/-ES: USE, PRONUNCIATION, AND SPELLING

(a) NOUN + -s: *Friends* are important.
NOUN + -ES: I like my *classes*.
	A final **-s** or **-es** is added to a noun to make the noun plural.
	
	    friend = *a singular noun*
	    friends = *a plural noun*

(b) VERB + -s: Mary *works* at the bank. VERB + -ES: John *watches* birds.	A final **-s** or **-es** is added to a simple present verb when the subject is a singular noun (e.g., *Mary, my father, the machine*) or third person singular pronoun (*she, he, it*). ***Mary works*** = *singular* ***She works*** = *singular* ***The students work*** = *plural* ***They work*** = *plural*

PRONUNCIATION OF -S/-ES

(c) seats → *seat*/s/ ropes → *rope*/s/ backs → *back*/s/	Final **-s** is pronounced /s/ after voiceless sounds, as in (c): "t," "p," and "k" are examples of voiceless sounds.★
(d) seeds → *seed*/z/ robes → *robe*/z/ bags → *bag*/z/ sees → *see*/z/	Final **-s** is pronounced /z/ after voiced sounds, as in (h): "d," "b," "g," and "ee" are examples of voiced sounds.★
(e) dishes → *dish*/əz/ catches → *catch*/əz/ kisses → *kiss*/əz/ mixes → *mix*/əz/ prizes → *prize*/əz/ edges → *edge*/əz/	Final **-s** and **-es** are pronounced /əz/ after "-sh," "-ch," "-s," "-z," and "-ge"/"-dge" sounds. The /əz/ ending adds a syllable. All of the words in (e) are pronounced with two syllables. COMPARE: All of the words in (c) and (d) are pronounced with one syllable.

SPELLING: FINAL -S vs. -ES

(f) sing → *sings* song → *songs*	For most words (whether a verb or a noun), simply a final **-s** is added to spell the word correctly.
(g) wash → *washes* watch → *watches* class → *classes* buzz → *buzzes* box → *boxes*	Final **-es** is added to words that end in **-sh, -ch, -s, -z,** and **-x.**
(h) toy → *toys* buy → *buys* (i) baby → *babies* cry → *cries*	For words that end in **-y:** In (h): If **-y** is preceded by a vowel, only **-s** is added. In (i): If **-y** is preceded by a consonant, the **-y** is changed to **-i** and **-es** is added.

★See Chart 2-6, p. 20, for an explanation of voiced vs. voiceless sounds.

☐ EXERCISE 2. Pronunciation of final -S/-ES. (Chart 6-1)

Directions: Practice pronouncing the following words. Say the final **-s/-es** sounds loudly and clearly. Then write the pronunciation of final **-s/-es** after each word. Work in pairs, in groups, or as a class.

GROUP A.

1. cats → /s/
2. feeds _____
3. hates _____
4. lids _____
5. sleeps _____
6. robs _____

7. trips _____
8. grabs _____
9. wishes _____
10. matches _____
11. guesses _____

GROUP B.

12. books _____
13. homes _____
14. occurs _____
15. fixes _____
16. sizes _____
17. pages _____

18. unlocks _____
19. fills _____
20. ashes _____
21. sniffs _____
22. miles _____
23. rugs _____

GROUP C.

24. arranges _____
25. itches _____
26. relaxes _____
27. rises _____
28. laughs _____
29. days _____

30. pies _____
31. agrees _____
32. faces _____
33. quizzes _____
34. judges _____
35. asks _____

☐ EXERCISE 3. Spelling of final -S/-ES. (Chart 6-1)

Directions: Add **-s** or **-es** to these words to spell them correctly, and give the pronunciation of the ending.

1. passenger s /z/
2. tax es /əz/
3. talk_____ _____
4. blush_____ _____
5. discover_____ _____
6. develop_____ _____
7. season_____ _____
8. flash_____ _____
9. hall_____ _____

10. touch_____ _____
11. cough_____ _____
12. press_____ _____
13. method_____ _____
14. mix_____ _____
15. try_____ _____
16. tray_____ _____
17. enemy_____ _____
18. guy_____ _____

☐ EXERCISE 4. Pronunciation and spelling of final -S/-ES. (Chart 6-1)
Directions: On a separate sheet of paper, draw three vertical columns. Write /s/ at the top of the first column, /z/ at the top of the second, and /əz/ at the top of the third. Using words of their own choosing, your teacher and/or your classmates in turn will say a word that has a final **-s/-es**. Write that word in the appropriate column according to how the ending is pronounced.

Example:
SPEAKER A: Number one: *windows*
SPEAKER B: Number two: *reaches*
SPEAKER C: Number three: *students*
SPEAKER D: Number four: *passes*
Etc.

	/s/	/z/	/əz/
1.		windows	
2.			reaches
3.	students		
4.			passes
5.			
Etc.			

☐ EXERCISE 5. Pronunciation of final -S/-ES. (Chart 6-1)
Directions: Practice the pronunciation of final **-s/-es** by reading these sentences aloud.

1. The teacher encourages the students to speak freely.
2. Chickens, ducks, and turkeys lay eggs.
3. He possesses many fine qualities.
4. My wages are low, but my taxes are high.
5. The cafeteria serves good sandwiches.
6. He coughs, sneezes, and wheezes.
7. People come in many shapes and sizes.
8. He practices pronunciation by reading sentences aloud.
9. She bought some shirts, shoes, socks, dresses, slacks, blouses, earrings, and necklaces.
10. She scratches her chin when it itches.

☐ EXERCISE 6. Use of final -S/-ES. (Chart 6-1)

Directions: What do the following people or things do? Follow the pattern in the example. Say final *-s/-es* sounds loudly and clearly. Work in pairs, in groups, or as a class.

Example: a birdwatcher

SPEAKER A *(book open):* What does a birdwatcher do?

SPEAKER B *(book closed):* A birdwatcher watches birds.

1. a stamp collector
2. an animal trainer
3. a bank robber
4. a dog catcher
5. a book publisher
6. a tax collector
7. a ticket taker
8. a fire extinguisher
9. a mind reader
10. a bullfighter
11. a wage earner
12. a storyteller

☐ EXERCISE 7. Use of final -S/-ES. (Chart 6-1)

Directions: What do these people, animals, and things do? Respond in complete sentences. Say the final *-s/-es* sounds loudly and clearly.

Example: a bird

SPEAKER A *(book open):* What does a bird do?

SPEAKER B *(book closed):* A bird flie**s** /sing**s** /build**s** nest**s** /etc.

1. a baby
2. a telephone
3. a star
4. a dog
5. a duck
6. a ball
7. a heart
8. a river
9. a cat
10. a door
11. a clock
12. an airplane
13. a doctor
14. a teacher
15. a psychologist

☐ EXERCISE 8. Preview: subject–verb agreement. (Charts 6-2 → 6-5)

Directions: Choose the correct answer in parentheses.

1. The results of Dr. Noll's experiment *(was,* were*)* published in a scientific journal.
2. The weather in the southern states *(gets, get)* very hot during the summer.
3. A woman and her child *(is, are)* waiting to see Dr. Chang.
4. Every man, woman, and child *(is, are)* protected under the law.
5. Washing the dishes *(is, are)* the children's job.
6. A lot of the students *(is, are)* already here.
7. Some of the furniture in our apartment *(is, are)* secondhand.
8. Some of the desks in the classroom *(is, are)* broken.
9. At least three-quarters of that book on famous Americans *(is, are)* about people who lived in the nineteenth century.
10. One of the countries I would like to visit *(is, are)* Italy.
11. Some of the cities I would like to visit *(is, are)* Rome and Venice.
12. Each student in the class *(has, have)* to have a book.
13. Each of the students *(has, have)* a notebook.
14. None of the students *(was, were)* late today.
15. The number of students in this room right now *(is, are)* twenty.

16. A number of students in the class *(speaks, speak)* English very well.
17. There *(is, are)* some interesting pictures in today's paper.
18. There *(is, are)* an incorrect statement in that newspaper article.
19. The United States *(is, are)* located in North America.
20. Economics *(is, are)* Dan's favorite subject.
21. Ten minutes *(is, are)* more than enough time to complete this exercise.
22. Most people *(likes, like)* to go to the zoo.
23. The police *(is, are)* coming. I've already called them.
24. Japanese *(is, are)* very difficult for English speakers to learn.
25. The Japanese *(has, have)* a long and interesting history.
26. The elderly in my country *(is, are)* cared for by their children and grandchildren.
27. My cousin, along with my aunt and uncle, *(works, work)* in my grandpa's hardware store.
28. Cattle *(is, are)* considered sacred in India.
29. Anna, as well as her two older sisters, *(is, are)* in college.
30. This exercise on singular–plural agreement of subjects and verbs *(is, are)* easy.

6-2 BASIC SUBJECT–VERB AGREEMENT

SINGULAR VERB	PLURAL VERB	
(a) My *friend* **lives** in Boston.	(b) My *friends* **live** in Boston.	*verb* + **-s/-es** = third person singular in the simple present tense *noun* + **-s/-es** = plural
	(c) My *brother* **and** *sister* **live** in Boston. (d) My *brother, sister,* **and** *cousin* **live** in Boston.	Two or more subjects connected by **and** require a plural verb.
(e) **Every** *man, woman,* **and** *child* **needs** love. (f) **Each** *book* **and** *magazine* **is** listed in the card catalog.		EXCEPTION: **Every** and **each** are always followed immediately by singular nouns. (See Chart 7-13, p. 128.) In this case, even when there are two (or more) nouns connected by **and**, the verb is singular.
(g) That *book* on political parties *is* interesting. (i) My *dog,* as well as my cats, *likes* cat food. (k) The *book* that I got from my parents *was* very interesting.	(h) The *ideas* in that book *are* interesting. (j) My *dogs,* as well as my cat, *like* cat food. (l) The *books* I bought at the bookstore *were* expensive.	Sometimes a phrase or clause separates a subject from its verb. These interrupting structures do not affect basic agreement. For example, in (g) the interrupting prepositional phrase **on political parties** does not change the fact that the verb **is** must agree with the subject **book**. In (k) and (l): The subject and verb are separated by an adjective clause. (See Chapter 13.)
(m) *Growing* flowers *is* her hobby.		A gerund used as the subject of the sentence requires a singular verb. (See Chart 14-11, p. 323.)

☐ **EXERCISE 9. Subject–verb agreement. (Chart 6-2)**
  Directions: Choose the correct answer in parentheses.

1. The extent of Jane's knowledge on various complex subjects *(astounds, astound)* me.
2. The subjects you will be studying in this course *(is, are)* listed in the syllabus.
3. Lettuce *(is, are)* good for you.
4. Oranges, tomatoes, fresh strawberries, cabbage, and lettuce *(is, are)* rich in vitamin C.
5. The professor and the student *(agrees, agree)* on that point.
6. Almost every professor and student at the university *(approves, approve)* of the choice of Dr. Brown as the new president.
7. Each girl and boy in the sixth-grade class *(has, have)* to do a science project.
8. Making pies and cakes *(is, are)* Mrs. Reed's specialty.★
9. Getting to know students from all over the world *(is, are)* one of the best parts of my job.
10. Annie had a hard time when she was coming home from the store because the bag of groceries *(was, were)* too heavy for her to carry.

11. Where *(does, do)* your parents live?
12. Why *(was, were)* Susan and Alex late for the meeting?
13. *(Is, Are)* having the responsibility for taking care of pets good for young children?
14. Alex, as well as his two older brothers, *(has, have)* a good full-time job.

6-3 SUBJECT–VERB AGREEMENT: USING EXPRESSIONS OF QUANTITY

SINGULAR VERB	PLURAL VERB	
(a) *Some of the **book is** good.* (c) *A lot of the **equipment is** new.* (e) *Two-thirds of the **money is** mine.*	(b) *Some of the **books are** good.* (d) *A lot of my **friends are** here.* (f) *Two-thirds of the **pennies are** mine.*	In most expressions of quantity, the verb is determined by the noun (or pronoun) that follows *of*. For example: In (a): ***Some of*** + *singular noun = singular verb.* In (b): ***Some of*** + *plural noun = plural verb.*
(g) ***One*** *of my friends **is** here.* (h) ***Each*** *of my friends **is** here.* (i) ***Every one*** *of my friends **is** here.*		EXCEPTIONS: ***One of, each of,*** and ***every one of*** take singular verbs. $\left.\begin{array}{l}\textit{one of}\\\textit{each of}\\\textit{every one of}\end{array}\right\}$ + *plural noun = singular verb*
(j) ***None*** *of the boys **is** here.*	(k) ***None*** *of the boys **are** here.* (informal)	Subjects with ***none of*** are considered singular in very formal English, but plural verbs are often used in informal speech writing.
(l) ***The number*** *of students* in the class ***is*** fifteen.	(m) ***A number of*** *students **were** late for class.*	COMPARE: In (l): ***The number*** is the subject. In (m): ***A number of*** is an expression of quantity meaning "a lot of." It is followed by a plural noun and a plural verb.

★*Specialty* = American English; *speciality* = British English.

□ EXERCISE 10. Using expressions of quantity. (Chart 6-3)
   Directions: Choose the correct answer in parentheses.

1. Some of the fruit in this bowl *(is, are)* rotten.
2. Some of the apples in that bowl *(is, are)* rotten.
3. Half of the students in the class *(is, are)* from Arabic-speaking countries.
4. Half of this money *(is, are)* yours.
5. A lot of the students in the class *(is, are)* from Southeast Asia.
6. A lot of clothing in those stores *(is, are)* on sale this week.
7. One of my best friends *(is, are)* coming to visit me next month.
8. Each boy in the class *(has, have)* his own notebook.
9. Each of the boys in the class *(has, have)* his own notebook.
10. Every one of the students *(is, are)* required to take the final test.
11. None of the animals at the zoo *(is, are)* free to roam. All of them *(is, are)* in enclosures.
12. A number of students *(is, are)* absent today.
13. The number of employees in my company *(is, are)* approximately ten thousand.
14. One of the chief materials in bones and teeth *(is, are)* calcium.
15. *(Does, Do)* all of the children have their books?
16. *(Does, Do)* all of this homework have to be finished by tomorrow?
17. Why *(was, were)* some of the students excused from the examination?
18. Why *(was, were)* one of the students excused from the examination?
19. What percentage of the people in the world *(is, are)* illiterate?
20. What percentage of the earth's surface *(is, are)* covered by water?
21. *(Does, Do)* any of you know the answer to that question?

6-4 SUBJECT–VERB AGREEMENT: USING *THERE* + *BE*

(a) *There are* twenty students in my class. (b) *There's* a fly in the room.	In the structure *there* + *be*, *there* is called an "expletive." It has no meaning as a vocabulary word. It introduces the idea that something exists in a particular place. Pattern: *there* + *be* + *subject* + *expression of place*
(c) *There are* seven continents.	Sometimes the expression of place is omitted when the meaning is clear. In (c): The implied expression of place is clearly *in the world*.

SINGULAR VERB	**PLURAL VERB**	
(d) There *is* *a book* on the shelf.	(e) There *are* *some books* on the shelf.	The subject follows *be* when *there* is used. In (d): The subject is *book*. In (e): The subject is *books*.
(f) INFORMAL: There's *some books* on the shelf.		In very informal spoken English, some native speakers use a singular verb even when the subject is plural, as in (f). The use of this form is fairly frequent but is not generally considered to be grammatically correct.

□ **EXERCISE 11. Using THERE and BE. (Chart 6-4)**

Directions: Choose the correct answer in parentheses.

1. There *(isn't, aren't)* any letters in the mail for you today.
2. There *(isn't, aren't)* any mail for you today.
3. There *(is, are)* a lot of problems in the world.
4. There *(is, are)* a hole in his sock.

5. There *(is, are)* over 600,000 kinds of insects in the world.
6. How many kinds of birds *(is, are)* there in the world?
7. Why *(isn't, aren't)* there a hospital close to those villages?
8. There *(was, were)* a terrible earthquake in Iran last year.
9. Why *(is, are)* there a shortage of available apartments for rent in this city at present?
10. There *(is, are)* more women than men in my office.
11. There *(has been, have been)* a line in front of that theater every night for the past two weeks.
12. How many wars do you suppose there *(has been, have been)* in the history of the world since the dawn of civilization?

□ **EXERCISE 12. Using THERE and BE. (Chart 6-4)**

Directions: Using ***there*** and ***be,*** name some things that exist:

1. in this room
2. in this city
3. in this country
4. in the world
5. in the universe

SINGULAR VERB	
(a) *The United States **is** big.* (b) *The Philippines **consists** of more than 7,000 islands.* (c) *The United Nations **has** its headquarters in* New York City. (d) *Sears **is** a department store.*	Sometimes a proper noun that ends in **-s** is singular. In the examples, if the noun is changed to a pronoun, the singular pronoun **it** is used (not the plural pronoun **they**) because the noun is singular. In (a): **The United States = it** (not **they**).
(e) The *news **is*** interesting.	**News** is singular.
(f) *Mathematics **is** easy for her. Physics **is** easy for her* too.	Fields of study that end in **-ics** require singular verbs.
(g) *Diabetes **is** an illness.*	Certain illnesses that end in **-s** are singular: *diabetes, measles, mumps, rabies, rickets, shingles.*
(h) *Eight hours of sleep **is** enough.* (i) *Ten dollars **is** too much to pay.* (j) *Five thousand miles **is** too far to travel.*	Expressions of *time, money,* and *distance* usually require a singular verb.
(k) *Two and two **is** four.* *Two and two **equals** four.* *Two plus two **is**/**equals** four.* (l) *Five times five **is** twenty-five.*	Arithmetic expressions require singular verbs.

PLURAL VERB	
(m) *Those people **are** from Canada.* (n) *The police **have** been called.* (o) *Cattle **are** domestic animals.*	**People,** ★ **police,** and **cattle** do not end in **-s,** but are plural nouns and require plural verbs.

SINGULAR VERB	PLURAL VERB	
(p) *English **is** spoken in* many countries. (r) *Chinese **is** his native* language.	(q) *The English **drink** tea.* (s) *The Chinese **have** an* interesting history.	In (p): **English** = language. In (q): **The English** = people from England. Some nouns of nationality that end in **-sh, -ese,** and **-ch** can mean either language or people, e.g., *English, Spanish, Chinese, Japanese, Vietnamese, Portuguese, French.*
	(t) *The poor **have** many* problems. (u) *The rich **get** richer.*	A few adjectives can be preceded by **the** and used as a plural noun (without final **-s**) to refer to people who have that quality. Other examples: *the young, the elderly, the living, the dead, the blind, the deaf, the disabled.*

★The word "people" has a final **-s** *(peoples)* only when it is used to refer to ethnic or national groups: *All the peoples of the world desire peace.*

☐ EXERCISE 13. Irregularities in subject–verb agreement. (Chart 6-5)
   Directions: Choose the correct answer in parentheses.

1. The United States *(has, have)* a population of around 250 million.
2. The news about Mr. Hogan *(is, are)* surprising.
3. Massachusetts *(is, are)* a state in the northeastern part of the United States.
4. Physics *(seeks, seek)* to understand the mysteries of the physical world.
5. Statistics *(is, are)* a branch of mathematics.
6. The statistics in that report on oil production *(is, are)* incorrect.★
7. Fifty minutes *(is, are)* the maximum length of time allowed for the exam.
8. Twenty dollars *(is, are)* an unreasonable price for the necklace.
9. Six and seven *(is, are)* thirteen.
10. Many people in the world *(does, do)* not have enough to eat.
11. The police *(is, are)* prepared in case there is a riot.
12. Rabies *(is, are)* an infectious and often fatal disease.
13. The English *(is, are)* proud, independent people.
14. English *(is, are)* not my native language.
15. Many Japanese *(commutes, commute)* to their places of work.
16. Portuguese *(is, are)* somewhat similar to Spanish, *(isn't, aren't)* it?
17. The poor *(is, are)* helped by government programs.
18. The effect of a honeybee's sting on a human being *(depends, depend)* on that person's susceptibility to the bee's venom. Most people *(is, are)* not in danger if they are stung, but there *(has, have)* been instances of allergic deaths from a single honeybee sting.

☐ EXERCISE 14. Review: subject–verb agreement. (Charts 6-2 → 6-5)
   Directions: Work in pairs, in groups, or as a class.
   Speaker A: Your book is open. Read the cue.
   Speaker B: Your book is closed. Respond with *is* or *are*.

   Examples:
   SPEAKER A *(book open):*   Some of my classmates . . . .
   SPEAKER B *(book closed):*   . . . are
   SPEAKER A *(book open):*   Some of that information . . . .
   SPEAKER B *(book closed):*   . . . is

1. His idea . . . .
2. His ideas . . . .
3. People . . . .
4. Each of the students . . . .
5. Most of the fruit . . . .
6. Most of the students . . . .
7. The United States . . . .
8. The news in this morning's paper . . . .
9. One of the girls . . . .
10. French . . . .
11. The Vietnamese . . . .
12. Two-thirds of the food . . . .
13. The number of students . . . .
14. Some of the people . . . .
15. Ninety-three million people . . . .
16. The story about his adventures . . . .
17. A lot of the chairs . . . .
18. A lot of the furniture . . . .

★*Statistics* is singular when it refers to a field of study: e.g., ***Statistics is** an interesting field of study.* When it refers to particular numbers, it is used as a count noun: *singular = one statistic* (no final *-s*); *plural = two statistics.* For example: ***This statistic is** correct. **Those statistics are** incorrect.*

19. Everyone in the English classes . . . .
20. The clothes in that store . . . .
21. Most of the information in those books . . . .
22. The news from home . . . .
23. Fifty percent of the people in the world . . . .
24. Fifty percent of the world's population . . . .
25. The clothing in those stores . . . .
26. Her husband's relatives . . . .
27. Over half of the books by that author . . . .
28. A million dollars . . . .
29. The rich . . . .
30. His method of doing things . . . .
31. A number of people . . . .
32. Most of the stores in this city . . . .
33. Mathematics . . . .
34. The police . . . .
35. Everybody in the whole world . . . .

☐ EXERCISE 15. Error analysis: subject–verb agreement. (Charts 6-2 → 6-5)
   Directions: Correct the errors in subject–verb agreement. Some sentences contain no errors.

                                    are
1. The books in my office ~~is~~ very valuable to me.

2. All of the windows in our house were broken in the earthquake. *(no errors)*

3. All of the employees in that company is required to be proficient in a second language.

4. A lot of the people in my class works during the day and attends class in the evening.

5. Listening to very loud music at rock concerts have caused hearing loss in some teenagers.

6. Many of the satellites orbiting the earth is used for communications.

7. The news about the long-range effects of air pollution on the development of children's lungs is disturbing.

8. Chinese have more than fifty thousand written characters.

9. About two-thirds of the Vietnamese works in agriculture.

10. A number of planes were delayed due to the snowstorm in Denver.

11. The number of passengers affected by the delays was great.

12. More men than women are left-handed.

13. Every girl and boy are required to have certain immunizations before enrolling in public school.

14. Seventy-five percent of the people in New York City lives in upstairs apartments, not on the ground floor.

15. Unless there are a profound and extensive reform of government policies in the near future, the economic conditions in that country will continue to deteriorate.

16. While I was in Paris, some of the best food I found were not at the well-known eating places, but in small out-of-the-way cafes.

17. Where's my gloves? Have you seen them anywhere? I can't find them.

18. Where's Kenya? Can you find it for me on the map?

19. Approximately 80 percent of all the data* in computers around the world is in English.

20. Why are the police here?

21. Studying a foreign language often lead students to learn about the culture of the countries where it is spoken.

22. Two hours is too long to wait, don't you think?

23. Some of the movie about the gangsters were surprisingly funny.

Data is an irregular plural noun. (See Chart 7-1, p. 100.) Even though it is grammatically plural, it typically takes a singular verb, but a plural verb is also used, especially in very formal English:
    The **data** in the census report **is** very interesting. OR The **data** in the census report **are** very interesting.

24. Some of the movies these days contain too much violence.

25. How many people is there in Canada?

26. What is the population of Canada?

27. Which one of the continents in the world are uninhabited?

28. One of the most common names for dogs in the United States are "Rover."

29. Everybody in my family enjoy music and reading.

30. Most of the mountain peaks in the Himalayan Range is covered with snow the year round.

☐ EXERCISE 16. Review: subject–verb agreement. (Charts 6-2 → 6-5)
Directions: Write the correct form of the given verb. Use only the simple present.

1. My alarm clock _____rings_____ at seven every morning. *(ring)*

2. There _____ a lot of sheep in the field. *(be)*

3. One of my friends _____ a goldfish bowl on her kitchen table. *(keep)*

4. Sensitivity to other people's feelings _____ him a kind and understanding person. *(make)*

5. Each car, truck, and motorcycle _____ stopped at the border by customs officials. *(be)*

6. My driver's license _____ in my wallet. *(be)*

7. _____ John's uncle live in the suburbs? *(do)*

8. _____ most of the students live in the dormitories? *(do)*

9. An orange and black bird _____ sitting in that tree. *(be)*

10. An orange bird and a black bird _____ sitting in that tree. *(be)*

11. The insurance rates on our car _____ high because we live in a city. *(be)*

12. _____ January and February the coldest months of the year in the Northern Hemisphere? *(be)*

13. Almost two-thirds of the land in the southwestern areas of the country _____ unsuitable for farming. *(be)*

14. A hummingbird's heart _____ 600 times a minute. *(beat)*

15. Four hours of skiing _____ plenty of exercise. *(provide)*

16. In many respects, this magazine article on wild animals in North America _____ the very real danger of extinction that many species face. *(oversimplify)*

17. A car with poor brakes and no brake lights _____ dangerous. *(be)*

18. A number of people from the company _____ to attend the conference. *(plan)*

19. Most of the news on the front pages of both daily newspapers _____ the progress of the peace conference. *(concern)*

20. The northernmost town in the forty-eight contiguous states _____ Angle Inlet, Minnesota. *(be)*

21. The number of human skeletons found at the archaeological site _____ seven. *(be)*

22. Almost all the information in those texts on the Aztec Indians and their civilization _____ to be well researched. *(appear)*

23. Every day there _____ more than a dozen traffic accidents in the city. *(be)*

24. No news _____ good news. *(be)*

25. Every member of this class _____ English very well. *(speak)*

☐ **EXERCISE 17. Review: subject–verb agreement.** (Charts 6-2 → 6-5)

Directions: Complete the following sentences with your own words. Use only PRESENT tenses. Work in pairs, in groups, or as a class.

Examples:

SPEAKER A *(book open):* One of my . . . .

SPEAKER B *(book closed):* One of my teachers knows Chinese.

SPEAKER A *(book open):* Some of my . . . .

SPEAKER B *(book closed):* Some of my friends are coming to visit me.

1. All of the rooms in . . . .
2. In my country, there . . . .
3. A lot of . . . .
4. The people in my country . . . .
5. The number of students . . . .
6. A number of students . . . .
7. Each of . . . .
8. The United States . . . .
9. The English language . . . .
10. The English . . . .
11. English . . . .
12. One of my . . . .
13. Most of the food . . . .
14. Most of my classmates . . . .
15. Linguistics . . . .
16. Linguists . . . .
17. The news about . . . .
18. There are . . . .
19. Greece, as well as Italy and Spain, ...
20. Fish . . . .

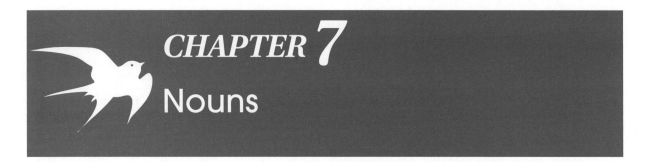

CHAPTER 7
Nouns

☐ EXERCISE 1. Preview: plural nouns.
    Directions: Write the plural form of the following nouns.

1. child   _____children_____

2. zero   _____zeroes/zeros_____

3. mouse   _____

4. monkey   _____

5. industry   _____

6. woman   _____

7. fox   _____

8. goose   _____

9. sheep   _____

10. series   _____

11. belief   _____

12. leaf   _____

13. self   _____

14. echo   _____

15. photo   _____

16. analysis   _____

17. hypothesis   _____

18. curriculum   _____

19. phenomenon   _____

20. stimulus   _____

21. offspring   _____

22. bacterium   _____

7-1 REGULAR AND IRREGULAR PLURAL NOUNS

(a) *song – songs*	The plural of most nouns is formed by adding final *-s.*★
(b) *box – boxes*	Final *-es* is added to nouns that end in *-sh, -ch, -s, -z,* and *-x.*★
(c) *baby – babies*	The plural of words that end in a consonant + *-y* is spelled *-ies.*★
(d) *man – men* *woman – women* *child – children* *ox – oxen* *foot – feet* *goose – geese* *tooth – teeth* *mouse – mice* *louse – lice*	The nouns in (d) have irregular plural forms that do not end in *-s.*
(e) *echo – echoes* *hero – heroes* *potato – potatoes* *tomato – tomatoes*	Some nouns that end in *-o* add *-es* to form the plural.
(f) *auto – autos* *ghetto – ghettos* *kangaroo – kangaroos* *kilo – kilos* *memo – memos* *photo – photos* *piano – pianos* *radio – radios* *solo – solos* *soprano – sopranos* *studio – studios* *tatoo – tatoos* *video – videos* *zoo – zoos*	Some nouns that end in *-o* add only *-s* to form the plural.
(g) *memento – mementoes/mementos* *mosquito – mosquitoes/mosquitos* *tornado – tornadoes/tornados* *volcano – volcanoes/volcanos* *zero – zeroes/zeros*	Some nouns that end in *-o* add either *-es* or *-s* to form the plural (with *-es* being the more usual plural form).
(h) *calf – calves* *half – halves* *knife – knives* *leaf – leaves* *life – lives* *loaf – loaves* *self – selves* *shelf – shelves* *thief – thieves* *wolf – wolves* *scarf – scarves/scarfs*	Some nouns that end in *-f* or *-fe* are changed to *-ves* to form the plural.
(i) *belief – beliefs* *chief – chiefs* *cliff – cliffs* *roof – roofs*	Some nouns that end in *-f* simply add *-s* to form the plural.
(j) *one deer – two deer* *one fish – two fish*★★ *one means – two means* *one offspring – two offspring* *one series – two series* *one sheep – two sheep* *one shrimp – two shrimp*★★★ *one species – two species*	Some nouns have the same singular and plural form: e.g., *One deer is . . . . Two deer are . . . .*
(k) *criterion – criteria* *phenomenon – phenomena* (l) *cactus – cacti/cactuses* *fungus – fungi* *nucleus – nuclei* *stimulus – stimuli* *syllabus – syllabi/syllabuses* (m) *formula – formulae/formulas* *vertebra – vertebrae* (n) *appendix – appendices/appendixes* *index – indices/indexes* (o) *analysis – analyses* *basis – bases* *crisis – crises* *hypothesis – hypotheses* *oasis – oases* *parenthesis – parentheses* *thesis – theses* (p) *bacterium – bacteria* *curriculum – curricula* *datum – data* *medium – media* *memorandum – memoranda*	Some nouns that English has borrowed from other languages have foreign plurals.

★For information about the pronunciation and spelling of words ending in *-s/-es*, see Chart 6-1, p. 84.

★★*Fishes* is also possible, but rarely used.

★★★Especially in British English, but also occasionally in American English, the plural of *shrimp* can be *shrimps.*

□ EXERCISE 2. Plural nouns. (Chart 7-1)

Directions: Write the correct form of the nouns in parentheses.

1. I met some interesting _____**men**_____ at the meeting last night. (man)

2. I need some ____**matches**____ to light the fire. (match)

3. The baby got two new _____. (tooth)

4. The farmer loaded his cart with _____ of fresh vegetables to take to market. His cart was pulled by two _____. (box, ox)

5. Alex saw some _____ running across the floor. (mouse)

6. The north side of the island has no _____. There are only steep _____. No one can climb these steep walls of rock. (beach, cliff)

7. If a houseplant is given too much water, its lower _____ turn yellow. (leaf)

8. Before Marie signed the contract, she talked to two _____. (attorney)

9. New scientific _____ are made every day in _____ throughout the world. (discovery, laboratory)

10. I caught several _____ in the lake. (fish)

11. On our trip in the mountainous countryside, we saw some _____, _____, _____, and wild _____. (wolf, fox, deer, sheep)

12. When we spoke in the cave, we could hear _____ of our voices. (echo)

13. The music building at the university has 27 _____. Students need to sign up for practice times. (piano)

14. Thunder and lightning are _____ of nature. (phenomenon)

15. People get most of their news about the world through the mass _____, that is, through radio, television, the Internet, newspapers, and magazines. (medium)

Nouns **101**

☐ EXERCISE 3. Plural nouns. (Chart 7-1)

Directions: Make the nouns plural where necessary. Do not change any other words.

Bacteria

(1) ~~Bacterium~~ are the smallest living thing. They are simple organism that consist of one cell.

(2) Bacterium exist almost everywhere. They are in the air, water, and soil,* as well as in the body of all living creature.

(3) There are thousand of kind of bacterium. Most of them are harmless to human beings, but some cause diseases such as tuberculosis and pneumonia.

(4) Virus are also microscopic organism, but virus live in the cell of other living thing. By themselves, they are lifeless particle that cannot reproduce, but inside a living cell they become active and can multiply hundred of time.

(5) Virus cause many disease. They infect human being with such illness as influenza, the common cold, measles, and AIDS (Acquired ImmunoDeficiency Syndrome).

(6) Virus are tiny. The virus that causes AIDS is so small that 230 million** of them could fit on the period at the end of this sentence.

(7) Today health official are expressing great concern about our health* in the future. They feel that today there is an epidemic of infectious condition that are difficult or impossible to treat, such as AIDS.

(8) In addition to this concern about new life-threatening viral infections, health official have discovered that bacterial infection that were once easily handled by antibiotics now pose a serious threat to our health. Many common bacterium have developed resistance to antibiotics and are evolving into form that are unaffected by all known medications.

(9) In a world where antibiotics don't work, the simplest infection are capable of escalating into fatal illnesses. Every year more people are dying of infection that resist every drug doctor try. The potential ineffectiveness of antibiotics is a frightening prospect.

---

*Air, water, soil, and health are used as noncount nouns and thus have no plural form. See Chart 7-4, p. 107, for information about noncount nouns.

When the words hundred, thousand, million, and billion are used with numerals, they remain in their singular form: **Six hundred employees will attend the company picnic this year. There are **three thousand** entrants in the photo contest. When they are used without numerals to indicate an indefinite but large number of something, they are used in their plural form: **Hundreds** of people came to the concert. There are **thousands** of earthquakes in the world every year. **Millions** of people in the world are starving.

7-2 POSSESSIVE NOUNS

SINGULAR NOUN	POSSESSIVE FORM	
(a) *the girl*	*the girl's*	To show possession, add an apostrophe (') and *-s* to a singular noun: *The **girl's** book is on the table.*
(b) *Tom*	*Tom's*	
(c) *my wife*	*my wife's*	If a singular noun ends in *-s*, there are two possible forms:
(d) *a lady*	*a lady's*	1. Add an apostrophe and *-s*: ***Thomas's** book.*
(e) *Thomas*	*Thomas's/Thomas'*	2. Add only an apostrophe: ***Thomas'** book.*

PLURAL NOUN	POSSESSIVE FORM	
(f) *the girls*	*the girls'*	Add only an apostrophe to a plural noun that ends in *-s*: *The **girls'** books are on the table.*
(g) *their wives*	*their wives'*	
(h) *the ladies*	*the ladies'*	
(i) *the men*	*the men's*	Add an apostrophe and *-s* to plural nouns that do not end in *-s*: *The **men's** books are on the table.*
(j) *my children*	*my children's*	

☐ **EXERCISE 4. Possessive nouns. (Chart 7-2)**

Directions: Complete the sentences with the possessive form of the nouns in parentheses.

1. *(Mrs. Smith)* ___Mrs. Smith's___ husband often gives her flowers.

2. *(boy)* The _____ hat is red.

3. *(boys)* The _____ hats are red.

4. *(children)* The _____ toys are all over the floor.

5. *(child)* I fixed the _____ bicycle.

6. *(baby)* The _____ toys are in the crib.

7. *(babies)* The _____ toys are in their cribs.

8. *(wives)* Tom and Bob are married. Their _____ names
   are Cindy and Judy, respectively.

9. *(wife)* That is my _____ coat.

10. *(Sally)* _____ last name is White.

11. *(Phyllis)* _____ last name is Young.

12. *(boss)* That's my _____ office.

13. *(bosses)* Those are my _____ offices.

14. *(woman)* This is a _____ purse.

15. *(women)* That store sells _____ clothes.

16. *(sister)* Do you know my _____ husband?

17. *(sisters)* Do you know my _____ husbands?

18. *(yesterday)* Did you read _____ newspaper?

19. *(today)* There are many problems in _____ world.

20. *(month)* It would cost me a _____ salary to buy that
    refrigerator.

□ EXERCISE 5. Possessive nouns. (Chart 7-2)

Directions: Correct the mistakes in the use of possessive nouns by adding apostrophes and final *-s/-es* as necessary.

1. I enjoy visiting ~~friend~~ *friends'* houses.

2. When I was in Chicago, I stayed at a ~~friend~~ *friend's* house.

3. My uncle is my father brother.

4. I have four aunts. All of my aunt homes are within walking distance of my mother apartment.

5. Mike's aunt oldest son is a violinist.

6. Five astronauts were aboard the space shuttle. The astronaut safe return to earth was a welcome sight to millions of television viewers.

7. The children favorite part of the circus was the trapeze act.

8. When the child toy broke, I fixed it.

9. I borrowed the secretary pen to fill out the application form.

10. It is the people right to know what the city is going to do about the housing problem.

11. Bill wife is a factory worker.

12. Bess husband is a housepainter.

13. Quite a few diplomats are assigned to our city. Almost all of the diplomat children attend a special school.

14. A diplomat work invariably involves numerous meetings.

□ EXERCISE 6. Using apostrophes. (Chart 7-2; Appendix Chart C)

Directions: Add apostrophes as necessary to mark a possessive noun or a contraction.

1. I borrowed my sister's car. It's old but reliable.

2. A polar bears sense of smell is keen. Its ability to smell prey over a mile away is important to its survival in the vast expanses of snow and ice where it lives.

3. Texas is a leading producer of petroleum and natural gas. Its one of the worlds largest storage areas for petroleum.

4. Psychologists have developed many different kinds of tests. A "personality test" is used to evaluate an individuals personal characteristics, such as friendliness or trustworthiness.

5. Many mythological stories tell of heroes encounters with giants or dangerous animals. In one story, the heros encounter with a dragon saves a village from destruction.

6. Childrens play is an important part of their lives. It teaches them about their environment while theyre having fun. For instance, they can learn that boats float and can practice ways to make boats move across water. Toys are not limited to children. Adults have their own toys, such as pleasure boats, and children have theirs, such as miniature boats. Adults toys are usually much more expensive than childrens toys.

7-3 USING NOUNS AS MODIFIERS

(a) The soup has vegetables in it. It is *vegetable soup*.	When a noun is used as a modifier, it is in its singular form.* In (a): *vegetable* modifies *soup*.
(b) The building has offices in it. It is an *office building*.	In (b): *office* modifies *building*.
(c) The test lasted two hours. It was a *two-hour test*.	When a noun used as a modifier is combined with a number expression, the noun is singular and a hyphen (-) is used.
(d) Her son is five years old. She has a *five-year-old son*.	INCORRECT: She has a *five years old* son.

*Adjectives never take a final **-s**. (INCORRECT: *beautifuls pictures*) See Appendix Chart A-3, p. A4. Similarly, nouns used as adjectives never take a final **-s**. (INCORRECT: *vegetables soup*)

☐ EXERCISE 7. Using nouns as modifiers. (Chart 7-3)
Directions: Complete the sentences with the words in parentheses. Use the singular or plural form as appropriate. Include hyphens (-) as necessary.

1. *(shoe)* They sell _____shoes_____ at that store. It is a _____shoe_____ store.

2. *(flower)* My garden has _____ in it. It is a _____ garden.

3. *(bean)* This soup is made from black _____. It is black _____ soup.

4. *(baby)* People can buy special food in small jars for _____. It is called _____ food.

5. *(child)* Dr. Adams is trained as a psychologist for _____. She is a _____ psychologist.

6. *(salad)* At a formal dinner, there are usually two forks on the table. The smaller fork is for _____. It is a _____ fork.

7. *(fax)* In our office we have a machine that sends and receives _____. It is called a _____ machine.

8. *(can)* A kitchen tool that opens _____ is called a _____ opener.
   (potato) A tool that peels _____ is called a _____ peeler.

9. *(airplane)* Seats on _____ are uncomfortable. _____ seats should be made more comfortable and convenient for the passengers.

10. *(mosquito)* In tropical climates, sometimes it is necessary to hang a net over a bed to protect the sleeper from _____ . It is called a _____ net.

11. *(two + hour)* The plane was late. We had a _____ wait. We had to wait for _____ .

12. *(ten + year + old)* My brother is _____ . I have a _____ brother.

13. *(ten + speed)* Joe can shift his bicycle into _____ different _____ . He has a _____ bike.

14. *(six + game)* The basketball team has won _____ in a row (i.e., they haven't lost one of their last six games). They have a _____ winning streak.

15. *(three + letter)* "Arm" and "dog" are _____ words. Each word has _____ .

□ **EXERCISE 8. Using nouns as modifiers. (Chart 7-3)**

Directions: Think of common expressions in which the given nouns are used to modify other nouns. Work in pairs, in groups, or as a class.

Example: flower → *a flower vase, a flower garden, a flower shop, etc.*

1. cotton	6. telephone	11. silk	16. kitchen
2. grammar	7. mountain	12. morning	17. baby
3. birthday	8. government	13. street	18. vegetable
4. chicken	9. football	14. newspaper	19. office
5. airplane	10. bedroom	15. hotel	20. bicycle

7-4 COUNT AND NONCOUNT NOUNS

(a) I bought *a chair.* Sam bought *three chairs.*
(b) We bought *some furniture.*
  INCORRECT: We bought some *furnitures.*
  INCORRECT: We bought a *furniture.*
	Chair is a count noun; chairs are items that can be counted.
	Furniture is a noncount noun. In grammar, furniture cannot be counted.

	SINGULAR	PLURAL	
COUNT NOUN	*a chair* *one chair*	Ø *chairs*★ *two chairs* *some chairs* *a lot of chairs* *many chairs*	A count noun: (1) may be preceded by *a/an* in the singular. (2) takes a final *-s/-es* in the plural.
NONCOUNT NOUN	Ø *furniture*★ *some furniture* *a lot of furniture* *much furniture*		A noncount noun: (1) is not immediately preceded by *a/an*. (2) has no plural form, so does not take a final *-s/-es*.

★Ø = nothing.

□ **EXERCISE 9. Count and noncount nouns. (Chart 7-4)**

Directions: Look at the *italicized* nouns in the sentences. Write "c" above the count nouns and "NC" above the noncount nouns.

1. I bought some *chairs, tables,* and *desks.* In other words, I bought some *furniture.*
   (C   C   C   NC)

2. Ann likes to wear *jewelry.* Today she is wearing four *rings,* six *bracelets,* and a *necklace.*

3. We saw beautiful *mountains, fields,* and *lakes* on our trip. In other words, we saw beautiful *scenery.*

4. *Gold* and *iron* are metals.

5. I used an *iron* to press my wrinkled shirt.

6. In the United States, *baseball* is called the national pastime. To play it, you need a *baseball* and a bat.

7-5 NONCOUNT NOUNS

(a) I bought some chairs, tables, and desks. In other words, I bought some *furniture*. (b) I put some *sugar* in my *coffee*.	Many noncount nouns refer to a "whole" that is made up of different parts. In (a): ***furniture*** represents a whole group of things that is made up of similar but separate items. In (b): ***sugar*** and ***coffee*** represent whole masses made up of individual particles or elements.★
(c) I wish you *luck*.	Many noncount nouns are abstractions. In (c): ***luck*** is an abstract concept, an abstract "whole." It has no physical form; you can't touch it. You can't count it.
(d) *Sunshine* is warm and cheerful.	A phenomenon of nature, such as ***sunshine,*** is frequently used as a noncount noun, as in (d).
(e) NONCOUNT: Ann has brown *hair*. COUNT: Tom has a *hair* on his jacket. (f) NONCOUNT: I opened the curtains to let in some *light*. COUNT: Don't forget to turn off the *light* before you go to bed.	Many nouns can be used as either noncount or count nouns, but the meaning is different; e.g., ***hair*** in (e) and ***light*** in (f). (Dictionaries written especially for learners of English as a second language are a good source of information on count/noncount usages of nouns.)

★To express a particular quantity, some noncount nouns may be preceded by unit expressions: *a spoonful of sugar, a glass of water, a cup of coffee, a quart of milk, a loaf of bread, a grain of rice, a bowl of soup, a bag of flour, a pound of meat, a piece of furniture, a piece of paper, a piece of jewelry.*

7-6 SOME COMMON NONCOUNT NOUNS

This list is a sample of nouns that are commonly used as noncount nouns. Many other nouns can also be used as noncount nouns.

(a) WHOLE GROUPS MADE UP OF SIMILAR ITEMS: *baggage, clothing, equipment, food, fruit, furniture, garbage, hardware, jewelry, junk, luggage, machinery, mail, makeup, money/cash/change, postage, scenery, traffic, etc.*

(b) FLUIDS: *water, coffee, tea, milk, oil, soup, gasoline, blood, etc.*

(c) SOLIDS: *ice, bread, butter, cheese, meat, gold, iron, silver, glass, paper, wood, cotton, wool, etc.*

(d) GASES: *steam, air, oxygen, nitrogen, smoke, smog, pollution, etc.*

(e) PARTICLES: *rice, chalk, corn, dirt, dust, flour, grass, hair, pepper, salt, sand, sugar, wheat, etc.*

(f) ABSTRACTIONS:
—*beauty, confidence, courage, education, enjoyment, fun, happiness, health, help, honesty, hospitality, importance, intelligence, justice, knowledge, laughter, luck, music, patience, peace, pride, progress, recreation, significance, sleep, truth, violence, wealth, etc.*
—*advice, information, news, evidence, proof, etc.*
—*time, space, energy, etc.*
—*homework, work, etc.*
—*grammar, slang, vocabulary, etc.*

(g) LANGUAGES: *Arabic, Chinese, English, Spanish, etc.*

(h) FIELDS OF STUDY: *chemistry, engineering, history, literature, mathematics, psychology, etc.*

(i) RECREATION: *baseball, soccer, tennis, chess, bridge, poker, etc.*

(j) ACTIVITIES: *driving, studying, swimming, traveling,★ walking, etc.* (and other gerunds)

(k) NATURAL PHENOMENA: *weather, dew, fog, hail, heat, humidity, lightning, rain, sleet, snow, thunder, wind, darkness, light, sunshine, electricity, fire, gravity, etc.*

★British spelling: *travelling.*

☐ EXERCISE 10. Count and noncount nouns. (Charts 7-5 and 7-6)
   Directions: Complete the sentences with the given nouns, adding final **-s/-es** if necessary. Use each noun only once.

advice	*homework*	*music*	*stuff*
✓*change*	*information*	*progress*	*thunder*
garbage	*junk*	✓*river*	*traffic*
hardware	*luggage/baggage*	*screwdriver*	

1. I have some coins in my pocket. In other words, I have some ____change____ in my pocket.

2. The Mississippi, the Amazon, and the Nile are well-known ____rivers____.

3. I like to listen to operas, symphonies, and folk songs. I enjoy _____.

4. The street is full of cars, trucks, and buses. It is full of _____.

5. I put some banana peels, empty juice cartons, and broken bottles in the waste can. The can is full of _____.

6. They have a rusty car without an engine, broken chairs, and an old refrigerator in their front yard. Their yard is full of _____.

7. Paul has books, pens, papers, notebooks, a clock, scissors, a tape recorder, and some other things on his desk. He has a lot of _____ on his desk.★

★As a noncount noun, **stuff** usually means "a group of various things." It is an inexact term used primarily in very informal spoken English. (*Junk* sometimes has the same meaning.)
   Examples: *I keep a lot of stuff in my desk drawers.*
   Look at all the stuff in this room!

8. The children got scared when they heard _____ during the storm.

9. Tools that are used for turning screws are called _____.

10. I went to the store to get some nails, hammers, and screws. In other words, I bought some _____.

11. Tonight I have to read 20 pages in my history book, do 30 algebra problems, and write a composition. In other words, I have a lot of _____ to do tonight.

12. Ann took three suitcases, a shoulder bag, and a cosmetics case. In other words, she took a lot of _____ on her trip.

13. Toronto is 365 ft./109 m. above sea level. The average annual precipitation in Toronto is 32 in./81 cm. The population of the metropolitan area is over 3,000,000. I found *(this, these)* _____ in the encyclopedia.

14. I didn't feel good. Ann said, "You should see a doctor." Nick said, "You should go home and go to bed." Martha said, "You should drink fruit juice and rest." I got _____ from three people.

15. My English is slowly getting better. My vocabulary is increasing. It's getting easier for me to write, and I make fewer mistakes. I can often understand people even when they talk fast. I'm satisfied with the _____ I've made in learning English.

☐ **EXERCISE 11. Count and noncount nouns; nouns as modifiers.**
    (Charts 7-3, 7-5, and 7-6)
Directions: Add final *-s/-es* to the nouns in *italics* if necessary. Do not add or change any other words.

1. Isabel always has fresh *egg* available because she raises *chicken* in her yard.

2. I had *chicken* and *rice* for dinner last night. *(no change)*

3. Outside my window, I can see a lot of *tree, bush, grass, dirt,* and *flower.*

4. Abdullah gave me some good *advice.* Nadia also gave me some good *suggestion.*

5. Yoko learned several new *word* today. She increased her *vocabulary* today.

6. I drank two *glass* of *water.*

7. *Window* are made of *glass.*

8. Mr. Chu wears *glass* because he has poor *eyesight.*

9. It took me a lot of *time* to finish my *homework*. I had a lot of *assignment*.

10. I have been in Mexico three *time*. I've spent a lot of *time* there.

11. There are *typewriter, copier, telephone,* and *stapler* in a typical business office. A business office needs a lot of *equipment*.

12. The *air* is full of *smoke, dust,* carbon *monoxide,* and many other harmful *substance*. We must seek to reduce air *pollution*.

13. I like to read good *literature*. I especially like to read *novel, poetry,* and *essay*. My favorite *poet* are Longfellow and Wordsworth. I have always liked their *poem*.

14. I like to experience different *season*. I like both hot and cold *weather*.

15. Being a parent has brought me a lot of *happiness*. Parenting requires a lot of *patience,* but it provides many *reward*.

16. You can find a lot of time-saving *machine* in a modern *factory*. Modern *factory* need modern *machinery*.

17. Experienced *traveler* learn to travel with minimal *luggage*. My globe-trotting aunt can pack everything she needs into two small *suitcase,* whether her trip will last for three *day* or three *month*. I'm not an experienced *traveler*. When I travel, I invariably take along too much *stuff*. Last month I took a three-*day* trip to Chicago with twice as many clothes as I needed.

18. Recycling is important. Regular *garbage* will typically contain many things that can be recycled: *magazine, envelope,* cardboard *box,* old *phone book, glass bottle, jar, copper, brass, tin can,* etc.

19. There are more *star* in the universe than there are *grain* of *sand* on all the beaches on earth.

7-7 BASIC ARTICLE USAGE

I. USING *A* or Ø: GENERIC NOUNS

SINGULAR COUNT NOUN	(a) *A banana* is yellow.★	A speaker uses generic nouns to make generalizations. A generic noun represents a whole class of things; it is not a specific, real, concrete thing, but rather a symbol of a whole group.
PLURAL COUNT NOUN	(b) *Ø Bananas* are yellow.	In (a) and (b): The speaker is talking about any banana, all bananas, bananas in general. In (c): The speaker is talking about any and all fruit, fruit in general.
NONCOUNT NOUN	(c) *Ø Fruit* is good for you.	Notice that no article (Ø) is used to make generalizations with plural count nouns, as in (b), and with noncount nouns, as in (c).

II. USING *A* or *SOME*: INDEFINITE NOUNS

SINGULAR COUNT NOUN	(d) I ate *a banana*.	Indefinite nouns are actual things (not symbols), but they are not specifically identified.
PLURAL COUNT NOUN	(e) I ate **some** *bananas*.	In (d): The speaker is not referring to "this banana" or "that banana" or "the banana you gave me." The speaker is simply saying that s/he ate one banana. The listener does not know nor need to know which specific banana was eaten; it was simply one banana out of that whole group of things in this world called bananas.
NONCOUNT NOUN	(f) I ate **some** *fruit*.	In (e) and (f): **Some** is often used with indefinite plural count nouns and indefinite noncount nouns. In addition to **some**, a speaker might use **two**, **a few**, **several**, **a lot of**, etc., with plural count nouns, or **a little**, **a lot of**, etc., with noncount nouns. (See Chart 7-4, p. 107.)

III. USING *THE*: DEFINITE NOUNS

SINGULAR COUNT NOUN	(g) Thank you for *the banana*.	A noun is definite when both the speaker and the listener are thinking about the same specific thing.
PLURAL COUNT NOUN	(h) Thank you for *the bananas*.	In (g): The speaker uses *the* because the listener knows which specific banana the speaker is talking about, i.e., that particular banana which the listener gave to the speaker.
NONCOUNT NOUN	(i) Thank you for *the fruit*.	Notice that *the* is used with both singular and plural count nouns and with noncount nouns.

★Usually *a/an* is used with a singular generic count noun. Examples:
A window is made of glass. **A doctor** heals sick people. *Parents must give* **a child** *love.* **A box** *has six sides.* **An apple** *can be red, green, or yellow.*

However, *the* is sometimes used with a singular generic count noun (not a plural generic count noun, not a generic noncount noun). "Generic *the*" is commonly used with, in particular:
(1) species of animals: **The blue whale** *is the largest mammal on earth.*
              The elephant *is the largest land mammal.*
(2) inventions: *Who invented* **the telephone?** **the wheel?** **the refrigerator?** **the airplane?**
          The computer *will play an increasingly large role in all of our lives.*
(3) musical instruments: *I'd like to learn to play* **the piano.**
          Do you play **the guitar?**

☐ EXERCISE 12. Article usage with generic nouns. (Chart 7-7)
Directions: Add *a/an* if necessary. Write **Ø** in the blank if the noun is noncount. Capitalize as appropriate.

1. __A__ *bird* has wings.

2. __An__ *animal* needs a regular supply of food.

3. __Ø__ ~~F~~*food* is a necessity of life.

4. _____ *concert* is a musical performance.

5. _____ *opera* is a musical play.

6. _____ *music* consists of a series of pleasant sounds.

7. _____ *cup* is a small container used for liquids.

8. _____ *milk* is nutritious.

9. _____ *island* is a piece of land surrounded by water.

10. _____ *gold* is a metal.

11. _____ *bridge* is a structure that spans a river.

12. _____ *valley* is an area of low land between two mountains.

13. _____ *health* is one of the most important things in life.

14. _____ *adjective* is a word that modifies a noun.

15. _____ *knowledge* is a source of power.

16. _____ *tennis* is a sport.

17. _____ tennis *player* has to practice long hours.

18. _____ *tree* needs water to survive.

19. _____ *water* is composed of oxygen and hydrogen.

20. _____ *homework* is a necessary part of a course of study.

21. _____ *grammar* is interesting and fun.

22. _____ *sentence* usually contains a subject and a verb.

23. _____ *English* is used in airports throughout much of the world.

24. _____ *air* is free.

25. _____ *orange* is green until it ripens.

26. _____ *fruit* is good for you.

27. _____ *iron* is a metal.

28. _____ *iron* is an instrument used to take wrinkles out of cloth fabric.

29. _____ *basketball* is round.

30. _____ *basketball* is a sport.

☐ EXERCISE 13. Article usage with indefinite nouns. (Chart 7-7)
Directions: Add *a/an* or *some* to these sentences.

1. The teacher made _____an_____ announcement.

2. I saw _____a_____ bird.

3. I saw _____some_____ birds.

4. Rosa borrowed _____some_____ money from her uncle.

5. I had _____ accident.

6. I have _____ homework to do tonight.

7. There is _____ table in the room.

8. There is _____ furniture in the room.

9. There are _____ chairs in the room.

10. My father gave me _____ advice.

11. Sonya is carrying _____ suitcase.

12. Sonya is carrying _____ luggage.

13. There was _____ earthquake in California.

14. I got _____ letters in the mail.

15. Helen got _____ letter from her mother.

16. Jerry got _____ mail yesterday.

17. A computer is _____ machine that can solve problems.

18. The factory bought _____ new machinery.

19. _____ machines are powered by electricity. Some use other sources of energy.

20. I threw away _____ junk.

21. I threw away _____ old basket that was falling apart.

22. I threw away _____ old boots that had holes in them.

☐ **EXERCISE 14. Count and noncount nouns. (Charts 7-4 → 7-7)**

Directions: A favorite game for adults and children alike is called "My Grandfather's Store." It is played with a group of people. Each person begins his/her turn by saying "I went to my grandfather's store and bought . . . . " The first person names something that begins with the letter "A." The second person repeats what the first person said, and then names something that begins with the letter "B." The game continues to the letter "Z," the end of the alphabet. The people in the group have to listen carefully and remember all the items previously named.

Example:
   1st person: *I went to my grandfather's store and bought **an apple**.*
   2nd person: *I went to my grandfather's store and bought **an apple** and **some bread**.*
   3rd person: *I went to my grandfather's store and bought **an apple**, **some bread**, and **a camel**.*
   4th person: *I went to my grandfather's store and bought **an apple**, **some bread**, **a camel**, and **some dark socks**.*
   5th person: *Etc.*

Assume that "grandfather's store" sells just about anything anyone would ever think of. Pay special attention to the use of **a**, **an**, and **some**.

Alternative beginnings:
         Tomorrow I'm going to (name of a place). In my suitcase, I will pack . . . .
         If I lived on a deserted island, I would need . . . .

7-8 GENERAL GUIDELINES FOR ARTICLE USAGE

(a) *The sun* is bright today. Please hand this book to *the teacher*. Please open *the door*. Omar is in *the kitchen*.	GUIDELINE: Use *the* when you know or assume that your listener is familiar with and thinking about the same specific thing or person you are talking about.
(b) Yesterday I saw *some dogs*. *The dogs* were chasing *a cat*. *The cat* was chasing *a mouse*. *The mouse* ran into *a hole*. *The hole* was very small.	GUIDELINE: Use *the* for the second mention of an indefinite noun.★ In (b): first mention = *some dogs, a cat, a mouse, a hole;* second mention = *the dogs, the cat, the mouse, the hole.*
(c) CORRECT: *Apples* are my favorite fruit. INCORRECT: *The apples* are my favorite fruit. (d) CORRECT: *Gold* is a metal. INCORRECT: *The gold* is a metal.	GUIDELINE: Do NOT use *the* with a plural count noun (e.g., *apples*) or a noncount noun (e.g., *gold*) when you are making a generalization.
(e) CORRECT: (1) I drove *a car*. (2) I drove *the car*. (3) I drove *that car*. (4) I drove *Jim's car*. INCORRECT: I drove *car*.	GUIDELINE: A singular count noun (e.g., *car*) is preceded by a marker: (1) *a* or *an* (or another singular marker such as *one, each,* or *every*); (2) *the*; (3) *this* or *that*; (4) a possessive (e.g., *my, Jim's*)

★*The* is not used for the second mention of a generic noun. COMPARE:
    (1) *What color is* ***a banana*** *(generic noun)?* ***A banana*** *(generic noun) is yellow.*
    (2) *Joe offered me* ***a banana*** *(indefinite noun) or an apple. I chose* ***the banana*** *(definite noun).*

☐ **EXERCISE 15. Article usage. (Charts 7-7 and 7-8)**
    Directions: In these dialogues, decide whether the speakers would probably use *a/an* or *the*.

1. A: I have __an__ idea. Let's go on __a__ picnic Saturday.
   B: Okay.

2. A: Did you have fun at __the__ picnic yesterday?
   B: Sure did. And you?

3. A: You'd better have _____ good reason for being late!
   B: I do.

4. A: Did you think _____ reason Mike gave for being late was believable?
   B: Not really.

5. A: Where's my blue shirt?
   B: It's in _____ washing machine.
   A: That's okay. I can wear _____ different shirt.

6. A: I wish we had _____ washing machine.
   B: So do I. It would make it a lot easier to do our laundry.

7. A: Can you repair my car for me?
   B: What's wrong with it?
   A: _____ radiator has _____ leak, and one of _____ windshield wipers doesn't work.
   B: Can you show me where _____ leak is?

8. A: What happened to your bicycle? _____ front wheel is bent.

   B: I ran into _____ parked car when I swerved to avoid _____ big pothole in the street.

   A: Did you damage _____ car?

   B: A little.

   A: What did you do?

   B: I left _____ note for _____ owner of _____ car.

   A: What did you write on _____ note?

   B: My name and address. I also wrote _____ apology.

9. A: Have you seen my boots?

   B: They're in _____ closet in _____ front hallway.

□ EXERCISE 16. Article usage. (Charts 7-7 and 7-8)
   Directions: Complete the sentences with *a/an*, *the*, or **Ø**. Capitalize as appropriate.

1. __Ø__ Beef is a kind of __Ø__ meat.
                    B

2. __The__ beef we had for dinner last night was excellent.

3. Jim is wearing __a__ straw hat today.

4. Jim likes to wear _____ hats.

5. _____ hat is _____ article of clothing.

6. _____ hats are _____ articles of clothing.

7. _____ brown hat on that hook over there belongs to Mark.

8. Everyone has _____ problems in _____ life.

9. My grandfather had _____ long life.

10. That book is about _____ life of Helen Keller.

11. Tommy wants to be _____ engineer when he grows up.

12. The Brooklyn Bridge was designed by _____ engineer.

13. John Roebling is _____ name of _____ engineer who designed the Brooklyn Bridge. He died in 1869 from _____ infection before _____ bridge was completed.

14. _____ people wear _____ jewelry to make themselves more attractive.

15. _____ jewelry Diana is wearing today is beautiful.

□ EXERCISE 17. Article usage. (Charts 7-7 and 7-8)
　　　Directions: Complete the sentences with **a/an**, **the**, or **Ø**.

1. We need to get _____ new phone.

2. Alex, would you please answer _____ phone?

3. _____ people use _____ plants in _____ many different ways. Plants supply us
with oxygen. They are a source of _____ lifesaving medicines. We use plant
products to build _____ houses and to make _____ paper and _____ textiles.

4. When you look at _____ sandy shore, it might seem practically empty of _____
animals. This appearance is deceptive, however. Beneath _____ surface, the sand
is full of _____ life. It is teeming with _____ crabs, _____ shrimp, _____
worms, _____ snails, and _____ other kinds of _____ marine animals.

5. Our children enjoyed going to the beach yesterday. When they dug in _____ sand,
they found various kinds of _____ animals. Susie found _____ crab, and so did
Johnny. _____ crab Johnny found pinched him, which made him cry. But he had
_____ good time at _____ beach anyway.

6. The biggest bird in the world is the ostrich. It eats just about anything it can reach,
including _____ stones, _____ glass, and _____ keys. It can kill _____
person with one kick.

7. Do you ever gaze into _____ space and wonder if _____ other life forms exist in
_____ universe?

8. _____ most mirrors are made from _____ glass to which _____ thin layer of
_____ silver or _____ aluminum has been applied.

9. In _____ recent newspaper article, I read about _____ Australian swimmer who was saved from _____ shark by _____ group of dolphins. When _____ shark attacked _____ swimmer, _____ dolphins chased it away. They saved _____ swimmer's life.

10. I heard on the radio that there is _____ evidence that _____ dolphins suffer in captivity. Dolphins that are free in _____ nature live around 40 years. Captive dolphins live _____ average of 12 years. It is believed that some captive dolphins commit _____ suicide.

11. _____ phonograph records have become old-fashioned. They have been supplanted by _____ compact discs, which are commonly referred to as CDs.

12. Look. There's _____ fly walking on _____ ceiling. It's upside down. Do you suppose _____ fly was flying rightside up and flipped over at the last second, or was it flying upside down when it landed on _____ ceiling?

☐ EXERCISE 18. Preview: expressions of quantity. (Chart 7-9)
    Directions: Before you look at the next chart, try this exercise. Draw a line through the expressions that CANNOT be used to complete the sentence correctly.

    Example: I bought _____ furniture.
        a. some
        b. a couple of
        c. several
        d. too much
        e. too many

    1. I received _____ letters.
        a. two
        b. a couple of
        c. both
        d. several
        e. some
        f. a lot of
        g. plenty of
        h. too many
        i. too much
        j. a few
        k. a little
        l. a number of
        m. a great deal of
        n. hardly any
        o. no

    2. I received _____ mail.
        a. two
        b. a couple of
        c. both
        d. several
        e. some
        f. a lot of
        g. plenty of
        h. too many
        i. too much
        j. a few
        k. a little
        l. a number of
        m. a great deal of
        n. hardly any
        o. no

7-9 EXPRESSIONS OF QUANTITY

EXPRESSIONS OF QUANTITY	USED WITH COUNT NOUNS	USED WITH NONCOUNT NOUNS	
(a) *one* *each* *every*	*one* apple *each* apple *every* apple	Ø★ Ø Ø	An expression of quantity may precede a noun. Some expressions of quantity are used only with count nouns, as in (a) and (b).
(b) *two, etc.* *both* *a couple of* *a few* *several* *many* *a number of*	*two* apples *both* apples *a couple of* apples *a few* apples *several* apples *many* apples *a number of* apples	Ø Ø Ø Ø Ø Ø	
(c) *a little* *much* *a great deal of*	Ø Ø Ø	*a little* rice *much* rice *a great deal of* rice	Some are used only with noncount nouns, as in (c).
(d) *no* *some/any* *a lot of/lots of* *plenty of* *most* *all*	*no* apples *some/any* apples *a lot of/lots of* apples *plenty of* apples *most* apples *all* apples	*no* rice *some/any* rice *a lot of/lots of* rice *plenty of* rice *most* rice *all* rice	Some are used with both count and noncount nouns, as in (d).

★Ø = not used. For example, you can say *"I ate one apple"* but NOT *"I ate one rice."*

☐ **EXERCISE 19. Expressions of quantity. (Chart 7-9)**

Directions: Draw a line through the expressions that CANNOT be used to complete the sentence correctly. Item 1 has been started for you.

1. Jake has _____ homework.
   a. ~~three~~
   b. several
   c. some
   d. a lot of
   e. too much
   f. too many
   g. a few
   h. a little
   i. a number of
   j. a great deal of
   k. hardly any
   l. no

2. Isabel has _____ assignments.
   a. three
   b. several
   c. some
   d. a lot of
   e. too much
   f. too many
   g. a few
   h. a little
   i. a number of
   j. a great deal of
   k. hardly any
   l. no

□ EXERCISE 20. MUCH vs. MANY. (Chart 7-9)

Directions: Write **much** or **many**. Also write the plural form of the *italicized* nouns as necessary. In some sentences, you will need to choose the correct verb in parentheses.

1. I haven't visited _____many_____ *city* (cities) in the United States.

2. There (isn't/aren't) _____isn't_____ _____much_____ *money* in my bank account.

3. I haven't gotten _____ *mail* lately.

4. I don't get _____ *letter*.

5. There (isn't/aren't) _____ _____ *hotel* in my hometown.

6. There (is/are) _____ too _____ *furniture* in Anna's living room.

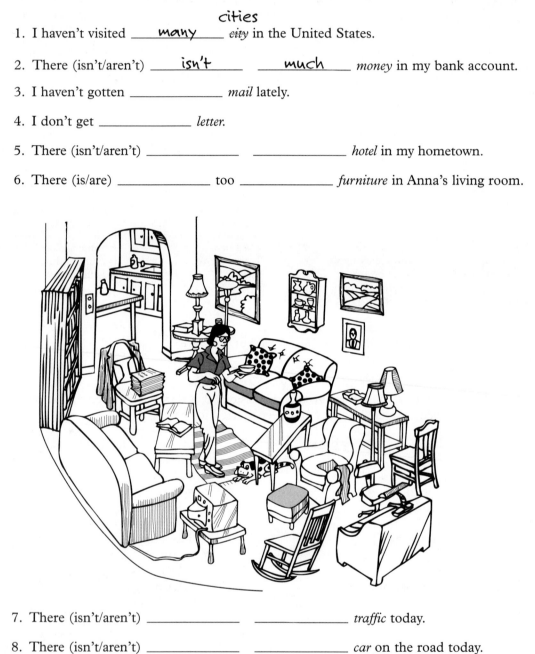

7. There (isn't/aren't) _____ _____ *traffic* today.

8. There (isn't/aren't) _____ _____ *car* on the road today.

9. I can't go with you because I have too _____ *work* to do.

10. A: How _____ *side* does a pentagon have?

    B: Five.

11. I couldn't find _____ *information* in that book.

12. How _____ *homework* did the teacher assign?

13. I haven't met _____ *people* since I came here.

14. How _____ *postage* does this letter need?

15. I think there (is/are) _____ too _____ *violence* on television.

16. I don't have _____ *patience* with incompetence.

17. The doctor has so _____ *patient* that she has to work at least twelve hours a day.

18. A: How _____ *tooth* does the average person have?

    B: Thirty-two.

19. There (isn't/aren't) _____ _____ international *news* in the local paper.

20. How _____ *fish* (is/are) _____ there in the ocean?

21. How _____ *continent* (is/are) _____ there in the world?

22. How _____ *progress* has your country made in improving the quality of medical care available to the average citizen?

□ EXERCISE 21. Expressions of quantity. (Chart 7-9)

    Directions: If the given noun can be used to complete the sentence, write it in its correct form (singular or plural). If the given noun cannot be used to complete the sentence, write **Ø**.

1. Helen bought several . . . .

    lamp   lamps

    furniture   Ø

    jewelry   Ø

    necklace   necklaces

2. Jack bought too much . . . .

    shoe   Ø

    salt   salt

    equipment   equipment

    tool   Ø

3. Sam bought a lot of . . . .

    stamp   stamps

    rice   rice

    stuff   stuff

    thing   things

4. Alice bought a couple of . . . .

    bread   _____

    loaf of bread   _____

    honey   _____

    jar of honey   _____

5. I read a few . . . .

   novel   _____

   literature   _____

   poem   _____

   poetry   _____

6. I bought some . . . .

   orange juice _____

   light bulb   _____

   hardware   _____

   computer software   _____

7. We need plenty of . . . .

   sleep   _____

   information _____

   fact   _____

   help   _____

8. I saw both . . . .

   woman   _____

   movie   _____

   scene   _____

   scenery   _____

9. Nick has a number of . . . .

   shirt   _____

   homework   _____

   pen   _____

   chalk   _____

10. I don't have a great deal of . . . .

   patience   _____

   wealth   _____

   friend   _____

   pencil   _____

11. I need a little . . . .

   luck   _____

   money   _____

   advice   _____

   new hat   _____

12. The author has many . . . .

   idea   _____

   theory   _____

   hypothesis   _____

   knowledge   _____

☐ EXERCISE 22. Expressions of quantity. (Chart 7-9)

Directions: Use ***many*** or ***much**** with the following words, changing the words to plural if necessary. Pronounce final *-s/-es* loudly and clearly. The cuer's book is open. The responder's book is closed. If you use this exercise in pairwork, switch roles after Item 14.

Examples: sentence → many sentences
water → much water
thief → many thieves

1. furniture	8. piece	15. music	22. hypothesis
2. desk	9. mouse	16. progress	23. mail
3. branch	10. advice	17. race	24. office
4. equipment	11. sheep	18. knowledge	25. slang
5. machinery	12. homework	19. marriage	26. roof
6. machine	13. prize	20. information	27. shelf
7. woman	14. goose	21. luck	28. tooth

*You may want to practice some of these words in sentences. **Much** is usually not used in affirmative sentences; instead, **a lot of** or **a great deal of** is frequently used. **Much** is used primarily in negative sentences and questions.

7-10 USING *A FEW* AND *FEW; A LITTLE* AND *LITTLE*

a few a little	(a) She has been here only two weeks, but she has already made ***a few friends***. (Positive idea: *She has made some friends.*) (b) I'm very pleased. I've been able to save ***a little money*** this month. (Positive idea: *I have saved some money instead of spending all of it.*)	***A few*** and ***a little*** give a positive idea; they indicate that something exists, is present, as in (a) and (b).
few little	(c) I feel sorry for her. She has *(very)* ***few friends***. (Negative idea: *She does not have many friends; she has almost no friends.*) (d) I have *(very)* ***little money***. I don't even have enough money to buy food for dinner. (Negative idea: *I do not have much money; I have almost no money.*)	***Few*** and ***little*** (without ***a***) give a negative idea; they indicate that something is largely absent. ***Very*** (+ ***few/little***) makes the negative stronger, the number/amount smaller.

*A few and *few* are used with plural count nouns. *A little* and *little* are used with noncount nouns.

☐ EXERCISE 23. Using A FEW and FEW; A LITTLE and LITTLE. (Chart 7-10)

Directions: Without substantially changing the meaning of the sentence, replace the *italicized* words with ***a few***, *(very)* ***few***, ***a little***, or *(very)* ***little***.

a little
1. I think that ~~some~~ lemon juice on fish makes it taste better.

(very) few
2. Many people are multilingual, but ~~not many~~ people speak more than ten languages.

3. *Some* sunshine is better than none.

4. January is a cold and dreary month in the northern states. There is *not much* sunshine during that month.

5. My parents like to watch TV. Every evening they watch *two or three* programs on TV before they go to bed.

6. I don't watch TV very much because there are *hardly any* television programs that I enjoy.

7. If a door squeaks, *several* drops of oil in the right places can prevent future trouble.

8. If your door squeaks, put *some* oil on the hinges.

9. Mr. Adams doesn't like to wear rings on his fingers. He wears *almost no* jewelry.

☐ EXERCISE 24. Using A FEW and FEW; A LITTLE and LITTLE. (Chart 7-10)

Directions: Complete the sentences with ***a few***, ***(very) few***, ***a little***, or ***(very) little***.

1. Do you have _____ a few _____ minutes? I'd like to ask you _____ a few _____ questions. I need _____ a little _____ more information.

2. Diana's previous employer gave her a good recommendation because she makes _____ very few _____ mistakes in her work.

3. After Steve tasted the soup, he added _____ salt to it.

4. I don't like a lot of salt on my food. I add _____ salt to my food.

5. I like music. I like to listen to _____ music after dinner before I begin studying.

6. Driving downtown to the stadium for the baseball game was easy. We got there quickly because there was _____ traffic.

7. Jim is having a lot of trouble adjusting to eighth grade. He seems to be unpopular. Unfortunately, he has _____ friends.

8. We're looking forward to our vacation. We're planning to spend _____ days with my folks and then _____ days with my husband's folks. After that, we're going to go to a fishing resort in Canada.

9. A: Are you finished?

   B: Not yet. I need _____ more minutes.

10. A: Are you finished?

    B: Not yet. I need _____ more time.

11 I was hungry, so I ate _____ nuts.

12. Because the family is very poor, the children have _____ toys.

13. Into each life, _____ rain must fall. *(a saying)*

14. Natasha likes sweet tea. She usually adds _____ honey to her tea. Sometimes she adds _____ milk, too.

15. Has anyone ever called you on the phone and tried to sell you something you didn't want? I have _____ patience with people who interrupt my dinner to try to sell me a magazine.

16. He's a lucky little boy. Because his parents have taken good care of him, he has had _____ problems in his young life.

7-11 USING *OF* IN EXPRESSIONS OF QUANTITY

(a) CORRECT: *A lot of books* are paperbacks. (b) CORRECT: *A lot of my books* are paperbacks. (c) INCORRECT: *A lot books* are paperbacks.	Some expressions of quantity (such as *a lot of*) always contain *of*, as in (a) and (b). See GROUP ONE below.
(d) CORRECT: *Many of my books* are paperbacks. (e) INCORRECT: *Many my books* are paperbacks. (f) CORRECT: *Many books* are paperbacks. (g) INCORRECT: *Many of books* are paperbacks.	Sometimes *of* is used with an expression of quantity, as in (d), and sometimes *of* is NOT used with the same expression of quantity, as in (f). See GROUP TWO below.

GROUP ONE: EXPRESSIONS OF QUANTITY THAT ALWAYS CONTAIN *OF*		
a lot of *lots of*	*a number of* *a great deal of*	*a majority of* *plenty of*

GROUP TWO: EXPRESSIONS OF QUANTITY THAT SOMETIMES CONTAIN *OF* AND SOMETIMES NOT				
all (of) *most (of)* *almost all (of)*	*many (of)* *much (of)* *a few (of)* *a little (of)*	*one (of)* *two (of)* *three (of)* *etc.*	*both (of)* *several (of)*	*some (of)* *any (of)*

(h) *Many **of my** books* are in English.
(i) *Many **of those** books* are in English.
(j) *Many **of the** books* on that shelf are in English.
	Of is used with the expressions of quantity in GROUP TWO when the noun is specific. A noun is specific when it is preceded by:
	   1. *my, John's* (or any possessive), as in (h).
	   2. *this, that, these,* or *those,* as in (i).
	   3. *the,* as in (j)

(k) *Many books* are in English.	*Of* is NOT used with the expressions of quantity in GROUP TWO if the noun it modifies is *nonspecific*. In (k): The noun ***books*** is nonspecific; ie., the speaker is not referring to "your books" or "these books" or "the books on that desk." The speaker is not referring to specific books, but to books in general.

☐ **EXERCISE 25. Using OF in expressions of quantity. (Chart 7-11)**
    Directions: Add *of* if necessary. Write Ø if *of* is not necessary.

1. I know several __of__ Jack's friends.

2. I've made several __Ø__ friends lately.

3. Some _____ students are lazy. Most _____ students are hard-working.

4. Some _____ the students in Mrs. Gray's class are a little lazy.

5. Most _____ books have an index.

6. Most _____ Ali's books are written in Arabic.

7. I bought a few _____ books yesterday.

8. I've read a few _____ those books.

9. I'm new here. I don't know many _____ people yet.

10. I've just moved into a new apartment. I don't know many _____ my neighbors yet.

11. Have you taken any _____ trips lately?

12. Sam hasn't met any _____ the students in the other class.

13. I usually get a lot _____ mail.

14. A lot _____ the mail I get is junk mail.

15. Our class has 30 students. Mr. Freeman's class has 25 students. Ms. North's class has 20 students. Of the three classes, our class has the most _____ students.*

16. Most _____ the students in our class are very smart.*

17. Out of all the students, Ali usually asks the most _____ questions during class. Most _____ his questions are about grammar.

18. Most _____ people need six to eight hours of sleep every night.

19. Most _____ the people in this class always hand in their assignments on time.

20. China has the most _____ people of any country in the world.

7-12 *ALL (OF)* AND *BOTH (OF)*

(a) CORRECT: *All of the students* in my class are here. (b) CORRECT: *All the students* in my class are here.	When a noun is specific (e.g., *the students)*, using *of* after *all* is optional as in (a) and (b).
(c) CORRECT: *All students* must have an I.D. card. (d) INCORRECT: *All of students* must have an I.D. card.	When a noun is nonspecific, *of* does NOT follow *all*, as in (c).
(e) I know *both (of) those men*.	Similarly, using *of* after *both* is optional when the noun is specific, as in (e).
(f) CORRECT: I know *both men*. (g) INCORRECT: I know *both of men*.	When a noun is nonspecific, *of* does NOT follow *both*, as in (f).

☐ EXERCISE 26. ALL (OF) and BOTH (OF). (Chart 7-12)
  Directions: *Of* is not necessary in any of these sentences. In the sentences in which the use of *of* is optional, write *(of)* in the blanks. If *of* is not possible because the noun is nonspecific, write **Ø**.

  1. All _(of)_ the children listened to the story.

  2. Almost all _Ø_ children like fairy tales.

---

*COMPARE:

(1) *The most* = superlative. The superlative is used to compare three or more persons or things. *The most* is never immediately followed by *of*. Example: *Out of all the boys, Tom ate the most food.*

(2) *Most* (not preceded by *the*) = an expression of quantity whose meaning ranges from "over fifty percent" to "almost all." Example: *Most of the food* at that restaurant is good, but not all of it.

3. Both _____ those books are mine.

4. I bought two books. Both _____ books were expensive.

5. Almost all _____ students study hard for exams.

6. All _____ birds have wings, but not all _____ birds can fly. Both _____ the birds in the picture are incapable of flight.

7. I have two brothers. Both _____ my brothers are in school.

emu   kiwi

8. Do you know all _____ the people in your biology class?

9. All _____ the students in my class are studying English.

10. Not all _____ people are friendly, but most _____ people have kind hearts.

☐ EXERCISE 27. Using OF in expressions of quantity. (Charts 7-11 and 7-12)
Directions: Add *of* and/or write **Ø**.

1. Some ___Ø___ fish are surface feeders. Others are bottom feeders.

2. Some ___of___ the fish we caught were too small to keep.

3. Almost all _of OR Ø_ the fish in Jennifer's aquarium died. She finally had to admit that she didn't know much about taking care of tropical fish.

4. I bought several _____ books at the used book sale.

5. Several _____ my friends and I have volunteered to clean up the litter left on the school grounds by thoughtless students.

6. The airline was crippled by a strike last month, but now it's over. All _____ the pilots were happy to get back to work after the strike.

7. Most _____ people have a little _____ trouble using the currency in a foreign country for a few _____ days after they first arrive.

8. There's nothing I like better than a good book, but I haven't done much reading for pleasure lately. Most _____ the reading I do is related to my work.

9. It's important for young people to have goals in their lives. My mother always told me that any _____ dream is worth pursuing if I know in my heart it is what I want to do. Few _____ people have made great accomplishments in life without first having a dream—a personal, inner vision of what is possible.

10. Square dancing is a traditional folk dance in the United States. We all had a lot _____ fun learning to square dance at the party. Many _____ the people at the party had never done any square dancing before.

11. When my parents were young, they had little _____ opportunity to travel.

12. A few _____ children are given their first watch by the time they are six years old. However, most _____ these children cannot tell time correctly.

7-13 SINGULAR EXPRESSIONS OF QUANTITY: ONE, EACH, EVERY

(a) **One student** was late to class. (b) **Each student** has a schedule. (c) **Every student** has a schedule.	**One**, **each**, and **every** are followed immediately by *singular count nouns* (never plural nouns, never noncount nouns).
(d) **One of the students** was late to class. (e) **Each (one) of the students** has a schedule. (f) **Every one of the students** has a schedule.	**One of**, **each of**, and **every one of*** are followed by *specific plural count nouns* (never singular nouns; never noncount nouns).

*COMPARE:
    Every one (two words) is an expression of quantity; e.g., *I have read **every one** of those books.*
    Everyone (one word) is an indefinite pronoun; it has the same meaning as ***everybody***; e.g., ***Everyone/Everybody*** *has a schedule.*
NOTE: **Each** and **every** have essentially the same meaning.
    Each is used when the speaker is thinking of one person/thing at a time: *Each student has a schedule. = Mary has a schedule. Hiroshi has a schedule. Carlos has a schedule. Sabrina has a schedule. (etc.)*
    Every is used when the speaker means "all": *Every student has a schedule. = All of the students have schedules.*

□ EXERCISE 28. Using ONE, EACH, and EVERY. (Chart 7-13)
    Directions: Complete the sentences with the correct form, singular or plural, of the noun in parentheses.

1. There is only one _____*girl*_____ on the sixth-grade soccer team. *(girl)*

2. Only one of the _____ in the sixth grade is on the soccer team. *(girl)*

3. Each of the _____ got a present. *(child)*

4. Mr. Hoover gave a present to each _____. *(child)*

5. We invited every _____ of the club. *(member)*

6. Every one of the _____ came. *(member)*

□ EXERCISE 29. Using ONE, EACH, and EVERY. (Chart 7-13)
Directions: Some (but not all) of the following sentences contain errors. Find and correct the errors.

student

1. It's important for every ~~students~~ to have a book.

2. Each of the students in my class has a book. (*no change*)

3. Spain is one of the country I want to visit.

4. The teacher gave each of students a test paper.

5. Every student in the class did well on the test.

6. Every furniture in that room is made of wood.

7. One of the equipment in our office is broken.

8. I gave a present to each of the woman in the room.

9. One of my favorite place in the world is an island in the Caribbean Sea.

10. Each one of your suitcases will be checked when you go through customs.

11. It's impossible for one human being to know every languages in the world.

12. I found each of the error in this exercise.

□ EXERCISE 30. Activity: expressions of quantity. (Charts 7-9 → 7-13)
Directions: Conduct an opinion poll among your classmates. Report your findings using expressions of quantity. Prepare five yes/no questions that ask for opinions or information about the respondents' likes, dislikes, habits, or experiences.

Possible questions:

1. Do you read an English language newspaper every day?
2. Do you like living in this city?
3. Do you have a car?
4. Have you ever ridden a horse?
5. Are you going to be in bed before midnight tonight?

Record your classmates' responses. Then in your report, make generalizations about this information by using expressions of quantity. For example:

1. Only a few of the people in this class read an English newspaper every day.
2. Most of them like living in this city.
3. Three of the people in this class have cars.
4. About half of them have ridden a horse at some time in their lifetime.
5. Almost all of them are going to be in bed before midnight tonight.

□ EXERCISE 31. Review: expressions of quantity. (Charts 7-9 → 7-13)

Directions: Most of the statements below are inaccurate overgeneralizations. Make each statement clearer or more accurate by adding an expression of quantity. Add other words to the sentence or make any changes you wish. The following list suggests expressions of quantity you might use. Work in pairs, in groups, or as a class.

all (of)	*many (of)*	*one (of)*	*some (of)*
each (of)	*much (of)*	*two (of)*	*several (of)*
every	*a number of*	*half of*	*(a) few (of)*
almost all (of)	*a great deal of*	*50 percent of*	*(a) little (of)*
most (of)	*a lot of*	*three fourths of*	*hardly any (of)*
		a majority of	*none of*
		hundreds of	*no*
		thousands of	
		millions of	

Example: My classmates are from Japan.
Possible sentences: → *Most of my classmates are from Japan.*
      → *All (of) my classmates are from Japan.*
      → *One of my classmates is from Japan.*
      → *Hardly any of my classmates are from Japan.*
      → *None of my classmates is from Japan.*

1. My classmates speak Arabic.
2. People are friendly.
3. The pages in this book contain illustrations.
4. Babies are born bald.
5. The students in my class are from South America.
6. People like to live alone.
7. The people I know like to live alone.
8. The countries in the world are in the Northern Hemisphere.
9. The citizens of the United States speak English.
10. Children like to read scary stories.
11. The children in my country go to school.
12. Airplanes depart and arrive precisely on time.
13. The rivers in the world are polluted.
14. The pollution in the world today is caused by human beings.
15. City dwellers do not have cars.
16. The food at *(name of the place you usually eat)* is very good.

CHAPTER 8
Pronouns

CONTENTS			

☐ EXERCISE 1. Preview: personal pronouns. (Chart 8-1)
Directions: Correct the errors you find in pronoun usage.

1. Some North American food is very good, but I don't like most of them.

2. When we were schoolgirls, my sister and me used to play badminton after school every day.

3. If you want to pass you're exams, you had better study very hard for it.

4. The work had to be finished by my boss and I after the store had closed for the night.

5. A hippopotamus spends most of it's time in the water of rivers and lakes.

6. After work, Mr. Gray asked to speak to Tim and I about the company's new policies. He explained it to us and asked for ours opinions.

7. A child should learn to respect other people. They need to learn how to treat other people politely, including their playmates.

8. My friends asked to borrow my car because their's was in the garage for repairs.

8-1 PERSONAL PRONOUNS

	SUBJECT PRONOUN	OBJECT PRONOUN	POSSESSIVE PRONOUN	POSSESSIVE ADJECTIVE
SINGULAR	*I* *you* *she, he, it*	*me* *you* *her, him, it*	*mine* *yours* *hers, his, its*	*my* name *your* name *her, his, its* name
PLURAL	*we* *you* *they*	*us* *you* *them*	*ours* *yours* *theirs*	*our* names *your* names *their* names

(a) I read *a book*. *It* was good. (b) I read *some books*. *They* were good.	A pronoun is used in place of a noun. The noun it refers to is called the "antecedent." In (a): The pronoun *it* refers to the antecedent noun *book*. A singular pronoun is used to refer to a singular noun, as in (a). A plural pronoun is used to refer to a plural noun, as in (b).
(c) *I* like tea. Do *you* like tea too?	Sometimes the antecedent noun is understood, not explicitly stated. In (c): *I* refers to the speaker, and *you* refers to the person the speaker is talking to.
(d) John has a car. *He drives* to work.	Subject pronouns are used as subjects of sentences, as *he* in (d).
(e) John works in my office. I *know him* well. (f) I talk *to him* every day.	Object pronouns are used as the objects of verbs, as in (e), or as the objects of prepositions, as in (f).

(g) That book is *hers*.
    Yours is over there.
 (h) *INCORRECT:* That book is *her's*.
    Your's is over there.
	Possessive pronouns are not followed immediately by a noun; they stand alone, as in (g).
	 In (h): Possessive pronouns do NOT take apostrophes. (See Chart 7-2, p. 103, for the use of apostrophes with possessive nouns.)

(i) *Her book* is here. *Your book* is over there.	Possessive adjectives are followed immediately by a noun; they do not stand alone.
(j) A bird uses *its* wings to fly. (k) *INCORRECT:* A bird uses *it's* wings to fly. (l) *It's* cold today. (m) The Harbour Inn is my favorite old hotel. *It's been* in business since 1933.	COMPARE: *Its* has NO APOSTROPHE when it is used as a possessive, as in (j). *It's* has an apostrophe when it is used as a contraction of *it is,* as in (l), or *it has* when *has* is part of the present perfect tense, as in (m).

☐ EXERCISE 2. Personal pronouns: antecedents. (Chart 8-1)
Directions: Identify the personal pronouns and their antecedents.

1. Jack has a part-time job. He works at a fast-food restaurant.
   → *(he = a pronoun; Jack = the antecedent)*
2. Most monkeys don't like water, but they can swim well when they have to.
3. The teacher graded the students' papers last night. She returned them during class today.

4. Nancy took an apple with her to work. She ate it at lunch time.

5. A dog makes a good pet if it is properly trained.

6. Tom's cat is named Maybelle Alice. She★ is very independent. She never obeys Tom. His dogs, on the other hand, obey him gladly. They like to please him.

☐ EXERCISE 3. Possessive pronouns and adjectives. (Chart 8-1)
Directions: Choose the correct words in *italics*.

1. This is (my) \ *mine* umbrella. (Your) \ *Yours* umbrella is over there.

2. This umbrella is *my* \ *mine*. The other one is *your* \ *yours*.

3. Mary and Bob have *their* \ *theirs* books. In other words, Mary has
   her \ *hers* and Bob has *his* \ *him*.

4. A honeybee has two wings on each side of *its* \ *it's* body.

5. *Its* \ *It's* true that a homing pigeon will find *its* \ *it's* way home even though it begins
   its \ *it's* trip in unfamiliar territory.

6. I have a pet. *Its* \ *It's* name is Squeak. *Its* \ *It's* a turtle. *Its* \ *It's* been my pet for two years.

7. *Our* \ *Ours* house is almost the same as *our* \ *ours* neighbors' house. The only
   difference in appearance is that *our* \ *ours* is gray and *their* \ *theirs* is white.

8. When I was in Florida, I observed an interesting fish-eating bird called an anhinga.
   It \ *They* dives into the water and spears *its* \ *it's* prey on *its* \ *it's* long, pointed bill.
   After emerging from the water, *it* \ *they* tosses the fish into the air and catches *it* \ *them*
   in mid-air, then swallows *it* \ *them* headfirst. *Its* \ *It's* interesting to watch anhingas in
   action. I enjoy watching *it* \ *them*.

★If the sex of a particular animal is known, usually **she** or **he** is used instead of **it**.

8-2 PERSONAL PRONOUNS: AGREEMENT WITH GENERIC NOUNS AND INDEFINITE PRONOUNS

(a) *A student* walked into the room. *She* was looking for the teacher. (b) *A student* walked into the room. *He* was looking for the teacher.	In (a) and (b): The pronouns refer to particular individuals whose gender is known. The nouns are not generic.
(c) *A student* should always do *his* assignments. (d) *A student* should always do *his/her* assignments. *A student* should always do *his or her* assignments.	A generic noun* does not refer to any person or thing in particular; rather, it represents a whole group. In (c): *A student* is a generic noun; it refers to *anyone who is a student.* With a generic noun, a singular masculine pronoun has been used traditionally, but many English speakers now use both masculine and feminine pronouns to refer to a singular generic noun, as in (d). The use of both masculine and feminine pronouns can create awkward-sounding sentences.
(e) *Students* should always do *their* assignments.	Problems with choosing masculine and/or feminine pronouns can often be avoided by using a plural rather than a singular generic noun, as in (e).

INDEFINITE PRONOUNS

everyone	*someone*	*anyone*	*no one***
everybody	*somebody*	*anybody*	*nobody*
everything	*something*	*anything*	*nothing*

(f) *Somebody* left *his* book on the desk. (g) *Everyone* has *his or her* own ideas. (h) INFORMAL: *Somebody* left *their* book on the desk. *Everyone* has *their* own ideas.	A singular pronoun is used in formal English to refer to an indefinite pronoun, as in (f) and (g). In everyday informal English, a plural personal pronoun is often used to refer to an indefinite pronoun, as in (h).

*See Chart 7-7, p. 112, *Basic Article Usage.*

***No one* can also be written with a hyphen in British English: *No-one* heard me.

☐ EXERCISE 4. Personal pronoun use with generic nouns. (Chart 8-2)

Directions: Use plural instead of singular generic nouns where possible. Change pronouns and verbs as necessary. Discuss the advantages of using plural rather than singular generic nouns.

1. When a student wants to study, he or she should find a quiet place.

   → *When students want to study, they should find a quiet place.*

2. I talked to a student in my chemistry class. I asked to borrow his notes from the class

   I missed. He gave them to me gladly. *(no change)*

3. Each student in Biology 101 has to spend three hours per week in the laboratory,

   where he or she does various experiments by following the directions in his or her lab

   manual.

4. A pharmacist fills prescriptions, but s/he is not allowed to prescribe medicine.

5. When the pharmacist handed my prescription to me, he made sure I understood how to take the medicine.

6. A citizen has two primary responsibilities. He should vote in every election, and he should serve willingly on a jury.

7. We listened to a really interesting lecturer last night. She discussed her experiences as an archaeologist in Argentina.

8. A lecturer needs to prepare his or her notes carefully so that he or she does not lose his or her place while he or she is delivering his or her speech.

☐ EXERCISE 5. Personal pronoun use with indefinite pronouns. (Chart 8-2)
   Directions: Complete the sentences with pronouns, choosing the correct verb in parentheses as necessary. Discuss formal vs. informal pronoun usage.

1. Somebody left ___*his; his or her; her or his; their*___ books on my desk.

2. Anyone can learn how to dance if _____ (*wants, want*) to.

3. Hmmm. Someone forgot _____ umbrella. I wonder whose it is.

4. Everyone who came to the picnic brought _____ own food.

5. A: Is that your notebook?

   B: No. It belongs to one of the other students.

   A: Look on the inside cover. Did _____ write _____ name there?

6. If anyone calls, please ask _____ to leave a message.

7. Everyone was shocked when _____ heard the news. Nobody opened _____ mouth. No one made a sound.

8. Nobody can always do whatever _____ (*pleases, please*) in life.

8-3 PERSONAL PRONOUNS: AGREEMENT WITH COLLECTIVE NOUNS

EXAMPLES OF COLLECTIVE NOUNS

audience	couple	family	public
class	crowd	government	staff
committee	faculty	group	team

(a) *My family* is large. *It* is composed of nine members.	When a collective noun refers to a single impersonal unit, a singular gender-neutral pronoun *(it, its)* is used, as in (a).
(b) *My family* is loving and supportive. *They* are always ready to help me.	When a collective noun refers to a collection of various individuals, a plural pronoun *(they, them, their)* is used, as in (b).*

*NOTE: When the collective noun refers to a collection of individuals, the verb may be either singular or plural: *My family is* OR *are loving and supportive.* A singular verb is generally preferred in American English. A plural verb is used more frequently in British English, especially with the words *government* or *public.* (American: ***The government is*** *planning many changes.* British: ***The government are*** *planning many changes.)*

☐ EXERCISE 6. Personal pronoun use with collective nouns. (Chart 8-3)
Directions: Complete the sentences with pronouns. In some of the sentences, there is more than one possibility. Choose the appropriate singular or plural verb in parentheses where necessary.

1. I have a wonderful family. I love _____them_____ very much, and ___they love___
   (loves, love) me.

2. I looked up some information about the average American family. I found out that
   _____ *(consists, consist)* of 2.3 children.

3. The crowd at the soccer game was huge. _____ exceeded 100,000 people.

4. The crowd became more and more excited as the premier's motorcade approached.
   _____ began to shout and wave flags in the air.

5. The soccer team felt unhappy because _____ had lost in the closing moments of the game.

6. A basketball team is relatively small. _____ *(doesn't, don't)* have as many members as a baseball team.

7. The audience clapped enthusiastically. Obviously _____ had enjoyed the concert.

8. The audience filled the room to overflowing. _____ *(was, were)* larger than I had expected.

9. The class is planning a party for the last day of school. _____ *(is, are)* going to bring many different kinds of food and invite some of _____ friends to celebrate with _____ .

10. The class is too small. _____ *(is, are)* going to be canceled.

☐ EXERCISE 7. Preview of reflexive pronouns. (Chart 8-4)
Directions: Draw a self-portrait. Show it to the rest of the class. Answer the questions in complete sentences.

1. Who drew a picture of herself? Name someone.
2. Who drew pictures of themselves?
3. (. . .), did you and (. . .) draw pictures of yourselves?
4. (. . .), what did you draw?
5. Who drew a picture of himself? Name someone.

SELF-PORTRAIT

☐ EXERCISE 8. Preview of reflexive pronouns. (Chart 8-4)
Directions: Complete the sentences with appropriate reflexive pronouns.

1. Everyone drew self-portraits. I drew a picture of _____myself_____ .

2. Ali drew a picture of _____ .

3. Rosa drew a picture of _____ .

4. The children drew pictures of _____ .

5. We drew pictures of _____ .

6. Olga, you drew a picture of _____, didn't you?

7. All of you drew pictures of _____, didn't you?

8. When one draws a picture of _____, it is called a self-portrait.

8-4 REFLEXIVE PRONOUNS

SINGULAR **myself** **yourself** **herself, himself, itself, oneself**	PLURAL **ourselves** **yourselves** **themselves**

(a) Larry was in the theater. I *saw him*. I talked *to him*. (b) *I saw myself* in the mirror. *I* looked *at myself* for a long time. (c) INCORRECT: I saw *me* in the mirror.	Compare (a) and (b): Usually an object pronoun is used as the object of a verb or preposition, as *him* in (a). (See Chart 8-1, p. 132.) A *reflexive pronoun* is used as the object of a verb or preposition when the subject of the sentence and the object are the same person, as in (b).* *I* and *myself* are the same person.
—Did someone fax the report to Mr. Lee? —Yes. —Are you sure? (d) —Yes. *I myself* faxed the report to him. (e) —*I* faxed the report to him *myself*.	Reflexive pronouns are also used for emphasis. In (d): The speaker would say "I myself" strongly, with emphasis. The emphatic reflexive pronoun can immediately follow a noun or pronoun, as in (d), or come at the end of the clause, as in (e).
(f) Anna lives *by herself*.	The expression *by* + *a reflexive pronoun* means "alone."

*Sometimes, but relatively infrequently, an object pronoun is used as the object of a preposition even when the subject and object pronoun are the same person. Examples: *I took my books with* **me**. **Bob** *brought his books with* **him**. *I looked around* **me**. **She** *kept her son close to* **her**.

☐ **EXERCISE 9. Reflexive pronouns. (Chart 8-4)**
Directions: Complete the sentences with appropriate reflexive pronouns.

1. Tommy told a lie. He was ashamed of _____ himself _____.

2. Masako cut _____ while she was chopping vegetables.

3. People surround _____ with friends and family during holidays.

4. Rita is careful about her weight, but she allows _____ one piece of candy a day.

5. Alex, you need to eat better and get more exercise. You should take better care of _____. Your father takes care of _____, and I take care of _____. Your father and I are healthy because we take good care of _____. People who take care of _____ have a better chance of staying healthy than those who don't.

6. Omar thinks Oscar is telling the truth. So does Ricardo. I _____ don't believe Oscar's story for a minute!

7. A: Did Mr. Yun's secretary answer the phone?
   B: No. Mr. Yun _____ answered the phone. I was very surprised.

8. A: Should I marry Steve?

    B: No one can make that decision for you, Ann. Only you _____ can make such an important decision about your own life.

9. Now that their children are grown, Mr. and Mrs. Grayson live by _____.

10. Nadia didn't join the rest of us. She sat in the back of the room by _____.

□ EXERCISE 10. Reflexive pronouns. (Chart 8-4)
   Directions: Complete the sentences with a word or expression from the list and an appropriate reflexive pronoun.

angry at	introduced	promised
enjoy	killed	proud of
entertained	laugh at	talking to
feeling sorry for	pat	✓taught

1. Karen Williams never took lessons. She __taught herself__ how to play the piano.

2. Did Roberto have a good time at the party? Did he _____?

3. All of you did a good job. You should be _____.

4. You did a good job, Barbara. You should _____ on the back.

5. A man down the street committed suicide. We were all shocked by the news that he had _____.

6. The children played very well without adult supervision. They _____ _____ by playing school.

7. I had always wanted to meet Mr. Anderson. When I saw him at a party last night, I walked over and _____ to him.

8. Nothing good ever comes from self-pity. You should stop _____ _____, George, and start doing something to solve your problems.

9. People might think you're a little crazy, but _____ is one way to practice using English.

10. Humor can ease the trials and tribulations of life. Sometimes we have to be able to _____.

11. Carol made several careless mistakes at work last week, and her boss is getting impatient with her. Carol has _____ to do better work in the future.

12. Yesterday Fred's car ran out of gas. He had to walk a long way to a gas station.

He is still _____ for forgetting to fill the tank.

8-5 USING *YOU, ONE,* AND *THEY* AS IMPERSONAL PRONOUNS

(a) *One* should always be polite. (b) How does *one* get to 5th Avenue from here? (c) *You* should always be polite. (d) How do *you* get to 5th Avenue from here?	In (a) and (b): *One* means "any person, people in general." In (c) and (d): *You* means "any person, people in general." *One* is much more formal than *you*. Impersonal *you,* rather than *one,* is used more frequently in everyday English.
(e) *One* should take care of *one's* health. (f) *One* should take care of *his* health. (g) *One* should take care of *his or her* health.	Notice the pronouns that may be used in the same sentence to refer back to *one:* (e) is typical in British usage and formal American usage. (f) is principally American usage. (g) is stylistically awkward.

(h) — Did Ann lose her job?
     — Yes. *They* fired her.
(i) — *They* mine graphite in Brazil, don't they?
     — Yes. Brazil is one of the leading graphite producers in the world.
	They is used as an impersonal pronoun in spoken or very informal English to mean "some people or somebody."*
	They has no stated antecedent. The antecedent is implied. In (h): *They* = the people Ann worked for.

*In written or more formal English, the passive is generally preferred to the use of impersonal *they:*

Active: *They fired her.*   Active: *They mine graphite in Brazil, don't they?*
Passive: *She was fired.*   Passive: *Graphite is mined in Brazil, isn't it?*

☐ EXERCISE 11. Impersonal YOU and THEY. (Chart 8-5)
    Directions: Discuss the meanings of the pronouns in *italics.*

1. I agree with Jim's decision to quit his corporate job and go to art school. I think *you* need to follow *your* dreams.

    → *The pronouns refer to everyone, anyone, people in general, all of us.*

2. Jake, if *you* really want my advice, I think *you* should find a new job.

    → *The pronouns refer to Jake, a specific person.*

3. Wool requires special handling. If *you* wash wool in hot water, it will shrink. *You* shouldn't throw a wool sweater into a washing machine with *your* cottons.

4. Alex, I told *you* not to wash *your* sweater in hot water. Now look at it. It's ruined!

5. Generosity is its own reward. *You* always get back more than *you* give.

6. Sonya, let's make a deal. If *you* wash the dishes, I'll take out the garbage.

7. The earth's environment is getting worse. *They* say that the ozone layer is being depleted more and more every year.

8. Memory is selective. Often *you* remember only what *you* want to remember. If *you* ask two people to tell *you* about an experience they shared, they might tell *you* two different stories.

9. I would have loved to go to the concert last night. *They* played Beethoven's Seventh Symphony. I heard it was wonderful.

10. I've grown to dislike airplane travel. *They* never give *you* enough room for *your* legs. And if the person in front of *you* puts his seat back, *you* can barely move. *You* can't even reach down to pick up something from the floor.

☐ EXERCISE 12. Review of nouns and pronouns, singular and plural. (Chapters 7 and 8)
    Directions: Choose the correct words in *italics.*

1. *Penguin \ ⟨Penguins⟩* are interesting *creature \ ⟨creatures⟩* They are *bird \ ⟨birds⟩* but *it \ ⟨they⟩* cannot fly.

2. *Million \ Millions* of *year \ years* ago, they had *wing \ wings.* *This \ These* wings changed as the birds adapted to *its \ their* environment.

3. *Penguin's \ Penguins'* principal food *was \ were* *fish \ fishes.* Penguins needed to be able to swim to find their food, so eventually their *wing \ wings* evolved into *flipper \ flippers* that enabled *it \ them* to swim through water with speed and ease.

4. Penguins *spends \ spend* most of their lives in *water \ waters.* However, they lay their *egg \ eggs* on *land \ lands.*

5. Emperor penguins have interesting egg-laying *habit \ habits.*

6. The female *lays \ lay* one *egg \ eggs* on the *ice \ ices* in Arctic regions, and then immediately *returns \ return* to the ocean.

7. After the female lays the egg, the male *takes \ take* over. *He \ They   covers \ cover* the egg with *his \ their* body until *she \ he \ it \ they   hatches \ hatch.*

8. *This \ These* process *takes \ take* seven to eight *week \ weeks.* During *this \ these* time, the male *doesn't \ don't* eat.

9. After the egg *hatches \ hatch,* the female returns to take care of the chick, and the male *goes \ go* to the ocean to find food for *himself \ herself,* his mate, and their offspring.

10. Although the *penguin's \ penguins'* natural habitat is in polar regions, we can see them in most major zoos in the world. *They \ It   seem \ seems* to adapt well to life in confinement, so we can enjoy watching *their \ its* antics without feeling sorry about *their \ its* loss of freedom.

8-6 FORMS OF *OTHER*

	ADJECTIVE	**PRONOUN**	Forms of *other* are used as either adjectives or pronouns. Notice: A final *-s* is used only for a plural pronoun (***others***).
SINGULAR PLURAL	***another*** book (is) ***other*** books (are)	***another*** (is) ***others*** (are)	
SINGULAR PLURAL	***the other*** book (is) ***the other*** books (are)	***the other*** (is) ***the others*** (are)	
(a) The students in the class come from many countries. One of the students is from Mexico. ***Another student is*** from Iraq. ***Another is*** from Japan. ***Other students are*** from Brazil. ***Others are*** from Algeria.			The meaning of ***another:*** *one more in addition to the one(s) already mentioned.* The meaning of ***other / others*** (without ***the***): *several more in addition to the one(s) already mentioned.*
(b) I have three books. Two are mine. ***The other book*** is yours. (***The other*** is yours.) (c) I have three books. One is mine. ***The other books*** are yours. (***The others*** are yours.)			The meaning of ***the other(s):*** *all that remains from a given number; the rest of a specific group.*
(d) I will be here for ***another three years.*** (e) I need ***another five dollars.*** (f) We drove ***another ten miles.***			***Another*** is used as an adjective with expressions of time, money, and distance, even if these expressions contain plural nouns. ***Another*** means "an additional" in these expressions.

□ **EXERCISE 13. Using OTHER.** (Chart 8-6)

Directions: Complete the sentences with a form of ***other***.

1. I got three letters. One was from my father. _____Another_____ one was from my sister. ____The other____ letter was from my girlfriend.

2. Look at your hand. You have five fingers. One is your thumb. _____ is your index finger. _____ one is your middle finger. _____ finger is your ring finger. And _____ finger (the last of the five) is your little finger.

3. Look at your hands. One is your right hand. _____ is your left hand.

4. I invited five people to my party. Of those five people, only John and Mary can come. _____ can't come.

5. I invited five people to my party. Of those five people, only John and Mary can come. _____ people can't come.

6. I would like some more books on this subject. Do you have any _____ that you could lend me?

7. I would like to read more about this subject. Do you have any _____ books that you could lend me?

8. There are many means* of transportation. The airplane is one means* of transportation. The train is _____ .

9. There are many means of transportation. The airplane is one. _____ are the train, the automobile, and the horse.

10. There are two women standing on the corner. One is Helen Jansen, and _____ _____ is Pat Hendricks.

11. Alice reads *The New York Times* every day. She doesn't read any _____ newspapers.

12. Some people prefer classical music, but _____ prefer rock music.

13. Individual differences in children must be recognized. Whereas one child might have a strong interest in mathematics and science, _____ child might tend toward more artistic endeavors.

14. I'm almost finished. I just need _____ five minutes.

_____

*Means is used as both a singular and a plural noun. See Chart 7-1, p. 100.

15. One of the most important inventions in the history of the world was the printing press. _____ was the electric light. _____ were the telephone, television, and the computer.

16. Some babies begin talking as early as six months; _____ don't speak until they are more than two years old.

17. One common preposition is *from*. _____ common one is *in*. _____ are *by, for,* and *of*. The most frequently used prepositions in English are *at, by, for, from, in, of, to,* and *with*. What are some _____ prepositions?

18. That country has two basic problems. One is inflation, and _____ is the instability of the government.

19. I have been in only three cities since I came to the United States. One is New York, and _____ are Washington, D. C., and Chicago.

20. When his alarm went off this morning, he shut it off, rolled over, and slept for _____ twenty minutes.

21. They have three children. One has graduated from college and has a job. _____ is at Yale University. _____ is still living at home.

☐ EXERCISE 14. Using OTHER. (Chart 8-6)
Directions: Complete the sentences orally, using an appropriate form of ***other***. Work in pairs, in groups, or as a class. If working in pairs, switch roles after Item 6.

Example:
SPEAKER A *(book open):* There are two books on my desk. One is . . . .
SPEAKER B *(book closed):* One is red. The other is blue.

1. I speak two languages. One is . . . .
2. I speak three languages. One is . . . .
3. I lost my textbook, so I had to buy . . . .
4. Some people have straight hair, but . . . .
5. George Washington is one American hero. Abraham Lincoln . . . .
6. I have two books. One is . . . .
7. Some TV programs are excellent, but . . . .
8. Some people need at least eight hours of sleep each night, but . . . .
9. Only two of the students failed the quiz. All of . . . .
10. There are three colors that I especially like. One is . . . .
11. I have two candy bars. I want only one of them. Would you like . . . .
12. There are three places in particular I would like to visit while I am in *(this city/country)*. One is . . . .

8-7 COMMON EXPRESSIONS WITH *OTHER*

(a) We write to *each other* every week. We write to *one another* every week.	*Each other* and *one another* indicate a reciprocal relationship.* In (a): I write to him every week, and he writes to me every week.
(b) Please write on *every other* line. I see her *every other* week.	*Every other* can give the idea of "alternate." In (b): Write on the first line. Do not write on the second line. Write on the third line. Do not write on the fourth line. (Etc.)
(c) —Have you seen Ali recently? —Yes. I saw him just *the other day*.	*The other* is used in time expressions such as *the other day, the other morning, the other week, etc.*, to refer to the recent past. In (c): *the other day* means "a few days ago, not long ago."
(d) The ducklings walked in a line behind the mother duck. Then the mother duck slipped into the pond. The ducklings followed her. They slipped into the water *one after the other*. (e) They slipped into the water *one after another*.	In (d): *one after the other* expresses the idea that separate actions occur very close in time. In (e): *one after another* has the same meaning as *one after the other*.

(f) No one knows my secret *other than* Rosa. (g) No one knows my secret *except* *(for)* Rosa.	In (f): *other than* is usually used after a negative to mean "except." (g) has the same meaning.
(h) Fruit and vegetables are full of vitamins and minerals. *In other words*, they are good for you.	In (h): *In other words* is used to explain, usually in simpler or clearer terms, the meaning of the preceding sentence(s).

*In typical usage, *each other* and *one another* are interchangeable; there is no difference between them. Some native speakers, however, use *each other* when they are talking about only two persons or things, and *one another* when there are more than two.

□ EXERCISE 15. Using OTHER. (Charts 8-6 and 8-7)
  Directions: Supply a form of *other*.

  1. Two countries border on the United States. One is Canada. ___The other___ is

   Mexico.

  2. One of the countries I would like to visit is Sweden. _____ is Mexico.

   Of course, besides these two countries, there are many _____

   places I would like to see.

3. Louis and I have been friends for a long time. We've known _____ since we were children.

4. A: I talked to Sam _____ day.

   B: Oh? How is he? I haven't seen him for ages.

5. In the Southwest there is a large area of land that has little or no rainfall, no trees, and very few plants _____ than cactuses. In _____ words, this area of the country is a desert.

6. Thank you for inviting me to the picnic. I'd like to go with you, but I've already made _____ plans.

7. Some people are tall; _____ are short. Some people are fat; _____ are thin. Some people are nearsighted; _____ people are farsighted.

8. Mr. and Mrs. Jay love _____. They support _____ _____. They like _____. In _____ words, they are a happily married couple.

9. A: How often do you travel to Portland?

   B: Every _____ month. I go there to visit my grandmother in a nursing home.

10. Could I borrow your pen? I need to write a check, but I have nothing to write with _____ than this pencil.

11. My niece, Kathy, ate one cookie after _____ until she finished the whole box. That's why she had a bad stomachache.

EXERCISE 16. Using OTHER. (Charts 8-6 and 8-7)
  Directions: Write sentences that include the given words. Punctuate carefully.

Examples:
  I . . . two . . . one . . . (+ form of *other*) . . .
  → **I** have **two** brothers. **One** of them is in high school, and **the other** is in college.

  Some . . . like coffee . . . while* (+ form of *other*) . . .
  → **Some** people **like coffee** with their breakfasts, **while others** prefer tea.

  One city . . . (+ form of *other*) is . . .
  → **One city** I would like to visit is Paris. **Another** is Rome.

1. My . . . has two . . . one of them . . . (+ form of *other*) . . .
2. Some people . . . in their free time . . . while (+ form of *other*) . . .
3. . . . national hero . . . (+ form of *other*) . . .
4. . . . three . . . two of . . . (+ form of *other*) . . .
5. . . . more time . . . (+ form of *other*) . . . minutes . . .
6. There are three . . . that I especially like . . . one is . . . (+ form of *other*) . . .
7. I lost . . . bought (+ form of *other*) . . .
8. Some movies . . . while (+ form of *other*) . . .
9. . . . speak . . . (+ form of *other*) . . .
10. . . . is one of the longest rivers in the world . . . is (+ form of *other*) . . .
11. Nobody . . . other than . . .
12. . . . each other during . . .

EXERCISE 17. Summary review. (Chapters 6 → 8)
  Directions: Correct the errors.

1. That book contain many different kind of story and article.

2. The English is one of the most important language in the world.

3. She is always willing to help her friends in every possible ways.

4. In the past, horses was the principal mean of transportation.

5. He succeeded in creating one of the best army in the world.

6. There are many equipments in the research laboratory, but undergraduates
   are not allowed to use them.

7. All of the guest enjoyed themself at the reception.

8. I have a five years old daughter and a three years old son.

9. Each states in the country have a different language.

While is similar in meaning to *but* in this situation. See Chart 17-4, p. 366.

10. Most of people in my apartment building is friendly.

11. A political leader should have the ability to adapt themselves to a changing world.

12. In my opinion, an international student should live in a dormitory because they will meet many people and can practice their English every day. Also, if you live in a dormitory, your food is provided for you.

13. When I lost my passport, I had to apply for the another one.

14. When I got to class, all of the others students were already in their seats.

15. Everyone seek the happiness in their life.

16. In my country, there is a lots of schools.

17. Writing compositions are very hard for me.

18. It's difficult for me to understand English when people uses a lot of slangs.

19. A student at the university should attend class regularly and hand in their assignments on time.

20. In my opinion, the english is a easy language to learn.

☐ EXERCISE 18. Summary review. (Chapters 6 → 8)
Directions: Correct the errors.

1. There is many different kind of animal in the world.

2. My cousin and her husband want to move to other city because they don't like a cold weather.

3. I like to travel because I like to learn about other country and custom.

4. Collecting stamps is one of my hobby.

5. I came here three and a half month ago. I think I have made a good progress in English.

6. I was looking for my keys, but I couldn't find it.

7. When my mother was child, she lived in a small town. Now this town is big city with tall building and many highway.

8. English has borrowed quite a few of word from another languages.

9. There is many student from differents countries in this class.

10. Thousand of athlete take part in the Olympics.

11. Education is one of the most important aspect of life. Knowledges about many different things allow us to live fuller lives.

12. All of the students names were on the list.

13. I live in a two rooms apartment.

14. Many of people prefer to live in small towns. Their attachment to their communities prevent them from moving from place to place in search of works.

15. Todays news is just as bad as yesterdays news.

16. Almost of the students in our class speaks English well.

17. The teacher gave us several homework to hand in next Tuesday.

18. Today womans work as doctor, pilot, archeologist, and many other thing. Both my mother and father are teacher's.

19. Every employees in our company respect Mr. Ward.

20. A child needs to learn how to get along with another people, how to spend his or her time wisely, and how to depend on yourself.

☐ EXERCISE 19. Writing: nouns and pronouns. (Chapters 7 and 8)
Directions: Choose any object you wish. Write a short paragraph about it, but do NOT include the name of the object in your writing; always use a pronoun to refer to it, not the noun itself.

Describe the object (What does it look like? What is it made of? What does it feel like? Does it make a noise? Does it have a smell? etc.), and explain why people use it or how it is used. Begin with its general characteristics, then gradually get more specific.

Then read your paragraph aloud to the class or to a group, who will guess what the object is.

Example:

It is usually made of metal. It is hollow. It is round on one end. It can be very small, small enough to fit in your pocket, or large, but not as large as a car. It is used to make noise. It can be used to give a signal. Sometimes it's part of an orchestra. Sometimes it is electric and you push a button to make it ring.

What is it?

☐ EXERCISE 20. Writing: agreement. (Chapters 6 → 8)

Directions: Write a paragraph about a subject you are familiar with. Choose a subject such as your country, your family, your job, your field of study — or anything you know something about: ducks, motorcycles, gardening, etc.

In this paragraph, purposely make mistakes in the use of final *-s/-es* subject–verb agreement, and pronoun agreement. Be sure your paragraph contains these kinds of mistakes.

Use only or mostly present tenses.

Give your completed paragraph to a classmate, who will correct the singular-plural errors you made (as well as any unintended errors).

☐ EXERCISE 21. Writing: nouns. (Chapters 6 → 8)

Directions: Write a paragraph on one of the topics below. Write as quickly as you can. Write whatever comes into your mind. Try to write 100 words in ten minutes.

When you finish your paragraph, exchange it with a classmate. Correct each other's errors before giving it to your teacher.

Topics:
1. food
2. English
3. this room
4. animals

CHAPTER 9
Modals, Part 1

CONTENTS

9-1   INTRODUCTION

The modal auxiliaries in English are *can, could, had better, may, might, must, ought (to), shall, should, will, would*.

Modal auxiliaries generally express speakers' attitudes. For example, modals can express that a speaker feels something is necessary, advisable, permissible, possible, or probable; and, in addition, they can convey the strength of those attitudes.

Each modal has more than one meaning or use. See Chart 10-10, p. 199, for a summary overview of modals.

(a) BASIC MODALS	
I You He She It We You They + { *can* do it. *could* do it. *had better* do it. *may* do it. *might* do it. *must* do it. *ought to* do it. *shall* do it. *should* do it. *will* do it. *would* do it. }	Modals do not take a final *-s*, even when the subject is *she, he,* or *it*. CORRECT: **She can** do it. INCORRECT: She *cans* do it.
	Modals are followed immediately by the simple form of a verb. CORRECT: **She can do it.** INCORRECT: She can *to* do it. / She can *does* it. / She can *did* it. The only exception is *ought*, which is followed by an infinitive (*to + the simple form of a verb*). CORRECT: He **ought to go** to the meeting.
(b) PHRASAL MODALS *be able to* do it *be going to* do it *be supposed to* do it *have to* do it *have got to* do it *used to* do it	Phrasal modals are common expressions whose meanings are similar to those of some of the modal auxiliaries. For example: **be able to** is similar to **can**; **be going to** is similar to **will**. An infinitive *(to + the simple form of a verb)* is used in these similar expressions.

        Directions: All of these contain errors in the forms of modals. Correct the errors.

1. She can to see it.	5. Can you please to pass the rice?
2. She cans see it.	6. Do you can see it?*
3. She can sees it.	7. They don't can go there.**
4. She can saw it.	

9-2   POLITE REQUESTS WITH *"I"* AS THE SUBJECT

MAY I COULD I	(a) *May I* (please) *borrow* your pen? (b) *Could I borrow* your pen (please)?	*May I* and *could I* are used to request permission. They are equally polite.† Note in (b): In a polite request, *could* has a present or future meaning, not a past meaning.
CAN I	(c) *Can I borrow* your pen?	*Can I* is used informally to request permission, especially if the speaker is talking to someone s/he knows fairly well. *Can I* is usually considered a little less polite than *may I* or *could I*.
	TYPICAL RESPONSES Certainly. Yes, certainly. Of course. Yes, of course. Sure. *(informal)*	Often the response to a polite request is an action, such as a nod or shake of the head, or a simple "uh-huh."

†*Might* is also possible: *Might I borrow* your pen? *Might I* is quite formal and polite; it is used much less frequently than *may I* or *could I*.

9-3   POLITE REQUESTS WITH *"YOU"* AS THE SUBJECT

WOULD YOU WILL YOU	(a) *Would you pass* the salt (please)? (b) *Will you* (please) *pass* the salt?	The meaning of *would you* and *will you* in a polite request is the same. *Would you* is more common and is often considered more polite. The degree of politeness, however, is often determined by the speaker's tone of voice.
COULD YOU	(c) *Could you pass* the salt (please)?	Basically, *could you* and *would you* have the same meaning. The difference is slight: *Would you* = *Do you want to do this please?* *Could you* = *Do you want to do this please, and is it possible for you to do this?* *Could you* and *would you* are equally polite.
CAN YOU	(d) *Can you* (please) *pass* the salt?	*Can you* is often used informally. It usually sounds less polite than *could you* or *would you*.
	TYPICAL RESPONSES Yes, I'd (I would) be happy to/be glad to. Certainly. Sure. *(informal)*	A person usually responds in the affirmative to a polite request. If a negative response is necessary, a person might begin by saying "I'd like to, but . . . " (e.g., "I'd like to pass the salt, but I can't reach it").
	(e) *INCORRECT: May you* pass the salt?	*May* is used only with *I* or *we* in polite requests.

---

*See Appendix Chart B-1, p. A8, for question forms with modals.
**See Appendix Chart D-1, p. A18, for negative forms with modals.

☐ EXERCISE 2. Polite requests. (Charts 9-2 and 9-3)

Directions: Ask and answer polite requests.

Speaker A: Your book is open. Present the situation to Speaker B.

Speaker B: Your book is closed. Make a polite request for the situation.

Speaker A: Give a typical response.

Example:

SPEAKER A *(book open):* You and I are co-workers. We don't know each other well. We're at a lunch table in a cafeteria. You want the pepper.

SPEAKER B *(book closed): Would/Could* you please pass me the pepper? (Note: *Will* is also possible because the speaker uses *please,* but *can* is probably not appropriate in this situation.)

SPEAKER A: Certainly. I'd be glad to. Here you are.

1. You and I are good friends. We're in my apartment. You want to use the phone.

2. I'm your instructor. You want to leave class early.

3. You call your friend. Her name is (. . .). I answer the phone. You and I don't know each other.

4. I'm your supervisor at work. You knock on my half-open office door. I'm sitting at my desk. You want to come in.

5. I'm Dr. North's secretary. You want to make an appointment to see Dr. North.

6. We're roommates. You want me to tape *(a particular program)* on the VCR tonight while you're away at a meeting.

7. I'm a stranger next to you at an airport check-in line. You want me to save your place in line and keep an eye on your luggage while you get a drink of water.

9-4   POLITE REQUESTS WITH *WOULD YOU MIND*

ASKING PERMISSION (a) *Would you mind **if I closed** the window?* (b) *Would you mind **if I used** the phone?*	Notice in (a): ***Would you mind if I*** is followed by the simple past.★ The meaning in (a): *May I close the window? Is it all right if I close the window? Will it cause you any trouble or discomfort if I close the window?*
TYPICAL RESPONSES No, not at all/of course not. No, that would be fine.	Another typical response might be "unh-unh," meaning "no."
ASKING SOMEONE TO DO SOMETHING (c) *Would you mind **closing** the window?* (d) Excuse me. *Would you mind **repeating** that?*	Notice in (c): ***Would you mind*** is followed by ***-ing*** (a gerund). The meaning in (c): *I don't want to cause you any trouble, but would you please close the window? Would that cause you any inconvenience?*
TYPICAL RESPONSES No. I'd be happy to. Not at all. I'd be glad to. Sure./Okay. *(informal)*	The informal responses of "Sure" and "Okay" are common, but are not logical: the speaker means "No, I wouldn't mind" but seems to be saying "Yes, I would mind." Native speakers understand that the response "Sure" or "Okay" in this situation means that the speaker agrees to the request.

★Sometimes, in informal spoken English, the simple present is used: *Would you mind if I **close** the window?*
(NOTE: The simple past does not refer to past time after ***would you mind;*** it refers to present or future time. See Chart 20-3, p. 415, for more information.)

□ **EXERCISE 3. Polite requests with WOULD YOU MIND. (Chart 9-4)**
Directions: Using the verb in parentheses, fill in the blank either with ***if I*** + *the past tense* or with the ***-ing*** *form of the verb.* In some of the sentences, either response is possible but the meaning is different.

1. I'm getting tired. I'd like to go home and go to bed. Would you mind *(leave)*
_____**if I left**_____ early?

2. I'm sorry. I didn't understand what you said. Would you mind *(repeat)*
_____**repeating**_____ that?

3. A: Are you going to the post office?
   B: Yes.
   A: Would you mind *(mail)* _____ this letter for me?
   B: Not at all.

4. A: Are you coming with us?
   B: I know I promised to go with you, but I'm not feeling very good. Would you mind
      (stay) _____ home?
   A: Of course not.

5. A: It's getting hot in here. Would you mind *(open)* _____ the
      window?
   B: No.

6. A: This is probably none of my business, but would you mind *(ask)* _____
      you a personal question?
   B: It depends.

7. A: Would you mind *(smoke)*

      _____ ?
   B: I'd really rather you didn't.

8. A: Excuse me. Would you mind

      (speak) _____ a
      little more slowly? I didn't
      catch what you said.
   B: Oh, of course. I'm sorry.

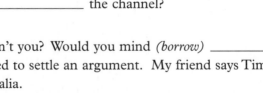

9. A: I don't like this TV program. Would you mind
      (change) _____ the channel?
   B: Unh-unh.

10. A: You have an atlas, don't you? Would you mind *(borrow)* _____
       it for a minute? I need to settle an argument. My friend says Timbuktu is in Asia,
       and I say it's in Australia.
    B: You're both wrong. It's in Africa. Here's the atlas. Look it up for yourself.

□ EXERCISE 4. Polite requests with WOULD YOU MIND. (Chart 9-4)
    Directions: Pair up and make dialogues.
    Speaker A: Make a polite request using **would you mind**.
    Speaker B: Give a typical response.

    Example: You have a library book. You want the other person to take it back to the library
        for you.
    SPEAKER A: Are you going to the library?
    SPEAKER B: Yes.
    SPEAKER A: This book is due. Would you mind taking it back to the library for me?
    SPEAKER B: Not at all. I'd be glad to.

    1. You've finished dinner. You're about to wash the dinner dishes. You want the other
       person to dry them.
    2. You're watching TV together. One of you has the remote control and wants to turn up
       the volume.
    3. One of you says that you're going to a particular store. The other one wants
       something from that store, too, but doesn't have time to go there.
    4. One of you wants to ask the other a personal question.
    5. You're in a computer lab at a language school. One of you knows how to run the
       computers, and the other doesn't. The one who doesn't wants to see a CD-ROM
       program.

□ EXERCISE 5. Polite requests. (Charts 9-2 → 9-4)
    Directions: Complete the polite requests with your own words. Try to imagine what the
    speaker might say in the given situation.

    1.   JACK: What's the trouble, Officer?
         OFFICER: You made an illegal U-turn.
            JACK: I did?
         OFFICER: Yes. May _I see your driver's license_?
            JACK: Certainly. It's in my wallet.
         OFFICER: Would _you please remove it from your wallet_?

    2.   WAITER: Good evening. Are you ready to order?
        CUSTOMER: No, we're not. Could _____?
          WAITER: Certainly. And if you have any questions, I'd be happy to tell you about
                  anything on the menu.

    3.   SALLY: Are you driving to the meeting tonight?
            MIKE: Uh-huh, I am.
           SALLY: Could _____?
            MIKE: Sure. I'll pick you up at 7:00.

    4. MR. PENN: Something's come up, and I can't meet with you Tuesday. Would you
                 mind _____?
        MS. GRAY: Let me check my calendar.

5. MECHANIC: What seems to be the trouble with your car?

CUSTOMER: Something's wrong with the brakes, I think. Could _____?

_____?

MECHANIC: Sure. Just pull the car into the garage.

6. CLERK: May _____?

CUSTOMER: Yes, please. Could _____?

CLERK: Surely. Do you have a particular color in mind?

7. SHELLEY: Are you enjoying the movie?

MIKE: Yeah, you?

SHELLEY: Yes, but I can't see over the man in front of me. Would you mind

_____?

MIKE: Not at all. I see two empty seats across the aisle.

8. CARLO: I have to leave now, but I'd like to continue this conversation later. May

_____?

ANNE: Of course. My phone number is 555-1716. I'll look forward to hearing from you.

□ EXERCISE 6. Polite requests. (Charts 9-2 → 9-4)
Directions: For each situation, make up a short dialogue between two speakers. The dialogue should contain a polite request and a response to that request.

Example: Names of the speakers: Janet and Sara
Janet doesn't have enough money to go to a movie tonight. She wants to borrow some from Sara, who is her roommate and good friend.

Possible dialogue:
JANET: There's a movie I really want to see tonight, but I'm running a little low on money right now. Could I borrow a few dollars? I'll pay you back Friday.
SARA: Sure. No problem. How much do you need?

1. Names of the speakers: Mike and Elena
Mike is walking down the hall of his office building. He needs to know what time it is. He asks Elena, a co-worker he's seen before but has never met.

2. Names of the speakers: Larry and Matt
Larry is trying to study. His roommate, Matt, is playing a CD very loudly, and this is bothering Larry, who is trying to be polite even though he feels frustrated and a little angry.

3. Names of the speakers: Kate and Jason
Kate is phoning her friend Tom. Jason answers and tells her that Tom is out. Kate wants to leave a message.

4. Names of the speakers: Ms. Jackson and a friendly stranger
Ms. Jackson is in the middle of the city. She's lost. She's trying to find the bus station. She stops someone on the street to ask for directions.

5. Names of the speakers: Paul and Jack
   Paul just arrived at work and remembered that he left his stove on back in his apartment. His neighbor Jack has a key to the front door, and Paul knows that Jack hasn't left for work yet. Anxiously, he telephones Jack for help.

6. Names of the speakers: your name and your partner's name
   One of you has a minor problem that requires the other's help.

☐ **EXERCISE 7. Polite requests. (Charts 9-2 → 9-4)**
   Directions: What are some polite requests you have heard or have said in the following places? Create typical dialogues.

1. in this classroom
2. at a service station
3. at a restaurant
4. at a clothing store
5. at an airport
6. on the telephone

9-5   EXPRESSING NECESSITY: *MUST, HAVE TO, HAVE GOT TO*

(a) All applicants *must take* an entrance exam. (b) All applicants *have to take* an entrance exam.	*Must* and *have to* both express necessity. In (a) and (b): It is necessary for every applicant to take an entrance exam. There is no other choice. The exam is required.
(c) I'm looking for Sue. I *have to talk* to her about our lunch date tomorrow. I can't meet her for lunch because I *have to go* to a business meeting at 1:00. (d) Where's Sue? I *must talk* to her right away. I have an urgent message for her.	In everyday statements of necessity, *have to* is used more commonly than *must*. *Must* is usually stronger than *have to* and can indicate urgency or stress importance. In (c): The speaker is simply saying, "I need to do this, and I need to do that." In (d): The speaker is strongly saying, "This is very important!"
(e) I *have to* ("hafta") be home by eight. (f) He *has to* ("hasta") go to a meeting tonight.	Note: *have to* is usually pronounced "hafta"; *has to* is usually pronounced "hasta."
(g) I *have got to go* now. I have a class in ten minutes. (h) I *have to go* now. I have a class in ten minutes.	*Have got to* also expresses the idea of necessity: (g) and (h) have the same meaning. *Have got to* is informal and is used primarily in spoken English. *Have to* is used in both formal and informal English.
(i) I *have got to go* ("I've gotta go/I gotta go") now.	Usual pronunciation of *got to* is "gotta." Sometimes *have* is dropped in speech: "I gotta do it."
(j) PRESENT or FUTURE I *have to / have got to / must study* tonight. (k) PAST I *had to study* last night.	The idea of past necessity is expressed by *had to*. There is no other past form for *must* (when it means necessity) or *have got to*.

☐ EXERCISE 8. MUST, HAVE TO, HAVE GOT TO. (Chart 9-5)

Directions: Answer the questions. Practice pronouncing the usual spoken forms of **have to** and **have got to**.

1. What are some of the things you have to do today or tomorrow?
2. What does (. . .) have to do today?
3. What have you got to do after class?
4. What has (. . .) got to do after class?
5. Can you think of something very important that you must do today or tomorrow?
6. What is something that you had to do yesterday?
7. Ask a classmate a question using *have to* and *what time/where/how often/why.*★

9-6 LACK OF NECESSITY AND PROHIBITION: *HAVE TO* AND *MUST* IN THE NEGATIVE

LACK OF NECESSITY	When used in the negative, **must** and **have to** have different meanings.
(a) Tomorrow is a holiday. We **don't have to go** to class. (b) I can hear you. You **don't have to shout.**†	**do not have to** = lack of necessity In (a): It is not necessary for us to go to class tomorrow because it is a holiday.
PROHIBITION (c) You **must not look** in the closet. Your birthday present is hidden there. (d) You **must not tell** anyone my secret. Do you promise?	**must not** = prohibition (DO NOT DO THIS!) In (c): Do not look in the closet. I forbid it. Looking in the closet is prohibited. Negative contraction: **mustn't**. (The first "t" is silent: "muss-ənt.")

†Lack of necessity may also be expressed by **need not** + *the simple form of a verb:* You **needn't shout**. The use of **needn't** as an auxiliary is chiefly British except in certain common expressions such as "You needn't worry."

☐ EXERCISE 9. HAVE TO and MUST in the negative. (Chart 9-6)

Directions: Use **must not** or **do not have to** in the following.

1. I've already finished all my work, so I ___*don't have to*___ study tonight. I think I'll read for a while.

2. I ___*must not*___ forget to take my key with me.

3. You _____ introduce me to Dr. Gray. We've already met.

4. In order to be a good salesclerk, you _____ be rude to a customer.

5. A person _____ become rich and famous in order to live a successful life.

★A form of **do** is used with **have to** in questions: e.g., *When does he have to leave?*

6. Johnny! You _____ play with sharp knives. Put that knife down immediately!

7. I _____ go to the doctor. I'm feeling much better.

8. We _____ go to the concert if you don't want to, but it might be good.

9. Robin! What are you doing? No, no, no. You _____ put your vitamin pill in your nose!

10. Bats _____ see in order to avoid obstacles. They can navigate in complete darkness.

11. If you encounter a growling dog, you _____ show any signs of fear. If a dog senses fear, it is more likely to attack a person.

12. A person _____ get married in order to lead a happy and fulfilling life.

☐ **EXERCISE 10. HAVE TO and MUST in the negative. (Chart 9-6)**
Directions: Complete the sentences with your own words.

Example: Students don't have to . . . .
Possible response: Students in elementary school don't have to pay tuition.

Example: Students must not . . . .
Possible response: Students must not cheat during tests.

1. Children must not . . . .
2. Children don't have to . . . .
3. Drivers must not . . . .
4. Drivers don't have to . . . .
5. We don't have to . . . .
6. We must not . . . .
7. (. . .) doesn't have to . . . .
8. (. . .) must not . . . .
9. Waiters must not . . . .
10. Waiters don't have to . . . .
11. I don't have to . . . .
12. I must not . . . .

9-7 ADVISABILITY: *SHOULD, OUGHT TO, HAD BETTER*

(a) You *should study* harder. You *ought to study* harder. (b) Drivers *should obey* the speed limit. Drivers *ought to obey* the speed limit.	*Should* and *ought to* have the same meaning: they express advisability. The meaning ranges in strength from a suggestion ("This is a good idea") to a statement about responsibility or duty ("This is a very important thing to do"). In (a): "This is a good idea. This is my advice." In (b): "This is an important responsibility."
(c) You *shouldn't leave* your keys in the car.	Negative contraction: *shouldn't.*★
(d) I *ought to* ("otta") *study* tonight, but I think I'll watch TV instead.	*Ought to* is often pronounced "otta" in informal speaking.
(e) The gas tank is almost empty. We *had better stop* at the next service station. (f) You *had better take* care of that cut on your hand soon, or it will get infected.	In meaning, *had better* is close to *should/ought to*, but *had better* is usually stronger. Often *had better* implies a warning or a threat of possible bad consequences. In (e): If we don't stop at a service station, there will be a bad result. We will run out of gas. Notes on the use of *had better:* • It has a present or future meaning. • It is followed by the simple form of a verb. • It is more common in speaking than writing.
(g) You*'d better* take care of it. (h) You *better* take care of it.	Contraction: *'d better,* as in (g). Sometimes in speaking, *had* is dropped, as in (h).
(i) You*'d better not* be late.	Negative form: *had better + not*.

★*Ought to* is not commonly used in the negative. If it is used in the negative, the *to* is sometimes dropped: *You oughtn't (to) leave your keys in the car.*

☐ EXERCISE 11. SHOULD, OUGHT TO, HAD BETTER. (Chart 9-7)
Directions: Work in pairs, in groups, or as a class.
Speaker A: Your book is open. Present the problem as given in the text.
Speaker B: Your book is closed. Give advice by using *should, ought to,* or *had better.*

Example:
SPEAKER A *(book open):*   I have a test tomorrow.
SPEAKER B *(book closed):* You should (ought to, had better) study tonight.

1. I'm writing a composition, and there is a word I don't know how to spell.
2. I don't feel well. I think I'm catching a cold.
3. I can't see the chalkboard when I sit in the back row.
4. I'm cold.
5. My foot is asleep.
6. My roommate snores, and I can't get to sleep.
7. My friend is arriving at the airport this evening. I'm supposed to pick him up, but I've forgotten what time his plane gets in.
8. My apartment is a mess, and my mother is coming to visit tomorrow!

9. There's no food in the house, and some guests are coming to dinner tonight.
10. I can't stop yawning.
11. I have a toothache.
12. I need to improve my English.
13. I have the hiccups.
14. When William gets out of college, his parents expect him to manage the family business, a shoe store, but he wants to be an architect.
15. Pam's younger brother, who is 18, is using illegal drugs. How can she help him?
16. The Taylors' daughter is very excited about going to Denmark to study for four months. You've been an international student, haven't you? Could you give her some advice?

☐ EXERCISE 12. SHOULD, OUGHT TO, HAD BETTER. (Chart 9-7)
Directions: Complete the dialogues with your own words.

1. A: Oops! I spilled _coffee on my shirt._

   B: You'd better _run it under hot water before the stain sets._

2. A: The shoes I bought last week _____

   B: Oh? You ought to _____

3. A: Jimmy, you'd better _____

      or I'm going to _____

   B: Okay, Mom. I'll do it right now.

4. A: I'd better _____

   B: I agree. It'll be winter soon.

5. A: I've been studying for three days straight.

   B: I know. You should _____

   A: I know, but _____

6. A: Kids, your dad and I work hard all day long. Don't you think you should _____

      _____

   B: _____

7. A: My doctor said I should _____ , but I

      _____

   B: Well, I think you'd better _____

8. A: You should _____ if you _____

   B: Thanks for reminding me. I'd better _____

9. A: Have you _____

   B: No, not yet.

   A: You really ought to _____

10. A: Mary's always wanted to learn how to _____

    B: Isn't your brother _____

    You should _____

11. A: Do you think I ought to _____ or _____

    B: I think you'd better _____ . If you don't,

    _____

12. A: Lately I can't seem to concentrate on anything, and I feel _____

    _____

    B: Maybe you should _____

    Or have you thought about _____

☐ EXERCISE 13. Necessity, advisability, and prohibition. (Charts 9-5 → 9-7)
Directions: Which sentence in the following pairs is stronger? Discuss situations in which a speaker might say these sentences.

1. a. You *should go* to a doctor.
   b. You'*d better go* to a doctor.
2. a. Mary *should go* to work today.
   b. Mary *must go* to work today.
3. a. We'*ve got to go* to class.
   b. We *ought to go* to class.
4. a. I *have to go* to the post office.
   b. I *should go* to the post office.
5. a. We *shouldn't go* into that room.
   b. We *must not go* into that room.
6. a. You'*d better not go* there alone.
   b. You *shouldn't go* there alone.

☐ EXERCISE 14. SHOULD vs. MUST/HAVE TO. (Charts 9-5 → 9-7)
Directions: Use either ***should*** or ***must*** / ***have to*** in the following. In some sentences either is possible, but the meaning is different. Discuss the meanings of the completions.

1. A person ___must/has to___ eat in order to live.

2. A person _____should_____ eat a balanced diet.

3. If you want to become a doctor, you _____ go to medical school for many years.

4. I don't have enough money to take the bus, so I _____ walk home.

5. Walking is good exercise. You say you want to get more exercise. You _____ walk to and from work instead of taking the bus.

6. We _____ go to Colorado for our vacation.

7. According to my advisor, I _____ take another English course.

8. Rice _____ have water in order to grow.

9. This pie is very good. You _____ try a piece.

10. This pie is excellent! You _____ try a piece.★

9-8 THE PAST FORM OF *SHOULD*

(a) I had a test this morning. I didn't do well on the test because I didn't study for it last night. I *should have studied* last night.	Past form: *should have* + *past participle*.★
	In (a): *I should have studied* means that studying was a good idea, but I didn't do it. I made a mistake.
(b) You were supposed to be here at 10 P.M., but you didn't come until midnight. We were worried about you. You *should have called* us. (You did not call.)	Usual pronunciation of *should have:* "should-əv" or "should-ə."
(c) My back hurts. I *should not have carried* that heavy box up two flights of stairs. (I carried the box, and now I'm sorry.)	In (c): *I should not have carried* means that I carried something, but it turned out to be a bad idea. I made a mistake.
(d) We went to a movie, but it was a waste of time and money. We *should not have gone* to the movie.	Usual pronunciation of *should not have:* "shouldn't-əv" or "shouldn't-ə."

★The past form of *ought to* is *ought to have* + *past participle*. (*I ought to have studied.*) It has the same meaning as the past form of *should*. In the past, *should* is used more commonly than *ought to*. *Had better* is used only rarely in a past form (e.g., *He had better have taken care of it*) and usually only in speaking, not writing.

☐ EXERCISE 15. The past form of SHOULD. (Chart 9-8)

Directions: Work in pairs, in groups, or as a class.
Speaker A: Your book is open. Present the situation given in the book.
Speaker B: Your book is closed. Comment on the situation using *should have* + *past participle*.

Example: I didn't invite (. . .) to my party. That made him/her feel bad. I'm sorry I didn't invite him/her.

SPEAKER A *(book open):*   I didn't invite Sonya to my party. That made her feel bad. I'm sorry I didn't invite her.

SPEAKER B *(book closed):*   You should have invited Sonya to your party.

1. (. . .) made a mistake yesterday. He/She left the door to his/her house open, and a bird flew in. He/She had a terrible time catching the bird.

2. There was an important meeting yesterday afternoon, but you decided not to go. That was a mistake. Now your boss is angry.

3. (. . .) didn't feel good a couple of days ago. I told him/her to see a doctor, but he/she didn't. That was a mistake. Now he/she is very sick.

4. (. . .) sold her/his car. That was a mistake because now she/he can't take trips to see her/his friends and relatives.

5. (. . .) signed a contract to buy some furniture without reading it thoroughly. Now she/he has discovered that she/he is paying a higher interest rate than she/he expected. She/he made a mistake.

★Sometimes in speaking, *must* has the meaning of a very enthusiastic *should*.

☐ EXERCISE 16. The past form of SHOULD. (Chart 9-8)

Directions: Work in pairs.
Speaker A: Your book is open. Present the situation.
Speaker B: Your book is closed. Use ***should have*** + *past participle* in your response.

Example:

SPEAKER A *(book open):*   You failed the test because you didn't study.

SPEAKER B *(book closed):* I should have studied.

1. You are cold because you didn't wear a coat.
2. You misspelled a word because you didn't look it up in the dictionary.
3. Your friend is upset because you didn't write him a letter.
4. You are broke now because you spent all your money foolishly.
5. The room is full of flies because you opened the window.
6. You don't have any food for dinner because you didn't go to the grocery store.
7. You overslept this morning because you didn't set your alarm clock.
8. Your friends went to (New Orleans) over vacation. They had a good time. You didn't go with them, and now you are sorry.

Switch roles.

9. You didn't have a cup of coffee. Now you are sleepy.
10. John loved Mary, but he didn't marry her. Now he is unhappy.
11. John loved Mary, and he married her. But now he is unhappy.
12. You were sick yesterday, but you went to class anyway. Today you feel worse.
13. The weather was beautiful yesterday, but you stayed inside all day.
14. You bought your girlfriend/boyfriend a box of candy for her/his birthday, but she/he doesn't like candy.
15. The little girl told a lie. She got into a lot of trouble.
16. You lent your car to (. . .), but s/he had an accident because s/he was driving on the wrong side of the road.

☐ EXERCISE 17. The past form of SHOULD. (Chart 9-8)

Directions: Discuss or write what you think the people in the following situations ***should have done*** and ***should not have done***.

Example:

   Tom didn't study for the test. During the exam he panicked and started looking at other students' test papers. He didn't think the teacher saw him, but she did. She warned him once to stop cheating, but he continued. As a result, the teacher took Tom's test paper, told him to leave the room, and failed him on the exam.

→ *Tom should have studied for the test.*
→ *He shouldn't have panicked during the test.*
→ *He shouldn't have started cheating.*
→ *He should have known the teacher would see him cheating.*
→ *He should have stopped cheating after the first warning.*
→ *The teacher should have ripped up Tom's paper and sent him out of the room the first time she saw him cheating.*

1. John and his wife, Julie, had good jobs as professionals in New York City. John was offered a high-paying job in Chicago, which he immediately accepted. Julie was shocked when he came home that evening and told her the news. She liked her job and the people she worked with, and did not want to move away and look for another job.

2. Ann agreed to meet her friend Carl at the library to help him with his chemistry homework. On the way, she stopped at a cafe where her boyfriend worked. Her boyfriend told her he could get off work early that night, so the two of them decided to go to a movie. Ann didn't cancel her plans with Carl. Carl waited for three hours at the library.

3. For three years, Donna had been saving her money for a trip to Europe. Her brother, Larry, had a good job, but spent all of his money on expensive cars, clothes, and entertainment. Suddenly, Larry was fired from his job and had no money to support himself while he looked for another one. Donna lent him nearly all of her savings, and within three weeks he spent it all on his car, more clothes, and expensive restaurants.

4. Sarah often exaggerated and once told a co-worker that she was fluent in French even though she had studied only a little and could not really communicate in the language. A few days later, her boss asked her to come to his office to interpret a meeting with a French businessman who had just arrived from Paris to negotiate a major contract with the company. After an embarrassed silence, Sarah told her boss that she was feeling ill and had to go home immediately.

9-9 EXPECTATIONS: *BE SUPPOSED TO*

(a) The game *is supposed to begin* at 10:00. (b) The committee *is supposed to vote* by secret ballot.	*Be supposed to* expresses the idea that someone (I, we, they, the teacher, lots of people, my father, etc.) expects something to happen. *Be supposed to* often expresses expectations about scheduled events, as in (a), or correct procedures, as in (b).
(c) I *am supposed to go* to the meeting. My boss told me that he wants me to attend. (d) The children *are supposed to put away* their toys before they go to bed.	*Be supposed to* also expresses expectations about behavior. In (c) and (d): *be supposed to* gives the idea that someone else expects (requests or requires) certain behavior.
(e) Jack *was supposed to call* me last night. I wonder why he didn't.	*Be supposed to* in the past *(was/were supposed to)* expresses unfulfilled expectations. In (e): The speaker expected Jack to call, but he didn't.

☐ **EXERCISE 18. Error analysis: BE SUPPOSED TO. (Chart 9-9)**
Directions: Correct the errors.

1. The building custodian supposed to unlock the classrooms every morning.

2. We're not suppose to open that door.

3. Where are we suppose to meet?

4. I have a meeting at seven tonight. I suppose to be there a little early to discuss the agenda.

5. When we go to the store, Annie, you not suppose to handle the glassware. It might break, and then you'd have to pay for it out of your allowance.

6. I'm suppose to be at the meeting. I suppose* I'd better go.

7. Where have you been? You suppose be here an hour ago!

8. A: I can't remember what the boss said. Should I supposed to work in the mail order room tomorrow morning and then the shipping department tomorrow afternoon? Or the other way around?

   B: How am I supposing to remember what you suppose to do? I have enough trouble remembering what I supposed doing.

---

*COMPARE: *I suppose* = *I guess, I think, I believe.*
I'm supposed to = *I am expected to.*

□ **EXERCISE 19. BE SUPPOSED TO. (Chart 9-9)**

Directions: Answer the questions in complete sentences, using **be supposed to**. Switch roles after Item 6 if you work in pairs.

Example:

SPEAKER A *(book open):* If you're driving and a traffic light turns red, what are you supposed to do?

SPEAKER B *(book closed):* You're supposed to come to a complete stop.*

1. What are you supposed to do if you're involved in a traffic accident?
2. What are you supposed to do prior to take-off in an airplane?
3. What are some things athletes in training are supposed to do, and some things they're not supposed to do?
4. What are you supposed to do later today or this week?
5. If you're driving and an ambulance with flashing lights and blaring sirens comes up behind you, what are you supposed to do?
6. Can you think of something you were supposed to do yesterday (or sometime in the past) but didn't do?
7. What are we supposed to be doing right now?
8. Tell me about any job you've had. What were you supposed to do on a typical day?
9. Where are you supposed to be at _____ o'clock tomorrow?
10. What were you supposed to do sometime last week that you didn't do?
11. If someone tells you a secret, what are you not supposed to do?
12. In the place you live or work, who is supposed to do what? In other words, what are the duties or responsibilities of the people who live or work with you?

□ **EXERCISE 20. Necessity, advisability, and expectations. (Charts 9-5 → 9-9)**

Directions: Which sentence in each pair is stronger?

1. a. You *have got to wear* your seatbelt.
   b. You *should wear* your seatbelt.

2. a. You *had better wear* your seatbelt.
   b. You *ought to wear* your seatbelt.

3. a. You *must wear* your seatbelt.
   b. You *had better wear* your seatbelt.

4. a. You *have to wear* your seatbelt.
   b. You *are supposed to wear* your seatbelt.

5. a. We *are supposed to bring* our own pencils.
   b. We *have to bring* our own pencils.

6. a. We *ought to bring* our own pencils.
   b. We *have got to bring* our own pencils.

7. a. We *had better bring* our own pencils.
   b. We *should bring* our own pencils.

---

*Note the use of impersonal **you.** See Chart 8-5, p. 140.

☐ EXERCISE 21. Necessity, advisability, and expectations. (Charts 9-5 → 9-9)
Directions: Complete the following and discuss the meaning you wish to express by giving reasons for your statement.

Example: I'd better . . . .
→ *I'd better write my mother a letter. (Reason:* If I don't, there will be a bad result: she'll be angry or start worrying about me or feel hurt.)

1. I should . . . .
2. I'm supposed to . . . .
3. I ought to . . . .
4. I'd better . . . .
5. I have to . . . .
6. I've got to . . . .
7. I must . . . .
8. I shouldn't . . . .
9. I'm not supposed to . . . .
10. I'd better not . . . .
11. I don't have to . . . .
12. I must not . . . .

☐ EXERCISE 22. Necessity, advisability, and expectations. (Charts 9-5 → 9-9)
Directions: Choose one (or more) of the following topics for writing, group discussion, or role-playing. Include these words and expressions.

a. should
b. have to
c. be supposed to
d. shouldn't
e. be not supposed to
f. had better
g. must
h. ought to
i. must not
j. do not have to
k. have got to

Topics:

1. Pretend that you are the supervisor of a roomful of young children. The children are in your care for the next six hours. What would you say to them to make sure they understand your expectations and your rules so that they will be safe and cooperative?
   a. You **should** pick up your toys when you are finished playing with them.
   b. You **have to** stay in this room. Do not go outside without my permission.
   c. You're **supposed to** take a short nap at one o'clock.
   d. Etc.

2. Pretend that you are teaching your younger sister/brother how to drive a car. This is her/his first time behind the wheel, and she/he knows little about driving regulations and the operation of an automobile.

3. Pretend that you are a travel agent and you are helping two students who are traveling abroad for a vacation. You want them to understand the travel arrangements you have made, and you want to explain some of the local customs of the countries they will be visiting.

4. Pretend that you are the supervisor of salesclerks in a large department store and that you are talking to two new employees. You want to acquaint them with their job and your expectations.

5. Pretend that you are instructing the babysitter who will watch your three young children while you are out for the evening. They haven't had dinner, and they don't like to go to bed when they're told to.

9-10 MAKING SUGGESTIONS: *LET'S, WHY DON'T, SHALL I/WE*

(a) *Let's go* to a movie. (b) *Let's not go* to a movie. *Let's stay* home instead.	*Let's* = *let us*. *Let's* is followed by the simple form of a verb. Negative form: *let's* + *not* + *simple verb* The meaning of *let's:* "I have a suggestion for us."
(c) *Why don't we go* to a movie? (d) *Why don't you come* around seven? (e) *Why don't I give* Mary a call?	*Why don't* is used primarily in spoken English to make a friendly suggestion. In (c): *Why don't we go* = *let's go*. In (d): I suggest that you come around seven. In (e): Should I give Mary a call? Do you agree with my suggestion?
(f) *Shall I open* the window? Is that okay with you? (g) *Shall we leave* at two? Is that okay? (h) Let's go, *shall we?* (i) Let's go, *okay?*	When *shall* is used with *I* or *we* in a question, the speaker is usually making a suggestion and asking another person if s/he agrees with this suggestion. This use of *shall* is relatively formal and infrequent. Sometimes "shall we?" is used as a tag question after *let's,* as in (h). More informally, "okay?" is used as a tag question, as in (i).

□ **EXERCISE 23. LET'S, WHY DON'T, SHALL I/WE. (Chart 9-10)**
    Directions: Complete the dialogues with your own words.

1. A: A new Japanese restaurant just opened downtown.

       Let's _eat there tonight._

    B: Great idea! I'd like some good sushi.

    A: Why don't _you call and make a reservation?_

       Make it for about 7:30.

    B: No, let's _make it for 8:00._ I'll be working until 7:30 tonight.

2. A: I don't feel like staying home today.

    B: Neither do I. Why don't _____

    A: Hey, that's a great idea! What time shall _____

    B: How about in an hour?

    A: Good.

3. A: Shall _____ or _____first?

    B: Let's _____ first, then we can take our time over

       dinner.

    A: Why don't _____

    B: Yes. Then we'll be sure _____

4. A: Let's _____ over the weekend.

       The fresh air would do us both good.

    B: I agree. Why don't _____

    A: No. Sleeping in a tent is too uncomfortable. Let's _____

       It won't be that expensive, and we'll have hot water and a TV in the room. All

       the comforts of home.

5. A: How are we ever going to prepare for tomorrow's exam? There's so much to know!

    B: Why don't _____

    A: All right. And then let's _____

    B: Okay, but after that we should _____

9-11 MAKING SUGGESTIONS: *COULD* vs. *SHOULD*

—*What should we do tomorrow?* (a) Why don't we go on a picnic? (b) We *could go* on a picnic.	***Could*** can be used to make suggestions. (a) and (b) are similar in meaning: the speaker is suggesting a picnic.
—*I'm having trouble in math class.* (c) You *should talk* to your teacher. (d) *Maybe* you *should talk* to your teacher.	***Should*** gives definite advice. In (c), the speaker is saying: "I believe it is important for you to do this. This is what I recommend." In (d), the use of ***maybe*** softens the strength of the advice.
—*I'm having trouble in math class.* (e) You *could talk* to your teacher. Or you *could ask* Ann to help you with your math lessons. Or I *could try* to help you.	***Could*** offers suggestions or possibilities. In (e), the speaker is saying: "I have some possible suggestions for you. It is possible to do this. Or it is possible to do that."*
—*I failed my math class.* (f) You *should have talked* to your teacher and gotten some help from her during the term.	***Should have*** gives "hindsight advice."** In (f), the speaker is saying: "It was important for you to talk to the teacher, but you didn't do it. You made a mistake."
—*I failed my math class.* (g) You *could have talked* to your teacher. Or you *could have asked* Ann to help you with your math. Or I *could have tried* to help you.	***Could have*** offers "hindsight possibilities."** In (g), the speaker is saying: "You had the chance to do this or that. It was possible for this or that to happen. You missed some good opportunities."

*****Might*** (but not ***may***) can also be used to make suggestions (*You **might talk** to your teacher*), but the use of ***could*** is more common.

**"Hindsight" refers to looking at something after it happens.

☐ EXERCISE 24. Making suggestions. (Chart 9-11)

Directions: Discuss Speaker B's use of ***should*** and ***could*** in the dialogues. In your own words, what is Speaker B saying?

1. A: Ted doesn't feel good. He has a bad stomachache.
   B: He *should see* a doctor.

2. A: Ted doesn't feel good. He has a bad stomachache. What do you think he should do?
   B: Well, I don't know. He *could call* a doctor. He *could call* Dr. Smith. Or he *could call* Dr. Jones. Or he *could* simply *stay* in bed for a day and hope he feels better tomorrow.

3. A: I need to get to the airport.
   B: You *should take* the airport bus. It's cheaper than a taxi.

4. A: I need to get to the airport.
   B: Well, you *could take* the airport bus. Or you *could take* a taxi. Maybe Matt *could take* you. He has a car.

5. A: I took a taxi to the airport, and it cost me a fortune.
   B: You *should have taken* the airport bus.

6. A: I took a taxi to the airport, and it cost me a fortune.
   B: You *could have taken* the airport bus. Or maybe Matt *could have taken* you.

☐ EXERCISE 25. Activity: making suggestions. (Charts 9-7 → 9-11)

Directions: Form a group of four.
Speaker A: Your book is open. Present the given situation.
Speakers B, C, and D: Your books are closed. Make suggestions or give advice. Use ***could*** to suggest possibilities. Use ***should*** only if you want to give strong, definite advice.
Speaker A: When the other students are finished, pass the open book to the next student.

Example:
SPEAKER A *(book open):*   I need to get to the airport. Any suggestions?
SPEAKER B *(book closed):* You could take a taxi or the airport bus.
SPEAKER C *(book closed):* I could take you if I can borrow my brother's car.
SPEAKER D *(book closed):* In my opinion, you should take the airport bus.

1. I don't have any plans for this weekend. I need some suggestions.
2. (. . .) and I want to go to a nice restaurant for dinner tonight. Any suggestions?
3. I need to get from here to *(name of a place in this city/town)*. Any suggestions?
4. I need to buy an umbrella, but I don't know where to go. I need some suggestions.
5. I'm hungry. I'd like to eat an egg, but I've never cooked an egg before. What should I do?
6. I need to get a car, but it can't be very expensive because I don't have a lot of money to spend on it. Any suggestions?
7. I bought a *(name of a car)*, but I'm unhappy with it. In hindsight, can you suggest other possibilities for a kind of car I could have bought?
8. I went to *(name of a place)* for my vacation last summer, but I didn't enjoy it. In hindsight, can you suggest some other possibilities that I didn't think of? (I had only five days and a limited amount of money.)
9. (. . .) went to *(name of a restaurant)* for dinner last night, but the food was terrible. Do you have any hindsight suggestions?

☐ EXERCISE 26. Activity: making suggestions. (Charts 9-7 → 9-11)

Directions: With another student, make up a short dialogue.
Speaker A: Begin the dialogue with "What's the matter?" or "Is something the matter?"
Speaker B: Present a problem. Suggestions of words to include in the dialogue are given in the numbered list.
Speaker A: Offer suggestions by using ***why don't you***, ***(maybe) you should***, and/or ***you could***.
Speaker B: Reject the first two or three suggestions and give your reasons. Then finally accept a suggestion.
Present your dialogue to the class.

Example: I don't feel very good.
SPEAKER A: Is something the matter, Carlos? You don't look good.
SPEAKER B: That's because I don't feel very good.
SPEAKER A: Oh? What's wrong?
SPEAKER B: My stomach feels a little upset.
SPEAKER A: Maybe it's something you ate. *Why don't you* go home and rest for a while?
SPEAKER B: I can't. I have an important meeting in fifteen minutes.
SPEAKER A: *Maybe you should* drink a carbonated beverage. That sometimes helps me when my stomach feels funny.

SPEAKER B: A carbonated beverage? I don't think so. I don't like carbonated drinks.
SPEAKER A: Well, *you could* take an antacid. I have some antacids in my office. Want me to get them for you?
SPEAKER B: Please. I think I'll try that. Maybe it'll help. Thanks.

Suggestions of words for Speaker B to include in the dialogue:

1. . . . but I really don't want to go.
2. . . . but I can't afford it.
3. . . . is angry with me.
4. I don't have enough . . . .
5. I don't know what . . . .
6. My . . . is broken.
7. I lost . . . .
8. I don't like my . . . .
9. *(Use your own words.)*

☐ EXERCISE 27. Activity: writing. (Chapter 9)
Directions: Write a letter to an advice columnist in a newspaper. Make up a personal problem for the columnist to solve. Then give your letter to a classmate, who will write an answer.

Example letter:

Dear Abby,

My husband and my sister had an argument over a year ago, and they haven't spoken to each other since. My husband accused my sister of insulting him about his baldness. Then he told my sister that her hair looked like straw. He said he'd rather be bald than have that kind of hair. My sister insists on an apology. My husband refuses until she apologizes to him first.

The problem is that I'm planning a graduation party for my daughter. My husband insists that I not invite my sister. I tell him I have to invite her. He says he'll leave the party if my sister walks in the door. My daughter is very close to my sister and very much wants her to come to the celebration.

What should I do? I feel I must include my sister in the graduation party, but I don't want to anger my husband.

Yours truly,
Confused and Torn

Example response:

Dear Confused and Torn,

Tell your husband that this party is your daughter's time to have her whole family around her and that you're going to invite your sister to the family celebration. This is certainly and clearly a time he has to put his daughter's needs first.

And you should tell both your husband and your sister that it's time to get past their silly argument and act like grownups instead of ten-year-olds. You could offer to serve as an intermediary to get them together to apologize to each other. If you present a reasonable, adult way of handling the problem, they may start behaving like adults. Good luck.

CHAPTER 10
Modals, Part 2

CONTENTS

☐ EXERCISE 1. Preview. (Chapter 10)

Directions: Which completion do you think the speaker would probably say? Choose the best one.

1. — Is Jeff a good student?
   — He __A__. I don't know him well, but I heard he was offered a scholarship for next year.
        A. must be   B. could be   C. is

2. — Do you know where Eva is?
   — She _____ at Barbara's house. She said something about wanting to visit after work today, but I'm really not sure.
        A. must be   B. could be   C. is

3. — I stayed up all night finishing this report for the boss.
   —You _____ really tired.
   — I do.
        A. must feel   B. might feel   C. feel

4. — Do you think the grocery store is still open?
   — It _____ . I can't ever remember what their hours are.
        A. must be   B. could be   C. is

5. —Where's the left-over chicken from dinner last night?
   — I just saw it when I got some ice cubes. It _____ in the freezer.
        A. must be   B. might be   C. is

6. — It's supposed to rain tomorrow.
   — I know, but the forecast _____ wrong. Weather forecasts are far from 100 percent accurate.
      A. must be   B. could be   C. is

7. — I heard that Jane has received a scholarship and will be able to attend the university in the fall.
   —Wonderful! That's good news. She _____ very happy to have the matter finally settled.
      A. must be   B. may be   C. is

8. — Excuse me. Could you tell me which bus I should take to get to City Hall?
   — Hmmm. Bus number 63 _____ there. But you'd better ask the driver.
      A. must go   B. might go   C. goes

9. —Which bus should I take to get to the main post office?
   — Bus number 39. It _____ right to the post office.
      A. must go   B. could go   C. goes

10. — Do you suppose Mrs. Chu is sick?
    — She _____. I can't think of anything else that would have kept her from coming to this meeting.
       A. must be   B. may be   C. is

11. — Is that Adam's brother standing with him in the cafeteria line?
    — It _____, I suppose. He does look a little like Adam.
       A. must be   B. could be   C. is

12. — Let's be really quiet when we go into the baby's room. The baby _____, and we don't want to wake her up.
    — Okay.
       A. might sleep   B. might be sleeping   C. might have been sleeping

13. — I wonder why the radio is on in the den. No one's in there.
    — Grandma _____ to turn it off. She was in the den earlier and was probably listening to it.
       A. must forget   B. must have forgotten   C. must be forgetting

14. —When Ms. White answered the door, I noticed her hands and clothes were dirty.
    — Really? That's odd.
    — Not really. I figured she _____ in her garden when she heard the doorbell, and came inside to answer it. She's an avid gardener, you know.
       A. must work   B. must have worked   C. must have been working

10-1 DEGREES OF CERTAINTY: PRESENT TIME

—Why isn't John in class? **100% sure**: He *is* sick. **95% sure**: He *must be* sick. **less than 50% sure**: { He *may be* sick. He *might be* sick. He *could be* sick.	"Degree of certainty" refers to how sure we are—what we think the chances are—that something is true. If we are sure something is true in the present, we don't need to use a modal. For example, if I say, "John is sick," I am sure; I am stating a fact that I am sure is true. My degree of certainty is 100%.
—Why isn't John in class? (a) He *must be* sick. (Usually he is in class every day, but when I saw him last night, he wasn't feeling good. So my best guess is that he is sick today. I can't think of another possibility.)	**Must** expresses a strong degree of certainty about a present situation, but the degree of certainty is still less than 100%.
	In (a): The speaker is saying, "Probably John is sick. I have evidence to make me believe that he is sick. That is my logical conclusion, but I do not know for certain."
—Why isn't John in class? (b) He *may be* sick. (c) He *might be* sick. (d) He *could be* sick. (I don't really know. He may be at home watching TV. He might be at the library. He could be out of town.)	**May, might,** and **could** express a weak degree of certainty.
	In (b), (c), and (d): The speaker is saying, "Perhaps, maybe,* possibly John is sick. I am only making a guess. I can think of other possibilities." (b), (c), and (d) have the same meaning.

*Maybe (one word) is an adverb: *Maybe he is sick.*
May be (two words) is a verb form: *He **may be** sick.*

☐ EXERCISE 2. Degrees of certainty: present time. (Chart 10-1)
Directions: From the given information, make your "best guess" by using **must**. This exercise can be done in pairs, in small groups, or as a class. If the exercise is done in pairs, A and B should switch roles halfway through.

Example:
SPEAKER A *(book open):* Alice always gets the best grades in the class. Why?
SPEAKER B *(book closed):* She must study hard. / She must be intelligent.

1. (. . .) is yawning. Why?
2. (. . .) is sneezing and coughing. Why?
3. (. . .) is wearing a wedding ring. Why?
4. (. . .) is shivering and has goose bumps. Why?
5. (. . .)'s stomach is growling. Why?
6. (. . .) is scratching his arm. Why?
7. (. . .) has already had two glasses of water, but now he/she wants another. Why?
8. (. . .) is smiling. Why?
9. (. . .) is crying. Why?
10. There is a restaurant in town that is always packed (full). Why?
11. I am in my car. I am trying to start it, but the engine won't turn over. I left my lights on all day. What's wrong?
12. Every night there is a long line of people waiting to get into *(a particular movie).* Why?
13. Don't look at your watch. What time is it?

□ **EXERCISE 3. Degrees of certainty: present time. (Chart 10-1)**
Directions: Respond by using "I don't know" + ***may/might/could***.

Example:
SPEAKER A *(book open):* (. . .)'s grammar book isn't on her desk. Where is it?
SPEAKER B *(book closed):* I don't know. It may/might/could be in her book bag.

1. (. . .) isn't in class today. Where is s/he? *(I don't know. S/he . . . .)*
2. Where does (. . .) live? *(I don't know. S/he . . . .)*
3. What do you think I have in my briefcase/pocket/purse?
4. What kind of watch is (. . .) wearing?
5. I can't find my pen. Do you know where it is?
6. How old do you think *(someone famous)* is?

□ **EXERCISE 4. Degrees of certainty: present time. (Chart 10-1)**
Directions: Complete the sentences by using ***must*** or ***may/might/could*** with the expressions in the list or with your own words.

be about ten	be very proud	✓like green
be at a meeting	feel terrible	miss them very much
be crazy	fit Jimmy	
be rich	have the wrong number	

1. A: Have you noticed that Professor Adams wears something green every day?
   B: I know. He _____ must like green. _____

2. A: Ed just bought his wife a diamond necklace with matching earrings.
   B: That's expensive! He _____
   A: He is.

3. A: Look at the man standing outside the window on the fifteenth floor of the building!
   B: He _____

4. A: Where's Ms. Adams? She's not in her office.
   B: I don't know. She _____, or maybe she's in the employee lounge.
   A: If you see her, would you tell her I'm looking for her?
   B: Certainly, Mr. French.

5. A: Hello?
   B: Hello. May I speak to Ron?
   A: I'm sorry. You _____
   There's no one here by that name.

6. A: I've heard that your daughter recently graduated from law school and that your son
   has gotten a scholarship to the state university. You _____
   B: We are.

7. A: You're coughing and sneezing, blowing your nose, and running a fever. You _____

    _____

    B: I do.

8. A: This winter jacket is still in good shape, but Tommy has outgrown it. Do you think it would fit one of your sons?
    B: Well, it's probably too small for Johnny, too, but it _____

    _____

9. A: How long has it been since you last saw your family?
    B: More than a year.

    A: You _____
    B: I do.

10. A: How old is their daughter now?
    B: Hmmm. I think she was born around the same time our daughter was born.

    She _____

10-2 DEGREES OF CERTAINTY: PRESENT TIME NEGATIVE

100% sure:	Sam *isn't* hungry.
99% sure:	⎰ Sam *couldn't be* hungry. ⎱ Sam *can't be* hungry.
95% sure:	Sam *must not be* hungry.
less than 50% sure:	⎰ Sam *may not be* hungry. ⎱ Sam *might not be* hungry.

(a) Sam doesn't want anything to eat. He *isn't* hungry. He told me his stomach is full. I heard him say that he isn't hungry. I believe him.	In (a): The speaker is sure that Sam is not hungry.
(b) Sam *couldn't/can't be* hungry! That's impossible! I just saw him eat a huge meal. He has already eaten enough to fill two grown men. Did he really say he'd like something to eat? I don't believe it.	In (b): The speaker believes that there is no possibility that Sam is hungry (but the speaker is not 100% sure). When used in the negative to show degree of certainty, *couldn't* and *can't* forcefully express the idea that the speaker believes something is impossible.
(c) Sam isn't eating his food. He *must not be* hungry. That's the only reason I can think of.	In (c): The speaker is expressing a logical conclusion, a "best guess."
(d) I don't know why Sam isn't eating his food. He *may not/might not be* hungry right now. Or maybe he doesn't feel well. Or perhaps he ate just before he got here. Who knows?	In (d): The speaker uses *may not/might not* to mention a possibility.

□ EXERCISE 5. Degrees of certainty: present time negative. (Chart 10-2)
   Directions: Complete the sentences with your "best guess."

   1. A: Yuko has flunked every test so far this semester.
      B: She must not . . . .
         → *She must not study very hard.*

   2. A: Who are you calling?
      B: Tarek. The phone is ringing, but there's no answer.
      A: He must not . . . .

   3. A: I'm trying to be a good host. I've offered Rosa a glass of water, a cup of coffee or
         tea, a soft drink. She doesn't want anything.
      B: She must not . . . .

   4. A: I offered Mr. Chang some nuts, but he refused them. Then I offered him some
         candy, and he accepted.
      B: He must not . . . .

   5. A: Rosa seems very lonely to me.
      B: I agree. She must not . . . .

□ EXERCISE 6. Degrees of certainty: present time negative. (Chart 10-2)
   Directions: Give possible reasons for Speaker B's conclusions.

   1. A: Someone is knocking at the door. It might be Mary.
      B: It couldn't be Mary. *(Reason? Mary is in Moscow. / Mary went to a movie
         tonight. / Etc.)*

   2. A: Someone left this wool hat here. I think it belongs to Alex.
      B: It couldn't belong to him. *(Reason?)*

   3. A: Someone told me that Karen is in Norway.
      B: That can't be right. She couldn't be in Norway. *(Reason?)*

   4. A: Look at that big animal! Is it a wolf?
      B: It couldn't be a wolf. *(Reason?)*

   5. A: Someone told me that Marie quit her job.
      B: You're kidding! That can't be true. *(Reason?)*

□ EXERCISE 7. Degrees of certainty: present time. (Charts 10-1 and 10-2)
   Directions: Discuss the meaning of the *italicized* verbs.

   1. SITUATION: Anna looks at some figures in her business records: 3456 + 7843 = 11,389.
      a. At first glance, she says to herself, "Hmmm. That *may not* be right."
      b. Then she looks at it again and says, "That *must not be* right. 6 + 3 is 9,
         but 5 + 4 isn't 8."
      c. So she says to herself, "That *couldn't be* right!"
      d. Finally, she adds the figures herself and says, "That *isn't* right."

2. SITUATION: Some people are talking about Ed.

    a. Tim says, "Someone told me that Ed quit his job, sold his house, and moved to an island in the Pacific Ocean."

    b. Lucy says, "That *may not be* true."

    c. Linda says, "That *must not be* true."

    d. Frank says, "That *can't be* true."

    e. Ron says, "That *isn't* true."

3. SITUATION: Tom and his young son hear a noise on the roof.

    a. Tom says, "I wonder what that noise is."

    b. His son says, "It *may be* a bird."

    c. Tom: "It *can't be* a bird. It's running across the roof. Birds don't run across roofs."

    d. His son: "Well, some birds do. It *could be* a big bird that's running fast."

    e. Tom: "No, I think it *must be* some kind of animal. It *might be* a mouse."

    f. His son: "It sounds much bigger than a mouse. It *may be* a dragon!"

    g. Tom: "Son, it *couldn't be* a dragon. We don't have any dragons around here. They exist only in story books."

    h. His son: "It *could be* a little dragon that you don't know about."

    i. Tom: "Well, I suppose it *might be* some kind of lizard."

    j. His son: "I'll go look."

    k. Tom: "That's a good idea."

    l. His son comes back and says, "Guess what, Dad. It*'s* a rat!"

☐ EXERCISE 8. Degrees of certainty: present time. (Charts 10-1 and 10-2)
    Directions: Pair up and create a dialogue.

    SITUATION: You and your friend are at your home. You hear a noise. You discuss the noise: what *may / might / could / must / may not / couldn't / must not* be the cause. Then you finally find out what is going on.

10-3 DEGREES OF CERTAINTY: PAST TIME

PAST TIME: AFFIRMATIVE	In (a): The speaker is sure.
—*Why wasn't Mary in class?*	In (b): The speaker is making a logical conclusion, e.g., "I saw Mary yesterday and found out that she was sick. I assume that is the reason why she was absent. I can't think of any other good reason."
(a) **100%**: She *was* sick.	
(b) **95%**: She *must have been* sick.	
(c) **less than 50%**: { She *may have been* sick. She *might have been* sick. She *could have been* sick.	In (c): The speaker is mentioning one possibility.

PAST TIME: NEGATIVE	In (d): The speaker is sure.
—*Why didn't Sam eat?*	In (e): The speaker believes that it is impossible for Sam to have been hungry.
(d) **100%**: Sam *wasn't* hungry.	
(e) **99%**: { Sam *couldn't have been* hungry. Sam *can't have been* hungry.	In (f): The speaker is making a logical conclusion.
(f) **95%**: Sam *must not have* been hungry.	In (g): The speaker is mentioning one possibility.
(g) **less than 50%**: { Sam *may not have been* hungry. Sam *might not have been* hungry.	

☐ EXERCISE 9. Degrees of certainty: past time. (Chart 10-3)

Directions: Work in pairs, in groups, or as a class.

Speaker A: Your book is open. Give the first cue. After the response, give the second cue.

Speaker B: Your book is closed. Respond to the first cue with ***may have*** / ***might have*** / ***could have***. Then after you get more information in the second cue, use ***must have***.

Example:

SPEAKER A *(book open):*   *1st cue:* Jack was absent yesterday afternoon. Where was he?

SPEAKER B *(book closed):*   I don't know. He may have been at home. He might have gone to a movie. He could have decided to go to the zoo because the weather was so nice.

SPEAKER A: *2nd cue:* What if you overhear him say, "My sister's plane was late yesterday afternoon. I had to wait almost three hours." Now what do you think?

SPEAKER B: He must have gone to the airport to meet his sister's plane.

1. *1st cue:* (. . .) didn't stay home last night. Where did she/he go?
   2nd cue: What if you overhear her/him say, "I usually go there to study in the evening because it's quiet, and if I need to use any reference books, they're right there."

2. *1st cue:* How did (. . .) get to school today?
   2nd cue: What if you see her/him pull some car keys out of her/his pocket?

3. *1st cue:* (. . .) took a vacation in a warm, sunny place. Where do you suppose she/he went?
   2nd cue: What if you then overhear her/him say, "Honolulu is a nice city"?

4. *1st cue:* (. . .) visited a person in this class yesterday. Do you know who she/he visited?
   2nd cue: What if I say this person *(supply a certain distinguishing characteristic)*?

5. *1st cue:* (. . .) walked into class this morning with a broken arm. What happened?
   2nd cue: Then you overhear her/him say, "After this I'm going to watch where I'm going when I'm riding my bicycle."

□ **EXERCISE 10. Degrees of certainty: past time. (Chart 10-3)**

Directions: Form groups of five and assume the roles of Speakers A, B, C, D, and E. Complete the conversation by giving possible reasons for the speakers' conclusions. Create a scenario by using the given information (some of which is irrelevant) and information you make up from your imaginations. After your group has completed your version of the story, write an account of what happened at the mansion late last night.

SITUATION: Last night in an old mansion, someone killed Mrs. Peacock with a revolver in the dining room at approximately ten o'clock. These people, and maybe others, were in the mansion last night: *Colonel Mustard, Mrs. White, Miss Scarlet, Mr. Green, Professor Plum, plus Speakers A, B, C, D, and E.*

Colonel Mustard is in his 70s. He usually goes to bed early. He has asthma. He has a gun. He argued with Mrs. Peacock at the dinner table. He is married, but his wife was not with him last night. He was angry last night. He has a gray mustache. He likes to play cards.

Mrs. White is in her 50s. She has four children. Her bedroom was next to Mrs. Peacock's. Mrs. White believed that Mr. White, her husband, was in love with Mrs. Peacock. Mrs. White is an account executive with an advertising agency. She was in the living room playing cards last night. She stays up late. She usually reads before she goes to sleep at night.

Miss Scarlet is in her late 20s. She's had a difficult life and is deeply in debt. She lives alone and has four cats. She's in love with her dentist. She is Mrs. Peacock's niece and only living relative. Mrs. Peacock was a wealthy woman. Miss Scarlet doesn't play cards. Miss Scarlet has huge dental bills.

*(Supply your own information about **Mr. Green**, **Professor Plum**, and the others at the mansion last night.)*

CONVERSATION:

A: Who killed Mrs. Peacock?

B: It might have been Colonel Mustard.

A: Why do you say that?

B: Because . . . .

C: Yes, that's true. But it could have been Mrs. White.

B: Oh? Why do you think that?

C: Because . . . .

D: No, it couldn't have been Colonel Mustard. And it can't have been Mrs. White.

A: How do you know? Why not?

D: Because . . . .

A: Well, then it must have been Miss Scarlet.

D: Really? Why?

A: Because . . . .

E: All of you are wrong.   It wasn't Miss Scarlet or Colonel Mustard or Mrs. White.

A: Oh? How do you know that? And if none of them did it, who did?

E: . . . .

☐ EXERCISE 11. Degrees of certainty. (Charts 10-1 → 10-3)

Directions: Complete the dialogues. Use an appropriate form of **must** with the verbs in parentheses. Use the negative if necessary.

1. A: Paula fell asleep in class this morning.

    B: She *(stay up)* ___must have stayed up___ up too late last night.

2. A: Jim is eating everything in the salad but the onions. He's pushed all of the onions to the side of his plate.

    B: He *(like)* _____ onions.

3. A: George had to give a speech in front of five hundred people.

    B: Whew! That's a big audience. He *(be)* _____ nervous.
    A: He was, but no one could tell.

4. A: What time is it?
    B: Well, we came at seven, and I'm sure we've been here for at least an hour. So it

    (be) _____ around eight o'clock.

5. A: My favorite magazine doesn't come in the mail anymore. I wonder why.

    B: Did your subscription run out?
    A: That's probably the problem. I *(forget)* _____ to renew it.

6. A: I met Marie's husband at the reception and we said hello to each other, but when I asked him a question in English, he just smiled and nodded.

    B: He *(speak)* _____ much English.

7. A: Where's Nadia? I've been looking all over for her.
   B: I saw her about ten minutes ago in the living room. Have you looked there?

   A: Yes, I've looked everywhere. She *(leave)* _____ .

8. A: Listen! Do you hear a noise downstairs?
   B: No, I don't hear a thing.
   A: You don't? Then something *(be)* _____ wrong with your hearing.

9. A: You have a black eye! What happened?
   B: I walked into a door.
   A: Ouch! That *(hurt)* _____ .
   B: It did.

10. A: Who is your teacher?
    B: I think his name is Mr. Rock, or something like that.

    A: Mr. Rock? Oh, you *(mean)* _____ Mr. Stone.

11. A: I grew up in a small town.

    B: That *(be)* _____ dull.
    A: It wasn't at all. You can't imagine the fun we had.

12. A: Why are you here so early?
    B: Sam told me that the party started at seven o'clock.
    A: No, it doesn't start until eight o'clock. You *(misunderstand)* _____

    _____ .

10-4 DEGREES OF CERTAINTY: FUTURE TIME

100% sure:	Kay *will do* well on the test.	→ The speaker feels sure.
90% sure:	Kay *should do* well on the test. Kay *ought to do* well on the test.	→ The speaker is almost sure.
less than 50% sure:	She *may do* well on the test. She *might do* well on the test. She *could do* well on the test.	→ The speaker is guessing.

(a) Kay has been studying hard. She *should do / ought to do* well on the test tomorrow.	**Should / ought to** can be used to express expectations about future events. In (a): The speaker is saying, "Kay will probably do well on the test. I expect her to do well. That is what I think will happen."
(b) I wonder why Sue hasn't written us. We *should have heard / ought to have heard* from her last week.	The past form of **should / ought to** is used to mean that the speaker expected something that did not occur.

☐ EXERCISE 12. Degrees of certainty. (Charts 4-2, 10-1, and 10-4)
   Directions: Use **will**, **should**/**ought to**, or **must** in the following. In some, more than one modal is possible. Discuss the meanings that the modals convey.*

1. Look at all the people standing in line to get into that movie. It _____ *must* _____ be a good movie.

2. Let's go to the lecture tonight. It _____ *should*/*ought to* OR *will* _____ be interesting.

3. Look. Jack's car is in front of his house. He _____ be at home. Let's stop and visit him.

4. A: Hello. May I speak to Jack?
   B: He isn't here right now.
   A: What time do you expect him?
   B: He _____ be home around nine or so.

5. A: Who do you think is going to win the game tomorrow?
   B: Well, our team has better players, so we _____ win, but you never know. Anything can happen in sports.

6. A: It's very important for you to be there on time.
   B: I _____ be there at seven o'clock. I promise!

7. A: What time are you going to arrive?
   B: Well, the trip takes about four hours. I think I'll leave sometime around noon, so I _____ get there around four.

8. A: Here are your tickets, Mr. Anton. Your flight _____ depart from Gate 15 on the Blue Concourse at 6:27.
   B: Thank you. Could you tell me where the Blue Concourse is?

9. A: Susie is yawning and rubbing her eyes.
   B: She _____ be sleepy. Let's put her to bed early tonight.

10. A: Martha has been working hard all day. She left for work before dawn this morning.
    B: She _____ be really tired when she gets home this evening.

11. A: Where can I find the address for the University of Chicago?
    B: I'm not sure, but you _____ be able to find that information at the library. The library carries catalogues of most of the universities in the U.S.

12. A: When's dinner?
    B: We're almost ready to eat. The rice _____ be done in five minutes.

---

*COMPARE: **Must** expresses a strong degree of certainty about a present situation. (See Chart 10-1, p. 176.) **Should** and **ought to** express a fairly strong degree of certainty about a future situation. (See Chart 10-4, p. 184.) **Will** indicates that there is no doubt in the speaker's mind about a future event. (See Chart 4-2, p. 52.)

13. A: Where's your dictionary?

   B: Isn't it on my desk?

   A: No, I don't see it there.

   B: Okay. Then it must be in the bookcase. You _____ find it on the second shelf. Is it there?

14. Ed has been acting strangely lately.

   He _____ be in love.

15. Hmmm. I wonder what's causing the delay.

   Ellen's plane _____ been here an hour ago.

16. I thought I had some money in my billfold, but I don't. I _____ spent it.

☐ EXERCISE 13. Degrees of certainty. (Charts 10-1 → 10-4)

   Directions: Using the information about each situation, complete the sentences.

1. *Situation:*   Someone's knocking at the door. I wonder who it is.
   Information: **Tom** is out of town.
                  Fred called half an hour ago and said he would stop by this afternoon.
                  Alice is a neighbor who sometimes drops by in the middle of the day.

   a. It must be _____ Fred. _____

   b. It couldn't be _____ Tom. _____

   c. I suppose it might be _____ Alice. _____

2. *Situation:*   Someone ran into the tree in front of our house. I wonder who did it.
   Information: **Sue** has a car, and she was out driving last night.
                  Jane doesn't have a car and doesn't know how to drive.
                  Ron has a car, but I'm pretty sure he was at home last night.
                  Ann was out driving last night, and today her car has a big dent in the front.

   a. It couldn't have been _____

   b. It must not have been _____

   c. It could have been _____

   d. It must have been _____

3. *Situation:* There is a hole in the bread. It looks like something ate some of the bread. The bread was in a closed drawer until I opened it.

Information: **A mouse** likes to eat bread and is small enough to crawl into a drawer.
A cat can't open a drawer. And most cats don't like bread.
A rat can sometimes get into a drawer, but I'm pretty sure we don't have rats in our house.

a. It could have been _____

b. It couldn't have been _____

c. It must have been _____

4. *Situation:* My friends Mark and Carol were in the next room with my neighbor. I heard someone playing a very difficult piece on the piano.

Information: **Mark** has no musical ability at all and doesn't play any instrument.
Carol is an excellent piano player.
I don't think **my neighbor** plays the piano, but I'm not sure.

a. It couldn't have been _____

b. I suppose it could have been _____

c. It must have been _____

5. *Situation:* The meeting starts in fifteen minutes. I wonder who is coming.

Information: I just talked to **Bob** on the phone. He's on his way.
Sally rarely misses a meeting.
Andy comes to the meetings sometimes, and sometimes he doesn't.
Janet is out of town.

a. _____ won't be at the meeting.

b. _____ should be at the meeting.

c. _____ will be here.

d. _____ might come.

☐ **EXERCISE 14. Degrees of certainty. (Charts 10-1 → 10-4)**

Directions: Work in pairs. Choose one of the given situations and create a dialogue of 10 to 20 sentences or more. Then present your dialogue to the rest of the class. For each situation, the beginning of the dialogue is given. Try to include modals in your conversation.

1. *Situation:* The two of you are roommates or a married couple. It is late at night. All of the lights are turned off. You hear a strange noise. You try to figure out what it might or must be, what you should or should not do, etc.

A: Psst. Are you awake?
B: Yes. What's the matter?
A: Do you hear that noise?
B: Yes. What do you suppose it is?
A: I don't know. It . . . .
B: . . . .

2. *Situation:* Your teacher is always on time, but today it is fifteen minutes past the time class begins and he/she still isn't here. You try to figure out why he/she isn't here yet and what you should do.

A: Mr./Mrs./Ms.*/Miss/Dr./Professor/(Jack)/etc. _____ should have been here fifteen minutes ago. I wonder where he/she is. Why do you suppose he/she hasn't arrived yet?

B: Well, ...

3. *Situation:* The two of you are supposed to meet Anita and Po at the park for a picnic. You are almost ready to leave when you hear a loud noise. It sounds like thunder.

A: Is the picnic basket all packed?

B: Yes. Everything's ready.

A: Good. Let's get going.

B: Wait. Did you hear that?

A: . . . .

4. *Situation:* It is late at night. The weather is very bad. Your eighteen-year-old son, who had gone to a party with some friends, was supposed to be home an hour ago. (The two of you are either a married couple or a parent and his/her friend.) You are getting worried. You are trying to figure out where he might be, what might or must have happened, and what you should do, if anything.

A: It's already _____ o'clock and _____ isn't home yet. I'm getting worried.

B: So am I. Where do you suppose he is?

A: . . . .

10-5 PROGRESSIVE FORMS OF MODALS

(a) Let's just knock on the door lightly. Tom **may be sleeping**. *(right now)* (b) All of the lights in Ann's room are turned off. She **must be sleeping**. *(right now)*	Progressive form, present time: *modal* + **be** + **-ing** Meaning: *in progress right now*
(c) Sue wasn't at home last night when we went to visit her. She **might have been studying** at the library. (d) Joe wasn't at home last night. He has a lot of exams coming up soon, and he is also working on a term paper. He **must have been studying** at the library.	Progressive form, past time: *modal* + **have been** + **-ing** Meaning: *in progress at a time in the past*

*In American English, a period is used with the abbreviations Mr./Mrs./Ms. British English does not use a period with these abbreviations.
American: *Mr. Black/Mrs. Green/Ms. Brown*
British: *Mr Black/Mrs Green/Ms Brown*

☐ EXERCISE 15. Progressive forms of modals. (Chart 10-5)
    Directions: Complete the sentences with the verbs in parentheses. Use the appropriate progressive forms of *must*, *should*, or *may/might/could*.

1. Look. Those people who are coming in the door are carrying wet umbrellas. It *(rain)*
       __must be raining__.

2. A: Why is Margaret in her room?
      B: I don't know. She *(do)* ___may be doing___ her homework.

3. A: Do you smell smoke?
      B: I sure do. Something *(burn)* _____ in the kitchen.

4. A: The line's been busy for over an hour. Who do you suppose Frank is talking to?
      B: I don't know. He *(talk)* _____ to his parents. Or he
       (talk) _____ to his sister in Chicago.

5. A: What's all that noise upstairs? It sounds like a herd of elephants.
      B: The children *(play)* _____ some kind of game.
      A: That's what it sounds like to me, too. I'll go see.

6. A: I need to call Howard. Do you know which hotel he's staying at in Boston?
      B: Well, he *(stay)* _____ at the Hilton, but I'm not sure.
      He *(stay)* _____ at the Holiday Inn.

7. A: What are you doing?
      B: I'm writing a letter to a friend, but I *(study)* _____.
      I have a test tomorrow.

8. A: Did you know that Andy just quit school and started to hitchhike to Alaska?
      B: What? You *(kid)* _____!

9. A: Did Ed mean what he said about Andy yesterday?
      B: I don't know. He *(kid)* _____ when he said that, but
      who knows?

10. A: Did Ed really mean what he said yesterday?
       B: No, I don't think so. I think he *(kid)* _____.

□ **EXERCISE 16. Progressive forms of modals. (Chart 10-5)**
Directions: Discuss what the students on the bus *should* and *should not be doing.*

Example: The student in the middle of the bus *shouldn't be climbing* out of the window to the top of the bus.

□ **EXERCISE 17. Progressive and past forms of modals. (Charts 9-8 and 10-1 → 10-5)**
Directions: Complete the sentences with the appropriate form of the words in parentheses. Add ***not*** if necessary for a sentence to make sense.

1. Alex has a test tomorrow that he needs to study for. He *(should + watch)*
   ___*shouldn't be watching*___ TV right now.

2. There's Tom. He's standing at the bus stop. He *(must + wait)* _____
   _____ for the two o'clock bus.

3. Kathy lost her way while driving to River City. She *(should + leave)* _____
   _____ her road map at home.

4. My tweed jacket isn't in my closet. I think my roommate *(might + borrow)* _____
   _____ it. He often borrows my clothes without asking me.

5. When I walked into the room, the TV was on but the room was empty. Dad *(must +
   watch)* _____ TV a short while before I came into
   the room. He *(must + forget)* _____ to turn it off
   before he left the room.

6. A: Why wasn't Pamela at the meeting last night?
   B: She *(may + attend)* _____ the lecture at Shaw Hall.
   I know she really wanted to hear the speaker.

7. A: Why didn't Diane come to the phone? I know she was home when I called.

   B: I don't know. She *(might + wash)* _____

   her hair when you called. Who knows?

8. A: Where's that cold air coming from?

   B: Someone *(must + leave)* _____ the door open.

9. A: Where's Jane? I haven't seen her for weeks.

   B: I'm not sure. She *(might + travel)* _____ in Europe.

   I think I heard her mention something about spending a few weeks in Europe this

   spring.

10. A: When I arrived, Dennis looked surprised.

    B: He *(must + expect)* _____ you.

11. A: Why didn't Jack answer the teacher when she asked him a question?

    B: He was too busy staring out the window. He *(must + daydream)* _____

    _____ . He *(should + pay)* _____

    _____ attention. He *(should + stare)* _____

    out the window during class.

12. A: The roads are treacherous this morning. In places they're nothing but a sheet of

    ice. I *(should + take)* _____ the bus to work today

    instead of driving my car. I thought I'd never make it!

    B: I know. It's terrible outside. Jake still hasn't arrived. He *(must + walk)*

    _____ to work right now. He doesn't live too far

    away, but I know he hates to drive on icy roads.

    A: He *(might + decide)* _____ not to come in at all. He

    (could + work) _____ on his report at home this morning.

    I'll check with his secretary. He *(may + call)* _____ her

    by now.

☐ EXERCISE 18. Degrees of certainty. (Charts 10-1 → 10-5)

Directions: Go to a public place where there are people whom you do not know (a cafeteria, store, street corner, park, zoo, lobby, etc.) or imagine yourself to be in such a place. Choose three of the people to write a composition about. Using a paragraph for each person, describe his/her appearance briefly and then make guesses about the person: age, occupation, personality, activities, etc.

Example:

I'm in a hotel lobby. I'm looking at a man who is wearing a blue pin-striped suit and carrying a briefcase. He is talking to someone at the registration desk, so he must be registering to stay in the hotel. He could be checking out, but I don't think so. He might be simply asking a question, but I doubt it. Judging from his clothes, I'd say he's probably a businessman. But he could be something else. He might be a doctor, a funeral director, or a professor. He has salt-and-pepper hair and not too many wrinkles. He must be about 50 or 55. He doesn't have any luggage with him. The porter must have taken his luggage. The hotel clerk just handed the man a key. Aha! I was right. He is registering to stay at the hotel.

☐ EXERCISE 19. Degrees of certainty. (Charts 10-1 → 10-5)

Directions: Discuss and/or write about the people and activities in the picture. Include any factual information you can get from the picture, and also make guesses about the people: their ages, occupations, activities, etc.

□ EXERCISE 20. Degrees of certainty. (Charts 10-1 → 10-5)

Directions: In pairs or small groups, discuss the dialogue. Make guesses about the two people and what's happening. What possibilities can you think of?

Situation: A man and woman are sitting at a table.

MAN: I don't think you should do this alone.

WOMAN: But you don't understand. I have to.

MAN: Let me go with you. *(fumbling with his wallet)* Just give me a minute to pay the bill.

WOMAN: No, I'll be fine.

MAN: You must let me help.

WOMAN: There's nothing you can do. *(standing)* This is something I need to do for myself.

MAN: Okay. If that's the way you want it.

WOMAN: *(leaving)* I'll call you.

Possible discussion questions:
1. Where are the man and woman?
2. Who are they? What is the relationship between them?
3. Where's the woman going?
4. Why does she want to go alone?
5. Why does the man want to go with her?
6. Etc.

10-6 ABILITY: *CAN* AND *COULD*

(a) Tom is strong. He *can lift* that heavy box.	*Can* is used to express physical ability, as in (a).
(b) I *can see* Central Park from my apartment.	*Can* is frequently used with verbs of the five senses: *see, hear, feel, smell, taste,* as in (b).
(c) Maria *can play* the piano. She's been taking lessons for many years.	*Can* is used to express an acquired skill. In (c), *can play = knows how to play.*
(d) You *can buy* a hammer at the hardware store.	*Can* is used to express possibility. In (d), *you can buy = it is possible for one to buy.*
COMPARE (e) I'm not quite ready to go, but you *can leave* if you're in a hurry. I'll meet you later. (f) When you finish the test, you *may leave.*	*Can* is used to give permission in informal situations, as in (e). In formal situations, *may* rather than *can* is usually used to give permission, as in (f).
(g) Dogs *can bark,* but they *cannot / can't talk.*	Negative form: *cannot* or *can't.*
(h) Tom *could lift* the box, but I *couldn't.*	The past form of *can* meaning "ability" is *could,* as in (h). Negative = *could not* or *couldn't.*

Directions: **Can** is typically pronounced /kən/ in normal spoken English, but may also be pronounced /kæn/. **Can't** is usually pronounced /kænt/. Try to determine whether the teacher is saying **can** or **can't** in the sentences.*

1. The secretary *can/can't* help you.
2. My mother *can/can't* speak English.
3. My friend *can/can't* meet you at the airport.
4. Mr. Smith *can/can't* answer your question.
5. We *can/can't* come to the meeting.
6. *Can/Can't* you come?**
7. You *can/can't* take that course.
8. I *can/can't* cook.
9. Our son *can/can't* count to ten.
10. I *can/can't* drive a stick-shift car.

□ EXERCISE 22. CAN and COULD. (Chart 10-6)

Directions: Make sentences, answer questions, and/or discuss meanings as suggested in the following. Work in pairs, in groups, or as a class.

1. Name a physical ability that you have and a physical ability you don't have.

2. Name an acquired skill that you have and an acquired skill you don't have.

3. There's no class tomorrow.
   a. What can you do tomorrow?
   b. What may (might) you do tomorrow?
   c. What are you going to do tomorrow?

4. a. What are the possible ways you can get to school?
   b. What are the possible ways you may get to school tomorrow?

5. What is the difference in the use of **can** and **may** in the following?
   a. Sure! You can borrow five dollars from me. You can pay me back later.
   b. You may pay the bill either in person or by mail.

6. Compare the following, using **can** and **can't**:
   a. people and animals
      (Example: Birds can fly, but people can't.)
   b. adults and children
   c. women and men

7. Plan your next vacation and describe what you . . .
   a. may do on your vacation.
   b. can do on your vacation.
   c. will do on your vacation.

8. What is something you could do as a child that you can't do now?

---

*Sometimes even native speakers have difficulty distinguishing between **can** and **can't**. Also, British and American pronunciations of **can't** are different. British: **can't** = /kant/ (cawhnt). American: **can't** = /kaent/ (rhymes with *rant*).

**NOTE: "t" + "you" = "chu" (*can't you* = /kænču/).

☐ **EXERCISE 23. Degrees of certainty; ability.** (Charts 10-1 → 10-6)
> *Directions:* Discuss the following in groups or as a class.

A researcher into human behavior conducted an experiment. First she talked to a group of four-year-olds.

"How many of you can dance?" All of the children raised their hands.

"How many of you can sing?" All of the hands shot up.

"And finally, how many of you can draw?" Every child's hand was raised.

Next the researcher went to a college class of twenty-five students in their late teens and early twenties.

"How many of you can dance?" she asked. About a third of the students raised their hands.

"How many of you can sing?" Some hands were raised, but fewer than were raised for the first question.

"How many of you can draw?" Only two hands went up.

Discussion question:
What do you think accounts for the different responses in the two groups, and what conclusions might you make if you were the researcher?

10-7 USING *WOULD* TO EXPRESS A REPEATED ACTION IN THE PAST

(a) When I was a child, my father *would read* me a story at night before bedtime. (b) When I was a child, my father *used to read* me a story at night before bedtime.	*Would* can be used to express an *action* that was repeated regularly in the past. When *would* is used to express this idea, it has the same meaning as *used to* (*habitual past*). (a) and (b) have the same meaning.
(c) I *used to live* in California. He *used to be* a Boy Scout. They *used to have* a Ford.	*Used to* expresses an habitual situation that existed in the past, as in (c). In this case, *would* may not be used as an alternative. *Would* is used only for regularly repeated actions in the past.

☐ **EXERCISE 24. Using WOULD and USED TO.** (Chart 10-7)
> *Directions:* In these sentences, use ***would*** whenever possible to express a repeated action in the past. Otherwise, use ***used to***.

1. I *(be)* _____used to be_____ very shy. Whenever a stranger came to our house, I

   (hide) _____would hide_____ in a closet.

2. I remember my Aunt Susan very well. Every time she came to our house, she *(give)*

   _____ me a big kiss and pinch my cheek.

3. Illiteracy is still a problem in my country, but it *(be)* _____ much

   worse.

4. I (be) _____ afraid of flying. My heart (start) _____ _____ pounding every time I stepped on a plane. But now I'm used to flying and enjoy it.

5. I (be) _____ an anthropology major. Once I was a member of an archaeological expedition. Every morning, we (get) _____ up before dawn. After breakfast, we (spend) _____ our entire day in the field. Sometimes one of us (find) _____ a particularly interesting item, perhaps an arrowhead or a piece of pottery. When that happened, other members of the group (gather) _____ around to see what had been unearthed.

6. I got a new bicycle when I was ten. My friends (ask) _____ to ride it, but for a long time I (let, never) _____ anyone else use it.

7. When my grandfather was a boy and had a cold, his mother (make) _____ _____ him go to bed. Then she (put) _____ goose fat on his chest.

8. Last summer, my sister and I took a camping trip in the Rocky Mountains. It was a wonderful experience. Every morning, we (wake) _____ up to the sound of singing birds. During the day, we (hike) _____ through woods and along mountain streams. Often we (see) _____ deer. On one occasion we saw a bear and quickly ran in the opposite direction.

9. When I was a child, I (take) _____ a flashlight to bed with me so that I could read comic books without my parents' knowing about it.

10. I remember Mrs. Sawyer's fifth grade class well. When we arrived each morning, she

(sit) _____ at her desk. She (smile, always) _____

_____ hello to each student as he or she entered. When the bell rang,

she (stand) _____ up and (clear) _____ her

throat. That was our signal to be quiet. Class was about to begin.

10-8 EXPRESSING PREFERENCE: *WOULD RATHER*

(a) I *would rather go* to a movie tonight *than study* grammar. (b) I'*d rather study* history than *(study)* biology.	*Would rather* expresses preference. In (a): Notice that the simple form of a verb follows both *would rather* and *than*. In (b): If the verb is the same, it usually is not repeated after *than*.
—*How much do you weigh?* (c) I'*d rather not tell* you.	Contraction: *I would = I'd* Negative form: *would rather + not*
(d) The movie was okay, but I *would rather have gone* to the concert last night.	The past form: *would rather have + past participle* Usual pronunciation: "I'd rather-əv"
(e) I'*d rather be lying* on a beach in India than *(be) sitting* in class right now.	Progressive form: *would rather + be + -ing*

☐ EXERCISE 25. Expressing preference: WOULD RATHER. (Chart 10-8)
   Directions: Use *would rather* to complete the sentences.

   1. A: Do you want to go to the concert tonight?
      B: Not really. I . . . .
   2. A: Did you go to the concert last night?
      B: Yes, but I . . . .
   3. A: What are you doing right now?
      B: I'm studying grammar, but I . . . .
   4. A: Do you want to come with us to the museum tomorrow?
      B: Thanks, but I . . . .
   5. A: I . . . than . . . .
      B: Not me. I . . . than . . . .

☐ EXERCISE 26. Expressing preference: WOULD RATHER. (Chart 10-8)
   Directions: Answer in complete sentences.

   1. You are in *(name of place)* right now. Where would you rather be?
   2. What would you rather do than go to class?
   3. What did you do last night? What would you have rather done?*
   4. What are you doing right now? What would you rather be doing?

_____
*Also possible: *What would you **rather have** done?*

Begin your answer with "No, I'd rather . . . . "

5. Do you want to go to a movie tonight? (to a concert?) (to the zoo tomorrow?)
6. Do you want to play tennis this afternoon? (go bowling?) (shoot pool?)
7. Do you want to eat at the cafeteria? (at a Chinese restaurant?)
8. Would you like to live in *(name of a city)?*

10-9   COMBINING MODALS WITH PHRASAL MODALS

(a) INCORRECT: Janet *will can* help you tomorrow.	A modal cannot be immediately followed by another modal. In (a): The modal *will* cannot be followed by *can*, which is another modal.
(b) CORRECT: Janet *will be able to* help you tomorrow.	A modal can, however, be followed by the phrasal modals *be able to* and *have to*. In (b): The modal *will* is correctly followed by the phrasal modal *be able to*.
(c) CORRECT: Tom *isn't going to be able to* help you tomorrow.	It is also sometimes possible for one phrasal modal to follow another phrasal modal. In (c): *be going to* is followed by *be able to*.

☐ EXERCISE 27. Combining modals with BE ABLE TO and HAVE TO. (Chart 10-9)
Directions: Use the given combinations in sentences or short dialogues.

1. might not be able to
2. be going to have to
3. have to be able to
4. shouldn't have to
5. must not have been able to
6. would rather not have to
7. not be going to be able to
8. may have had to

10-10 SUMMARY CHART OF MODALS AND SIMILAR EXPRESSIONS

AUXILIARY	USES	PRESENT/FUTURE	PAST
may	(1) polite request *(only with* I *or* we)	*May* I *borrow* your pen?	
	(2) formal permission	You *may leave* the room.	
	(3) less than 50% certainty	—*Where's John?* He *may be* at the library.	He *may have been* at the library.
might	(1) less than 50% certainty	—*Where's John?* He *might be* at the library.	He *might have been* at the library.
	(2) polite request *(rare)*	*Might* I *borrow* your pen?	
should	(1) advisability	I *should study* tonight.	I *should have studied* last night, but I didn't.
	(2) 90% certainty *(expectation)*	She *should do* well on the test. *(future only, not present)*	She *should have done* well on the test.
ought to	(1) advisability	I *ought to study* tonight.	I *ought to have studied* last night, but I didn't.
	(2) 90% certainty *(expectation)*	She *ought to do* well on the test. *(future only, not present)*	She *ought to have done* well on the test.
had better	(1) advisability with threat of bad result	You *had better be* on time, or we will leave without you.	*(past form uncommon)*
be supposed to	(1) expectation	Class *is supposed to begin* at 10:00.	
	(2) unfulfilled expectation		Class *was supposed to begin* at 10:00, but it didn't begin until 10:15.
must	(1) strong necessity	I *must go* to class today.	(I *had to go* to class yesterday.)
	(2) prohibition *(negative)*	You *must not* open that door.	
	(3) 95% certainty	Mary isn't in class. She *must be* sick. *(present only)*	Mary *must have been* sick yesterday.
have to	(1) necessity	I *have to go* to class today.	I *had to go* to class yesterday.
	(2) lack of necessity *(negative)*	I *don't have to go* to class today.	I *didn't have to go* to class yesterday.
have got to	(1) necessity	I *have got to go* to class today.	(I *had to go* to class yesterday.)
will	(1) 100% certainty	He *will be* here at 6:00. *(future only)*	
	(2) willingness	—*The phone's ringing.* I*'ll get* it.	
	(3) polite request	*Will* you please *pass* the salt?	

AUXILIARY	USES	PRESENT/FUTURE	PAST
be going to	(1) 100% certainty *(prediction)*	He *is going to be* here at 6:00. *(future only)*	
	(2) definite plan *(intention)*	I*'m going to paint* my bedroom. *(future only)*	
	(3) unfulfilled intention		I *was going to paint* my room, but I didn't have time.
can	(1) ability/possibility	I *can run* fast.	I *could run* fast when I was a child, but now I can't.
	(2) informal permission	You *can use* my car tomorrow.	
	(3) informal polite request	*Can* I *borrow* your pen?	
	(4) impossibility *(negative only)*	That *can't be* true!	That *can't have been* true!
could	(1) past ability		I *could run* fast when I was a child.
	(2) polite request	*Could* I *borrow* your pen? *Could* you *help* me?	
	(3) suggestion *(affirmative only)*	—I need help in math. You *could talk* to your teacher.	You *could have talked* to your teacher.
	(4) less than 50% certainty	—Where's John? He *could be* at home.	He *could have been* at home.
	(5) impossibility *(negative only)*	That *couldn't be* true!	That *couldn't have been* true!
be able to	(1) ability	I *am able to help* you. I *will be able to help* you.	I *was able to help* him.
would	(1) polite request	*Would* you please *pass* the salt? *Would* you *mind* if I left early?	
	(2) preference	I *would rather go* to the park than *stay* home.	I *would rather have gone* to the park.
	(3) repeated action in the past		When I was a child, I *would visit* my grandparents every weekend.
	(4) polite for "want" *(with* like*)*	I *would like* an apple, please.	
	(5) unfulfilled wish		I *would have liked* a cookie, but there were none in the house.
used to	(1) repeated action in the past		I *used to visit* my grandparents every weekend.
	(2) past situation that no longer exists		I *used to live* in Spain. Now I live in Korea.
shall	(1) polite question to make a suggestion	*Shall* I *open* the window?	
	(2) future with "I" or "we" as subject	I *shall arrive* at nine. *(will = more common)*	

NOTE: Use of modals in reported speech is discussed in Chart 12-7, p. 254. Use of modals in conditional sentences is discussed in Chapter 20.

☐ EXERCISE 28. Review: modals and similar expressions. (Chapters 9 and 10)
Directions: Discuss the differences in meaning, if any, in each group of sentences.

1. a. May I use your phone?
   b. Could I use your phone?
   c. Can I use your phone?

2. a. You should take an English course.
   b. You ought to take an English course.
   c. You're supposed to take an English course.
   d. You must take an English course.

3. a. You should see a doctor about that cut on your arm.
   b. You had better see a doctor about that cut on your arm.
   c. You have to see a doctor about that cut on your arm.

4. a. You must not use that door.
   b. You don't have to use that door.

5. a. I will be at your house by six o'clock.
   b. I should be at your house by six o'clock.

6. —*There is a knock at the door. Who do you suppose it is?*
   a. It might be Sally.
   b. It may be Sally.
   c. It could be Sally.
   d. It must be Sally.

7. —*There's a knock at the door. I think it's Mike.*
   a. It may not be Mike.
   b. It couldn't be Mike.
   c. It can't be Mike.

8. —*Where's Jack?*
   a. He might have gone home.
   b. He must have gone home.
   c. He had to go home.

9. a. Each student should have health insurance.
   b. Each student must have health insurance.

10. a. If you're having a problem, you could talk to Mrs. Anderson.
    b. If you're having a problem, you should talk to Mrs. Anderson.

11. a. I've got to go.
    b. I have to go.
    c. I should go.
    d. I'm supposed to go.
    e. I'd better go.
    f. I'd rather go.

12. —*I needed some help.*
    a. You should have asked Tom.
    b. You could have asked Tom.

13. a. When I was living at home, I would go to the beach every weekend with my friends.
    b. When I was living at home, I used to go to the beach every weekend with my friends.

☐ EXERCISE 29. Review: modals and similar expressions. (Chapters 9 and 10)

Directions: Use a modal or phrasal modal with each verb in parentheses. More than one auxiliary may be possible. Use the one that seems most appropriate to you and explain why you chose that one rather than another.

1. It looks like rain. We *(shut)* _____ the windows.

2. Ann, *(you, hand)* _____ me that dish? Thanks.

3. Spring break starts on the thirteenth. We *(go, not)* _____ to classes again until the twenty-second.

4. The baby is only a year old, but she *(say, already)* _____ a few words.

5. In the United States, elementary education is compulsory. All children *(attend)* _____ six years of elementary school.

6. There was a long line in front of the theater. We *(wait)* _____ almost an hour to buy our tickets.

7. A: I'd like to go to a warm, sunny place next winter. Any suggestions?
   B: You *(go)* _____ to Hawaii or Mexico. Or how about Indonesia?

8. I don't feel like going to the library to study this afternoon. I *(go)* _____ _____ to the shopping mall than to the library.

9. A: Mrs. Wilson got a traffic ticket. She didn't stop at a stop sign.
   B: That's surprising. Usually she's a very cautious driver and obeys all the traffic laws. She *(see, not)* _____ the sign.

10. Annie, you *(clean)* _____ this mess before Dad gets home. He'll be mad if he sees all this stuff all over the living room floor.

11. A: This is Steve's laptop, isn't it?
    B: It *(be, not)* _____ his. He doesn't have a laptop computer, at least not that I know of. It *(belong)* _____ to Lucy or to Linda. They sometimes bring their laptops to class.

12. In my country, a girl and boy *(go, not)* _____ out on a date unless they are accompanied by a chaperone.

13. Jimmy was serious when he said he wanted to be a cowboy when he grew up. We *(laugh, not)* _____ at him. We hurt his feelings.

14. A: *(I, speak)* _____ to Peggy?

B: She *(come, not)* _____ to the phone right now. *(I, take)*
_____ message?

15. A: How are you planning to get to the airport?

B: By taxi.

A: You *(take)* _____ a shuttle bus instead. It's cheaper than a

taxi. You *(get)* _____ one in front of the hotel. It picks up

passengers there on a regular schedule.

16. A: Why didn't you come to the party last night?

B: I *(study)* _____ .

A: You *(come)* _____ . We had a good time.

17. A: The phone's ringing again. Let's not answer it. Just let it ring.

B: No, we *(answer)* _____ it. It *(be)* _____
important. We *(get)* _____ an answering machine.

18. It's not like Tony to be late. He *(be)* _____ here an hour ago.
I hope nothing bad has happened.

19. A: This is a great open-air market. Look at all this wonderful fresh fish! What kind of
fish is this?

B: I'm not sure. It *(be)* _____ ocean perch. Let's ask.

20. The teacher called on Sam in class yesterday, but he kept looking out the window and
didn't respond. He *(daydream)* _____ .

□ EXERCISE 30. Error analysis: modals. (Chapters 9 and 10)
Directions: Correct the errors. Some of the sentences contain spelling or singular-plural errors.

1. If you have a car, you can traveled around the United State.

2. During class the students must to sit quitely. When the student have questions, they must to raise their hands.

3. When you send for the brochure, you should included a self-addressed, stamped envelope.

4. A film director must has control over every aspect of a movie.

5. When I was a child, I can went to the roof of my house and saw all the other houses and streets.

6. While I was working in the fields, my son would brought me oranges or candy.

7. I used to brake my leg in a soccer game three month ago.

8. May you please help me with this?

9. Many student would rather to study on their own than going to classes.

10. We supposed to bring our books to class every day.

11. You can having a very good time as a tourist in my country. My country have many diferent wheather area, so you have better plan ahead before you came.

12. When you visit big city in my country, you must to be paying attention to your wallet when you are in a crowdy place because there's a lot of thief.

□ EXERCISE 31. Activity: modals. (Chapters 9 and 10)
Directions: Complete the dialogues with your own words. Work in pairs.

Example:
SPEAKER A: Why don't . . . *we go to Luigi's Restaurant for lunch?*
SPEAKER B: Thanks, but I can't. I have to . . . *stay and finish this report during lunchtime.*
SPEAKER A: That's too bad.
SPEAKER B: I should have . . . *come early this morning to finish it,* but I couldn't. I had to . . . *drop my daughter off at school and meet with her teacher.*

1. A: I . . . .
   B: You shouldn't have done that!
   A: I know, but . . . .
   B: Well, why don't . . . .

2. A: . . . .
   B: No, he had to . . . .
   A: Why?
   B: . . . .

3. A: Did you hear the news? We don't
      have to . . . .
   B: Why not?
   A: . . . .
   B: Well, then, why don't . . . .

4. A: Whose . . . .
   B: I don't know. It . . . or it . . . .
   A: Can . . . .
   B: I'll try.

5. A: . . . .
   B: Not at all. I'd be happy to.
   A: Thank you. Maybe sometime . . . .

6. A: . . . .
   B: I would have liked to, but I . . . .

7. A: You must not . . . .
   B: Why not?
   A: . . . .

8. A: . . . .
   B: Well, you'd better . . . or . . . .
   A: I know, but . . . .

9. A: . . . .
   B: . . . , but I'd rather not have gone.
      I'd rather . . . .

10. A: May I . . . .
    B: Please do. I . . . .
    A: We could, but it's going to . . . .

11. A: . . . .
    B: That can't be true! She couldn't
       have . . . .
    A: Oh? Why not? Why do you say
       that?
    B: Because . . . .

12. A: Did you have to . . . .
    B: Yes.
    A: Are you going to have to . . . .
    B: I think so. So I'm probably not
       going to be able to . . . . But I
       might be able to . . . .

☐ EXERCISE 32. Activity: modals. (Chapters 9 and 10)
   Directions: In small groups, debate one, some, or all of the following statements. At the
   end of the discussion time, choose one member of your group to summarize for the rest of
   the class the principal ideas expressed during your discussion.

   Do you agree with the following statements? Why or why not?

   1. Violence on television influences people to act violently.
   2. Cigarette smoking should be banned from all public places.
   3. No family should have more than two children.
   4. Books, films, and news should be censored by government agencies.
   5. People of different religions should not marry.
   6. People shouldn't marry until they are at least twenty-five years old.
   7. All nuclear weapons in the possession of any nation should be eliminated.
   8. The United Nations is a productive and essential organization.
   9. All people of the world should speak the same language.

☐ EXERCISE 33. Review of verb forms. (Chapters 1 → 5, 9, and 10)

Directions: Complete the sentences with the words in parentheses. Use any appropriate tense or modal.

A: Yesterday I (1. *have*) _____ a bad day.

B: Oh? What (2. *happen*) _____ ?

A: I was supposed to be at a job interview at ten, but I didn't make it because while I

(3. *drive*) _____ down the freeway, my car (4. *break*) _____

down.

B: What (5. *you, do*) _____ ?

A: I (6. *pull*) _____ over to the side of the road, (7. *get*) _____

out, and (8. *start*) _____ walking.

B: You (9. *do, not*) _____ that! Walking alone along a

highway can be dangerous. You (10. *stay*) _____ in

your car until help came.

A: You (11. *be, probably*) _____ right, but I (12. *start*) _____

walking down the highway. After I (13. *walk*) _____ for about

20 minutes, I got to an exit ramp. Near the bottom of the exit ramp, there was a

restaurant with a public phone. I (14. *go*) _____ to the phone and

(15. *discover*) _____ that I had left my purse in the car, so I

(16. *have, not*) _____ any money to make a phone call.

B: What did you do then?

A: What do you think I should have done?

B: I don't know. I (17. *think*) _____ of several things. You (18. *go*)

_____ back to your car for your purse. You (19. *try*)

_____ to borrow some change from a customer in the

restaurant. You (20. *ask*) _____ to use the private phone in

the restaurant. What did you actually do?

A: I (21. *ask*) _____ to speak with the manager of the restaurant.

B: That was a good idea. That's exactly what you should have done. What did the

manager do?

A: When I (22. *tell*) _____ her my tale of woe, she (23. *be*) _____ very

sympathetic. She (24. *allow*) _____ me to use her private phone to call

my friend Bill, who (25. *drive*) _____ to the restaurant.

B: You (26. *feel*) _____ really glad when you saw Bill.

A: I did. First he (27. *take*) _____ me to my job interview, and then he

(28. *take*) _____ care of the car.

B: Good friends are important, aren't they?

A: They sure are.

B: Did you get the job you interviewed for?

A: I don't know yet. I (29. *get*) _____ it, or I might not. I just don't

know. I (30. *know*) _____ in a couple more days.

B: Good luck!

A: Thanks! I need it! Well, I (31. *leave*) _____ now. I (32. *be*)

_____ at a meeting in 45 minutes. (33. *I, use*) _____

your phone? I (34. *need*) _____ to call a taxi. My car is still in the

garage, and I (35. *have, not*) _____ time to wait for a bus.

B: I (36. *take*) _____ you to your meeting.

A: Really? Thanks. As you said, good friends are important!

☐ EXERCISE 34. Writing: modals. (Chapters 9 and 10)
  Directions: Write a short paragraph on one or more of the topics.

  Topics:
  1. Write about when, where, and why you should (or should not) have done
     something in your life.
  2. Write about a time in your life when you did something you did not want to do.
     Why did you do it? What could you have done differently? What should you have
     done? What would you rather have done?
  3. Look at your future. What will, might, should it be like? Write about what you
     should, must, can do now in order to make your life what you want it to be.
  4. Write about one embarrassing incident in your life. What could, should, might you
     have done to avoid it?
  5. Look at the world situation and the relationships between nations. What could,
     should (or should not), must (or must not) be done to improve understanding?
  6. Choose one of the environmental problems we are facing today. What could,
     should, may, must, might be done to solve this problem?

CHAPTER *11*
The Passive

CONTENTS

11-1   FORMING THE PASSIVE

<table>
<tr>
<td>
ACTIVE: (a)
 subject verb object
 Mary *helped* the boy.

 PASSIVE: (b)
 subject verb
 The boy *was helped* by Mary.
</td>
<td>
In the passive, *the object* of an active verb becomes *the subject* of the passive verb: ***the boy*** in (a) becomes the subject of the passive verb in (b).

Notice that the subject of an active verb follows ***by*** in a passive sentence. The noun that follows ***by*** is called the "agent." In (b): ***Mary*** is the agent.

(a) and (b) have the same meaning.
</td>
</tr>
<tr>
<td>
ACTIVE: (c) An accident *happened*.
PASSIVE: (d) (none)
</td>
<td>
Only transitive verbs (verbs that can be followed by an object) are used in the passive. It is not possible to use intransitive verbs (such as *happen, sleep, come, seem*) in the passive. (See Appendix Chart A-1, p. A1.)
</td>
</tr>
</table>

Form of the passive: ***be*** + *past participle*

	ACTIVE			PASSIVE		
simple present	Mary	***helps***	the boy.	The boy	***is***	***helped*** by Mary.
present progressive	Mary	***is helping***	the boy.	The boy	***is being***	***helped*** by Mary.
present perfect★	Mary	***has helped***	the boy.	The boy	***has been***	***helped*** by Mary.
simple past	Mary	***helped***	the boy.	The boy	***was***	***helped*** by Mary.
past progressive	Mary	***was helping***	the boy.	The boy	***was being***	***helped*** by Mary.
past perfect★	Mary	***had helped***	the boy.	The boy	***had been***	***helped*** by Mary.
simple future★	Mary	***will help***	the boy.	The boy	***will be***	***helped*** by Mary.
be going to	Mary	***is going to help***	the boy.	The boy	***is going to be***	***helped*** by Mary.
future perfect★	Mary	***will have helped***	the boy.	The boy	***will have been***	***helped*** by Mary.

<table>
<tr>
<td>
(e) ***Was the boy*** *helped* by Mary?
(f) ***Is the boy*** *being helped* by Mary?
(g) ***Has the boy*** *been helped* by Mary?
</td>
<td>
In the question form of passive verbs, an auxiliary verb precedes the subject. (See Appendix Chart B-1, p. A8, for information about question forms.)
</td>
</tr>
</table>

★The progressive forms of the *present perfect, past perfect, future,* and *future perfect* are very rarely used in the passive.

□ EXERCISE 1. Forming the passive. (Chart 11-1)

Directions: Change the active to the passive.

1. Tom *opens* the door. → The door _____is opened_____ by Tom.

2. Tom *is opening* the door. → The door _____ by Tom.

3. Tom *has opened* the door. → The door _____ by Tom.

4. Tom *opened* the door. → The door _____ by Tom.

5. Tom *was opening* the door. → The door _____ by Tom.

6. Tom *had opened* the door. → The door _____ by Tom.

7. Tom *will open* the door. → The door _____ by Tom.

8. Tom *is going to open* the door. → The door _____ by Tom.

9. Tom *will have opened* the door. → The door _____ by Tom.

10. *Is* Tom *opening* the door? → _____ the door _____ by Tom?

11. *Did* Tom *open* the door? → _____ the door _____ by Tom?

12. *Has* Tom *opened* the door? → _____ the door _____ by Tom?

□ EXERCISE 2. Forming the passive. (Chart 11-1)

PART I. Change the active to passive.

1. Shakespeare *wrote* that play. → *That play was written by Shakespeare.*

2. Waitresses and waiters *serve* customers.

3. The teacher *is going to explain* the lesson.

4. Shirley *has suggested* a new idea.

5. Bill *will invite* Ann to the party.

6. Alex *is preparing* that report.

7. Two horses *were pulling*

the farmer's wagon.

8. Kathy *had returned* the book to the library.

9. By this time tomorrow, the president *will have made* the announcement.

10. I *didn't write* that note. Jim *wrote* it.

11. Alice *didn't make* that pie. *Did* Mrs. French *make* it?

12. *Does* Prof. Jackson *teach* that course? I know that Prof. Adams *doesn't teach* it.

13. Mrs. Andrews *hasn't signed* those papers yet. *Has* Mr. Andrews *signed* them yet?

14. *Is* Mr. Brown *painting* your house?

15. His tricks *won't fool* me.

PART II. Change the passive to active.

16. That sentence *was written* by Omar.

17. Our papers *are going to be collected* by the teacher.

18. *Was* the electric light bulb *invented* by Thomas Edison?

19. The speed limit on Highway 5 *isn't obeyed* by most drivers.

20. *Have* you *been informed* of a proposed increase in our rent by the building superintendent?

☐ EXERCISE 3. Forming the passive. (Chart 11-1)
Directions: Change the active to passive if possible. Some verbs are intransitive and cannot be changed.

1. A strange thing happened yesterday. *(no change)*
2. Jackie scored the winning goal. → *The winning goal was scored by Jackie.*
3. My cat died.
4. I agree with Dr. Ikeda's theory.
5. Dr. Ikeda developed that theory.
6. Timmy dropped the cup.
7. The cup fell to the floor.
8. The assistant manager interviewed me.
9. It rained hard yesterday.
10. A hurricane destroyed the small fishing village.
11. Dinosaurs existed millions of years ago.
12. A large vase stands in the corner of our front hallway.
13. The children seemed happy when they went to the zoo.
14. After class, one of the students always erases the chalkboard.

15. The solution to my problem appeared to me in a dream.
16. Our plan succeeded at last.
17. Barbara traveled to Uganda last year.
18. Lightning didn't cause the fire.
19. A special committee is going to settle the dispute.
20. Did the army surround the enemy?
21. What happened in class yesterday?
22. The Persians invented windmills around 1500 years ago.

11-2 USING THE PASSIVE

(a) Rice *is grown* in India. (b) Our house *was built* in 1980. (c) This olive oil *was imported* from Crete.	Usually the passive is used without a *by*-phrase. The passive is most frequently used when it is not known or not important to know exactly who performs an action. In (a): Rice is grown in India by people, by farmers, by someone. It is not known or important to know exactly who grows rice in India. (a), (b), and (c) illustrate the most common use of the passive, i.e., without the *by*-phrase.
(d) *Life on the Mississippi was written* by Mark Twain.	The *by*-phrase is included only if it is important to know who performs an action, as in (d), where **by Mark Twain** is important information.
(e) My aunt *made* this rug. *(active)*	If the speaker knows who performs an action, usually the active is used, as in (e).
(f) This rug *was made* by my aunt. That rug *was made* by my mother.	Sometimes, even when the speaker knows who performs an action, s/he chooses to use the passive with the *by*-phrase because s/he wants to focus attention on the subject of a sentence. In (f): The focus of attention is on two rugs.

☐ EXERCISE 4. Using the passive. (Charts 11-1 and 11-2)
  Directions: Discuss why the use of the passive is appropriate in the sentences. For purposes of comparison, form possible active equivalents, and discuss probable reasons why the speakers/writers would choose to use the passive.

  1. My sweater was made in England.
  2. The new highway will be completed sometime next month.
  3. Language skills are taught in every school in the country.
  4. Beethoven's Seventh Symphony was performed at the concert last night.
  5. The World Cup soccer games are being televised all over the world this year.

6. This composition was written by Ali. That one was written by Yoko.

7. The Washington Monument is visited by hundreds of people every day.

8. Bananas originated in Asia but now are grown in the tropics of both hemispheres of the world. They were introduced to the Americas in 1516.

9. Ink has been used for writing and drawing throughout history. No one knows when the first ink was developed. The ancient Egyptians and Chinese made ink from various natural substances, such as berries, soot, and tree bark. Through the centuries, thousands of different formulas have been developed for ink. Most ink today is made from synthetic chemicals.

10. The chief writing material of ancient times was papyrus. It was used in Egypt, Greece, and other Mediterranean lands. Parchment, another writing material that was widely used in ancient times, was made from the skins of animals such as sheep and goats. After the hair had been removed, the skins were stretched and rubbed smooth so that they could be written on. Paper, the main writing material today, was invented by the Chinese.

☐ EXERCISE 5. Using the passive. (Charts 11-1 and 11-2)
Directions: Change the active sentences to passive sentences if possible. (Some of the verbs are intransitive and cannot be changed.) Keep the same tense. Include the *by*-phrase only if necessary.

1. People grow corn in Iowa. → *Corn is grown in Iowa.*

2. Peter came here two months ago. *(no change)*

3. Someone made this antique table in 1734.

4. An accident happened at the corner of Fifth and Main.

5. Someone stole my purse.

6. Someone was making the coffee when I walked into the kitchen.

7. Translators have translated that book into many languages.

8. Jim's daughter drew that picture. My son drew this picture.

9. The judges will judge the applicants on the basis of their originality.

10. My sister's plane will arrive at 10:35.

11. Is Professor Rivers teaching that course this semester?

12. When did someone invent the radio?

13. The mail carrier had already delivered the mail by the time I left for school this morning.

14. When is someone going to announce the results of the contest?

15. After the concert was over, hundreds of fans mobbed the rock music star outside the theater.

16. Ever since I arrived here, I have been living in the dormitory because someone told me that it was cheaper to live there than in an apartment.

17. They★ are going to build the new hospital next year. They have already built the new elementary school.

18. If you★ expose a film to light while you are developing it, you will ruin the negative.

★In Item 17, *they* is an impersonal pronoun; it refers to "some people" but to no people in particular.
   In Item 18, *you* is an impersonal pronoun; it refers to any person or people in general. See Chart 8-5, p. 140.

11-3 INDIRECT OBJECTS AS PASSIVE SUBJECTS

	I.O.	D.O.	I.O. = *indirect object*; D.O. = *direct object*
(a) Someone gave	*Mrs. Lee*	an award.	Either an indirect object or a direct object may become the subject of a passive sentence.
(b) *Mrs. Lee* was given an award.			(a), (b), (c), and (d) have the same meaning.
	D.O.	I.O.	
(c) Someone gave	*an award*	to Mrs. Lee.	Notice in (d): When the direct object becomes the subject, *to* is usually kept in front of the indirect object.*
(d) *An award* was given to Mrs. Lee.			

*The omission of *to* is more common in British English than American English: *An award was given Mrs. Lee.*

☐ **EXERCISE 6. Indirect objects as passive subjects. (Chart 11-3)**
Directions: Find the indirect object in each sentence and make it the focus of attention by using it as the subject of a passive sentence. Use the *by*-phrase only if necessary.

1. Someone handed Ann a menu at the restaurant.
   (indirect object = Ann) → Ann was handed a menu at the restaurant.

2. Indiana University has awarded Peggy a scholarship.

3. Some company paid Fred three hundred dollars in consulting fees for a job he did last week.

4. Someone has given Maria a promotion at her job as a computer programmer at Microsoft.

5. They will send you a bill at the end of the month.

6. Someone will give the starving people a week's supply of rice as soon as the food supplies arrive in the famine-stricken area.

☐ **EXERCISE 7. Using the passive. (Charts 11-1 → 11-3)**
Directions: Change active to passive. Work in pairs, in groups, or as a class.

Example:
SPEAKER A *(book open):* Someone built that house ten years ago.
SPEAKER B *(book closed):* That house was built ten years ago.

1. Someone invited you to a party.
2. People grow rice in many countries.
3. Someone is televising the game.
4. Teachers teach reading in the first grade.
5. Someone told you to be here at ten.
6. Someone made that hat in Mexico.
7. Someone is going to serve dinner at six.
8. Someone will announce the news tomorrow.
9. Someone has made a mistake.
10. The teacher is giving a test in the next room right now.

□ **EXERCISE 8. Using the passive.** (Charts 11-1 → 11-3)

Directions: Form groups of three.

Speaker A: Your book is open. Give the first cue to Speaker B.
Speaker B: Your book is closed. Change the cue to a passive sentence.
Speaker A: Give the second cue, a question.
Speaker C: Your book is closed. Answer the question, using the passive if possible.

Examples:

SPEAKER A *(book open):* Someone stole your watch.

SPEAKER B *(book closed):* My watch was stolen.

SPEAKER A *(book open):* What happened to (. . .)'s watch?

SPEAKER C *(book closed):* It was stolen.

SPEAKER A *(book open):* People speak Arabic in many countries.

SPEAKER B *(book closed):* Arabic is spoken in many countries.

SPEAKER A *(book open):* Is Arabic a common language?

SPEAKER C *(book closed):* Yes. It is spoken in many countries.

1. *1st cue:* Someone stole your pen.
   2nd cue: What happened to (. . .)'s pen?
2. *1st cue:* People speak Spanish in many countries.
   2nd cue: Is Spanish a common language?
3. *1st cue:* People play soccer in many countries.
   2nd cue: Is soccer a popular sport?
4. *1st cue:* Mark Twain wrote that book.
   2nd cue: Who is the author of that book?
5. *1st cue:* You went to a movie last night, but it bored you.
   2nd cue: Why did (. . .) leave the movie before it ended?
6. *1st cue:* Someone returned your letter.
   2nd cue: (. . .) sent a letter last week, but he/she put the wrong address on it. What happened to the letter?
7. *1st cue:* Someone established this school in 1950.
   2nd cue: How long has this school been in existence?

Switch roles.

8. *1st cue:* Someone robbed the bank.
   2nd cue: What happened to the bank?
9. *1st cue:* The police caught the bank robber.
   2nd cue: Did the bank robber get away?
10. *1st cue:* A judge sent the bank robber to jail.
    2nd cue: What happened to the bank robber?
11. *1st cue:* The government requires international students to have visas.
    2nd cue: Is it necessary for international students to have visas?
12. *1st cue:* Someone had already made the coffee by the time you got up this morning.
    2nd cue: Did (. . .) have to make the coffee when he/she got up?
13. *1st cue:* Something confused you.
    2nd cue: Why did (. . .) ask you a question?
14. *1st cue:* Someone discovered gold in California in 1848.
    2nd cue: What happened in California in 1848?

Switch roles.

15. *1st cue:* I read about a village in the newspaper. Terrorists attacked the village.
    2nd cue: What happened to the village?

16. *1st cue:* People used candles for light in the 17th century.
    2nd cue: Was electricity used for light in the 17th century?

17. *1st cue:* The pilot flew the hijacked plane to another country.
    2nd cue: What happened to the hijacked plane?

18. *1st cue:* When you had car trouble, a passing motorist helped you.
    2nd cue: Yesterday (. . .) was driving down *(Highway 40)* when suddenly her/his car started to make a terrible noise. So she/he pulled over to the side of the road. Then what happened?

19. *1st cue:* There is a party tomorrow night. Someone invited you to go.
    2nd cue: Is (. . .) going to the party?

20. *1st cue:* You wanted to buy a chair, but you needed time to make up your mind. Finally you decided to buy it, but someone had already sold the chair by the time you returned to the store.
    2nd cue: Did (. . .) buy the chair?

☐ EXERCISE 9. Using the passive. (Charts 11-1 → 11-3)

Directions: Use the words in the list to complete these passive sentences. Use any appropriate tense.

build	frighten	report
cause	✓invent	spell
confuse	kill	surprise
divide	offer	surround
expect	order	wear

1. The electric light bulb _____ **was invented** _____ by Thomas Edison.

2. An island _____ by water.

3. The *-ing* form of "sit" _____ with a double *t*.

4. Even though construction costs are high, a new dormitory _____ next year.

5. The class was too large, so it _____ into two sections.

6. A bracelet _____ around the wrist.

7. The Johnsons' house burned down. According to the inspector, the fire _____ _____ by lightning.

8. Al got a ticket for reckless driving. When he went to traffic court, he _____ _____ to pay a large fine.

9. I read about a hunter who _____ accidently _____ by another hunter.

10. The hunter's fatal accident _____ in the newspaper yesterday.

11. I didn't expect Lisa to come to the meeting last night, but she was there. I _____ to see her.

12. Last week I _____ a job at a local bank, but I didn't accept it.

13. The children _____ in the middle of the night when they heard strange noises in the house.

14. Could you explain this math problem to me? Yesterday in class I _____ _____ by the teacher's explanation.

15. A: Is the plane going to be late?

B: No. It _____ to be on time.

☐ EXERCISE 10. Using the passive. (Charts 11-1 → 11-3)
Directions: Use either active or passive, in any appropriate tense, for the verbs in parentheses.

1. The Amazon valley is extremely important to the ecology of the earth. Forty percent of the world's oxygen *(produce)* _____ there.

2. Right now Roberto is in the hospital.* He *(treat)* _____ for a bad burn on his hand and arm.

3. The game *(win, probably)* _____ by the other team tomorrow. They're a lot better than we are.

4. There was a terrible accident on a busy downtown street yesterday. Dozens of people *(see)* _____ it, including my friend, who *(interview)* _____ _____ by the police.

5. In my country, certain prices, such as the price of medical supplies, *(control)* _____ _____ by the government. Other prices *(determine)* _____ _____ by how much consumers are willing to pay for a product.

6. Yesterday a purse-snatcher *(catch)* _____ by a dog. While the thief *(chase)* _____ by the police, he *(jump)* _____ over a fence into someone's yard, where he encountered a ferocious dog. The dog *(keep)* _____ the thief from escaping.

---

*in the hospital = American English; *in hospital* = British English

7. The first fish (appear) _____ on the earth about 500 million years ago. Up to now, more than 20,000 kinds of fish (name) _____ and (describe) _____ by scientists. New species (discover) _____ every year, so the total increases continually.

8. Richard Anderson is a former astronaut. Several years ago, when he was 52, Anderson (inform) _____ by his superior at an aircraft corporation that he could no longer be a test pilot. He (tell) _____ that he was being relieved of his duties because of his age. Anderson took the corporation to court for age discrimination.

9. Frostbite may occur when the skin (expose) _____ to extreme cold. It most frequently (affect)★ _____ the skin of the cheeks, chin, ears, fingers, nose, and toes.

10. In 1877, a network of lines (discover) _____ on the surface of Mars by an Italian astronomer, Giovanni Schiaparelli. The astronomer (call) _____ these lines "channels," but when the Italian word (translate) _____ into English, it became "canals." As a result, some people thought the lines were waterways that (build) _____ by some unknown creatures. We now know that the lines are not really canals. Canals (exist, not) _____ on Mars.

11. Carl Gauss (recognize) _____ as a mathematical genius when he was ten. One day a professor gave him an arithmetic problem. Carl (ask) _____ to add up all the numbers from 1 to 100 (1 + 2 + 3 + 4 + 5, etc.). It (take) _____ him only eight seconds to solve the problem. How could he do it so quickly? Can you do it quickly?

   Carl could do it quickly because he (know) _____ that each pair of numbers — 1 plus 100, 2 plus 99, 3 plus 98, and so on to 50 plus 51 — equaled 101. So he (multiply) _____ 50 times 101 and (come) _____ up with the answer: 5,050.

★NOTE: **affect** = a verb (e.g., *The weather affects my moods.*)
  effect = a noun (e.g., *The weather has an effect on my moods.*)

12. Captain Cook, a British navigator, was the first European to reach Australia's east coast. While his ship was lying off Australia, his sailors *(bring)* _____ a strange animal on board. Cook wanted to know the name of this unusual creature, so he *(send)* _____ his men ashore to ask the native inhabitants. When the natives *(ask)* _____ in impromptu sign language to name the animal, they said, "Kangaroo." The sailors, of course, believed "kangaroo" was the animal's name. Years later, the truth *(discover)* _____. "Kangaroo" means "What did you say?" But today the animal *(call, still)* _____ _____ a kangaroo in English.

11-4 THE PASSIVE FORM OF MODALS AND PHRASAL MODALS

THE PASSIVE FORM:		modal*	+	*be*	+	past participle	

(a)	Tom	*will*	*be*	*invited*	to the picnic.
(b)	The window	*can't*	*be*	*opened.*	
(c)	Children	*should*	*be*	*taught*	to respect their elders.
(d)		*May I*	*be*	*excused*	from class?
(e)	This book	*had better*	*be*	*returned*	to the library before Friday.
(f)	This letter	*ought to*	*be*	*sent*	before June 1st.
(g)	Mary	*has to*	*be*	*told*	about our change in plans.
(h)	Fred	*is supposed to*	*be*	*told*	about the meeting.

THE PAST-PASSIVE FORM:	modal + *have been* + past participle

(i)	The letter	*should*	*have been*	*sent*	last week.
(j)	This house	*must*	*have been*	*built*	over 200 years ago.
(k)	Jack	*ought to*	*have been*	*invited*	to the party.

*See Chapters 9 and 10 for a discussion of the form, meaning, and use of modals and phrasal modals.

□ **EXERCISE 11. Passive modals.** (Chart 11-4)

Directions: Complete the sentences with the given words, active or passive.

1. James *(should + tell)* ___should be told___ the news as soon as possible.

2. Someone *(should + tell)* ___should tell___ James the news immediately.

3. James *(should + tell)* ___should have been told___ the news a long time ago.

4. Meat *(must + keep)* _____ in a refrigerator or it will spoil.

5. You *(must + keep)* _____ meat in a refrigerator or it will spoil.

6. We tried, but the window *(couldn't + open)* _____ . It was painted shut.

7. I tried, but I *(couldn't + open)* _____ the window.

8. Good news! I *(may + offer)* _____ a job soon. I had an interview at an engineering firm yesterday.

9. Chris has good news. The engineering firm where she had an interview yesterday *(may + offer)* _____ her a job soon.

10. I hope Chris accepts our job offer, but I know she's been having interviews with several companies. She *(may + already + offer*)* _____ a job by a competing firm before we made our offer.

11. A competing firm *(may + already + offer*)* _____ Chris a job before we made our offer.

12. The class for next semester is too large. It *(ought to + divide)* _____ _____ in half, but there's not enough money in the budget to hire another teacher.

13. Last semester's class was too large. It *(ought to + divide)* _____ _____ in half.

14. These books *(have to + return)* _____ to the library by tomorrow.

15. Polly *(have to + return)* _____ these books by next Friday. If she doesn't return them, she *(will + have to + pay)* _____ a fine to the library.

---

*A midsentence adverb such as **already** may be placed after the first auxiliary (e.g., *might already have come*) or after the second auxiliary (e.g., *might have already come*).

16. A: Andy, your chores *(had better + finish)* _____

   by the time I get home, including taking out the garbage.

   B: Don't worry, Mom. I'll do everything you told me to do.

17. A: Andy, you *(had better + finish)* _____ your chores before

   Mom gets home.

   B: I know. I'll do them in a minute. I'm busy right now.

18. This application *(be supposed to + send)* _____

   to the personnel department soon.

19. Ann's birthday was on the 5th, and today is the 8th. Her birthday card *(should + send)*

   _____ a week ago. Maybe we'd better give her a

   call to wish her a belated happy birthday.

20. A: Ann didn't expect to see her boss at the labor union meeting.

   B: She *(must + surprise)* _____ when she saw him.

   A: She was.

☐ **EXERCISE 12. Passive modals. (Chart 11-4)**
   Directions: Use the verb in parentheses with the modal or phrasal modal that sounds best
   to you. All of the sentences are passive.

   1. The entire valley *(see)* _____**can be seen**_____ from their mountain home.

   2. He is wearing a gold band on his fourth finger. He *(marry)* _____

   _____ .

   3. According to our teacher, all of our compositions *(write)* _____

   _____ in ink. He won't accept papers written in pencil.

   4. I found this book on my desk when I came to class. It *(leave)* _____

   _____ by one of the students in the earlier class.

   5. Five of the committee members will be unable to attend the next meeting. In my

   opinion, the meeting *(postpone)* _____ .

   6. A child *(give, not)* _____ everything he or she wants.

   7. Your daughter has a good voice. Her interest in singing *(encourage)* _____

   _____ .

   8. Try to speak slowly when you give your speech. If you don't, some of your words

   (misunderstand) _____ .

9. Some UFO sightings (explain, not) _____ easily. They are inexplicable.

10. What? You tripped over a chair at the party and dropped your plate of food into a woman's lap? You (embarrass) _____.

11. She is very lazy. If you want her to do anything, she (push) _____ _____.

12. The hospital in that small town is very old and can no longer serve the needs of the community. A new hospital (build) _____ years ago.

13. Blue whales and other endangered species (save) _____ from extinction. Do you agree?

14. We can't wait any longer! Something (do) _____ immediately!

15. In my opinion, Ms. Hansen (elect) _____ because she is honest, knowledgeable, and competent.

☐ EXERCISE 13. Passive modals. (Chart 11-4)
Directions: Create dialogues that include one (or more) of the given verb phrases. Use other passive modals if you can. Present your dialogues to the class.

1. should have been changed
2. must be submitted
3. ought to have been told
4. could have been damaged
5. will be announced
6. may be required
7. must have been surprised
8. had better be sent
9. is/are supposed to be worn
10. can't be estimated

☐ **EXERCISE 14. Using the passive.** (Charts 11-1 → 11-4)

Directions: Use active or passive, in any appropriate tense, for the verbs in parentheses.

1. It's noon. The mail should be here soon. It (deliver, usually) _____
   _____ sometime between noon and one o'clock.

2. Only five of us (work) _____ in the laboratory yesterday
   when the explosion (occur) _____. Luckily, no one (hurt)
   _____.

3. I was supposed to take a test yesterday, but I (admit, not) _____
   _____ to the testing room because the examination (begin, already)
   _____.

4. Before she graduated last May, Susan (offer, already) _____
   _____ a position with a law firm.

5. Right now a student trip to the planetarium (organize) _____
   _____ by Mrs. Hunt. You can sign up for it at her office.

6. He is a man whose name will go down in history. He (forget, never) _____
   _____.

7. A: Yesterday (be) _____ a terrible day.
   B: What (happen) _____?
   A: First, I (flunk) _____ a test, or at least I think I did. Then I (drop)
      _____ my books while I (walk) _____ across
      campus, and they (fall) _____ into a mud puddle. And finally, my bicycle
      (steal) _____.
   B: You should have stayed in bed.

8. Yesterday we went to look at an apartment. I really liked it, but by the time we got
   there, it (rent, already) _____.

9. During the family celebration, the little boy was crying because he (ignore) _____
   _____. He needed some attention, too.

10. A: Where (buy, you) _____ that beautiful necklace?
    B: I (buy, not) _____ it. It (give) _____ to
       me for my birthday. (you, like) _____ it?

11. The sun is just one of billions of stars in the universe. As it travels through space, it

    (circle) _____ by many other celestial bodies. The nine known

    planets (hold) _____ in orbit by the sun's gravitational field. The

    planets, in turn, (circle) _____ by their own satellites, or moons.

12. Early inhabitants of this region (worship*) _____ the sun and the

    moon. We know this from the jewelry, sculptures, and other artwork archaeologists

    have found.

13. Since the beginning of the modern industrial age, many of the natural habitats of

    plants and animals (destroy) _____ by industrial

    development and pollution.

14. The Olympic Games began more than 2,000 years ago in Olympia, a small town in

    Greece. At that time, only Greek men (allow) _____ to

    compete. People of other nationalities (invite, not) _____ to

    participate, and women (forbid) _____ to set foot in the area

    where the games (hold) _____.

15. Ever since it (build) _____ three centuries ago, the Taj Mahal in

    Agra, India, (describe, often) _____ as the most

    beautiful building in the world. It (design) _____ by a Turkish

    architect, and it (take) _____ 20,000 workers 20 years to complete it.

16. The photography competition that is taking place at the art museum today (judge)

    _____ by three well-known photographers. I've entered

    three of my pictures and have my fingers crossed. The results (announce) _____

    _____ later this afternoon.

---

*Spelling note: worshiped or worshipped = American English
                  worshipped = British English

☐ EXERCISE 15. Activity: the passive. (Charts 11-1 → 11-4)

Directions: Write a fill-in-the-blanks grammar exercise of 10 (or more) items on active vs. passive verb forms. Choose from the given subjects and verbs. Give your exercise to a classmate to complete.

Example: (name of a person)\offer

Possible item: When Sally *(offer)* ——————————————— a job at Microsoft last

week, she happily *(accept)* _____ it.

1. *(name of language)* \ speak
2. *(name of a person)* \ speak
3. *(kind of game)* \ play
4. my friends and I \ play
5. earthquake \ occur
6. news\ report
7. food \ serve
8. dark cloud \ appear
9. jeans \ wear
10. students \ wear
11. bill \ pay
12. I \ pay
13. *(name of a thing)* \ invent
14. *(name of a place/thing)* \ discover
15. *(kind of car)* \ manufacture
16. computer \ cost
17. newspaper \ sell
18. I \ eat
19. *(name of a person)* \ respect
20. friend \ agree
21. bride \ kiss
22. I \ influence
23. movie \ show
24. rice \ cook
25. rule \ obey
26. damage \ cause
27. automobile accident \ happen

☐ EXERCISE 16. Using the passive. (Charts 11-1 → 11-4)

Directions: Change the verbs to the passive as appropriate. Discuss why you decide that certain verbs should be in the passive but others should remain active.

(1) Paper is a common material. People use it everywhere in the world. [It is used] Throughout history, people have made it from various plants, such as rice and papyrus, but today wood is the chief source of paper. In the past, people made paper by hand, but now machines do most of the work.* Today people make paper from wood pulp by using either a mechanical or a chemical process.

(2) In the mechanical process, someone grinds the wood into small chips. During the grinding, someone sprays it with water to keep it from burning from the friction of the grinder. Then someone soaks the chips in water.

(3) In the chemical process, first someone washes the wood, and then someone cuts it into small pieces in a chipping machine. Then someone cooks the chips in certain chemicals. After someone cooks the wood, someone washes it to get rid of the chemicals.

———————————
*Whether or not to use the passive in the second half of this sentence is a stylistic choice. Either the active or the passive can appropriately be used. Some writers might prefer the passive so that both halves of the sentence are parallel in structure.

(4)   The next steps in making paper are the same for both the mechanical and the chemical processes. Someone drains the pulp to form a thick mass, bleaches it with chlorine, and then thoroughly washes it again. Next someone puts the pulp through a large machine that squeezes the water out and forms the pulp into long sheets. After the pulp sheets go through a drier and a press, someone winds them onto rolls. These rolls of paper are then ready for use.

(5)   The next time you use paper, you should think about its origin and how people make it. And you should ask yourself this question: What would the world be like without paper? If you can imagine how different today's world would be without paper, you will immediately understand how essential paper has been in the development of civilization.

☐ EXERCISE 17. Writing: the passive. (Charts 11-1 → 11-4)
Directions: In writing, describe how something is made. Choose one of the following:

1. Use a reference book such as an encyclopedia to find out how something is made, and then summarize this information. It's not necessary to go into technical details. Read about the process and then describe it in your own words. *Possible subjects:* a candle, a pencil, glass, steel, silk thread, bronze, leather, etc.
2. Write about something you know how to make. *Possible subjects:* a kite, a ceramic pot, a bookcase, a sweater, a bead necklace, a special kind of food, etc.

11-5   STATIVE PASSIVE

(a) The door is *old*. (b) The door is *green*. (c) The door is *locked*.	In (a) and (b): *old* and *green* are adjectives. They describe the door. In (c): *locked* is a past participle. It is used as an adjective. It describes the door.
(d) I locked the door five minutes ago. (e) The door was locked by me five minutes ago. (f) Now the door *is locked*.	When the passive form is used to describe an existing situation or state, as in (c), (f), and (i), it is called the "stative passive." In the stative passive: • no action is taking place; the action happened earlier. • there is no *by*-phrase. • the past participle functions as an adjective.
(g) Ann broke the window yesterday. (h) The window was broken by Ann. (i) Now the window *is broken*.	
(j) I *am interested in* Chinese art. (k) He *is satisfied with* his job. (l) Ann *is married to* Alex.	Prepositions other than *by* can follow stative passive verbs. (See Chart 11-6, p. 228.)
(m) I don't know where I am. I *am lost*. (n) I can't find my purse. It *is gone*. (o) I *am finished with* my work. (p) I *am done with* my work.	(m) through (p) are examples of idiomatic usage of the passive form in common, everyday English. These sentences have no equivalent active sentences.

☐ EXERCISE 18. Stative passive. (Chart 11-5)

Directions: Supply the stative passive of the given verbs. Use the SIMPLE PRESENT or the SIMPLE PAST.

1. Sarah is wearing a blouse. It *(make)* _____is made_____ of cotton.

2. The door to this room *(shut)* _____.

3. The lights in this room *(turn)* _____ on.

4. This room *(crowd, not)* _____.

5. Jim is sitting quietly. His elbows *(bend)* _____, and his hands

   (fold) _____ in front of him.

6. We can leave now because class *(finish)* _____.

7. It is hot in this room because the window *(close)* _____.

8. Yesterday it was hot in this room because the window *(close)* _____.

9. We can't go any farther. The car *(stick)* _____ in the mud.

10. We couldn't go any farther. The car *(stick)* _____ in the mud.

11. My room is very neat right now. The bed *(make)* _____, the floor

    (sweep) _____ , and the dishes *(wash)* _____.

12. We are ready to sit down and eat dinner. The table *(set)* _____, the

    meat and rice *(do)* _____ , and the candles *(light)* _____

    _____ .

13. Where's my wallet? It *(go)* _____! Did you take it?

14. Hmmm. My dress *(tear)* _____. I wonder how that happened.

15. Don't look in the hall closet. Your birthday present *(hide)* _____ there.

☐ EXERCISE 19. Stative passive. (Chart 11-5)

Directions: Complete the sentences with an appropriate form of the words in the list.

bear (born)★	*exhaust*	*plug in*
block	*go*	*qualify*
confuse	*insure*	*schedule*
crowd	*locate*	*spoil*
divorce	✓*lose*	*stick*
do	*marry*	*turn off*

1. Excuse me, sir. Could you give me some directions? I _____am lost._____

_____

*In the passive, **born** is used as the past participle of **bear** to express "given birth to."

2. Let's find another restaurant. This one _____ too _____. We would have to wait at least an hour for a table.

3. The meeting _____ for tomorrow at nine.

4. That's hard work! I _____. I need to rest for a while.

5. You told me one thing, and John told me another. I don't know what to think. I _____.

6. I can't open the window.

   It _____.

7. Louise is probably sleeping. The lights in her room _____.

8. Mrs. Wentworth's jewelry _____ _____ for $50,000.

9. Carolyn and Joe were married to each other for five years, but now they _____.

10. I thought I had left my book on this desk, but it isn't here. It _____. I wonder where it is.

11. I'm sorry. You _____ not _____ for the job. We need someone with a degree in electrical engineering.

12. I love my wife. I _____ to a wonderful woman.

13. We can't eat this fruit. It _____. We'll have to throw it out.

14. We'd better call a plumber. The water won't go down the drain. The drain _____.

15. Vietnam _____ in Southeast Asia.

16. A: How old is Jack?

    B: He _____ in 1980.

17. A: The TV set doesn't work.

    B: Are you sure? _____ it _____?

18. A: Is dinner ready?

    B: Not yet. The potatoes _____ not _____. They need another ten minutes.

11-6 COMMON STATIVE PASSIVE VERBS + PREPOSITIONS

(a) I'm *interested **in** Greek culture.* (b) He's *worried **about** losing his job.*	Many stative passive verbs are followed by prepositions other than **by**.

COMMON STATIVE PASSIVE VERBS + PREPOSITIONS

be accustomed to	be engaged to	be opposed to
be acquainted with	be equipped with	
be addicted to	be excited about	be pleased with
be annoyed with, by	be exhausted from	be prepared for
be associated with	be exposed to	be protected from
		be provided with
be bored with, by	be filled with	
	be finished with	be qualified for
be cluttered with	be frightened of, by	
be composed of		be related to
be concerned about	be gone from	be remembered for
be connected to		
be coordinated with	be interested in	be satisfied with
be covered with	be involved in	be scared of, by
be crowded with		
	be known for	be terrified of, by
be dedicated to		be tired of, from
be devoted to	be limited to	
be disappointed in, with	be located in	be worried about
be discriminated against		
be divorced from	be made of	
be done with	be married to	
be dressed in		

☐ **EXERCISE 20. Stative passive + prepositions. (Chart 11-6)**
Directions: Complete the sentences with appropriate prepositions.

1. Our high school soccer team was very excited __about__ going to the national finals.

2. I'm not acquainted _____ that man. Do you know him?

3. Mark Twain is known _____ his stories about life on the Mississippi.

4. A person who is addicted _____ drugs needs professional medical help.

5. Jack is married _____ Joan.

6. Could I please have the dictionary when you are finished _____ it?

7. A: Aren't you ready yet? We have to be at the ferry dock at 7:45.

   B: I'll never make it. I'm still dressed _____ my pajamas.

8. My car is equipped _____ air conditioning and a sun roof.

9. The school children were exposed _____ the measles by a student who had them.

10. Gandhi was committed _____ nonviolence. He believed in it all of his life.

11. The large table was covered _____ every kind of food you could imagine.

12. Barbara turned off the TV because she was tired _____ listening to the news.

13. The choices in that restaurant are limited _____ pizza and sandwiches.

14. A: Are you in favor of a worldwide ban on nuclear weapons, or are you opposed _____ it?

    B: I'm in favor of it. I'm terrified _____ the possibility of a nuclear war starting by accident. However, my wife is against disarmament.

15. The department store was filled _____ toys for the holiday sale.

16. John's bald head is protected _____ the hot sun when he's wearing his hat.

17. The store was crowded _____ last-minute shoppers on the eve of the holiday.

18. I think you're involved _____ too many activities. You don't have enough time to spend with your family.

19. Your leg bone is connected _____ your hip bone.

20. Their apartment is always messy. It's cluttered _____ newspapers, books, clothes, and dirty dishes.

21. Don't leave those seedlings outside tonight. If they're exposed _____ temperatures below freezing, they will die.

22. An interior decorator makes certain that the color of the walls is coordinated _____ the color of the carpets and window coverings.

23. We finished packing our sleeping bags, tent, first-aid kit, food, and warm clothes. We are finally prepared _____ our camping trip.

24. I was very disappointed _____ that movie. The whole first hour was devoted _____ historical background, with a cast of thousands fighting endless battles. I was bored _____ it before the plot took shape.

25. A: Are you still associated _____ the International Red Cross and Red Crescent?

   B: I was, until this year. Are you interested _____ working with them?

   A: I think I'd like to. They are dedicated _____ helping people in time of crisis, and I admire the work they have done. Can you get me some information?

☐ EXERCISE 21. Stative passive + prepositions. (Chart 11-6)
Directions: Work in pairs.
Speaker A: Your book is open. Give the cue. Don't lower your intonation.
Speaker B: Your book is closed. Supply the correct preposition and finish the sentence with your own words.

Example: I'm interested . . . .
SPEAKER A *(book open):* I'm interested . . . .
SPEAKER B *(book closed):* I'm interested in the history of architecture.

Switch roles.

1. Are you related . . . .
2. (. . .) is worried . . . .
3. I'm not accustomed . . . .
4. (. . .) is dressed . . . .
5. My foot is connected . . . .

6. The walls of this room are covered . . . .
7. This class is composed . . . .
8. (. . .) is married . . . .
9. I'm opposed . . . .
10. Are you acquainted . . . .

☐ EXERCISE 22. Stative passive + prepositions. (Chart 11-6)
Directions: Supply the correct form of the verb in parentheses and an appropriate preposition. Use the SIMPLE PRESENT.

1. *(interest)*   Carol ___is interested in___ ancient history.

2. *(compose)*   Water _____ hydrogen and oxygen.

3. *(accustom)*   I _____ living here.

4. *(terrify)*   Our son _____ dogs.

5. *(finish)*   Pat _____ her composition.

6. *(addict)*   Ann laughingly calls herself a "chocoholic." She says she

_____ chocolate.

7. *(cover)*   It's winter, and the ground _____ snow.

8. *(satisfy)*   I _____ the progress I have made.

9. *(marry)*   Jack _____ Ruth.

10. *(divorce)*   Elaine _____ Ed.

11. *(acquaint)*   I _____ not _____ that author's work.

12. *(tire)*   I _____ sitting here.

13. *(relate)*   Your name is Mary Smith. _____ you _____
John Smith?

14. *(dedicate)*   Mrs. Robinson works in an orphanage. She _____
_____ her work.

15. *(disappoint)*   Jim got a bad grade because he didn't study. He _____
_____ himself.

16. *(scare)*   Bobby is not very brave. He _____ his own
shadow.

17. *(commit)*   The administration _____ improving the
quality of education at our school.

18. *(devote)*   Mr. and Mrs. Miller _____ each other.

19. *(dress)*   Walter _____ his best suit for his wedding today.

20. *(do)*   We _____ this exercise.

11-7 THE PASSIVE WITH *GET*

GET + *ADJECTIVE* (a) I'***m getting hungry***. Let's eat soon. (b) You shouldn't eat so much. You'***ll get fat***. (c) I stopped working because I ***got sleepy***.	***Get*** may be followed by certain adjectives.* ***Get*** gives the idea of change — the idea of becoming, beginning to be, growing to be. In (a): ***I'm getting hungry*** = I wasn't hungry before, but now I'm beginning to be hungry.
GET + *PAST PARTICIPLE* (d) I stopped working because I ***got tired***. (e) They ***are getting married*** next month. (f) I ***got worried*** because he was two hours late.	***Get*** may also be followed by a past participle. The past participle functions as an adjective; it describes the subject. The passive with ***get*** is common in spoken English, but is often not appropriate in formal writing.

*Some of the common adjectives that follow ***get*** are:

angry	chilly	fat	hungry	old	thirsty
anxious	cold	full	late	rich	warm
bald	dark	good	light	sick	well
better	dizzy	heavy	mad	sleepy	wet
big	empty	hot	nervous	tall	worse
busy					

☐ **EXERCISE 23. The passive with GET. (Chart 11-7)**

Directions: Complete the sentences with any appropriate tense of ***get*** and an adjective from the list.

better	hot	nervous
busy	✓hungry	sleepy
dark	late	well
full	light	wet

1. What time are we going to eat? I ____*am getting hungry*____ .

2. A: I _____ .

   B: Why don't you take a nap? A couple of hours of sleep will do you good.

3. A: What time is it?

   B: Almost ten.

   A: I'd better leave soon. It _____ . I have to be at the airport by eleven.

4. I didn't have an umbrella, so I _____ while I was waiting for the bus yesterday.

5. Let's turn on the air conditioner. It _____ in here.

6. Every time I have to give a speech, I _____ .

7. Would you mind turning on the light? It _____ in here.

8. A: It's a long drive from Denver to here. I'm glad you finally arrived. What time did you leave this morning?

   B: At sunrise. We left as soon as it _____ outside.

9. A: Won't you have another helping?

   B: This dinner is delicious, but I really can't eat any more. I _____

   _____ .

10. Maria's English is improving. It _____ .

11. Shake a leg! We don't have all day to finish this work! Get moving! Let's step on it!

    _____ and finish your work. There's no time to waste.

12. My friend was sick, so I sent him a card. It said, "_____ soon."

☐ **EXERCISE 24. The passive with GET. (Chart 11-7)**

   Directions: Complete the sentences with an appropriate form of **get** and the given verbs.

   1. *(tire)*   I think I'll stop working. I _____ am getting tired _____ .

   2. *(hurt)*   There was an accident, but nobody _____ .

   3. *(lose)*   We didn't have a map, so we _____ .

   4. *(dress)*   We can leave as soon as you _____ .

   5. *(marry)*   When _____ you _____ ?

   6. *(accustom)* How long did it take you to _____ to living

                    here?

   7. *(worry)*   Sam was supposed to be home an hour ago, but he still isn't here. I

                    _____ .

   8. *(upset)*   Just try to take it easy. Don't _____ .

   9. *(confuse)*   I _____ because everybody gave me different

                    advice.

   10. *(do)*   We can leave as soon as I _____ with this work.

   11. *(depress)* Chris _____ when she lost her job, so I tried to

                    cheer her up.

   12. *(invite)*   _____ you _____ to the party?

   13. *(bore)*   I _____ , so I didn't stay for the end of the movie.

14. *(pack)*   I'll be ready to leave as soon as I _____.

15. *(pay)*   I _____ on Fridays. I'll give you the money I owe you next Friday. Okay?

16. *(hire)*   After Ed graduated, he _____ by an engineering firm.

17. *(fire)*   But later he _____ because he didn't do his work.

18. *(finish, not)* Last night I _____ with my homework until after midnight.

19. *(disgust)*   I _____ and left because the things they were saying at the meeting were ridiculous.

20. *(engage)*   First, they _____.

   (marry)   Then, they _____.

   (divorce)   Later, they _____.

   (remarry)   Finally, they _____.

   Today they are very happy.

☐ EXERCISE 25. The passive with GET. (Chart 11-7)
   Directions: Create sentences with ***get*** and the given words.

   Example: dizzy
   Possible response: I went on a really great ride at the carnival last summer. It was a lot of fun even though I got dizzy.

   1. sleepy
   2. confused
   3. married
   4. wet
   5. done
   6. full
   7. mad
   8. nervous
   9. excited
   10. scared
   11. dressed
   12. rich
   13. finished
   14. lost
   15. hurt
   16. cheated
   17. bored
   18. elected
   19. older
   20. worried
   21. worse
   22. prepared
   23. wrinkled
   24. better and better

11-8 PARTICIPIAL ADJECTIVES

—The problem confuses the students. (a) It is *a **confusing** problem*. —The students are confused by the problem. (b) They are ***confused** students*.	The *present participle* serves as an adjective with an active meaning. The noun it modifies performs an action. In (a): The noun **problem** does something; it **confuses**. Thus, it is described as a "confusing problem." The *past participle* serves as an adjective with a passive meaning. In (b): The students are confused by something. Thus, they are described as "confused students."
—The story amuses the children. (c) It is *an **amusing** story*. —The children are amused by the story. (d) They are ***amused** children*.	In (c): The noun **story** performs the action. In (d): The noun **children** receives the action.

☐ **EXERCISE 26. Participial adjectives. (Chart 11-8)**
Directions: Complete the sentences with the present or past participle of the verbs in *italics*.

1. The class *bores* the students. It is a _____boring_____ class.

2. The students *are bored* by the class. They are _____bored_____ students.

3. The game *excites* the people. It is an _____ game.

4. The people *are excited* by the game. They are _____ people.

5. The news *surprised* the man. It was _____ news.

6. The man *was surprised* by the news. He was a _____ man.

7. The child *was frightened* by the strange noise. The _____ child sought comfort from her father.

8. The strange noise *frightened* the child. It was a _____ sound.

9. The work *exhausted* the men. It was _____ work.

10. The men *were exhausted*. The _____ men sat down to rest under the shade of a tree.

☐ **EXERCISE 27. Participial adjectives. (Chart 11-8)**
Directions: Respond with a present or a past participle. Switch roles halfway through if you work in pairs.

Example:
SPEAKER A *(book open):* If a book confuses you, how would you describe the book?
SPEAKER B *(book closed):* confusing
SPEAKER A *(book open):* How would you describe yourself?
SPEAKER B *(book closed):* confused

1. If a story amazes you, how would you describe the story?
   How would you describe yourself?

2. If a story depresses you, how would you describe the story?
How would you describe yourself?

3. If some work tires you, how would you describe yourself?
How would you describe the work?

4. If a movie bores you, how would you describe the movie?
How would you describe yourself?

5. If a painting interests you, how would you describe yourself?
How would you describe the painting?

6. If a situation embarrasses you . . . .

7. If a book disappoints you . . . .

8. If a person fascinates you . . . .

9. If a situation frustrates you . . . .

10. If a noise annoys you . . . .

11. If an event shocks you . . . .

12. If an experience thrills you . . . .

☐ **EXERCISE 28. Participial adjectives. (Chart 11-8)**

Directions: Complete the sentences with the present or past participle of the verbs in parentheses.

1. The *(steal)* _____ stolen _____ jewelry was recovered.

2. Success in one's work is a *(satisfy)* _____ experience.

3. The dragon was a *(terrify)* _____ sight for the villagers.

4. The *(terrify)* _____ villagers ran for their lives.

5. I found myself in an *(embarrass)* _____ situation last night.

6. A kid accidentally threw a ball at one of the school windows. Someone needs to repair the *(break)* _____ window.

7. I elbowed my way through the *(crowd)* _____ room.

8. The thief tried to pry open the *(lock)* _____ cabinet.

9. The *(injure)* _____ woman was put into an ambulance.

10. That *(annoy)* _____ buzz is coming from the fluorescent light.

11. The teacher gave us a *(challenge)* _____ assignment, but we all enjoyed doing it.

12. The *(expect)* _____ event did not occur.

13. A *(grow)* _____ child needs a *(balance)* _____ diet.

14. No one appreciates a *(spoil)* _____ child.

15. There is an old saying: Let *(sleep)* _____ dogs lie.

16. We had a *(thrill)* _____ but hair-raising experience on our backpacking trip into the wilderness.

17. The *(abandon)* _____ car was towed away by a tow truck.

18. I still have five more *(require)* _____ courses to take.

19. *(Pollute)* _____ water is not safe for drinking.

20. I don't have any furniture of my own. Do you know where I can rent a *(furnish)* _____ apartment?

21. The equator is the *(divide)* _____ line between the Northern and Southern hemispheres.

22. We all expect our *(elect)* _____ officials to be honest.

23. The invention of the *(print)* _____ press was one of the most important events in the history of the world.

24. *(Experience)* _____ travelers pack lightly. They carry little more than necessities.

25. The psychologist spoke to us about some of the *(amaze)* _____ coincidences in the lives of twins living apart from each other from birth.

☐ EXERCISE 29. Error analysis: the passive. (Chapter 11)
Directions: Correct the errors in these sentences.

1. I am ~~interesting~~ *interested* in his ideas.

2. Two people got hurted in the accident and were took to the hospital by an ambulance.

3. The movie was so bored that we fell asleep after an hour.

4. The students helped by the clear explanation that the teacher gave.

5. That alloy is composing by iron and tin.

6. The winner of the race hasn't been announcing yet.

7. If you are interesting in modern art, you should see the new exhibit at the museum. It is fascinated.

8. Progress is been made every day.

9. When and where has the automobile invented?

10. My brother and I have always been interesting in learning more about our family tree.

11. I am not agree with you, and I don't think you'll ever to convince me.

12. Each assembly kit is accompany by detailed instructions.

13. Arthur was giving an award by the city for all of his efforts in crime prevention.

14. It was late, and I was getting very worry about my mother.

15. The problem was very puzzled. I couldn't figure it out.

16. Many strange things were happened last night.

17. How many peoples have you been invited to the party?

18. When I returned home, everything is quite. I walk to my room, get undress, and going to bed.

19. I didn't go to dinner with them because I had already been eaten.

20. In class yesterday, I was confusing. I didn't understand the lesson.

21. I couldn't move. I was very frighten.

22. When we were children, we are very afraid of caterpillars. Whenever we saw one of these monsters, we run to our house before the caterpillars could attack us. I am still scare when I saw a caterpillar close to me.

23. One day, while the old man was cutting down a big tree near the stream, his axe was fallen into the river. He sat down and begin to cry because he does not have enough money to buy another axe.

CHAPTER 12
Noun Clauses

CONTENTS

12-1 INTRODUCTION

independent clause (a) Sue lives in Tokyo. independent clause (b) Where does Sue live?	A clause is a group of words containing a subject and a verb.★ An *independent clause* (or *main clause*) is a complete sentence. It contains the main subject and verb of a sentence. Examples (a) and (b) are complete sentences. (a) is a statement, and (b) is a question.
dependent clause (c) where Sue lives	A *dependent clause* (or *subordinate clause*) is not a complete sentence. It must be connected to an independent clause. Example (c) is a dependent clause.
indep. cl. dependent cl. (d) I know *where Sue lives*.	Example (d) is a complete sentence. It has an independent clause with the main subject (*I*) and verb (*know*) of the sentence. ***Where Sue lives*** is a dependent clause connected to an independent clause. ***Where Sue lives*** is called a *noun clause*.
noun phrase (e) ***His story*** was interesting. noun clause (f) ***What he said*** was interesting.	A *noun phrase* is used as a subject or an object. A *noun clause* is used as a subject or an object. In other words, a noun clause is used in the same ways as a noun phrase. In (e): ***His story*** is a noun phrase. It is used as the subject of the sentence. In (f): ***What he said*** is a noun clause. It is used as the subject of the sentence. The noun clause has its own subject (*he*) and verb (*said*).
noun phrase (g) I heard ***his story***. noun clause (h) I heard ***what he said***.	In (g): ***his story*** is a noun phrase. It is used as the object of the verb ***heard***. In (h): ***what he said*** is a noun clause. It is used as the object of the verb ***heard***.
noun phrase (i) I listened to ***his story***. noun clause (j) I listened to ***what he said***.	In (i): ***his story*** is a noun phrase. It is used as the object of the preposition ***to***. In (j): ***what he said*** is a noun clause. It is used as the object of the preposition ***to***.

★A *phrase* is a group of words that does NOT contain a subject and a verb.

★★See Appendix Unit B for more information about question words and question forms.

□ **EXERCISE 1. Noun clauses. (Chart 12-1)**

Directions: Add the necessary punctuation and capitalization to the following. <u>Underline</u> the noun clauses.

1. I couldn't hear the teacher what did she say

   → *I couldn't hear the teacher.* ***What did she say?***

2. I couldn't hear <u>what the teacher said.</u>
                              ∧

3. Where did Tom go no one knows

4. No one knows where Tom went

5. Where Tom went is a secret

6. What does Anna want we need to know

7. We need to know what Anna wants

8. What does Alex need do you know

9. Do you know what Alex needs

10. What Alex needs is a new job

11. We talked about what Alex needs

12. What do you need did you talk to your parents about what you need

12-2 NOUN CLAUSES BEGINNING WITH A QUESTION WORD

QUESTION	NOUN CLAUSE	
Where does she live? What did he say?` When do they arrive?	(a) I don't know ***where she lives***. (b) I couldn't hear ***what he said***. (c) Do you know ***when they arrive?***	In (a): ***where she lives*** is the object of the verb ***know***. In a noun clause, the subject precedes the verb. Do not use question word order in a noun clause. Notice: ***does***, ***did***, and ***do*** are used in questions, but not in noun clauses. See Appendix Unit B for more information about question words and question forms.
S V Who lives there? What happened? Who is at the door?	S V (d) I don't know ***who lives there***. (e) Please tell me ***what happened***. (f) I wonder ***who is at the door***.	In (d): The word order is the same in both the question and the noun clause because ***who*** is the subject in both.
V S Who is she? Who are those men? Whose house is that?	S V (g) I don't know ***who she is***. (h) I don't know ***who those men are***. (i) I wonder ***whose house that is***.	In (g): ***she*** is the subject of the question, so it is placed in front of the verb ***be*** in the noun clause.★
What did she say? What should they do?	(j) ***What she said*** surprised me. (k) ***What they should do*** is obvious.	In (j): ***What she said*** is the subject of the sentence. Notice in (k): A noun clause subject takes a singular verb (e.g., ***is***).

★COMPARE: *Who is at the door?* = ***who*** is the subject of the question.
          Who are those men? = ***those men*** is the subject of the question, so ***be*** is plural.

□ **EXERCISE 2. Noun clauses beginning with a question word.** (Chart 12-2)
   Directions: Change the question in parentheses to a noun clause.

1. *(How old is he?)* I don't know _____how old he is_____.

2. *(What was he talking about?)* ___What he was talking about___

   was interesting.

3. *(Where do you live?)* Please tell me _____.

4. *(What did she say?)* _____ wasn't true.

5. *(When are they coming?)* Do you know _____?

6. *(How much does it cost?)* I can't remember _____.

7. *(Which one does he want?)* Let's ask him _____.

8. *(Who is coming to the party?)* I don't know _____.

9. *(Who are those people?)* I don't know _____.

10. *(Whose pen is this?)* Do you know _____?

11. *(Why did they leave the country?)* _____ is a secret.

12. *(What are we doing in class?)* _____ is easy.

13. *(Where did she go?)* _____ is none of your business.

14. *(How many letters are there in the English alphabet?)* I don't remember _____

    _____.

15. *(Who is the mayor of New York City?)* I don't know _____

    _____.

16. *(How old does a person have to be to get a driver's license?)* I need to find out _____

    _____.

17. *(What happened?)* I don't know _____.

18. *(Who opened the door?)* I don't know _____.

☐ **EXERCISE 3. Noun clauses beginning with a question word. (Chart 12-2)**

Directions: Work in pairs, in groups, or as a class.
Speaker A: Your book is open. Ask the question.
Speaker B: Your book is closed. Begin your response with "I don't know . . . ."

Example:
SPEAKER A *(book open):* What time is it?
SPEAKER B *(book closed):* I don't know what time it is.

(Switch roles if working in pairs.)

1. Where does (. . .) live?
2. What country is (. . .) from?
3. How long has (. . .) been living here?
4. What is (. . .)'s telephone number?
5. Where is the post office?
6. How far is it to (Kansas City)?
7. Why is (. . .) absent?
8. Where is my book?
9. What kind of watch does (. . .) have?
10. Why was (. . .) absent yesterday?
11. Where did (. . .) go yesterday?
12. What kind of government does (Italy) have?

13. What is (. . .)'s favorite color?
14. How long has (. . .) been married?
15. Why are we doing this exercise?
16. Who turned off the lights?
17. Where is (. . .) going to eat lunch/dinner?
18. When does (the semester) end?
19. Where did (. . .) go after class yesterday?
20. Why is (. . .) smiling?
21. How often does (. . .) go to the library?
22. Whose book is that?
23. How much did that book cost?
24. Who took my book?

☐ **EXERCISE 4. Noun clauses beginning with a question word.**
(Chart 12-2 and Appendix Unit B)

Directions: Make a question from the given sentence. The words in parentheses should be the answer to the question you make. Use a question word (**who, what, how,** *etc.*).★ Then change the question to a noun clause.

1. Tom will be here *(next week).*

   QUESTION: _____ When will Tom be here? _____

   NOUN CLAUSE: Please tell me _____ when Tom will be here. _____

2. He is coming *(because he wants to visit his friends).*

   QUESTION: _____

   NOUN CLAUSE: Please tell me _____

3. He'll be on flight *(645, not flight 742).*

   QUESTION: _____

   NOUN CLAUSE: Please tell me _____

---

*★See Appendix Unit B for information about forming questions.

4. *(Jim Hunter)* is going to meet him at the airport.

QUESTION: _____

NOUN CLAUSE: Please tell me _____

5. Jim Hunter is *(his roommate)*.

QUESTION: _____

NOUN CLAUSE: Please tell me _____

6. Tom's address is *(4149 Riverside Road)*.

QUESTION: _____

NOUN CLAUSE: Please tell me _____

7. He lives *(on Riverside Road in Columbus, Ohio, USA)*.

QUESTION: _____

NOUN CLAUSE: Please tell me _____

8. He was *(in Chicago)* last week.

QUESTION: _____

NOUN CLAUSE: Please tell me _____

9. He has been working for IBM* *(since 1998)*.

QUESTION: _____

NOUN CLAUSE: Do you know _____

10. He has *(an IBM)* computer at home.

QUESTION: _____

NOUN CLAUSE: Do you know _____

☐ EXERCISE 5. Noun clauses beginning with a question word.
   (Chart 12-2 and Appendix Unit B)

Directions: Use the words in parentheses to complete the sentences. Use any appropriate verb tense. Some of the completions contain noun clauses, and some contain questions.

1. A: Where *(Ruth, go)* _____ *did Ruth go* _____? She's not in her room.

   B: I don't know. Ask her friend Tina. She might know where *(Ruth, go)*
   _____ *Ruth went* _____ .

2. A: Oops! I made a mistake. Where *(my eraser, be)* _____?
   Didn't I lend it to you?

   B: I don't have it. Ask Sally where *(it, be)* _____. I think I saw
   her using it.

---

*IBM = the name of a corporation (**I**nternational **B**usiness **M**achines)

3. A: The door isn't locked! Why *(Fred, lock, not)* _____ it

   before he left?★

   B: Why ask me? How am I supposed to know why *(he, lock, not)* _____

   _____ it? Maybe he just forgot.

4. A: Mr. Lee is a recent immigrant, isn't he? How long *(he, be)* _____

   in this country?

   B: I have no idea, but I'll be seeing Mr. Lee this afternoon. Would you like me to ask

   him how long *(he, live)* _____ here?

5. A: Are you a student here? I'm a student here, too. Tell me what classes *(you, take)*

   _____ this term. Maybe we're in some of the same classes.

   B: Math 4, English 2, History 6, and Chemistry 101. What classes *(you, take)*

   _____?

6. A: Help! Quick! Look at that road sign! Which road *(we, be supposed)* _____

   _____ to take?

   B: You're the driver! Don't look at me! I don't know which road *(we, be supposed)*

   _____ to take. I've never been here before in my entire life.

_____

★Word order in negative questions:

    Usual: *Why didn't you call me?* (with *did* + *not* contracted)

    Very formal: *Why did you not call me?*

□ **EXERCISE 6. Information questions and noun clauses.**
    (Charts 12-1 and 12-2; Appendix Unit B)
Directions: Work in pairs. Switch roles after every group of five items.
Speaker A: Your book is open. Ask any question using the given words.
Speaker B: Your book is closed. To make sure you understood Speaker A correctly, repeat
            what s/he said, using a noun clause. Begin by saying "You want to know . . . ."
Listen to each other's grammar carefully, especially word order.

Example: who \ roommate
SPEAKER A *(book open):* Who is your roommate?
SPEAKER B *(book closed):* You want to know who my roommate is.

Example: where \ go
SPEAKER A *(book open):* Where did you go after class yesterday?
SPEAKER B *(book closed):* You want to know where I went after class yesterday.

Example: how far \ it
SPEAKER A *(book open):* How far is it from Bangkok to Rangoon?
SPEAKER B *(book closed):* You want to know how far it is from Bangkok to Rangoon.

1. whose \ that	11. who \ prime minister	21. when \ get
2. how much \ cost	12. which \ want	22. where \ located
3. what time \ get	13. why \ blue	23. who \ is
4. how long \ you	14. what \ after	24. who \ talk
5. what kind \ have	15. from whom \ borrow	25. how many \ go
6. when \ you	16. where \ born	26. what \ tomorrow
7. whcre \ last night	17. what color \ eyes	27. how far \ it
8. why \ didn't	18. whose \ is	28. what kind \ buy
9. what \ like	19. which \ you	29. how often \ you
10. where \ the teacher	20. why \ ask	30. to whom \ give

12-3 NOUN CLAUSES BEGINNING WITH *WHETHER* OR *IF*

YES/NO QUESTION	NOUN CLAUSE	
Will she come?	(a) I don't know *whether she will come.* I don't know *if she will come.*	When a yes/no question is changed to a noun clause, *whether* or *if* is used to introduce the clause.
Does he need help?	(b) I wonder *whether he needs help.* I wonder *if he needs help.*	(Note: *Whether* is more acceptable in formal English, but *if* is quite commonly used, especially in speaking.)
	(c) I wonder *whether or not* she will come. (d) I wonder *whether* she will come *or not.* (e) I wonder *if* she will come *or not.*	In (c), (d), and (e): Notice the patterns when *or not* is used.
	(f) *Whether she comes or not* is unimportant to me.	In (f): Notice that the noun clause is in the subject position.

☐ **EXERCISE 7. Noun clauses beginning with WHETHER or IF. (Chart 12-3)**

Directions: Work in pairs, in groups, or as a class. Begin all responses with "I wonder . . . ."

Examples:

SPEAKER A *(book open):* Does (. . .) need any help?
SPEAKER B *(book closed):* I wonder whether/if (. . .) needs any help.

SPEAKER A *(book open):* Where is (. . .)?
SPEAKER B *(book closed):* I wonder where (. . .) is.

1. Where is your friend?
2. Should we wait for him?
3. Should you call him?
4. Where is your dictionary?
5. Who took your dictionary?
6. Did (. . .) borrow your dictionary?
7. Who is that woman?
8. Does she need any help?
9. Why is the sky blue?
10. How long does a butterfly live?
11. What causes earthquakes?
12. When was the first book written?
13. Who is that man?
14. What is he doing?
15. Is he having trouble?
16. Should you offer to help him?
17. How far is it to (Florida)?
18. Do we have enough time to go to (Florida) over vacation?
19. Whose book is this?
20. Does it belong to (. . .)?
21. Why did dinosaurs become extinct?
22. Is there life on other planets?
23. How did life begin?
24. Will people live on the moon someday?

☐ **EXERCISE 8. Noun clauses. (Charts 12-2 and 12-3)**

Directions: Work in pairs, in groups, or as a class. Begin all responses with "Could you please tell me . . . ."

Example:

SPEAKER A *(book open):* What is this?
SPEAKER B *(book closed):* Could you please tell me what this is?

1. Does this bus go downtown?
2. How much does this book cost?
3. When is Flight 62 expected to arrive?
4. Where is the nearest phone?
5. Is this word spelled correctly?
6. What time is it?
7. Is this information correct?
8. How much does it cost to fly from (Chicago) to (New York)?
9. Where is the bus station?
10. Whose pen is this?

☐ **EXERCISE 9. Error analysis: noun clauses. (Charts 12-1 → 12-3)**
   Directions: Correct the errors.

   1. Please tell me what is your name. → *Please tell me what **your name is.***

   2. No one seems to know when will Maria arrive.

   3. I wonder why was Bob late for class.

   4. I don't know what does that word mean.

   5. I wonder does the teacher know the answer?

   6. What should they do about the hole in their roof is their most pressing problem.

   7. I'll ask her would she like some coffee or not.

   8. Be sure to tell the doctor where does it hurt.

   9. Why am I unhappy is something I can't explain.

   10. I wonder does Tom know about the meeting or not.

   11. I need to know who is your teacher.

   12. I don't understand why is the car not running properly.

   13. My young son wants to know where do the stars go in the daytime?

12-4 QUESTION WORDS FOLLOWED BY INFINITIVES

(a) I don't know *what I should do.* (b) I don't know **what to do.** (c) Pam can't decide *whether she should go or stay home.* (d) Pam can't decide **whether to go or (to) stay home.** (e) Please tell me *how I can get to the bus station.* (f) Please tell me **how to get to the bus station.** (g) Jim told us *where we could find it.* (h) Jim told us **where to find it.**	Question words (**when, where, how, who, whom, whose, what, which**) and **whether** may be followed by an infinitive. Each pair of sentences in the examples has the same meaning. Notice that the meaning expressed by the infinitive is either **should** or **can/could**.

☐ **EXERCISE 10. Question words followed by infinitives. (Chart 12-4)**
   Directions: Create sentences with the same meaning by using infinitives.

   1. He told me when I should come. → *He told me when to come.*
   2. The plumber told me how I could fix the leak in the sink.
   3. Please tell me where I should meet you.
   4. Don had an elaborate excuse for being late for their date, but Sandy didn't know whether she should believe him or not.
   5. Jim found two shirts he liked, but he had trouble deciding which one he should buy.
   6. I've done everything I can think of to help Andy get his life straightened out. I don't know what else I can do.

Complete the following; use infinitives in your completions.

7. I was tongue-tied. I didn't know what _____.

8. A: I can't decide _____ to the reception.

   B: How about your green suit?

9. A: Where are you going to live when you go to the university?

   B: I'm not sure. I can't decide whether _____.

10. A: Do you know how _____?

    B: No, but I'd like to learn.

11. A: I don't know what _____ for her birthday. Got any

    suggestions?

    B: How about a book?

12. My cousin has a dilemma. He can't decide whether _____ or

    _____. What do you think he should do?

13. Before you leave on your trip, read this tour book. It tells you where _____

    _____ and how _____.

12-5 NOUN CLAUSES BEGINNING WITH *THAT*

STATEMENT	NOUN CLAUSE	
He is a good actor.	(a) I think *that he is a good actor*. (b) I think *he is a good actor*.	In (a): *that he is a good actor* is a noun clause. It is used as the object of the verb *think*. The word *that*, when it introduces a noun clause, has no meaning in itself. It simply marks the beginning of the clause. Frequently it is omitted, as in (b), especially in speaking. (If used in speaking, it is unstressed.)
The world is round.	(c) We know *(that) the world is round*.	
She doesn't understand spoken English.	(d) *That she doesn't understand spoken English* is obvious. (e) *It* is obvious *(that)* she doesn't understand spoken English.	In (d): The noun clause (*That she doesn't understand spoken English*) is the subject of the sentence. The word *that* is not omitted when it introduces a noun clause used as the subject of a sentence, as in (d) and (f). More commonly, the word *it* functions as the subject and the noun clause is placed at the end of the sentence, as in (e) and (g).
The world is round.	(f) *That the world is round* is a fact. (g) *It* is a fact *that* the world is round.	

☐ EXERCISE 11. Noun clauses beginning with THAT. (Chart 12-5)
　　　　　Directions: Work in pairs, in groups, or as a class.
　　　　　Speaker A: Change the given sentence into a noun clause. Use *it* + any appropriate
　　　　　　　　　　expression from the list.
　　　　　Speaker B: Give the equivalent sentence by using a *that*-clause as the subject.

Example: The world is round.
SPEAKER A *(book open):* It is a fact that the world is round.
SPEAKER B *(book closed):* That the world is round is a fact.

a fact	*obvious*	*surprising*	*unfair*	*a shame*
a well-known fact	*apparent*	*strange*	*too bad*	*a pity*
true	*clear*		*unfortunate*	

　　1. Tim hasn't been able to make any friends.
　　2. Drug abuse can ruin one's health.
　　3. Some women do not earn equal pay for equal work.
　　4. The earth revolves around the sun.
　　5. Irene, who is an excellent student, failed her entrance examination.
　　6. Smoking can cause cancer.
　　7. English is the principal language of the business community throughout much of
　　　　the world.

☐ EXERCISE 12. Noun clauses beginning with THAT. (Chart 12-5)
　　　　　Directions: Work in pairs or as a class.
　　　　　Speaker A: Make an original sentence by using *it* and the given expression.
　　　　　Speaker B: Give the equivalent sentence by using a *that*-clause as the subject.

Example: true
SPEAKER A: It is true that plants need water in order to grow.
SPEAKER B: That plants need water in order to grow is true.

　　　　　　　　　　　　　　　　　(Switch roles if working in pairs)
　　1. a fact　　　　　　　　　　6. unfortunate
　　2. surprising　　　　　　　　7. true
　　3. obvious　　　　　　　　　8. strange
　　4. too bad　　　　　　　　　9. unlikely
　　5. a well-known fact　　　　10. undeniable

☐ EXERCISE 13. Noun clauses beginning with THAT. (Chart 12-5)
　　　　　Directions: Complete the sentences.

　　1. It is my belief that . . . *the war between*　　5. It is widely believed that . . . .
　　　　those two countries will end soon.　　　　6. It is thought that . . . .
　　2. It seems to me that . . . .　　　　　　　　7. It has been said that . . . .
　　3. It is my impression that . . . .　　　　　　8. It is a miracle that . . . .
　　4. It is my theory that . . . .

☐ EXERCISE 14. Noun clauses beginning with THAT. (Chart 12-5)
Directions: *That*-clauses may follow *be* + certain adjectives that express feelings or attitudes. Complete the following with your own words.

1. I'm sorry (that) . . . *I was late for class.*
2. I'm glad (that) . . . .
3. I'm disappointed (that) . . . .
4. I'm pleased (that) . . . .
5. I'm surprised (that) . . . .
6. I'm sure (that) . . . .
7. I'm amazed (that) . . . .
8. I'm happy (that) . . . .
9. Yesterday I was annoyed (that) . . . .
10. I'm afraid (that)★ . . . .

☐ EXERCISE 15. Noun clauses beginning with THAT. (Chart 12-5)
Directions: A *that*-clause may follow *be* directly. Complete the sentences with your own ideas by using *that*-clauses.

1. He says he is twenty-one, but the truth is . . . *that he is only eighteen.*
2. There are two reasons why I do not want to go out tonight.
   The first reason is . . . *that I have to study.*
   The second reason is . . . *that I do not have enough money.***
3. There are several reasons why I am studying English.
   One reason is . . . .
   Another reason is . . . .
   A third reason is . . . .
4. I have had three problems since I came here.
   One problem is that . . . .
   Another problem is that . . . .
   The third problem I have had is that . . . .
5. One advantage of owning your own car is . . . .
   Another advantage is . . . .
   One disadvantage, however, of owning your own car is . . . .

☐ EXERCISE 16. Noun clauses beginning with THAT. (Chart 12-5)
Directions: A *that*-clause is frequently used with **the fact**. Combine the sentences using "the fact that" to introduce a noun clause.

1. Ann was late. That didn't surprise me.
   → *The fact that Ann was late didn't surprise me.*
2. Rosa didn't come. *That* made me angry.
3. I'm a little tired. I feel fine except for *that*.
4. Natasha didn't pass the entrance examination. She was not admitted to the university due to *that*.
5. Many people in the world live in intolerable poverty. *That* must concern all of us.

★*To be afraid* has two possible meanings:
  (1) It can express fear: *I'm afraid of dogs. I'm afraid that his dog will bite me.*
  (2) In informal English, it often expresses a meaning similar to "*to be sorry*":
        I'm afraid that I can't accept your invitation.
        I'm afraid you have the wrong number.
**NOTE: *That* is used, not *because*, to introduce the clause. (*Because* might occur only in very informal spoken English: *The first reason is because I have to study.*)

6. Surasuk is frequently absent from class. *That* indicates his lack of interest in school.

7. I was supposed to bring my passport to the examination for identification. I was not aware of *that*.

8. The people of the town were given no warning of the approaching tornado. Due to *that*, there were many casualties.

12-6 QUOTED SPEECH

Quoted speech refers to reproducing words exactly as they were originally spoken.★
Quotation marks ("...") are used.★★

QUOTING ONE SENTENCE (a) She said, *"My* brother is a student." (b) "My brother is a student," she said. (c) "My brother," she said, *"i*s a student."	In (a): Use a comma after *she said*. Capitalize the first word of the quoted sentence. Put the final quotation marks outside the period at the end of the sentence. In (b): Use a comma, not a period, at the end of the quoted sentence when it precedes *she said*. In (c): If the quoted sentence is divided by *she said*, use a comma after the first part of the quote. Do not capitalize the first word after *she said*.
QUOTING MORE THAN ONE SENTENCE (d) *"*My brother is a student. He is attending a university," she said. (e) "My brother is a student," she said. *"H*e is attending a university."	In (d): Quotation marks are placed at the beginning and end of the complete quote. Notice: There are no quotation marks after **student**. In (e): If *she said* comes between two quoted sentences, the second sentence begins with quotation marks and a capital letter.
QUOTING A QUESTION OR AN EXCLAMATION (f) She asked, "When will you be here?" (g) "When will you be here?" she asked. (h) She said, "Watch out!"	In (f): The question mark is inside the quotation marks. In (g): If a question mark is used, no comma is used before *she asked*. In (h): The exclamation point is inside the quotation marks.
(i) "My brother is a student," *said Anna.* "My brother," *said Anna,* "is a student."	In (i): The noun subject *(Anna)* follows **said**. A noun subject often follows the verb when the subject and verb come in the middle or at the end of a quoted sentence. (Note: A pronoun subject almost always precedes the verb. Very rare: *"My brother's a student," said she.*)
(j) "Let's leave," *whispered* Dave. (k) "Please help me," *begged* the unfortunate man. (l) "Well," Jack *began*, "it's a long story."	*Say* and *ask* are the most commonly used quote verbs. Some others: *add, agree, announce, answer, beg, begin, comment, complain, confess, continue, explain, inquire, promise, remark, reply, respond, shout, suggest, whisper.*

★*Quoted speech* is also called "direct speech." *Reported speech* (discussed in Chart 12-7, p. 254) is also called "indirect speech."

★★In British English, quotation marks are called "inverted commas" and can consist of either double marks (") or a single mark ('): She said, 'My brother is a student.'

☐ EXERCISE 17. Quoted speech. (Chart 12-6)
   Directions: Add the necessary punctuation and capitalization.

1. Henry said   there is a phone call for you

2. There is a phone call for you   he said

3. There is   said Henry   a phone call for you

4. There is a phone call for you   it's your sister   said Henry

5. There is a phone call for you   he said   it's your sister

6. I asked him   where is the phone

7. Where is the phone   she asked

8. Stop the clock   shouted the referee   we have an injured player

9. Who won the game   asked the spectator

10. I'm going to rest for the next three hours   she said   I don't want to be disturbed

    That's fine   I replied   you get some rest   I'll make sure no one disturbs you

☐ EXERCISE 18. Quoted speech. (Chart 12-6)
   Directions: Add the necessary punctuation and capitalization. Notice that a new paragraph begins each time the speaker changes.

When the police officer came over to my car, he said   let me see your driver's license, please

What's wrong, Officer   I asked   was I speeding

No, you weren't speeding   he replied you went through a red light at the corner of Fifth Avenue and Main Street   you almost caused an accident

Did I really do that   I said   I didn't see a red light

☐ **EXERCISE 19. Activity: quoted speech. (Chart 12-6)**

Directions: Choose two of your classmates to have a brief conversation in front of the class, and decide upon a topic for them (what they did last night, what they are doing right now, sports, music, books, etc.). Give them a few minutes to practice their conversation. Then, while they are speaking, take notes so that you can write their exact conversation. Use quoted speech in your written report. Be sure to start a new paragraph each time the speaker changes.

☐ **EXERCISE 20. Activity: quoted speech. (Chart 12-6)**

Directions: Write fables using quoted speech.

1. In fables, animals have the power of speech. Discuss what is happening in the illustrations of the grasshopper and the ants. Then write a fable based on the illustrations. Use quoted speech in your fable.

2. Write a fable that is well known in your country. Use quoted speech.

12-7 REPORTED SPEECH: VERB FORMS IN NOUN CLAUSES

QUOTED SPEECH	REPORTED SPEECH	
(a) "I *watch* TV every day."	→ She said she *watched* TV every day.	*Reported speech* refers to using a noun clause to report what someone has said. No quotation marks are used.
(b) "I *am watching* TV."	→ She said she *was watching* TV.	
(c) "I *have watched* TV."	→ She said she *had watched* TV.	If the reporting verb (the main verb of the sentence, e.g., *said*) is simple past, the verb in the noun clause will usually also be in a past form, as in the examples.
(d) "I *watched* TV."	→ She said she *had watched* TV.	
(e) "I *had watched* TV."	→ She said she *had watched* TV.	
(f) "I *will watch* TV."	→ She said she *would watch* TV.	
(g) "I *am going to watch* TV."	→ She said she *was going to watch* TV.	
(h) "I *can watch* TV."	→ She said she *could watch* TV.	
(i) "I *may watch* TV."	→ She said she *might watch* TV.	
(j) "I *must watch* TV."	→ She said she *had to watch* TV.	
(k) "I *have to watch* TV."	→ She said she *had to watch* TV.	
(l) "I *should watch* TV."	→ She said she *should watch* TV.	In (l): *should*, *ought to*, and *might* do not change to a past form.
"I *ought to watch* TV."	→ She said she *ought to watch* TV.	
"I *might watch* TV."	→ She said she *might watch* TV.	
(m) Immediate reporting: —What did the teacher just say? I didn't hear him. —He said he *wants* us to read Chapter Six. (n) Later reporting: —I didn't go to class yesterday. Did Mr. Jones make any assignments? —Yes. He said he *wanted* us to read Chapter Six.		Changing verbs to past forms in reported speech is common in both speaking and writing. However, sometimes in spoken English, no change is made in the noun clause verb, especially if the speaker is reporting something immediately or soon after it was said.
(o) "The world *is* round."	→ She said the world *is* round.	Also, sometimes the present tense is retained even in formal English when the reported sentence deals with a general truth, as in (o).
(p) "I *watch* TV every day."	→ She *says* she *watches* TV every day.	When the reporting verb is simple present, present perfect, or future, the noun clause verb is not changed.
(q) "I *watch* TV every day."	→ She *has said* that she *watches* TV every day.	
(r) "I *watch* TV every day."	→ She *will say* that she *watches* TV every day.	
(s) "*Watch* TV."	→ She *told* me *to watch* TV.★	In reported speech, an imperative sentence is changed to an infinitive. *Tell* is used instead of *say* as the reporting verb. See Chart 14-7, p. 307, for other verbs followed by an infinitive that are used to report speech.

★NOTE: *Tell* is immediately followed by a (pro)noun object, but *say* is not: *He told **me** he would be late. He said he would be late.* Also possible: *He said **to me** he would be late.*

☐ EXERCISE 21. Reported speech. (Chart 12-7)
    Directions: Complete the sentences by reporting the speaker's words in a noun clause. Use past verb forms in noun clauses if appropriate.

    1. Pedro said, "I will help you."

       Pedro said   *(that) he would help me.*

    2. "Do you need a pen?" Annie asked.

       Annie asked me   *if I needed a pen.*

3. Jennifer asked, "What do you want?"

   Jennifer asked me ___what I wanted.___

4. Talal asked, "Are you hungry?"

   Talal wanted to know _____

5. "I want a sandwich," Elena said.

   Elena said _____

6. "I'm going to move to Ohio," said Bruce.

   Bruce informed me _____

7. "Did you enjoy your trip?" asked Kim.

   Kim asked me _____

8. Oscar asked, "What are you talking about?"

   Oscar asked me _____

9. Maria asked, "Have you seen my grammar book?"

   Maria wanted to know _____

10. Yuko said, "I don't want to go."

    Yuko said _____

11. Sam asked, "Where is Nadia?"

    Sam wanted to know _____

12. "Can you help me with my report?" asked David.

    David asked me _____

13. "I may be late," said Mike.

    Mike told me _____

14. Felix said, "You should work harder."

    Felix told me _____

15. Rosa said, "I have to go downtown."

    Rosa said _____

16. "Why is the sky blue?" my young daughter often asks.

    My young daughter often asks me _____

17. My mother asked, "Why are you tired?"

    My mother wondered _____

18. "I will come to the meeting," said Pedro.

    Pedro told me _____

19. Ms. Adams just asked Ms. Chang, "Will you be in class tomorrow?"

    Ms. Adams wanted to know _____

20. "The sun rises in the east," said Mr. Clark.

Mr. Clark, an elementary school teacher, explained to his students _____

_____

21. "Someday we'll be in contact with beings from outer space."

The scientist predicted _____

22. "I think I'll go to the library to study."

Joe said _____

23. "Does Omar know what he's doing?"

I wondered _____

24. "Is what I've heard true?"

I wondered _____

25. "Sentences with noun clauses are a little complicated."

Olga thinks _____

☐ EXERCISE 22. Activity: reported speech. (Chart 12-7)

Directions: Form groups of three and choose a leader. Only the leader's book is open.
Speaker A: You are the leader. Your book is open. Whisper a question to Speaker B.
Speaker B: Your book is closed. Make sure you understand the question.
Speaker C: Your book is closed. Ask Speaker B something like "What did Speaker A want to know/say/ask you?"
Speaker B: Begin your response with "He (She) asked me . . . ."

Example:

SPEAKER A to B *(whispered):* Where is your friend?

SPEAKER C to B *(aloud):* What did (Speaker A) want to know?

SPEAKER B to C *(aloud):* He (She) asked me where my friend was (OR is).

1. What time is it?
2. Can you speak Arabic?
3. Have you seen *(title of a movie)?*
4. Will you be here tomorrow?
5. What kind of camera do you have?
6. What courses are you taking?
7. Did you finish your assignment?
8. *(Make up your own question.)*

Switch roles.

9. Have you read any good books lately?
10. How do you like living here?
11. May I borrow your dictionary?
12. Where will you be tomorrow around three o'clock?
13. What are you going to do during vacation?

14. Did you go to a party last night?
15. Can I use your pen?
16. *(Make up your own question.)*

Switch roles.

17. How many people have you met in the last couple of months?
18. Where should I meet you after class?
19. Do you understand what I am saying?
20. Did you go to class yesterday?
21. Is what you said really true?
22. Is what you want to talk to me about important?
23. How do you know that what you said is true?
24. *(Make up your own question.)*

☐ EXERCISE 23. Activity: reported speech. (Chart 12-7)
Directions: With books closed, report to the class at least one question you were asked in the previous exercise and who asked it. Use a past verb form in the noun clause.

Example: Roberto asked me if I'd read any good books lately.

☐ EXERCISE 24. Reported speech: verb forms in noun clauses. (Chart 12-7)
Directions: Complete the sentences, using the information in the dialogue. Change the verbs to a past form as appropriate.

1. *Fred asked me, "Can we still get tickets to the game?"*
   I said, "I've already bought them."

   When Fred asked me if we ___could still get___

   tickets to the game, I told him that I

   ___had already bought___ them.

CAN WE STILL GET TICKETS TO THE GAME?

I'VE ALREADY BOUGHT THEM.

2. *Mrs. White said, "Janice, you have to clean up your room and empty the dishwasher before you leave for the game."*
   Janice said, "Okay, Mom. I will."

   Mrs. White told Janice that she ___had to clean up___

   her room and empty the dishwasher before she ___could leave___

   for the game. Janice promised her mom that she ___would___ .

3. *I asked the ticket seller, "Is the concert going to be rescheduled?"*
   The ticket seller said, "I don't know, Ma'am. I just work here."

   When I asked the ticket seller if the concert _____ to be

   rescheduled, she told me that she _____ and said that she just

   _____ there.

4. *I asked Boris, "Where will the next chess match take place?"*
   Boris replied, "It hasn't been decided yet."

   When I asked Boris _____ place, he replied that it

   _____ yet.

5. *I said to Alan, "I'm very discouraged. I don't think I'll ever speak English well."*
   Alan said, "Your English is getting better every day. In another year, you'll be speaking English with the greatest of ease."

   I complained that I _____ very discouraged. I said that I

   _____ I _____ ever _____ English

   well. Alan told me that my English _____ better every day. He

   assured me that in another year, I _____ English with the

   greatest of ease.

6. *A person in the audience asked the speaker, "Are the necessary means to increase the world's food supply presently available?"*
    The agronomy professor said, "It might be possible to grow 50 percent of the world's food in underwater cultivation if we can develop inexpensive methods."

    A person in the audience asked the agronomy professor if the necessary means to

    increase the world's food supply _____ presently available. The

    professor stated that it _____ possible to grow 50 percent of the

    world's food under water if we _____ inexpensive methods.

☐ EXERCISE 25. Reported speech. (Chart 12-7)
    Directions: Change the quoted speech to reported speech. Study the example carefully and use the same pattern: ***said that . . . and that*** OR ***said that . . . but that.***

    1. "My father is a businessman. My mother is an engineer."
        He said that ___ his father was a businessman and that his mother ___
        ___ was an engineer. ___

    2. "I'm excited about my new job. I've found a nice apartment."
        I got a letter from my sister yesterday. She said _____
        _____

    3. "Your Uncle Harry is in the hospital. Your Aunt Sally is very worried about him."
        The last time my mother wrote to me, she said _____
        _____

    4. "I expect you to be in class every day. Unexcused absences may affect your grades."
        Our sociology professor said _____
        _____

    5. "Highway 66 will be closed for two months. Commuters should seek alternate routes."
        The newspaper said _____
        _____

    6. "I'm getting good grades, but I have difficulty understanding lectures."
        My brother is a junior at a state university. In his last letter, he wrote _____
        _____

    7. "Every obstacle is a steppingstone to success. You should view problems in your life as opportunities to prove yourself."
        My father often told me _____
        _____

8. "I'll come to the meeting, but I can't stay for more than an hour."

Julia told me _____

_____

☐ EXERCISE 26. Activity: reported speech. (Charts 12-1 → 12-7)
Directions: Work in groups or as a class.
Speaker A: Ask a question on the given topic—whatever comes into your mind. Use a
        question word (***when, how, where, what, why***, *etc.*).
Speaker B: Answer the question in a complete sentence.
Speaker C: Report what Speaker A and Speaker B said.

Example: tonight
SPEAKER A (ROSA): What are you going to do tonight?
SPEAKER B (ALI): I'm going to study.
SPEAKER C (YUNG): Rosa asked Ali what he was going to do tonight, and Ali replied that
        he was going to study.

1. tonight	5. book	9. television
2. music	6. this city	10. dinner
3. courses	7. population	11. next year
4. tomorrow	8. last year	12. vacation

☐ EXERCISE 27. Review: noun clauses. (Charts 12-1 → 12-7)
Directions: Complete the sentences.

1. I cannot understand why . . . .
2. One of the students remarked that . . . .
3. I was not sure whose . . . .
4. What . . . surprised me.
5. That she . . . surprised me.
6. One of the students stated that . . . .
7. I could not . . . due to the fact that . . . .
8. What he said was that . . . .
9. No one knows who . . . .
10. The instructor announced that . . . .
11. What I want to know is why . . . .
12. What . . . is not important.
13. We discussed the fact that . . . .
14. I wonder whether . . . .

☐ EXERCISE 28. Activity: noun clauses. (Charts 12-1 → 12-7)
Directions: Read each dialogue and then write a report about it. The report should include
an accurate idea of the speakers' words, but doesn't have to use their exact words.

Example: Jack said, "I can't go to the game."
        Tom said, "Oh? Why not?"
        "I don't have enough money for a ticket," replied Jack.

Possible written reports of the above dialogue:
  a. Jack told Tom that he couldn't go to the game because he didn't have enough
     money for a ticket.
  b. When Tom asked Jack why he couldn't go to the game, Jack said he didn't have
     enough money for a ticket.
  c. Jack said he couldn't go to the game. When Tom asked him why not, Jack replied
     that he didn't have enough money for a ticket.

Write reports of the following dialogues:

1. "What are you doing?" Alex asked.
   "I'm drawing a picture," I said.

2. Ann said, "Do you want to go to a movie Sunday night?"
   Sue said, "I'd like to, but I have to study."

3. "How old are you, Mrs. Robinson?" the little boy asked.
   Mrs. Robinson said, "It's not polite to ask people their age."

4.   "Is there anything you especially want to watch on TV tonight?" my sister asked.
     "Yes," I replied. "There's a show at eight that I've been waiting to see for a long time."
     "What is it?" she asked.
     "It's a documentary on green sea turtles," I said.
     "Why do you want to see that?"
     "I'm doing a research paper on sea turtles. I think I might be able to get some good information from the documentary. Why don't you watch it with me?"
     "No, thanks," she said. "I'm not especially interested in green sea turtles."

☐ EXERCISE 29. Activity: noun clauses. (Charts 12-1 → 12-7)
   Directions: Make up a dialogue for the two characters waiting in the supermarket line, and then write a story about the picture. The events in the picture happened yesterday.

☐ **EXERCISE 30. Error analysis: noun clauses** (Charts 12-1 → 12-7)

Directions: Correct the errors.

1. Tell the taxi driver where do you want to go.

2. My roommate came into the room and asked me why aren't you in class? I said I am waiting for a telephone call from my family.

3. It was my first day at the university, and I am on my way to my first class. I wondered who else will be in the class. What the teacher would be like?

4. He asked me that what did I intend to do after I graduate?

5. Many of the people in the United States doesn't know much about geography. For example, people will ask you where is Japan located.

6. What does a patient tell a doctor it is confidential.

7. What my friend and I did it was our secret. We didn't even tell our parents what did we do.

8. The doctor asked that I felt okay. I told him that I don't feel well.

9. Is clear that the ability to use a computer it is an important skill in the modern world.

10. I asked him what kind of movies does he like, he said me, I like romantic movies.

11. Is true you almost drowned? my friend asked me. Yes, I said. I'm really glad to be alive. It was really frightening.

12. It is a fact that I almost drowned makes me very careful about water safety whenever I go swimming.

13. I didn't know where am I supposed to get off the bus, so I asked the driver where is the science museum. She tell me the name of the street. She said she will tell me when should I get off the bus.

14. My mother did not live with us. When other children asked me where was my mother, I told them she is going to come to visit me very soon.

15. When I asked the taxi driver to drive faster he said I will drive faster if you pay me more. At that time I didn't care how much would it cost, so I told him to go as fast as he can.

16. We looked back to see where are we and how far are we from camp. We don't know, so we decided to turn back. We are afraid that we wander too far.

17. After the accident, I opened my eyes slowly and realize that I am still alive.

18. My country is prospering due to it is a fact that it has become a leading producer of oil.

19. Is true that one must to know english in order to study at an american university.

20. My mother told me what it was the purpose of our visit.

☐ EXERCISE 31. Activity: noun clauses. (Charts 12-1 → 12-7)
Directions: Choose one of the following.

1. Think of a letter written in English that you have received recently. In a short paragraph, summarize some of the news or information in this letter. (If you have not recently received a letter written in English, invent one.) Include at least two sentences that use the pattern *said that . . . and that* OR *said that . . . but that*.
2. Student A: Write a letter to a classmate (Student B). Give it to Student B.
   Student B: Write a report summarizing Student A's letter.

☐ EXERCISE 32. Activity: noun clauses. (Charts 12-1 → 12-7)
Directions: Form small groups and discuss one (or more) of the following topics. Then write a report of the main points made by each speaker in your group. (Do not attempt to report every word that was spoken.)

In your report, use words such as *think*, *believe*, *say*, *remark*, and *state* to introduce noun clauses. When you use *think* or *believe*, you will probably use present tenses (e.g., *Omar thinks that money is the most important thing in life.*). When you use *say*, *remark*, or *state*, you will probably use past tenses (e.g., *Olga **said** that many other things **were** more important than money.*).

Do you agree with the given statements? Why or why not?

1. Money is the most important thing in life.
2. A woman can do any job a man can do.
3. When a person decides to get married, his or her love for the other person is the only important consideration.
4. A world government is both desirable and necessary. Countries should simply become the states of one nation, the Earth. In this way, wars could be eliminated and wealth could be equally distributed.

☐ EXERCISE 33. Activity: noun clauses. (Charts 12-1 → 12-7)
Directions: Give a one-minute impromptu speech on any topic that comes to mind (pollution, insects, soccer, dogs, etc.). Your classmates will take notes as you speak. Then, in a short paragraph or orally, they will report what you said.

□ **EXERCISE 34. Activity: noun clauses. (Charts 12-1 → 12-7)**

Directions: You and your classmates are newspaper reporters at a press conference. You will all interview your teacher or a person whom your teacher invites to class. Your assignment is to write a newspaper article about the person whom you interviewed.

Take notes during the interview. Write down some of the important sentences so that you can use them for quotations in your article. Ask for clarification if you do not understand something the interviewee has said. It is important to report information accurately.

In your article, try to organize your information into related topics. For example, if you interview your teacher:

I. General introductory information
II. Professional life
   A. Present teaching duties
   B. Academic duties and activities outside of teaching
   C. Past teaching experience
   D. Educational background
III. Personal life
   A. Basic biographical information (e.g., place of birth, family background, places of residence)
   B. Spare-time activities and interests
   C. Travel experiences

The above outline only suggests a possible method of organization. You must organize your own article, depending upon the information you have gained from your interview.

When you write your report, most of your information will be presented in reported speech; use quoted speech only for the most important or memorable sentences. When you use quoted speech, be sure you are presenting the interviewee's *exact words*. If you are simply paraphrasing what the interviewee said, do not use quotation marks.

12-8   USING THE SUBJUNCTIVE IN NOUN CLAUSES

(a) The teacher **demands** that we **be** on time. (b) I **insisted** that he **pay** me the money. (c) I **recommended** that she **not go** to the concert. (d) **It is important** that they **be told** the truth.	A subjunctive verb uses the simple form of a verb. It does not have present, past, or future forms; it is neither singular nor plural. Sentences with subjunctive verbs generally *stress importance or urgency*. A subjunctive verb is used in *that*-clauses that follow the verbs and expressions listed below. In (a): **be** is a subjunctive verb; its subject is **we**. In (b): **pay** (not *pays*, not *paid*) is a subjunctive verb; it is in its simple form, even though its subject (**he**) is singular. Negative: **not** + *simple form*, as in (c). Passive: *simple form of **be** + past participle*, as in (d).
(e) I **suggested** that she **see** a doctor. (f) I **suggested** that she **should see** a doctor.	**Should** is also possible after **suggest** and **recommend.***

COMMON VERBS AND EXPRESSIONS FOLLOWED BY THE SUBJUNCTIVE IN A NOUN CLAUSE			
advise (that)	*propose (that)*	*it is essential (that)*	*it is critical (that)*
ask (that)	*recommend (that)*	*it is imperative (that)*	*it is necessary (that)*
demand (that)	*request (that)*	*it is important (that)*	*it is vital (that)*
insist (that)	*suggest (that)*		

*The subjunctive is more common in American English than British English. In British English, **should** + *simple form* is more usual than the subjunctive: *The teacher **insists** that we **should be** on time.*

☐ EXERCISE 35. Using the subjunctive in noun clauses. (Chart 12-8)
    Directions: Complete the sentences. There is often more than one possible completion.

1. Mr. Adams insists that we _____ *be* _____ careful in our writing.

2. They requested that we not _____ after midnight.

3. She demanded that I _____ her the truth.

4. I recommended that Jane _____ to the head of the department.

5. I suggest that everyone _____ a letter to the governor.

6. It is essential that I _____ you tomorrow.

7. It is important that he _____ the director of the English program.

8. It is necessary that everyone _____ here on time.

☐ EXERCISE 36. Using the subjunctive in noun clauses. (Chart 12-8)
    Directions: Give the correct form of the verb in parentheses. Some of the verbs are passive.

1. Her advisor recommended that she *(take)* _____ five courses.

2. Roberto insisted that the new baby *(name)* _____ after his grandfather.

3. The doctor recommended that she *(stay)* _____ in bed for a few days.

4. The students requested that the test *(postpone)* _____, but the instructor decided against a postponement.

5. It is essential that no one *(admit)* _____ to the room without proper identification.

6. It is critical that pollution *(control)* _____ and eventually *(eliminate)* _____.

7. It was such a beautiful day that one of the students suggested we *(have)* _____ class outside.

8. The movie director insisted that everything about his productions *(be)* _____ authentic.

9. It is vital that no one else *(know)* _____ about the secret government operation.

10. Mrs. Wah asked that we *(be)* _____ sure to lock the door behind us.

11. I requested that I *(permit)* _____ to change my class.

12. It is important that you *(be, not)* _____ late.

13. It is imperative that he *(return)* _____ home immediately.

14. The governor proposed that a new highway *(build)* _____.

15. Fumiko specifically asked that I *(tell, not)* _____ anyone else about it.

    She said it was important that no one else *(tell)* _____ about it.

12-9 USING *-EVER* WORDS

The following *-ever* words give the idea of "any." Each pair of sentences in the examples has the same meaning.

whoever	(a)	***Whoever*** wants to come is welcome. *Anyone who* wants to come is welcome.
who(m)ever	(b)	He makes friends easily with ***who(m)ever*** he meets.* He makes friends easily with *anyone who(m)* he meets.
whatever	(c)	He always says ***whatever*** comes into his mind. He always says *anything that* comes into his mind.
whichever	(d)	There are four good programs on TV at eight o'clock. We can watch ***whichever program*** (***whichever one***) you prefer. We can watch *any of the four programs that* you prefer.
whenever	(e)	You may leave ***whenever*** you wish. You may leave *at any time that* you wish.
wherever	(f)	She can go ***wherever*** she wants to go. She can go *anyplace that* she wants to go.
however	(g)	The students may dress ***however*** they please. The students may dress *in any way that* they please.

*In (b): ***whomever*** is the object of the verb ***meets***. In American English, ***whomever*** is rare and very formal. In British English, ***whoever*** (not ***whomever***) is used as the object form: *He makes friends easily with whoever he meets.*

☐ EXERCISE 37. Using -EVER words. (Chart 12-9)
   Directions: Complete the following by using *-ever* words.

1. Mustafa is free to go anyplace he wishes. He can go ____**wherever**____ he wants.

2. Mustafa is free to go anytime he wishes. He can go _____ he wants.

3. I don't know what you should do about that problem. Do _____
   seems best to you.

4. There are five flights to Chicago every day. I don't care which one we take. We can
   take _____ one fits in best with your schedule.

5. I want you to be honest. I hope you feel free to say _____ is on your
   mind.

6. _____ leads a life full of love and happiness is rich.

7. No one can tell him what to do. He does _____ he wants.

8. If you want to rearrange the furniture, go ahead. You can rearrange it _____ you want. I don't care one way or the other.

9. Those children are wild! I feel sorry for _____ has to be their babysitter.

10. I have a car. I can take you _____ you want to go.

11. Scott likes to tell people about his problems. He will talk to _____ will listen to him. But he bores _____ he talks to.

12. To Ellen, the end justifies the means. She will do _____ she has to do in order to accomplish her objective.

13. I have four. Take _____ one pleases you most.

14. My wife and I are going to ride our bicycles across the country. We'll ride for six to seven hours every day, then stop for the night _____ we happen to be.

15. Irene does _____ she wants to do, goes _____ she wants to go, gets up _____ she wants to get up, makes friends with _____ she meets, and dresses _____ she pleases.

CHAPTER *13*
Adjective Clauses

CONTENTS

13-1   INTRODUCTION

CLAUSE:	*A clause* is a group of words containing a subject and a verb.
INDEPENDENT CLAUSE:	*An independent clause* is a complete sentence. It contains the main subject and verb of a sentence. (It is also called "a main clause.")
DEPENDENT CLAUSE:	*A dependent clause* is not a complete sentence. It must be connected to an independent clause.
ADJECTIVE CLAUSE:	*An adjective clause* is a dependent clause that modifies a noun. It describes, identifies, or gives further information about a noun. (An adjective clause is also called "a relative clause.")
ADJECTIVE CLAUSE PRONOUNS:	An adjective clause uses pronouns to connect the dependent clause to the independent clause. The *adjective clause pronouns* are *who, whom, which, that,* and *whose*. (Adjective clause pronouns are also called "relative pronouns.")

13-2 ADJECTIVE CLAUSE PRONOUNS USED AS THE SUBJECT

I thanked the woman. **She** helped me. ↓	In (a): *I thanked the woman* = an independent clause; *who helped me* = an adjective clause. The adjective clause modifies the noun **woman**.
(a) I thanked the woman **who** *helped me*. (b) I thanked the woman **that** *helped me*.	In (a): **who** is the subject of the adjective clause. In (b): **that** is the subject of the adjective clause. Note: (a) and (b) have the same meaning. (c) and (d) have the same meaning.
The book is mine. **It** is on the table. ↓	
(c) The book **which** *is on the table* is mine. (d) The book **that** *is on the table* is mine.	**who** = used for people **which** = used for things **that** = used for both people and things
(e) *INCORRECT:* *The book is mine that is on the table.*	An adjective clause closely follows the noun it modifies.

☐ EXERCISE 1. Adjective clause pronouns used as subjects. (Chart 13-2)

Directions: Combine the two sentences. Use the second sentence as an adjective clause.

1. I saw the man. He closed the door. → *I saw the man* $\begin{Bmatrix} who \\ that \end{Bmatrix}$ *closed the door.*
2. The girl is happy. She won the race.
3. The student is from China. He sits next to me.
4. The students are from China. They sit in the front row.
5. We are studying sentences. They contain adjective clauses.
6. I am using a sentence. It contains an adjective clause.
7. Algebra problems contain letters. They stand for unknown numbers.
8. The taxi driver was friendly. He took me to the airport.

13-3 ADJECTIVE CLAUSE PRONOUNS USED AS THE OBJECT OF A VERB

The man was Mr. Jones. I saw **him**. ↓	Notice in the examples: The adjective clause pronouns are placed at the beginning of the clause.
(a) The man **who(m)** *I saw* was Mr. Jones. (b) The man **that** *I saw* was Mr. Jones. (c) The man **Ø** *I saw* was Mr. Jones.	In (a): **who** is usually used instead of **whom**, especially in speaking. **Whom** is generally used only in very formal English.
The movie wasn't very good. We saw **it** last night. ↓	In (c) and (f): An object pronoun is often omitted from an adjective clause. (A subject pronoun, however, may not be omitted.)
(d) The movie **which** *we saw last night* wasn't very good. (e) The movie **that** *we saw last night* wasn't very good. (f) The movie **Ø** *we saw last night* wasn't very good.	**who(m)** = used for people **which** = used for things **that** = used for both people and things
(g) *INCORRECT:* The man who(m) I saw *him* was Mr. Jones. The man that I saw *him* was Mr. Jones. The man I saw *him* was Mr. Jones.	In (g): The pronoun **him** must be removed. It is unnecessary because *who(m)*, *that*, or Ø functions as the object of the verb **saw**.

☐ **EXERCISE 2. Adjective clause pronouns used as the object of a verb. (Chart 13-3)**
Directions: Combine the sentences, using the second sentence as an adjective clause. Give all the possible patterns.

1. The book was good. I read it.
2. I liked the woman. I met her at the party last night.
3. I liked the composition. You wrote it.
4. The people were very nice. We visited them yesterday.
5. The man is standing over there. Ann brought him to the party.

13-4 ADJECTIVE CLAUSE PRONOUNS USED AS THE OBJECT OF A PREPOSITION

She is the woman. I told you **about her**. (a) She is the woman **about whom** I told you. (b) She is the woman **who(m)** I told you **about**. (c) She is the woman **that** I told you **about**. (d) She is the woman Ø I told you **about**.	In very formal English, the preposition comes at the beginning of the adjective clause, as in (a) and (e). Usually, however, in everyday usage, the preposition comes after the subject and verb of the adjective clause, as in the other examples.
The music was good. We listened **to it** last night. (e) The music **to which** we listened last night was good. (f) The music **which** we listened **to** last night was good. (g) The music **that** we listened **to** last night was good. (h) The music Ø we listened **to** last night was good.	Note: If the preposition comes at the beginning of the adjective clause, only **whom** or **which** may be used. A preposition is never immediately followed by **that** or **who**.*

*⋆*INCORRECT:* She is the woman *about who* I told you.
INCORRECT: The music *to that* we listened last night was good.

☐ **EXERCISE 3. Adjective clause pronouns used as the object of a preposition. (Chart 13-4)**
Directions: Combine the sentences, using the second sentence as an adjective clause. Give all the possible patterns.

1. The meeting was interesting. I went to it.
2. The man was very kind. I talked to him yesterday.
3. I must thank the people. I got a present from them.
4. The picture was beautiful. She was looking at it.
5. The man is standing over there. I was telling you about him.
6. I ran into a woman. I had gone to elementary school with her.
7. The topic was interesting. Omar talked about it.
8. The people were friendly. I spoke to them.
9. Olga wrote on a topic. She knew nothing about it.
10. The candidate didn't win the election. I voted for her.

☐ **EXERCISE 4. Adjective clauses. (Charts 13-2 → 13-4)**
Directions: Identify the adjective clause in each sentence. Then give the other possible patterns.

Example: The dress which she is wearing is new.
→ Adjective clause: *which she is wearing.*

Other possible patterns: *The dress* $\begin{Bmatrix} that \\ \emptyset \end{Bmatrix}$ *she is wearing is new.*

1. Did I tell you about the woman I met last night?

2. The woman I was dancing with stepped on my toe.

3. The report Joe is writing must be finished by Friday.

4. The doctor who examined the sick child was gentle.

5. The people I was waiting for were late.

6. Did you hear about the earthquake that occurred in California?

13-5   USUAL PATTERNS OF ADJECTIVE CLAUSES

(a) USUAL: I like the people *who live next to me.* LESS USUAL: I like the people *that live next to me.*	In everyday informal usage, often one adjective clause pattern is used more commonly than another.* In (a): As a subject pronoun, *who* is more common than *that*.
(b) USUAL: I like books *that have good plots.* LESS USUAL: I like books *which have good plots.*	In (b): As a subject pronoun, *that* is more common than *which*.
(c) USUAL: I liked the people Ø *I met last night.* (d) USUAL: I liked the book Ø *I read last week.*	In (c) and (d): Object pronouns are commonly omitted, especially in speaking.

*See Chart 13-10, p. 281, for patterns of pronoun usage when an adjective clause requires commas.

☐ **EXERCISE 5. Adjective clauses. (Charts 13-2 → 13-5)**
Directions: Combine the sentences, using the second sentence as an adjective clause. Give all the possible adjective clause patterns. Discuss which patterns are used more commonly than others.

Example: The scientist is well known for her research. We met her yesterday.

→ *The scientist* $\begin{Bmatrix} \emptyset \\ who(m) \\ that \end{Bmatrix}$ *we met yesterday is well known for her research.*

1. She lectured on a topic. I know very little about it.

2. The students missed the assignment. They were absent from class.

3. Yesterday I ran into an old friend. I hadn't seen him for years.

4. The young women are all from Japan. We met them at the meeting last night.

5. I am reading a book. It was written by Jane Austen.

6. The man gave me good advice. I spoke to him.

7. I returned the money. I had borrowed it from my roommate.

8. The dogcatcher caught the dog. It had bitten my neighbor's daughter.

9. I read about a man. He keeps chickens in his apartment.

☐ EXERCISE 6. Adjective clauses. (Charts 13-2 → 13-5)
   Directions: All of these sentences contain errors in adjective clause structures. Correct the errors.

1. In our village, there were many people didn't have much money.

2. I enjoyed the book that you told me to read it.

3. I still remember the man who he taught me to play the violin when I was a boy.

4. I showed my father a picture of the car I am going to buy it as soon as I save enough money.

5. The woman about who I was talking about suddenly walked into the room. I hope she didn't hear me.

6. Almost all of the people appear on television wear makeup.

7. I don't like to spend time with people which loses their temper easily.

8. The boy drew pictures of people at an airport which was waiting for their planes.

9. People who works in the hunger program they estimate that 3500 people in the world die from starvation every day of the year.

10. In one corner of the marketplace, an old man who was playing a violin.

□ **EXERCISE 7. Adjective clauses. (Charts 13-2 → 13-5)**

Directions: Work in pairs (switching roles after item 6), in groups, or as a class.

Speaker A: Your book is open. Ask the questions. Use the names of classmates.

Speaker B: Your book is closed. Begin your answer with "Yes, she/he did. She/He told me about **the** . . . ." Use an adjective clause in the completion. Omit the object pronoun.

Example: Did (. . .) write a report?

SPEAKER A *(book open):* Did Carmen write a report?

SPEAKER B *(book closed):* Yes, she did. She told me about **the** report she wrote.

1. Did (. . .) get a letter from (her/his) brother yesterday?
2. Did (. . .) write a letter to *(name of a person)?*
3. Did (. . .) go to a party yesterday?
4. Did (. . .) meet some people at that party?
5. Did (. . .) take a trip to *(name of a country)* last summer?
6. Did (. . .) have some experiences in *(name of that country)?*
7. Did (. . .) use to live in a small town?
8. Did (. . .) watch a program on TV last night?
9. Did (. . .) interview for a job?
10. Did (. . .) have to write a report for (her/his) boss?
11. Did (. . .) talk to a person about health insurance?
12. Did (. . .) go to the meeting for new employees?

☐ EXERCISE 8. Adjective clauses. (Charts 13-2 → 13-5)
   Directions: Work in pairs.
   Speaker A: Your book is open. Look at a cue briefly. Then, without looking at the text, say the cue sentence to Speaker B.
   Speaker B: Your book is closed. Begin your answer with "Yes."

Examples:
SPEAKER A: You read **a** book. Was it interesting?
SPEAKER B: Yes, **the** book I read was interesting.

SPEAKER A: You drank **some** tea. Did it taste good?
SPEAKER B: Yes, **the** tea I drank tasted good.

SPEAKER A: **A** stranger gave you directions to the post office. Did she speak too fast?
SPEAKER B: Yes, **the** stranger who gave me directions to the post office spoke too fast.

SPEAKER A: **A** police officer helped you. Did you thank her?
SPEAKER B: Yes, I thanked **the** police officer who helped me.

1. You are sitting in a chair. Is it comfortable?
2. You saw a man. Was he wearing a brown suit?
3. You talked to a woman. Did she answer your question?
4. A woman stepped on your toe. Did she apologize?
5. Some students took a test. Did most of them pass?
6. You had some meat for dinner last night. Was it good?
7. A woman shouted at you. Was she angry?
8. A person is sitting next to you. Do you know him/her?
9. A woman came into the room. Did you recognize her?
10. You bought a coat. Does it keep you warm?
11. You watched a TV program last night. Was it good?
12. You were reading a book. Did you finish it?

Switch roles.
13. You stayed at a hotel. Was it in the middle of the city?
14. We are doing an exercise. Is it easy?
15. A waiter served you at a restaurant. Was he polite?
16. A student stopped you in the hall. Did he ask you for the correct time?
17. Some students are sitting in this room. Can all of them speak English?
18. You were looking for a book. Did you find it?
19. You are wearing (boots/tennis shoes/loafers). Are they comfortable?
20. A taxi driver took you to the bus station. Did you have a conversation with her?
21. A man opened the door for you. Did you thank him?
22. A clerk cashed your check. Did he ask for identification?
23. You got a package in the mail. Was it from your parents?
24. A man stopped you on the street. Did he ask you for directions?

☐ EXERCISE 9. Adjective clauses. (Charts 13-4 → 13-5)

Directions: Work in pairs or as a class.

Speaker A: Your book is open. Give the cues from the text.

Speaker B: Your book is closed. Repeat the cue, changing "you" to "I" as necessary. Then make a second sentence with an adjective clause. The adjective clause should modify the noun at the end of the first sentence, as in the examples.

Examples:

SPEAKER A *(book open):* You're looking at a person.

SPEAKER B *(book closed):* I'm looking at **a person**. **The person** I'm looking at is Peter Lo.

SPEAKER A *(book open):* You're sitting at a desk.

SPEAKER B *(book closed):* I'm sitting at **a desk**. **The desk** I'm sitting at has many scratches on it.

(Switch roles if working in pairs.)

1. You're studying at a school.
2. You're living in a (city/town).
3. That book belongs to a student.★
4. (. . .) and you listened to some music.
5. (. . .) went to a movie last night.
6. You are sitting next to a person.
7. You're living with some people.
8. (. . .) was talking about a movie.
9. You're interested in a field of study.
10. That (bookbag/backpack/bag) belongs to a person.
11. You spoke to some people.
12. You went to a doctor to get some medicine.

13-6 USING *WHOSE*

I know the man.
His bicycle was stolen.
↓
(a) I know the man *whose bicycle was stolen.*
	Whose is used to show possession. It carries the same meaning as other possessive pronouns used as adjectives: *his, her, its,* and *their.* Like *his, her, its,* and *their,* ***whose*** is connected to a noun:
	    his bicycle → *whose bicycle*
	    her composition → *whose composition*
	Both ***whose*** and the noun it is connected to are placed at the beginning of the adjective clause. ***Whose*** cannot be omitted.

The student writes well. I read ***her composition***. ↓ (b) The student *whose composition I read* writes well.	
Mr. Catt has a painting. ***Its value*** is inestimable. ↓ (c) Mr. Catt has a painting *whose value is inestimable.*	***Whose*** usually modifies people, but it may also be used to modify things, as in (c).

★Sometimes a sentence has "that that": *I've read the book that that man wrote.* In this example, the first ***that*** is an adjective clause pronoun. The second ***that*** is a demonstrative adjective, like *this* or *those.*

□ **EXERCISE 10. Using WHOSE in adjective clauses. (Chart 13-6)**

Directions: Combine the sentences, using the second sentence as an adjective clause.

1. I know a man. His last name is Goose.

   → *I know a man whose last name is Goose.*

2. I apologized to the woman. I spilled her coffee.

3. The man called the police. His wallet was stolen.

4. I met the woman. Her husband is the president of the corporation.

5. The professor is excellent. I am taking her course.

6. Mr. North teaches a class for students. Their native language is not English.

7. The people were nice. We visited their house.

8. I live in a dormitory. Its residents come from many countries.

9. I have to call the man. I accidentally picked up his umbrella after the meeting.

10. The man poured a glass of
    water on his face. His beard
    caught on fire when he lit a
    cigarette.

□ **EXERCISE 11. Using WHOSE in adjective clauses. (Chart 13-6)**

Directions: Work in pairs (switching roles after item 4), in groups, or as a class.
Speaker A: Your book is open. Give the cues from the text.
Speaker B: Your book is closed. Repeat the cue, changing "you" to "I" as necessary. Then
combine the two sentences into one that contains an adjective clause with **whose**.

Example:
SPEAKER A *(book open):* Dr. Jones is a professor. You're taking his course.
SPEAKER B *(book closed):* Dr. Jones is **a** professor. I'm taking his course.
              Dr. Jones is **the** professor whose course I'm taking.

1. Maria is a student. You found her book.
2. Omar is a student. You borrowed his dictionary.
3. You used a woman's phone. You thanked her.
4. You broke a child's toy. He started to cry.
5. You stayed at a family's house. They were very kind.
6. A woman's purse was stolen. She called the police.
7. *(Name of a famous singer)* is a singer. You like his/her music best.
8. Everyone tried to help a family. Their house had burned down.

☐ **EXERCISE 12. Using WHOSE in adjective clauses. (Chart 13-6)**

Directions: Pair up. Pretend you are in a room full of people. You and your classmate are speaking. Together, you are identifying various people in the room. Begin each sentence with "There is . . . ." Alternate items, with Speaker A doing Item 1, Speaker B doing Item 2, Speaker A doing Item 3, etc.

1. That man's wife is your teacher.
   → SPEAKER A: *There is the man whose wife is my teacher.*

2. That woman's husband is a football player.
   → SPEAKER B: *There is the woman whose husband is a football player.*

3. That boy's father is a doctor.

4. That girl's mother is a dentist.

5. That person's picture was in the newspaper.

6. That woman's car was stolen.

7. That man's daughter won a gold medal at the Olympic Games.

8. You found that woman's keys.

9. You are in that teacher's class.

10. We met that man's wife.

11. You read that author's book.

12. You borrowed that student's lecture notes.

☐ **EXERCISE 13. Using WHOSE in adjective clauses. (Chart 13-6)**

Directions: Combine the sentences, using ***whose*** in an adjective clause.

1. The man's wife had been admitted to the hospital. I spoke to him.
   → *I spoke to the man whose wife had been admitted to the hospital.*

2. I read about a child. Her life was saved by her pet dog.
   → *I read about a child whose life was saved by her pet dog.*

3. The students raised their hands. Their names were called.

4. Jack knows a man. The man's name is William Blueheart Duckbill, Jr.

5. The woman's purse was stolen outside the supermarket. The police came to question her.

6. The day care center was established to take care of children. These children's parents work during the day.

7. We couldn't find the person. His car was blocking the driveway.

8. Three students' reports were turned in late. The professor told them he would accept the papers this time but never again.

13-7 USING *WHERE* IN ADJECTIVE CLAUSES

				Where is used in an adjective clause to modify a place *(city, country, room, house, etc.)*.
	The building is very old. He lives **there (in that building)**.			If **where** is used, a preposition is NOT included in the adjective clause, as in (a). If **where** is not used, the preposition must be included, as in (b).
(a)	The building	*where*	*he lives*	is very old.
(b)	The building	*in which*	*he lives*	is very old.
	The building	*which*	*he lives in*	is very old.
	The building	*that*	*he lives in*	is very old.
	The building	Ø	*he lives in*	is very old.

☐ **EXERCISE 14. Using WHERE in adjective clauses. (Chart 13-7)**
Directions: Combine the sentences, using the second sentence as an adjective clause.

1. The city was beautiful. We spent our vacation there (in that city).
2. That is the restaurant. I will meet you there (at that restaurant).
3. The town is small. I grew up there (in that town).
4. That is the drawer. I keep my jewelry there (in that drawer).

13-8 USING *WHEN* IN ADJECTIVE CLAUSES

				When is used in an adjective clause to modify a noun of time *(year, day, time, century, etc.)*.
	I'll never forget the day. I met you **then (on that day)**.			The use of a preposition in an adjective clause that modifies a noun of time is somewhat different from that in other adjective clauses: a preposition is used preceding **which**, as in (b). Otherwise, the preposition is omitted.
(a)	I'll never forget the day	*when*	*I met you.*	
(b)	I'll never forget the day	*on which*	*I met you.*	
(c)	I'll never forget the day	*that*	*I met you.*	
(d)	I'll never forget the day	Ø	*I met you.*	

☐ **EXERCISE 15. Using WHEN in adjective clauses. (Chart 13-8)**
Directions: Combine the sentences, using the second sentence as an adjective clause.

1. Monday is the day. We will come then (on that day).
2. 7:05 is the time. My plane arrives then (at that time).
3. July is the month. The weather is usually the hottest then (in that month).
4. 1960 is the year. The revolution took place then (in that year).

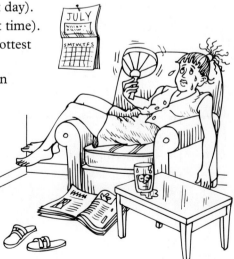

☐ **EXERCISE 16. Using WHERE and WHEN in adjective clauses. (Charts 13-7 and 13-8)**

Directions: Combine the sentences by using either **where** or **when** to introduce an adjective clause.

1. That is the place. The accident occurred there.
   → *That is the place **where** the accident occurred.*

2. There was a time. Movies cost a dime then.
   → *There was a time **when** movies cost a dime.*

3. A cafe is a small restaurant. People can get a light meal there.

4. Every neighborhood in Brussels has small cafes. Customers drink coffee and eat pastries there.

5. There was a time. Dinosaurs dominated the earth then.

6. The house was destroyed in an earthquake ten years ago. I was born and grew up there.

7. Summer is the time of year. The weather is the hottest then.

8. The miser hid his money in a place. It was safe from robbers there.

9. There came a time. The miser had to spend his money then.

10. His new shirt didn't fit, so Dan took it back to the store. He'd bought it there.

☐ **EXERCISE 17. Adjective clauses. (Charts 13-2 → 13-8)**

Directions: Work in pairs, in groups, or as a class. Begin your response to the cue with either "I'll never forget the . . . " or "I'll always remember the . . . ."

Example: trip
Response: I'll never forget the trip . . . *I took to France.*

1. trip
2. experiences
3. day
4. first day
5. time
6. first time
7. person
8. people
9. woman
10. man
11. house
12. story
13. accident
14. wonderful food
15. room
16. friends

□ EXERCISE 18. Activity: adjective clauses. (Charts 13-2 → 13-8)
Directions: Work in groups of four or as a class. Only the leader's book is open.
Leader: Direct the questions to the group as a whole, or sometimes to a particular student.
Speaker A: Answer the questions, inventing your answers if necessary.
Leader: Ask another student to summarize the information in Speaker A's responses in one sentence beginning with "The . . . ."
Speaker B: Begin with "The . . . ." Use an adjective clause.

Example:
LEADER TO GROUP: Who got a letter yesterday?
SPEAKER A: I did.
LEADER TO A: Who was it from?
SPEAKER A: My brother.
LEADER TO B: Can you summarize this information? Begin with "The."
SPEAKER B: The letter (Ali) got yesterday was from his brother.

Change leaders.

1. Who got a letter last week?
   Where was it from?

2. Who is wearing earrings?
   What are they made of?

3. Who lives in an apartment?
   Is it close to school?

4. Pick up something that doesn't belong to you. What is it?
   Whose is it?

Change leaders.

5. Who grew up in a small town?
   In what part of the country is it located?

6. Who has bought something recently?
   What have you bought recently?
   Was it expensive?

7. Hold up a book.
   What is the title?

8. Who went to a bar/restaurant last night?
   Was it crowded?

Change leaders.

9. What did you have for dinner last night?
   Was it good?

10. Who watched a TV program last night?
    What was it about?

11. Who has borrowed something recently?
    What did you borrow?
    Who does it belong to?

12. Who shops for groceries?
    What is the name of the store?

Change leaders.

13. Who eats lunch away from home?
    Where do you usually eat?
    Does it have good food?

14. Who took the bus to class today?
    Was it late or on time?

15. Who read a newspaper today?
    Which newspaper?

16. Point at a person.
    Who are you pointing at?

13-9 USING ADJECTIVE CLAUSES TO MODIFY PRONOUNS

(a) There is **someone** *(whom) I want you to meet.* (b) **Everything** *he said* was pure nonsense. (c) **Anybody** *who wants to come* is welcome.	Adjective clauses can modify indefinite pronouns (e.g., *someone, everybody*). Object pronouns (e.g., *who(m), that, which*) are usually omitted in the adjective clause.
(d) Paula was **the only one** *I knew at the party.* (e) Scholarships are available for **those** *who need financial assistance.*	Adjective clauses can modify **the one(s)** and **those.***
(f) INCORRECT: *I who am a student at this school* come from a country in Asia. (g) It is **I** *who am responsible.* (h) **He** *who laughs last* laughs best.	Adjective clauses are almost never used to modify personal pronouns. Native English speakers would not write the sentence in (f). (g) is possible, but very formal and uncommon. (h) is a well-known saying in which **he** is used as an indefinite pronoun (meaning "anyone," "any person").

*An adjective clause with **which** can also be used to modify the demonstrative pronoun **that**. For example:
   We sometimes fear **that which** *we do not understand.*
   The bread my mother makes is much better than **that which** *you can buy at a store.*

☐ EXERCISE 19. Using adjective clauses to modify pronouns. (Chart 13-9)
   Directions: Complete the sentences with adjective clauses.

1. Ask Jack. He's the only one _____ who knows the answer. _____

2. I have a question. There is something _____

3. He can't trust anyone. There's no one _____

4. I'm powerless to help her. There's nothing _____

5. I know someone _____

6. Susan makes a good first impression. She charms everyone _____

7. What was Mrs. Wood talking about? I didn't understand anything _____

8. I listen to everything _____

9. You can believe him. Everything _____

10. All of the students are seated. The teacher is the only one _____

11. The test we took yesterday was easier than the one _____

12. The courses I'm taking this term are more difficult than the ones _____

13. The concert had already begun. Those _____
    had to wait until intermission to be seated.

14. The class was divided in half. Those _____
    were assigned to Section A. Those _____
    were assigned to Section B.

☐ EXERCISE 20. Review: adjective clauses. (Charts 13-1 → 13-9)
Directions: Create sentences in which you use the given groups of words. Each sentence should contain an adjective clause.

Examples: the people that I
→ One of **the people that I** admire most in the history of the world is Gandhi.
the people with whom we
→ I enjoyed talking to **the people with whom we** had dinner last night.

1. the things I
2. the people who
3. a person who
4. the man to whom I
5. the place I
6. a book that
7. the time my
8. a person whose
9. a woman I
10. employees who
11. the restaurant where
12. someone that I
13. everything you
14. those who
15. the only one who
16. nothing I
17. everyone she
18. the doctor he

13-10 PUNCTUATING ADJECTIVE CLAUSES

General guidelines for the punctuation of adjective clauses:
(1) **DO NOT USE COMMAS IF** the adjective clause is necessary to identify the noun it modifies.*
(2) **USE COMMAS IF** the adjective clause simply gives additional information and is not necessary to identify the noun it modifies.**

(a) **The professor** *who teaches Chemistry 101* is an excellent lecturer. (b) **Professor Wilson,** *who teaches Chemistry 101,* is an excellent lecturer.	In (a): No commas are used. The adjective clause is necessary to identify which professor is meant. In (b): Commas are used. The adjective clause is not necessary to identify Professor Wilson. We already know who he is: he has a name. The adjective clause simply gives additional information.
(c) **Hawaii,** *which consists of eight principal islands,* is a favorite vacation spot. (d) **Mrs. Smith,** *who is a retired teacher,* does volunteer work at the hospital.	Guideline: Use commas, as in (b), (c), and (d), if an adjective clause modifies a proper noun. (A proper noun begins with a capital letter.) Note: A comma reflects a pause in speech.
(e) **The man** $\begin{cases} who(m) \\ that \\ \varnothing \end{cases}$ *I met* teaches chemistry. (f) **Mr. Lee,** *whom I met yesterday,* teaches chemistry.	In (e): If no commas are used, any possible pronoun may be used in the adjective clause. Object pronouns may be omitted. In (f): When commas are necessary, the pronoun *that* may not be used (only **who, whom, which, whose, where,** and **when** may be used), and object pronouns cannot be omitted.
COMPARE THE MEANING (g) We took some children on a picnic. **The children, who wanted to play soccer,** ran to an open field as soon as we arrived at the park. (h) We took some children on a picnic. **The children who wanted to play soccer** ran to an open field as soon as we arrived at the park. The others played a different game.	In (g): The use of commas means that *all* of the children wanted to play soccer and *all* of the children ran to an open field. The adjective clause is used only to give additional information about the children. In (h): The lack of commas means that *only some* of the children wanted to play soccer. The adjective clause is used to identify which children ran to the open field.

*Adjective clauses that do not require commas are called "essential" or "restrictive" or "identifying."

**Adjective clauses that require commas are called "nonessential" or "nonrestrictive" or "nonidentifying."

NOTE: Nonessential adjective clauses are more common in writing than in speaking.

☐ **EXERCISE 21. Punctuating adjective clauses.** (Chart 13-10)

Directions: Add commas where necessary. Change the adjective clause pronoun to ***that*** if possible.

1. Alan and Jackie, who did not come to class yesterday, explained their absence to the teacher. *("Who" cannot be changed to "that.")*

2. The students who did not come to class yesterday explained their absence to the teacher. *(No commas; "who" can be changed to "that.")*

3. Only people who speak Russian should apply for the job.

4. Matthew who speaks Russian applied for the job.

5. The rice which we had for dinner last night was very good.

6. Rice which is grown in many countries is a staple food throughout much of the world.

7. The newspaper article was about a man who died two years ago of a rare tropical disease.

8. Paul O'Grady who died two years ago was a kind and loving man.

9. I have fond memories of my hometown which is situated in a valley.

10. I live in a town which is situated in a valley.

11. The Mississippi River which flows south from Minnesota to the Gulf of Mexico is the major commercial river in the United States.

12. A river which is polluted is not safe for swimming.

13. Mr. Brown whose son won the spelling contest is very proud of his son's achievement. The man whose daughter won the science contest is also very pleased and proud.

14. Goats which were first tamed more than 9,000 years ago in Asia have provided people with milk, meat, and wool since prehistoric times.

15. Mrs. Clark has two goats. She's furious at the goat which got on the wrong side of the fence and is eating her flowers.

☐ EXERCISE 22. Punctuating adjective clauses. (Chart 13-10)
    Directions: Circle the correct explanation (a. or b.) of the meaning of each sentence.

1. The teacher thanked the students, who had given her some flowers.
    a. The flowers were from *only some* of the students.
    (b.) The flowers were from *all* of the students.

2. The teacher thanked the students who had given her some flowers.
    (a.) The flowers were from *only some* of the students.
    b. The flowers were from *all* of the students.

3. There was a terrible flood. The villagers who had received a warning of the impending flood escaped to safety.
    a. *Only some* of the villagers had been warned; only some escaped.
    b. *All* of the villagers had been warned; all escaped.

4. There was a terrible flood. The villagers, who had received a warning of the impending flood, escaped to safety.
    a. *Only some* of the villagers had been warned; only some escaped.
    b. *All* of the villagers had been warned; all escaped.

5. Roberto reached down and picked up the grammar book, which was lying upside down on the floor.
    a. There was *only one* grammar book near Roberto.
    b. There was *more than one* grammar book near Roberto.

6. Roberto reached down and picked up the grammar book which was lying upside down on the floor.
    a. There was *only one* grammar book near Roberto.
    b. There was *more than one* grammar book near Roberto.

Discuss the differences in meaning in the following pairs of sentences.
7. He reached in the basket and threw away the apples that were rotten.
8. He reached in the basket and threw away the apples, which were rotten.

9. The students who had done well on the test were excused from class early.
10. The students, who had done well on the test, were excused from class early.

11. Cindy was delighted when she opened the present, which was from her grandmother.
12. Cindy was delighted when she opened the present that was from her grandmother.

13. The teacher pointed to the maps that were hanging on the rear wall of the classroom.
14. The teacher pointed to the maps, which were hanging on the rear wall of the classroom.

☐ EXERCISE 23. Punctuating adjective clauses. (Chart 13-10)
    Directions: Add commas where necessary.

1. We enjoyed the city where we spent our vacation.

2. We enjoyed Mexico City where we spent our vacation.

3. An elephant which is the earth's largest land mammal has few natural enemies other than human beings.

4. One of the elephants which we saw at the zoo had only one tusk.

5. At the botanical gardens, you can see a Venus's-flytrap which is an insectivorous plant.

6. In Venezuela, there are plants that eat insects with their roots.

7. One of the most useful materials in the world is glass which is made chiefly from sand, soda, and lime.

8. Glaciers which are masses of ice that flow slowly over land form in the cold polar regions and in high mountains.

9. A rebel is a person who resists or fights against authority.

10. Petroleum which some people refer to as black gold is one of the most valuable resources in the world today.

11. You don't need to take heavy clothes when you go to Bangkok which has one of the highest average temperatures of any city in the world.

12. A political party is an organized group of people who control or seek to control a government.

13. Child labor was a social problem in late eighteenth-century England where employment in factories became virtual slavery for children.

14. We had to use a telephone, so we went to the nearest house. The woman who answered our knock listened cautiously to our request.

15. According to a newspaper article which I read, the police arrested the man who had robbed the First National Bank. The man who was wearing a plaid shirt and blue jeans was caught shortly after he had left the bank.

16. I watched a scientist conduct an experiment on bees. The research scientist who was well protected before she stepped into the special chamber holding the bees was not stung. A person who was unprotected by the special clothing could have gotten 300 to 400 bee stings within a minute.

13-11 USING EXPRESSIONS OF QUANTITY IN ADJECTIVE CLAUSES

In my class there are 20 students. *Most of **them*** are from the Far East. (a) In my class there are 20 students, *most of **whom*** are from Asia.	An adjective clause may contain an expression of quantity with ***of****: some of, many of, most of, none of, two of, half of, both of, neither of, each of, all of, several of, a few of, little of, a number of*, etc.
He gave several reasons. *Only a few of **them*** were valid. (b) He gave several reasons, *only a few of **which*** were valid.	The expression of quantity precedes the pronoun. Only ***whom***, ***which***, and ***whose*** are used in this pattern.
The teachers discussed Jim. *One of **his** problems* was poor study habits. (c) The teachers discussed Jim, *one of **whose** problems* was poor study habits.	Adjective clauses that begin with an expression of quantity are more common in writing than speaking. Commas are used.

☐ **EXERCISE 24. Using expressions of quantity in adjective clauses. (Chart 13-11)**
Directions: Combine the two sentences. Use the second sentence as an adjective clause.

1. The city has sixteen schools. Two of them are junior colleges.

   → *The city has sixteen schools, two of which are junior colleges.*

2. Last night the orchestra played three symphonies. One of them was Beethoven's Seventh.
3. I tried on six pairs of shoes. I liked none of them.
4. The village has around 200 people. The majority of them are farmers.
5. That company currently has five employees. All of them are computer experts.
6. After the riot, over one hundred people were taken to the hospital. Many of them had been innocent bystanders.

☐ **EXERCISE 25. Using expressions of quantity in adjective clauses. (Chart 13-11)**
Directions: Complete the sentences.

1. Al introduced me to his roommates, both of ___whom are from California.___

2. The Paulsons own four automobiles, one of _____

3. I have three brothers, all of _____

4. I am taking four courses, one of _____

5. I have two roommates, neither of _____

6. This semester I had to buy fifteen books, most of _____

7. The company hired ten new employees, some of _____

8. In my apartment building, there are twenty apartments, several of _____

   _____

13-12 USING NOUN + *OF WHICH*

We have an antique table. *The top of it* has jade inlay. (a) We have an antique table, *the top of which* has jade inlay.	An adjective clause may include *a noun + of which* (e.g., *the top of which*). This pattern carries the meaning of *whose* (e.g., *We have an antique table whose top has jade inlay.*). This pattern is used in an adjective clause that modifies a thing and occurs primarily in formal written English. A comma is used.

☐ EXERCISE 26. Using noun + OF WHICH. (Chart 13-12)

Directions: Combine the two sentences. Use the second sentence as an adjective clause.

1. We toured a 300-year-old house. The exterior of the house consisted of logs cemented with clay.

    → *We toured a 300-year-old house, the exterior of which consisted of logs cemented with clay.*

2. They own an original Picasso painting. The value of the painting is more than a million dollars.
3. I bought a magazine. The title of the magazine is *Contemporary Architectural Styles.*
4. My country is dependent upon its income from coffee. The price of coffee varies according to fluctuations in the world market.
5. The genetic engineers are engaged in significant experiments. The results of the experiments will be published in the *Journal of Science.*
6. The professor has assigned the students a research paper. The purpose of the research paper is to acquaint them with methods of scholarly inquiry.

13-13 USING *WHICH* TO MODIFY A WHOLE SENTENCE

(a) Tom was late. (b) *That* surprised me. (c) Tom was late, *which surprised me.*	The pronouns *that* and *this* can refer to the idea of a whole sentence which comes before. In (b): The word *that* refers to the whole sentence "Tom was late."
(d) The elevator is out of order. (e) *This* is too bad. (f) The elevator is out of order, *which is too bad.*	Similarly, an adjective clause with *which* may modify the idea of a whole sentence. In (c): The word *which* refers to the whole sentence "Tom was late." Using *which* to modify a whole sentence is informal and occurs most frequently in spoken English. This structure is generally not appropriate in formal writing. Whenever it is written, however, it is preceded by a comma to reflect a pause in speech.

☐ EXERCISE 27. Using WHICH to modify a whole sentence. (Chart 13-13)

Directions: Use the second sentence as an adjective clause.

1. Max isn't home yet. That worries me.

    → *Max isn't home yet, which worries me.*

2. My roommate never picks up after herself. This irritates me.
3. Mrs. Anderson responded to my letter right away. I appreciated that very much.

4. There's been an accident on Highway 5. That means I'll be late to work this morning.
5. I shut the door on my necktie. That was really stupid of me.

6. Sally lost her job. That wasn't surprising.
7. She usually came to work late. That upset her boss.
8. So her boss fired her. That made her angry.
9. She hadn't saved any money. That was unfortunate.
10. So she had to borrow some money from me. I didn't like that.
11. She has found a new job. That is lucky.
12. So she has repaid the money she borrowed from me. I appreciate that.
13. She has promised herself to be on time to work every day. That is a good idea.

☐ EXERCISE 28. Using WHICH to modify a whole sentence. (Chart 13-13)
Directions: Make up a sentence to precede the given sentence. Then combine the two sentences, using the second sentence as an adjective clause.

1. _The student next to me kept cracking his knuckles._ That bothered

me a lot. → *The student next to me kept cracking his knuckles, which bothered me a lot.*

2. _____ That disappointed me.

3. _____ That made me nervous.

4. _____ That shocked all of us.

5. _____ That means he's probably in
trouble.

6. _____ That was a pleasant surprise.

7. _____ That made her very unhappy.

8. _____ I appreciated that very much.

9. _____ That made it difficult for me
to concentrate.

10. _____ That bothered me so much
that I couldn't get to sleep.

☐ EXERCISE 29. Special adjective clauses. (Charts 13-11 → 13-13)
Directions: Create sentences that contain the following groups of words. Do not change the order of the words as they are given. Add words only before and after the group of words. Add punctuation as necessary.

Examples: . . . yesterday which surprised . . . .
→ Tom didn't come to class **yesterday, which surprised** me.

. . . people to my party some of whom . . . .
→ I invited ten **people to my party, some of whom** are my classmates.

1. . . . brothers all of whom . . . .
2. . . . early which was fortunate . . . .
3. . . . students three of whom . . . .
4. . . . ideas none of which . . . .
5. . . . jewelry the value of which . . . .
6. . . . teachers some of whom . . . .
7. . . . mother which made me . . . .
8. . . . a little money all of which . . . .
9. . . . sisters each of whom . . . .
10. . . . new car the inside of which . . . .
11. . . . clothes some of which . . . .
12. . . . two days ago which surprised . . . .

☐ EXERCISE 30. Adjective clauses. (Charts 13-1 → 13-13)
Directions: Combine the sentences. Use formal written English. Use (b) as an adjective clause. Punctuate carefully.

1. (a) An antecedent is a word.
   (b) A pronoun refers to this word.
   → *An antecedent is a word to which a pronoun refers.*

2. (a) The blue whale is considered the largest animal that has ever lived.
   (b) It can grow to 100 feet and 150 tons.

3. (a) The plane was met by a crowd of three hundred people.
   (b) Some of them had been waiting for more than four hours.

4. (a) In this paper, I will describe the basic process.
   (b) Raw cotton becomes cotton thread by this process.

5. (a) The researchers are doing case studies of people to determine the importance of heredity in health and longevity.
   (b) These people's families have a history of high blood pressure and heart disease.

6. (a) At the end of this month, scientists at the institute will conclude their AIDS research.
   (b) The results of this research will be published within six months.

7. (a) According to many education officials, "math phobia" (that is, a fear of mathematics) is a widespread problem.
   (b) A solution to this problem must and can be found.

8. (a) The art museum hopes to hire a new administrator.
   (b) Under this person's direction it will be able to purchase significant pieces of art.

9. (a) The giant anteater licks up ants for its dinner.
   (b) Its tongue is longer than 30 centimeters (12 inches).

10. (a) The anteater's tongue is sticky.
    (b) It can go in and out of its mouth 160 times a minute.

□ EXERCISE 31. Activity: adjective clauses. (Charts 13-1 → 13-13)
     Directions: Discuss and/or write definitions for one or more of these people. Include an adjective clause in your definition. Include several qualities of each person. If you are writing, expand your definition to a whole paragraph.

     1. the ideal friend
     2. the ideal mother
     3. the ideal father
     4. the ideal wife
     5. the ideal husband

     6. the ideal teacher
     7. the ideal student
     8. the ideal political leader
     9. the ideal doctor
     10. the ideal *(use your own words)*

□ EXERCISE 32. Activity: adjective clauses. (Charts 13-1 → 13-13)
     Directions: Discuss and/or write about one or more of these topics.

     1. the ideal vacation
     2. the ideal job
     3. the ideal school
     4. the ideal system of government

13-14 REDUCING ADJECTIVE CLAUSES TO ADJECTIVE PHRASES: INTRODUCTION

CLAUSE: *A clause* is a group of related words that contains a subject and a verb.
PHRASE: *A phrase* is a group of related words that does not contain a subject and a verb.

(a) ADJECTIVE CLAUSE: The girl *who is sitting next to me* is Maria. (b) ADJECTIVE PHRASE: The girl *sitting next to me* is Maria.	An adjective phrase is a reduction of an adjective clause. It modifies a noun. It does not contain a subject and verb. The adjective clause in (a) can be reduced to the adjective phrase in (b). (a) and (b) have the same meaning.
(c) CLAUSE: The boy *who is playing the piano* is Ben. (d) PHRASE: The boy *playing the piano* is Ben.	Only adjective clauses that have a subject pronoun—*who*, *which*, or *that*—are reduced to modifying adjective phrases.
(e) CLAUSE: The boy *(whom) I saw* was Tom. (f) PHRASE: *(none)*	The adjective clause in (e) cannot be reduced to an adjective phrase.

13-15 CHANGING AN ADJECTIVE CLAUSE TO AN ADJECTIVE PHRASE

(a) CLAUSE: The man *who is talking* to John is from Korea. PHRASE: The man Ø Ø *talking* to John is from Korea.	There are two ways in which an adjective clause is changed to an adjective phrase.
(b) CLAUSE: The ideas *which are presented* in that book are good. PHRASE: The ideas Ø Ø *presented* in that book are good. (c) CLAUSE: Ann is the woman *who is responsible* for the error. PHRASE: Ann is the woman Ø Ø *responsible* for the error. (d) CLAUSE: The books *that are on that shelf* are mine. PHRASE: The books Ø Ø *on that shelf* are mine.	1. If the adjective clause contains the *be* form of a verb, omit the pronoun and the *be* form, as in examples (a), (b), (c), and (d).
(e) CLAUSE: English has an alphabet *that consists* *of 26 letters.* PHRASE: English has an alphabet Ø *consisting* *of 26 letters.* (f) CLAUSE: Anyone *who wants* *to come with us* is welcome. PHRASE: Anyone Ø *wanting* *to come with us* is welcome.	2. If there is no *be* form of a verb in the adjective clause, it is sometimes possible to omit the subject pronoun and change the verb to its *-ing* form, as in (e) and (f).
(g) George Washington, *who was the first president of the United States,* was a wealthy colonist and a general in the army. (h) George Washington, *the first president of the United States,* was a wealthy colonist and a general in the army.	If the adjective clause requires commas, as in (g), the adjective phrase also requires commas, as in (h).
(i) *Paris, the capital of France,* is an exciting city. (j) I read a book by *Mark Twain, a famous American author.*	Adjective phrases in which a noun follows another noun, as in (h), (i), and (j), are called "appositives."

*If an adjective clause that contains *be* + *a single adjective* is changed, the adjective is moved to its normal position in front of the noun it modifies.

    CLAUSE: **Fruit that is fresh** *tastes better than old, soft, mushy fruit.*
    CORRECT PHRASE: **Fresh fruit** *tastes better than old, soft, mushy fruit.*
    INCORRECT PHRASE: *Fruit fresh tastes better than old, soft, mushy fruit.*

□ EXERCISE 33. Adjective phrases. (Charts 13-14 and 13-15)
Directions: Change the adjective clauses to adjective phrases.

1. Do you know the woman who is coming toward us?
   → *Do you know the woman coming toward us?*
2. The people who are waiting for the bus in the rain are getting wet.
3. I come from a city that is located in the southern part of the country.
4. The children who attend that school receive a good education.
5. The scientists who are researching the causes of cancer are making progress.
6. The fence which surrounds our house is made of wood.
7. They live in a house that was built in 1890.
8. We have an apartment which overlooks the park.

□ EXERCISE 34. Adjective phrases. (Charts 13-14 and 13-15)
Directions: Change the adjective clauses to adjective phrases.

1. Dr. Stanton, ~~who is~~ the president of the university, will give a speech at the commencement ceremonies.
2. Be sure to follow the instructions that are given at the top of the page.
3. The rules that allow public access to wilderness areas need to be reconsidered.
4. The photographs which were published in the newspaper were extraordinary.
5. There is almost no end to the problems that face a head of state.
6. The psychologists who study the nature of sleep have made important discoveries.
7. The experiment which was conducted at the University of Chicago was successful.
8. Kuala Lumpur, which is the capital city of Malaysia, is a major trade center in Southeast Asia.
9. Antarctica is covered by a huge ice cap that contains 70 percent of the earth's fresh water.
10. When I went to Alex's house to drop off some paperwork, I met Jerry, who is his longtime partner.
11. Our solar system is in a galaxy that is called the Milky Way.
12. Two out of three people who are struck by lightning survive.
13. Simon Bolivar, who was a great South American general, led the fight for independence early in the 19th century.
14. Many of the students who hope to enter the university will be disappointed because only one-tenth of those who apply for admission will be accepted.
15. There must exist in a modern community a sufficient number of persons who possess the technical skill that is required to maintain the numerous devices upon which our physical comforts depend.
16. Many famous people did not enjoy immediate success in their early lives. Abraham Lincoln, who was one of the truly great presidents of the United States, ran for public office 26 times and lost 23 of the elections. Walt Disney, who was the creator of Mickey Mouse and the founder of his own movie production company, once was fired by a newspaper editor because he had no good ideas. Thomas Edison, who was the inventor of the light bulb and the phonograph, was believed by his teachers to be too stupid to learn. Albert Einstein, who was one of the greatest scientists of all time, performed badly in almost all of his high school courses and failed his first college entrance exam.

☐ EXERCISE 35. Adjective phrases. (Charts 13-14 and 13-15)
Directions: Change the adjective phrases to adjective clauses.

1. We visited Barcelona, a city in northern Spain.
   → *We visited Barcelona, which is a city in northern Spain.*
2. Corn was one of the agricultural products introduced to the European settlers by the Indians. Some of the other products introduced by the Indians were potatoes, peanuts, and tobacco.
3. He read *The Old Man and the Sea*, a novel written by Ernest Hemingway.
4. Mercury, the nearest planet to the sun, is also the smallest of the nine planets orbiting the sun.
5. The pyramids, the monumental tombs of ancient Egyptian pharaohs, were constructed more than 4,000 years ago.
6. The sloth, a slow-moving animal found in the tropical forests of Central and South America, feeds entirely on leaves and fruit.
7. Two-thirds of those arrested for car theft are under twenty years of age.
8. St. Louis, Missouri, known as "The Gateway to the West," traces its history to 1763, when Pierre Laclède, a French fur trader, selected this site on the Mississippi River as a fur-trading post.
9. Any student not wanting to go on the trip should inform the office.
10. I just purchased a volume of poems written by David Keller, a contemporary poet known for his sensitive interpretations of human relationships.

☐ EXERCISE 36. Adjective phrases. (Charts 13-14 and 13-15)
Directions: Complete the sentences in *PART II* with adjective phrases by using the information in *PART I*. Use commas as necessary.

PART I.

A. It is the lowest place on the earth's surface.
✔B. It is the highest mountain in the world.
C. It is the capital of Iraq.
D. It is the capital of Argentina.
E. It is the largest city in the Western Hemisphere.
F. It is the largest city in the United States.
G. It is the most populous country in Africa.
H. It is the northernmost country in Latin America.
I. It is an African animal that eats ants and termites.
J. It is a small animal that spends its entire life underground.
K. They are sensitive instruments that measure the shaking of the ground.
L. They are devices that produce a powerful beam of light.

PART II.

1. Mt. Everest __, the highest mountain in the world,__ is in the Himalayas.

2. One of the largest cities in the Middle East is Baghdad _____

3. Earthquakes are recorded on seismographs _____

4. The Dead Sea _____

   is located in the Middle East between Jordan and Israel.

5. The newspaper reported an earthquake in Buenos Aires _____

6. Industry and medicine are continually finding new uses for lasers _____

   _____

7. Mexico _____

   lies just south of the United States.

8. The nation Nigeria _____ consists

   of over 250 different cultural groups even though English is the official language.

9. Both Mexico City _____ and New York

   City _____ face challenging futures.

10. The mole _____ is almost blind. The

    aardvark _____ also lives

    underground but hunts for its food above ground.

☐ **EXERCISE 37. Review: adjective clauses and phrases. (Chapter 13)**
   Directions: Combine each group of short, choppy sentences into one sentence. Use the
   underlined sentence as the independent clause; build your sentence around the
   independent clause. Use adjective clauses and adjective phrases wherever possible.

   1. Chihuahua is divided into two regions. It is the largest Mexican state. One region is a
      mountainous area in the west. The other region is a desert basin in the north and east.
      → ***Chihuahua,*** *the largest Mexican state,* ***is divided into two regions,*** *a mountainous*
      area in the west and a desert basin in the north and east.

   2. Disney World covers a large area of land. It is an amusement park. It is located in
      Orlando, Florida. The land includes lakes, golf courses, campsites, hotels, and a
      wildlife preserve.

   3. Jamaica is one of the world's leading producers of bauxite. It is the third largest island
      in the Caribbean Sea. Bauxite is an ore. Aluminum is made from this ore.

   4. Robert Ballard made headlines in 1985. He is an oceanographer. In 1985 he discovered
      the remains of the *Titanic*. The *Titanic* was the "unsinkable" passenger ship. It has
      rested on the floor of the Atlantic Ocean since 1912. It struck an iceberg in 1912.

   5. William Shakespeare's father was a glove maker and a town official. William Shakespeare's
      father was John Shakespeare. He owned a shop in Stratford-upon-Avon. Stratford-upon-
      Avon is a town. It is about 75 miles (120 kilometers) northwest of London.

   6. The Republic of Yemen is an ancient land. It is located at the southwestern tip of the
      Arabian Peninsula. This land has been host to many prosperous civilizations. These
      civilizations include the Kingdom of Sheba and various Islamic empires.

☐ EXERCISE 38. Error analysis: adjective clauses and phrases. (Chapter 13)

Directions: Correct the errors.

1. One of the people which I admire most is my uncle.

2. Baseball is the only sport in which I am interested in it.

3. My favorite teacher, Mr. Chu, he was always willing to help me after class.

4. It is important to be polite to people who lives in the same building.

5. She lives in a hotel is restricted to senior citizens.

6. My sister has two childrens, who their names are Ali and Talal.

7. He comes from Venezuela that is a Spanish-speaking country.

8. There are some people in the government who is trying to improve the lives of poor people.

9. I have some good advice for anyone who he wants to learn a second language.

10. My classroom is located on the second floor of Carver Hall that is a large brick building in the center of the campus.

11. A myth is a story expresses traditional beliefs.

12. There is an old legend telling among people in my country about a man lived in the seventeenth century saved a village from destruction.

13. An old man was fishing next to me on the pier was muttering to himself.

14. When I was a child, I was always afraid of the beggars whom they went from house to house in my neighborhood.

15. At the national park, there is a path leads to a spectacular waterfall.

16. The road that we took it through the forest it was narrow and steep.

17. There are ten universities in Thailand, seven of them locate in Bangkok is the capital city.

18. I would like to write about several problem which I have faced them since I come to United State.

19. There is a small wooden screen separates the bed from the rest of the room.

20. At the airport, I was waiting for some relatives which I had never met them before.

21. It is almost impossible to find two persons who their opinions are the same.

22. On the wall, there is a colorful poster which it consists of a group of young people who dancing.

23. The sixth member of our household is Alex that is my sister's son.

24. Before I came here, I didn't have the opportunity to speak with people who English is their native tongue.

☐ EXERCISE 39. Activity: adjective clauses. (Chapter 13)

Directions: A discovery and an invention are different, but they are related. A discovery occurs when something that exists in nature is recognized for the first time. Fire is an example of a discovery. An invention is something that is made for the first time by a creator. An invention never existed before the act of creation. The telephone and the automobile are two examples of important 20th-century inventions.

Either in a group or by yourself, draw up a list of inventions made in the 20th century. After your list is finished, discuss the inventions you have named, using the following questions as guidelines:

1. What are the three most important 20th-century inventions that you have listed? Why? In other words, why do you rate these as the most influential/important inventions?
2. What were some important inventions prior to the 20th century? Why?
3. Which invention has brought the most happiness to people? Which has caused the most unhappiness?
4. Are any of the inventions you have listed luxury items? Which of the inventions you have listed have become accepted as necessities?
5. What would your world be like without a certain invention? How has your life been influenced by these inventions? Would you like to go back to 1900 when none of these things existed? Can you visualize life as it was then?
6. What would you like to see invented now? What do you think will be one of the most important inventions that will be made in the future? What are you going to invent?

☐ EXERCISE 40. Activity: adjective clauses. (Chapter 13)

Directions: Form a group of three people. Together, make up one sentence with as many adjective clauses as possible. In other words, make the most awkward sentence you can while still using grammatically correct sentence structure. Count the number of adjective clauses you use. See which group can make the worst sentence by using the largest number of adjective clauses.

Example of a stylistically terrible, but grammatically correct, sentence:

The man who was sitting at a table which was at the restaurant where I usually eat dinner, which is something I do every evening, was talking to a woman who was wearing a dress which was blue, which is my favorite color.

☐ EXERCISE 41. Writing: adjective clauses and phrases. (Chapter 13)

Directions: Write on one or more of these topics. Try to use adjective clauses and phrases.

1. Write about three historical figures from your country. Give your reader information about their lives and accomplishments.
2. Write about your favorite TV shows. What are they? What are they about? Why do you enjoy them?
3. Who are some people in your country who are popular with young people (e.g., singers, movie stars, political figures, etc.)? Tell your readers about these people. Assume your readers are completely unfamiliar with them.
4. You are a tourist agent for your hometown/country. Write a descriptive brochure that would make your readers want to visit your hometown/country.
5. What kind of people do you like? What kind of people do you avoid?
6. What kind of person do you want to marry? What kind of person do you not want to marry? If you are already married: What kind of person did you marry?

☐ EXERCISE 42. Activity: speaking and writing.

Directions: Form a group of volunteers who are interested in performing a short play. Work together outside of class to prepare a performance for the rest of the class. Choose a scene from a published play, or write your own.

If you write your own, choose a situation in which there is some kind of conflict, for example, people who are facing a problem. Perhaps the characters or situations can be based on current movies or TV programs, or possibly on historical events. Write down the dialogue so that each member of the group has the exact same script.

Then present your play to the rest of the class.

Possible follow-up activities:

1. Write a synopsis of the play your classmates presented.
2. Write a letter to a character in one of the plays, giving advice on how to handle the conflict in the play.
3. With a group, discuss the relationships and the conflict in the play.
4. With others, re-enact the play you saw, without looking at a script.

CONTENTS

14-1 GERUNDS: INTRODUCTION

(a) *Playing* tennis is fun.
     S   V

(b) We enjoy *playing* tennis.
     S   V   O

(c) He's excited about *playing* tennis.
           PREP   O

A *gerund* is the *-ing* form of a verb used as a noun.★ A gerund is used in the same ways as a noun, i.e., as a subject or as an object.

In (a): *playing* is a gerund. It is used as the subject of the sentence. *Playing tennis* is a *gerund phrase*.

In (b): *playing* is a gerund used as the object of the verb *enjoy*.

In (c): *playing* is a gerund used as the object of the preposition *about*.

★COMPARE the uses of the *-ing* form of verbs:
(1) *Walking* is good exercise.
    → *walking* = a gerund used as the subject of the sentence.
(2) *Bob and Ann are* **playing** *tennis.*
    → *playing* = a present participle used as part of the present progressive tense.
(3) *I heard some* **surprising** *news.*
    → *surprising* = a present participle used as an adjective.

14-2 USING GERUNDS AS THE OBJECTS OF PREPOSITIONS

(a) We talked *about going* to Canada for our vacation. (b) Sue is in charge *of organizing* the meeting. (c) I'm interested *in learning* more about your work.	A gerund is frequently used as the object of a preposition.
(d) I*'m used to sleeping* with the window open. (e) I*'m accustomed to sleeping** with the window open. (f) I *look forward to going* home next month. (g) They *object to changing* their plans at this late date.	In (d) through (g): *to* is a preposition, not part of an infinitive form, so a gerund follows.
(h) We *talked about not going* to the meeting, but finally decided we should go.	Negative form: *not* precedes a gerund.

*Possible in British English: *I'm accustomed to sleep* with the window open.

☐ EXERCISE 1. Preview. (Chart 14-3)

Directions: Without referring to Chart 14-3, see how many of the preposition combinations you already know by completing these sentences with an appropriate preposition and verb form.

1. Alice isn't interested ___in___ *(look)* ___looking___ for a new job.

2. Henry is excited _____ *(leave)* _____ for India.

3. You are capable _____ *(do)* _____ better work.

4. I have no excuse _____ *(be)* _____ late.

5. I'm accustomed _____ *(have)* _____ a big breakfast.

6. The rain prevented us _____ *(complete)* _____ the work.

7. Fred is always complaining _____ *(have)* _____ a headache.

8. Instead _____ *(study)* _____, Margaret went to a ballgame with some of her friends.

9. Thank you _____ *(help)* _____ me carry my suitcases.

10. Mrs. Grant insisted _____ *(know)* _____ the whole truth.

11. I believe _____ *(be)* _____ honest at all times.

12. You should take advantage _____ *(live)* _____ here.

13. Fatima had a good reason _____ *(go, not)* _____ to class yesterday.

14. Everyone in the neighborhood participated _____ *(search)* _____ for the lost child.

15. I apologized to Yoko _____ *(make)* _____ her wait for me.

16. The weather is terrible tonight. I don't blame you _____ *(want, not)* _____ _____ to go to the meeting.

17. Who is responsible _____ *(wash)* _____ and *(dry)* _____ the dishes after dinner?

18. In addition _____ *(go)* _____ to school full time, Spiro has a part-time job.

19. I stopped the child _____ *(run)* _____ into the street.

20. Where should we go for dinner tonight? Would you object _____ *(go)* _____ to an Italian restaurant?

21. The mayor made another public statement for the purpose _____ *(clarify)* _____ the new tax proposal.

22. The thief was accused _____ *(steal)* _____ a woman's purse.

23. The jury found Mr. Adams guilty _____ *(take)* _____ money from the company he worked for and *(keep)* _____ it for himself.

24. Larry isn't used _____ *(wear)* _____ a suit and tie every day.

25. I'm going to visit my family during the school vacation. I'm looking forward _____ *(eat)* _____ my mother's cooking and *(sleep)* _____ in my own bed.

14-3 COMMON PREPOSITION COMBINATIONS FOLLOWED BY GERUNDS

be excited *be* worried } ***about*** *doing* it	keep (someone) prevent (someone) prohibit (someone) stop (someone) } ***from*** *doing* it	insist ***on*** *doing* it
complain dream talk think } ***about/of*** *doing* it	believe *be* interested participate succeed } ***in*** *doing* it	*be* accustomed in addition *be* committed *be* devoted look forward object *be* opposed *be* used } ***to*** *doing* it
apologize blame (someone) forgive (someone) have an excuse have a reason *be* responsible thank (someone) } ***for*** *doing* it	*be* accused *be* capable for the purpose *be* guilty instead take advantage take care *be* tired } ***of*** *doing* it	

☐ EXERCISE 2. Using gerunds as the objects of prepositions. (Charts 14-2 and 14-3)
Directions: Using the words in parentheses, complete the sentences.

1. Kostas went to bed instead ___*of finishing his work.*___ *(finish)*

2. I thanked my friend _____ *(lend)*

3. I'm excited _____ *(go)*

4. I'm not accustomed _____ *(live)*

5. Omar didn't feel good. He complained _____ *(have)*

6. I don't blame you _____ *(want, not)*

7. I have a good reason _____ *(be)*

8. It's getting late. I'm worried _____ *(miss)*

9. I'm interested _____ *(find out about)*

10. I'm thinking _____ *(go)*

11. I apologized to my friend _____ *(be)*

12. I am/am not used _____ *(drive)*

13. Nothing can stop me _____ *(go)*

14. In that office, who is responsible _____ *(take care of)*

15. I look forward _____ *(go)*

16. The thief was guilty _____ *(steal)*

17. Sonya has two jobs. In addition _____ *(work)*

18. Please forgive me _____ *(write, not)*

19. Sarah is an honest person. She's not capable _____ *(tell)*

20. Ill health keeps my grandfather _____ *(travel)*

☐ EXERCISE 3. Using gerunds as the objects of prepositions. (Charts 14-2 and 14-3)
Directions: To practice using gerunds following prepositions, answer the questions in complete sentences. If working in pairs, switch roles after Item 7.

Example:
SPEAKER A *(book open):* Your friend was late. Did she apologize?
SPEAKER B *(book closed):* Yes, she apologized OR No, she didn't apologize *for being* late.

1. You were late for class yesterday. Did you have a good excuse?

2. You are going to *(a city)* to visit your friends this weekend. Are you looking forward to that?

3. (. . .) picked up your pen when you dropped it. Did you thank him/her?

4. You're living in a cold/warm climate. Are you accustomed to that?

5. You're going to *(a place)* for a vacation. Are you excited?

6. You interrupted (. . .) while s/he was speaking. Did you apologize?

7. The students in the class did pantomimes. Did all of them participate?

8. Someone broke the window. Do you know who is responsible?

9. Americans usually have their biggest meal in the evening. Are you used to doing that?

10. The weather is hot/cold. What does that prevent you from doing?

11. (. . .) has to do a lot of homework. Does s/he complain?

12. (. . .) was sick last week, so s/he stayed home in bed. Do you blame her/him?

13. (. . .) didn't study grammar last night. What did s/he do instead?

14. You studied last night. What did you do in addition?

☐ EXERCISE 4. Using gerunds as the objects of prepositions. (Chart 14-2)
Directions: Complete the following using **by** + *a gerund or gerund phrase* to express how something is done.

1. Pat turned off the tape recorder ____by pushing the stop button.____

2. We show people we are happy ____by smiling.____

3. We decided who should get the last piece of pie ____by flipping a coin.____

4. We satisfy our hunger _____

5. We quench our thirst _____

6. I found out what "quench" means _____

7. Tony improved his listening comprehension _____

8. Alex caught my attention _____

9. They got rid of the rats in the building _____

10. My dog shows me she is happy _____

11. He accidentally electrocuted himself _____

12. Sometimes teenagers get into trouble with their parents _____

_____

14-4 COMMON VERBS FOLLOWED BY GERUNDS

(a) I <u>enjoy</u> <u>playing</u> tennis. 　　verb　+　gerund	Gerunds are used as the objects of certain verbs. In (a), **enjoy** is followed by a gerund (**playing**). **Enjoy** is not followed by an infinitive. INCORRECT: I enjoy to play tennis. Common verbs that are followed by gerunds are given in the list below.
(b) Joe **quit smoking**. (c) Joe **gave up smoking**.	(b) and (c) have the same meaning. Some phrasal verbs,* e.g., **give up**, are followed by gerunds. These phrasal verbs are given in parentheses in the list below.

VERB + GERUND

enjoy	quit (give up)	avoid	consider
appreciate	finish (get through)	postpone (put off)	discuss
mind	stop**	delay	mention
		keep (keep on)	suggest

*A *phrasal verb* consists of a verb and a particle (a small word such as a preposition) that together have a special meaning. For example, *put off* means "postpone."

Stop can also be followed immediately by an infinitive of purpose (**in order to**). See Chart 15-1, p. 326.
COMPARE the following:
(1) **stop** + *gerund:* When the professor entered the room, the students **stopped talking**. The room became quiet.
(2) **stop** + *infinitive of purpose:* While I was walking down the street, I ran into an old friend. I **stopped to talk** to him.
　　(I stopped walking *in order to talk* to him.)

☐ **EXERCISE 5. Verbs followed by gerunds. (Chart 14-4)**
　　Directions: Create sentences from the given words, using any tense and subject. Work in pairs, in groups, or as a class. The cuer's book is open. The responder's book is closed.

　　Example: enjoy + read the newspaper
　　SPEAKER A *(book open):*　"enjoy" (pause) "read the newspaper"
　　SPEAKER B *(book closed):*　I enjoy reading the newspaper every morning while I'm having my first cup of coffee.

1. enjoy + watch TV
2. mind + open the window
3. quit + eat desserts
4. give up + eat desserts
5. finish + eat dinner
6. get through + eat dinner
7. stop + rain
8. avoid + answer my question
9. postpone + do my work
10. put off + do my work
11. delay + leave on vacation
12. keep + work
13. keep on + work
14. consider + get a job
15. think about + get a job
16. discuss + go to a movie
17. talk about + go to a movie
18. mention + go to a concert
19. suggest + go on a picnic*
20. enjoy + listen to music

---

*For other ways of expressing ideas with *suggest*, see Chart 12-8, p. 263.

☐ **EXERCISE 6. Verbs followed by gerunds. (Chart 14-4)**

Directions: Complete each sentence with any appropriate gerund.

1. When Beth got tired, she stopped ___working/studying___.

2. Would you mind _____ the door? Thanks.

3. The weather will get better soon. We can leave as soon as it quits _____.

4. The police officer told him to stop, but the thief kept _____.

5. I enjoy _____ a long walk every morning.

6. I have a lot of homework tonight, but I'd still like to go with you later on. I'll call you when I get through _____.

7. I would like to have some friends over. I'm thinking about _____ a dinner party.

8. He told a really funny joke. We couldn't stop _____!

9. Jack almost had an automobile accident. He barely avoided _____ another car at the intersection of 4th and Elm.

10. Where are you considering _____ for vacation?

11. Sometimes I put off _____ my homework.

12. You have to decide where you want to go to school next year. You can't postpone _____ that decision much longer.

13. I wanted to go to Mexico. Sally suggested _____ to Hawaii.

14. Tony mentioned _____ the bus to school instead of walking.

15. I appreciate _____ able to study in peace and quiet.

14-5 *GO* + GERUND

(a) Did you *go shopping?* (b) We *went fishing* yesterday.	*Go* is followed by a gerund in certain idiomatic expressions to express, for the most part, recreational activities.

GO + GERUND

go birdwatching	go fishing*	go sailing	go skinnydipping
go boating	go hiking	go shopping	go sledding
go bowling	go hunting	go sightseeing	go snorkeling
go camping	go jogging	go skating	go swimming
go canoeing/kayaking	go mountain climbing	go skateboarding	go tobogganing
go dancing	go running	go skiing	go window shopping

*Also, in British English: *go angling*

□ EXERCISE 7. GO + gerund. (Chart 14-5)
Directions: Discuss the activities listed in Chart 14-5.

1. Which ones have you done? When? Briefly describe your experiences.
2. Which ones do you like to do?
3. Which ones do you never want to do?
4. Which ones have you not done but would like to do?

□ EXERCISE 8. GO + gerund. (Chart 14-5)
Directions: Create sentences from the given words, using any tense and subject. Work in pairs, in groups, or as a class. The cuer's book is open. The responder's book is closed.

Example: enjoy + go
SPEAKER A *(book open):* "enjoy" (pause) "go"
SPEAKER B *(book closed):* I enjoy going to the zoo. / My friend and I enjoyed going to a rock concert last weekend. / Where do you enjoy going in *(this city)* when you have some free time?

1. finish + study	7. go + fish	13. give up + ask
2. go + dance	8. talk about + go + swim	14. discuss + go + birdwatch
3. keep + work	9. stop + fight	15. appreciate + hear
4. go + bowl	10. postpone + go + camp	16. mind + wait
5. think about + wear	11. quit + rain	17. think about + not go
6. enjoy + play	12. avoid + go + shop	18. talk about + go + run

14-6 SPECIAL EXPRESSIONS FOLLOWED BY -*ING*

(a) We *had fun*
We *had a good time* } *playing* volleyball.
	-*ing* forms follow certain special expressions:
	   have fun/a good time + -*ing*
	   have trouble/difficulty + -*ing*
	   have a hard time/difficult time + -*ing*

(b) I *had trouble* I *had difficulty* I *had a hard time* I *had a difficult time* } *finding* his house.	
(c) Sam *spends most of his time studying*. (d) I *waste a lot of time watching* TV.	*spend* + expression of time or money + -*ing* *waste* + expression of time or money + -*ing*
(e) She *sat at her desk writing* a letter. (f) I *stood there wondering* what to do next. (g) He *is lying in bed reading* a novel.	*sit* + expression of place + -*ing* *stand* + expression of place + -*ing* *lie* + expression of place + -*ing*
(h) When I walked into my office, I *found George using* my telephone. (i) When I walked into my office, I *caught a thief looking* through my desk drawers.	*find* + (pro)noun + -*ing* *catch* + (pro)noun + -*ing* In (h) and (i): Both *find* and *catch* mean "discover." *Catch* often expresses anger or displeasure.

□ EXERCISE 9. Special expressions followed by -ING. (Chart 14-6)
Directions: Complete the sentences.

1. We had a lot of fun _____playing_____ games at the picnic.

2. I have trouble _____ Mrs. Maxwell when she speaks. She talks too fast.

3. I spent five hours _____ my homework last night.

4. Olga is standing at the corner _____ for the bus.

5. Ricardo is sitting in class _____ notes.

6. It was a beautiful spring day. Dorothy was lying under a tree _____ to the birds sing.

7. We wasted our money _____ to that movie. It was very boring.

8. Omar spent all day _____ ready to leave on vacation.

9. Ted is an indecisive person. He has a hard time _____ up his mind about anything.

10. I wondered what the children were doing while I was gone. When I got home, I found them _____ TV.

11. When Mr. Chan walked into the kitchen, he caught the children _____ some candy even though he'd told them not to spoil their dinners.

12. Ms. Gray is a commuter. Every work day, she spends almost two hours _____ to and from work.

13. A: My friend is going to Germany next month, but he doesn't speak German. What do you suppose he will have difficulty _____?

    B: Well, he might have trouble _____.

14. A: Did you enjoy your trip to New York City?

    B: Very much. We had a good time _____.

15. A: This is your first semester at this school. Have you had any problems?

    B: Not really, but sometimes I have a hard time _____.

16. A: What did you do yesterday?

    B: I spent almost all day _____.

☐ EXERCISE 10. Special expressions followed by -ING. (Chart 14-6)
Directions: Create sentences from the given verb combinations. Work in pairs, in groups, or as a class. The cuer's book is open. The responder's book is closed.

Example: have a difficult time + understand
SPEAKER A *(book open):* "have a difficult time" (pause) "understand"
SPEAKER B *(book closed):* I have a difficult time understanding the teacher's explanations in calculus.

Example: spend *(time)* + polish
SPEAKER A *(book open):* "spend an hour" (pause) "polish"
SPEAKER B *(book closed):* The soldier spent an hour polishing his boots.

1. have trouble + remember

2. stand *(place)* + wait

3. have a hard time + learn

4. sit *(place)* + think

5. have a good time + play

6. lie *(place)* + dream

7. have difficulty + pronounce

8. have fun + sing and dance

9. find *(someone)* + study

10. spend *(time)* + chat

11. waste *(money)* + try

12. catch *(someone)* + take

14-7 COMMON VERBS FOLLOWED BY INFINITIVES

VERB + INFINITIVE (a) I *hope to see* you again soon. (b) He *promised to be* here by ten. (c) He *promised not to be* late.	An *infinitive* = *to* + *the simple form of a verb (to see, to be, to go, etc.).* Some verbs are followed immediately by an infinitive, as in (a) and (b). See Group A below. Negative form: *not* precedes the infinitive, as in (c).
VERB + (PRO)NOUN + INFINITIVE (d) Mr. Lee *told me to be* here at ten o'clock. (e) The police *ordered the driver to stop*. (f) I *was told to be* here at ten o'clock. (g) The driver *was ordered to stop*.	Some verbs are followed by a (pro)noun and then an infinitive, as in (d) and (e). See Group B below. These verbs are followed immediately by an infinitive when they are used in the passive, as in (f) and (g).

(h) I *expect to pass* the test.
(i) I *expect Mary to pass* the test.
	Ask, expect, would like, want, and *need* may or may not be followed by a (pro)noun object.
	COMPARE
	   In (h): I think I will pass the test.
	   In (i): I think Mary will pass the test.

GROUP A: VERB + INFINITIVE			
hope to *(do something)*	*promise* to	*seem* to	*expect* to
plan to	*agree* to	*appear* to	*would like* to
intend to★	*offer* to	*pretend* to	*want* to
decide to	*refuse* to	*ask* to	*need* to

GROUP B: VERB + (PRO)NOUN + INFINITIVE			
tell someone to	*permit* someone to	*force* someone to	*need* someone to
advise someone to★★	*allow* someone to	*ask* someone to	
encourage someone to	*warn* someone to	*expect* someone to	
remind someone to	*require* someone to	*would like* someone to	
invite someone to	*order* someone to	*want* someone to	

  ★*Intend* is usually followed by an infinitive *(I intend to go to the meeting)*, but sometimes may be followed by a gerund *(I intend going to the meeting)* with no change in meaning.

  ★★A gerund is used after *advise* (active) if there is no (pro)noun object.
    COMPARE:
      (1) He *advised buying* a Fiat.
      (2) He *advised me to buy* a Fiat. I *was advised to buy* a Fiat.

☐ EXERCISE 11. Verb + gerund or infinitive. (Charts 14-4 and 14-7)
    Directions: Use a gerund or an infinitive to complete each sentence.

    1. We're going out for dinner. Would you like _____to join_____ us?

    2. Jack avoided _____looking at_____ me.

    3. Fred didn't have any money, so he decided _____ a job.

    4. The teacher reminded the students _____ their assignments.

    5. Do you enjoy _____ soccer?

    6. I was broke, so Jenny offered _____ me a little money.

    7. Mrs. Allen promised _____ tomorrow.

8. My boss expects me _____ this work ASAP.*

9. Would you mind _____ the door for me?

10. Even though I asked the people in front of me at the movie _____ quiet, they kept _____.

11. Joan and David were considering _____ married in June, but they finally decided _____ until August.

12. Our teacher encourages us _____ a dictionary whenever we are uncertain of the spelling of a word.

13. Before I went away to college, my mother reminded me _____ her a letter at least once a week.

14. Mrs. Jackson had warned her young son

_____

the hot stove.

15. I don't mind _____ alone.

16. The teacher seems _____ in a good mood today, don't you think?

17. Lucy pretended _____ the answer to my question.

18. Paulo intends _____ his friend a letter.

19. Residents are not allowed _____ pets in my apartment building.

20. All applicants are required _____ an entrance examination.

21. Someone asked me _____ this package.

22. I was asked _____ this package.

23. Jack advised me _____ a new apartment.

24. I was advised _____ a new apartment.

25. Jack advised _____ a new apartment.

26. Jack suggested _____ a new apartment.

27. Ann advised her sister _____ the plane instead of driving to Oregon.

28. Ann advised _____ the plane instead of driving to Oregon.

_____

*ASAP = *as soon as possible*

☐ EXERCISE 12. Verbs followed by infinitives. (Chart 14-7)

Directions: Use an infinitive phrase to create active and passive sentences using the given ideas and the verbs in parentheses. (Omit the *by*-phrase in passive sentences.)

1. The teacher said to me, "You may leave early."

   (permit) The teacher permitted me to leave early. (active)

   I was permitted to leave early. (passive)

2. The secretary said to me, "Please give this note to Sue."

   (ask)

3. My advisor said to me, "You should take Biology 109."

   (advise)

4. When I went to traffic court, the judge said to me, "You must pay a fine."

   (order)

5. During the test, the teacher said to Greg, "Keep your eyes on your own paper."

   (warn)

6. During the test, the teacher said to Greg, "Don't look at your neighbor's paper."

   (warn)

7. At the meeting, the head of the department said to the faculty, "Don't forget to turn in your grade reports by the 15th."

   (remind)

8. Mr. Lee said to the children, "Be quiet."

   (tell)

9. The hijacker said to the pilot, "You must land the plane."

   (force)

10. When I was growing up, my parents said to me, "You may stay up late on Saturday night."

    (allow)

11. The teacher said to the students, "Speak slowly and clearly."

    (encourage)

12. The teacher always says to the students, "You are supposed to come to class on time."

    (expect)

□ EXERCISE 13. Using infinitives to report speech. (Chart 14-7)
Directions: Report what someone said by using one of the verbs in the list to introduce an infinitive phrase.

advise	*expect*	*remind*
allow	*force*	*require*
ask	*order*	*tell*
encourage	*permit*	*warn*

1. The professor said to Alan, "You may leave early."
   → *The professor allowed Alan to leave early.* OR
   → *Alan was allowed to leave early.*
2. The general said to the soldiers, "Surround the enemy!"
3. Nancy said to me, "Would you please open the window?"
4. Bob said to me, "Don't forget to take your book back to the library."
5. Paul thinks I have a good voice, so he said to me, "You should take singing lessons."
6. Mrs. Anderson was very stern and a little angry. She shook her finger at the children and said to them, "Don't play with matches!"
7. I am very relieved because the Dean of Admissions said to me, "You may register for school late."
8. The law says, "Every driver must have a valid driver's license."
9. My friend said to me, "You should get some automobile insurance."
10. The robber had a gun. He said to me, "Give me all of your money."
11. Before the examination began, the teacher said to the students, "Work quickly."
12. My boss said to me, "Come to the meeting ten minutes early."

□ EXERCISE 14. Common verbs followed by infinitives. (Chart 14-7)
Directions: Work in groups of three. The cuer's book is open. The responders' books are closed.
Speaker A: Your book is open. Give the cue.
Speaker B: Your book is closed. Make an active sentence from the verb combination.
Speaker C: Your book is closed. Change the sentence to the passive; omit the *by*-phrase as appropriate.

Example: allow me + leave
SPEAKER A *(book open):* "allow me" (pause) "leave"
SPEAKER B *(book closed):* The teacher allowed me to leave class early last Friday because I had an appointment with my doctor.
SPEAKER C *(book closed):* (. . .) was allowed to leave class early last Friday because he/she had an appointment with his/her doctor.

	Switch roles.	*Switch roles.*
1. remind me + finish	4. expect me + be	7. tell me + open
2. ask me + go	5. warn me + not go	8. encourage me + visit
3. permit me + have	6. advise me + take	9. require us + take

14-8 COMMON VERBS FOLLOWED BY EITHER INFINITIVES OR GERUNDS

Some verbs can be followed by either an infinitive or a gerund, sometimes with no difference in meaning, as in Group A below, and sometimes with a difference in meaning, as in Group B below.

GROUP A: VERB + INFINITIVE OR GERUND, WITH NO DIFFERENCE IN MEANING			The verbs in Group A may be followed by either an infinitive or a gerund with little or no difference in meaning.
begin	*like*	*hate*	
start	*love*	*can't stand*	
continue	*prefer*★	*can't bear*	

(a) It *began to rain*. / It *began raining*.	In (a): There is no difference between *began to rain* and *began raining*.
(b) I *started to work*. / I *started working*.	
(c) It *was beginning to rain*.	If the main verb is progressive, an infinitive (not a gerund) is usually used, as in (c).

GROUP B: VERB + INFINITIVE OR GERUND, WITH A DIFFERENCE IN MEANING		The verbs in Group B may be followed by either an infinitive or a gerund, but the meaning is different.
remember	*regret*	
forget	*try*	

(d) Judy always *remembers to lock* the door.	*Remember* + *infinitive* = remember to perform responsibility, duty, or task, as in (d).
(e) Sam often *forgets to lock* the door.	*Forget* + *infinitive* = forget to perform a responsibility, duty, or task, as in (e).
(f) I *remember seeing* the Alps for the first time. The sight was impressive.	*Remember* + *gerund* = remember (recall) something that happened in the past, as in (f).
(g) I'*ll never forget seeing* the Alps for the first time.	*Forget* + *gerund* = forget something that happened in the past, as in (g).★★

(h) I *regret to tell* you that you failed the test.	*Regret* + *infinitive* = regret to say, to tell someone, to inform someone of some bad news, as in (h).
(i) I *regret lending* him some money. He never paid me back.	*Regret* + *gerund* = regret something that happened in the past, as in (i).

(j) I'*m trying to learn* English.	*Try* + *infinitive* = make an effort, as in (j).
(k) The room was hot. I *tried opening* the window, but that didn't help. So I *tried turning* on the fan, but I was still hot. Finally, I turned on the air conditioner.	*Try* + *gerund* = experiment with a new or different approach to see if it works, as in (k).

★Notice the patterns with *prefer:*

    prefer + *gerund:* I *prefer staying* home *to going* to the concert.

    prefer + *infinitive:* I'd *prefer to stay* home (rather) *than (to) go* to the concert.

★★*Forget* followed by a gerund usually occurs in a negative sentence or in a question: e.g., *I'll never forget, I can't forget, Have you ever forgotten,* and *Can you ever forget* are often followed by a gerund phrase.

☐ EXERCISE 15. Gerund vs. infinitive. (Chart 14-8)

Directions: Complete the sentences with the correct form(s) of the verbs in parentheses.

1. I like *(go)* _____to go / going_____ to the zoo.

2. The play wasn't very good. The audience started *(leave)* _____ before it was over.

3. After a brief interruption, the professor continued *(lecture)* _____ _____.

4. The children love *(swim)* _____ in the ocean.

5. I hate *(see)* _____ any living being suffer. I can't bear it.

6. I'm afraid of flying. When a plane begins *(move)* _____ down the runway, my heart starts *(race)* _____. Oh-oh! The plane is beginning *(move)* _____, and my heart is starting *(race)* _____.

7. When I travel, I prefer *(drive)* _____ to *(take)* _____ a plane.

8. I prefer *(drive)* _____ rather than *(take)* _____ _____ a plane.

9. I always remember *(turn)* _____ off all the lights before I leave my house.

10. I can remember *(be)* _____ very proud and happy when I graduated.

11. Did you remember *(give)* _____ Jake my message?

12. I remember *(play)* _____ with dolls when I was a child.

13. What do you remember *(do)* _____ when you were a child?

14. What do you remember *(do)* _____ before you leave for class every day?

15. What did you forget *(do)* _____ before you left for class this morning?

16. I'll never forget *(carry)* _____ my wife over the threshold when we moved into our first home.

17. I can't ever forget *(watch)* _____ our team score the winning goal in the last seconds of the championship game.

18. Don't forget *(do)* _____ your homework tonight!

19. I regret *(inform)* _____ you that your loan application has not been approved.

20. I regret *(listen, not)* _____ to my father's advice. He was right.

21. When a student asks a question, the teacher always tries *(explain)* _____ _____ the problem as clearly as possible.

22. I tried everything, but the baby still wouldn't stop crying. I tried *(hold)* _____ _____ him, but that didn't help. I tried *(feed)* _____ _____ him, but he refused the food and continued to cry. I tried *(burp)* _____ him. I tried *(change)* _____ his diapers. Nothing worked. The baby wouldn't stop crying.

☐ EXERCISE 16. Gerund vs. infinitive. (Charts 14-4 → 14-8)

Directions: Supply an appropriate form, gerund or infinitive, of the verbs in parentheses.

1. Mary reminded me *(be, not)* _____ not to be _____ late for the meeting.

2. We went for a walk after we finished *(clean)* _____ up the kitchen.

3. I forgot *(take)* _____ a book back to the library, so I had to pay a fine.

4. When do you expect *(leave)* _____ on your trip?

5. The baby started *(talk)* _____ when she was about eighteen months old.

6. I don't mind *(wait)* _____ for you. Go ahead and finish *(do)*
    _____ your work.

7. I've decided *(stay)* _____ here over vacation and *(paint)*
    _____ my room.

8. We discussed *(quit)* _____ our jobs and *(open)* _____
    our own business.

9. I'm getting tired. I need *(take)* _____ a break.

10. Sometimes students avoid *(look)* _____ at the teacher if they don't
    want *(answer)* _____ a question.

11. The club members discussed *(postpone)* _____ the next meeting until
    March.

12. Most children prefer *(watch)* _____ television to *(listen)*
    _____ to the radio.

13. My grandfather prefers *(read)* _____ .

14. Did Carol agree *(go)* _____ *(camp)* _____ with you?

15. As the storm approached, the birds quit *(sing)* _____.

16. The taxi driver refused *(take)* _____ a check. He wanted the passenger
    (pay) _____ cash.

17. The soldiers were ordered *(stand)* _____ at attention.

18. The travel agent advised us *(wait, not)* _____ until August.

☐ EXERCISE 17. Gerund vs. infinitive. (Charts 14-4 → 14-8)
Directions: Use the correct form of the verbs in parentheses and complete the sentences. Include a (pro)noun object between the two verbs if necessary. Work in pairs, in groups, or as a class.

Examples: The fire marshal *(tell + unlock)*
→ *The fire marshall told us to unlock the back doors of the school to provide a fast exit in the event of an emergency.*

(. . .) *(be asked + lead)*
→ *Maria was asked to lead a group discussion in class yesterday.*

1. (. . .) *(remind + finish)*
2. We *(have fun + swim)*
3. Students *(be required + have)*
4. The counselor *(advise + take)*
5. I *(try + learn)*
6. (. . .) *(warn + not open)*
7. I *(like + go + camp)*
8. (. . .) *(invite + go)*

9. (. . .) *(promise + not tell)*
10. We *(not be permitted + take)*
11. My friend *(ask + tell)*
12. When the wind *(begin + blow)*
13. I *(remember + call)*
14. (. . .) *(tell + not worry about + be)*
15. (. . .) *(be told + be)*
16. I *(spend + write)*

☐ EXERCISE 18. Gerund vs. infinitive. (Charts 14-4 → 14-8)
Directions: Work in pairs or small groups.
SPEAKER A: Your book is open. Give the cues.
SPEAKER B: Your book is closed. Make sentences from the verb combinations. Use "I" or the name of another person in the room. Use any verb tense or modal.

Examples:
SPEAKER A *(book open):*   like + go
SPEAKER B *(book closed):* I like to go (OR: going) to the park.

SPEAKER A *(book open):*   ask + open
SPEAKER B *(book closed):* Kostas asked me to open the window.

1. enjoy + listen
2. offer + lend
3. start + laugh
4. remind + take

Switch roles.
5. postpone + go
6. look forward to + see
7. forget + bring
8. remember + go

Switch roles.
9. prefer + live
10. finish + do
11. encourage + go
12. can't stand + have to wait

Switch roles.
13. continue + walk
14. stop + walk
15. be interested in + learn
16. be used to + speak

Switch roles.
17. suggest + go
18. advise + go
19. be allowed + have
20. like + go + swim

Switch roles.
21. regret + take
22. consider + not go
23. keep + put off + do
24. decide + ask + come

☐ EXERCISE 19. Gerund vs. infinitive. (Charts 14-4 → 14-8)
    Directions: Supply an appropriate form, gerund or infinitive, of the verbs in parentheses.

1. Keep *(talk)* _____. I'm listening to you.

2. The children promised *(play)* _____ more quietly. They promised *(make, not)* _____ so much noise.

3. Linda offered *(look after)* _____ my cat while I was out of town.

4. You shouldn't put off *(pay)* _____ your bills.

5. Alex's dog loves *(chase)* _____ sticks.

6. Mark mentioned *(go)* _____ to the market later today. I wonder if he's still planning *(go)* _____.

7. Igor suggested *(go)* _____ *(ski)* _____ in the mountains this weekend. How does that sound to you?

8. The doctor ordered Mr. Gray *(smoke, not)* _____.

9. Don't tell me his secret. I prefer *(know, not)* _____.

10. Could you please stop *(whistle)* _____? I'm trying *(concentrate)* _____ on my work.

11. Recently, Jo has been spending most of her time *(do)* _____ research for a book on pioneer women.

12. Nadia finally decided *(quit)* _____ her present job and *(look for)* _____ another one.

13. Did you remember *(turn off)* _____ the stove?

14. Toshi was allowed *(renew)* _____ his student visa.

15. Pat told us *(wait, not)* _____ for her.

16. Mr. Buck warned his daughter *(play, not)* _____ with matches.

17. Would you please remind me *(call)* _____ Gina tomorrow?

18. The little boy had a lot of trouble *(convince)* _____ anyone he had seen a mermaid.

19. Liz encouraged me *(throw away)* _____ my old running shoes with holes in the toes and *(buy)* _____ a new pair.

20. I'm considering *(drop out of)* _____ school, *(hitchhike)* _____ to New York, and *(try)* _____ *(find)* _____ a job.

21. Don't forget *(tell)* _____ Jane *(call)* _____ me about *(go)* _____ *(swim)* _____ tomorrow.

22. Sally reminded me *(ask)* _____ you *(tell)* _____ Bob *(remember)* _____ *(bring)* _____ his soccer ball to the picnic.

14-9 REFERENCE LIST OF VERBS FOLLOWED BY GERUNDS

Verbs with a bullet (•) can also be followed by infinitives. See Chart 14-10.

1.	*admit*	He *admitted stealing* the money.
2.	*advise•*	She *advised waiting* until tomorrow.
3.	*anticipate*	I *anticipate having* a good time on vacation.
4.	*appreciate*	I *appreciated hearing* from them.
5.	*avoid*	He *avoided answering* my question.
6.	*can't bear•*	I *can't bear waiting* in long lines.
7.	*begin•*	It *began raining*.
8.	*complete*	I finally *completed writing* my term paper.
9.	*consider*	I *will consider going* with you.
10.	*continue•*	He *continued speaking*.
11.	*delay*	He *delayed leaving* for school.
12.	*deny*	She *denied committing* the crime.
13.	*discuss*	They *discussed opening* a new business.
14.	*dislike*	I *dislike driving* long distances.
15.	*enjoy*	We *enjoyed visiting* them.
16.	*finish*	She *finished studying* about ten.
17.	*forget•*	I*'ll never forget visiting* Napoleon's tomb.
18.	*hate•*	I *hate making* silly mistakes.
19.	*can't help*	I *can't help worrying* about it.
20.	*keep*	I *keep hoping* he will come.
21.	*like•*	I *like going* to movies.
22.	*love•*	I *love going* to operas.
23.	*mention*	She *mentioned going* to a movie.
24.	*mind*	*Would* you *mind helping* me with this?
25.	*miss*	I *miss being* with my family.
26.	*postpone*	Let's *postpone leaving* until tomorrow.
27.	*practice*	The athlete *practiced throwing* the ball.
28.	*prefer•*	Ann *prefers walking* to driving to work.
29.	*quit*	He *quit trying* to solve the problem.
30.	*recall*	I *don't recall meeting* him before.
31.	*recollect*	I *don't recollect meeting* him before.
32.	*recommend*	She *recommended seeing* the show.
33.	*regret•*	I *regret telling* him my secret.
34.	*remember•*	I *can remember meeting* him when I was a child.
35.	*resent*	I *resent her interfering* in my business.
36.	*resist*	I *couldn't resist eating* the dessert.
37.	*risk*	She *risks losing* all of her money.
38.	*can't stand•*	I *can't stand waiting* in long lines.
39.	*start•*	It *started raining*.
40.	*stop*	She *stopped going* to classes when she got sick.
41.	*suggest*	She *suggested going* to a movie.
42.	*tolerate*	She *won't tolerate cheating* during an examination.
43.	*try•*	I *tried changing* the light bulb, but the lamp still didn't work.
44.	*understand*	I *don't understand his leaving* school.

14-10 REFERENCE LIST OF VERBS FOLLOWED BY INFINITIVES

Verbs with a bullet (•) can also be followed by gerunds. See Chart 14-9.

A. VERBS FOLLOWED IMMEDIATELY BY AN INFINITIVE

1. *afford*	I *can't afford to buy* it.	24. *love•*	I *love to go* to operas.
2. *agree*	They *agreed to help* us.	25. *manage*	She *managed to finish* her work early.
3. *appear*	She *appears to be* tired.	26. *mean*	I *didn't mean to hurt* your feelings.
4. *arrange*	I'll *arrange to meet* you at the airport.	27. *need*	I *need to have* your opinion.
5. *ask*	He *asked to come* with us.	28. *offer*	They *offered to help* us.
6. *can't bear•*	I *can't bear to wait* in long lines.	29. *plan*	I *am planning to have* a party.
7. *beg*	He *begged to come* with us.	30. *prefer•*	Ann *prefers to walk* to work.
8. *begin•*	It *began to rain*.	31. *prepare*	We *prepared to welcome* them.
9. *care*	I *don't care to see* that show.	32. *pretend*	He *pretends not to understand*.
10. *claim*	She *claims to know* a famous movie star.	33. *promise*	I *promise not to be* late.
11. *consent*	She finally *consented to marry* him.	34. *refuse*	I *refuse to believe* his story.
12. *continue•*	He *continued to speak*.	35. *regret•*	I *regret to tell* you that you failed.
13. *decide*	I *have decided to leave* on Monday.	36. *remember•*	I *remembered to lock* the door.
14. *demand*	I *demand to know* who is responsible.	37. *seem*	That cat *seems to be* friendly.
15. *deserve*	She *deserves to win* the prize.	38. *can't stand•*	I *can't stand to wait* in long lines.
16. *expect*	I *expect to enter* graduate school in the fall.	39. *start•*	It *started to rain*.
17. *fail*	She *failed to return* the book to the library on time.	40. *struggle*	I *struggled to stay* awake.
18. *forget•*	I *forgot to mail* the letter.	41. *swear*	She *swore to tell* the truth.
19. *hate•*	I *hate to make* silly mistakes.	42. *threaten*	She *threatened to tell* my parents.
20. *hesitate*	*Don't hesitate to ask* for my help.	43. *try•*	I'm *trying to learn* English.
21. *hope*	Jack *hopes to arrive* next week.	44. *volunteer*	He *volunteered to help* us.
22. *learn*	He *learned to play* the piano.	45. *wait*	I *will wait to hear* from you.
23. *like•*	I *like to go* to the movies.	46. *want*	I *want to tell* you something.
		47. *wish*	She *wishes to come* with us.

B. VERBS FOLLOWED BY A (PRO)NOUN + AN INFINITIVE

48. *advise•*	She *advised me to wait* until tomorrow.	61. *instruct*	He *instructed them to be* careful.
49. *allow*	She *allowed me to use* her car.	62. *invite*	Harry *invited the Johnsons to come* to his party.
50. *ask*	I *asked John to help* us.	63. *need*	We *needed Chris to help* us figure out the solution.
51. *beg*	They *begged us to come*.	64. *order*	The judge *ordered me to pay* a fine.
52. *cause*	Her laziness *caused her to fail*.	65. *permit*	He *permitted the children to stay* up late.
53. *challenge*	She *challenged me to race* her to the corner.	66. *persuade*	I *persuaded him to come* for a visit.
54. *convince*	I couldn't *convince him to accept* our help.	67. *remind*	She *reminded me to lock* the door.
55. *dare*	He *dared me to do* better than he had done.	68. *require*	Our teacher *requires us to be* on time.
56. *encourage*	He *encouraged me to try* again.	69. *teach*	My brother *taught me to swim*.
57. *expect*	I *expect you to be* on time.	70. *tell*	The doctor *told me to take* these pills.
58. *forbid*	I *forbid you to tell* him.	71. *urge*	I *urged her to apply* for the job.
59. *force*	They *forced him to tell* the truth.	72. *want*	I *want you to be* happy.
60. *hire*	She *hired a boy to mow* the lawn.	73. *warn*	I *warned you not to drive* too fast.

☐ EXERCISE 20. Gerund vs. infinitive. (Charts 14-9 and 14-10)

Directions: Work in pairs.

Speaker A: Your book is open. Give the cue. Don't lower your intonation at the end of the cue.

Speaker B: Your book is closed. Complete the sentence with **doing it** or **to do it**.

Speaker A: If you are unsure about the correctness of B's completion, refer to Charts 14-9 and 14-10.

Example:

SPEAKER A *(book open):* I promise . . . .

SPEAKER B *(book closed):* . . . to do it.

1. I enjoyed . . . .
2. I can't afford . . . .
3. She didn't allow me . . . .
4. We plan . . . .
5. Please remind me . . . .
6. I am considering . . . .
7. Our director postponed . . . .
8. He persuaded me . . . .
9. I don't mind . . . .
10. Everyone avoided . . . .

Switch roles.

11. I refused . . . .
12. I hope . . . .
13. She convinced me . . . .
14. He mentioned . . . .
15. I expect . . . .
16. I encouraged him . . . .
17. I warned him not . . . .
18. We prepared . . . .
19. I don't recall . . . .
20. We decided . . . .

Switch roles.

21. Did someone offer . . . .
22. When will you finish . . . .
23. Did you practice . . . .
24. She agreed . . . .
25. Keep . . . .

26. Stop . . . .
27. I didn't force him . . . .
28. I couldn't resist . . . .
29. Somehow, the cat managed . . . .
30. Did the little boy admit . . . .

Switch roles.

31. He denied . . . .
32. I didn't mean . . . .
33. She swore . . . .
34. I volunteered . . . .
35. He suggested . . . .
36. He advised me . . . .
37. He struggled . . . .
38. I don't want to risk . . . .
39. Do you recommend . . . .
40. I miss . . . .

Switch roles.

41. I can't imagine . . . .
42. She threatened . . . .
43. He seems to dislike . . . .
44. The children begged . . . .
45. She challenged me . . . .
46. Did he deny . . . .
47. Don't hesitate . . . .
48. Do you anticipate . . . .
49. Why did she fail . . . .
50. I'll arrange . . . .

□ EXERCISE 21. Gerund vs. infinitive. (Charts 14-9 and 14-10)

Directions: Complete the sentences with the correct form, gerund or infinitive, of the words in parentheses.

1. Hassan volunteered *(bring)* _____ some food to the reception.

2. The students practiced *(pronounce)* _____ the "th" sound in the phrase "these thirty-three dirty trees."

3. In the fairy tale, the wolf threatened *(eat)* _____ a girl named Little Red Riding Hood.

4. Susie! How many times do I have to remind you *(hang up)* _____ your coat when you get home from school?

5. The horses struggled *(pull)* _____ the wagon out of the mud.

6. Anita demanded *(know)* _____ why she had been fired.

7. My skin can't tolerate *(be)* _____ in the sun all day. I get sunburned easily.

8. I avoided *(tell)* _____ Mary the truth because I knew she would be angry.

9. Fred Washington claims *(be)* _____ a descendant of George Washington.

10. Mr. Kwan broke the antique vase. I'm sure he didn't mean *(do)* _____ it.

11. I urged Omar *(return)* _____ to school and *(finish)* _____ his education.

12. Mrs. Freeman can't help *(worry)* _____ about her children.

13. Children, I forbid you *(play)* _____ in the street. There's too much traffic.

14. My little cousin is a blabbermouth! He can't resist *(tell)* _____ everyone my secrets!

15. I appreciate your *(take)* _____ the time to help me.

16. I can't afford *(buy)* _____ a new car.

17. Kim managed *(change)* _____ my mind.

18. I think Sam deserves *(have)* _____ another chance.

19. Olga finally admitted *(be)* _____ responsible for the problem.

20. I don't recall ever *(hear)* _____ you mention his name before.

21. Nadia keeps *(promise)* _____ *(visit)* _____ us, but she never does.

22. Margaret challenged me *(race)* _____ her across the pool.

23. Oscar keeps *(hope)* _____ and *(pray)* _____ that things will get better.

24. I finally managed *(persuade)* _____ Yoko *(stay)* _____ in school and *(finish)* _____ her degree.

☐ **EXERCISE 22. Activity: gerund vs. infinitive. (Charts 14-9 and 14-10)**
Directions: Return to Exercise 20, but this time use your own words instead of **to do it** or **doing it**. Work with a partner.

Example:
SPEAKER A *(book open):*   I promise . . . .
SPEAKER B *(book closed):*   . . . to be on time for our meeting tomorrow.

☐ **EXERCISE 23. Activity: gerund vs. infinitive. (Charts 14-9 and 14-10)**
Directions: Divide into two teams. Your teacher will begin a sentence by using any of the verbs in Charts 14-9 and 14-10 or by using the verbs in Exercise 20. Complete the sentence with a gerund or infinitive phrase. Each correct completion scores one point.

14-11 *IT* + INFINITIVE; GERUNDS AND INFINITIVES AS SUBJECTS

(a) *It* is difficult *to learn a second language.*	Often an infinitive phrase is used with *it* as the subject of a sentence. The word *it* refers to and has the same meaning as the infinitive phrase at the end of the sentence. In (a): *It* = *to learn a second language.*
(b) *Learning a second language* is difficult.	A gerund phrase is frequently used as the subject of a sentence, as in (b).
(c) *To learn a second language* is difficult.	An infinitive can also be used as the subject of a sentence, as in (c), but far more commonly an infinitive phrase is used with *it*, as in (a).
(d) It is easy *for young children* to learn a second language. *Learning a second language* is easy *for young children.* *To learn a second language* is easy *for young children.*	The phrase *for (someone)* may be used to specify exactly who the speaker is talking about, as in (d).

☐ **EXERCISE 24. IT + infinitive. (Chart 14-11)**
   Directions: Create sentences beginning with *it*. Use a form of the given expression in your sentence, followed by an infinitive phrase.

   1. be dangerous → *It's dangerous to ride a motorcycle without wearing a helmet.*
   2. be important
   3. not be easy
   4. be foolish
   5. must be interesting
   6. be always a pleasure
   7. be clever of you
   8. not cost much money
   9. be necessary
   10. take time

☐ **EXERCISE 25. IT + infinitive. (Chart 14-11)**
   Directions: Add *for (someone)* and any other words to give a more specific and accurate meaning to the sentences.

   1. It isn't possible to be on time.
      → *It isn't possible for me to be on time for class if the bus drivers are on strike and I have to walk to class in a rainstorm.*
   2. It's easy to speak Spanish.
   3. It's important to learn English.
   4. It is essential to get a visa.
   5. It's important to take advanced math courses.
   6. It's difficult to communicate.
   7. It was impossible to come to class.
   8. It is a good idea to study gerunds and infinitives.

□ **EXERCISE 26. Gerunds as subjects. (Chart 14-11)**
Directions: Complete the sentences. Use gerund phrases as subjects.

1. . . . isn't easy. → *Climbing to the top of a mountain isn't easy.*
2. . . . is hard.
3. . . . can be interesting.
4. . . . was a good experience.
5. Does . . . sound like fun to you?
6. . . . demands patience and a sense of humor.
7. . . . is a complicated process.
8. . . . is considered impolite in my country.

□ **EXERCISE 27. IT + infinitive; gerunds as subjects. (Chart 14-11)**
Directions: Work in pairs.
Speaker A: Your book is open. Give the cue.
Speaker B: Your book is closed. Complete the sentence with an infinitive phrase.
Speaker A: Create a sentence with the same meaning by using a gerund phrase as the subject.

Example:
SPEAKER A *(book open):*   It's fun . . . .
SPEAKER B *(book closed):*   . . . to ride a horse.
SPEAKER A: Riding a horse is fun.

Switch roles.

1. It's dangerous . . . .
2. It's easy . . . .
3. It's impolite . . . .
4. It is important . . . .
5. It is wrong . . . .
6. It takes a lot of time . . . .
7. It's a good idea . . . .
8. Is it difficult . . . ?

□ **EXERCISE 28. Activity: gerunds and infinitives. (Chapter 14)**
Directions: Form a group of three to five members. Choose one of the story beginnings or make up your own. Each group member continues the story by adding a sentence or two. At least one of the sentences should contain words from the given list, plus a gerund or infinitive phrase (but it is okay simply to continue the story without using a gerund or infinitive if it works out that way). As a group, use as many of the words in the list which follows as you can.

Example: (Yoko) had a bad night last night. First, when she got home, she discovered that . . . .
SPEAKER A: . . . her door was unlocked. She didn't *recall leaving* her door unlocked. She always *remembers to lock* her door and in fact specifically *remembered locking* it that morning. So she became afraid that someone had broken into her apartment.
SPEAKER B: She *thought about going* inside, but then decided *it* would be better *not to go* into her apartment alone. What if there was a burglar inside?
SPEAKER C: *Instead of going* into her apartment alone, Yoko walked to her next-door neighbor's door and knocked.
SPEAKER D: Her neighbor answered the door. He could see that something was the matter. "Are you all right?" he asked her.
SPEAKER A: Etc.

Story beginnings:

1. (. . .) is having trouble with (her/his) roommate, whose name is (. . .). (Her/His) roommate keeps many pets even though the lease they signed forbids residents to keep animals in their apartments. Yesterday, one of these pets, a/an . . . .

2. Not long ago, (. . .) and (. . .) were walking home together after dark. They heard a strange whooshing sound. When they looked up in the night sky, they saw a huge hovering aircraft. It glowed! It was round and green! (. . .) was frightened and curious at the same time. (She/He) wanted to . . . , but . . . .

3. Once upon a time, (. . .) lived in a faraway village in a remote mountainous region. All of the villagers were terrified because of the dragon that lived nearby. At least once a week, the dragon would descend on the village and . . . .

4. It was a dark and stormy night. (. . .) was all alone at home. Suddenly . . . .

5. (. . .) had a bad day yesterday. First of all, when (she/he) got up in the morning, (she/he) discovered that . . . .

List of words and phrases to work into the story:

PREPOSITIONAL EXPRESSIONS FOLLOWED BY GERUNDS	VERBS FOLLOWED BY GERUNDS OR INFINITIVES		IT + INFINITIVE OR A GERUND SUBJECT
be accused of	admit	mind	be a bad experience
be accustomed to	advise	need	be a bad idea
in addition to	afford	offer	be better
be afraid	agree	permit	be clever
apologize (to someone) for	ask	persuade	be dangerous
believe in	avoid	plan	be difficult
blame (someone) for	beg	postpone	be easy
be capable of	begin	prefer	be essential
be committed to	consider	prepare	be foolish
complain about	continue	pretend	be a good experience
dream of	convince	promise	be a good idea
forgive (someone) for	decide	quit	be fun
be excited about	demand	recall	be hard
be guilty of	deny	refuse	be important
instead of	discuss	regret	be impossible
be interested in	dislike	remember	be interesting
look forward to	encourage	remind	be necessary
be opposed to	enjoy	risk	be a pleasure
prevent (someone) from	expect	seem	be possible
be scared of	fail	start	be relaxing
stop (someone) from	force	stop	take effort
succeed in	forget	struggle	take energy
take advantage of	hesitate	suggest	take money
be terrified of	hope	threaten	take patience
thank (someone) for	invite	wait	take time
think of	learn	want	
be tired of	like	warn	
be worried about	manage		

CHAPTER 15

Gerunds and Infinitives, Part 2

15-1 INFINITIVE OF PURPOSE: *IN ORDER TO*

(a) He came here *in order to study* English. (b) He came here *to study* English.	*In order to* is used to express *purpose*. It answers the question "Why?" *In order* is often omitted, as in (b).
(c) *INCORRECT:* He came here *for studying* English. (d) *INCORRECT:* He came here *for to study* English. (e) *INCORRECT:* He came here *for study* English.	To express purpose, use *(in order) to*, not *for*, with a verb.★
(f) I went to the store *for* some bread. (g) I went to the store *to buy* some bread.	*For* can be used to express purpose, but it is a preposition and is followed by a noun object, as in (f).

★Exception: The phrase *be used for* expresses the typical or general purpose of a thing. In this case, the preposition *for* is followed by a gerund: *A saw is used for cutting wood.* Also possible: *A saw is used to cut wood.*

However, to talk about a particular thing and a particular situation, *be used* + *an infinitive* is used: *A chain saw was used to cut* (NOT *for cutting*) *down the old oak tree.*

☐ **EXERCISE 1. Error analysis: IN ORDER TO. (Chart 15-1)**
Directions: Correct the errors.

1. I went to the library ~~for~~ to study last night.

2. Helen borrowed my dictionary for to look up the spelling of "occurred."

3. The teacher opened the window for letting some fresh air in the room.

4. I came to this school for learn English.

5. I traveled to Osaka for to visit my sister.

☐ EXERCISE 2. IN ORDER TO vs. FOR. (Chart 15-1)
　　　　Directions: Make up completions. Express the *purpose* of the action.

1. I went to Chicago to _____ visit my relatives. _____

2. Tom went to Chicago for _____ a business conference. _____

3. I went to the market for _____

4. Mary went to the market to _____

5. I went to the doctor to _____

6. My son went to the doctor for _____

7. I swim every day to _____

8. My friend swims every day for _____

9. I drove into the service station to _____

10. They stopped at the service station for _____

☐ EXERCISE 3. IN ORDER TO. (Chart 15-1)
　　　　Directions: Add *in order* wherever possible. If nothing should be added, write Ø.

1. I went to the garden center _____ in order _____ to get some fertilizer for my flowers.

2. When the teacher asked him a question, Jack pretended _____ Ø _____ to
understand what she was saying.

3. My roommate asked me _____ to clean up the dishes after dinner.

4. I bought a new screwdriver _____ to repair my bicycle.

5. My mother always said I should eat lots of green vegetables _____ to
make my body strong.

6. Mustafa climbed onto a chair _____ to change a light bulb in the
ceiling.

7. I really want _____ to learn Italian before I visit Venice next year.

8. I jog three times a week _____ to stay healthy.

9. It is a good idea _____ to know where your children are at all times.

10. I need to find her _____ to talk to her.

11. Rita has to work at two jobs _____ to support herself and her three
children.

12. Jim finally went to the dentist _____ to get some relief from his toothache.

13. It's easier for me _____ to understand written English than it is to understand spoken English.

14. I practice speaking English into a tape recorder _____ to improve my pronunciation.

15. It isn't important _____ to speak English without an accent as long as people understand what you're saying.

15-2 ADJECTIVES FOLLOWED BY INFINITIVES

(a) We *were sorry to hear* the bad news. (b) I *was surprised to see* Tim at the meeting.	Certain adjectives can be immediately followed by infinitives, as in (a) and (b). In general, these adjectives describe a person (or persons), not a thing. Many of these adjectives describe a person's feelings or attitudes.

SOME COMMON ADJECTIVES FOLLOWED BY INFINITIVES

glad to (do it)	*sorry to★*	*ready to*	*careful to*	*surprised to★*
happy to	*sad to★*	*prepared to*	*hesitant to*	*amazed to★*
pleased to	*upset to★*	*anxious to*	*reluctant to*	*astonished to★*
delighted to	*disappointed to★*	*eager to*	*afraid to*	*shocked to★*
content to		*willing to*		*stunned to★*
relieved to	*proud to*	*motivated to*	*likely to*	
lucky to	*ashamed to*	*determined to*	*certain to*	
fortunate to				

★The expressions with asterisks are usually followed by infinitive phrases with verbs such as *see, learn, discover, find out, hear.*

☐ EXERCISE 4. Adjectives followed by infinitives. (Chart 15-2)
Directions: Complete the sentences, using the expressions listed in Chart 15-2 and your own words. Use infinitive phrases in your completions.

1. Maria always speeds on the expressway. She's . . . .
   → *She's certain to get stopped by the police.*
   → *She's likely to get a ticket.*

2. There have been a lot of burglaries in my neighborhood recently, so I have started taking precautions. Now I am always very . . . .

3. I've worked hard all day long. Enough's enough! I'm . . . .

4. Next month, I'm going to a family reunion—the first one in 25 years. I'm very much looking forward to it. I'm . . . .

5. Some children grow up in unhappy homes. My family, however, has always been loving and supportive. I'm . . . .

6. Ivan's run out of money again, but he doesn't want anyone to know his situation. He needs money desperately, but he's . . . .

7. Rosalyn wants to become an astronaut. That has been her dream since she was a little girl. She has been working hard toward her goal and is . . . .

8. Mr. Wah was offered an excellent job in another country, but his wife and children don't want to move. He's not sure what to do. Although he would like the job, he's . . . .

9. Our neighbors had extra tickets to the ballet, so they invited us to go with them. Since both of us love the ballet, we were . . . .

10. Sally recently told me what my wayward brother is up to these days. I couldn't believe my ears! I was . . . .

☐ **EXERCISE 5. Adjectives followed by infinitives. (Chart 15-2)**
Directions: Work in pairs.
Speaker A: Your book is open. Give the cues.
Speaker B: Your book is closed. Answer "yes" to the question. Use an infinitive phrase in your response.

Example:
SPEAKER A *(book open):* You saw your friend at the airport. Were you happy?
SPEAKER B *(book closed):* Yes. I was happy to see my friend at the airport.

1. (. . .) has a lot of good friends. Is he/she fortunate?
2. You're leaving on vacation soon. Are you eager?
3. You met (. . .)'s wife/husband. Were you delighted?
4. You went to *(name of a faraway place in the world)* last summer. You saw (. . .) there. Were you surprised?

Switch roles.
5. You're going to take a test tomorrow. Are you prepared?
6. You're thinking about asking (. . .) a personal question. Are you hesitant?
7. Your friend was ill. Finally you found out that she was okay. Were you relieved?
8. You heard about (. . .)'s accident. Were you sorry?

☐ **EXERCISE 6. Adjectives followed by infinitives. (Chart 15-2)**
Directions: Work in pairs, in groups, or as a class.
Speaker A: Your book is open. Ask the questions.
Speaker B: Your book is closed. Answer in complete sentences.

1. What are you careful to do before you cross a busy street?
2. What are children sometimes afraid to do?
3. When you're tired in the evening, what are you content to do?
4. If one of your friends has a problem, what are you willing to do?
5. Sometimes when people don't know English very well, what are they reluctant to do?
6. If the teacher announces there is a test tomorrow, what will you be motivated to do?
7. What are you determined to do before you are 70 years old?
8. What are some things people should be ashamed to do?
9. Is there anything you are eager to do today or tomorrow?
10. In what ways are you a fortunate person?
11. Can you tell me something you were shocked to find out?/astonished to learn?
12. Can you tell me something you were disappointed to discover?/sad to hear?

15-3 USING INFINITIVES WITH *TOO* AND *ENOUGH*

COMPARE	In the speaker's mind, the use of *too* implies a negative result.
(a) That box is *too heavy* for Bob to lift. (b) That box is *very heavy*, but Bob can lift it.	In (a): *too heavy* = It is *impossible* for Bob to lift that box. In (b): *very heavy* = It is *possible but difficult* for Bob to lift that box.
(c) I am *strong enough to lift* that box. I can lift it. (d) I have *enough strength to lift* that box. (e) I have *strength enough to lift* that box.	*Enough* follows an adjective, as in (c). Usually *enough* precedes a noun, as in (d). In formal English, it may follow a noun, as in (e).

☐ **EXERCISE 7. Using infinitives with TOO and ENOUGH. (Chart 15-3)**
Directions: Think of a negative result, and then complete the sentence with an infinitive phrase.

1. That ring is too expensive. → Negative result: *I can't buy it. That ring is too expensive for me to buy.*

2. I'm too tired. → Negative result: *I can't/don't want to go to the meeting. I'm too tired to go to the meeting.*

3. It's too late. → Negative result: . . . .

4. It's too cold.

5. Nuclear physics is too difficult.

6. I'm too busy.

7. My son is too young.

8. The mountain cliff is too steep.

Now think of a positive result, and complete the sentence with an infinitive phrase.

9. That ring is very expensive, but it isn't too expensive → Positive result: *I can buy it. That ring isn't too expensive for me to buy.*

10. I'm very tired, but I'm not too tired → Positive result: . . . .

11. My suitcase is very heavy, but it's not too heavy.

12. I'm very busy, but I'm not too busy.

☐ **EXERCISE 8. Activity: using infinitives with TOO and ENOUGH. (Chart 15-3)**
Directions: Discuss the questions.

1. (. . .)'s daughter is 18 months old. Is she too young or very young?
2. What is a child too young to do but an adult old enough to do?
3. Who had a good dinner last night? Was it too good or very good?
4. Is it very difficult or too difficult to learn English?
5. After you wash your clothes, are they too clean or very clean?
6. Who stayed up late last night? Did you stay up too late or very late?
7. What is your pocket big enough to hold? What is it too small to hold?

8. Compare a mouse with an elephant. Is a mouse too small or very small?
9. What is the highest mountain in *(this country/the world)*? Is it too high or very high?
10. What did you have enough time to do before class today?
11. What's the difference between the following situations?
    a. We don't have enough big envelopes.
    b. We don't have big enough envelopes.
12. If you apologize for something, do you say you're very sorry or too sorry?
13. What is the sun too bright for you to do?
14. What can't you do if a room is too dark?
15. In what circumstances would you say your cup of tea or coffee is too full?

15-4 PASSIVE AND PAST FORMS OF INFINITIVES AND GERUNDS

FORMS

	SIMPLE	PAST
ACTIVE	*to see* *seeing*	*to have seen* *having seen*
PASSIVE	*to be seen* *being seen*	*to have been seen* *having been seen*

PAST INFINITIVE: ***to have*** + *past participle* (a) The rain seems *to have stopped*.	The event expressed by a past infinitive or past gerund happened before the time of the main verb. In (a): *The rain seems now to have stopped a few minutes ago.*★
PAST GERUND: ***having*** + *past participle* (b) I appreciate *having had* the opportunity to meet the king.	In (b): I met the king yesterday. *I appreciate now having had the opportunity to meet the king yesterday.*★
PASSIVE INFINITIVE: ***to be*** + *past participle* (c) I didn't expect *to be invited* to his party.	In (c): *to be invited* is passive. The understood *by*-phrase is "by him": *I didn't expect to be invited by him.*
PASSIVE GERUND: ***being*** + *past participle* (d) I appreciated *being invited* to your home.	In (d): ***being invited*** is passive. The understood *by*-phrase is "by you": *I appreciated being invited by you.*
PAST-PASSIVE INFINITIVE: ***to have been*** + *past participle* (e) Nadia is fortunate *to have been given* a scholarship.	In (e): Nadia was given a scholarship last month by her government. She is fortunate. *Nadia is fortunate now to have been given a scholarship last month by her government.*
PAST-PASSIVE GERUND: ***having been*** + *past participle* (f) I appreciate *having been told* the news.	In (f): I was told the news yesterday by someone. I appreciate that. *I appreciate now having been told the news yesterday by someone.*

★If the main verb is past, the action of the past infinitive or gerund happened before a time in the past:
*The rain **seemed to have stopped**.* = The rain seemed at six P.M. to have stopped before six P.M.
*I **appreciated having had** the opportunity to meet the king.* = I met the king in 1995. In 1997 I appreciated having had the opportunity to meet the king in 1995.

☐ EXERCISE 9. Passive and past forms of infinitives and gerunds. (Chart 15-4)
Directions: Supply an appropriate form for each verb in parentheses.

1. I don't enjoy *(laugh)* __being laughed__ at by other people.

2. I'm angry at him for *(tell, not)* __not telling / not having told*__ me the truth.

3. It is easy *(fool)* __to be fooled__ by his lies.

4. I expected *(invite)* _____ to the party, but I wasn't.

5. Sometimes adolescents complain about not *(understand)* _____
   _____ by their parents.

6. Your compositions are supposed *(write)* _____ in ink.

7. Jin Won had a narrow escape. He was almost hit by a car. He barely avoided *(hit)*
   _____ by a speeding automobile.

8. Ms. Thompson is always willing to help if there is a problem in the office, but she
   doesn't want *(call)* _____ at home unless there is an emergency.

9. Jack Welles has a good chance of *(elect)* _____. I know I'm
   going to vote for him.

10. Carlos appears *(lose)* _____ some weight. Has he been ill?

11. You must tell me the truth. I insist on *(tell)* _____ the truth.

12. Don't all of us want *(love)* _____ and *(need)* _____
    by other people?

13. Dear Hiroki,
    I feel guilty about *(write, not)* _____ to you sooner, but
    I've been swamped with work lately.

14. A: You know Jim Frankenstein, don't you?
    B: Jim Frankenstein? I don't think so. I don't recall ever *(meet)* _____
    _____ him.

15. Mr. Gow mentioned *(injure)* _____ in an accident as a child,
    but he never told us the details.

16. Tim was in the army during the war. He was caught by the enemy, but he managed to
    escape. He is lucky *(escape)* _____ with his life.

_____

*The past gerund is used to emphasize that the action of the gerund took place before that of the main verb.
However, often there is little difference in meaning between a simple gerund and a past gerund.

17. A: Is Abdul a transfer student?

B: Yes.

A: Where did he go to school before he came here?

B: I'm not sure, but I think he mentioned something about *(go)* _____ _____ to UCLA or USC.

18. We would like *(invite)* _____ to the president's reception at the Pearl Hotel last week, but we weren't.*

15-5 USING GERUNDS OR PASSIVE INFINITIVES FOLLOWING *NEED*

(a) I *need to borrow* some money. (b) John *needs to be told* the truth.	Usually an infinitive follows *need*, as in (a) and (b).
(c) The house *needs painting*. (d) The house *needs to be painted*.	In certain circumstances, a gerund may follow *need*. In this case, the gerund carries a passive meaning. Usually the situations involve fixing or improving something. (c) and (d) have the same meaning.

☐ **EXERCISE 10. Using gerunds or passive infinitives following NEED. (Chart 15-5)**
Directions: Supply an appropriate form of the verbs in parentheses.

1. The chair is broken. I need *(fix)* _____to fix_____ it. The chair needs *(fix)* __fixing / to be fixed__ .

2. The baby's diaper is wet. It needs *(change)* _____.

3. What a mess! This room needs *(clean)* _____ up. We need *(clean)* _____ it up before the company arrives.

4. My shirt is wrinkled. It needs *(iron)* _____.

5. There is a hole in our roof. The roof needs *(repair)* _____.

6. I have books and papers all over my desk. I need *(take)* _____ some time to straighten up my desk. It needs *(straighten)* _____ up.

7. The apples on the tree are ripe. They need *(pick)* _____.

8. The dog's been digging in the mud. He needs *(wash)* _____.

---

*Sometimes native speakers use both a past modal and a past infinitive even though only one past form is necessary: *We would have liked to have been invited* . . . . Also possible, with the same meaning: *We would have liked to be invited* . . . .

□ **EXERCISE 11. Gerunds vs. infinitives following NEED. (Chart 15-5)**

Directions: Look at the picture.
What needs doing/to be done?

15-6 USING A POSSESSIVE TO MODIFY A GERUND

We came to class late. Mr. Lee complained about that fact. (a) FORMAL: Mr. Lee complained about *our coming* to class late.* (b) INFORMAL: Mr. Lee complained about *us coming* to class late.	In formal English, a possessive adjective (e.g., ***our***) is used to modify a gerund, as in (a). In informal English, the object form of a pronoun (e.g., ***us***) is frequently used, as in (b).
(c) FORMAL: Mr. Lee complained about *Mary's coming* to class late. (d) INFORMAL: Mr. Lee complained about *Mary coming* to class late.	In very formal English, a possessive noun (e.g., ***Mary's***) is used to modify a gerund. The possessive form is often not used in informal English, as in (d).

**Coming to class late occurred before Mr. Lee complained, so a past gerund is also possible: Mr. Lee complained about our having come to class late.*

□ **EXERCISE 12. Using a possessive to modify a gerund. (Chart 15-6)**

Directions: Combine the pairs of sentences. Change *that fact* to a gerund phrase. Use formal English. Discuss informal usage.

1. Mary won a scholarship. We are excited about *that fact.*
   → *We are excited about Mary's (Mary) winning a scholarship.*

2. He didn't want to go. I couldn't understand *that fact.*
   → *I couldn't understand his (him) not wanting to go.*

3. You took the time to help us. We greatly appreciate *that fact.*

4. We talked about him behind his back. The boy resented *that fact.*

5. They ran away to get married. *That fact* shocked everyone.

6. You are late to work every morning. I will no longer tolerate *that fact.*

7. Ann borrowed Sally's clothes without asking her first. Sally complained about *that fact.*

8. Helen is here to answer our questions about the company's new insurance plan. We should take advantage *of that fact.*

☐ EXERCISE 13. Review: verb forms. (Charts 14-1 → 15-6)

Directions: Supply an appropriate form for each verb in parentheses.

1. Alice didn't expect *(ask)* _____ to Bill's party.

2. I'm not accustomed to *(drink)* _____ coffee with my meals.

3. I'll help you with your homework as soon as I finish *(wash)* _____ the dishes.

4. She took a deep breath *(relax)* _____ herself before she got up to give her speech.

5. I'm prepared *(answer)* _____ any question that might be asked during my job interview tomorrow.

6. Matthew left without *(tell)* _____ anyone.

7. It's useless. Give up. Enough's enough. Don't keep *(beat)* _____ your head against a brick wall.

8. His *(be, not)* _____ able to come is disappointing.

9. I hope *(award)* _____ a scholarship for the coming semester.

10. We are very pleased *(accept)* _____ your invitation.

11. I have considered *(get)* _____ a part-time job *(help)* _____ pay for my school expenses.

12. It is exciting *(travel)* _____ to faraway places and *(leave)* _____ one's daily routine behind.

13. *(Help)* _____ the disadvantaged children learn how to read was a rewarding experience.

14. He wants *(like)* _____ and *(trust)* _____ by everyone.

15. I can't help *(wonder)* _____ why Larry did such a foolish thing.

16. Mr. Carson is very lucky *(choose)* _____ by the committee as their representative to the meeting in Paris.

17. *(Live)* _____ in a city has certain advantages.

18. Keep on *(do)* _____ whatever you were doing. I didn't mean

    (interrupt) _____ you.

19. It is very kind of you *(take)* _____ care of that problem for me.

20. She opened the window *(let)* _____ in some fresh air.

21. They agreed *(cooperate)* _____ with us to the fullest extent.

22. Jack wastes a lot of time *(hang)* _____ out with his friends on street corners.

23. Did you remember *(turn)* _____ in your assignment?

24. I don't remember ever *(hear)* _____ that story before.

25. Does your son regret *(leave)* _____ home and *(go)* _____ to a foreign country *(study)* _____?

26. I appreciate your *(ask)* _____ my opinion on the matter.

27. You should stop *(drive)* _____ if you get sleepy. It's dangerous *(drive)* _____ when you're not alert.

28. I have trouble *(fall)* _____ asleep at night.

29. After driving for three hours, we stopped *(get)* _____ something to eat.

30. Please forgive me for *(be, not)* _____ here to help you yesterday.

☐ **EXERCISE 14. Review: gerunds and infinitives. (Charts 14-1 → 15-6)**
Directions: Complete the sentences with your own words. Each sentence should contain a GERUND or an INFINITIVE.

Example: You are required . . . .
→ *You are required to stop at the border when entering Canada by car.*

1. Your not wanting . . . .
2. It's important for . . . .
3. I'll never forget . . . .
4. Jack advised not . . . .
5. I'm not willing . . . .
6. My apartment needs . . . .
7. . . . enough energy . . . .
8. . . . in order to save . . . .
9. . . . to be told about . . . .
10. . . . had just begun . . . when . . . .
11. Do you think it is easy . . . ?
12. . . . my having been . . . .
13. Have you ever considered . . . ?
14. . . . is likely . . . .
15. Most people object . . . .
16. . . . try to avoid . . . .

15-7 USING VERBS OF PERCEPTION

(a) I *saw* my friend *run* down the street. (b) I *saw* my friend *running* down the street. (c) I *heard* the rain *fall* on the roof. (d) I *heard* the rain *falling* on the roof.	Certain verbs of perception are followed by either *the simple form*★ or *the -ing form*★★ of a verb. There is often little difference in meaning between the two forms, except that the *-ing* form usually gives the idea of "while." In (b): I saw my friend while she was running down the street.
(e) When I walked into the apartment, I *heard* my roommate *singing* in the shower. (f) I *heard* a famous opera star *sing* at the concert last night.	Sometimes (not always) there is a clear difference between using the simple form or the *-ing* form. The use of the *-ing* form gives the idea that an activity is already in progress when it is perceived, as in (e): The singing was in progress when I first heard it. In (f): I heard the singing from beginning to end. It was not in progress when I first heard it.

VERBS OF PERCEPTION FOLLOWED BY THE SIMPLE FORM OR THE *-ING* FORM

see	*look at*	*hear*	*feel*	*smell*
notice	*observe*	*listen to*		
watch				

★*The simple form of a verb* = the infinitive form without "to." INCORRECT: I saw my friend *to run* down the street.

★★*The -ing form* refers to the present participle.

☐ **EXERCISE 15. Using verbs of perception. (Chart 15-7)**

PART I. Complete the sentences with any appropriate verbs. Both the simple form and the *-ing* form are possible with little, if any, difference in meaning.

1. Polly was working in her garden, so she didn't hear the phone ___ring / ringng___.

2. I like to listen to the birds _____ when I get up early in the morning.

3. The guard observed a suspicious-looking person _____ into the bank.

4. There was an earthquake in my hometown last year. It was just a small one, but I could feel the ground _____.

5. I was almost asleep last night when I suddenly heard someone _____ on the door.

6. While I was waiting for my plane, I watched other planes _____ and _____.

PART II. Both the simple form and the *-ing* form are grammatically correct, so you can't make a grammar mistake. But a speaker might choose one over the other. Read the situation, then decide which form seems better to you in the sentence that contains a verb of perception. Remember that the *-ing* form gives the idea that an activity is in progress when it is perceived.

1. SITUATION: *I was downtown yesterday. I saw the police. They were chasing a thief.*

   When I was downtown yesterday, I saw the police ___chasing___ a thief.

2. SITUATION: *The front door slammed. I got up to see if someone had come in.*

   When I heard the front door _____, I got up to see if someone had come in.

3. SITUATION: *Uncle Jake is in the bedroom. He is snoring.*

   I know Uncle Jake is in the bedroom because I can hear him _____.

4. SITUATION: *When I walked past the park, some children were playing softball.*

   When I walked past the park, I saw some children _____ softball.

5. SITUATION: *It was graduation day in the auditorium. When the school principal called my name, I walked to the front of the room.*

   When I heard the school principal _____ my name, I walked to the front of the auditorium to receive my diploma.

6. SITUATION: *I glanced out the window. Jack was walking toward the house. I was surprised.*

   I was surprised when I glanced out the window and saw Jack _____ toward the house.

7. SITUATION: *Someone is calling for help in the distance. I suddenly hear that.*

   Listen! Do you hear someone _____ for help? I do.

8. SITUATION: *My daughter's team plays soccer every weekend. I always watch the team when they play a game.*

   I enjoy watching my daughter _____ soccer every weekend.

9. SITUATION: *I went to bed around eleven. At that time, the people in the next apartment were singing and laughing.*

   When I went to bed last night around eleven, I could hear the people in the next

   apartment _____ and _____. I had trouble getting to sleep because they were making so much noise.

10. SITUATION: *A fly landed on the table. I swatted it with a rolled up newspaper.*

    As soon as I saw the fly _____ on the table, I swatted it with a rolled up newspaper.

11. SITUATION: *I smell smoke. Something must be burning.*

    Do you smell something _____? I do.

12. SITUATION: *I was sitting in class. Suddenly someone touched my shoulder.*

    I was startled in class yesterday when I felt someone _____ my shoulder. I didn't mind. It just surprised me. It was Olga. She wanted to borrow my dictionary.

☐ EXERCISE 16. Activity: using verbs of perception. (Chart 15-7)
   Directions: Describe what you see and hear.

   1. What do you see happening around you right now?
   2. Ask (. . .) to stand up and sit back down. What did you just see (. . .) do?
   3. Close your eyes. What do you hear happening right now?
   4. Ask (. . .) to say something. What did you just hear (. . .) say?
   5. Ask (. . .) to do something. As he/she continues to do this, describe what you see and hear him/her doing.

15-8 USING THE SIMPLE FORM AFTER *LET* AND *HELP*

(a) My father *lets* me *drive* his car. (b) I *let* my friend *borrow* my bicycle. (c) *Let's go* to a movie.	*Let* is followed by the simple form of a verb, not an infinitive. *INCORRECT:* My father lets me *to drive* his car.
(d) My brother *helped* me *wash* my car. (e) My brother *helped* me *to wash* my car.	*Help* is often followed by the simple form of a verb, as in (d). An infinitive is also possible, as in (e). Both (d) and (e) are correct.

□ **EXERCISE 17. Using the simple form after LET and HELP.** (Chart 15-8)

Directions: Complete the sentences with verb phrases.

1. Don't let me _forget to take my keys to the house with me._

2. The teacher usually lets us _____

3. Why did you let your roommate _____

4. You shouldn't let other people _____

5. A stranger helped the lost child _____

6. It was very kind of my friend to help me _____

7. Keep working. Don't let me _____

8. Could you help me _____

15-9 USING CAUSATIVE VERBS: *MAKE, HAVE, GET*

(a) I *made* my brother *carry* my suitcase. (b) I *had* my brother *carry* my suitcase. (c) I *got* my brother *to carry* my suitcase.	*Make*, *have*, and *get* can be used to express the idea that "X" causes "Y" to do something. When they are used as causative verbs, their meanings are similar but not identical. In (a): My brother had no choice. I insisted that he carry my suitcase. In (b): My brother carried my suitcase because I asked him to. In (c): I managed to persuade my brother to carry my suitcase.
FORMS X *makes* Y *do* something. (simple form) X *has* Y *do* something. (simple form) X *gets* Y *to do* something. (infinitive)	
CAUSATIVE *MAKE* (d) Mrs. Lee *made* her son *clean* his room. (e) Sad movies *make* me *cry*.	Causative *make* is followed by the simple form of a verb, not an infinitive. (*INCORRECT:* She made him *to clean* his room.) *Make* gives the idea that "X" **forces** "Y" to do something. In (d): Mrs. Lee's son had no choice.
CAUSATIVE *HAVE* (f) I *had* the plumber *repair* the leak. (g) Jane *had* the waiter *bring* her some tea.	Causative *have* is followed by the simple form of a verb, not an infinitive. (*INCORRECT:* I had him *to repair* the leak.) *Have* gives the idea that "X" **requests** "Y" to do something. In (f): The plumber repaired the leak because I asked him to.
CAUSATIVE *GET* (h) The students *got* the teacher *to dismiss* class early. (i) Jack *got* his friends *to play* soccer with him after school.	Causative *get* is followed by an infinitive. *Get* gives the idea that "X" **persuades** "Y" to do something. In (h): The students managed to persuade the teacher to let them leave early.
PASSIVE CAUSATIVES (j) I *had* my watch *repaired* (by someone). (k) I *got* my watch *repaired* (by someone).	The past participle is used after *have* and *get* to give a passive meaning. In this case, there is usually little or no difference in meaning between *have* and *get*. In (j) and (k): I caused my watch to be repaired by someone.

☐ **EXERCISE 18. Causative verbs. (Chart 15-9)**

Directions: Complete the sentences with the words in parentheses.

1. The doctor made the patient *(stay)* _____ stay _____ in bed.

2. Mrs. Crane had her house *(paint)* _____ painted _____ .

3. The teacher had the class *(write)* _____ a 2000-word research paper.

4. I made my son *(wash)* _____ the windows before he could go outside
   to play.

5. Kostas got some kids in the neighborhood *(clean)* _____ out his garage.

6. I went to the bank to have a check *(cash)* _____ .

7. Tom had a bad headache yesterday, so he got his twin brother, Tim, *(go)*
   _____ to class for him. The teacher didn't know the difference.

8. When Scott went shopping, he found a jacket that he really liked. After he had the
   sleeves *(shorten)* _____ , it fit him perfectly.

9. My boss made me *(redo)* _____ my report because he wasn't satisfied
   with it.

10. Alice stopped at the service station to have the tank *(fill)* _____ .

11. I got Rosa *(lend)* _____ me some money so I could go to a movie last
    night.

12. Mr. Fields went to a doctor to have a wart on his nose *(remove)* _____ .

13. I spilled some tomato sauce on my suit coat. Now I need
    to get my suit *(clean)* _____ .

14. Peeling onions always makes me *(cry)*
    _____ .

15. Tom Sawyer was supposed to paint the fence, but
    he didn't want to do it. He was a very clever boy.
    Somehow he got his friends *(do)*
    _____ it for him.

16. We had a professional photographer *(take)*
    _____ pictures of everyone
    who participated in our wedding.

☐ EXERCISE 19. Causative verbs. (Chart 15-9)
    Directions: Complete the sentences with verb phrases.

1. I got my friend _____ to translate a letter for me. _____

2. Sometimes parents make their children _____

3. When I was at the restaurant, I had the waiter _____

4. Many people take their cars to service stations to get the oil _____

5. Teachers sometimes have their students _____

6. I'm more than willing to help you _____

7. Before I left on my trip, I had the travel agent _____

8. My cousin's jokes always make me _____

9. When I was a child, my parents wouldn't let me _____

10. We finally got our landlady _____

☐ EXERCISE 20. Activity: causative verbs. (Chart 15-9)
    Directions: Answer the questions in complete sentences.

1. Who has had something fixed recently? What was it? Who fixed it? Where did you go to get it repaired?

2. What did your parents make you do when you were a child? What did they let you do? What did they help you do?

3. In one of the jobs you've held in the past, what did your boss have you do?

4. Have you persuaded someone to do something recently? What did you get him/her to do?

5. Where do you usually go to get . . .
    a. a check cashed?
    b. your clothes drycleaned?
    c. your laundry done?
    d. your blood pressure checked?
    e. your hair cut?

☐ EXERCISE 21. Error analysis: gerunds, infinitives, causatives. (Chapters 14 and 15)
    Directions: Correct the errors.

1. Stop tell me what to do! Let me to make up my own mind.

2. My English is pretty good, but sometimes I have trouble to understand lectures at school.

3. When I entered the room, I found my wife to cry over the broken vase that had belonged to her great-grandmother.

4. Sara is going to spend next year for studying Chinese at a university in Taiwan.

5. I went to the pharmacy for having my prescription to be filled.

6. You shouldn't let children playing with matches.

7. When I got home, Irene was lying in bed think about what a wonderful time she'd had.

8. When Shelley needed a passport photo, she had her picture taking by a professional photographer.

9. I've finally assembled enough information for beginning writing my thesis.

10. Omar is at the park right now. He is sit on a park bench watch the ducks swiming in the pond. The sad expression on his face makes me to feel sorry for him.

☐ EXERCISE 22. Review: verb forms. (Chapters 14 and 15)
Directions: Supply an appropriate form for each verb in parentheses.

1. As he contemplated the meaning of life, Edward stood on the beach *(look)* _____*looking*_____ out over the ocean.

2. It was a hot day, and the work was hard. I could feel sweat *(trickle)* _____ down my back.

3. It is foolish *(ignore)* _____ physical ailments.

4. You can lead a horse to water, but you can't make him *(drink)* _____ .

5. My cousins helped me *(move)* _____ into my new apartment.

6. I was tired, so I just watched them *(play)* _____ volleyball instead of *(join)* _____ them.

7. Many people think Mr. Peel will win the election. He has a good chance of *(elect)* _____ .

8. If you hear any news, I want *(tell)* _____ immediately.

9. Let's *(have)* _____ Ron and Maureen *(join)* _____ us for dinner tonight, okay?

10. I was getting sleepy, so I had my friend *(drive)* _____ the car.

11. We sat in his kitchen (sip) _____ very hot, strong tea and (eat) _____ chunks of hard cheese.

12. Emily stopped her car (let) _____ a black cat (run) _____ across the street.

13. He's a terrific soccer player! Did you see him (make) _____ that goal?

14. We spent the entire class period (talk) _____ about the revolution.

15. I don't like (force) _____
    (leave) _____ the room (study)
    _____ whenever my roommate feels
    like (have) _____ a party.

16. Yuko got along very well in France despite not (be)
    _____ able to speak French. She used
    English a lot.

17. He's at an awkward age. He's old enough (have)
    _____ adult problems but too young
    (know) _____ how (handle) _____
    _____ them.

18. (Look) _____ at the car after the accident made him (realize)
    _____ that he was indeed lucky (be) _____ alive.

19. I'm tired. I wouldn't mind just (stay) _____ home tonight and (get)
    _____ to bed early.

20. I don't anticipate (have) _____ any difficulties (adjust)
    _____ to a different culture when I go abroad.

☐ EXERCISE 23. Review: verb forms. (Chapters 14 and 15)
   Directions: Complete the sentence with an appropriate form of the verb in parentheses.

1. My children enjoy (allow) _____ to stay up late when there's something special on TV.

2. (Observe) _____ the sun (climb) _____ above the horizon at dawn makes one (realize) _____ the earth is indeed turning.

3. John admitted (surprise) _____ by the unexpected birthday party last night. We had a lot of fun (plan) _____ it.

4. I don't understand how you got the wrong results. When I look over your notes, your chemistry experiment seems *(perform)* _____ correctly. But something is wrong somewhere.

5. The witness to the murder asked not *(identify)* _____ in the newspaper. She wanted her name kept secret.

6. It is generally considered impolite *(pick)* _____ your teeth at the dinner table.

7. I don't recall *(meet)* _____ Mr. Tanaka before. I'm sure I haven't. I'd like *(introduce)* _____ to him. Would you do the honors?

8. Ed's boss recommended him for the job. Ed was pleased *(consider)* _____ _____ for the job even though he didn't get it.

9. I wasn't tired enough *(sleep)* _____ last night. For a long time, I just lay in bed *(think)* _____ about my career and my future.

10. It is the ancient task of the best artists among us *(force)* _____ us *(use)* _____ our ability *(feel)* _____ and *(share)* _____ _____ emotions.

11. Jeff applied to medical school many months ago. Now he's so concerned about *(accept)* _____ into medical school that he's having a difficult time *(concentrate)* _____ on the courses he's taking this term.

12. It may be impossible *(persuade)* _____ my mother *(give)* _____ _____ up her job even though she's having health problems. We can't even get her *(cut)* _____ down on her working hours. She enjoys *(work)* _____ so much that she refuses *(retire)* _____ and *(take)* _____ it easy. I admire her for *(dedicate)* _____ _____ to her work, but I also want her to take care of her health.

13. Traffic has become too heavy for the Steinbergs *(commute)* _____ easily to their jobs in the city. They're considering *(move)* _____ to an apartment close to their places of work. They don't want *(give)* _____ up their present home, but they need *(live)* _____ in the city *(be)* _____ closer to their work so they can spend more time *(do)* _____ the things they really enjoy *(do)* _____ in their free time.

14. Last week I was sick with the flu. It made me *(feel)* _____ awful. I

    didn't have enough energy *(get)* _____ out of bed. I just lay there

    (feel) _____ sorry for myself. When my father heard me *(sneeze)*

    _____ and *(cough)* _____, he opened my bedroom

    door *(ask)* _____ me if I needed anything. I was really happy *(see)*

    _____ his kind and caring face, but there wasn't anything he could do

    to make the flu *(go)* _____ away.

15. Fish don't use their teeth for *(chew)* _____. They use them for *(grab)*

    _____, *(hold)* _____, or *(tear)* _____.

    Most fish *(swallow)* _____ their prey whole.

16. I can't seem *(get)* _____ rid of the cockroaches in my apartment.

    Every night I see them *(run)* _____ all over my kitchen counters. It

    drives me crazy. I'm considering *(have)* _____ the whole apartment

    (spray) _____ by a professional pest control expert.

17. The employees were unhappy when the new management took over. They weren't

    accustomed to *(treat)* _____ disrespectfully by the managers of the

    production departments. By *(threaten)* _____ *(stop)* _____

    (work) _____, they got the company *(listen)* _____

    to their grievances. In the end, a strike was averted.

18. According to some estimates, well over half of the world's population is functionally

    illiterate. Imagine *(be)* _____ a parent with a sick child and *(be)*

    _____ unable to read the directions on a medicine bottle. We all know

    that it is important for medical directions *(understand)* _____

    clearly. Many medical professionals are working today *(bridge)* _____

    the literacy gap by *(teach)* _____ health care through pictures.

☐ EXERCISE 24. Error analysis: gerunds, infinitives, causatives. (Chapters 14 and 15)
Directions: Correct the errors.

1. My parents made me to promise to write them once a week.

2. I don't mind to have a roommate.

3. Most students want return home as soon as possible.

4. When I went to shopping last Saturday, I saw a man to drive his car onto the sidewalk.

5. I asked my roommate to let me to use his shoe polish.

6. To learn about another country it is very interesting.

7. I don't enjoy to play card games.

8. I heard a car door to open and closing.

9. I had my friend to lend me his car.

10. I tried very hard to don't make any mistakes.

11. You should visit my country. It is too beautiful.

12. The music director tapped his baton for beginning the rehearsal.

13. Some people prefer to save their money to spend it.

14. The task of find a person who could help us wasn't difficult.

15. All of us needed to went to the cashier's window.

16. I am looking forward to go to swim in the ocean.

17. When your planting a garden, it's important to be known about soils.

18. My mother always make me to be slow down if she think I am driving to fast.

19. One of our fights ended up with me having to sent to the hospital for getting stitches.

20. Please promise not telling anybody my secret.

21. I would appreciate having heard from you soon.

22. Maria has never complained about have a handicap.

23. Lillian deserves to be tell the truth about what happened last night.

24. Barbara always makes me laughing. She has a great sense of humor.

25. Ali no speak Spanish, and Juan not know Arabic. But they communicate well by speak English when they be together.

26. I enjoyed to talk to her on the phone. I look forward to see her next week.

27. During a fire drill, everyone is required leaving the building.

28. Ski in the Alps was a big thrill for me.

29. Don't keep to be asking me the same questions over and over.

30. When I entered the room, I found my young son stand on the kitchen table.

☐ **EXERCISE 25. Writing. (Chapters 14 and 15)**

Directions: Choose one to write about.

1. Write about your first day or week here (in this city/at this school/etc.). Did you have any unusual, funny, or difficult experiences? What were your first impressions and reactions? Whom did you meet?

2. Write about your childhood. What are some of the pleasant memories you have of your childhood? Do you have any unpleasant memories?

3. Whom do you like to spend some of your free time with? What do you enjoy doing together? Include an interesting experience the two of you have had.

☐ **EXERCISE 26. Writing. (Chapters 14 and 15)**

Directions: Write a composition for me, your reader, in which you explain exactly how to do something. Choose any topic that you know well. Assume that I know almost nothing about your topic. I have not had the experiences you have had. I don't know what you know. You must teach me. In your composition, use the words "I" and "you." Explain why/how you know about this topic. Address your information directly to your reader.

Possible topics:

How to: buy a used car
          travel to a particular place
          open a bank account
          get a job
          design a bridge
          plant a garden
          rent an apartment
          register at a hotel
          breed dairy cows
          interpret an X-ray
          change a flat tire
          play a guitar
          catch a fish

prepare a meal
write a story
paint a room
repair a car
study a language
organize a meeting
decorate a home
teach a class
maintain a farm
start a business
live abroad
play a game
take care of someone who has the flu

Example of an introductory paragraph:

    Have you ever thought about buying a used car? When I was in my late teens, I decided I had to have a car. I worked hard and saved my money. When the time came, I convinced my best friend to accompany me to a used car lot. I didn't really know what I was doing, so I knew I needed him to help me. When we got to the lot, the salesman had us look at lots of cars. Suddenly we came upon the car of my dreams: a small, black sports convertible. It was classy, comfortable, shiny, and it had leather seats, not to mention a powerful engine and lots of speed. My friend urged me to think it over, but I was so excited I handed the salesman my check for the first of many payments. Of course, I had no idea that the car was simply a beautiful pile of junk. I learned that later when everything started to go wrong with it. I'm older and wiser now, and even though I'm not an expert on automobiles, I'd like to share my experiences with you and discuss what you should consider before you buy a used car.

CHAPTER 16
Coordinating Conjunctions

16-1 PARALLEL STRUCTURE

One use of a conjunction is to connect words or phrases that have the same grammatical function in a sentence. This use of conjunctions is called "parallel structure." The conjunctions used in this pattern are **and**, **but**, **or**, **nor**. These words are called "coordinating conjunctions."

(a) *Steve* **and** his *friend* are coming to dinner.	In (a): *noun* + **and** + *noun*
(b) Susan *raised* her hand **and** *snapped* her fingers.	In (b): *verb* + **and** + *verb*
(c) He *is waving* his arms **and** *(is) shouting* at us.	In (c): *verb* + **and** + *verb* (The second auxiliary may be omitted if it is the same as the first auxiliary.)
(d) These shoes are *old* **but** *comfortable*.	In (d): *adjective* + **but** + *adjective*
(e) He wants *to watch* TV **or** *(to) listen* to some music.	In (e): *infinitive* + **or** + *infinitive* (The second **to** is usually omitted.)
(f) *Steve, Joe,* **and** *Alice* are coming to dinner.	A parallel structure may contain more than two parts. In a series, commas are used to separate each unit.
(g) Susan *raised* her hand, *snapped* her fingers, **and** *asked* a question.	The final comma that precedes the conjunction is optional; also correct: *Steve, Joe and Alice* are coming to dinner.
(h) The colors in that fabric are *red, gold, black,* **and** *green*.	
(i) INCORRECT: *Steve, and Joe* are coming to dinner.	Note: No commas are used if there are only two parts to a parallel structure.

☐ EXERCISE 1. Parallel structure. (Chart 16-1)
> *Directions:* <u>Underline</u> the parallel structure in each sentence and give the pattern that is used, as shown in the examples.

1. The old man is extremely <u>kind</u> and <u>generous</u>. <u>*adjective* + and + *adjective*</u>

2. He received a pocket <u>calculator</u> and a wool <u>sweater</u> for his birthday. <u>*noun* + and + *noun*</u>

3. She spoke angrily and bitterly about the war.   _____ + and +

4. I looked for my book but couldn't find it.   _____ + but +

5. I hope to go to that university and study under Dr. Liu.   _____ + and +

6. In my spare time, I enjoy reading novels or watching television.   _____ + or +

7. He will leave at eight and arrive at nine.   _____ + and +

8. He should have broken his engagement to Beth and married Sue instead.   _____ + and +

☐ EXERCISE 2. Parallel structure. (Chart 16-1)

Directions: Parallel structure makes repeating the same words unnecessary.★ Combine the given sentences into one concise sentence that contains parallel structure. Punctuate carefully.

1. Mary opened the door. Mary greeted her guests.
   → *Mary opened the door and greeted her guests.*
2. Mary is opening the door. Mary is greeting her guests.
3. Mary will open the door. Mary will greet her guests.
4. Alice is kind. Alice is generous. Alice is trustworthy.
5. Please try to speak more loudly. Please try to speak more clearly.
6. He gave her flowers on Sunday. He gave her candy on Monday. He gave her a ring on Tuesday.
7. While we were in New York, we attended an opera. While we were in New York, we ate at marvelous restaurants. While we were in New York, we visited some old friends.
8. He decided to quit school. He decided to go to California. He decided to find a job.
9. I am looking forward to going to Italy. I am looking forward to eating wonderful pasta every day.
10. I should have finished my homework. I should have cleaned up my room.
11. The boy was old enough to work. The boy was old enough to earn some money.
12. He preferred to play baseball. Or he preferred to spend his time in the streets with other boys.
13. I like coffee. I do not like tea.
    → *I like coffee but not tea.*★★
14. I have met his mother. I have not met his father.
15. Jake would like to live in Puerto Rico. He would not like to live in Iceland.

_____

★This form of parallel structure, in which unnecessary words are omitted but are understood, is called "ellipsis."

★★Sometimes a comma precedes **but not**: *I like coffee, but not tea.*

☐ EXERCISE 3. Parallel structure. (Chart 16-1)

Directions: In each group, complete the unfinished sentence. Then combine the sentences into one concise sentence that contains parallel structure. Punctuate carefully.

1. The country lane was narrow.
   The country lane was steep.
   The country lane was _____ muddy. _____
   _____ The country lane was narrow, steep, and muddy. _____

2. I like to become acquainted with the people of other countries.
   I like to become acquainted with the customs of other countries.

   I like to become acquainted with _____ of other countries.

   _____

3. I dislike living in a city because of the air pollution.
   I dislike living in a city because of the crime.

   I dislike living in a city because of _____

   _____

4. We discussed some of the social problems of the United States.
   We discussed some of the political problems of the United States.

   We discussed some of the _____ problems of the United States.

   _____

   _____

5. Hawaii has _____
   Hawaii has many interesting tropical trees.
   Hawaii has many interesting tropical flowers.
   Hawaii has beautiful beaches.

   _____

   _____

6. Mary Hart would make a good president because she _____
   Mary Hart would make a good president because she works effectively with others.
   Mary Hart would make a good president because she has a reputation for integrity.
   Mary Hart would make a good president because she has a reputation for independent thinking.

   _____

   _____

   _____

□ EXERCISE 4. Parallel structure. (Chart 16-1)
Directions: With your own words, complete each sentence, using parallel structure.

1. Judge Holmes served the people of this country with impartiality, ability, and
   ___integrity___.

2. Ms. Polanski has proven herself to be a sincere, hardworking, and
   _____ supervisor.

3. The professor walked through the door and _____.

4. I was listening to music and _____ when I heard a
   knock at the door.

5. I get up at seven every morning, eat a light breakfast, and _____.

6. _____ and attending concerts in the park are two
   of the things my wife and I like to do on summer weekends.

7. Our whole family enjoys camping. We especially enjoy fishing in mountain streams
   and _____.

8. Resolve to be tender with the young, compassionate with the aged, understanding of
   those who are wrong, and _____.
   Sometime in your life, you will have been all of these.

□ EXERCISE 5. Error analysis: parallel structure. (Chart 16-1)
Directions: Correct the errors.

1. By obeying the speed limit, we can save energy, lives, and it costs us less.

2. My home offers me a feeling of security, warm, and love.

3. The pioneers labored to clear away the forest and planting crops.

4. When I refused to help her, she became very angry and shout at me.

5. In my spare time, I enjoy taking care of my aquarium and to work on my stamp
   collection.

6. With their keen sight, fine hearing, and they have a refined sense of smell, wolves hunt
   elk, deer, moose, and caribou.

7. All plants need light, to have a suitable climate, and an ample supply of water and
   minerals from the soil.

8. Slowly and being cautious, the firefighter ascended the burned staircase.

9. The Indian cobra snake and the king cobra use poison from their fangs in two ways: by injecting it directly into their prey or they spit it into the eyes of the victim.

10. On my vacation I lost a suitcase, broke my glasses, and I missed my flight home.

11. When Anna moved, she had to rent an apartment, make new friends, and to find a job.

☐ **EXERCISE 6. Error analysis: parallel structure. (Chart 16-1)**
Directions: Correct the errors.

What do people in your country think of bats? Are they mean and scary creatures, or are they symbols of happiness and lucky?

In Western countries, many people have an unreasoned fear of bats. According to scientist Dr. Sharon Horowitz, bats are beneficial mammals and harmless. "When I was a child, I believed that a bat would attack me and tangled itself in my hair. Now I know better," said Dr. Horowitz.

Contrary to popular Western myths, bats do not attack humans and not blind. Although a few bats may be infected, they are not major carriers of rabies or carry other dread diseases. Bats help natural plant life by pollinating plants, spreading seeds, and they eat insects. If you get rid of bats that eat overripe fruit, then fruit flies can flourish and destroying the fruit industry.

According to Dr. Horowitz, bats make loving pets, and they are trainable, and are gentle pets. Not many people, however, are known to have bats as pets, and bats themselves prefer to avoid people.

16-2 PAIRED CONJUNCTIONS: *BOTH . . . AND; NOT ONLY . . . BUT ALSO; EITHER . . . OR; NEITHER . . . NOR*

(a) **Both** my mother **and** my sister **are** here.	Two subjects connected by **both . . . and** take a plural verb, as in (a).
(b) **Not only** my mother **but also** my sister **is** here. (c) **Not only** my sister **but also** my parents **are** here. (d) **Neither** my mother **nor** my sister **is** here. (e) **Neither** my sister **nor** my parents **are** here.	When two subjects are connected by **not only . . . but also**, **either . . . or**, or **neither . . . nor**, the subject that is closer to the verb determines whether the verb is singular or plural.
(f) The research project will take **both** *time* **and** *money*. (g) Yesterday it **not only** *rained* **but (also)** *snowed*. (h) I'll take **either** *chemistry* **or** *physics* next quarter. (i) That book is **neither** *interesting* **nor** *accurate*.	Notice the parallel structure in the examples. The same grammatical form should follow each part of the paired conjunctions.* In (f): **both** + *noun* + **and** + *noun* In (g): **not only** + *verb* + **but also** + *verb* In (h): **either** + *noun* + **or** + *noun* In (i): **neither** + *adjective* + **nor** + *adjective*

*Paired conjunctions are also called "correlative conjunctions."

☐ **EXERCISE 7. Paired conjunctions. (Chart 16-2)**
Directions: Add **is** or **are** to each sentence.

1. Both the teacher and the student ___*are*___ here.

2. Neither the teacher nor the student _____ here.

3. Not only the teacher but also the student _____ here.

4. Not only the teacher but also the students _____ here.

5. Either the students or the teacher _____ planning to come.

6. Either the teacher or the students _____ planning to come.

7. Both the students and the teachers _____ planning to come.

8. Both the students and the teacher _____ planning to come.

☐ **EXERCISE 8. Error analysis: paired conjunctions. (Chart 16-2)**
Directions: What is wrong with these sentences?

1. Either John will call Mary or Bob.

2. Not only Sue saw the mouse but also the cat.

3. Both my mother talked to the teacher and my father.

4. Either Mr. Anderson or Ms. Wiggins are going to teach our class today.

5. I enjoy not only reading novels but also magazines.

6. Oxygen is plentiful. Both air contains oxygen and water.

□ EXERCISE 9. Paired conjunctions. (Chart 16-2)

Directions: Answer the questions, using paired conjunctions. Work in pairs, in groups, or as a class.

PART I. Use **both . . . and**.
1. You have met his father. Have you met his mother?
   → *Yes, I have met both his father and his mother.*
2. The driver was injured in the accident. Was the passenger injured in the accident?
3. Wheat is grown in Kansas. Is corn grown in Kansas?
4. He buys used cars. Does he sell used cars?
5. You had lunch with your friends. Did you have dinner with them?
6. The city suffers from air pollution. Does it suffer from water pollution?

PART II. Use **not only . . . but also**.
7. I know you are studying math. Are you studying chemistry too?
   → *Yes, I'm studying not only math but also chemistry.*
8. I know his cousin is living with him. Is his mother-in-law living with him too?
9. I know your country has good universities. Does the United States have good universities too?
10. I know you lost your wallet. Did you lose your keys too?
11. I know she goes to school. Does she have a full-time job too?
12. I know he bought a coat. Did he buy a new pair of shoes too?

PART III. Use **either . . . or**.
13. Omar has your book, or Rosa has your book. Is that right?
    → *Yes, either Omar or Rosa has my book.*
14. You're going to give your friend a book for her birthday, or you're going to give her a pen. Is that right?
15. Your sister will meet you at the airport, or your brother will meet you there. Right?
16. They can go swimming, or they can play tennis. Is that right?
17. You're going to vote for Mr. Smith, or you're going to vote for Mr. Jones. Right?
18. You'll go to New Orleans for your vacation, or you'll go to Miami. Right?

PART IV. Use **neither . . . nor**.
19. He doesn't like coffee. Does he like tea?
    → *No, he likes neither coffee nor tea.*
20. Her husband doesn't speak English. Do her children speak English?
21. The students aren't wide awake today. Is the teacher wide awake today?
22. They don't have a refrigerator for their new apartment. Do they have a stove?
23. She doesn't enjoy hunting. Does she enjoy fishing?
24. The result wasn't good. Was the result bad?

Directions: Combine the following into sentences that contain parallel structure. Use ***both ... and; not only ... but also; either ... or; neither ... nor.***

1. He does not have a pen. He does not have paper.
   → *He has neither a pen nor paper.*
2. Ron enjoys horseback riding. Bob enjoys horseback riding.
3. You can have tea, or you can have coffee.
4. Arthur is not in class today. Ricardo is not in class today.
5. Arthur is absent. Ricardo is absent.
6. We can fix dinner for them here, or we can take them to a restaurant.
7. She wants to buy a Chevrolet, or she wants to buy a Toyota.
8. The leopard faces extinction. The tiger faces extinction.
9. The library doesn't have the book I need. The bookstore doesn't have the book I need.
10. We could fly, or we could take the train.
11. The president's assistant will not confirm the story. The president's assistant will not deny the story.
12. Coal is an irreplaceable natural resource. Oil is an irreplaceable natural resource.
13. Smallpox is a dangerous disease. Malaria is a dangerous disease.
14. Her roommates don't know where she is. Her brother doesn't know where she is.
15. According to the news report, it will snow tonight, or it will rain tonight.

16-3 COMBINING INDEPENDENT CLAUSES WITH COORDINATING CONJUNCTIONS

(a) It was raining hard. There was a strong wind. (b) INCORRECT PUNCTUATION: It was raining hard**,** there was a strong wind.	Example (a) contains two *independent clauses* (i.e., two complete sentences). Notice the punctuation. A period,* NOT A COMMA, is used to separate two independent clauses. The punctuation in (b) is not correct; the error in (b) is called "a run-on sentence."
(c) It was raining hard, *and* there was a strong wind. (d) It was raining hard *and* there was a strong wind. (e) It was raining hard. *And* there was a strong wind.	A *conjunction* may be used to connect two independent clauses. PUNCTUATION: Usually a comma immediately precedes the conjunction, as in (c). In short sentences, the comma is sometimes omitted, as in (d). In informal writing, a conjunction sometimes begins a sentence, as in (e).

(f) He was tired, *so* he went to bed.
 (g) The child hid behind his mother's skirt, *for* he was afraid of the dog.
 (h) She did not study, *yet* she passed the exam.
	In addition to ***and***, ***but***, ***or***, and ***nor***, other conjunctions are used to connect two independent clauses: ***so*** (meaning "therefore, as a result")
	      for (meaning "because")
	      yet (meaning "but, nevertheless")
	 A comma almost always precedes ***so***, ***for***, and ***yet*** when they are used as coordinating conjunctions.**

* In British English, a period is called "a full stop."

** ***So***, ***for***, and ***yet*** have other meanings in other structures: e.g., *He is not **so** tall as his brother.* (**so** = as) *We waited **for** the bus.* (**for** = a preposition) *She hasn't arrived **yet**.* (**yet** = an adverb meaning "up to this time")

☐ **EXERCISE 11. Combining independent clauses with coordinating conjunctions. (Chart 16-3)**

Directions: Punctuate the sentences by adding commas or periods. Do not add any words. Capitalize where necessary.

1. The boys walked the girls ran. → *The boys walked. The girls ran.*

2. The teacher lectured the students took notes.

3. The teacher lectured and the students took notes.

4. Elena came to the meeting but Pedro stayed home.

5. Elena came to the meeting her brother stayed home.

6. Her academic record was outstanding yet she was not accepted by the university.

7. I have not finished writing my term paper yet I will not be finished until sometime next week.

8. We had to go to the grocery store for some milk and bread.

9. We had to go to the grocery store for there was nothing in the house to fix for dinner.

10. Kostas didn't have enough money to buy an airplane ticket so he couldn't fly home for the holiday.

☐ **EXERCISE 12. Combining independent clauses with coordinating conjunctions. (Chart 16-3)**

Directions: Punctuate the sentences by adding commas or periods. Do not add any words. Capitalize where necessary.

1. A thermometer is used to measure temperature a barometer measures air pressure.

2. Daniel made many promises but he had no intention of keeping them.

3. I always enjoyed mathematics in high school so I decided to major in it in college.

4. Anna is in serious legal trouble for she had no car insurance at the time of the accident.

5. Last night Martha had to study for a test so she went to the library.

6. The ancient Egyptians had good dentists archaeologists have found mummies that had gold fillings in their teeth.

7. Both John and I had many errands to do yesterday John had to go to the post office and the bookstore I had to go to the post office the travel agency and the bank.

8. I did not like the leading actor yet the movie was quite good on the whole.

9. The team of researchers has not finished compiling the statistics yet their work will not be made public until later.

10. We have nothing to fear for our country is strong and united.

11. He slapped his desk in disgust he had failed another examination and had ruined his chances for a passing grade in the course.

12. I struggled to keep my head above water I tried to yell for help but no sound came from my mouth.

13. The earthquake was devastating tall buildings crumbled and fell to the earth.

14. It was a wonderful picnic the children waded in the stream collected rocks and insects and flew kites the teenagers played an enthusiastic game of baseball the adults busied themselves preparing the food supervising the children and playing a game or two of volleyball.

15. Some people collect butterflies for a hobby these collectors capture them with a net and put them in a jar that has poison in it the dead butterflies are then mounted on a board.

16. Caterpillars eat plants and cause damage to some crops but adult butterflies feed principally on nectar from flowers and do not cause any harm.

17. The butterfly is a marvel it begins as an ugly caterpillar and turns into a work of art.

18. The sight of a butterfly floating from flower to flower on a warm sunny day brightens anyone's heart a butterfly is a charming and gentle creature.

19. When cold weather comes some butterflies travel great distances to reach tropical climates.*

20. Butterflies are admired throughout the world because they are beautiful they can be found on every continent except Antarctica.*

---

*See Chart 5-1, p. 70, for ways to punctuate sentences that contain adverb clauses.

□ EXERCISE 13. Writing. (Chapter 16)

Directions: Write two descriptive paragraphs on one of the topics below. The first paragraph should be a draft, and the second should be a "tightened" revision of the first. Look for places where two or three sentences can be combined into one by using parallel structure. Pay special attention to punctuation, and be sure all of your commas and periods are used correctly.

Topics:

1. Give a physical description of your place of residence (apartment, dorm room, etc.)
2. Describe the characteristics and activities of a successful student.
3. Give your reader directions for making a particular food dish.

Example:

FIRST DRAFT

To make spaghetti sauce, you will need several ingredients. First, you will need some ground beef. Probably about one pound of ground beef will be sufficient. You should also have an onion. If the onions are small, you should use two. Also, find a green pepper and put it in the sauce. Of course, you will also need some tomato sauce or tomatoes.

REVISION

To make spaghetti sauce you will need one pound of ground beef, one large or two small onions, a green pepper, and some tomato sauce or tomatoes.

CHAPTER 17
Adverb Clauses

CONTENTS

17-1 INTRODUCTION

(a) *When we were in New York,* we saw several plays. (b) We saw several plays *when we were in New York*.	*When we were in New York* is an adverb clause. PUNCTUATION: When an adverb clause precedes an independent clause, as in (a), a comma is used to separate the clauses. When the adverb clause follows, as in (b), usually no comma is used.
(c) *Because he was sleepy,* he went to bed. (d) He went to bed *because he was sleepy*.	Like *when*, *because* introduces an adverb clause. *Because he was sleepy* is an adverb clause.
(e) INCORRECT: *When we were in New York. We saw several plays.* (f) INCORRECT: *He went to bed. Because he was sleepy.*	Adverb clauses are dependent clauses. They cannot stand alone as a sentence in written English. They must be connected to an independent clause.*

SUMMARY LIST OF WORDS USED TO INTRODUCE ADVERB CLAUSES**

TIME		CAUSE AND EFFECT	CONTRAST	CONDITION
after	*by the time (that)*	*because*	*even though*	*if*
before	*once*	*now that*	*although*	*unless*
when	*as/so long as*	*since*	*though*	*only if*
while	*whenever*			*whether or not*
as	*every time (that)*		DIRECT CONTRAST	*even if*
as soon as	*the first time (that)*		*while*	*in case*
since	*the last time (that)*		*whereas*	*in the event that*
until	*the next time (that)*			

*See Chart 13-1, p. 267, for the definition of dependent and independent clauses.

**Words that introduce adverb clauses are called "subordinating conjunctions."

□ **EXERCISE 1. Adverb clauses. (Chart 17-1)**

Directions: Add periods, commas, and capitalization. Do not change, add, or omit any words. <u>Underline</u> each adverb clause. (NOTE: Item 12 contains an adjective clause. Item 13 contains an adjective clause and a noun clause. Can you find these other dependent clauses?)

1. Sue was in the other room when the phone rang as soon as she heard it she ran to the front room to answer it.

    → *Sue was in the other room <u>when the phone rang</u>.* **As** <u>soon as she heard it</u> *, she ran to the front room to answer it.*

2. When it began to rain he closed the windows.

3. He closed the windows when it began to rain.

4. As soon as the rain began the children wanted to go outdoors they love to play outside in the warm summer rain I used to do the same thing when I was a child.

5. Jack got to the airport early after he checked in at the airline counter he went to the waiting area near his gate he sat and read until his flight was announced.

6. Jack walked onto the plane found his seat and stowed his bag in an overhead compartment.

7. Before the plane took off he fastened his seat belt and put his seat in an upright position.

8. Jack's wife doesn't like to fly because she gets nervous on airplanes.

9. When Jack and his wife go on vacation they have to drive or take the train because his wife is afraid of flying.

10. I had a cup of tea before I left for work this morning but I didn't have anything to eat I rarely eat breakfast.

11. After Ellen gets home from work she likes to read the newspaper she follows the same routine every day after work as soon as she gets home she changes her clothes gets a snack and a drink and sits down in her favorite chair to read the newspaper in peace and quiet she usually has about half an hour to read the paper before her husband arrives home from his job.

12. When you speak to someone who is hard of hearing you do not have to shout it is important to face the person directly and speak clearly my elderly father is hard of hearing but he can understand me if I face him speak slowly and say each word clearly.

13. Greg Adams has been blind since he was two years old today he is a key scientist in a computer company he is able to design complex electronic equipment because he has a special computer that reads writes and speaks out loud his blindness neither helps nor hinders him it is irrelevant to how well he does his job.

☐ EXERCISE 2. Review of adverb clauses of time. (Chapter 5 and Chart 17-1)
Directions: Complete the sentences. Punctuate carefully. Pay special attention to verb tense usage.

1. Since I came to . . . .
2. Just as I was falling asleep last night . . . .
3. I'll help you with your homework as soon as I . . . .
4. I was late. By the time I got to the airport . . . .
5. One of my friends gets nervous every time . . . .
6. I will be here until I . . . .
7. . . . as long as I live.
8. I heard . . . while I . . . .
9. Once summer/winter comes . . . .
10. Shortly before I . . . .
11. I have been in . . . for . . . . By the time I leave, I . . . .
12. The last time I . . . .
13. The next time you . . . .
14. I . . . just as soon as . . . .
15. Not long after I . . . .
16. I had already . . . when . . . .
17. Whenever . . . .
18. Ever since . . . .

17-2 USING ADVERB CLAUSES TO SHOW CAUSE AND EFFECT

because	(a) *Because he was sleepy,* he went to bed. (b) He went to bed *because he was sleepy.*	An adverb clause may precede or follow the independent clause. Notice the punctuation in (a) and (b).
now that	(c) *Now that the semester is over,* I'm going to rest a few days and then take a trip. (d) Jack lost his job. *Now that he's unemployed,* he can't pay his bills.	***Now that*** means "because now." In (c): *Now that the semester is over* means "because the semester is now over." ***Now that*** is used for present causes of present or future situations.
since	(e) *Since Monday is a holiday,* we don't have to go to work. (f) *Since you're a good cook and I'm not,* you should cook the dinner.	When ***since*** is used to mean "because," it expresses a known cause; it means "because it is a fact that" or "given that it is true that." Cause and effect sentences with ***since*** say: "Given the fact that X is true, Y is the result." In (e): "Given the fact that Monday is a holiday, we don't have to go to work." Note: ***Since*** has two meanings. One is "because." It is also used in time clauses: e.g., *Since I came here, I have met many people.* See Chart 5-2, p. 72.

☐ EXERCISE 3. Using adverb clauses to show cause and effect. (Chart 17-2)
Directions: Combine the sentences, using the word or phrase in parentheses. Add commas where necessary.

1. We can go swimming every day. The weather is warm. *(now that)*
   → *We can go swimming every day now that the weather is warm.*

2. All of the students had done poorly on the test. The teacher decided to give it again. *(since)*
   → *Since all of the students had done poorly on the test, the teacher decided to give it again.*

3. Cold air hovers near the earth. It is heavier than hot air. *(because)*

4. You paid for the theater tickets. Please let me pay for our dinner. *(since)*

5. Larry is finally caught up on his work. He can start his vacation tomorrow. *(now that)*

6. Our TV set was broken. We listened to the news on the radio. *(because)*

7. My brother got married last month. He's a married man now, so he has more responsibilities. *(now that)*

8. Oil is an irreplaceable natural resource. We must do whatever we can in order to conserve it. *(since)*

9. Do you want to go for a walk? The rain has stopped. *(now that)*

10. Many young people move to the cities in search of employment. There are few jobs available in the rural areas. *(since)*

11. The civil war has ended. A new government is being formed. *(now that)*

12. Ninety-two thousand people already have reservations with an airline company for a trip to the moon. I doubt that I'll get the chance to go on one of the first tourist flights. *(since)*

☐ EXERCISE 4. Using adverb clauses to show cause and effect. (Chart 17-2)
  Directions: Complete the sentences. Punctuate carefully.

1. Now that I've finally finished . . . .
2. The teacher didn't . . . because . . . .
3. Since it's too expensive to . . . .
4. Jack can't stay out all night with his friends now that . . . .
5. Since we don't have class tomorrow . . . .

17-3 EXPRESSING CONTRAST (UNEXPECTED RESULT): USING *EVEN THOUGH*

(a) ***Because*** the weather was cold, I *didn't go* swimming.	***Because*** is used to express expected results.
(b) ***Even though*** the weather was cold, I *went* swimming.	***Even though*** is used to express unexpected results.
(c) ***Because*** I wasn't tired, I *didn't go* to bed.	Note: Like ***because***, ***even though*** introduces an adverb clause.
(d) ***Even though*** I wasn't tired, I *went* to bed.	

☐ EXERCISE 5. Using EVEN THOUGH. (Chart 17-3)
 Directions: Complete the sentences by using either *even though* or *because*.

1. Tim's in good shape physically _____*even though*_____ he doesn't get much exercise.

2. Larry's in good shape physically _____*because*_____ he gets a lot of exercise.

3. I put on my sunglasses _____ it was a dark, cloudy day.

4. I put on my sunglasses _____ the sun was bright.

5. _____ Maria has a job, she doesn't make enough money to support her four children.

6. _____ Anna has a job, she is able to pay her rent and provide food for her family.

7. Susan didn't learn Spanish _____ she lived in Mexico for a year.

8. Joe speaks Spanish well _____ he lived in Mexico for a year.

9. Jing-Won jumped into the river to rescue the little girl who was drowning _____ he wasn't a good swimmer.

10. A newborn kangaroo can find its mother's pouch _____ its eyes are not yet open.

11. Some people protest certain commercial fishing operations _____ dolphins, considered to be highly intelligent mammals, are killed unnecessarily.

12. _____ the earthquake damaged the bridge across Skunk River, the Smiths were able to cross the river _____ they had a boat.

☐ EXERCISE 6. Using EVEN THOUGH. (Chart 17-3)
 Directions: Work in pairs, in groups, or as a class.
 Speaker A: Your book is open. Give Student B the cues in the text.
 Speaker B: Your book is closed. Answer each question by using a sentence with *even though*. Begin your response with either *yes* or *no*.

Examples:
SPEAKER A *(book open):* It was raining. Did you go to the zoo anyway?
SPEAKER B *(book closed):* Yes, even though it was raining, I went to the zoo.

SPEAKER A *(book open):* You studied hard. Did you pass the test?
SPEAKER B *(book closed):* No, even though I studied hard, I didn't pass the test.

1. You weren't tired. Did you go to bed anyway?
2. The telephone rang many times, but did . . . wake up?
3. The food was terrible. Did you eat it anyway?
4. You didn't study. Did you pass the test anyway?

5. The weather is terrible today. Did you stay home?
6. You fell down the stairs. Did you get hurt?
7. You took a nap. Do you still feel tired?

(Switch roles if working in pairs.)
8. You told the truth, but did anyone believe you?
9. You turned on the air conditioner. Is it still hot in here?
10. You mailed the letter three days ago. Has it arrived yet?
11. You have a lot of money. Can you afford to buy an airplane?
12. Your grandmother is ninety years old. Is she still young at heart?
13. (. . .) told a joke. You didn't understand it. Did you laugh anyway?
14. Your house burned down. You lost your job. Your wife/husband left you. Are you still cheerful?

☐ EXERCISE 7. Using EVEN THOUGH and BECAUSE. (Charts 17-2 and 17-3)
Directions: Write sentences that include the verbs in parentheses. Use any verb tense or modal.

1. Because the bus drivers went on strike, I *(walk)* ___had to walk___ all the way home.

2. Even though I was dead tired, I *(walk)* ___walked___ all the way home.

3. Because _____, I *(go)* _____ fishing.

4. Even though _____, I *(go)* _____ fishing.

5. Even though there *(be)* _____ very few customers in the store,

_____

6. Because there *(be)* _____ very few customers in the store,

_____

7. I *(wear)* _____ heavy gloves because _____

8. Even though my feet *(be)* _____ killing me and my head *(be)* _____ pounding, I _____

9. Even though _____, I *(get, not)* _____ a traffic ticket.

10. Even though I *(be)* _____ tired, I _____

because _____

11. Even though _____ when _____,

I _____ because _____

12. Because _____ while _____, I

_____ even though _____

17-4 SHOWING DIRECT CONTRAST: *WHILE* AND *WHEREAS*

(a) Mary is rich, ***while*** *John is poor.* (b) John is poor, ***while*** *Mary is rich.* (c) Mary is rich, ***whereas*** *John is poor.* (d) ***Whereas*** *Mary is rich,* John is poor.	***While*** and ***whereas*** are used to show direct contrast: "this" is exactly the opposite of "that." ***While*** and ***whereas*** may be used with the idea of either clause with no difference in meaning. ***Whereas*** mostly occurs in formal written English. Note: A comma is usually used even if the adverb clause comes second.
COMPARE (e) ***While*** *I was studying,* the phone rang.	***While*** is also used in time clauses and means "during the time that," as in (e). See Chart 5-2, p. 72.

☐ EXERCISE 8. Using WHILE and WHEREAS. (Chart 17-4)
Directions: Choose the best completion.

1. Some people are tall, whereas others are __C__ .
   A. intelligent
   B. thin
   C. short
   D. large

2. A box is square, whereas _____ .
   A. a rectangle has four sides
   B. my village has a town square in the center
   C. we use envelopes for letters
   D. a circle is round

3. While some parts of the world get an abundance of rain, others _____ .
   A. are warm and humid
   B. are cold and wet
   C. get little or none
   D. get a lot

4. In some nations the favorite beverage is coffee, while _____ .
   A. I like tea
   B. it has caffeine
   C. in others it is tea
   D. tea has caffeine too

5. Some people like cream and sugar in their coffee, while _____ .
   A. others drink hot coffee
   B. others like it black
   C. milk is good in coffee, too
   D. sugar can cause cavities

6. Jack is an interesting storyteller and conversationalist, whereas his brother _____ .
   A. is a newspaper reporter
   B. bores other people by talking about himself all the time
   C. has four children
   D. knows a lot of stories, too

☐ EXERCISE 9. Using WHILE and WHEREAS. (Chart 17-4)
Directions: Complete the sentences. Discuss other ways of expressing the same idea by moving the position of ***while*** or ***whereas***.

1. Some people are fat, whereas . . .
   → *Some people are fat, whereas others are thin.*
   → *Whereas some people are fat, others are thin.*
   → *Some people are thin, whereas others are fat.*

2. Some people are tall, whereas . . . .

3. Some people prefer to live in the country, while . . . .

4. While some people know only their native language . . . .

5. A mouse is small, whereas . . . .

6. The climate at sea level at the equator is always hot, whereas the climate at the North

and South poles . . . .

7. Some people . . . , while . . . .

8. Some countries . . . , whereas . . . .

17-5 EXPRESSING CONDITIONS IN ADVERB CLAUSES: *IF*-CLAUSES

(a) *If it rains*, the streets get wet.	*If*-clauses (also called "adverb clauses of condition") present possible conditions. The main clause expresses results. In (a): POSSIBLE CONDITION = *it rains* RESULT = *the streets get wet*
(b) *If it **rains** tomorrow*, I will take my umbrella.	A present tense, not a future tense, is used in an *if*-clause even though the verb in the *if*-clause may refer to a future event or situation, as in (b).*

WORDS THAT INTRODUCE ADVERB CLAUSES OF CONDITION (*IF*-CLAUSES)		
if *whether or not* *even if*	*in case* *in the event that*	*unless* *only if*

*See Chapter 20 for uses of other verb forms in sentences with *if*-clauses.

☐ EXERCISE 10. IF-clauses. (Chart 17-5)
   Directions: Make sentences from the given possibilities. Use *if*.

1. It may be cold tomorrow.
   → *If it's cold tomorrow, I'm going to stay home.*
   → *If it's cold tomorrow, let's go skating.*
   → *If it's cold tomorrow, you should wear your wool sweater.*
   → *We can't go on a picnic if it's cold tomorrow.*

2. Maybe it will be hot tomorrow.

3. Maybe you will have some free time tomorrow.

4. Maybe you will lock yourself out of your apartment.

5. Maybe the sun will be shining when you get up tomorrow morning.

6. You will probably be too tired to finish your work today.

7. You might not have enough money to take your trip next month.

8. We might continue to destroy our environment.

17-6 ADVERB CLAUSES OF CONDITION: USING *WHETHER OR NOT* AND *EVEN IF*

WHETHER OR NOT	
(a) I'm going to go swimming tomorrow *whether or not it is cold*. (OR: *whether it is cold or not*.)	***Whether or not*** expresses the idea that neither this condition nor that condition matters; the result will be the same. In (a): "If it is cold, I'm going swimming. If it is not cold, I'm going swimming. I don't care about the temperature. It doesn't matter."
EVEN IF	
(b) I have decided to go swimming tomorrow. *Even if the weather is cold*, I'm going to go swimming.	Sentences with ***even if*** are close in meaning to those with ***whether or not***. ***Even if*** gives the idea that a particular condition does not matter. The result will not change.

☐ EXERCISE 11. Using WHETHER OR NOT and EVEN IF. (Chart 17-6)
   Directions: Use the given information to complete the sentences.

1. *Usually people need to graduate from school to get a good job. But it's different for Ed. Maybe Ed will graduate from school, and maybe he won't. It doesn't matter because he has a good job waiting for him in his father's business.*

   a. Ed will get a good job whether or not . . . *he graduates.*
   b. Ed will get a good job even if . . . *he doesn't graduate.*

2. *Sam's uncle tells a lot of jokes. Sometimes they're funny, and sometimes they're not. It doesn't matter.*

   a. Sam laughs at the jokes whether . . . or not.
   b. Sam laughs at the jokes even if . . . .

3. *Maybe you are finished with the exam, and maybe you're not. It doesn't matter. The time is up.*

   a. You have to hand in your examination paper whether . . . or not.
   b. You have to hand in your examination paper even if . . . .

4. *It might snow, or it might not. We don't want to go camping in the snow, but it doesn't matter.*

   a. We're going to go camping in the mountains whether . . . or not.
   b. We're going to go camping in the mountains even if . . . .

5. *Max's family doesn't have enough money to send him to college. He would like to get a scholarship, but it doesn't matter because he's saved some money to go to school and has a part-time job.*

   a. Max can go to school whether or not . . . .
   b. Max can go to school even if . . . .

6. *Sometimes the weather is hot, and sometimes the weather is cold. It doesn't matter. My grandfather always wears his gray sweater.*

   a. My grandfather wears his gray sweater whether or not . . . .
   b. My grandfather always wears his gray sweater even if . . . .

7. *Your approval doesn't matter to me.*

   a. I'm going to marry Harry whether . . . or not.
   b. I'm going to marry Harry even if . . . .

☐ **EXERCISE 12. Using WHETHER OR NOT and EVEN IF.** (Chart 17-6)

Directions: Complete the sentences with your own words.

Examples: Even if . . . , I'm not going to go.
→ *Even if I get an invitation to the reception, I'm not going to go.*

. . . whether I feel better or not.
→ *I have to go to work tomorrow whether I feel better or not.*

1. . . . even if the weather improves.
2. Even if . . . , Maria may lose her job.
3. Getting that job depends on whether or not . . . .
4. . . . whether you want me to or not.
5. I won't tell you even if . . . .
6. I'm really angry! Maybe he'll apologize, and maybe he won't. It doesn't matter. Even if . . . , I won't forgive him!
7. I'm exhausted. Please don't wake me up even if . . . .
8. I'm not going to . . . even if . . . .
9. Even if . . . , I'm going to . . . .
10. I'm going to . . . whether . . . or not.

17-7 ADVERB CLAUSES OF CONDITION: USING *IN CASE* AND *IN THE EVENT THAT*

(a) I'll be at my uncle's house *in case* you (should) *need to reach me.*	*In case* and *in the event that* express the idea that something probably won't happen, but it might. *In case/in the event that* means "if by chance this should happen."
(b) *In the event that* you (should) *need to reach me,* I'll be at my uncle's house.	Notes: *In the event that* is more formal than *in case*. The use of *should* in the adverb clause emphasizes the speaker's uncertainty that something will happen.

☐ **EXERCISE 13. Using IN CASE and IN THE EVENT THAT.** (Chart 17-7)

Directions: Show the relationship between the ideas in the two sentences by using *in case* and/or *in the event that*.

1. You probably won't need to get in touch with me, but maybe you will. If so, I'll give you my phone number.
   → *I'll give you my phone number in case you (should) need to get in touch with me/in the event that you (should) need to get in touch with me.*
2. You probably won't need to see me, but maybe you will. If so, I'll be in my office tomorrow morning around ten.
3. I don't think you need any more information, but maybe you do. If so, you can call me.
4. You probably don't have any more questions, but maybe you do. If so, ask Dr. Smith.
5. Jack probably won't call, but maybe he will. If so, please tell him that I'm at the library.

6. You will probably be satisfied with your purchase, but maybe not. If not, you can return it to the store.

Complete the following.

7. I've told you all I know. In the event that you need more information, ...

8. It's a good idea for you to keep a written record of your credit card numbers in case . . . .

9. I think I'd better clean up the apartment in case . . . .

10. I have my umbrella with me just in case . . . .

11. In the event that the two countries agree to a peace treaty, ...

12. I'll try to be there on time, but in case I'm not, ...

13. According to the manufacturer's guarantee, I should return my new camera to the factory in the event that . . . .

17-8 ADVERB CLAUSES OF CONDITION: USING *UNLESS*

(a) I'll go swimming tomorrow *unless* it's cold. (b) I'll go swimming tomorrow *if* it isn't cold.	*unless* = *if . . . not* In (a): *unless it's cold* means "if it isn't cold." (a) and (b) have the same meaning.

☐ EXERCISE 14. Using UNLESS. (Chart 17-8)
Directions: Make sentences with the same meaning by using *unless*.

1. I will go to the zoo if it isn't cold.
   → *I will go to the zoo unless it's cold.*

2. You can't travel abroad if you don't have a passport.

3. You can't get a driver's license if you're not at least sixteen years old.

4. If I don't get some film, I won't be able to take pictures when Ann and Rob get here.

5. You'll get hungry during class if you don't eat breakfast.

□ EXERCISE 15. Using UNLESS. (Chart 17-8)
    Directions: Complete the sentences.

1. Your letter won't be delivered unless . . . .
   → *Your letter won't be delivered unless it has the correct postage.*
2. I'm sorry, but you can't see the doctor unless . . . .
3. I can't graduate from school unless . . . .
4. . . . unless you put it in the refrigerator.
5. Unless it rains, ...
6. Certain species of animals will soon become extinct unless . . . .
7. . . . unless I get a raise in salary.
8. Tomorrow I'm going to . . . unless . . . .
9. The political situation in . . . will continue to deteriorate unless . . . .
10. Ivan never volunteers in class. He doesn't say anything unless . . . .
11. Unless you . . . .

17-9 ADVERB CLAUSES OF CONDITION: USING *ONLY IF*

(a) The picnic will be canceled *only if* it rains.
    If it's windy, we'll go on the picnic.
    If it's cold, we'll go on the picnic.
    If it's damp and foggy, we'll go on the picnic.
    If it's unbearably hot, we'll go on the picnic.
	Only if expresses the idea that there is only one condition that will cause a particular result.

(b) *Only if* it rains *will the picnic be canceled.*	When *only if* begins a sentence, the subject and verb of the main clause are inverted, as in (b).* No commas are used.

*Other subordinating conjunctions and prepositional phrases fronted by *only* at the beginning of a sentence require subject-verb inversion in the main clause:
    Only when the teacher dismisses us *can we stand* and *leave* the room.
    Only after the phone rang *did I realize* that I had fallen asleep in my chair.
    Only in my hometown *do I feel* at ease.

□ EXERCISE 16. Using ONLY IF. (Chart 17-9)
    Directions: Use the given information to complete the sentences.

1. John must get a scholarship in order to go to school. That is the only condition under which he can go to school. If he doesn't get one, he can't go to school.
   He can go to school only if . . . he gets a scholarship.

2. You have to have an invitation in order to go to the party. That is the only condition under which you will be admitted. If you don't have an invitation, you can't go.
   You can go to the party only if . . . .

3. You have to have a student visa in order to study here. Unless you have a student visa, you can't go to school here.
   You can attend this school only if . . . .

4. Jimmy's mother doesn't want him to chew gum, but sometimes he chews it anyway.
   Jimmy . . . only if he's sure his mother won't find out.

5. If you want to go to the movie, we'll go. If you don't want to go, we won't go.
We . . . only if you want to.

6. The temperature has to reach 32°F / 0°C before water will freeze.
Water will freeze only if . . . .

7. You must study hard. Then you will pass the exam.
Only if you study hard . . . .

8. You have to have a ticket. Then you can get into the soccer stadium.
Only if you have a ticket . . . .

9. My parents make Jake finish his homework before he can watch TV in the evening.
Only if Jake's homework is finished . . . .

10. I have to get a job. Then I will have enough money to go to school.
Only if I get a job . . . .

Complete the following.

11. Yes, John, I will marry you—but only if . . . .

12. I . . . . only if . . . .

13. Only if . . . .

☐ **EXERCISE 17. Using UNLESS and ONLY IF.** (Charts 17-8 and 17-9)
Directions: Create sentences with the same meaning as the given ones. Use ***only if*** and ***unless***.

1. If you don't study hard, you won't pass the test.
   → *You will pass the test only if you study hard.*
   → *You won't pass the test unless you study hard.*
2. If I don't get a job, I can't pay my bills.
3. Your clothes won't get clean if you don't use soap.
4. I can't take any pictures if I don't buy some film.
5. I don't wake up if the alarm clock doesn't ring.
6. If eggs aren't kept at the proper temperature, they won't hatch.
7. Don't borrow money from friends if you don't absolutely have to.
8. Anita doesn't talk in class if the teacher doesn't ask her specific questions.

☐ **EXERCISE 18. Adverb clauses of condition.** (Charts 17-6 → 17-9)
Directions: Using the given words, combine the following two ideas.

It may or may not rain. The party will be held inside/outside.

1. if → *If it rains, the party will be held inside.*
   → *If it doesn't rain, the party will be held outside.*

2. whether or not   5. in the event that
3. even if   6. unless
4. in case   7. only if

☐ EXERCISE 19. Activity: adverb clauses. (Chapter 17)

Directions: Work in pairs.
Speaker A: Your book is open. Say the given words, then add your own words to complete the adverb clause (but do not complete the whole sentence).
Speaker B: Your book is closed. Complete Speaker A's sentence.

Example: Although I . . . .
SPEAKER A *(book open):* Although I wanted to go to the park and fly a kite . . . .
SPEAKER B *(book closed):* Although I wanted to go to the park and fly a kite, I went to my English class because I really need to improve my English.

1. Even if I . . . .
2. Because I . . . .
3. By the time I . . . .
4. Even though I . . . .
5. The next time I . . . .
6. Until I . . . .
7. Every time I . . . .

Switch roles.

8. In the event that you . . . .
9. Unless I . . . .
10. Since I . . . .
11. Only if I . . . .
12. Now that I . . . .
13. While some people are . . . .
14. While I was walking . . . .

CHAPTER 18

Reduction of Adverb Clauses to Modifying Adverbial Phrases

CONTENTS

18-1 INTRODUCTION

(a) ADVERB CLAUSE:	*While **I was walking** to class,* I ran into an old friend.	In Chapter 13, we discussed changing adjective clauses to modifying phrases (see Chart 13-13, p. 286). Some adverb clauses may also be changed to modifying phrases, and the ways in which the changes are made are the same:
(b) MODIFYING PHRASE:	*While **walking** to class,* I ran into an old friend.	
(c) ADVERB CLAUSE:	*Before **I left** for work,* I ate breakfast.	1. Omit the subject of the dependent clause and the **be** form of the verb, as in (b). OR
(d) MODIFYING PHRASE:	*Before **leaving** for work,* I ate breakfast.	2. If there is no **be** form of a verb, omit the subject and change the verb to **-ing**, as in (d).
(e) CHANGE POSSIBLE:	*While **I** was sitting in class, **I**** fell asleep.* *While sitting in class, **I** fell asleep.*	An adverb clause can be changed to a modifying phrase **only when the subject of the adverb clause and the subject of the main clause are the same**. A *modifying adverbial phrase* that is the reduction of an adverb clause *modifies the subject* of the main clause.
(f) CHANGE POSSIBLE:	*While **Ann** was sitting in class, **she** fell asleep. (clause)* *While sitting in class, **Ann** fell asleep.*	
(g) NO CHANGE POSSIBLE:	*While **the teacher** was lecturing to the class, **I** fell asleep.★*	No reduction (i.e., change) is possible if the subjects of the adverb clause and the main clause are different, as in (g) and (h).
(h) NO CHANGE POSSIBLE:	*While **we** were walking home, **a frog** hopped across the road in front of us.*	
(i) *INCORRECT:*	*While walking home, a frog hopped across the road in front of us.*	In (i): *While walking home* is called a "dangling modifier" or a "dangling participle," i.e., a modifier that is incorrectly "hanging alone" without an appropriate noun or pronoun subject to modify.
(j) *INCORRECT:*	*While watching TV last night, the phone rang.*	

★*While lecturing to the class, I fell asleep* means "While **I** was lecturing to the class, **I** fell asleep."

18-2 CHANGING TIME CLAUSES TO MODIFYING ADVERBIAL PHRASES

(a) CLAUSE: *Since Maria came to this country,* she has made many friends. (b) PHRASE: *Since coming to this country,* Maria has made many friends.	Adverb clauses beginning with *after*, *before*, *while*, and *since* can be changed to modifying adverbial phrases.
(c) CLAUSE: *After he (had) finished his homework,* Peter went to bed. (d) PHRASE: *After finishing his homework,* Peter went to bed. (e) PHRASE: *After having finished his homework,* Peter went to bed.	In (c): There is no difference in meaning between *After he finished* and *After he had finished*. (See Chart 3-3, p. 45.) In (d) and (e): There is no difference in meaning between *After finishing* and *After having finished*.
(f) PHRASE: Peter went to bed *after finishing his homework*.	A modifying adverbial phrase may follow the main clause, as in (f).

☐ **EXERCISE 1. Changing time clauses to modifying adverbial phrases.**
        (Charts 18-1 and 18-2)
    Directions: Underline the subject of the adverb clause and the subject of the main clause. Change the adverb clauses to modifying adverbial phrases if possible.

1. While Joe was driving to school yesterday, he had an accident.
    → *While driving to school yesterday, Joe had an accident.*

2. While Joe was watching TV last night, the telephone rang. *(no change)*

3. Before I came to class, I had a cup of coffee.

4. Before the student came to class, the teacher had already given a quiz.

5. Since I came here, I have learned a lot of English.

6. Since Bob opened his new business, he has been working 16 hours a day.

7. After Omar (had) finished breakfast, he left the house and went to his office.

8. Alex hurt his back while he was chopping wood.

9. You should always read a contract before you sign your name.

10. Before the waiter came to our table, I had already made up my mind to order shrimp.

11. Before you ask the librarian for help, you should make every effort to find the materials yourself.

12. While Jack was trying to sleep last night, a mosquito kept buzzing in his ear.

13. While Susan was climbing the mountain, she lost her footing and fell onto a ledge several feet below.

14. The Wilsons have experienced many changes in their lifestyle since they adopted twins.

15. After I heard Mary describe how cold it gets in Minnesota in the winter, I decided not to go there for my vacation in January.

18-3 EXPRESSING THE IDEA OF "DURING THE SAME TIME" IN MODIFYING ADVERBIAL PHRASES

(a) *While I was walking* down the street, *I* ran into an old friend. (b) *While walking* down the street, *I* ran into an old friend. (c) *Walking* down the street, *I* ran into an old friend. (d) *Hiking* through the woods yesterday, *we* saw a bear. (e) *Pointing* to the sentence on the board, *the teacher* explained the meaning of modifying phrases.	Sometimes *while* is omitted but the *-ing* phrase at the beginning of the sentence gives the same meaning (i.e., "during the same time"). (a), (b), and (c) have the same meaning.

18-4 EXPRESSING CAUSE AND EFFECT IN MODIFYING ADVERBIAL PHRASES

(f) *Because she needed* some money to buy a book, *Sue* cashed a check. (g) *Needing* some money to buy a book, *Sue* cashed a check. (h) *Because he lacked* the necessary qualifications, *he* was not considered for the job. (i) *Lacking* the necessary qualifications, *he* was not considered for the job.	Often an *-ing* phrase at the beginning of a sentence gives the meaning of "because." (f) and (g) have the same meaning. *Because* is not included in a modifying phrase. It is omitted, but the resulting phrase expresses a cause and effect relationship, as in (g) and (i).
(j) *Having seen* that movie before, *I don't want* to go again. (k) *Having seen* that movie before, *I didn't want* to go again.	*Having* + *past participle* gives the meaning not only of "because" but also of "before."
(l) *Because she was unable* to afford a car, *she* bought a bicycle. (m) *Being unable* to afford a car, *she* bought a bicycle. (n) *Unable* to afford a car, *she* bought a bicycle.	A form of *be* in the adverb clause may be changed to *being*. The use of *being* makes the cause and effect relationship clear. (l), (m), and (n) have the same meaning.

☐ EXERCISE 2. Modifying adverbial phrases. (Charts 18-3 and 18-4)

Directions: Discuss the meaning of these sentences. Which ones give the meaning of *because?* Which ones give the meaning of *while?* Do some of the sentences give the idea of both *because* and *while?*

1. Sitting on the airplane and watching the clouds pass beneath me, I let my thoughts wander to the new experiences that were in store for me during the next two years of living abroad.

2. Being a self-supporting widow with three children, she has no choice but to work.

3. Lying on her bed in peace and quiet, she soon forgot her troubles.

4. Having already spent all of his last paycheck, he does not have any money to live on for the rest of the month.

5. Watching the children's energetic play, I felt like an old man even though I am only forty.

6. Having brought up ten children of their own, the Smiths may be considered experts on child behavior.

7. Being totally surprised by his proposal of marriage, Carol could not find the words to reply.

8. Driving to my grandparents' house last night, we saw a young woman who was selling flowers. We stopped so that we could buy some for my grandmother.

9. Struggling against fatigue, I forced myself to put one foot in front of the other.

10. Having guessed at the correct answers for a good part of the test, I did not expect to get a high score.

11. Realizing that I had made a dreadful mistake when I introduced him as George Johnson, I walked over to him and apologized. I know his name is John George.

12. Tapping his fingers loudly on the desk top, he made his impatience and dissatisfaction known.

☐ **EXERCISE 3. Modifying adverbial phrases. (Chart 18-4)**
Directions: Change the adverb clauses to modifying adverbial phrases.

1. Because Sam didn't want to hurt her feelings, he didn't tell her the bad news.
   → *Not wanting to hurt her feelings, Sam didn't tell her the bad news.*

2. Because the little boy believed that no one loved him, he ran away from home.

3. Because she was not paying attention to where she was going, Rosa stepped into a hole and sprained her ankle.

4. Because I had forgotten to bring a pencil to the examination, I had to borrow one.

5. Because Chelsea is a vegetarian, she does not eat meat.

6. Because he has already flunked out of school once, Mike is determined to succeed this time.

☐ **EXERCISE 4. Modifying adverbial phrases. (Charts 18-2 → 18-4)**
Directions: Change the adverb clauses to modifying adverbial phrases.

1. Before I talked to you, I had never understood that formula.

2. Because he did not want to spend any more money this month, Larry decided against going to a restaurant for dinner. He made himself a sandwich instead.

3. After I read the chapter four times, I finally understood the author's theory.

4. Because I remembered that everyone makes mistakes, I softened my view of his seemingly inexcusable error.

5. Since he completed his Bachelor's degree, he has had three jobs, each one better than the last.

6. While I was traveling across the United States, I could not help being impressed by the great differences in terrain.

7. Before he gained national fame, the union leader had been an electrician in a small town.

8. Because we were enjoying the cool evening breeze and listening to the sounds of nature, we lost track of time.

9. Because she had never flown in an airplane before, the little girl was surprised and a little frightened when her ears popped.

10. Before he became vice-president of marketing and sales, Peter McKay worked as a sales representative.

□ EXERCISE 5. Modifying adverbial phrases. (Charts 18-3 and 18-4)
Directions: Combine the two sentences, making a modifying phrase out of the first sentence if possible.

1. The children had nothing to do. They were bored.
   → *Having nothing to do, the children were bored.*
2. I heard that Nadia was in the hospital. I called her family to find out what was wrong.
3. We slowly approached the door to the hospital. The nurse stepped out to greet us.
4. I live a long distance from my work. I have to commute daily by train.
5. Heidi lives a long distance from her work. She has to commute daily by train.
6. Abdul lives a long distance from his work. His car is essential.
7. I did not want to inconvenience my friend by asking her to drive me to the airport. I decided to take a taxi.
8. I was sitting on a large rock at the edge of a mountain stream. I felt at peace with the world.
9. I am a married man. I have many responsibilities.
10. The little boy was trying his best not to cry. He swallowed hard and began to speak.
11. Anna kept one hand on the steering wheel. She opened a can of soda pop with her free hand.
12. Anna kept one hand on the steering wheel. Bob handed her a can of pop to hold in the other hand.
13. I recognized his face, but I had forgotten his name. I just smiled and said, "Hi."
14. Martha was picking strawberries in the garden. A bumblebee stung her.
15. Ann was convinced that she could never learn to play the piano. She stopped taking lessons.

□ EXERCISE 6. Modifying adverbial phrases. (Charts 18-3 and 18-4)
Directions: Make sentences by combining the ideas in Column A and Column B. Use the idea in Column A as a modifying adverbial phrase. Show logical relationships.

Examples:

Column A	**Column B**
1. She was looking in the want ads in the Sunday newspaper.	A. Mary has a lot of responsibilities.
2. She had grown up overseas.	B. Ann found a good used car at a price she could afford to pay.
3. She is the vice-president of a large company.	C. Alice enjoys trying foods from other countries.

→ 1. *Looking in the want ads in the Sunday newspaper, Ann found a good used car at a price she could afford to pay.*

→ 2. *Having grown up overseas, Alice enjoys trying foods from other countries.*

→ 3. *Being the vice-president of a large company, Mary has a lot of responsibilities.*

Column A	Column B
1. They have sticky pads on their feet.	A. Sally didn't know what to expect when she went to the Thai restaurant for dinner.
2. He has worked with computers for many years.	B. Mice can hide in almost any part of a house.
3. She was born two months prematurely.	C. Rhinos are protected by law from poachers who kill them solely for their horns.
4. He had done everything he could for the patient.	D. The doctor left to attend other people.
5. She had never eaten Thai food before.	E. Nancy expects to be hired by a top company after graduation.
6. He had no one to turn to for help.	F. Diamonds are used extensively in industry to cut other hard minerals.
7. They are endangered species.	G. Flies can easily walk on the ceiling.
8. They are able to crawl into very small places.	H. Sam was forced to work out the problem by himself.
9. She has done very well in her studies.	I. Mary needed special care for the first few days of her life.
10. They are extremely hard and nearly indestructible.	J. Ed has an excellent understanding of their limitations as well as their potential.

☐ EXERCISE 7. Modifying adverbial phrases. (Charts 18-1 → 18-4)

Directions: Some (but not all) of the sentences contain DANGLING MODIFIERS (i.e., incorrectly used modifying adverbial phrases). Correct these errors.

1. After leaving the theater, we stopped at a coffee shop for a late night snack. *(no change)*

2. After leaving the theater, Tom's car wouldn't start, so we had to take a taxi home.

 → *After we left the theater, Tom's car wouldn't start, so we had to take a taxi home.*

 → *After leaving the theater, we discovered that Tom's car wouldn't start, so we took a taxi home.*

3. Not wanting to interrupt the conversation, I stood quietly and listened until I could have a chance to talk.

4. Being too young to understand death, my mother gave me a simple explanation of where my grandfather had gone.

5. When asked to explain his mistake, the new employee cleared his throat nervously.

6. While working in my office late last night, someone suddenly knocked loudly at my door and nearly scared me to death!

7. After hurrying to get everything ready for the picnic, it began to rain just as we were leaving.

8. While walking across the street at a busy intersection, a truck nearly ran over my foot.

18-5 USING *UPON + -ING* IN MODIFYING ADVERBIAL PHRASES

(a) *Upon reaching* the age of 21, I received my inheritance. (b) *When I reached* the age of 21, I received my inheritance.	Modifying adverbial phrases beginning with *upon + -ing* usually have the same meaning as adverb clauses introduced by *when*. (a) and (b) have the same meaning.
(c) *On reaching* the age of 21, I received my inheritance.	*Upon* can be shortened to *on*. (a), (b), and (c) all have the same meaning.

☐ **EXERCISE 8. Using UPON + -ING. (Chart 18-5)**

Directions: Using the given information, make sentences with *upon + -ing*.

1. When Tom saw his wife and child get off the airplane, he broke into a big smile.
   → *Upon seeing his wife and child get off the airplane, Tom broke into a big smile.*

2. When Tina crossed the marathon finish line, she fell in exhaustion.

3. When I looked in my wallet, I discovered I didn't have enough money to pay my restaurant bill.

4. I bowed my head when I met the king.

5. When Sam re-read the figures, he found that he had made a mistake.

6. The small child reached toward the lighted candle. When he discovered it was hot, he jerked his hand back, held it in front of himself, and stared at it curiously. Then he began to scream.

7. Mrs. Alexander nearly fainted when she learned that she had won the lottery.

8. When you finish the examination, bring your paper to the front of the room.

9. There must have been 300 students in the room on the first day of class. The professor slowly read through the list of names. When I heard my name, I raised my hand to identify myself.

10. Captain Cook had been sailing for many weeks with no land in sight. Finally, one of the sailors shouted, "Land ho!" When he heard this, Cook grabbed his telescope and searched the horizon.

☐ **EXERCISE 9. Review: modifying adverbial phrases. (Chapter 18)**

Directions: Change the adverb clause in each sentence to a modifying adverbial phrase if possible. Make any necessary changes in punctuation, capitalization, or word order.

1. After it spends some time in a cocoon, a caterpillar will emerge as a butterfly.

    → *After spending some time in a cocoon, a caterpillar will emerge as a butterfly.*

2. When the movie started, it suddenly got very quiet inside the theater. *(no change)*

3. When we entered the theater, we handed the usher our tickets.

    → *Upon entering the theater, we handed the usher our tickets.*

4. Because I was unprepared for the test, I didn't do well.

    → *Being unprepared for the test, I didn't do well.* OR: *Unprepared for the test, I didn't do well.*

5. Before I left on my trip, I checked to see what shots I would need.

6. Since Indians in the high Andes Mountains live in thin air, their hearts grow to be a larger than average size.

7. Because I hadn't understood the directions, I got lost.

8. My father reluctantly agreed to let me attend the game after he had talked it over with my mother.

9. When I discovered I had lost my key to the apartment, I called the building superintendent.

10. Jane's family hasn't received any news from her since she arrived in Australia two weeks ago.

11. Garcia Lopez de Cardenas accidentally discovered the Grand Canyon while he was looking for the legendary Lost City of Gold.

12. Because the forest area is so dry this summer, it is prohibited to light campfires.

13. After we had to wait for more than half an hour, we were finally seated at the restaurant.

14. Before Maria got accepted on her country's Olympic running team, she had spent most of the two previous years in training.

15. Because George wasn't paying attention to his driving, he didn't see the large truck until it was almost too late.

□ EXERCISE 10. Review: modifying adverbial phrases. (Chapter 18)

Directions: <u>Underline</u> the adverb clauses in the following. Change the adverb clauses to adverb phrases if possible. Make any necessary changes in punctuation, capitalization, or word order.

1.   Alexander Graham Bell, a teacher of the deaf in Boston, invented the first telephone. One day in 1875, <u>while ~~he was~~ running a test on his latest attempt to create a machine</u> that could carry voices, he accidentally spilled acid on his coat. Naturally, he called for his assistant, Thomas A. Watson, who was in another room. Bell said, "Mr. Watson, come here. I want you." When Watson heard words coming from the machine, he immediately realized that their experiments had at last been successful. He rushed excitedly into the other room to tell Bell that he had heard his words over the machine.

After Bell had successfully tested the new apparatus again and again, he confidently announced his invention to the world. For the most part, scientists appreciated his accomplishment, but the general public did not understand the revolutionary nature of Bell's invention. Because they believed the telephone was a toy with little practical application, most people paid little attention to Bell's announcement.

2.   Wolves are much misunderstood animals. Because many people believe that wolves eagerly kill human beings, they fear them. However, the truth is that wolves avoid any contact with human beings. Wildlife biologists in the United States say there is no documented case of wolves attacking humans in the lower 48 states. More people are hurt and killed by buffaloes in Yellowstone Park than have ever been hurt by wolves in North America.

Because they are strictly carnivorous, wolves hunt large animals such as elk and deer, as well as their mainstay, small animals such as mice and rabbits. And they are particularly fond of sheep. Killing ranchers' livestock has helped lead to wolves' bad reputation among people.

Because it was relentlessly poisoned, trapped, and shot by ranchers and hunters, the timber wolf, a subspecies of the gray wolf, was eradicated in the lower 48 states by the 1940s. Not one wolf remained. In the 1970s, after they realized a mistake had been made, U.S. lawmakers passed laws to protect wolves.

Long ago, wolves could be found in almost all areas of the Northern Hemisphere throughout Asia, Europe, and North America. Today, after they have been unremittingly destroyed for centuries, they are found in few places, principally in sparsely populated areas of Alaska, Minnesota, Canada, and the northernmost regions of Russia and China.

□ EXERCISE 11. Review: modifying adverbial phrases. (Chapter 18)
Directions: Complete the sentences. Punctuate carefully.

1. After having finished my . . . .
2. Before going to . . . .
3. Since coming to . . . .
4. Sitting in the park the other day . . . .
5. Having heard a strange noise in the other room . . . .
6. Being new on the job . . . .
7. Being the largest city in the United States . . . .
8. Upon reaching our destination . . . .
9. Receiving no answer when he knocked on the door . . . .
10. Exhausted by the long hours of work . . . .

Directions: Correct the errors.

1. I was very tired, go to bed.

    → *I was very tired, so I went to bed.* OR: *I was very tired and went to bed.*

2. Because our leader could not attend the meeting, so it was canceled.

3. I and my wife likes to travel.

4. I always fasten my seat belt before to start the engine.

5. I don't like our classroom. Because it is hot and crowded. I hope we can change to a different room.

6. The day was very warm and humid, for that I turned on the air conditioner.

7. Upon I learned that my car couldn't be repaired for three days, I am very distressed.

8. Having missed the final examination because, the teacher gave me a failing grade.

9. Both my sister and my brother is going to be at the family reunion.

10. I hope my son will remain in school until he will finish his degree.

11. My brother has succeeded in business because of he works hard.

12. Luis stood up, turned toward me, and speaking so softly that I couldn't hear what he said.

13. I was lost. I could not find my parents neither my brother.

14. Having studied Greek for several years, Sarah's pronunciation was easy to understand.

CHAPTER 19
Connectives That Express Cause and Effect, Contrast, and Condition

CONTENTS

☐ **EXERCISE 1. Preview. (Charts 19-1 → 19-3)**
Directions: Correct the errors.

1. Because of Rosa's computer skills were poor she was not considered for the job.

2. Rosa's computer skills were poor therefore she was not considered for the job.

3. Because Rosa's computer skills were poor, therefore she was not considered for the job.

4. Because Rosa's computer skills were poor, so she was not considered for the job.

5. Due to her poor computer skills, Rosa was not considered for the job therefore.

6. Consequently Rosa's computer skills were poor, she was not considered for the job.

19-1 USING *BECAUSE OF* AND *DUE TO*

(a) *Because the weather was cold,* we stayed home.	*Because* introduces an adverb clause; it is followed by a subject and verb, as in (a).
(b) *Because of the cold weather,* we stayed home. (c) *Due to the cold weather,* we stayed home.	*Because of* and *due to* are phrasal prepositions; they are followed by a noun object, as in (b) and (c).
(d) *Due to the fact that the weather was cold,* we stayed home.	Sometimes, usually in more formal writing, *due to* is followed by a noun clause introduced by *the fact that*.
(e) We stayed home *because of the cold weather.* We stayed home *due to the cold weather.* We stayed home *due to the fact that the weather was cold.*	Like adverb clauses, these phrases can also follow the main clause, as in (e).

☐ EXERCISE 2. Using BECAUSE and BECAUSE OF. (Charts 17-2 and 19-1)
  Directions: Complete the sentences with either *because* or *because of*.

  1. We postponed our trip ___because of___ the bad driving conditions.

  2. Sue's eyes were red ___because___ she had been swimming in a chlorinated pool.

  3. We can't visit the museum tomorrow _____ it isn't open.

  4. Jim had to give up jogging _____ his sprained ankle.

  5. _____ heavy fog at the airport, we had to stay in London an extra day.

  6. _____ the elevator was broken, we had to walk up six flights of stairs.

  7. Thousands of Irish people emigrated to the United States _____ the potato famine in Ireland in the mid-19th century.

  8. The young couple decided not to buy the house _____ its dilapidated condition.

☐ EXERCISE 3. Using BECAUSE OF and DUE TO. (Chart 19-1)
  Directions: Using the ideas given in parentheses, complete the sentences.

  1. *(Our parents are generous.)* Because of ___our parents' generosity___, all of the children in our family have received the best of everything.

  2. *(The traffic was heavy.)* We were late to the meeting due to _____ _____ .

3. *(Bill's wife is ill.)* Bill has to do all of the cooking and cleaning because of

   _____ .

4. *(Dr. Robinson has done excellent research on wolves.)* Due to _____

   _____ , we know much more

   today about that endangered species than we did even five years ago.

5. *(It was noisy in the next apartment.)* I couldn't get to sleep last night because of

   _____ .

6. *(Circumstances are beyond my control.)* Due to _____

   _____ , I regret to say that I cannot be present at your daughter's

   wedding.

19-2 USING TRANSITIONS TO SHOW CAUSE AND EFFECT: *THEREFORE* AND *CONSEQUENTLY*

(a) Al failed the test because he didn't study. (b) Al didn't study. ***Therefore,*** he failed the test. (c) Al didn't study. ***Consequently,*** he failed the test.	(a), (b), and (c) have the same meaning. ***Therefore*** and ***consequently*** mean "as a result." In grammar, they are called *transitions* (or *conjunctive adverbs)*. Transitions connect the ideas between two sentences.

(d) Al didn't study. ***Therefore,*** he failed the test.
(e) Al didn't study. He, ***therefore,*** failed the test.
(f) Al didn't study. He failed the test, ***therefore.***
 	
POSITIONS OF A TRANSITION
    transition + s + v (+ rest of sentence)
    s + *transition* + v (+ rest of sentence)
    s + v (+ rest of sentence) + *transition*
	A transition occurs in the second of two related sentences. Notice the patterns and punctuation in the examples. A period (NOT a comma) is used at the end of the first sentence.* The transition has several positions in the second sentence. The transition is separated from the rest of the sentence by commas.

(g) Al didn't study, *so* he failed the test.	COMPARE: A *transition* (e.g., ***therefore***) has several possible positions within the second sentence of the pair, as in (d), (e), and (f). A *conjunction* (e.g., ***so***) has only one possible position: between the two sentences. (See Chart 16-3, p. 355.) ***So*** cannot move around in the second sentence as ***therefore*** can.

*A semicolon is also possible in this situation. See the footnote to Chart 19-3, p. 389.

☐ EXERCISE 4. Using THEREFORE and CONSEQUENTLY. (Chart 19-2)
    Directions: Restate the sentences, using the given transitions. Use three alternative positions for the transitions, as shown in Chart 19-2. Punctuate carefully.

    1. The children stayed home because a storm was approaching. *(therefore)*

        _____

        _____

        _____

2. I didn't have my umbrella, so I got wet. *(consequently)*

_____

_____

_____

☐ EXERCISE 5. Showing cause and effect. (Charts 16-3, 17-2, 19-1, and 19-2)
Directions: Punctuate the sentences. Add capital letters if necessary.

    1. *adverb clause:*   Because it was cold she wore a coat.

    2. *adverb clause:*   She wore a coat because it was cold.

    3. *prepositional phrase:*   Because of the cold weather she wore a coat.

    4. *prepositional phrase:*   She wore a coat because of the cold weather.

    5. *transition:*   The weather was cold therefore she wore a coat.

    6. *transition:*   The weather was cold she therefore wore a coat.

    7. *transition:*   The weather was cold she wore a coat therefore.

    8. *conjunction:*   The weather was cold so she wore a coat.

☐ EXERCISE 6. Showing cause and effect. (Charts 17-2, 19-1, and 19-2)
Directions: Punctuate the sentences. Add capital letters if necessary.

    1. Pat always enjoyed studying sciences in high school therefore she decided to major in biology in college.

    2. Due to recent improvements in the economy fewer people are unemployed.

    3. Last night's storm damaged the power lines consequently the town was without electricity for several hours.

    4. Because of the snowstorm only five students came to class the teacher therefore canceled the class.

    5. Anna always makes numerous spelling mistakes in her compositions because she does not use a dictionary when she writes.

19-3   SUMMARY OF PATTERNS AND PUNCTUATION

ADVERB CLAUSE	(a) **Because** it was hot, we went swimming. (b) We went swimming **because** it was hot.	An *adverb clause* may precede or follow an independent clause. PUNCTUATION: A comma is used if the adverb clause comes first.
PREPOSITION	(c) **Because of** the hot weather, we went swimming. (d) We went swimming **because of** the hot weather.	A *preposition* is followed by a noun object, not by a subject and verb. PUNCTUATION: A comma is usually used if the prepositional phrase precedes the subject and verb of the independent clause.
TRANSITION	(e) It was hot. ***Therefore,*** *we went swimming.* (f) It was hot. *We,* ***therefore,*** *went swimming.* (g) It was hot. *We went swimming,* ***therefore.***	A *transition* is used with the second sentence of a pair. It shows the relationship of the second idea to the first idea. A transition is movable within the second sentence. PUNCTUATION: A period is used between the two independent clauses.* A comma may NOT be used to separate the clauses. Commas are usually used to set the transition off from the rest of the sentence.
CONJUNCTION	(h) It was hot, *so we went swimming.*	A conjunction comes between two independent clauses. PUNCTUATION: Usually a comma is used immediately in front of a conjunction.

*A semicolon (;) may be used instead of a period between the two independent clauses.
> *It was hot; therefore, we went swimming.*
> *It was hot; we, therefore, went swimming.*
> *It was hot; we went swimming, therefore.*

In general, a semicolon can be used instead of a period between any two sentences that are closely related in meaning.
Example: *Peanuts are not nuts; they are beans.* Notice that a small letter, not a capital letter, immediately follows a semicolon.

☐ EXERCISE 7. Showing cause and effect. (Chart 19-3)
> *Directions:* Using the given words, combine the two ideas.

PART I. **We postponed our trip. The weather was bad.**

1. because   → *We postponed our trip because the weather was bad.*
   → *Because the weather was bad, we postponed our trip.*

2. therefore   5. because of
3. since   6. consequently
4. so   7. due to (the fact that)

PART II. **She missed class. She was ill.**

1. because of   4. so
2. because   5. due to (the fact that)
3. consequently   6. therefore

☐ **EXERCISE 8. Showing cause and effect. (Charts 19-2 and 19-3)**

Directions: Combine ideas, using the words in parentheses.

1. We stayed home. The weather was bad. *(because)*

   → *We stayed home because the weather was bad.* OR
   → *Because the weather was bad, we stayed home.*

2. Emily has never wanted to return to the Yukon to live. The winters are too severe. *(because of)*

3. It is important to wear a hat on cold days. We lose sixty percent of our body heat through our head. *(since)*

4. When I was in my teens and twenties, it was easy for me to get into an argument with my father. Both of us can be stubborn and opinionated. *(for)*

5. A camel can go completely without water for eight to ten days. It is an ideal animal for desert areas. *(due to the fact that)*

6. Bill couldn't pick us up after the concert. His car wouldn't start. *(therefore)*

7. Robert had to ask many of the same questions again the next time he talked to the travel agent. He did not pay close attention to what she said when he went to see her at her office last week. *(so)*

8. A tomato is classified as a fruit, but most people consider it a vegetable. It is often eaten in salads along with lettuce, onions, cucumbers, and other vegetables. *(since)*

9. There is consumer demand for ivory. Many African elephants are being slaughtered ruthlessly. Many people who care about saving these animals from extinction refuse to buy any item made from ivory. *(due to, consequently)*

10. Most 15th-century Europeans believed the world was flat and that a ship could conceivably sail off the end of the earth. Many sailors of the time refused to venture forth with explorers into unknown waters. *(because)*

19-4 OTHER WAYS OF EXPRESSING CAUSE AND EFFECT: *SUCH . . . THAT* AND *SO . . . THAT*

(a) Because the weather was nice, we went to the zoo. (b) It was *such nice weather that* we went to the zoo. (c) The weather was *so nice that* we went to the zoo.	Examples (a), (b), and (c) have the same meaning.
(d) It was *such good coffee that* I had another cup. (e) It was *such a foggy day that* we couldn't see the road.	*Such . . . that* encloses a modified noun: *such* + *adjective* + *noun* + *that*
(f) The coffee is *so hot that* I can't drink it. (g) I'm *so hungry that* I could eat a horse. (h) She speaks *so fast that* I can't understand her. (i) He walked *so quickly that* I couldn't keep up with him.	*So . . . that* encloses an adjective or adverb: *so* + { *adjective* or *adverb* } + *that*
(j) She made *so many mistakes that* she failed the exam. (k) He has *so few friends that* he is always lonely. (l) She has *so much money that* she can buy whatever she wants. (m) He had *so little trouble* with the test *that* he left twenty minutes early.	*So . . . that* is used with *many*, *few*, *much*, and *little*.
(n) It was *such a good book* *(that)* I couldn't put it down. (o) I was *so hungry* *(that)* I didn't wait for dinner to eat something.	Sometimes, primarily in speaking, *that* is omitted.

☐ **EXERCISE 9. Using SUCH . . . THAT and SO . . . THAT. (Chart 19-4)**
Directions: Combine the sentences by using *so . . . that* or *such . . . that*.

1. This tea is good. I think I'll have another cup.
   → *This tea is so good that I think I'll have another cup.*

2. This is good tea. I think I'll have another cup.
   → *This is such good tea that I think I'll have another cup.*

3. It was an expensive car. We couldn't afford to buy it.

4. The car was expensive. We couldn't afford to buy it.

5. The weather was hot. You could fry an egg on the sidewalk.

6. During the summer, we had hot and humid weather. It was uncomfortable just sitting in a chair doing nothing.

7. I don't feel like going to work. We're having beautiful weather.

8. Ivan takes everything in life too seriously. He is unable to experience the small joys and pleasures of daily living.

9. I've met too many people in the last few days. I can't possibly remember all of their names.

10. Tommy ate too much candy. He got a stomachache.

11. It took us only ten minutes to get there. There was little traffic.

12. In some countries, few students are accepted by the universities. As a result, admission is virtually a guarantee of a good job upon graduation.

☐ EXERCISE 10. Using SUCH . . . THAT and SO . . . THAT. (Chart 19-4)
Directions: Make sentences using *such* or *so* by combining the ideas in Column A and Column B.

Example: The wind was strong. → *The wind was so strong that it blew my hat off my head.*

Column A
1. The wind was strong.
2. Karen is a good pianist.
3. The radio was too loud.
4. Small animals in the forest move about quickly.
5. Olga did poor work.
6. The food was too hot.
7. There are many leaves on a single tree.
8. The tornado struck with great force.
9. Grandpa held me tightly when he hugged me.
10. Few students showed up for class.
11. Sally used too much paper when she was writing her report.

Column B
A. It burned my tongue.
B. She was fired from her job.
✔ C. It blew my hat off my head.
D. The teacher postponed the test.
E. It is impossible to count them.
F. It lifted automobiles off the ground.
G. I couldn't hear what Michael was saying.
H. I'm surprised she didn't go into music professionally.
I. The wastepaper basket overflowed.
J. One can barely catch a glimpse of them.
K. I couldn't breathe for a moment.

☐ EXERCISE 11. Using SO . . . THAT. (Chart 19-4)
Directions: Work in pairs, in groups, or as a class.
Speaker A: Your book is open. Give the cue and engage Speaker B in conversation.
Speaker B: Your book is closed. Answer the *how*-question using *so . . . that*.

Example: Think of a time you were tired. How tired were you?
SPEAKER A: Think of a time you were very tired. Can you remember one particular time?
SPEAKER B: There was one time when I'd stayed up all night writing a paper.
SPEAKER A: And you were very tired the next morning, right? How tired were you?
SPEAKER B: I was so tired that I almost fell asleep in my morning classes.

Think of a time you were
1. . . . nervous. How nervous were you?
2. . . . angry. How angry were you?
3. . . . happy. How happy were you?
4. . . . surprised. How surprised were you?
5. . . . exhausted. How exhausted were you?
6. . . . unhappy/embarrassed/glad/sick/sad/ frightened/excited/disappointed/etc.

19-5 EXPRESSING PURPOSE: USING *SO THAT*

(a) I turned off the TV *in order to* enable my roommate to study in peace and quiet.	*In order to* expresses *purpose*. (See Chart 15-1, p. 326.) In (a): I turned off the TV for a purpose. The purpose was to make it possible for my roommate to study in peace and quiet.
(b) I turned off the TV *so (that)* my roommate could study in peace and quiet.	*So that* also expresses *purpose*.* It expresses the same meaning as *in order to*. The word "that" is often omitted, especially in speaking.
SO THAT + *CAN* or *COULD* (c) I'm going to cash a check *so that I can* buy my textbooks. (d) I cashed a check *so that I could* buy my textbooks.	*So that* is often used instead of *in order to* when the idea of ability is being expressed. *Can* is used in the adverb clause for a present/future meaning. In (c): *so that I can buy* = in order to be able to buy. *Could* is used after *so that* in past sentences.**
SO THAT + *WILL* /SIMPLE PRESENT or *WOULD* (e) I'll take my umbrella *so that I won't* get wet. (f) I'll take my umbrella *so that I don't* get wet. (g) Yesterday I took my umbrella *so that I wouldn't* get wet.	In (e): *so that I won't get wet* = in order to make sure that I won't get wet. In (f): It is sometimes possible to use the simple present after *so that* in place of *will;* the simple present expresses a future meaning. *Would* is used in past sentences; as in (g).

*NOTE: *In order that* has the same meaning as *so that* but is less commonly used.
   Example: *I turned off the TV in order that my roommate could study in peace and quiet.*
   Both *so that* and *in order that* introduce adverb clauses. It is unusual, but possible, to put these adverb clauses at the beginning of a sentence: *So that my roommate could study in peace and quiet, I turned off the TV.*

**Also possible but less common: the use of *may* or *might* in place of *can* or *could*: e.g., *I cashed a check so that I might buy my textbooks.*

☐ EXERCISE 13. Using SO THAT. (Chart 19-5)
   Directions: Combine the ideas by using *so (that)*.

   1. Please turn down the radio. I want to be able to get to sleep.
      → *Please turn down the radio so (that) I can get to sleep.*

   2. My wife turned down the radio. I wanted to be able to get to sleep.
      → *My wife turned down the radio so (that) I could get to sleep.*

   3. Put the milk in the refrigerator. We want to make sure it won't (OR doesn't) spoil.
      → *Put the milk in the refrigerator so (that) it won't (OR doesn't) spoil.*

   4. I put the milk in the refrigerator. I wanted to make sure it didn't spoil.
      → *I put the milk in the refrigerator so (that) it wouldn't spoil.*

   5. Please be quiet. I want to be able to hear what Sharon is saying.

   6. I asked the children to be quiet. I wanted to be able to hear what Sharon was saying.

   7. I'm going to cash a check. I want to make sure that I have enough money to go to the market.

   8. I cashed a check yesterday. I wanted to make sure that I had enough money to go to the market.

   9. Ann and Larry have a six-year-old child. Tonight they're going to hire a babysitter. They want to be able to go out with some friends.

   10. Last week Ann and Larry hired a babysitter. They wanted to be able to go to a dinner party at the home of Larry's boss.

11. Be sure to put the meat in the oven at 5:00. You want to be sure that it will be (OR is) ready to eat by 6:30.

12. Yesterday I put the meat in the oven at 5:00. I wanted it to be ready to eat by 6:30.

13. I'm going to leave the party early. I want to be able to get a good night's sleep tonight.

14. When it started to rain, Harry opened his umbrella. He wanted to be sure he didn't get wet.

15. The little boy pretended to be sick. He wanted to stay home from school.

16. A lot of people were standing in front of me. I stood on tiptoes. I wanted to see the parade better.

☐ EXERCISE 14. Using SO THAT. (Chart 19-5)

Directions: Complete the sentences in Column A with the ideas in Column B. Pay special attention to the verb forms following **so that**.

Example: Ali borrowed an eraser so that . . . .
→ *Ali borrowed an eraser so that he could erase a mistake in his composition.*

Column A

1. Ali borrowed an eraser so that . . . .
2. I turned on the radio so that . . . .
3. I need to buy some detergent so that . . . .
4. Roberto fixed the leak in the boat so that . . . .
5. Mr. Kwan is studying the history and government of Canada so that . . . .
6. Ms. Gow put on her reading glasses so that . . . .
7. Jane is taking a course in auto mechanics so that . . . .
8. Omar is working hard to impress his supervisor so that . . . .
9. Po is saving his money so that . . . .
10. During the parade, Toshi lifted his daughter to his shoulder so that . . . .

Column B

A. wash my clothes
B. read the fine print at the bottom of the contract
C. not sink
✔ D. erase a mistake in his composition
E. travel in Europe next summer
F. listen to the news
G. see the dancers in the street
H. fix her own car
I. become a Canadian citizen
J. be considered for a promotion at his company

☐ EXERCISE 15. Using SO THAT. (Chart 19-5)

Directions: Complete the sentences with your own words.

Examples: Sam took lots of pictures on his vacation so (that) . . . .
→ *Sam took lots of pictures on his vacation so (that) he could show us where he'd been.*

. . . so (that) I could see better.
→ *I moved to the front of the room so (that) I could see better.*

1. I need a pen so (that) . . . .
2. . . . so (that) he can improve his English.
3. I turned on the TV so (that) . . . .
4. Mary hurried to get the child out of the road so (that) . . . .
5. . . . so (that) he wouldn't miss his important appointment.
6. I'm taking a bus instead of flying so (that) . . . .
7. . . . so (that) I could tell him the news in person.

8. . . . so (that) his children will have a better life.

9. Martina is trying to improve her English so (that) . . . .

10. . . . so (that) the celebration would be a great success.

11. Tarek borrowed some money from his friend so (that) . . . .

12. . . . so (that) you can be ready to leave on time.

☐ EXERCISE 16. Summary: cause and effect. (Charts 19-2 → 19-5)
Directions: Using the given words, make sentences about yourself, your friends, your family, your classes, today's weather, current events in the world, etc.

1. now that
2. therefore
3. for (meaning *because*)
4. consequently
5. so (meaning *therefore*)
6. since (meaning *because*)
7. in order to
8. so that
9. so . . . that
10. such . . . that
11. because
12. because of
13. due to
14. due to the fact that

19-6 SHOWING CONTRAST (UNEXPECTED RESULT)

All these sentences have the same meaning. The idea of cold weather is contrasted with the idea of going swimming. Usually if the weather is cold, one does not go swimming, so going swimming in cold weather is an "unexpected result." It is surprising that the speaker went swimming in cold weather.

ADVERB CLAUSES	*even though* *although* *though*	(a) ***Even though** it was cold*, I went swimming. (b) ***Although** it was cold*, I went swimming. (c) ***Though** it was cold*, I went swimming.
CONJUNCTIONS	*but . . . anyway* *but . . . still* *yet . . . still*	(d) It was cold, ***but*** I went swimming ***anyway***. (e) It was cold, ***but*** I ***still*** went swimming. (f) It was cold, ***yet*** I ***still*** went swimming.
TRANSITIONS	*nevertheless* *nonetheless* *however . . . still*	(g) It was cold. ***Nevertheless***, I went swimming. (h) It was cold; ***nonetheless***, I went swimming. (i) It was cold. ***However***, I ***still*** went swimming.
PREPOSITIONS	*despite* *in spite of* *despite the fact that* *in spite of the fact that*	(j) I went swimming ***despite*** the cold weather. (k) I went swimming ***in spite of*** the cold weather. (l) I went swimming ***despite the fact that*** the weather was cold. (m) I went swimming ***in spite of the fact that*** the weather was cold.

☐ EXERCISE 17. Showing contrast (unexpected result). (Chart 19-6)
Directions: Complete the sentences with the given words. Pay close attention to the given punctuation and capitalization.

PART I. Complete the sentences with ***but***, ***even though***, or ***nevertheless***.

1. Bob ate a large dinner. _____Nevertheless_____, he is still hungry.

2. Bob ate a large dinner, _____but_____ he is still hungry.

3. Bob is still hungry _____ *even though* _____ he ate a large dinner.

4. I had a lot of studying to do, _____ I went to a movie anyway.

5. I had a lot of studying to do. _____, I went to a movie.

6. _____ I had a lot of studying to do, I went to a movie.

7. I finished all of my work _____ I was very sleepy.

8. I was very sleepy, _____ I finished all of my work anyway.

9. I was very sleepy. _____, I finished all of my work.

PART II. Complete the sentences with *yet*, *although*, or *however*.

10. I washed my hands. _____, they still looked dirty.

11. I washed my hands, _____ they still looked dirty.

12. _____ I washed my hands, they still looked dirty.

13. Diana didn't know how to swim, _____ she jumped into the swimming pool.

14. _____ Diana didn't know how to swim, she jumped into the swimming pool.

15. Diana didn't know how to swim. _____, she jumped into the swimming pool.

☐ **EXERCISE 18. Showing contrast (unexpected result). (Chart 19-6)**
Directions: Add commas, periods, and capital letters as necessary. Do not add, omit, or change any words.

1. Anna's father gave her some good advice nevertheless she did not follow it.

   → *Anna's father gave her some good advice. Nevertheless, she did not follow it.*

2. Anna's father gave her some good advice but she didn't follow it.

3. Even though Anna's father gave her some good advice she didn't follow it.

4. Anna's father gave her some good advice she did not follow it however.

5. Thomas was thirsty I offered him some water he refused it.

6. Thomas refused the water although he was thirsty.

7. Thomas was thirsty nevertheless he refused the glass of water I brought him.

8. Thomas was thirsty yet he refused to drink the water that I offered him.

☐ EXERCISE 19. Showing contrast (unexpected result). (Chart 19-6)
   Directions: Combine the ideas in the two sentences, using the given words. Discuss correct punctuation. Use the negative if necessary to make a logical statement.

   1. *We went for a walk. It was raining.*
      even though
      but . . . anyway
      nevertheless
      in spite of
      because

   2. *His grades were low. He was admitted to the university.*
      although
      yet . . . still
      nonetheless
      despite
      because of

☐ EXERCISE 20. Showing opposition (unexpected result). (Chart 19-6)
   Directions: Complete the sentences with your own words. Add commas where appropriate.

   1. I had a cold but I _____ anyway.

   2. Even though I had a cold I _____

   3. Although I didn't study _____

   4. I didn't study but _____ anyway.

   5. I got an "A" on the test even though _____

   6. Even though Howard is a careful driver _____

   7. Even though the food they served for dinner tasted terrible _____

   8. My shirt still has coffee stains on it even though _____

   9. I still trust him even though _____

   10. Even though he was drowning no one _____

   11. Although I tried to be very careful _____

   12. Even though Ruth is one of my best friends _____

   13. It's still hot in here even though _____

   14. Even though I had a big breakfast _____

□ EXERCISE 21. Showing contrast (unexpected result). (Chart 19-6)
Directions: Create sentences with the same meaning by using *in spite of* or *despite*.

1. Even though her grades were low, she was admitted to the university.
   → *In spite of her low grades,*
   → *Despite her low grades,*
   → *In spite of the fact that her grades were low,* } she was admitted to the university.
   → *Despite the fact that her grades were low,*
2. I like living in the dorm even though it is noisy.
3. Even though the work was hard, they enjoyed themselves.
4. They wanted to climb the mountain even though it was dangerous.
5. Although the weather was extremely hot, they went jogging in the park.
6. He is unhappy even though he has a vast fortune.

□ EXERCISE 22. Showing contrast (unexpected result). (Chart 19-6)
Directions: Complete the sentences, punctuating carefully. (Correct punctuation is not indicated in the given cues.) Capitalize as necessary.

1. I didn't . . . but . . . anyway.

2. He is very old yet he still . . . .

3. . . . nevertheless we arrived on schedule.

4. Even though she wanted . . . .

5. I wanted . . . however I . . . because . . . .

6. The teacher . . . even though . . . .

7. Although . . . only . . . years old . . . .

8. She never went to school however she . . . despite her lack of education.

9. Despite the fact that my . . . .

10. I have decided to . . . even though . . . .

19-7 SHOWING DIRECT CONTRAST

All of the sentences have the same meaning.

ADVERB CLAUSES	*while* *whereas*	(a) Mary is rich, *while John is poor.* (b) John is poor, *while Mary is rich.* (c) Mary is rich, *whereas John is poor.* (d) *Whereas Mary is rich,* John is poor.
CONJUNCTION	*but*	(e) Mary is rich, *but* John is poor. (f) John is poor, *but* Mary is rich.
TRANSITIONS	*however* *on the other hand*	(g) Mary is rich; *however*, John is poor. (h) John is poor; Mary is rich, *however*. (i) Mary is rich. John, *on the other hand*, is poor. (j) John is poor. Mary, *on the other hand*, is rich.

□ **EXERCISE 23. Showing direct contrast. (Chart 19-7)**

Directions: Create sentences with the same meaning by using **however** or **on the other hand**. Punctuate carefully.

1. Florida has a warm climate, whereas Alaska has a cold climate.
2. While Fred is a good student, his brother is lazy.
3. In the United States, gambling casinos are not legal in most places, while in my country it is possible to gamble in any city or town.
4. Sue and Ron are expecting a child. Sue is hoping for a boy, whereas Ron is hoping for a girl.
5. Old people in my country usually live with their children, whereas the old in the United States often live by themselves.

□ **EXERCISE 24. Showing direct contrast. (Chart 19-7)**

Directions: Complete the sentences with your own words.

1. Some people really enjoy swimming, while others . . . *are afraid of water.*

2. In the United States, people drive on the right-hand side of the road. However, people in . . . .

3. While my apartment always seems to be a mess, my . . . .

4. Marge keeps to herself and has few friends. Carol, on the other hand, ...

5. People who grew up on farms are accustomed to dealing with various kinds of animals. However, city people like myself . . . .

6. Teak is a hard wood that is difficult to cut. Balsa, on the other hand, ...

7. My oldest son is shy, while my youngest son . . . .

8. I'm right-handed. That means that I can accomplish difficult manipulations with my right hand. However, ...

□ **EXERCISE 25. Activity: expressing direct contrast. (Chart 19-7)**

Directions: What aspects of your country and the United States or Canada are in contrast? Use **while, whereas, however, on the other hand**.

1. Size?
2. Population?
3. Food?
4. Time of meals?
5. Climate?
6. Political system?
7. Economic system?
8. Educational system?
9. Religion?
10. Student life?
11. Coffee/tea?
12. Role of women?
13. Language?
14. Educational costs?
15. Medical care?
16. Family relationships?
17. Public transportation?
18. Length of history?
19. Dating customs?
20. Predictability of the weather?

☐ EXERCISE 26. Showing cause and effect and contrast.
(Charts 19-1, 19-2, 19-7, and 19-8)

Directions: Complete the sentences, using the words and phrases below. There may be more than one possible completion. Add any necessary punctuation and capitalization.

although	*despite the fact that*	*nevertheless*
because	*even though*	*now that*
because of	*however*	*therefore*
but		

1. It was cold and wet ___. **Nevertheless,** Bob put on his swimming suit and went to the beach.

2. I can't ride my bicycle _____ there isn't any air in one of the tires.

3. I got to class on time _____ I had missed my bus.

4. Brian used to be an active person, but now he has to limit his activities _____ problems with his health.

5. It should be easy for Bob to find more time to spend with his children _____ he no longer has to work in the evenings and on weekends.

6. Jake is a very good student of languages. His brother Michael _____ has never been able to master another language.

7. The ancient Aztecs of Mexico had no technology for making tools from metal _____ they had sharp knives and spears. They made them from a stone called obsidian.

8. Garlic was believed in ancient Rome to make people courageous _____ Roman soldiers ate large quantities of it before a battle.

9. I usually enjoy attending amateur productions in small community theaters. The play we attended last night _____ was so bad that I wanted to leave after the first act.

10. Some snakes are poisonous _____ others are harmless.

11. Roberta missed the meeting without a good reason _____ she had been told that it was critical that she be there. I wouldn't want to be in her shoes at work tomorrow.

19-8 EXPRESSING CONDITIONS: USING *OTHERWISE* AND *OR (ELSE)*

ADVERB CLAUSE	(a) **If** *I don't eat breakfast,* I get hungry. (b) You'll be late **if** *you don't hurry.* (c) You'll get wet **unless** *you take your umbrella.*	**If** and **unless** state conditions that produce certain results. (See Charts 17-5 and 17-8, pp. 367 and 370.)
TRANSITION	(d) I always eat breakfast. **Otherwise,** I get hungry during class. (e) You'd better hurry. **Otherwise,** you'll be late. (f) Take your umbrella. **Otherwise,** you'll get wet.	**Otherwise** expresses the idea "if the opposite is true, then there will be a certain result." In (d): **otherwise** = *if I don't eat breakfast.*
CONJUNCTION	(g) I always eat breakfast, *or (else)* I get hungry during class. (h) You'd better hurry, *or (else)* you'll be late. (i) Take your umbrella, *or (else)* you'll get wet.	**Or else** and **otherwise** have the same meaning.

☐ **EXERCISE 27. Using OTHERWISE and OR (ELSE). (Chart 19-8)**
Directions: Create sentences with the same meaning by using **otherwise** or **or else**.

1. If I don't call my mother, she'll start worrying about me.

   → *I am going to / should / had better / have to / must call my mother. Otherwise, she'll start worrying about me.*

2. If you don't leave now, you'll be late for class.

3. If you don't go to bed, your cold will get worse.

4. Unless you have a ticket, you can't get into the theater.

5. You can't enter that country unless you have a passport.

6. If Tom doesn't get a job soon, his family won't have enough money for food.

7. Only if you speak both Japanese and Chinese fluently will you be considered for that job.★

8. Mary can go to school only if she gets a scholarship.

9. If I don't wash my clothes tonight, I won't have any clean clothes to wear tomorrow.

★Notice that the subject and verb in the main clause are inverted because the sentence begins with *only if.* See Chart 17-9, pp. 371.

□ EXERCISE 28. Expressing conditions. (Charts 17-5 17-9 and 19-8)
Directions: Complete the sentences, punctuating correctly. Use capital letters where appropriate.

1. I am going to . . . even if . . . .
2. We have no choice we have to . . . whether . . . .
3. I will go to . . . only if . . . .
4. . . . is very inconsiderate he plays his record player even if . . . .

5. I can't . . . unless . . . .
6. Tomorrow I'd better . . . otherwise . . . .
7. You should . . . in case . . . .
8. I will . . . only if . . . .
9. I will . . . unless . . . .
10. . . . must . . . otherwise . . . .

19-9 SUMMARY OF CONNECTIVES: CAUSE AND EFFECT, CONTRAST, CONDITION

	ADVERB CLAUSE WORDS		TRANSITIONS	CONJUNCTIONS	PREPOSITIONS
CAUSE AND EFFECT	*because* *since* *now that*	*so (that)*	*therefore* *consequently*	*so* *for*	*because of* *due to*
CONTRAST	*even though* *although* *though*	*whereas* *while*	*however* *nevertheless* *nonetheless* *on the other hand*	*but (. . . anyway)* *yet (. . . still)*	*despite* *in spite of*
CONDITION	*if* *unless* *only if* *even if* *whether or not*	*in case* *in the event that*	*otherwise*	*or (else)*	

□ EXERCISE 29. Summary of connectives. (Chart 19-9)
Directions: Using the two ideas of *to study* and *to pass or fail the exam*, complete the sentences. Punctuate and capitalize correctly.

1. Because I did not study _____, I failed the exam._____

2. I failed the exam because _____

3. Although I studied _____

4. I did not study   therefore _____

5. I did not study   however _____

6. I studied   nevertheless _____

7. Even though I did not study _____

8. I did not study   so _____

9. Since I did not study _____

10. If I study for the test _____

11. Unless I study for the test _____

12. I must study   otherwise _____

13. Even if I study _____

14. I did not study   consequently _____

15. I did not study   nonetheless _____

16. I will probably fail the test whether _____

17. I failed the exam   for _____

18. I have to study so that _____

19. Only if I study _____

20. I studied hard   yet _____

21. You'd better study   or else _____

☐ EXERCISE 30. Summary of connectives. (Chart 19-9)
   Directions: Using the ideas of *to be hungry* (or *not to be hungry*) and *to eat breakfast* (or *not to eat breakfast*), complete the following. Punctuate and capitalize correctly.

1. Because I was not hungry this morning _____

2. Because I ate breakfast this morning _____ now.

3. Because I was hungry this morning _____

4. I did not eat breakfast this morning even though _____

5. Although I was hungry this morning _____

6. I was hungry this morning   therefore _____

7. I was hungry this morning   nevertheless _____

8. I was so hungry this morning _____

9. I was not hungry this morning   but _____

10. I ate breakfast this morning even though _____

11. Since I did not eat breakfast this morning _____

12. I ate breakfast this morning   nonetheless _____

13. I was not hungry   so _____

14. Even though I did not eat breakfast this morning _____

15. I never eat breakfast unless _____

16. I always eat breakfast whether or not _____

17. I eat breakfast even if _____

18. Now that I have eaten breakfast _____

19. I eat breakfast only if _____

20. I ate breakfast this morning   yet _____

21. Even if I am hungry _____

22. I was not hungry   however _____

☐ EXERCISE 31. Summary of connectives.   (Chart 19-9)
   Directions: Using the given words, combine the following two ideas. The time is now, so use present and future tenses.

   (a) **to go (or not to go) to the beach**   (b) **hot, cold, nice weather**

   1. because → *Because the weather is cold, we aren't going to go to the beach.*
            → *We're going to go to the beach because the weather is hot.*

2. so . . . that	9. because of	16. therefore
3. so	10. consequently	17. only if
4. nevertheless	11. as soon as	18. nonetheless
5. despite	12. such . . . that	19. in spite of
6. now that	13. since	20. even if
7. once	14. but . . . anyway	21. yet . . . still
8. although	15. unless	22. whether . . . or not

☐ EXERCISE 32. Summary of connectives.   (Chart 19-9)
   Directions: Complete the sentences, adding punctuation and capitalization.

   1. While some people are optimists . . . .

   2. Even though he drank a glass of water . . . still . . . .

   3. Even if she invites me to her party . . . .

   4. I have never been to Hawaii my parents however . . . .

   5. I couldn't . . . for my arms were full of packages.

   6. I need to borrow some money so that . . . .

   7. The airport was closed due to fog therefore . . . .

   8. . . . therefore the airport was closed.

   9. As soon as the violinist played the last note at the concert . . . .

10. Since neither my roommate nor I know how to cook . . . .

11. I am not a superstitious person nevertheless . . . .

12. The crops will fail unless . . . .

13. Just as I was getting ready to eat dinner last night . . . .

14. We must work quickly otherwise . . . .

15. Some children are noisy and wild my brother's children on the other hand . . . .

16. According to the newspaper, now that . . . .

17. Ever since I can remember . . . .

18. Although my . . . .

19. The United States . . . whereas . . . .

20. I was tired however I . . . because . . . .

21. You must . . . whether . . . .

22. . . . nevertheless I could not understand what the person who . . . because . . . .

☐ EXERCISE 33. Error analysis: general review. (Chapters 16 → 19)
Directions: Correct the errors.

1. Unless I study very hard, I will pass all of my exams.

2. My shoes and pants got muddy. Even though I walked carefully through the wet streets.

3. My neighborhood is quiet and safe however I always lock my doors.

4. Although I usually don't like Mexican food, but I liked the food I had at the Mexican restaurant last night.

5. Although my room in the dormitory is very small, but I like it. Because it is a place where I can be by myself and studying in peace and quiet.

6. Despite I prefer to be a history teacher, I am studying in the Business School in order for I can get a job in industry.

7. A little girl approached the cage however when the tiger shows its teeth and growls she run to her mother. Because she was frightened.

8. Many of the people working to save our environment think that they are fighting a losing battle. Because big business, and the government have not joined together to eliminate pollution.

9. The weather was so cold that I don't like to leave my apartment.

10. I have to study four hour every day because of my courses are difficult.

11. On the third day of our voyage, we sailed across a rough sea before to reach the shore.

12. I can't understand the lectures in my psychology class therefore my roommate lets me borrow her notes.

13. According to this legend, a man went in search of a hidden village, he finally found it after walk two hundred mile.

14. Because my country it is located in a subtropical area, so the weather is hot.

15. I will stay at the united state for two more year. Because I want finish my degree before go home.

☐ EXERCISE 34. Activity: connectives.   (Chart 19-9)
Directions: Form a group of four people. One of you will begin a "chain sentence" by speaking the given words plus one, two, or three additional words. Each of the others should add one, two, or three words until the sentence is completed. The maximum number of words a person can add is three. When you complete your sentence, one person in the group should write it down (with correct punctuation, spelling, and capitalization).

Example: Although education is . . . .
SPEAKER A: Although education is **important,** . . . .
SPEAKER B: Although education is important, **some students** . . . .
SPEAKER C: Although education is important, some students **would rather** . . . .
SPEAKER D: Although education is important, some students would rather **fly a kite** . . . .
SPEAKER A: Although education is important, some students would rather fly a kite **than** . . . .
SPEAKER B: Although education is important, some students would rather fly a kite than **go to class**.
FINAL SENTENCE: → *Although education is important, some students would rather fly a kite than go to class.*

1. Because we are . . . .
2. Unless you . . . .
3. Students have to study. Otherwise, ...
4. In spite of the fact that students . . . .
5. Even if we . . . .
6. Only if . . . .
7. An educated populace is important to a nation's future. Therefore, ...
8. I was so confused when the teacher . . . .
9. Now that we . . . .
10. Even though students who . . . .

☐ EXERCISE 35. Review: punctuation and capitalization. (Chapters 13 and 16 → 19)

Directions: Add appropriate punctuation and capitalization. Notice how these clarify meaning in written English.

1. I did not expect to get a pay raise nevertheless I accepted when my boss offered it.
   → *I did not expect to get a pay raise. Nevertheless, I accepted when my boss offered it.*

2. Although a computer has tremendous power and speed it cannot think for itself a human operator is needed to give a computer instructions for it cannot initially tell itself what to do.

3. Being a lawyer in private practice I work hard but I do not go into my office on either Saturday or Sunday if clients insist upon seeing me on those days they have to come to my home.

4. Whenever the weather is nice I walk to school but when it is cold or wet I either take the bus or get a ride with one of my friends even though my brother has a car I never ask him to take me to school because he is very busy he has a new job and has recently gotten married so he doesn't have time to drive me to and from school anymore I know he would give me a ride if I asked him to but I don't want to bother him.

5. The common cold which is the most widespread of all diseases continues to plague humanity despite the efforts of scientists to find its prevention and cure even though colds are minor illnesses they are one of the principal causes of absence from school and work people of all ages get colds but children and adults who live with children get them the most colds can be dangerous for elderly people because they can lead to other infections I have had three colds so far this year I eat the right kinds of food get enough rest and exercise regularly nevertheless I still get at least one cold a year.

MARTY'S FISH AND SEAFOOD

REDFISH FILETS

RAINBOW TROUT

6. Whenever my father goes fishing we know we will have fish to eat for dinner for even if he doesn't catch any he stops at the fish market on his way home and buys some.

☐ **EXERCISE 36. Review: showing relationships.** (Chapters 5 and 16 → 19)

Directions: Using the words in parentheses, combine the sentences to show relationships between the ideas. Punctuate and capitalize correctly.

1. a. Jack hates going to the dentist.
   b. He should see his dentist soon.
   c. He has a very bad toothache.
   (even though, because)
   → *Even though Jack hates going to the dentist, he should see his dentist soon because he has a very bad toothache.*

2. a. You may really mean what you say.
   b. I'll give you one more chance.
   c. You have to give me your best effort.
   d. You'll lose your job.
   (if, but, otherwise)

3. a. The weather is bad.
   b. I'm going to stay home.
   c. The weather may change.
   d. I don't want to go to the picnic.
   (due to, even if)

4. a. The children had eaten lunch.
   b. They got hungry in the middle of the afternoon.
   c. I took them to the market.
   d. They wanted to get some fruit for a snack.
   e. We went home for dinner.
   (even though, therefore, so that, before)

5. a. Robert is totally exhausted after playing tennis.
   b. Marge isn't even tired.
   c. She ran around a lot more during the game.
   (whereas, in spite of the fact that)

6. a. Many animals are most vulnerable to predators when they are grazing.
   b. Giraffes are most vulnerable when they are drinking.
   c. They must spread their legs awkwardly in order to lower their long necks to the water in front of them.
   d. It is difficult and time-consuming for them to stand up straight again to escape a predator.
   e. Once they are up and running, they are faster than most of their predators.
   (while, consequently, however)

7. a. My boss promised me that I could have two full weeks.
   b. It seems that I can't take my vacation after all.
   c. I have to train the new personnel this summer.
   d. I may not get a vacation in the fall either.
   e. I will be angry.
   (even though, because, if)

8. a. Education, business, and government are all dependent on computers.
   b. It is advisable for all students to have basic computer skills.
   c. They graduate from high school and enter the work force or college.
   d. A course called "Computer Literacy" has recently become a requirement for graduation from Westside High School.
   e. Maybe you will want more information about this course.
   f. You can call the academic counselor at the high school.
   (since, before, therefore, if)

□ EXERCISE 37. Review: showing relationships. (Chapters 5 and 13 → 19)
   Directions: Write out the sentences on another piece of paper, completing them with your own words. Some punctuation is given; add other punctuation as necessary. (NOTE: Some of your sentences will have to get a little complicated.)

   Examples: I have trouble _____ , so I _____ when I _____

   → *I have trouble **remembering people's names**, so I **concentrate** when I **first meet someone.***

   I wanted to _____ . Nevertheless, I _____ because _____

   → *I wanted to **go to Chicago**. Nevertheless, I **stayed home** because **I had to study for final exams.***

1. _____ sore throat. Nevertheless, _____ .

2. I _____ . My _____ , on the other hand, _____ .

3. When a small, black insect _____ , I _____ because _____ .

4. I _____ because _____ . However, _____ .

5. Even though I told _____ that _____ , _____ .

6. According to the newspaper, now that _____ . Therefore, _____ .

7. Since neither the man who _____ nor _____ , I _____ .

8. When people who _____ , _____ because _____ .

9. Since I didn't know whose _____ , I _____ .

10. Even though the book which _____ , I _____ .

11. What did the woman who _____ when you _____ ?

12. If what he said _____ .

13. Because the man who _____ .

14. Even though she didn't understand what the man who _____ .

15. Now that all of the students who _____ .

16. Since the restaurant where we _____ .

☐ **EXERCISE 38. Error analysis: general review.** (Chapters 1 → 19)
Directions: These passages are taken from student writing. You are the editor for these students. Rewrite the passages, correcting errors and making whatever revisions in phrasing or vocabulary you feel will help the writers say what they intended to say.

Example: My idea of the most important thing in life. It is to be healthy. Because a person can't enjoy life without health.
→ *In my opinion, the most important thing in life is good health, for a person cannot enjoy life fully without it.*

1. We went shopping after ate dinner. But the stores were closed. We had to go back home even we hadn't found what were we looking for.

2. I want explain that I know alot of grammers but is my problem I haven't enough vocabularies.

3. When I got lost in the bus station a kind man helped me, he explained how to read the huge bus schedule on the wall. Took me to the window to buy a ticket and showed me where was my bus, I will always appreciate his kindness.

4. I had never understand the important of know English language. Until I worked at a large international company.

5. Since I was young my father found an American woman to teach me and my brothers English, but when we move to other town my father wasn't able to find other teacher for other five years.

6. I was surprised to see the room that I was given at the dormitory. Because there aren't any furniture, and dirty.

7. When I meet Mr. Lee for the first time, we played ping pong at the student center even though we can't communicate very well, but we had a good time.

8. Because the United States is a large and also big country. It means that they're various kinds of people live there and it has a diverse population.

9. My grammar class was start at 10:35. When the teacher was coming to class, she returned the last quiz to my classmates and I. After we have had another quiz.

10. If a wife has a work, her husband should share the houseworks with her. If both of them help, the houseworks can be finish much faster.

11. The first time I went skiing. I was afraid to go down the hill. But somewhere from a little corner of my head kept shouting, "Why not! Give it a try. You'll make it!" After stand around for ten minutes without moving. Finally, I decided go down that hill.

12. This is a story about a man. He had a big garden. One day he was sleeping in his garden. Then he woke up. He ate some fruit. Then he picked some apples and he walked to a small river and he saw a beautiful woman was on the other side. And he gave her some apples and then she gave him a loaf of bread. The two of them walked back to the garden. Then some children came and were playing games with him. Everyone was laughing and smiling. Then one child destroyed a flower and the man became angry and he said to them, "Get out of here." Then the children left and the beautiful woman left. Then the man built a wall around his garden and would not let anyone in. He stayed in his garden all alone for the rest of his life.

☐ **EXERCISE 39. Activity: general review. (Chapters 1 → 19)**
Directions: Read and discuss.

In prehistoric times, humans probably spoke between 10,000 and 15,000 languages. Today about 6,000 languages are spoken around the world. Experts predict that up to 50 percent of these languages will probably become extinct during the 21st century.

Question for discussion and/or writing:
What do you think accounts for the decrease in the number of languages in the world?

CHAPTER 20
Conditional Sentences and Wishes

A conditional sentence typically consists of an *if*-clause (which presents a condition) and a result clause.* Example: *If it rains, the streets get wet.*

*See Charts 17-1 (p. 359) and 17-5 (p. 367) for the basic structure of adverb clauses of condition.

☐ EXERCISE 1. Preview: conditional sentences. (Charts 20-1 → 20-4)
    Directions: Answer the questions with "yes" or "no."

1. *If the weather had been good yesterday, our picnic would not have been canceled.*

    a. Was the picnic canceled? ___yes___

    b. Was the weather good? ___no___

2. *If I had an envelope and a stamp, I would mail this letter right now.*

    a. Do I have an envelope and a stamp right now? _____

    b. Do I want to mail this letter right now? _____

    c. Am I going to mail this letter right now? _____

3. *Ann would have made it to class on time this morning if the bus hadn't been late.*

    a. Did Ann try to make it to class on time? _____

    b. Did Ann make it to class on time? _____

    c. Was the bus late? _____

4. *If the hotel had been built to withstand an earthquake, it would not have collapsed.*

    a. Was the hotel built to withstand an earthquake? _____

    b. Did the hotel collapse? _____

5. *If I were a carpenter, I would build my own house.*

   a. Do I want to build my own house? _____

   b. Am I going to build my own house? _____

   c. Am I a carpenter? _____

6. *If I didn't have any friends, I would be lonely.*

   a. Am I lonely? _____

   b. Do I have friends? _____

7. *If Bob had asked me to keep the news a secret, I wouldn't have told anybody.*

   a. Did I tell anybody the news? _____

   b. Did Bob ask me to keep it a secret? _____

8. *If Ann and Jan, who are twins, dressed alike and had the same hairstyle, I wouldn't be able to tell them apart.*

   a. Do Ann and Jan dress alike? _____

   b. Do they have the same hairstyle? _____

   c. Can I tell them apart? _____

20-1 OVERVIEW OF BASIC VERB FORMS USED IN CONDITIONAL SENTENCES

SITUATION	IF-CLAUSE	RESULT CLAUSE	EXAMPLES
True in the present/future	**simple present**	**simple present** *will* + *simple form*	If I *have* enough time, I *watch* TV every evening. If I *have* enough time, I *will watch* TV later on tonight.
Untrue in the present/future	**simple past**	*would* + *simple form*	If I *had* enough time, I *would watch* TV now or later on.
Untrue in the past	**past perfect**	*would have* + *past participle*	If I *had had* enough time, I *would have watched* TV yesterday.

☐ **EXERCISE 2. Basic verb forms in conditional sentences. (Chart 20-1)**

   Directions: Complete the sentences with the verbs in parentheses.

   1. SITUATION: *I usually write my parents a letter every week. That is a true fact. In other words:*

      If I *(have)* ____have____ enough time, I *(write)* ____write____ my parents a letter **every week**.

2. SITUATION: *I may have enough time to write my parents a letter later tonight. I want to write them a letter tonight. Both of those things are true. In other words:*

If I *(have)* _____ enough time, I *(write)* _____ my

parents a letter **later tonight**.

3. SITUATION: *I don't have enough time right now, so I won't write my parents a letter. I'll try to do it later. I want to write them, but the truth is that I just don't have enough time right now. In other words:*

If I *(have)* _____ enough time **right now**, I *(write)* _____

my parents a letter.

4. SITUATION: *I won't have enough time tonight, so I won't write my parents a letter. I'll try to do it tomorrow. I want to write them, but the truth is that I just won't have enough time. In other words:*

If I *(have)* _____ enough time **later tonight**, I *(write)* _____

my parents a letter.

5. SITUATION: *I wanted to write my parents a letter last night, but I didn't have enough time. In other words:*

If I *(have)* _____ enough time, I *(write)* _____

my parents a letter **last night**.

20-2 TRUE IN THE PRESENT OR FUTURE

(a) If I *don't eat* breakfast, I always *get* hungry during class.	In conditional sentences that express true, factual ideas in the present/future, the *simple present* (not the simple future) is used in the *if*-clause.
(b) Water *freezes* OR **will freeze** if the temperature *reaches* 32°F/0°C.	The result clause has various possible verb forms. A result clause verb can be:
(c) If I *don't eat* breakfast tomorrow morning, I **will get** hungry during class.	1. the *simple present*, to express a habitual activity or situation, as in (a).
(d) If it *rains*, we **should stay** home. If it *rains*, I **might decide** to stay home. If it *rains*, we **can't go**. If it *rains*, we **'re going to stay** home.	2. either the *simple present* or the *simple future*, to express an established, predictable fact or general truth, as in (b). 3. the *simple future*, to express a particular activity or situation in the future, as in (c). 4. *modals* and *phrasal modals* such as **should**, **might**, **can**, **be going to**, as in (d).★
(e) If anyone *calls*, please *take* a message.	5. an imperative verb, as in (e).
(f) If anyone **should** *call*, please take a message.	Sometimes **should** is used in an *if*-clause. It indicates a little more uncertainty than the use of the simple present, but basically the meaning of examples (e) and (f) is the same.

★See Chart 9-1, p. 151, for a list of modals and phrasal modals.

Directions: Answer the questions. Pay special attention to the verb forms in the result clauses. Work in pairs, in groups, or as a class.

1. If it rains, what always happens?*
2. If it rains tomorrow, what will happen?
3. If it should rain tomorrow, what will you do or not do?
4. If it's cold tomorrow, what are you going to wear to class?
5. Fish can't live out of water. If you take a fish out of water, what will happen? / If you take a fish out of water, what happens?
6. If I want to learn English faster, what should I do?
7. If you run up a hill, what does/will your heart do?**
8. Tell me what to do, where to go, and what to expect if I visit your hometown as a tourist.

20-3 UNTRUE (CONTRARY TO FACT) IN THE PRESENT OR FUTURE

(a) If I *taught* this class, I *wouldn't give* tests. (b) If he *were* here right now, he *would help* us. (c) If I *were* you, I *would accept* their invitation.	In (a): In truth, I don't teach this class. In (b): In truth, he is not here right now. In (c): In truth, I am not you. Note: **Were** is used for both singular and plural subjects. **Was** (with *I, he, she, it*) is sometimes used in informal speech: *If I **was** you, I'd accept their invitation.*
COMPARE (d) If I had enough money, I *would* buy a car. (e) If I had enough money, I *could* buy a car.	In (d): The speaker wants a car, but doesn't have enough money. **Would** expresses desired or predictable results. In (e): The speaker is expressing one possible result. **Could** = *would be able to.* **Could** expresses possible options.

□ EXERCISE 4. Present or future conditional sentences. (Charts 20-2 and 20-3)
Directions: Complete the sentences with the verbs in parentheses.

1. If I have enough apples, I *(bake)* _____will bake_____ an apple pie this afternoon.

2. If I had enough apples, I *(bake)* _____ an apple pie this afternoon.

3. I will fix your bicycle if I *(have)* _____ a screwdriver of the proper size.

4. I would fix your bicycle if I *(have)* _____ a screwdriver of the proper size.

5. Sally always answers the phone if she *(be)* _____ in her office.

6. Sally would answer the phone if she *(be)* _____ in her office right now.

---

*In true conditional sentences that express a habitual activity or general truth, *if* is very close in meaning to **when** or **whenever**. These sentences have essentially the same meaning:
    If it rains, the streeets get wet.
    When it rains, the streets get wet.
    Whenever it rains, the streets get wet.
**In this sentence, *you* is an impersonal pronoun. Begin the response to this question with *"If you run . . . ."*

7. I (be, not) _____ a student in this class if English (be) _____ my native language.

8. Most people know that oil floats on water. If you pour oil on water, it (float) _____.

9. If there (be) _____ no oxygen on earth, life as we know it (exist, not) _____.

10. My evening newspaper has been late every day this week. If the paper (arrive, not) _____ on time today, I'm going to cancel my subscription.

11. If I (be) _____ a bird, I (want, not) _____ to live my whole life in a cage.

12. How old (human beings, live) _____ _____ to be if all diseases in the world (be) _____ completely eradicated?

13. If you boil water, it (disappear) _____ _____ into the atmosphere as vapor.

14. If people (have) _____ paws instead of hands with fingers and opposable thumbs, the machines we use in everyday life (have to) _____ _____ be constructed very differently. We (be, not) _____ _____ able to turn knobs, push small buttons, or hold tools and utensils securely.

☐ EXERCISE 5. Activity: present or future untrue conditions. (Chart 20-3)
Directions: In small groups or as a class, discuss the questions.

Under what conditions, if any, would you . . .
1. exceed the speed limit while driving?
2. lie to your best friend?
3. disobey an order from your boss?
4. steal food?
5. carry a friend on your back for a long distance?
6. not pay your rent?
7. *(Make up other conditions for your classmates to discuss.)*

☐ EXERCISE 6. Activity: present conditionals. (Chart 20-3)

Directions: Use the statistics in *PART I* to answer the question in *PART II*. Work in pairs, in groups, or as a class.

PART I. POPULATION STATISTICS

1. 51% of the world's population is female.
2. 57% of the people in the world are from Asia, the Middle East, and the South Pacific.
3. 21% are Europeans.
4. 14% are from the Western Hemisphere.
5. 8% are from Africa.
6. 50% of the world's population suffers from malnutrition.
7. 30% of the world's population is illiterate. 60% of the people who are illiterate are women.
8. 1% of the world's population has a college education.
9. 6% of the people in the world own half of the world's wealth.
10. One person in three is below 15 years of age. One person in ten is over 65 years old.

PART II. QUESTION

If there were only one village on earth and it had exactly 100 people, who would it consist of? Assuming that the village would reflect global population statistics, describe the people in this imaginary village. Use the illustration to point out the number of people who fit each description you make.

→ *If there were only one village on earth and it had exactly 100 people, 51 of them would be women and 49 of them would be men. More than half of the people in the village (57 of them) would . . .* (continue describing the village).

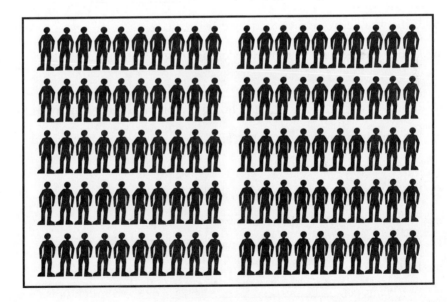

A village of 100 people

20-4 UNTRUE (CONTRARY TO FACT) IN THE PAST

(a) If you *had told* me about the problem, I *would have helped* you.	In (a): In truth, you did not tell me about it.
(b) If they *had studied*, they *would have passed* the exam.	In (b): In truth, they did not study. Therefore, they failed the exam.
(c) If I *hadn't slipped* on the stairs, I *wouldn't have broken* my arm.	In (c): In truth, I slipped on the stairs. I broke my arm.
	Note: The auxiliary verbs are almost always contracted in speech. "If you'd told me, I would've helped you (OR I'd've helped you)."*
COMPARE	In (d): *would* expresses a desired or predictable result.
(d) If I had had enough money, I *would* have bought a car.	In (e): *could* expresses a possible option; *could have bought = would have been able to buy.*
(e) If I had had enough money, I *could* have bought a car.	

*In casual, informal speech, some native speakers sometimes use *would have* in an *if*-clause: *If you would've told* me *about the problem, I would've helped you.* This verb form usage is generally considered not to be grammatically correct standard English, but it occurs fairly commonly.

☐ **EXERCISE 7. Conditional sentences. (Charts 20-1 → 20-4)**

Directions: Complete the sentences with the verbs in parentheses.

1. If I *(have)* _____ enough money, I will go with you.

2. If I *(have)* _____ enough money, I would go with you.

3. If I *(have)* _____ enough money, I would have gone with you.

4. If the weather is nice tomorrow, we *(go)* _____ to the zoo.

5. If the weather were nice today, we *(go)* _____ to the zoo.

6. If the weather had been nice yesterday, we *(go)* _____ to the zoo.

7. If Sally *(be)* _____ at home tomorrow, I am going to visit her.

8. Jim isn't home right now. If he *(be)* _____ at home right now, I *(visit)* _____ him.

9. Linda wasn't at home yesterday. If she *(be)* _____ at home yesterday, I *(visit)* _____ her.

10. A: Shh! Your father is taking a nap. Uh-oh. You woke him up.

    B: Gee, I'm sorry, Mom. If I *(realize)* _____ he was sleeping, I *(make, not)* _____ so much noise when I came in. But how was I supposed to know?

11. Last night Alex ruined his sweater when he washed it. If he *(read)*

_____ the label, he *(wash, not)*

_____ it in hot water.

12. A: Ever since I broke my foot, I haven't been

able to get down to the basement to wash

my clothes.

B: Why didn't you say something? I *(come)*

_____ over and

(wash) _____ them for you

if you *(tell)* _____ me.

A: I know you *(come)* _____

right away if I *(call)* _____ you. I guess

I didn't want to bother you.

B: Nonsense! What are good neighbors for?

☐ EXERCISE 8. Untrue in the past. (Chart 20-4)
Directions: Work in pairs.
Speaker A: Your book is open. Give the cue.
Speaker B: Your book is closed. Begin your response with "But if I had known . . . ."

Example:
SPEAKER A *(book open):* There was a test yesterday. You didn't know that, so you didn't study.
SPEAKER B *(book closed):* But if I had known (that there was a test yesterday), I would have studied.

1. Your friend was in the hospital. You didn't know that, so you didn't visit her.
2. I've never met your friend. You didn't know that, so you didn't introduce me.
3. There was a meeting last night. You didn't know that, so you didn't go.
4. Your friend's parents are in town. You didn't know that, so you didn't invite them to dinner.

Switch roles.
5. I wanted to go to the soccer game. You didn't know that, so you didn't buy a ticket for me.
6. I was at home last night. You didn't know that, so you didn't visit me.
7. Your sister wanted a gold necklace for her birthday. You didn't know that, so you didn't buy her one.
8. I had a problem. You didn't know that, so you didn't offer to help.

☐ EXERCISE 9. Untrue conditionals. (Charts 20-3 and 20-4)
    Directions: Change the statements into conditional sentences.

1. Roberto came, so I wasn't disappointed. But . . . .
    → *But if he hadn't come, I would have been disappointed.*

2. There are so many bugs in the room because there
    isn't a screen on the window. But . . . .

3. I didn't buy a bicycle because I didn't have
    enough money. But . . . .

4. I won't buy a bicycle because I don't have
    enough money. But . . . .

5. You got into so much trouble because you
    didn't listen to me. But . . . .

6. The woman didn't die because she received
    immediate medical attention. But . . . .

7. Nadia didn't pass the entrance examination, so
    she wasn't admitted to the university. But . . . .

8. We ran out of gas because we didn't stop at the
    service station. But . . .

☐ EXERCISE 10. Untrue conditional sentences. (Charts 20-3 and 20-4)
    Directions: Make an *if*-clause from the given information and then supply a result clause
    using your own words.

    Examples: I wasn't late to work yesterday.
                → *If I had been late to work yesterday, I would have missed the regular morning
                meeting.*
                Tom asked my permission before he took my bicycle.
                → *If Tom hadn't asked my permission before he took my bicycle, I would have been
                angry.*

1. I wasn't absent from class yesterday.

2. I don't have enough energy today.

3. Ocean water is salty.

4. Our teacher likes his/her job.

5. People don't have wings.

6. You didn't ask for my opinion.

7. Water is heavier than air.

8. Most nations support world trade agreements.

□ EXERCISE 11. Review: conditional sentences. (Charts 20-1 → 20-4)
   Directions: Complete the sentences with the verbs in parentheses.

   1. You should tell your father exactly what happened. If I *(be)* _____ you, I
      (tell) _____ him the truth as soon as possible.

   2. If I *(have)* _____ my camera with me yesterday, I *(take)* _____
      _____ a picture of Alex standing on his head.

   3. I'm almost ready to plant my garden. I have a lot of seeds. Maybe I have more than I
      need. If I *(have)* _____ more seeds than I need, I *(give)* _____
      _____ some to my neighbor.

   4. George has only two pairs of socks. If he *(have)* _____ more than two pairs
      of socks, he *(have to, not)* _____ wash his socks so
      often.

   5. The cowboy pulled his gun to shoot at the rattlesnake, but he was
      too late. If he *(be)* _____
      quicker to pull the trigger, the snake *(bite, not)*
      _____ him on
      the foot. It's a good thing he was wearing
      heavy leather boots.

   6. What *(we, use)* _____
      to look at ourselves when we comb our hair
      if we *(have, not)* _____
      mirrors?

   7. It's been a long drought. It hasn't rained for over a month. If it *(rain, not)*
      _____ soon, a lot of crops *(die)* _____. If the
      crops *(die)* _____, many people *(go)* _____ hungry this
      coming winter.

   8. According to one scientific theory, an asteroid collided with the earth millions of years
      ago, causing great changes in the earth's climate. Some scientists believe that if this
      asteroid *(collide, not)* _____ with the earth, the dinosaurs
      (become, not) _____ extinct. Can you imagine what the
      world *(be)* _____ like today if dinosaurs *(exist, still)* _____
      _____ ? Do you think it *(be)* _____ possible for
      dinosaurs and human beings to coexist on the same planet?

☐ **EXERCISE 12. Untrue conditionals. (Charts 20-3 and 20-4)**

Directions: Make a true statement about the given topic. Then make a contrary-to-fact conditional sentence about that statement. Work in pairs, in groups, or as a class.

Examples: yourself
→ *I am twenty years old. If I were seventy years old, I would already have lived most of my life.*

ice
→ *Ice doesn't sink. If the polar ice caps sank, the level of the oceans would rise and flood coastal cities.*

Topics:

1. yourself	5. peace	9. a famous person
2. fire	6. your activities right now	10. your activities last night
3. space travel	7. air	11. dinosaurs
4. vegetables	8. a member of this class	12. a member of your family

☐ **EXERCISE 13. Conditional sentences. (Charts 20-1 → 20-4)**

Directions: Complete each sentence with an appropriate auxiliary verb.

1. I don't have a pen, but if I _____ *did* _____, I would lend it to you.

2. He is busy right now, but if he _____ *weren't* _____, he would help us.

3. I didn't vote in the last election, but if I _____ *had* _____, I would have voted for Senator Anderson.

4. I don't have enough money, but if I _____, I would buy that book.

5. The weather is cold today, but if it _____, I would go swimming.

6. She didn't come, but if she _____, she would have met my brother.

7. I'm not a good cook, but if I _____, I would make all of my own meals.

8. I have to go to class this afternoon, but if I _____, I would go downtown with you.

9. He didn't go to a doctor, but if he _____, the cut on his hand wouldn't have gotten infected.

10. I always pay my bills. If I _____, I would get in a lot of trouble.

11. Helium is lighter than air. If it _____, a helium-filled balloon wouldn't float upward.

12. I called my husband to tell him I would be late. If I _____, he would have gotten worried about me.

☐ **EXERCISE 14. Conditional sentences. (Charts 20-1 → 20-4)**

Directions: Work in pairs.
Speaker A: Your book is open. Ask the questions.
Speaker B: Your book is closed. Begin your answers with "No, but . . . ."

Example:
SPEAKER A *(book open):* Do you have a dollar?
SPEAKER B *(book closed):* No, but if I did (No, but if I had a dollar), I would lend it to you.

Switch roles.

1. Are you rich?
2. Do you have a car?
3. Are you a bird?
4. Are you in *(student's country/ hometown)?*
5. Do you live in a hotel?
6. Are you the teacher of this class?
7. Do you have your own airplane?
8. Did you watch TV last night?
9. Did you grow up in *(another country)?*

10. Are you tired?
11. Are you at home right now?
12. Are you married/single?
13. Do you speak *(another language)?*
14. Is the weather hot/cold today?
15. Are you hungry?
16. Do you live in *(a different city)?*
17. Did we eat dinner together last night?
18. Did you forget to bring your grammar book to class today?

20-5 USING PROGRESSIVE VERB FORMS IN CONDITIONAL SENTENCES

Notice the use of progressive verb forms in these examples. Even in conditional sentences, progressive verb forms are used in progressive situations. (See Chart 1-2, p. 3, for a discussion of progressive verbs.)

(a)	TRUE:	It *is raining* right now, so I *will not go for* a walk.
(b)	CONDITIONAL:	If it *were not raining* right now, I *would go* for a walk.
(c)	TRUE:	I *am not living* in Chile. I *am not working* at a bank.
(d)	CONDITIONAL:	If I *were living* in Chile, I *would be working* at a bank.
(e)	TRUE:	It *was raining* yesterday afternoon, so I *did not go* for a walk.
(f)	CONDITIONAL:	If it *had not been raining*, I *would have gone* for a walk.
(g)	TRUE:	I *was not living* in Chile last year. I *was not working* at a bank.
(h)	CONDITIONAL:	If I *had been living* in Chile last year, I *would have been working* at a bank.

☐ **EXERCISE 15. Using progressive verb forms in conditional sentences. (Chart 20-5)**

Directions: Change the statements into conditional sentences.

1. It is snowing, so I won't go with you. But . . . .
   → *But if it weren't snowing, I would go with you.*
2. The child is crying because his mother isn't here. But . . . .
3. You weren't listening, so you didn't understand the directions. But . . . .
4. Joe got a ticket because he was driving too fast. But . . . .

5. I was listening to the radio, so I heard the news bulletin. But . . . .

6. Grandpa is not wearing his hearing aid because it's broken. But . . . .

7. You were sleeping, so I didn't tell you the news as soon as I heard it. But . . . .

8. I'm enjoying myself, so I won't leave. But . . . .

20-6 USING "MIXED TIME" IN CONDITIONAL SENTENCES

Frequently the time in the *if*-clause and the time in the result clause are different: one clause may be in the present and the other in the past. Notice that past and present times are mixed in these sentences.

(a)	TRUE:	I *did not eat* breakfast several hours ago, so I *am* hungry now.
(b)	CONDITIONAL:	If I *had eaten* breakfast several hours ago, I *would not be* hungry now.
		(past) *(present)*

(c)	TRUE:	He *is not* a good student. He *did not study* for the test yesterday.
(d)	CONDITIONAL:	If he *were* a good student, he *would have studied* for the test yesterday.
		(present) *(past)*

☐ **EXERCISE 16. Using "mixed time" in conditional sentences. (Chart 20-6)**
   Directions: Change the statements into conditional sentences.

1. I'm hungry now because I didn't eat dinner. But . . . .
    → *But if I'd eaten dinner, I wouldn't be hungry now.*

2. The room is full of flies because you left the door open. But . . . .

3. You are tired this morning because you didn't go to bed at a reasonable hour last night. But . . . .

4. I didn't finish my report yesterday, so I can't begin a new project today. But . . . .

5. Anita is sick because she didn't follow the doctor's orders. But . . . .

6. I'm not you, so I didn't tell him the truth. But . . . .

7. I don't know anything about plumbing, so I didn't fix the leak in the sink myself. But . . . .

8. I received a good job offer from the oil company, so I won't seriously consider taking the job with the electronics firm. But . . . .

20-7 OMITTING *IF*

(a) *Were I* you, I wouldn't do that. (b) *Had I known* I would have told you. (c) *Should anyone call* please take a message.	With *were*, *had* (past perfect), and *should*, sometimes *if* is omitted and the subject and verb are inverted. In (a): *Were I you* = *if I were you.* In (b): *Had I known* = *if I had known.* In (c): *Should anyone call* = *if anyone should call.*

☐ **EXERCISE 17. Omitting IF. (Chart 20-7)**

Directions: Create sentences with the same meaning by omitting *if*.

1. If you should need more money, go to the bank before six o'clock.
   → *Should you need more money, go to the bank before six o'clock.*
2. If I were you, I wouldn't do that.
3. If they had realized the danger, they would have done it differently.
4. If I were your teacher, I would insist you do better work.
5. If you should change your mind, please let me know immediately.
6. She would have gotten the job if she had been better prepared.
7. Your boss sounds like a real tyrant. If I were you, I would look for another job.
8. I'll be out of the country until June 12. If you should need to reach me, I'll be at the Hilton Hotel in Seoul.
9. The artists and creative thinkers throughout the history of the world have changed all of our lives. If they had not dared to be different, the history of civilization would have to be rewritten.
10. If there should be a global nuclear war, life on earth as we know it would end forever.

20-8 IMPLIED CONDITIONS

(a) I *would have gone* with you, *but I had to study*. (b) I never *would have succeeded* without your help.	Often the *if*-clause is implied, not stated. Conditional verbs are still used in the result clause. In (a): the implied condition = *if I hadn't had to study*. In (b): the implied condition = *if you hadn't helped me*.
(c) She ran; *otherwise*, she *would have missed* her bus.	Conditional verbs are frequently used following **otherwise**. In (c), the implied *if*-clause = *if she had not run*.

☐ **EXERCISE 18. Implied conditions. (Chart 20-8)**

Directions: Identify the implied conditions by creating sentences using *if*-clauses.

1. I would have visited you, but I didn't know that you were at home.
   → *I would have visited you if I had known you were at home.*
2. It wouldn't have been a good meeting without Rosa.
   → *It wouldn't have been a good meeting if Rosa hadn't been there.*
3. I would have answered the phone, but I didn't hear it ring.
4. I couldn't have finished the work without your help.
5. I like to travel. I would have gone to Nepal last summer, but I didn't have enough money.
6. I stepped on the brakes. Otherwise, I would have hit the child on the bicycle.
7. Olga turned down the volume on the tape player. Otherwise, the neighbors probably would have called to complain about the noise.
8. Tarek would have finished his education, but he had to quit school and find a job in order to support his family.

☐ EXERCISE 19. Implied conditions. (Chart 20-8)
     Directions: Complete the sentences with your own words.

1. I would have . . . , but I didn't have enough time.
2. I couldn't have . . . without my parents' help.
3. I would . . . , but I don't have enough money.
4. I ran out of time. Otherwise, I would have . . . .
5. I could . . . , but I don't want to.
6. I would have . . . , but I didn't know about it.
7. Without water, all life on earth would . . . .
8. I set my alarm for six every day. Otherwise, I would . . . .
9. I set my alarm for six this morning. Otherwise, I would have . . . .
10. I would have . . . , but I didn't . . . .

☐ EXERCISE 20. Review: conditional sentences. (Charts 20-1 → 20-8)
     Directions: Complete the sentences with the verbs in parentheses. Some of the verbs are passive.

1. If I could speak Japanese, I *(spend)* _____ next year studying in Japan.

2. Had I known Mr. Jung was in the hospital, I *(send)* _____ him a note and some flowers.

3. We will move into our new house next month if it *(complete)* _____ _____ by then.

4. It's too bad that it's snowing. If it *(snow, not)* _____, we could go for a drive.

5. I was very tired. Otherwise, I *(go)* _____ to the party with you last night.

6. I'm glad I have so many friends and such a wonderful family. Life without friends or family *(be)* _____ lonely for me.

7. My grandfather is no longer alive, but if he *(be)* _____, I'm sure he *(be)* _____ proud of me.

8. If you *(sleep, not)* _____ last night when we arrived, I would have asked you to go with us, but I didn't want to wake you up.

9. Bill has such a bad memory that he *(forget)* _____ his head if it *(be, not)* _____ attached to his body.

10. According to one report, the average hen lays 247 eggs a year, and the average person eats 255 eggs a year. If hens *(outnumber, not)* _____ people, the average person *(eat, not)* _____ 255 eggs a year.

11. A: What would you be doing right now if you *(be, not)* _____ in class?

    B: I *(sleep)* _____ .

12. A: Boy, is it ever hot today!

    B: You said it! If there *(be)* _____ only a breeze, it *(be, not)* _____ _____ quite so unbearable.

13. A: Why isn't Peggy Anderson in class today?

    B: I don't know, but I'm sure she *(be, not)* _____ absent unless *

    she *(have)* _____ a good reason.

14. A: Hi. Sorry I'm late.

    B: That's okay.

    A: I *(be)* _____ here sooner, but I had car trouble.

15. A: Want to ride on the roller coaster?

    B: No way! I *(ride, not)* _____ on the roller coaster even if you paid me a million dollars!

16. A: Hi, Pat. Come on in.

    B: Oh, I didn't know you had company. I *(come, not)* _____ if *(I, know)* _____ someone was here.

    A: That's okay. Come in and let me introduce you to my friends.

17. A: Are you coming to the party?

    B: I don't think so, but if I change my mind, I *(tell)* _____ you.

□ **EXERCISE 21. Review: conditional sentences. (Charts 20-1 → 20-8)**
Directions: Complete the sentences. Add commas where necessary.

1. If it hadn't rained . . . .
2. If it weren't raining . . . .
3. You would have passed the test had . . . .

_____

*unless = if not (See Chart 17-8, p. 370.)

4. It's a good thing we took a map with us. Otherwise . . . .

5. Without electricity modern life . . . .

6. If you hadn't reminded me about the meeting tonight . . . .

7. Should you need any help . . . .

8. If I could choose any profession I wanted . . . .

9. If I were at home right now . . . .

10. Without your help yesterday . . . .

11. Were I you . . . .

12. What would you do if . . . .

13. If I had the chance to live my childhood over again . . . .

14. Had I known . . . .

15. Can you imagine what life would be like if . . . .

□ **EXERCISE 22. Activity: conditional sentences. (Charts 20-1 → 20-8)**

Directions: Explain what you would do in these situations. Work in pairs, in groups, or as a class.

Example:

SPEAKER A *(book open):* Suppose the student sitting next to you drops her pen. What would you do?

SPEAKER B *(book closed):* I would pick it up for her.

1. Suppose (pretend) there is a fire in this building right now. What would you do?

2. Suppose there is a fire in your room or apartment or house. You have time to save only one thing. What would you save?

3. Suppose you go to the bank to cash a check for (twenty dollars). The bank teller cashes your check and you leave, but when you count the money, you find she gave you (thirty dollars) instead of (twenty). What would you do?

4. Same situation, but she gave you only (fifteen dollars) instead of (twenty).

5. John was cheating during an examination. Suppose you were the teacher and you saw him. What would you have done?

6. You are at a party. A man starts talking to you, but he is speaking so fast that you can't catch what he is saying. What would you do?

7. Late at night you're driving your car down a deserted street. You're all alone. In an attempt to avoid a dog in the road, you swerve and hit a parked car. You know that no one saw you. What would you do?

8. (. . .) goes to a friend's house for dinner. Her/His friend serves a dish that (. . .) can't stand, doesn't like at all. What if you were (. . .)?

9. My friend borrowed (ten dollars) from me and told me he would repay it in a couple of days, but it's been three weeks. I think he has forgotten about it. I really need the money, but I don't want to ask him for it. Give me some advice.

10. John was driving over the speed limit. A police car began to chase him, with lights flashing. John stepped on the accelerator and tried to escape the police car. Put yourself in his position.

11. Suppose you are walking down the street at night all by yourself. A man suddenly appears in front of you. He has a gun. He says, "Give me your money!" Would you try to take his gun away?

12. Suppose you go to (Chicago) to visit a friend. You have never been there before. Your friend said he would meet you at the airport, but he's not there. You wait a long time, but he never shows up. You try to call him, but nobody answers the phone. Now what?

☐ EXERCISE 23. Activity: conditional sentences. (Charts 20-1 → 20-8)

Directions: Discuss the situations. Use the given information to make conditional sentences.

Example:

Jan is working for a law firm, but she has been trying to find a different job for a long time. She doesn't like her job at the law firm. Recently she was offered a job with a computer company closer to her home. She wanted to accept it, but the salary was too low.
→ *If Jan liked her job at the law firm, she wouldn't be trying to find a different job.*
→ *Jan would have accepted the job at the computer company if the salary hadn't been too low.*
→ Etc.

1. Jim: Why don't we go to the ball game after work tonight?
   Ron: I'd like to, but I can't.
   Jim: Why not?
   Ron: I have a dinner meeting with a client.
   Jim: Well, maybe some other time.

2. Tommy had a pet mouse. He took it to school. His friend Jimmy put the mouse in the teacher's desk drawer. When the teacher found the mouse, she jumped in surprise and tried to kill it with a book. Tommy ran to the front of the room and saved his pet mouse. Tommy and Jimmy got into a lot of trouble with their teacher.

3. Ivan's axe was broken, and he wanted to borrow his neighbor Dan's axe so that he could chop some wood. Then Ivan remembered that he had already borrowed Dan's saw and had never returned it. He has since lost the saw, and he's too embarrassed to tell Dan. Because of that, Ivan decided not to ask Dan for his axe.

□ EXERCISE 24. Activity: conditional sentences. (Charts 20-1 → 20-8)
Directions: Discuss and/or write about one or more of the topics.

1. If, beginning tomorrow, you had a two-week holiday and unlimited funds, what would you do? Why?

2. If you had to teach your language to a person who knew nothing at all about your language, how would you begin? What would you do so that this person could learn your language as quickly and easily as possible?

3. If you were Philosopher-King of the world, how would you govern? What would you do? What changes would you make? (A "Philosopher-King" may be defined as a person who has ideal wisdom and unlimited power to shape the world as s/he wishes.)

4. Suppose you had only one year to live. What would you do?

5. Describe your activities if you were in some other place (in this country or in the world) at present. Describe your probable activities today, yesterday, and tomorrow. Include the activities of other people you would be with if you were in that place.

20-9 USING *AS IF/AS THOUGH*

(a) It looks *like* rain. (b) It looks *as if* it is going to rain. (c) It looks *as though* it is going to rain. (d) It looks *like* it is going to rain. *(informal)*	Notice in (a): *like* is followed by a noun object. Notice in (b) and (c): *as if* and *as though* are followed by a clause. Notice in (d): *like* is followed by a clause. This use of *like* is common in informal English, but is not generally considered appropriate in formal English; *as if* or *as though* is preferred. (a), (b), (c), and (d) all have the same meaning.

"TRUE" STATEMENT (FACT)	VERB FORM AFTER *AS IF/AS THOUGH*	
(e) He *is not* a child.	She talked to him *as if* he *were* a child.	Usually the idea following *as if/as though* is "untrue." In this case, verb usage is similar to that in conditional sentences.
(f) She *did not take* a shower with her clothes on.	When she came in from the rainstorm, she looked *as if* she *had taken* a shower with her clothes on.	
(g) He *has met* her.	He acted *as though* he *had never met* her.	
(h) She *will be* here.	She spoke *as if* she *wouldn't be* here.	

□ EXERCISE 25. Using AS IF/AS THOUGH. (Chart 20-9)
Directions: Using the given idea, complete each sentence with *as if/as though*.

1. *I wasn't run over by a ten-ton truck.*

   I feel terrible. I feel ___as if (as though) I had been run over by a ten-ton truck.___

2. *English is not her native tongue.*

   She speaks English _____

3. *You didn't see a ghost.*

   What's the matter? You look _____

4. *His animals aren't people.*

   I know a farmer who talks to his animals

   _____

   _____

5. *His father is not a general in the army.*

   Sometimes his father gives orders _____

   _____

6. *I didn't climb Mt. Everest.*

   When I reached the fourth floor, I was

   winded. I felt _____

   instead of just three flights of stairs.

7. *He does have a brain in his head.*

   Sometimes he acts _____

8. *We haven't known each other all of our lives.*

   We became good friends almost immediately. After talking to each other for only a

   short time, we felt _____

9. *A giant bulldozer didn't drive down Main Street.*

   After the tornado, the town looked _____

10. *I don't have wings and can't fly.*

    I was so happy that I felt _____

11. *The child won't burst.*

    The child was so excited that he looked _____

12. NOTE: The following sentiments were expressed by Helen Keller, a woman who was
    both blind and deaf but who learned to speak and to read (Braille★). Complete these
    sentences.

    Use your eyes as if tomorrow you _____ become blind. Hear the music

    of voices, the song of a bird, as if you _____ become deaf tomorrow. Touch

    each object as if tomorrow you _____ never be able to feel anything again.

    Smell the perfume of the flowers and taste with true enjoyment each bite of food as if

    tomorrow you _____ never be able to smell and taste again.

★A system of writing for the blind devised by the Frenchman Louis Braille. Blind people read Braille by
 placing the tips of their fingers on raised dots that represent letters, punctuation, etc.

20-10 VERB FORMS FOLLOWING *WISH*

Wish is used when the speaker wants reality to be different, to be exactly the opposite.

	"TRUE" STATEMENT	VERB FORM FOLLOWING *WISH*	*Wish* is followed by a noun clause. (See Chart 12-5, p. 248.) Past verb forms, similar to those in conditional sentences, are used in the noun clause. For example, in (a): *would*, the past form of *will*, is used to make a wish about the future. In (d): the simple past *(knew)* is used to make a wish about the present. In (g): the past perfect *(had come)* is used to make a wish about the past.
A wish about the future	(a) She *will not tell* me. (b) He *isn't going to be* here. (c) She *can't come* tomorrow.	I *wish* (that) she *would tell* me. I *wish* he *were going to be* here. I *wish* she *could come* tomorrow.	
A wish about the present	(d) I *don't know* French. (e) It *is raining* right now. (f) I *can't speak* Japanese.	I *wish* I *knew* French. I *wish* it *weren't raining* right now. I *wish* I *could speak* Japanese.	
A wish about the past	(g) John *didn't come.* (h) Mary *couldn't come.*	I *wish* John *had come.*★ I *wish* Mary *could have come.*	

★Sometimes in very informal speaking: *I wish John **would have come**.*

☐ **EXERCISE 26. Verb forms following WISH. (Chart 20-10)**
Directions: Complete the sentences with an appropriate verb form.

1. Our classroom doesn't have any windows. I wish our classroom _____*had*_____ windows.

2. The sun isn't shining. I wish the sun _____ right now.

3. I didn't go shopping. I wish I _____ shopping.

4. I don't know how to dance. I wish I _____ how to dance.

5. You didn't tell them about it. I wish you _____ them about it.

6. It's cold today. I'm not wearing a coat. I wish I _____ a coat.

7. I don't have enough money to buy that book. I wish I _____ enough money.

8. Elena is tired because she went to bed late last night. She wishes she _____ _____ to bed earlier last night.

9. I can't go with you tomorrow, but I wish I _____.

10. My friend won't ever lend me his car. I wish he _____ me his car for my date tomorrow night.

11. Mrs. Takasawa isn't coming to dinner with us tonight. I wish she _____ _____ to dinner with us.

12. The teacher is going to give an exam tomorrow. I wish he _____ _____ us an exam tomorrow.

13. You can't meet my parents. I wish you _____ them.

14. Khalid didn't come to the meeting. I wish he _____ to the meeting.

15. I am not lying on a beach in Hawaii. I wish I _____ on a beach in Hawaii.

☐ **EXERCISE 27. Activity: verb forms following WISH. (Chart 20-10)**
Directions: Discuss the questions.

1. What is something you can't do, but you wish you could do?
2. What do you wish you were doing right now?
3. What is something you don't have but wish you had?
4. What is something that didn't happen yesterday, but that you wish had happened?
5. What is something that has never happened in your life, but that you wish would happen?
6. What is something that happened in your life, but that you wish had not happened?
7. What is something you have to do but wish you didn't have to do?
8. What is something that will not happen tomorrow, but that you wish would happen?
9. What is something you don't know but wish you knew?
10. What is something you were unable to do yesterday, but you wish you could have done?

☐ **EXERCISE 28. Verb forms following WISH. (Chart 20-10)**
Directions: Complete the sentences with an appropriate auxiliary verb.

1. I'm not at home, but I wish I _____ *were* _____.

2. I don't know her, but I wish I _____ *did* _____.

3. I can't sing well, but I wish I _____ *could* _____.

4. I didn't go, but I wish I _____ *had* _____.

5. He won't talk about it, but I wish he _____ *would* _____.

6. I didn't read that book, but I wish I _____.

7. I want to go, but I can't. I wish I _____.

8. I don't have a bicycle, but I wish I _____.

9. He didn't buy a ticket to the game, but he wishes he _____.

10. She can't speak English, but she wishes she _____.

11. It probably won't happen, but I wish it _____.

12. He isn't old enough to drive a car, but he wishes he _____.

13. They didn't go to the movie, but they wish they _____.

14. I don't have a driver's license, but I wish I _____.

15. I'm not living in an apartment, but I wish I _____.

20-11 USING *WOULD* TO MAKE WISHES ABOUT THE FUTURE

(a) It is raining. I *wish* it **would stop**. *(I want it to stop raining.)* (b) I'm expecting a call. I *wish* the phone **would ring**. *(I want the phone to ring.)*	**Would** is usually used to indicate that the speaker wants something to happen or someone other than the speaker to do something in the future. The wish may or may not come true (be realized).
(c) It's going to be a good party. I *wish* you **would come**. (d) We're going to be late. I *wish* you **would hurry**.	In (c) and (d): ***I wish you would*** . . . is often used to make a request.

☐ **EXERCISE 29. Using WOULD to make wishes. (Chart 20-10 and 20-11)**

Directions: Use the given information to answer the questions.

Example:
TOM: *Why are you watching the telephone?*
SUE: *I'm waiting to hear from Sam. I want him to call me. I need to talk to him right now. We had an argument. I need to make sure everything's okay.*
TOM: *Watching the phone won't make it ring, you know.*

(a) What does Sue want to happen in the near future? (Use *wish + would*.)
   → *She wishes the phone* **would** *ring.*

(b) What else does Sue wish?
   → *She wishes Sam would call her. She wishes she could talk to Sam right now. She probably wishes she and Sam hadn't had an argument.*

1. RITA: *It's raining. I want to go for a walk, but not in the rain.*
    YOKO: *I want the rain to stop, too.*

    (a) What does Rita want to happen in the near future? (Use *wish + would*.)
    (b) What does Yoko wish?

2. ANNA: *Can't you come to the concert? Please change your mind. I'd really like you to come.*
    YOKO: *No, I can't. I have to work.*

    (a) What does Anna want Yoko to do? (Use *wish + would*.)
    (b) What else does Anna wish?

3. BOB'S MOTHER: *Do you really like how you look with a beard?*
              BOB: *Yes.*
    BOB'S MOTHER: *Don't you want to shave it off?*
              BOB: *Nope.*

    (a) What does Bob's mother want Bob to do? (Use *wish + would*.)
    (b) What does Bob probably wish?

4. *Helen is a neat and orderly person. Judy, her roommate, is messy. Judy never picks up after herself. She leaves dirty dishes in the sink. She drops her clothes all over the apartment. She clutters the apartment with her stuff everywhere. She never makes her bed. Helen nags Judy to pick up after herself.*

    (a) What does Helen want Judy to do? (Use *wish + would.*)
    (b) What does Judy probably wish?

☐ EXERCISE 30. Using WISH. (Charts 20-10 and 20-11)
    Directions: Complete the sentences with an appropriate form of the verbs in parentheses.

1. We need some help. I wish Alfred *(be)* _____ here now. If he *(be)* _____, we could finish this work very quickly.

2. We had a good time in Houston over vacation. I wish you *(come)* _____ with us. If you *(come)* _____ with us, you *(have)* _____ _____ a good time.

3. I wish it *(be, not)* _____ so cold today. If it *(be, not)* _____ so cold, I *(go)* _____ swimming.

4. I missed part of the lecture because I was daydreaming, and now my notes are incomplete. I wish I *(pay)* _____ more attention to the lecturer.

5. A: Did you study for that test?
   B: No, but now I wish I *(have)* _____ because I flunked it.

6. A: Is the noise from the TV in the next apartment bothering you?
   B: Yes. I'm trying to study. I wish he *(turn)* _____ it down.

7. A: What a beautiful day! I wish I *(lie)* _____ in the sun by a swimming pool instead of sitting in a classroom.
   B: I wish I *(be)* _____ anywhere but here!

8. A: I wish we *(have, not)* _____ to go to work today.
   B: So do I. I wish it *(be)* _____ a holiday.

9. A: He couldn't have said that! That's impossible. You must have misunderstood him.
   B: I only wish I *(have)* _____, but I'm sure I heard him correctly.

10. Alice doesn't like her job as a nurse. She wishes she *(go, not)* _____ to nursing school.

11. A: I know that something's bothering you. I wish you *(tell)* _____ me what it is. Maybe I can help.
   B: I appreciate it, but I can't discuss it now.

12. A: My feet are killing me! I wish I *(wear)* _____ more

     comfortable shoes.

    B: Yeah, me too. I wish I *(know)* _____ that we were going to

     have to walk this much.

☐ EXERCISE 31. Using WISH. (Charts 20-10 and 20-11)
    Directions: Answer the questions. Use **wish**. Work in pairs, in groups, or as a class.

1. Where do you wish you were right now? What do you wish you were doing?

2. Are you pleased with the weather today, or do you wish it were different?

3. Look around this room. What do you wish were different?

4. Is there anything you wish were different about the place you are living?

5. What do you wish were different about this city/town?

6. What do you wish were different about this country?

7. What do you wish were different about a student's life? about a worker's life?

8. Where do you wish you could go on your next vacation?

9. Your friend gave you his phone number, but you didn't write it down because you thought you would remember it. Now you have forgotten the number. What do you wish?

10. (. . .) kept all of his money in his wallet instead of putting it in the bank. Then he lost his wallet. What does he probably wish?

11. You didn't eat breakfast/lunch/dinner before you came to class. Now you are hungry. What do you wish?

12. (. . .) stayed up very late last night. Today she is tired and sleepy. What does she probably wish?

☐ EXERCISE 32. Using WISH. (Charts 20-10 and 20-11)
    Directions: Using the given ideas, create sentences with **wish**. Add something that explains why you are making that wish.

Examples: be different
      → *I wish my name were different. I've never liked having "Daffodil" as my first name.*

     go to the moon
      → *I wish I could go to the moon for a vacation. It would be fun to be able to leap long
       distances in the moon's lighter gravity.*

1. be different	6. travel by instant teleportation
2. know several world leaders personally	7. remember everything I read
3. speak every language in the world	8. be a big movie star
4. be more patient and understanding	9. read people's minds
5. interview some great people in history	10. be born in the last century

□ **EXERCISE 33. Activity: conditionals and wishes.** (Chapter 20)

    Directions: Answer the questions. Work in pairs, in groups, or as a class.

1. If you could have free service for the rest of your life from a chauffeur, cook, housekeeper, or gardener, which would you choose? Why?

2. If you had to leave your country and build a new life elsewhere, where would you go? Why?

3. If you had control of all medical research in the world and, by concentrating funds and efforts, could find the cure for only one disease in the next 25 years, which disease would you select? Why?

4. If you could stay one particular age for a span of 50 years, what age would you choose? Why? (At the end of the 50 years, you would suddenly turn 50 years older.)

5. You have promised to spend an evening with your best friend. Then you discover you have the chance to spend the evening with *(supply the name of a famous person)*. Your friend is not invited. What would you do? Why?

6. Assume that you have a good job. If your boss told you to do something that you think is wrong, would you do it? Why or why not? (You understand that if you don't do it, you will lose your job.)

7. If you had to choose among perfect health, a loving family, and wealth (and you could have only one of the three during the rest of your life), which would you choose? Why?

8. Just for fun, what do you wish were or could be different in the world? What about animals being able to speak? people being able to fly? there being only one language in the world? being able to take a vacation on the moon? speed of transportation?

9. Is there anything in your past life that you would change? What do you wish you had or had not done? Why?

10. Suppose you were offered the opportunity to be a crew member on a spaceship that would travel to far points in the universe. There would be no guarantee that you would ever return to earth. Would you go? Why or why not?

APPENDIX
Supplementary Grammar Units

CONTENTS

UNIT A: Basic Grammar Terminology

A-1   SUBJECTS, VERBS, AND OBJECTS

(a) *Birds* *fly*. **S** **V** (NOUN) (VERB)	Almost all English sentences contain a subject (**s**) and a verb (**v**). The verb may or may not be followed by an object (**o**).
(b) The *baby* *cried*. **S** **V** (NOUN) (VERB)	VERBS: Verbs that are not followed by an object, as in (a) and (b), are called "intransitive verbs." Common intransitive verbs: *agree, arrive, come, cry, exist, go, happen, live, occur, rain, rise, sleep, stay, walk.* Verbs that are followed by an object, as in (c) and (d), are called "transitive verbs." Common transitive verbs: *build, cut, find, like, make, need, send, use, want.* Some verbs can be either intransitive or transitive. intransitive: *A student studies.* transitive: *A student studies books.*
(c) The *student* *needs* a *pen*. **S** **V** **O** (NOUN) (VERB) (NOUN)	
(d) My *friend* *enjoyed* the *party*. **S** **V** **O** (NOUN) (VERB) (NOUN)	SUBJECTS AND OBJECTS: The subjects and objects of verbs are nouns (or pronouns). Examples of nouns: *person, place, thing, John, Asia, pen, information, appearance, amusement.*

☐ EXERCISE 1. Subjects, verbs, and objects. (Chart A-1)

Directions: <u>Underline</u> the subject (**s**), verb (**v**), and object of the verb (**o**) in each sentence.

           S   V   O

1. The <u>politician</u> <u>supported</u> new <u>taxes</u>.

2. The mechanic repaired the engine.

3. Those boxes contain old photographs.

4. The teacher canceled the test.

5. An earthquake destroyed the village.

6. All birds have feathers.

List all of the nouns in the above sentences.

politician, taxes

_____

☐ EXERCISE 2. Transitive vs. intransitive verbs. (Chart A-1)

Directions: <u>Underline</u> each verb in the sentences. Write **vt** if it is transitive. Write **vi** if it is intransitive.

               VT

1. Mr. West <u>repeated</u> his question.

         VI

2. Smoke <u>rises</u>.

3. The children divided the candy.

4. I sneezed.

5. A strange thing happened.

6. The customer bought some butter.

7. Our team won the game.

8. Our team won yesterday.

9. The fog disappeared, and the sun shone.

10. Omar boiled some water. We made tea and drank it.

A-2 PREPOSITIONS AND PREPOSITIONAL PHRASES

COMMON PREPOSITIONS

about	at	beyond	into	since	up
above	before	by	like	through	upon
across	behind	despite	near	throughout	with
after	below	down	of	till	within
against	beneath	during	off	to	without
along	beside	for	on	toward(s)	
among	besides	from	out	under	
around	between	in	over	until	

(a) **S** **V** **PREP** **O of PREP** The student studies *in* the *library*. (NOUN)	An important element of English sentences is the prepositional phrase. It consists of a preposition (**PREP**) and its object (**O**). The object of a preposition is a noun or pronoun. In (a): ***in the library*** is a prepositional phrase.
(b) **S** **V** **O** **PREP** **O of PREP** We enjoyed the party *at* your *house*. (NOUN)	
(c) We went *to the zoo* *in the afternoon*. (place) (time)	In (c): In most English sentences, "place" comes before "time."
(d) ***In the afternoon***, we went to the zoo.	In (d): Sometimes a prepositional phrase comes at the beginning of a sentence.

☐ **EXERCISE 3. Identifying prepositions. (Chart A-2)**

Directions: Underline the prepositional phrases in the following. Identify the preposition (**P**) and the noun that is used as the object of the preposition (**O of P**).

                    P   O of P

1. Grasshoppers destroyed the wheat in the field.

2. The waiter cleared the dirty dishes from our table.

3. I parked my car in the garage.

4. Trees fell during the violent storm.

5. Cowboys depended on horses for transportation.

6. We walked to the park after class.

☐ **EXERCISE 4. Sentence elements. (Charts A-1 and A-2)**

Directions: Underline the subjects (**S**), verbs (**VT** or **VI**), objects of verbs (**O**), and prepositional phrases (**PP**) in the following sentences.

       S   VT   O   PP

1. Alex needs new batteries for his camera.

        S   VI   PP

2. A bomb exploded in the road.

3. Sally wore her blue suit to the meeting.

4. Beethoven wrote nine symphonies.

5. Bells originated in Asia.

6. Plants need a reliable supply of water.

7. We enjoyed the view of snowy mountains from the window of our hotel room.

8. The child sat between her parents on the sandy beach. Above her, an eagle flew across the cloudless sky.

A-3 ADJECTIVES

(a) Ann is an *intelligent* student.
        (ADJECTIVE) (NOUN)
(b) The *hungry* child ate fruit.
    (ADJECTIVE) (NOUN)
	Adjectives describe nouns. In grammar, we say that adjectives modify nouns. The word "modify" means "change a little." Adjectives give a little different meaning to a noun: *intelligent student, lazy student, good student.* Examples of adjectives: *young, old, rich, beautiful, brown, French, modern.*

(c) I saw some *beautiful* pictures. *INCORRECT*: *beautifuls pictures*	An adjective is neither singular nor plural. A final *-s* is never added to an adjective.

A-4 ADVERBS

(a) He walks *quickly*.
       (ADVERB)
(b) She opened the door *quietly*.
           (ADVERB)
	Adverbs modify verbs. Often they answer the question *"How?"* In (a): *How does he walk?* Answer: *Quickly.*
	Adverbs are often formed by adding *-ly* to an adjective.
	    adjective: **quick**
	    adverb: **quickly**

(c) I am *extremely* happy. (ADVERB) (ADJECTIVE)	Adverbs are also used to modify adjectives, i.e., to give information about adjectives, as in (c).
(d) Ann will come *tomorrow*. (ADVERB)	Adverbs are also used to express time or frequency. Examples: *tomorrow, today, yesterday, soon, never, usually, always, yet.*

MIDSENTENCE ADVERBS
(e) Ann *always* comes on time.
(f) Ann *is always* on time.
(g) Ann *has always come* on time.
(h) *Does she always come* on time?
	Some adverbs may occur in the middle of a sentence. Midsentence adverbs have usual positions; they
	    (1) come in front of simple present and simple past verbs (except **be**), as in (e);
	    (2) follow **be** (simple present and simple past), as in (f);
	    (3) come between a helping verb and a main verb, as in (g).
	In a question, a midsentence adverb comes directly after the subject, as in (h).

COMMON MIDSENTENCE ADVERBS

ever	*usually*	*generally*	*seldom*	*never*	*already*
always	*often*	*sometimes*	*rarely*	*not ever*	*finally*
	frequently	*occasionally*	*hardly ever*		*just*
					probably

☐ EXERCISE 5. Nouns, verbs, adjectives, adverbs. (Charts A-1 → A-4)
   Directions: <u>Underline</u> the adjectives (**ADJ**) and adverbs (**ADV**) in the sentences.

         ADJ   ADV   ADJ
1. A <u>terrible</u> fire spread <u>rapidly</u> through the <u>old</u> house.

2. A small child cried noisily in the third row of the theater.

3. The eager player waited impatiently for the start of the game.

4. An unusually large crowd came to the concert.

5. Arthur carefully repaired the antique vase with special glue.

6. On especially busy days, the telephone in the main office rings constantly.

The above six sentences have 10 adjectives and 7 adverbs.

Count the total number of nouns in the above six sentences: _____

Count the total number of verbs in the above six sentences: _____

☐ EXERCISE 6. Adjectives and adverbs. (Charts A-3 and A-4)
   Directions: Choose the correct adjective or adverb in parentheses.

1. George is a *(careless, carelessly)* writer. He writes *(careless, carelessly)*.
2. Frank asked me an *(easy, easily)* question. I answered it *(easy, easily)*.
3. Sally speaks *(soft, softly)*. She has a *(soft, softly)* voice.
4. I entered the classroom *(quiet, quietly)* because I was late.
5. Ali speaks English very *(good, well)*. He has very *(good, well)* pronunciation.*

☐ EXERCISE 7. Midsentence adverbs. (Chart A-4)
   Directions: Put each adverb in parentheses in its usual midsentence position.

1. *(never)*   Erica has seen snow. → *Erica has never seen snow.*
2. *(often)*   Ted studies at the library in the evening.
3. *(often)*   Ann is at the library in the evening, too.
4. *(already)*   Fred has finished studying for tomorrow's test.
5. *(seldom)*   Jack is at home.
6. *(always)*   Does he stay there?
7. *(often)*   He goes into town to hang around with his buddies.
8. *(always)*   You should tell the truth.

---

*The word **well** can be either an adverb or an adjective.
    *Ron writes **well**.* **well** = an adverb meaning "in a good manner." It describes how Ron writes.
    *Mary was sick, but now she **is well**.* **well** = an adjective meaning "healthy, not sick." It follows the verb
    be and describes the subject "she"; i.e., Mary is a *well person*, not a sick person.
NOTE: After the linking verb *feel*, either **good** or **well** may be used:
    *I feel **good** and I feel **well*** have essentially the same meaning. However, **well** usually refers specifically to
    health, whereas **good** can refer to one's physical and/or emotional condition.

A-5 THE VERB *BE*

(a) John *is* **a student**. 　　(BE)　(NOUN) (b) John *is* **intelligent**. 　　(BE)　(ADJ) (c) John *was* **at the library**. 　　(BE)　(PREP. PHRASE)	A sentence with **be** as the main verb has three basic patterns: In (a): **be** + *a noun* In (b): **be** + *an adjective* In (c): **be** + *a prepositional phrase*
(d) Mary *is* writing a letter. (e) They *were* listening to some music. (f) That letter *was* written by Alice.	**Be** is also used as an auxiliary verb in progressive verb tenses and in the passive. In (d): **is** = *auxiliary*; **writing** = *main verb*

TENSE FORMS OF *BE*

	SIMPLE PRESENT	SIMPLE PAST	PRESENT PERFECT
SINGULAR	*I* **am** *you* **are** *he, she, it* **is**	*I* **was** *you* **were** *he, she, it* **was**	*I* **have been** *you* **have been** *he, she, it* **has been**
PLURAL	*we, you, they* **are**	*we, you, they* **were**	*we, you, they* **have been**

A-6 LINKING VERBS

(a) The soup　*smells*　　**good**. 　　(LINKING VERB)　(ADJECTIVE) (b) This food *tastes delicious*. (c) The children *feel happy*. (d) The weather *became cold*.	Other verbs like **be** that may be followed immediately by an adjective are called "linking verbs." An adjective following a linking verb describes the subject of a sentence.★ Common verbs that may be followed by an adjective: 　• *feel, look, smell, sound, taste* 　• *appear, seem* 　• *become* (and *get, turn, grow* when they mean "become")

★COMPARE:
> (1) *The man looks angry.* → An adjective *(angry)* follows **look**. The adjective describes the subject *(the man)*. **Look** has the meaning of "appear."
> (2) *The man looked at me angrily.* → An adverb *(angrily)* follows **look at**. The adverb describes the action of the verb. **Look at** has the meaning of "regard, watch."

☐ EXERCISE 8. Linking verbs. (Charts A-3 → A-6)
> *Directions:* Choose the correct adjective or adverb in parentheses.

> 1. This math problem looks *(easy, easily)*. I'm sure I can do it *(easy, easily)*.
> 2. That chair looks *(comfortable, comfortably)*.
> 3. I looked at the problem *(careful, carefully)* and then solved it.
> 4. I felt *(sad, sadly)* when I heard the news.
> 5. Susan smiled *(cheerful, cheerfully)*. She seemed *(cheerful, cheerfully)*.
> 6. I tasted the soup *(careful, carefully)* because it was hot. The soup tasted *(good, well)*.
> 7. The room got *(quiet, quietly)* when the professor entered. The students sat *(quiet, quietly)* at their desks.
> 8. The sky grew *(dark, darkly)* as the storm approached.

□ EXERCISE 9. Nouns, verbs, adjectives, adverbs, prepositions. (Charts A-1 → A-6)

Directions: Identify each underlined word as a noun, verb, adjective, adverb, or preposition.

          PREP   NOUN

1. Through the centuries, many people have confused whales with fish.

2. Whales are mammals, not fish. They breathe air and give birth to live young.

3. Some species of whales dive deeply beneath the surface of the ocean in order to feed and can stay under the water for more than an hour. All whales, however, must come to the surface for air.

4. Whales make the longest migrations known among mammals. Gray whales swim from the Pacific coast of Mexico, where they give birth in winter, to the icy Arctic for the summer.

5. Orca whales, which are black and white, are highly trainable. They are also called "killer whales," but trainers tell us that these whales are intelligent and sensitive. One time, a newly captured male orca refused to eat for a long time. Finally, he took a fish from the trainer. However, he didn't eat the fish immediately; he took it to another recently captured whale, a female who had also refused to eat, and shared it with her.

6. Whales have no sense of smell and poor eyesight. Their senses of touch and hearing, however, are highly developed. They can hear an extremely wide range of sounds and use sound to locate objects.

7. Whales do not have vocal chords, but they can communicate <u>with</u> each other. They have a wide range of <u>clicks</u>, <u>whistles</u>, and <u>songs</u>. When a whale is captured in a net, other whales <u>gather</u> <u>around</u> it and <u>communicate</u> <u>through</u> the net. They follow the captured whale for long distances.

UNIT B: Questions

B-1 FORMS OF YES/NO AND INFORMATION QUESTIONS

A yes/no question = a question that may be answered by *yes* or *no*.
A: Does he live in Chicago?
B: Yes, he does. OR No, he doesn't.

An information question = a question that asks for information by using a question word.
A: Where does he live?
B: In Chicago.

Question word order = *(Question word) + helping verb + subject + main verb*
Notice that the same subject-verb order is used in both yes/no and information questions.

(QUESTION WORD)	HELPING VERB	SUBJECT	MAIN VERB	(REST OF SENTENCE)	
(a)	*Does*	*she*	*live*	there?	If the verb is in the simple present, use **does** (with *he, she, it*) or **do** (with *I, you, we, they*) in the question. If the verb is simple past, use **did**. Notice: The main verb in the question is in its simple form; there is no final *-s* or *-ed*.
(b) Where	*does*	*she*	*live?*		
(c)	*Do*	*they*	*live*	there?	
(d) Where	*do*	*they*	*live?*		
(e)	*Did*	*he*	*live*	there?	
(f) Where	*did*	*he*	*live?*		
(g)	*Is*	*he*	*living*	there?	If the verb has an auxiliary (a helping verb), the same auxiliary is used in the question. There is no change in the form of the main verb. If the verb has more than one auxiliary, only the first auxiliary precedes the subject, as in (m) and (n).
(h) Where	*is*	*he*	*living?*		
(i)	*Have*	*they*	*lived*	there?	
(j) Where	*have*	*they*	*lived?*		
(k)	*Can*	*Mary*	*live*	there?	
(l) Where	*can*	*Mary*	*live?*		
(m)	*Will*	*he*	*be living*	there?	
(n) Where	*will*	*he*	*be living?*		
(o) Who	Ø	Ø	*lives*	there?	If the question word is the subject, usual question word order is not used; **does**, **do**, and **did** are not used. The verb is in the same form in a question as it is in a statement. Statement: *Tom came.* Question: *Who came?*
(p) Who	*can*	Ø	*come?*		
(q)	*Are*	*they*	Ø	there?	Main verb **be** in the simple present *(am, is, are)* and simple past *(was, were)* precedes the subject. It has the same position as a helping verb.
(r) Where	*are*	*they?*	Ø		
(s)	*Was*	*Jim*	Ø	there?	
(t) Where	*was*	*Jim?*	Ø		

☐ EXERCISE 10. Forms of yes/no and information questions. (Chart B-1)

Directions: For each of the following, first make a yes/no question. Then make an information question using **where**.

Example: They can stay there.
Yes/no question: Can they stay there?
Information question: Where can they stay?

1. She stays there.
2. She is staying there.
3. She will stay there.
4. She is going to stay there.
5. They stayed there.
6. They will be staying there.
7. They should stay there.
8. He has stayed there.
9. He has been staying there.
10. John is there.
11. John will be there.
12. John has been there.
13. Judy will have been there.
14. Ann and Tom were married there.
15. This package should have been taken there.

B-2 QUESTION WORDS

	QUESTION	ANSWER	
WHEN	(a) *When* did they arrive? *When* will you come?	Yesterday. Next Monday.	*When* is used to ask questions about *time*.
WHERE	(b) *Where* is she? *Where* can I find a pen?	At home. In that drawer.	*Where* is used to ask questions about *place*.
WHY	(c) *Why* did he leave early? *Why* aren't you coming with us?	Because he's ill. I'm tired.	*Why* is used to ask questions about *reason*.
HOW	(d) *How* did you come to school? *How* does he drive?	By bus. Carefully.	*How* generally asks about *manner*.
	(e) *How much* money does it cost? *How many* people came?	Ten dollars. Fifteen.	*How* is used with **much** and **many**.
	(f) *How old* are you? *How cold* is it? *How soon* can you get here? *How fast* were you driving?	Twelve. Ten below zero. In ten minutes. 50 miles an hour.	*How* is also used with adjectives and adverbs.
	(g) *How long* has he been here? *How often* do you write home? *How far* is it to Miami from here?	Two years. Every week. 500 miles.	*How long* asks about *length of time*. *How often* asks about *frequency*. *How far* asks about *distance*.

WHO	(h) *Who* can answer that question? *Who* came to visit you?	I can. Jane and Eric.	*Who* is used as the subject of a question. It refers to people.
	(i) *Who* is coming to dinner tonight? *Who* wants to come with me?	Ann, Bob, and Al. We do.	*Who* is usually followed by a singular verb even if the speaker is asking about more than one person.
WHOM	(j) *Who(m)* did you see? *Who(m)* are you visiting? (k) *Who(m)* should I talk *to*? *To whom* should I talk? *(formal)*	I saw George. My relatives. The secretary.	*Whom* is used as the object of a verb or preposition. In everyday spoken English, *whom* is rarely used; *who* is used instead. *Whom* is used only in formal questions. Note: *Whom*, not *who*, is used if preceded by a preposition.
WHOSE	(l) *Whose* book did you borrow? *Whose* key is this? (*Whose* is this?)	David's. It's mine.	*Whose* asks questions about *possession*.
WHAT	(m) *What* made you angry? *What* went wrong?	His rudeness. Everything.	*What* is used as the subject of a question. It refers to things.
	(n) *What* do you need? *What* did Alice buy? (o) *What* did he talk *about*? *About what* did he talk? *(formal)*	I need a pencil. A book. His vacation.	*What* is also used as an object.
	(p) *What kind of* soup is that? *What kind of* shoes did he buy?	It's bean soup. Sandals.	*What kind of* asks about the particular variety or type of something.
	(q) *What did* you *do* last night? *What is* Mary *doing*?	I studied. Reading a book.	*What* + *a form of do* is used to ask questions about activities.
	(r) *What countries* did you visit? *What time* did she come? *What color* is his hair?	Italy and Spain. Seven o'clock. Dark brown.	*What* may accompany a noun.
	(s) *What is* Ed *like*? (t) *What is* the weather *like*?	He's kind and friendly. Hot and humid.	*What* + *be like* asks for a general description of qualities.
	(u) *What does* Ed *look like*? (v) *What does* her house *look like*?	He's tall and has dark hair. It's a two-story,* red brick house.	*What* + *look like* asks for a physical description.
WHICH	(w) I have two pens. *Which pen* do you want? *Which one* do you want? *Which do* you want? (x) *Which book* should I buy?	The blue one. That one.	*Which* is used instead of *what* when a question concerns choosing from a definite, known quantity or group.
	(y) *Which countries* did he visit? *What countries* did he visit? (z) *Which class* are you in? *What class* are you in?	Peru and Chile. This class.	In some cases, there is little difference in meaning between *which* and *what* when they accompany a noun, as in (y) and (z).

*American English: *a two-story house.*
British English: *a two-storey house.*

☐ **EXERCISE 11. Information questions. (Charts B-1 and B-2)**

Directions: Work in pairs, in groups, or as a class.

Speaker A: Give the cues in the text. The first of the two cues is the answer to the question you want Speaker B to form. Your book is open.

Speaker B: Make an appropriate question for the answer Speaker A gives you. Your book is closed.

Examples:

SPEAKER A *(book open):* The teacher. The teacher opened the door.

SPEAKER B *(book closed):* Who opened the door?

SPEAKER A *(book open):* Opening the door. The teacher is opening the door.

SPEAKER B *(book closed):* What is the teacher doing?

1. My friend. That letter is from my friend.
2. Maria. Maria wrote that letter.
3. My mother's. That is my mother's coat.
4. In August. Alice and John are going to get married in August.
5. Gray. Her eyes are gray.
6. Black. Her hair is black.
7. Herb tea. I'd like some herb tea.
8. Coffee. I usually drink coffee with my breakfast.
9. The soap bubbles. The soap bubbles made her sneeze.
10. Ten minutes. It usually takes me ten minutes to eat breakfast.
11. By taxi. I got to the airport by taxi.
12. A ball. The boy has a ball in his pocket.*
13. Four. I have four brothers and sisters.
14. Florida. I grew up in Florida.
15. Five hours. It takes five hours to get there by plane.
16. Historical novels. I like to read historical novels.
17. Chapters 2 and 3. The test will cover Chapters 2 and 3.
18. Because the traffic was heavy. I was late because the traffic was heavy.**
19. For three days. She's been sick for three days.
20. Twenty. I'm going to invite twenty people to my party.
21. This one. You should buy this camera, not that one.
22. Marie Curie. Marie Curie discovered radium.
23. Practicing asking questions. We're practicing asking questions.
24. Great. Everything's going great.

---

*A form of **do** is usually used in questions when the main verb is **have** (especially in American English but also commonly in British English); e.g. *Do you have a car?* Using **have** without a form of **do** is also possible but less common; e.g., *Have you a car?*

  NOTE: Especially in British English but also in American English, the idiom **have got** is used to indicate possession instead of **have** alone; e.g., *Bob **has got** a car. **Have** you **got** a car?*

In informal spoken English, another way of asking **why is **how come**. Usual question word order is not used with **how come**; instead, the subject comes in front of the verb.

  Example: John isn't here *(because he is sick).* → *Why isn't John here?* OR

                       How come John isn't here?

☐ EXERCISE 12. Activity: asking questions. (Charts B-1 and B-2)

Directions: Pair up with another student. Together create a dialogue for one or more of the situations. One of you is Speaker A, and the other is Speaker B. If you don't have a partner, write a dialogue as you would imagine the conversation to go. The beginning of each dialogue is given.

1. *This conversation takes place after class is over.*
   Speaker A: You are a student. You have a problem.
   Speaker B: You are a teacher. You try to solve the problem.

   SPEAKER A: Excuse me, _____. Do you have a few minutes?
   SPEAKER B: Certainly.
   SPEAKER A: I'd like to talk to you about _____.
   SPEAKER B: _____.
   Etc.

2. *This conversation takes place on the telephone.*
   Speaker A: You work for a travel agency.
   Speaker B: You want to take a trip.

   SPEAKER A: Hello. Worldwide Travel Agency. May I help you?
   SPEAKER B: Yes. I need to make arrangements to go to _____.
   Etc.

3. *This conversation takes place at a job interview.*
   Speaker A: You are the interviewer.
   Speaker B: You are the interviewee.

   SPEAKER A: Mr./Ms. _____, isn't it?
   SPEAKER B: Yes.
   SPEAKER A: I'm Mr./Ms. _____. It's nice to meet you. Come in and have a seat.
   Etc.

4. *Choose a situation that involves one person asking another person a series of questions. Assign yourselves roles and make up a conversation.*

B-3 SHORTENED YES/NO QUESTIONS

(a) *Going to bed now? = Are you going to bed now?* (b) *Finish your work? = Did you finish your work?* (c) *Want to go to the movie with us? = Do you want to go to the movie with us?*	Sometimes in spoken English, the auxiliary and the subject *you* are dropped from a yes/no question, as in (a), (b), and (c).

☐ EXERCISE 13. Shortened yes/no questions. (Chart B-3)

Directions: Find the shortened questions, then give the complete question form.

1. A: Need some help? → *Do you need some help?*
   B: Thanks.

2. A: Why do you keep looking out of the window? Expecting someone?
   B: I'm waiting for the mail to come.

3. A: You look tired.
   B: I am.
   A: Stay up late last night?
   B: Yup.

4. A: I'm looking forward to going to Colorado over spring vacation.
   B: Ever been there before?

5. A: Why are you pacing the floor? Nervous?
   B: Who me?

6. A: Want a cup of coffee?
   B: Only if it's already made.

7. A: Heard any news about your scholarship?
   B: Not yet.

8. A: Hungry?
   B: Yeah. You?

B-4 NEGATIVE QUESTIONS

(a) ***Doesn't she live*** in the dormitory? (b) ***Does she not live*** in the dormitory? *(very formal)*	In a yes/no question in which the verb is negative, usually a contraction (e.g., *does* + *not* = *doesn't*) is used, as in (a). Example (b) is very formal and is usually not used in everyday speech. Negative questions are used to indicate the speaker's idea (i.e., what s/he believes is or is not true) or attitude (e.g., surprise, shock, annoyance, anger).

(c) Bob returns to his dorm room after his nine o'clock class. Matt, his roommate, is there. Bob is surprised.
   Bob says, *"What are you doing here?* ***Aren't you supposed to be in class now?"***
(d) Alice and Mary are at home. Mary is about to leave on a trip, and Alice is going to take her to the airport.
   Alice says, *"It's already two o'clock. We'd better leave for the airport.* ***Doesn't your plane leave at three?"***
	In (c): Bob believes that Matt is supposed to be in class now.
	Expected answer: **Yes.**
	
	In (d): Alice believes that Mary's plane leaves at three. She is asking the negative question to make sure that her information is correct.
	Expected answer: **Yes.**

(e) The teacher is talking to Jim about a test he failed. The teacher is surprised that Jim failed the test because he usually does very well.
   The teacher says: *"What happened?* ***Didn't you study?"***
(f) Barb and Ron are riding in a car. Ron is driving. He comes to a corner where there is a stop sign, but he does not stop the car. Barb is shocked.
   Barb says, *"What's the matter with you?* ***Didn't you see that stop sign?"***
	In (e): The teacher believes that Jim did not study.
	Expected answer: **No.**
	
	In (f): Barb believes that Ron did not see the stop sign.
	Expected answer: **No.**

☐ **EXERCISE 14. Negative questions. (Chart B-4)**

Directions: Sometimes the expected answer to a negative question is "yes" and sometimes "no." In the following dialogues, make negative questions from the words in parentheses and determine the expected response.

1. A: Why didn't you come too lunch with us? *(be hungry)* **Weren't you hungry** ?

   B: _____ . I had a late breakfast.

2. A: It's almost dinner time, and you haven't eaten since breakfast.

   (you, be) _____ hungry?

   B: _____ . I'm starving. Let's go eat.

3. A: You look tired this morning. *(you, sleep)* _____ well?

   B: _____ . I tossed and turned all night.

4. A: Daddy, Tommy said that the sun rises in the west. *(it, rise)* _____ in the east?

   B: _____ , Annie. You're right. Tommy is a little mixed up.

5. A: See that man over there, the one in the green shirt?

   B: Yes. Who is he?

   A: *(you, recognize)* _____ him?

   B: _____ . Am I supposed to?

6. A: I can't understand why David isn't here yet. *(he, say, not)* _____

   _____ he would be here by 4:00?

   B: _____ . Something must have delayed him. I'm sure he'll be here soon.

7. A: What's the matter? Everyone else at the party seems to be having fun, but you look bored. *(you, have, not)* _____ a good time?

   B: _____ . I'm thinking about going home pretty soon.

8. A: Did you know that the Missouri River is the longest river in the United States?

   B: Are you sure? *(the Mississippi, be, not)* _____ the longest?

   A: _____ . The Missouri is around 2,565 miles (4,130 kilometers) long. The Mississippi is around 2,350 miles (3,800 kilometers).

Missouri River

Mississippi River

B-5 TAG QUESTIONS

(a) Jack *can* come, *can't* he? (b) Fred *can't* come, *can* he?	A tag question is a question added at the end of a sentence. Speakers use tag questions chiefly to make sure their information is correct or to seek agreement.★

AFFIRMATIVE SENTENCE **+** NEGATIVE TAG → AFFIRMATIVE ANSWER EXPECTED

Mary *is* here,	*isn't* she?	Yes, she is.
You *like* tea,	*don't* you?	Yes, I do.
They *have left*,	*haven't* they?	Yes, they have.

NEGATIVE SENTENCE **+** AFFIRMATIVE TAG → NEGATIVE ANSWER EXPECTED

Mary *isn't* here	*is* she?	No, she isn't.
You *don't like* tea,	*do* you?	No, I don't.
They *haven't left*,	*have* they?	No, they haven't.

(c) *This/That* is your book, isn't *it?* *These/Those* are yours, aren't *they?*	The tag pronoun for *this/that* = *it*. The tag pronoun for *these/those* = *they*.
(d) *There is* a meeting tonight, *isn't there?*	In sentences with *there + be*, *there* is used in the tag.
(e) *Everything* is okay, isn't *it?* (f) *Everyone* took the test, didn't *they?*	Personal pronouns are used to refer to indefinite pronouns. *They* is usually used in a tag to refer to *everyone, everybody, someone, somebody, no one, nobody.*
(g) *Nothing is* wrong, *is* it? (h) *Nobody called* on the phone, *did* they? (i) You*'ve never been* there, *have* you?	Sentences with negative words take affirmative tags.
(j) *I am* supposed to be here, *am I not?* (k) *I am* supposed to be here, *aren't I?*	In (j): *am I not?* is formal English. In (k): *aren't I?* is common in spoken English.

★A tag question may be spoken:
   (1) with a rising intonation if the speaker is truly seeking to ascertain that his/her information, idea, belief is correct (e.g., *Ann lives in an apartment, doesn't she?*); OR
   (2) with a falling intonation if the speaker is expressing an idea with which s/he is almost certain the listener will agree (e.g., *It's a nice day today, isn't it?*).

☐ EXERCISE 15. Tag questions. (Chart B-5)
   Directions: Add tag questions.

   1. They want to come, ___*don't they*___?

   2. Elizabeth is a dentist, _____?

   3. They won't be there, _____?

   4. You'll be there, _____?

   5. There aren't any problems, _____?

   6. That's your umbrella, _____?

   7. George is a student, _____?

   8. He's learned a lot in the last couple of years, _____?

9. Larry has* a bicycle, _____?

10. Monkeys can't swim, _____?

11. Tina will help us later, _____?

12. Peggy would like to come with us to the party, _____?

13. Those aren't Tony's books, _____?

14. You've never been to Paris, _____?

15. There is something wrong with Jane today, _____?

16. Everyone can learn how to swim, _____?

17. Nobody cheated on the exam, _____?

18. Nothing went wrong while I was gone, _____?

19. I am invited, _____?

20. This grammar is easy, _____?

☐ EXERCISE 16. Tag questions. (Chart B-5)
   Directions: Add tag questions. Work in pairs, in groups, or as a class.

   Example: (Carlos) is a student . . . .
   SPEAKER A *(book open):* (Carlos) is a student . . . .
   SPEAKER B *(book closed):* . . . isn't he?

1. That's (. . .)'s pen . . . .
2. (. . .) is living in an apartment . . . .
3. (. . .) lives on (Main Street) . . . .
4. There isn't a test tomorrow . . . .
5. (. . .) has his/her book . . . .
6. You had a good time . . . .
7. (. . .) has been invited to the party . . . .
8. You didn't forget your key . . . .
9. Your parents haven't arrived yet . . . .
10. Turtles lay eggs . . . .
11. (. . .) can't speak (Arabic) . . . .
12. (. . .) is never late to class . . . .
13. Something will be done about that problem right away . . . .
14. These keys don't belong to you . . . .
15. You used to live in New York . . . .
16. There's a better way to solve that problem . . . .
17. (. . .) is going to come to class tomorrow . . . .
18. You should leave for the airport by six . . . .
19. (. . .) doesn't have a car . . . .
20. (. . .) sat next to (. . .) yesterday . . . .
21. We have class tomorrow . . . .
22. You've already seen that movie . . . .
23. (. . .) will help us . . . .
24. Nobody has told you the secret . . . .
25. I am right . . . .
26. Class ends at (ten) . . . .

---

*A form of *do* is usually used in the tag when *have* is the main verb: *Tom **has** a car, **doesn't** he?* Also possible, but less common: *Tom **has** a car, **hasn't** he?*

UNIT C: Contractions

C CONTRACTIONS

IN SPEAKING: In everyday spoken English, certain forms of *be* and auxiliary verbs are usually contracted with pronouns, nouns, and question words.

IN WRITING: (1) In written English, contractions with pronouns are common in informal writing, but not generally acceptable in formal writing.

(2) Contractions with nouns and question words are, for the most part, rarely used in writing. A few of these contractions may be found in quoted dialogue in stories or in very informal writing, such as a chatty letter to a good friend, but most of them are rarely if ever written.

In the following, quotation marks indicate that the contraction is frequently spoken, but rarely if ever written.

	WITH PRONOUNS	**WITH NOUNS**	**WITH QUESTION WORDS**
am	*I'm* reading a book.	Ø	*"What'm"* I supposed to do?
is	*She's* studying. *It's* going to rain.	My *"book's"* on the table. *Mary's* at home.	*Where's* Sally? *Who's* that man?
are	*You're* working hard. *They're* waiting for us.	My *"books're"* on the table. The *"teachers're"* at a meeting.	*"What're"* you doing? *"Where're"* they going?
has	*She's* been here for a year. *It's* been cold lately.	My *"book's"* been stolen! *Sally's* never met him.	*Where's* Sally been living? *What's* been going on?
have	*I've* finished my work. *They've* never met you.	The *"books've"* been sold. The *"students've"* finished the test.	*"Where've"* they been? *"How've"* you been?
had	*He'd* been waiting for us. *We'd* forgotten about it.	The *"books'd"* been sold. *"Mary'd"* never met him before.	*"Where'd"* you been before that? *"Who'd"* been there before you?
did	Ø	Ø	*"What'd"* you do last night? *"How'd"* you do on the test?
will	*I'll* come later. *She'll* help us.	The *"weather'll"* be nice tomorrow. *"John'll"* be coming soon.	*"Who'll"* be at the meeting? *"Where'll"* you be at ten?
would	*He'd* like to go there. *They'd* come if they could.	My *"friends'd"* come if they could. *"Mary'd"* like to go there, too.	*"Where'd"* you like to go?

☐ EXERCISE 17. Contractions. (Chart C)

Directions: Read the sentences aloud. Practice usual contracted speech.

Example: The streets are wet. → "The streets're wet."

PART I. CONTRACTIONS WITH NOUNS

1. My friend is here.
2. My friends are here.
3. Tom has been here since two.
4. The students have been here since one.
5. Bob had already left.
6. Bob would like to come with us.
7. Ron will be here soon.
8. The window is open.
9. The windows are open.
10. Jane has never seen a ghost.
11. The boys have been there before.
12. Sally had forgotten her book.
13. Sally would forget her book if I didn't remind her to take it.

14. Who is that woman?
15. Who are those people?
16. Who has been taking care of your house?
17. What have you been doing?
18. What had you been doing before that?
19. What would you like to do?

20. What did you do yesterday?
21. Why did you stay home?
22. When will I see you again?
23. How long will you be away?
24. Where am I supposed to go?
25. Where did you stay?

UNIT D: Negatives

D-1 USING *NOT* AND OTHER NEGATIVE WORDS

(a) AFFIRMATIVE: The earth is round. (b) NEGATIVE: The earth is *not* flat.	*Not* expresses a *negative* idea.

AUX + *NOT* + MAIN VERB (c) I *will* *not* *go* there. I *have* *not* *gone* there. I *am* *not* *going* there. I *was* *not* there. I *do* *not* *go* there. He *does* *not* *go* there. I *did* *not* *go* there.	*Not* immediately follows an auxiliary verb or *be*. (Note: If there is more than one auxiliary, *not* comes immediately after the first auxiliary: *I **will** **not be** going there.*) ***Do*** or ***does*** is used with ***not*** to make a simple present verb (except ***be***) negative. ***Did*** is used with ***not*** to make a simple past verb (except ***be***) negative.

CONTRACTIONS OF AUXILIARY VERBS WITH *NOT*

are not = aren't★ *cannot = can't* *could not = couldn't* *did not = didn't* *does not = doesn't* *do not = don't*	*has not = hasn't* *have not = haven't* *had not = hadn't* *is not = isn't* *must not = mustn't* *should not = shouldn't*	*was not = wasn't* *were not = weren't* *will not = won't* *would not = wouldn't*

(d) I almost *never* go there.
     I have *hardly ever* gone there.
 	
 (e) There's *no* chalk in the drawer.
	In addition to *not*, the following are negative adverbs:
	     never, rarely, seldom
	     hardly (ever), scarcely (ever), barely (ever)
	 No also expresses a negative idea.

COMPARE: *NOT* vs. *NO* (f) I *do not have* any money. (g) I have *no money*.	*Not* is used to make a verb negative, as in (f). *No* is used as an adjective in front of a noun (e.g., *money*), as in (g). Note: (f) and (g) have the same meaning.

★Sometimes in spoken English you will hear "ain't." It means "am not," "isn't," or "aren't." *Ain't* is not considered proper English, but many people use *ain't* regularly, and it is also frequently used for humor.

☐ EXERCISE 18. Using NOT and NO. (Chart D-1)
    Directions: Complete the sentences with ***not*** or ***no***.

1. There are ____no____ mountains in Iowa. You will ____not____ see any mountains in Iowa.

2. Fish have _____ eyelids. They are _____ able to shut their eyes, and although they rest, they do _____ actually go to sleep in the same way mammals do.

3. _____ automobiles are permitted in the park on Sundays.

4. I can do it by myself. I need _____ help.

5. The operation was _____ successful. The patient did _____ survive.

6. When I became ill, I had _____ choice but to cancel my trip.

7. The opera *Rigoletto* was _____ composed by Mozart; it was composed by Verdi.

8. I have _____ patience with cheaters.

9. Ask me _____ questions, and I'll tell you _____ lies.

10. You should _____ ask people embarrassing questions about their personal lives.

11. "Colour" is spelled with a "u" in British English, but there is _____ "u" in the American English spelling ("color").

12. I excitedly reeled in my fishing line, but the big fish I had expected to find did _____ appear. Instead, I pulled up an old rubber boot.

D-2 AVOIDING DOUBLE NEGATIVES

(a) INCORRECT: I *don't* have *no* money. (b) CORRECT: I ***don't*** have ***any*** *money.* CORRECT: I have ***no*** *money.*	(a) is an example of a "double negative," i.e., a confusing and grammatically incorrect sentence that contains two negatives in the same clause. One clause should contain only one negative.*

*NOTE: Negatives in two different clauses in the same sentence cause no problems; for example:
    *A person who **doesn't** have love **can't** be truly happy.*
    *I **don't** know why he **isn't** here.*

☐ EXERCISE 19. Error analysis: double negatives. (Chart D-2)
    Directions: Correct the sentences, all of which contain double negatives.

1. I don't need no help. → *I don't need any help.* OR *I need no help.*

2. I didn't see nobody.

3. I can't never understand him.

4. He doesn't like neither coffee nor tea.

5. I didn't do nothing.

6. I can't hardly hear the radio. Would you please turn it up?

7. The beach was deserted. We couldn't see nothing but sand.

8. Methods of horse training haven't barely changed at all in the last eight centuries.

D-3 BEGINNING A SENTENCE WITH A NEGATIVE WORD

(a) ***Never will I do*** that again! (b) ***Rarely have I eaten*** better food. (c) ***Hardly ever does he come*** to class on time.	When a negative word begins a sentence, the subject and verb are inverted (i.e., question word order is used).*

*Beginning a sentence with a negative word is relatively uncommon in everyday usage, but is used when the speaker/writer wishes to emphasize the negative element of the sentence and be expressive.

☐ EXERCISE 20. Negative words. (Chart D-3)
    Directions: Change each sentence so that it begins with a negative word.

1. We rarely go to movies. → *Rarely do we go to movies.*
2. I seldom sleep past seven o'clock.
3. I hardly ever agree with her.
4. I will never forget the wonderful people I have met here.
5. I have never known Rosa to be dishonest.
6. The mail scarcely ever arrives before noon.

UNIT E: Preposition Combinations

E PREPOSITION COMBINATIONS WITH ADJECTIVES AND VERBS

A
be absent from
be accused of
be accustomed to
be acquainted with
be addicted to
be afraid of
    agree with
be angry at, with
be annoyed with, by
    apologize for
    apply to, for
    approve of
    argue with, about
    arrive in, at
be associated with
be aware of

B
    believe in
    blame for
be blessed with
be bored with, by

C
be capable of
    care about, for
be cluttered with
be committed to
    compare to, with
    complain about, of
be composed of
be concerned about
be connected to
    consist of
be content with
    contribute to
be convinced of
be coordinated with
    count (up)on
be covered with
be crowded with

D
    decide (up)on
be dedicated to
    depend (up)on
be devoted to
be disappointed in, with
be discriminated against
    distinguish from
be divorced from

    be done with
    dream of, about
be dressed in

E
be engaged in, to
be envious of
be equipped with
    escape from
    excel in, at
be excited about
be exhausted from
    excuse for
be exposed to

F
be faithful to
be familiar with
    feel like
    fight for
be filled with
be finished with
be fond of
    forget about
    forgive for
be friendly to, with
be frightened of, by
be furnished with

G
be gone from
be grateful to, for
be guilty of

H
    hide from
    hope for

I
be innocent of
    insist (up)on
be interested in
    introduce to
be involved in

J
be jealous of

K
    keep from
be known for

L
be limited to
be located in
    look forward to

M
be made of, from
be married to

O
    object to
be opposed to

P
    participate in
be patient with
be pleased with
be polite to
    pray for
be prepared for
    prevent from
    prohibit from
be protected from
be proud of
    provide with

Q
be qualified for

R
    recover from
be related to
be relevant to
    rely (up)on
be remembered for
    rescue from
    respond to
be responsible for

S
be satisfied with
be scared of, by
    stare at
    stop from
    subscribe to
    substitute for
    succeed in

T
    take advantage of
    take care of
    talk about, of
be terrified of, by
    thank for
    think about, of
be tired of, from

U
be upset with
be used to

V
    vote for

W
be worried about

☐ EXERCISE 21. Prepositions. (Chart E)
Directions: Complete the sentences with appropriate prepositions.

1. Do you believe ——— *in* ——— ghosts?

2. Anthony is engaged _____ my cousin.

3. Ms. Ballas substituted _____ our regular teacher.

4. I can't distinguish one twin _____ the other.

5. Did you forgive him _____ lying to you?

6. Children rely _____ their parents for food and shelter.

7. Tim wore sunglasses to protect his eyes _____ the sun.

8. Chris excels _____ sports.

9. Andrea contributed her ideas _____ the discussion.

10. I hope you succeed _____ your new job.

11. I'm very fond _____ their children.

12. The firefighters rescued many people _____ the burning building.

13. I don't care _____ spaghetti. I'd rather eat something else.

14. Charles doesn't seem to care _____ his bad grades.

15. Sometimes Bobby seems to be jealous _____ his brother.

☐ EXERCISE 22. Prepositions. (Chart E)
Directions: Complete the sentences with appropriate prepositions.

1. Max is known _____ his honesty.

2. Mr. and Mrs. Jones have always been faithful _____ each other.

3. Do you promise to come? I'm counting _____ you to be here.

4. Trucks are prohibited _____ using residential streets.

5. The little girl is afraid _____ an imaginary
   bear that lives in her closet.

6. Do you take good care _____ your health?

7. I'm worried _____ this problem.

8. I don't agree _____ you.

9. We decided _____ eight o'clock as the
   time we should meet.

10. Who did you vote _____ in the last election?

11. How many students were absent _____ class yesterday?

12. It is important to be polite _____ other people.

13. The farmers are hoping _____ rain.

14. Jason was late because he wasn't aware _____ the time.

15. We will fight _____ our rights.

□ EXERCISE 23. Prepositions. (Chart E)
Directions: Complete the sentences with appropriate prepositions.

1. I am not familiar _____ that author's works.

2. He doesn't approve _____ smoking.

3. I subscribe _____ several magazines.

4. Water consists _____ oxygen and hydrogen.

5. I became uncomfortable because she was staring _____ me.

6. She hid the candy _____ the children.

7. He never argues _____ his wife.

8. I arrived _____ this country two weeks ago.

9. We arrived _____ the airport ten minutes late.

10. Has Mary recovered _____ her illness?

11. I pray _____ peace.

12. I am envious _____ people who can speak three or four languages fluently.

13. Why are you angry _____ me? Did I do something wrong?

14. They are very patient _____ their children.

15. The students responded _____ the questions.

□ EXERCISE 24. Prepositions. (Chart E)
Directions: Supply appropriate prepositions.

1. I am grateful _____ you _____ your assistance.

2. The criminal escaped _____ prison.

3. Elizabeth is not content _____ the progress she is making.

4. Paul's comments were not relevant _____ the topic under discussion.

5. Have you decided _____ a date for your wedding yet?

6. My boots are made _____ leather.

7. I'm depending _____ you to finish this work for me.

8. Patricia applied _____ admission _____ the university.

9. Daniel dreamed _____ some of his childhood friends last night.

10. Mr. Miller dreams _____ owning his own business someday.

11. The accused woman was innocent _____ the crime with which she was charged.

12. Ms. Sanders is friendly _____ everyone.

13. Benjamin was proud _____ himself for winning the prize.

14. The secretary provided me _____ a great deal of information.

15. Ivan compared the wedding customs in his country _____ those in the United States.

UNIT F: Connectives to Give Examples and to Continue an Idea

F-1 CONNECTIVES TO GIVE EXAMPLES

(a) There are many interesting places to visit in the city. *For example*, the botanical garden has numerous displays of plants from all over the world. (b) There are many interesting places to visit in the city. The art museum, *for instance*, has an excellent collection of modern paintings.	*For example* and *for instance* have the same meaning. They are often used as transitions. (See Chart 19-3, p. 389.)
(c) There are many interesting places to visit in the city, *e.g.*, the botanical garden and the art museum. (d) There are many interesting places to visit in the city, *for example*, the botanical garden or the art museum.	*e.g.* = *for example* (*e.g.* is an abbreviation of the Latin phrase *exempli gratia*.)★ (c) and (d) have the same meaning.
(e) I prefer to wear casual clothes, *such as* jeans and a sweatshirt. (f) Some countries, *such as* Brazil and Canada, are big. (g) Countries *such as* Brazil and Canada are big. (h) *Such* countries *as* Brazil and Canada are big.	*such as* = *for example* (f), (g), and (h) have essentially the same meaning even though the pattern varies.★★

★Punctuation note: Periods are used with *e.g.* in American English. Periods are generally not used with *eg* in British English.

★★Punctuation note:
  (1) When the "*such as* phrase" can be omitted without substantially changing the meaning of the sentence, commas are used.
      Example: Some words, such as *know* and *see*, are verbs. *(Commas are used.)*
  (2) No commas are used when the "*such as* phrase" gives essential information about the noun to which it refers.
      Example: Words such as *know* and *see* are verbs. *(No commas are used.)*

☐ EXERCISE 25. Giving examples. (Chart F-1)
   Directions: Add examples to the given sentences.

1. There are many simple kinds of exercise you could include in your life to improve your health. For example . . . .
   → *For example, you could walk briskly for half an hour three times a week.*

2. Some rock stars have international fame, for example, ...

3. The names of some newspapers are internationally known, e.g., ...

4. Some English words have the same pronunciation but different spelling, e.g., ...

5. Many English words have more than one meaning. For example, ...

6. If you are working too hard and not making time for pleasurable activities in your life, you should consciously schedule in relaxation time. For example, ...

7. Some natural phenomena, such as spring showers or moonlight, do not endanger human life. Other natural phenomena, however, have the potential to be life-threatening to humans, for example, ...

☐ EXERCISE 26. Using SUCH AS. (Chart F-1)
Directions: Complete the sentences with your own words. Use **such as**.

1. You need a hobby. There are many hobbies you might enjoy, ___*such as*___ ___*ceramics or stamp collecting.*___

2. There are certain products that almost everyone buys regularly, _____ _____

3. You should buy a small, economical car, _____

4. Medical science has made many advances, yet there are still serious diseases that have not been conquered, _____

5. Some countries, _____ and _____, are rich in oil.

6. I enjoy such sports _____

7. Such inventions _____ have contributed greatly to the progress of civilization. However, other inventions, _____ _____, have threatened human existence.

8. There are certain times when I wish to be alone, _____when _____ or when _____

9. Some subjects have always been easy and enjoyable for me, _____ _____. However, other subjects, _____ _____, _____

10. In certain situations, _____ when _____ _____ or when _____, my English still gives me a little trouble.

11. Numbers _____ are odd numbers, whereas numbers _____ are even numbers.

12. Some languages, _____ and _____, are closely related to English, while others, _____ and _____, are not.

F-2 CONNECTIVES TO CONTINUE THE SAME IDEA

(a) The city provides many cultural opportunities. It has an excellent art museum. *Moreover,* *Furthermore,* $\Big\}$ it has a fine symphony orchestra. *In addition,*	*Moreover*, *furthermore*, and *in addition* mean "also." They are *transitions*. (See Chart 19-3, p. 389.)
(b) The city provides many cultural opportunities. *In addition to* $\Big\}$ an excellent art museum, it has *Besides* a fine symphony orchestra.	In (b): *In addition to* and *besides*★ are used as prepositions. They are followed by an object (*museum*), not a clause.

★COMPARE: *Besides* means "in addition to."
         Beside means "next to"; e.g., *I sat beside my friend.*

☐ EXERCISE 27. Connectives to continue the same idea. (Chart F-2)
    Directions: Combine the ideas in these sentences by using *moreover*, *furthermore*, *in addition (to)*, *besides*, or *also* where appropriate.

1. I like to read that newspaper. One reason is that the news is always reported accurately. It has interesting special features.

2. There are many ways you can work on improving your English outside of class. For example, you should speak English as much as possible, even when you are speaking with friends who speak your native language. You should read as many magazines in English as you have time for. Watching television can be helpful.

3. Along with the increase in population in the city, there has been an increase in the rate of crime. A housing shortage has developed. There are so many automobiles in the city that the expressways are almost always jammed with cars, regardless of the time of day.

4. Good health is perhaps one's most valuable asset. To maintain good health, it is important to eat a balanced diet. The body needs a regular supply of vitamins, minerals, protein, carbohydrates, and other nutrients. Physical exercise is essential. Sleep and rest should not be neglected.

UNIT G: Verb Form Review Exercises

☐ EXERCISE 28. General review of verb forms. (Chapters 1 → 20)
    Directions: Complete the sentences with the correct form of the verbs in parentheses.

1. Some of the students *(speak, never)* _____
   English before they came here last fall.

2. I wish I *(come, not)* _____ here last year.

3. It is essential that you *(be)* _____ here tomorrow.

4. Had I known Dan wouldn't be here, I *(come, not)* _____ .

5. My passport *(stamp)* _____ at the airport when I arrived.

6. My seventy-year-old grandfather, who owns his own business, *(continue, probably)*
   _____ to work as long as he *(live)* _____ .

7. I arrived here in August 1999. By August 2009, I *(be)* _____ here for ten years.

8. Before *(go)* _____ to bed, I have to finish my homework.

9. *(Hear)* _____ that story many times before, I got bored when Jim began to tell it again.

10. Do you know that man *(sit)* _____ in the brown leather chair?

11. Many of the goods that *(produce)* _____ since the beginning of the twentieth century are totally machine-made.

12. The instructor said that she *(give)* _____ an exam next Friday.

13. I *(know)* _____ Beth for six years. When I *(meet)* _____ her, she *(work)* _____ in a law office.

14. If you *(be)* _____ here yesterday, you *(meet)* _____ my father and mother.

15. This evening the surface of the lake is completely still. It looks as if it *(make)* _____ of glass.

16. I don't know why the food service has to be so slow. We *(stand)* _____ _____ here in the cafeteria line for over half an hour, and there *(be)* _____ still a lot of people in front of us.

17. Sue says she can't come on the picnic with us. I wish she *(change)* _____ _____ her mind and *(decide)* _____ to come with us.

18. My dog turned her head toward me and looked at me quizzically, almost as if she *(understand)* _____ what I said.

19. *(Be)* _____ an excellent researcher, Dr. Barnes *(respect)* _____ _____ by the entire faculty.

20. Without the sun, life as we know it *(exist, not)* _____.

☐ EXERCISE 29. General review of verb forms. (Chapters 1 → 20)
   Directions: Fill in the blanks with the correct form of the verbs in parentheses.

1. Since *(come)* _____ to the United States six months ago, Maria *(learn)* _____ a lot of English.

2. Mrs. McKay *(give, already)* _____ birth to the child by the time her husband arrived at the hospital.

3. I recommended that he *(apply)* _____ to at least three universities.

4. Thank you for your help. I never *(be)* _____ able to finish this work without it.

5. Peggy told me she *(be)* _____ here at six tomorrow.

6. *(Sit)* _____ on a park bench and *(watch)* _____ the brightly colored leaves fall gently to the ground, he felt at peace with the world.

7. Why didn't you tell me about this before? I certainly wish I *(inform)* _____ _____ earlier.

8. The large dormitory *(destroy, completely)* _____ by fire last week. Since all of the students *(go)* _____ home for the holidays, there was no loss of life.

9. James blushed when his friend asked him an *(embarrass)* _____ question.

10. Anna is grown up now. You shouldn't speak to her as if she *(be)* _____ a child.

11. I asked all of the people *(invite)* _____ to the party to RSVP.

12. When the *(puzzle)* _____ student could not figure out the answer to the *(puzzle)* _____ problem, she demanded that I *(give)* _____ her the correct answer, but I insisted that she *(figure)* _____ it out for herself.

13. Ever since I can remember, mathematics *(be)* _____ my favorite subject.

14. The people *(work)* _____ to solve the problems of urban poverty are hopeful that many of these problems *(solve)* _____ within the next ten years.

15. It's a funny story. I'll tell you the details when I *(call)* _____ you tomorrow.

☐ EXERCISE 30. General review of verb forms. (Chapters 1 → 20)
Directions: This exercise is based on compositions written by students who were members of a multicultural class. Complete the sentences with the correct forms of the verbs in parentheses.

(1) Next week, when I _____ _____ my final examinations, I
                        (finish)   *(take)*

(2) _____ one of the best experiences I _____
    (finish, also)   *(have, ever)*

(3) in my lifetime. In the last four months, I _____ more about
                                      (learn)

(4) foreign cultures than I _____ before _____
                   (anticipate)   *(come)*

(5) to the United States. _____ in a foreign country and _____
                         (Live)   *(go)*

(6) to school with people from various parts of the world _____ me the
(give)

(7) opportunity _____ and _____ with people from
(encounter)   (interact)

(8) different cultures. I _____ to share some of my experiences and
(like)

thoughts with you.

(9)   When I first _____, I _____ no one and I
(arrive)   (know)

(10) _____ all of my fingers _____ what I was
(need)   (communicate)

trying to say in English. All of the international students were in the same situation.

(11) When we _____ the right word, we _____
(can, find, not)   (use)

(12) strange movements and gestures _____ our meaning.
(communicate)

(13) _____ some common phrases, such as "How are you?", "Fine, thank
(Know)

(14) you, and you?" and "What country are you from?", _____ enough in the
(be)

(15) beginning for us _____ friends with each other. The TV room in the
(make)

(16) dormitory _____ our common meeting place every evening after dinner.
(become)

(17) _____ _____ our English, many of us tried to
(Hope)   (improve)

(18) watch television and _____ what the people _____
(understand)   (appear)

(19) on the screen _____, but for the most part their words were just a
(say)

(20) strange mumble to us. After a while, _____ and a little sad, we slowly
(bore)

(21) began to disappear to our separate rooms. I _____ that all of us
(think)

(22) _____ some homesickness. However, despite my loneliness,
(experience)

(23) I had a good feeling within myself because I _____ what I
(do)

(24) _____ to do for many years: _____ and
(want)   (live)

(25) _____ in a foreign country.
(study)

(26)   After a few days, classes _____ and we _____
(begin)   (have)

(27) another meeting place: the classroom. _____ quite what
(know, not)

(28) _____ the first day of class, I was a bit nervous, but also
(expect)

(29) _____. After _____ the right building and the
(excite)   (find)

(30)   right room, I walked in and _____ an empty seat. I _____
                                        (choose)   (introduce)

(31)   myself to the person _____ next to me, and we sat _____ to
                                        (sit)   (talk)

(32)   each other for a few minutes. Since we _____ from different countries, we
                                                            (be)

(33)   _____ in English. At first, I was afraid that the other student
                    (speak)

(34)   _____ what I _____, but I _____
                    (understand, not)   (say)

(35)   _____ when she _____ to my questions easily.
                    (surprise, pleasantly)   (respond)

(36)   Together we _____ the first steps toward _____ a friendship.
                            (take)   (build)

(37)   As the semester _____, I _____ out more and more
                                    (progress)   (find)

         about my fellow students. Students from some countries were reticent and shy in class.

(38)   They almost never _____ questions and _____ very softly.
                                    (ask)   (speak)

(39)   Others of different nationalities _____ just the opposite: they spoke in
                                                    (be)

(40)   booming voices and never _____ _____ questions,
                                        (hesitate)   (ask)

(41)   and sometimes they _____ the teacher. I _____
                                (interrupt, even)   (be, never)

(42)   in a classroom with such a mixture of cultures before. I learned _____
                                                                                    (suprise, not)

(43)   by anything my classmates might say or do. The time spent _____ our
                                                                                (share)

(44)   ideas with each other and _____ about each other's customs and beliefs
                                        (learn)

(45)   _____ valuable and fun. As we progressed in our English, we slowly
                    (be)

         learned about each other, too.

(46)   Now, several months after my arrival in the United States, I _____ able
                                                                                    (be)

         to understand not only some English but also something about different cultures. If I

(47)   _____ here, I _____ able to attain these insights
                    (come, not)   (be, not)

(48)   into other cultures. I wish everyone in the world _____ the same experience.
                                                                    (have)

(49)   Perhaps if all the people in the world _____ more about cultures different
                                                        (know)

(50)   from their own and _____ the opportunity _____ friends
                                    (have)   (make)

(51)   with people from different countries, peace _____ secure.
                                                            (be)

Chapter 1: OVERVIEW OF VERB TENSES

EXERCISE 1, p. 1.

ACTIVITY A QUESTIONS: **1.** What is your name? **2.** How do you spell your (last) name? / How do you spell that? **3.** Where are you from? / What country are you from? / What is your hometown? / Where were you born? **4.** Where are you living? / Where do you live? **5.** How long have you been living (in this place/here)? How long do you plan to be / are you planning to be / are you going to be (in this place here)? **6.** Why did you (decide to) come here? **7.** [If a student]: What is your major / your field of study? / What are you studying? [If an employee]: What kind of work do you do? / What do you do? **8.** What do you like to do in your spare time? / Do you have any hobbies? **9.** How are you getting along? **10.** How do you like living here? / What do you think of (this place)?

EXERCISE 2, p. 2.

EXPECTED QUESTIONS: **1.** What do you do every day before you leave home? **2.** What did you do last night? **3.** What were you doing at (this exact time) yesterday? **4.** What are you doing right now? **5.** What have you done since you got up this morning? **6.** What have you been doing for the past five minutes? **7.** What will you do/are you going to do tomorrow? **8.** What will you be doing at (this exact time) tomorrow? **9.** What had you done by the time you got here today? **10.** What will you have done by the time you go to bed tonight?

EXERCISE 3, p. 3.

POSSIBLE RESPONSES: **1.** The sun rises in the east. Water and oil don't mix. **2.** Every day I get out of bed, get dressed, and have breakfast. **3.** Yesterday I took the bus to school, went to class, and cooked dinner. **4.** Tomorrow is Saturday, so I am going to do my laundry.

EXERCISE 4, p. 3.

POSSIBLE RESPONSES: **1.** Right now I am doing Exercise 4. My classmates are looking at their grammar books. It is raining outside the classroom. **2.** At two o'clock this morning, I was at home. I was sleeping. **3.** At two o'clock tomorrow morning, I will be at home. I will be sleeping.

EXERCISE 5, p. 4.

POSSIBLE RESPONSES: **1.** Yes, I have already eaten today. I had lunch at noon. **2.** Yes, I had eaten supper before I went to bed last night. **3.** Yes, by the time I go to bed tonight, I will have had dinner.

EXERCISE 6, p. 5.

POSSIBLE RESPONSES: **1.** Right now I am doing an exercise in my grammar book. I have been doing the exercise for ten minutes.   **2.** Last night at nine o'clock I was doing my English homework. I stopped doing my homework at ten o'clock. I stopped doing my homework because my eyes were tired. I had been doing my English homework for two hours before I stopped.   **3.** At nine o'clock tomorrow night, I am going to be doing my English homework. I am going to stop doing my English homework at ten o'clock. I need to go to sleep at ten o'clock. I will have been doing my English homework for one hour before I stop.

EXERCISE 7, p. 8.

ANSWERS: **2.** The speakers are discussing an activity that began and ended in the past. Tense: the simple past   **3.** The speakers are discussing an activity that is happening (is in progress) at the moment of speaking. Tense: the present progressive   **4.** The speakers are discussing an activity in progress at a particular time in the past. Tense: the past progressive   **5.** The speakers are discussing activities that have occurred (or not occurred) "before now," at unspecific times in the past. Tense: the present perfect   **6.** The speakers are discussing what will happen at a specific time in the future. Tense: the simple future   **7.** This question concerns an activity that will be in progress at a particular time in the future. Tense: the future progressive   **8.** This question concerns the duration of an activity that started in the past and is still in progress. Tense: the present perfect progressive   **9.** The speakers are talking about the duration of an activity that has already started and will end at a specific time in the future. Tense: the future perfect progressive   **10.** This question concerns an activity that started and ended before another time in the past. Tense: the past perfect   **11.** This question concerns an activity that will be finished before a particular time in the future. Tense: the future perfect **12.** This question concerns the duration of an activity that began before another time in the past. Tense: the past perfect progressive

EXERCISE 8, p. 9.

POSSIBLE ANSWERS: **1.** I brush my teeth every day.   **2.** I combed my hair yesterday.   **3.** Tomorrow I will hug my children and kiss my wife/husband.   **4.** Right now I am talking to you. [Note: The Answer Key gives the full, uncontracted forms of verbs rather than contracting them with pronoun subjects. Auxiliary verbs such as *will* and *am* are usually contracted in speech.   **5.** At this time yesterday, I was watching a game on TV.   **6.** At this time tomorrow, I will be sitting right here.   **7.** Since I got up this morning, I have eaten breakfast and have come to school.   **8.** Before I went to bed last night, I had eaten dinner, done my homework, and read the newspaper.   **9.** By the time I go to bed tonight, I will have watched the news on TV.   **10.** I am talking to you. I have been talking to you for ten minutes.   **11.** Before Ms. Foley walked into the classroom today, I was chatting with the student next to me. I had been doing that for five minutes. **12.** Tomorrow before Ms. Foley walks into the classroom, I will be talking to the student who sits next to me. I will have been talking to him/her for four or five minutes before Ms. Foley walks into the classroom.

EXERCISE 9, p. 9.

1. Does Pedro <u>walk</u> to work every morning?   **2.** What <u>are you</u> talking about? I <u>don't</u> understand you.   **3.** Did you <u>finish</u> your work?   **4.** My friend doesn't <u>like</u> her apartment.   **5.** Do you <u>work</u> for this company?   OR   <u>Are you</u> working for this company?   **6.** What time <u>did</u> your plane arrive?   **7.** How long have you <u>been</u> living in this city?   OR   How long have you <u>lived</u> in this city?   **8.** My brother <u>doesn't</u> have <u>a</u> job right now.   **9.** Ali <u>won't</u> ~~to~~ <u>be</u> in class tomorrow.   **10.** I <u>hadn't seen</u> snow before I moved to Canada last year.   OR   I <u>had</u> never <u>seen</u> snow before I moved to Canada last year.

EXERCISE 10, p. 10.

ANSWERS: **1.** hoped   **2.** dining   **3.** stopped   **4.** planning   **5.** rained   **6.** waiting   **7.** listening   **8.** happened   **9.** beginning   **10.** occurred   **11.** starting   **12.** warned   **13.** enjoyed   **14.** playing   **15.** studying   **16.** worried   **17.** died   **18.** lying

EXERCISES 11 and 12, p. 11.

EX. 11:

PART I. **2.** hiding   **3.** running   **4.** ruining   **5.** coming   **6.** writing   **7.** eating   **8.** sitting   **9.** acting   **10.** patting   **11.** opening   **12.** beginning   **13.** earning   **14.** frying   **15.** dying   **16.** employing

PART II. **2.** trying, tried   **3.** staying, stayed   **4.** taping, taped   **5.** tapping, tapped   **6.** offering, offered   **7.** preferring, preferred   **8.** gaining, gained   **9.** planning, planned   **10.** tying, tied   **11.** helping, helped   **12.** studying, studied   **13.** admitting, admitted   **14.** visiting, visited   **15.** hugging, hugged   **16.** raging, raged

EX. 12:

PART I. **2.** jarred   **3.** jeered   **4.** dotted   **5.** looted   **6.** pointed   **7.** exited   **8.** permitted   **9.** intensified   **10.** destroyed   **11.** suffered   **12.** occurred

PART II. **14.** riding   **15.** bidding   **16.** burying   **17.** decaying   **18.** tying   **19.** taming   **20.** teeming   **21.** trimming   **22.** harming   **23.** ripening   **24.** regretting

Chapter 2: PRESENT AND PAST, SIMPLE AND PROGRESSIVE

EXERCISE 1, p. 12.

ANSWERS: **2.** I <u>don't know</u> Sam's wife.   **3.** A: What <u>are you</u> talking about?   B: I <u>am</u> talking about the political situation in my country.   **4.** My roommate usually <u>watches</u> TV, <u>listens</u> to music, or <u>goes</u> out in the evening.   **5.** When I turned the ignition key, the car <u>started</u>.   **6.** This class <u>consists</u> of students who <u>want</u> to learn English.   **7.** The children <u>drew</u> some pictures in school this morning.   **8.** While Tom <u>was</u> reading in bed last night, his phone <u>rang</u>. When he <u>answered</u> it, the caller <u>hung</u> up.   **9.** Right now Sally <u>is</u> in the kitchen eating breakfast.   **10.** When the sun <u>rises</u>, it <u>appears</u> from below the horizon.

EXERCISE 4, p. 14.

ANSWERS: **2.** washes   **3.** usually sits . . . is sitting   **4.** am trying   **5.** Do you always lock   **6.** am still waiting   **7.** is shining   **8.** shines . . . wakes   **9.** is snowing . . . doesn't snow   **10.** A: am I doing   B: are rubbing . . . are rubbing

EXERCISE 6, p. 16.

   1. a. *smell* describes a state that exists, i.e., the flowers have a smell, and that smell is good.

      b. *is smelling* describes the action of using one's nose.

   2. a. *think* means "believe" in this sentence and describes a state.

      b. *am thinking* is an action; thoughts are going through the speaker's mind.

3. a. *see* describes a perception that exists right now as a result of the speaker using his/her eyes.

  b. *is seeing a doctor* means "is going to a doctor for help," a general activity in progress at present.

  c. *are seeing* means they are dating each other, a general activity in progress at present.

4. a. *looks* means "appears" or "seems to be" and describes an apparent state that exists: Kathy is apparently cold.

  b. *is looking* describes the action of using one's eyes.

5. a. *appears* means "seems" and describes an apparent state that exists.

  b. *is appearing* describes the action of performing on stage in a theater, a general activity in progress at present.

6. a. *is feeling* describes the action of using one's sense of touch. Sue is using her hands to touch the cat's fur. The activity is in progress at the present moment.

  b. *feels* describes a state that exists, the state of the cat's fur; i.e., it is soft.

  c. *am not feeling* describes the speaker's physical feelings of illness, in progress at the present. [Note: The simple present is also possible here with little difference in meaning *(I don't feel well today)* to describe a state that exists.]

  d. *feel* means "think" or "believe" in this sentence and describes a state.

7. a. *has* means "owns" here and describes a state that exists.

  b. *am having* and *is having* mean "experiencing" and describe activities in progress.

8. a. *remember* describes a state that exists.

  b. *is remembering* describes an activity in progress: memories are going through Aunt Sara's mind.

9. a. *weighs* describes a state that exists.

  b. *is weighing* describes an activity in progress: the grocer is putting the bananas on a scale and reading what the scale says.

EXERCISE 7, p. 17.

ANSWERS: **2.** careful, kind, responsible   **3.** polite, quiet   **4.** cruel, unfair, unpleasant   **5.** good, noisy

EXERCISE 8, p. 18.

ANSWERS: **2.** is beginning . . . don't have . . . is wearing   **3.** don't own . . . wear
4. sleep . . . get . . . study   **5.** is taking . . . don't want . . . needs   **6.** am looking
. . . looks . . . has . . . isn't having   **7.** am looking . . . is writing . . . is biting . . . is
scratching . . . is staring . . . seems . . . is thinking . . . do you think . . . is doing
8. want . . . know . . . means . . . does "sword" mean   **9.** is doing . . . is being . . .
doesn't want . . . is always

EXERCISE 10, p. 20.

ANSWERS: **2.** sob/d/   **3.** grade/əd/   **4.** ask/t/   **5.** help/t/   **6.** watch/t/
7. fill/d/   **8.** defend/əd/   **9.** pour/d/   **10.** wait/əd/   **11.** enjoy/d/
12. load/əd/   **13.** roam/d/   **14.** kiss/t/   **15.** halt/əd/   **16.** laugh/t/
17. dry/d/   **18.** believe/d/   **19.** judge/d/   **20.** count/əd/   **21.** add/əd/
22. box/t/   **23.** rest/əd/   **24.** push/t/

EXERCISE 11, p. 21.

ANSWERS: **2.** hope/t/   **3.** mop/t/ . . . vacuum/d/ . . . dust/əd/   **4.** last/əd/
5. tap/t   **6.** describe/d/   **7.** demand/əd/   **8.** push/t/ . . . pull/d/
9. hand/əd/   **10.** toot/əd/   **11.** ask/t/   **12.** flood/əd/   **13.** depart/əd/ . . .
land/əd/   **14.** jump/t/ . . . shout/əd/

EXERCISES 13–16, pp. 24–25.

EX. 13 PARTIAL ANSWERS: **1.** Yes, I drank . . . . **2.** brought **3.** forgot **4.** shook **5.** caught **6.** drove **7.** lost **8.** mislaid **9.** found **10.** understood **11.** told **12.** spread **13.** fell **14.** hurt **15.** flew **16.** wore **17.** hung **18.** ate **19.** took **20.** rode **21.** swore **22.** forgave **23.** wrote **24.** No! I didn't bite the dog. The dog bit me.

EX. 14 PARTIAL ANSWERS: **1.** No, someone else made . . . . **2.** broke **3.** stole **4.** took **5.** drew **6.** swept **7.** taught **8.** dug **9.** fed **10.** hid **11.** blew **12.** threw **13.** tore **14.** built **15.** spoke **16.** wove

EX. 15 PARTIAL ANSWERS: **1.** Yes, I gave . . . . **2.** stood **3.** chose **4.** ran **5.** slept **6.** heard **7.** withdrew **8.** woke up [also possible: *waked*] **9.** swam **10.** went **11.** bent **12.** sent **13.** sang **14.** stuck **15.** ground **16.** struck **17.** lit [also possible: *lighted*] **18.** meant **19.** held **20.** spoke

EX. 16 PARTIAL ANSWERS: **1.** Yes, it began . . . . **2.** rose **3.** cut [no change in form] **4.** bled **5.** grew **6.** stung **7.** rang **8.** froze **9.** quit [also possible in BrE: *quitted*] **10.** fought **11.** crept **12.** shot **13.** fled **14.** won **15.** slid **16.** swung **17.** blew **18.** burst **19.** broadcast **20.** knew

EXERCISE 17, p. 26.

ANSWERS: **1.** raised **2.** rises **3.** sat **4.** set **5.** lay **6.** lying **7.** laid **8.** lie **9.** lies **10.** raises **11.** rose **12.** lays **13.** laid **14.** set **15.** sat **16.** lies

EXERCISE 19, p. 28.

ANSWERS: **2.** didn't want . . . was raining **3.** called . . . wasn't . . . was studying **4.** didn't hear . . . was sleeping **5.** was shining . . . was blowing . . . were singing **6.** were arguing . . . walked **7.** opened . . . found **8.** was reading . . . fell . . . closed . . . tiptoed **9.** was waiting **10.** A: Did you hear B: wasn't listening . . . was thinking **11.** A: did you break B: slipped . . . was crossing **12.** was she wearing **13.** finally found . . . was already . . . were talking busily . . . were speaking . . . were conversing . . . were just sitting . . . chose . . . sat . . . walked . . . stopped **14.** was snowing . . . was shining . . . were shoveling . . . was lying

EXERCISE 23, p. 31.

ANSWERS: **2.** [e] He's always leaving his dirty dishes on the table. **3.** [c] He's forever borrowing my clothes without asking me. **4.** [a] He's constantly bragging about himself. **5.** [f] He's always trying to show me he's smarter than me. **6.** [g] He's constantly cracking his knuckles while I'm trying to study. **7.** [d] He's always forgetting to give me my phone messages. **8.** *(free response)*

EXERCISE 24, p. 32.

PART I QUESTIONS: **3.** He was in his bedroom watching TV. **4.** He was watching TV in his bedroom. **5.** He's taking a nap on the couch in the living room. **6.** He's on the couch in the living room taking a nap. **7.** She's in Singapore attending a conference.

PART II POSSIBLE COMPLETIONS: **9.** He's upstairs getting his books. **10.** She's in her office correcting test papers. **11.** She's in the kitchen washing dishes. **12.** He was at home resting from his long trip. **13.** He was in New York attending a basketball game.

15. I'm back to work now, but a month ago I was <u>on the beach</u> lying in the sun.   **16.** We are <u>in Ritter Hall</u> studying English grammar.   **17.** No one could see the thief because he was <u>in the garbage can</u> hiding from the police.
18. When I saw Diana, she was <u>in the Registrar's Office</u> trying to find out what she was supposed to do.

EXERCISE 25, p. 33.

1. <u>I</u> always <u>eat</u> breakfast.   **2.** <u>While</u> I was working in my office yesterday, my cousin <u>stopped</u> by to visit me.   **3.** Portual <u>lies</u> to the west of Spain.   **4.** Yuki <u>stayed</u> home because she <u>caught</u> / <u>was catching</u> / <u>had caught</u> a bad cold.   **5.** My brother <u>looks</u> like our father, but I <u>resemble</u> my mother.   **6.** As a verb, "sink" <u>means</u> "move downward." What <u>does</u> it <u>mean</u> as a noun?   **7.** Sang-Joon, are you <u>listening</u> to me? I am <u>talking</u> to you!
8. I <u>rewound</u> the rented video before I <u>returned</u> it to the store yesterday.
9. Abdallah <u>wants</u> a snack. <u>He's</u> ~~being~~ <u>hungry</u>.   **10.** Anna <u>raised</u> her eyebrows in surprise.   **11.** Yesterday I was working at my computer when Shelley <u>came</u> to the door of my office. I <u>didn't know</u> she was there. I was <u>concentrating</u> hard on my work. When she suddenly <u>spoke,</u> <u>I jumped.</u> She <u>startled</u> me.   **12.** While I was surfing the net yesterday, I <u>found</u> a really interesting website.

Chapter 3: PERFECT AND PERFECT PROGRESSIVE TENSES

EXERCISE 1, p. 34.

QUESTIONS ONLY: Have you ever . . . ?
1. bought   **2.** broken   **3.** hidden   **4.** taught   **5.** made   **6.** won
7. flown   **8.** spoken   **9.** stolen   **10.** fallen   **11.** held   **12.** fed
13. built   **14.** forgotten   **15.** understood   **16.** eaten

EXERCISE 2, p. 35.

QUESTIONS ONLY: Have you ever . . . ?
1. climbed   **2.** written   **3.** been   **4.** told   **5.** smoked   **6.** ridden
7. taught   **8.** seen   **9.** met   **10.** given   **11.** eaten   **12.** studied
13. played   **14.** gone   **15.** walked   **16.** watched   **17.** taken   **18.** driven
19. fallen   **20.** had   **21.** driven   **22.** read   **23.** drawn   **24.** ridden
25. caught   **26.** slept   **27.** written   **28.** lost   **29.** had   **30.** brought
31. worn   **32.** drunk   **33.** left   **34.** dug   **35.** shaken   **36.** sung

EXERCISE 3, p. 36.

ANSWERS: **2.** went   **3.** arrived   **4.** has been   **5.** have already missed . . .
missed   **6.** have had   **7.** has drawn . . . drew   **8.** has called . . .
called   **9.** has worn . . . wore   **10.** has risen . . . rose   **11.** saw
12. has never seen   **13.** have known   **14.** has just arrived / just arrived
15. haven't been . . . hasn't responded . . . started . . . have faxed . . .
have phoned . . . have sent

EXERCISE 4, p. 37.

POSSIBLE RESPONSES: **1.** I've bought six books . . . . OR I haven't bought
any . . . .   **2.** I've gotten two . . . . OR I haven't gotten any . . . .
3. I've written three . . . . OR I haven't written any . . . .   **4.** You've asked three
questions . . . .   **5.** I've flown many times . . . .   **6.** I have made dinner many
times . . . .   **7.** I've met lots of people . . . .   **8.** I haven't missed any
classes . . . .   **9.** I've had two cups . . . .   **10.** I've had four classes . . . .
11. I've eaten at a restaurant several times . . . .   **12.** I've ridden a bike lots of times.

EXERCISE 5, p. 38.

SAMPLE RESPONSES: **2.** two weeks . . . two weeks . . . the twenty-second of September   **3.** October 2. . . September 2   OR   one month ago . . . September 2 . . . one month   **4.** 1999 . . . 1981 . . . eighteen years . . . 1981   **5.** In October . . . three months . . . October

EXERCISE 7, p. 39.

ITEM NOTES: **3.** "weather's" been   **4.** "neighbors've" asked   **5.** "teacher's" never eaten   **6.** *(no contraction; "has" is the main verb)*   **7.** "parents've" lived   **8.** *(no contraction; "have" is the main verb)*   **9.** "Where've" you been?   **10.** "What've" you done

EXERCISE 8, p. 40.

ANSWERS: **1.** came . . . have you made   **2.** haven't had . . . have had   **3.** had . . . went   **4.** have gotten/got [*got* is principally British usage.] . . . saw . . . have also gotten/got   **5.** advanced   **6.** have made   **7.** have changed . . . were . . . have become . . . has also changed . . . were   **8.** have already taken . . . took   **9.** A: Have you ever met   B: haven't   **10.** have never eaten   **11.** Have you eaten . . . have already eaten . . . have just finished   OR   Did you eat . . . already ate . . . just finished   **12.** A: have you visited   B: have been   A: have never been . . . were you   B: also visited . . . took   A: did you visit   A: have always wanted . . . haven't had . . . went . . . haven't gone

EXERCISE 10, p. 42.

ANSWERS: **1.** They <u>have been</u> playing for almost two hours.   **2.** He <u>has been talking</u> on the phone for more than half an hour.   **3.** I <u>have been trying</u> to study for the last hour, but something always seems to interrupt me.   **4.** He <u>has been</u> waiting there for the last twenty minutes.

EXERCISE 11, p. 43.

ANSWERS: **1.** has been snowing   **2.** have had   **3.** have been studying   **4.** have written   **5.** has rung   **6.** has been ringing   **7.** Have you been . . . have been trying   **8.** haven't seen . . . have you been doing   **9.** have never had   **10.** Have you been crying?   **11.** A: has he been   B: has been teaching/has taught   **12.** has been playing

EXERCISE 15, p. 46.

ANSWERS: **1.** was/had been . . . became   **2.** felt . . . took/had taken   **3.** had already given . . . got   **4.** was . . . had stopped   **5.** roamed . . . had become . . . appeared   **6.** had never seen . . . visited   **7.** saw . . . hadn't seen . . . didn't recognize . . . had lost   **8.** emigrated . . . had never traveled . . . settled . . . grew . . . went . . . had always wanted

EXERCISE 17, p. 48.

ANSWERS: **3.** have been studying   **4.** had been studying   **5.** had been daydreaming   **6.** have been sleeping

EXERCISE 18, p. 48.

ANSWERS: **2.** Gloria   **3.** Ken   **4.** Mr. Sanchez   **5.** Alice   **6.** Joe   **7.** Carlos   **8.** Jane   **9.** Mr. Fox

EXERCISE 19, p. 49.

1. Since I came to this country, I <u>have learned</u> a lot about the way of life here.
2. Before I <u>came</u> here, I <u>had never bought</u> anything from a vending machine.   **3.** I <u>arrived</u> here only a short time ago. I <u>have been</u> here only since last Friday.   **4.** When I arrived here, I <u>didn't know</u> much about the United States. I <u>had seen</u> many movies about America, but that wasn't enough.   **5.** My understanding of this country <u>has</u> changed a lot since I arrived.   **6.** When I was in my country, I <u>coached</u> a children's soccer team. When I came here, I <u>wanted</u> to do the same thing. Now I am coaching a soccer team at a local elementary school. I <u>have been</u> coaching this team for the last two months.   **7.** My grandfather <u>lived</u> in a small village in Italy when he was a child. At nineteen, he <u>moved</u> to Rome, where he <u>met</u> and <u>married</u> my grandmother in 1947. My father <u>was</u> born in Rome in 1950. I <u>was</u> born in Rome in 1979.   **8.** I <u>have been living</u> / <u>have lived</u> in my cousin's apartment since I <u>arrived</u> here. I <u>haven't been</u> able to find my own apartment yet. I <u>have looked</u> at several places for rent, but I <u>haven't found</u> one that I can afford.   **9.** How long <u>have</u> you been living here? I <u>have</u> been here for almost two <u>years</u>.   **10.** Why <u>haven't</u> you been in class the last couple of days?

Chapter 4: FUTURE TIME

EXERCISE 1, p. 51.

ANSWERS: **6.** weather'll   **7.** Mary'll   **8.** Bill'll   **9.** children'll   **10.** Who'll
11. Where'll   **12.** long'll   **13.** Nobody'll   **14.** That'll   **15.** What'll

EXERCISE 2, p. 52.

PART I: **2.** will be/is going to be . . . will come/is going to come   **3.** will probably see/am probably going to see   **4.** A: won't be/isn't going to be . . . Who will be/Who's going to be   B: will teach/is going to teach . . . will be/am going to be   **5.** will the damage we do to our environment today affect/is the damage we do to our environment today going to affect

PART II: **8.** B: will do   C: will do   **9.** is going to erase   **10.** will meet   **11.** am going to meet   **12.** will get   **13.** am going to enroll . . . am going to take   **14.** will get   **15.** will go   **16.** am going to sell   **17.** will look

EXERCISE 3, p. 55.

ANSWERS: **2.** [After the rain <u>stops</u>,]   **3.** [before my wife <u>gets</u> home from work today.]   **4.** [until Jessica <u>comes</u>.]   **5.** [As soon as the war <u>is</u> over,]   **6.** [when the tide <u>comes</u> in,]   **7.** [While I'<u>m driving</u> to work tomorrow,]

EXERCISE 4, p. 55.

ANSWERS: **2.** eat [*have eaten* is also correct] . . . will probably take/am probably going to take   **3.** get . . . I'll call/am going to call   **4.** watch . . . will write/am going to write   **5.** will wait/am going to wait . . . comes   **6.** stops [also possible: *has stopped*] . . . will walk/am going to walk   **7.** graduate . . . intend . . . will go . . . get
8. am going to listen . . . sleep   **9.** A: are you staying/are you going to stay   B: plan/am planning . . . hope/am hoping   A: will you do/are you going to do . . . leave   B: will return/am going to return . . . get   A: will be/am going to be . . . return . . . get

EXERCISE 5, P. 57.

VERB FORMS IN ANSWERS: **2.** [simple present . . . future]   **3.** [future . . . simple present]   **4.** [future . . . simple present]   **5.** [simple present . . . future]   **6.** [future . . . simple present]   **7.** [simple present . . . future]   **8.** [*(someone)* . . . future]

EXERCISE 6, p. 57.

ANSWERS: **4.** in the future   **5.** in the future   **6.** now   **7.** in the future   **8.** habitually   **9.** in the future   **10.** in the future   **11.** habitually   **12.** A: now B: now   A: in the future   **13.** A: in the future   B: in the future   C: in the future   **14.** in the future   **15.** in the future   **16.** in the future   **17.** in the future   **18.** in the future

EXERCISE 7, p. 59.

EXPECTED COMPLETIONS: **2.** am taking   **3.** are having . . . are coming   **4.** am seeing   **5.** is going   **6.** are driving   **7.** is playing   **8.** am stopping

EXERCISE 10, p. 60.

ANSWERS: **1.** will be attending   **2.** arrive . . . will be waiting   **3.** get . . . will be shining . . . will be singing . . . will still be lying   **4.** B: will be lying   A: will be thinking   **5.** will be staying   **6.** will be doing . . . will be attending school . . . (will be) studying   **7.** is . . . will probably be raining   **8.** will be in Chicago visiting   **9.** will be at the library working   **10.** will be living . . . will be driving

EXERCISE 11, p. 62.

ANSWERS: **1.** have been . . . had been . . . will have been   **2.** get . . . will already have arrived / will have already arrived   **3.** got . . . had already arrived   **4.** have been sitting . . . had been sitting . . . will have been sitting   **5.** will have been driving [also possible: *will have driven*]   **6.** had been living / had lived . . . will have been living / will have lived   **7.** get . . . will have taken   **8.** will have been running   **9.** will have had . . . dies   **10.** will have been

EXERCISE 12, p. 63.

ANSWERS: **2.** He will shave and shower, and then make a light breakfast.   **3.** After he eats breakfast tomorrow, he will get ready to go to work.   **4.** By the time he gets to work tomorrow, he will have drunk three cups of coffee.   **5.** Between 8:00 and 9:00, Bill will answer his e-mail and (will) plan his day.   **6.** By 10:00 tomorrow, he will have called his new clients.   **7.** At 11:00 tomorrow, Bill will be attending a staff meeting.   **8.** He will go to lunch at noon and have a sandwich and a bowl of soup.   **9.** After he finishes eating, he will take a short walk in the park before he returns to the office.   **10.** He will work at his desk until he goes to another meeting in the middle of the afternoon.   **11.** By the time he leaves the office, he will have attended three meetings.   **12.** When Bill gets home, his children will be playing in the yard.   **13.** They will have been playing since 3:00 in the afternoon.   **14.** As soon as he finishes dinner, he will take the children for a walk to a nearby playground.   **15.** Afterward, the whole family will sit in the living room and discuss their day.   **16.** They will watch television for a while, then Bill and his wife will put the kids to bed.   **17.** By the time Bill goes to bed tomorrow, he will have had a full day and will be ready for sleep.

Chapter 5: ADVERB CLAUSES OF TIME AND REVIEW OF VERB TENSES

EXERCISE 1, p. 65.

ANSWERS: **2.** By the time I return to my country, I <u>will have been</u> away from home for more than three years.   **3.** As soon as I ~~will~~ graduate, I <u>am</u> going to return to my hometown.   **4.** By the end of the 21st century, scientists will <u>have</u> discovered the cure for the common cold.   **5.** I want to get married, but I <u>haven't met</u> the right person yet.   **6.** I have <u>seen</u> that movie three times, and now I <u>want</u> to see it again.   **7.** Last night, I ~~have~~ <u>had</u> dinner with two <u>friends</u>. I <u>have known</u> both of them for a long time. **8.** I <u>don't</u> like my job at the restaurant. My brother wants me to change it. I <u>think</u> he is right.   **9.** So far this week, the teachers <u>have given</u> us a lot of homework every day. **10.** There <u>have been</u> more than forty presidents of the United States since it became a country. George Washington <u>was</u> the first president. He <u>became</u> the president in 1789.   **11.** While I <u>am</u> studying tonight, I'm going to listen to Beethoven's Seventh Symphony.   **12.** We washed the dishes and <u>cleaned</u> up the kitchen after our dinner guests <u>left/had left</u>.   **13.** My neighbors are Mr. and Mrs. Jones. I <u>have known</u> them ever since I <u>was</u> a child.   **14.** It <u>will rain</u> tomorrow morning. / It is <u>probably going to rain</u> tomorrow morning.   **15.** Many scientists believe there <u>will be</u> / is <u>going to be</u> a major earthquake in California in the next few years.   **16.** When I got home to my apartment last night, I <u>used</u> my key to open the door as usual. But the door didn't open. I <u>tried</u> my key again and again with no luck. So I <u>knocked</u> on the door for my wife to let me in. Finally the door <u>opened</u>, but I <u>didn't see</u> my wife on the other side. I saw a stranger. I had been <u>trying</u> to get into the wrong apartment! I quickly <u>apologized</u> and <u>went</u> to my own apartment.

EXERCISE 4, p. 68.

ANSWERS: **1.** is studying . . . is also taking . . . begin   **2.** had already eaten . . . left . . . always eats . . . goes . . . goes . . . will eat/will have eaten   **3.** called . . . was attending   **4.** will be attending   **5.** got . . . was sleeping . . . had been sleeping **6.** is taking . . . fell . . . has been sleeping   **7.** started . . . hasn't finished . . . is reading   **8.** has read . . . is reading . . . has been reading . . . intends . . . has read . . . has ever read   **9.** eats . . . is going to go . . . will have eaten . . . goes

EXERCISE 6, p. 70.

[The adverb clauses are <u>underlined</u>.]   **1.** We went inside <u>when it began to rain</u>.   **2.** It began to rain. We went inside.   **3.** <u>When it began to rain</u>, we went inside.   **4.** <u>When the mail comes</u>, my assistant opens it.   **5.** My assistant opens the mail <u>when it comes</u>. **6.** The mail comes <u>around ten o'clock every morning</u>. My assistant opens it.

EXERCISE 7, p. 71.

EXPECTED COMPLETIONS: **2.** [after I <u>did</u> my homework.]   **3.** [after I <u>do/have done</u> my homework.]   **4.** [Ever since I was a child,] I <u>have been</u> afraid of dogs.   **5.** [while she <u>was playing</u> basketball]   **6.** [before you <u>hand</u> it in to the teacher tomorrow.]   **7.** [By the time I left my apartment this morning,] the mail carrier <u>had already delivered</u> the mail.   **8.** [since he <u>was</u> ten years old]   **9.** [as I <u>was driving</u> my car to work this morning.]   **10.** [By the time I leave this city,] I <u>will have been</u> here for four months. **11.** [Whenever Mark <u>gets</u> angry,]   **12.** I <u>used to go</u> to the beach [whenever the weather was nice,] but now I don't have time to do that [because I have to study.]   **13.** [when <u>my parents arrive from Moscow</u>.]   **14.** [The next time I <u>go</u> to Hawaii,]   **15.** [the last time I <u>ate</u> at that restaurant]

EXERCISE 8, p. 73.

ANSWERS: **3.** Whenever/Every time Susan feels nervous, she chews her nails. (~~before~~) **4.** The frying pan caught on fire while I was making dinner. (~~by the time, as soon as~~) **5.** Someone knocked on the door just as we were sitting down to eat. Just after we sat down to eat, someone knocked on the door. (~~just before~~) **6.** As soon as the singer finished her song, the audience burst into applause. The audience burst into applause immediately after the singer finished her song. (~~as long as~~) **7.** We have to wait here until Nancy comes. (~~as soon as, after~~) **8.** After / As soon as /When Nancy comes, we can leave for the theater. **9.** I knew that something was wrong just as soon as/when my roommate walked into the room yesterday. (~~whenever~~) **10.** Just before I stood up to give my speech, I got butterflies in my stomach. (~~until, while~~) **11.** The first time I saw the great pyramids of Egypt in the moonlight, I was speechless. (~~until, before~~) **12.** Jane has gotten three promotions since she started working at this company six months ago. (~~before, when~~) **13.** The phone rang shortly after / not long after / a short time after I had gone to bed. **14.** When/Once the weather gets warmer, we can start playing tennis again. (~~while~~) **15.** By the time Shakespeare died in 1616, he had written more than 37 plays. (~~while, once~~) **16.** The next time Sam goes to the movies, he'll remember to take his glasses. (~~as long as, by the time~~) **17.** As long as I live, I will not forget Mr. Tanaka. (~~as, so long as~~) **18.** Mohammad had never heard about Halloween before/until he came to the U.S. (~~since~~)

EXERCISE 9, p. 74.

ANSWERS: **1.** B **2.** D **3.** C **4.** D **5.** D **6.** A **7.** B **8.** C **9.** B **10.** B **11.** B **12.** A **13.** D **14.** B

EXERCISE 11, p. 76.

ANSWERS: **1.** am listening **2.** A: Have you met B: have never had **3.** A: are you doing B: am trying A: will electrocute / are going to electrocute **4.** A: is lying B: see . . . certainly looks **5.** A: went B: Was it A: enjoyed B: did you see A: had never seen B: have seen . . . saw . . . was . . . wasn't **6.** A: had never been B: were you doing A: were driving **7.** A: Are you taking B: am not A: Have you ever taken B: have A: did you take . . . was . . . is/was he B: is/was **8.** A: was . . . haven't received . . . don't have/haven't B: do you need A: will pay . . . get **9.** A: isn't B: will be sitting **10.** A: do you know . . . have been looking B: is seeing . . . received A: sounds . . . has . . . will be working

EXERCISE 12, p. 78.

ANSWERS: **(1)** Are you studying **(2)** am **(3)** have been . . . studied / was studying / had been studying **(4)** are you taking **(5)** am taking . . . are you taking **(6)** am studying . . . need . . . take **(7)** have you been **(8)** have been . . . arrived . . . have been studying . . . lived / was living **(9)** speak . . . Did you study / Had you studied . . . came **(10)** studied / had studied / had been studying . . . spent . . . picked . . . was living/lived **(11)** were . . . came . . . had never studied . . . started **(12)** do you plan / are you planning **(13)** I'm not . . . return . . . will have been **(14)** hope / am hoping

EXERCISE 13, p. 79.

ANSWERS: **(1)** received **(2)** have been trying . . . have been **(3)** have had **(4)** has been staying **(5)** and **(6)** have spent / have been spending **(7)** have been **(8)** went . . . watched **(9)** have barely had **(10)** is . . . am sitting **(11)** have been sitting **(12)** leaves . . . decided **(13)** am writing **(14)** am getting **(15)** will take / am going to take . . . get **(16)** are you getting **(17)** are your classes going

EXERCISE 15, p. 80.

ANSWERS: **(1)** has experienced **(2)** will experience / is going to experience **(3)** began **(4)** have occurred **(5)** causes **(6)** have developed **(7)** waves **(8)** hold **(9)** moves **(10)** know **(11)** happened **(12)** struck **(13)** were sitting **(14)** suddenly found **(15)** died . . . collapsed **(16)** sent **(17)** will the next earthquake occur / is the next earthquake going to occur **(18)** have often helped **(19)** are studying **(20)** and **(21)** also appear **(22)** seem **(23)** have developed **(24)** will be **(25)** strikes

EXERCISE 19, p. 81.

1. I <u>have been</u> living at 3371 **G**rand **A**venue since last September. **2.** I have been in New York **C**ity <u>for two weeks</u> ~~ago~~. OR I <u>was</u> in New York **C**ity two <u>weeks</u> ago. **3.** My country <u>has changed</u> its capital city five <u>times</u>. **4.** Dormitory life is not quiet. Everyone <u>shouts</u> and <u>makes</u> a lot of noise in the halls. **5.** My friends will meet me when I ~~will~~ <u>arrive</u> at the airport. **6.** Hasn't anyone ever <u>told</u> you to knock on the door before you enter someone else's room? Didn't your parents <u>teach</u> you that? **7.** When I was a child, I viewed <u>things</u> from a much lower height. Many physical objects around me <u>appeared</u> very large. When I <u>wanted</u> to move something such as a chair, I <u>needed</u> help. **8.** I ~~will~~ <u>intend</u> to go back home when I <u>finish</u> my education. **9.** The phone <u>rang</u> while I was doing the dishes. I <u>dried</u> my hands and <u>answered</u> it. When I <u>heard</u> my <u>husband's</u> voice, I <u>was</u> very happy. **10.** I <u>have been</u> in the United States for the last four months. During this time, I <u>have</u> done many <u>things</u> and <u>(have) seen</u> many <u>places</u>. **11.** When the old man started to walk back to his cave, the sun <u>had</u> already <u>hidden</u> itself behind the mountain. **12.** While I <u>was</u> writing my composition last night, someone <u>knocked</u> on the door. **13.** I'm <u>studying</u> English at an English conversation school two <u>times</u> a week. **14.** Getting accustomed to a different <u>culture is</u> not easy. **15.** I'm really glad you <u>visited / are going to visit / will visit / will be visiting</u> my hometown this year. **16.** While I was <u>visiting</u> my cousin in Los Angeles, **w**e went to a Thai restaurant and <u>ate</u> Thai food. **17.** <u>After</u> **w**e ate dinner, **w**e watched TV. OR We ate dinner. We watched TV <u>afterwards</u>. **18.** When I was in my country, I <u>was</u> afraid to come to the United States. I thought I couldn't walk outside at night because of the terrible crime. But now I <u>have</u> a different opinion. I <u>have lived</u> in this small town for three <u>months</u> and <u>(have) learned</u> that there is very little crime here. **19.** Before I came to the United <u>States</u>, I pictured the U.S. as an exciting place with <u>honest</u>, hard-working, well-mannered <u>people</u>. <u>Since</u> I came to the United <u>States</u> four <u>months</u> ago, this picture <u>has</u> changed. The manners of the students while [also possible: *when*] they are in the cafeteria are really bad. I also <u>think</u> that office workers here <u>are</u> lazy. People in my country <u>work</u> a lot harder.

Chapter 6: SUBJECT-VERB AGREEMENT

EXERCISE 1, p. 83.

2. works = *singular verb* **3.** consists = *singular verb*, planets = *plural noun* **4.** rotates = *singular verb* **5.** animals = *plural noun* **6.** needs = *singular verb* **7.** Students, tests = *plural nouns* **8.** wings = *plural noun* **9.** Swallows, creatures = *plural nouns* **10.** Butterflies = *plural noun* **11.** sunsets = *plural noun* **12.** contains = *singular verb*, books = *plural noun* **13.** Encyclopedias, things = *plural nouns* **14.** watches = *singular verb* **15.** changes = *singular verb*

EXERCISE 2, p. 85.

GROUP A ANSWERS: **2.** feeds /z/ **3.** hates /s/ **4.** lids /z/ **5.** sleep /s/ **6.** robs /z/ **7.** trips /s/ **8.** grabs /z/ **9.** wishes /əz/ **10.** matches /əz/ **11.** guesses /əz/

GROUP B ANSWERS: **12.** books /s/ **13.** homes /z/ **14.** occurs /z/ **15.** fixes /əz/ **16.** sizes /əz/ **17.** pages /əz/ **18.** unlocks /s/ **19.** fills /z/ **20.** ashes /əz/ **21.** sniffs /s/ **22.** miles /z/ **23.** rugs /z/

GROUP C ANSWERS: **24.** arranges /əz/ **25.** itches /əz/ **26.** relaxes /əz/ **27.** rises /əz/ **28.** laugh /s/ **29.** days /z/ **30.** pies /z/ **31.** agrees /z/ **32.** faces /əz/ **33.** quizzes /əz/ **34.** judges /əz/ **35.** asks /s/

EXERCISE 3, p. 85.

ANSWERS: **3.** talks /s/ **4.** blushes /əz/ **5.** discovers /z/ **6.** develops /s/ **7.** seasons /z/ **8.** flashes /əz/ **9.** halls /z/ **10.** touches /əz/ **11.** coughs /s/ **12.** presses /əz/ **13.** methods /z/ **14.** mixes /əz/ **15.** tries /z/ **16.** trays /z/ **17.** enemies /z/ **18.** guys /z/

EXERCISE 6, p. 87.

1. A stamp collector collects stamps. **2.** An animal trainer trains animals. **3.** A bank robber robs banks. **4.** A dog catcher catches dogs. **5.** A book publisher publishes books. **6.** A tax collector collects taxes. **7.** A ticket taker takes tickets. **8.** A fire extinguisher extinguishes fires. **9.** A mind reader reads minds. **10.** A bullfighter fights bulls. **11.** A wage earner earns wages. **12.** A storyteller tells stories.

EXERCISE 7, p. 87.

POSSIBLE ANSWERS: **1.** A baby cries / drinks milk / sleeps a lot. **2.** A telephone rings. **3.** A star shines / twinkles. **4.** A dog barks / runs / fetches. **5.** A duck quacks / swims. **6.** A ball bounces / rolls. **7.** A heart beats / pounds / races / pumps. **8.** A river flows / overflows / dries up. **9.** A cat purrs / chases mice. **10.** A door closes / shuts / opens / swings. **11.** A clock ticks / chimes / tells time. **12.** An airplane flies / lands / takes off. **13.** A doctor heals / sees patients / prescribes medicine. **14.** A teacher teaches / instructs / educates / lectures. **15.** A psychologist studies human behavior / helps people with problems.

EXERCISE 8, p. 87.

ANSWERS: **2.** gets **3.** are **4.** is **5.** is **6.** are **7.** is **8.** are **9.** is **10.** is **11.** are **12.** has **13.** has **14.** was/were **15.** is **16.** speak **17.** are [also possible and common, but informal and substandard: *is*] **18.** is **19.** is **20.** is **21.** is **22.** like **23.** are **24.** Japanese (language) is **25.** Japanese (people) have **26.** are **27.** works **28.** are **29.** is **30.** is

EXERCISE 9, p. 89.

ANSWERS: **1.** astounds **2.** are **3.** is **4.** are **5.** agree **6.** approves **7.** has **8.** is **9.** is **10.** was **11.** do **12.** were **13.** Is **14.** has

EXERCISE 10, p. 90.

ANSWERS: **1.** is **2.** are **3.** are **4.** is **5.** are **6.** is **7.** is **8.** has **9.** has **10.** is **11.** is/are . . . are **12.** are **13.** is **14.** is **15.** Do **16.** Does **17.** were **18.** was **19.** is **20.** is **21.** Do [Note: Approximately 70% of the earth's surface is covered by water.]

EXERCISE 11, p. 91.

ANSWERS: **1.** aren't **2.** isn't **3.** are **4.** is **5.** are **6.** are **7.** isn't **8.** was **9.** is **10.** are **11.** has been **12.** have been

EXERCISE 13, p. 93.

ANSWERS: **1.** The United States *(it)* has **2.** news *(it)* . . . is **3.** Massachusetts *(it)* is **4.** Physics *(it)* seeks **5.** Statistics *(it)* is **6.** The statistics *(they)* . . . are **7.** Fifty minutes *(It)* is **8.** Twenty dollars *(It)* is **9.** Six and seven *(It)* is **10.** Many people *(They)* . . . do **11.** police *(they)* are **12.** Rabies *(It)* is **13.** The English *(They)* are **14.** English *(It)* is **15.** Many Japanese *(They)* commute **16.** Portuguese *(It)* is . . . isn't **17.** The poor *(They)* are **18.** effect *(it)* . . . depends . . . Most people *(They)* are . . . there have been instances

EXERCISE 14, p. 93.

ANSWERS: **1.** is **2.** are **3.** are **4.** is **5.** is **6.** are **7.** is **8.** is **9.** is **10.** is **11.** are **12.** is **13.** is **14.** are **15.** are **16.** is **17.** are **18.** is **19.** is **20.** are **21.** is **22.** is **23.** are **24.** is **25.** is **26.** are **27.** are **28.** is/are **29.** are **30.** is **31.** are **32.** are **33.** is **34.** are **35.** is

EXERCISE 15, p. 94.

3. All of the employees in that company <u>are</u> required to be proficient in a second language. **4.** A lot of the people in my class <u>work</u> during the day and <u>attend</u> class in the evening. **5.** Listening to very loud music at rock concerts <u>has</u> caused hearing loss in some teenagers. **6.** Many of the satellites orbiting the earth <u>are</u> used for communications. **7.** *(no errors)* **8.** Chinese [the language] <u>has</u> more than fifty thousand written characters. **9.** About two-thirds of the Vietnamese <u>work</u> in agriculture. **10.** *(no errors)* **11.** *(no errors)* **12.** *(no errors)* **13.** Every girl and boy <u>is</u> required to have certain immunizations before enrolling in public school. **14.** Seventy-five percent of the people in New York City <u>live</u> in upstairs apartments, not on the ground floor. **15.** Unless there <u>is</u> a profound and extensive reform of government policies in the near future, the economic conditions in that country will continue to deteriorate. **16.** While I was in Paris, some of the best food I found <u>was</u> not at the well-known eating places, but in small out-of-the-way cafes. **17.** <u>Where are</u> my gloves? Have you seen them anywhere? I can't find them. **18.** *(no errors)* **19.** *(no errors)* OR [possible but extremely formal: *are*] **20.** *(no errors)* **21.** Studying a foreign language often <u>leads</u> students to learn about the culture of the <u>country</u> where it is spoken. **22.** *(no errors)* **23.** Some of the <u>movies</u> about ~~the~~ gangsters <u>are</u> surprisingly funny. **24.** *(no errors)* **25.** How many people <u>are</u> there in Canada? **26.** *(no errors)* **27.** Which one of the continents in the world <u>is</u> uninhabited? [*answer:* Antarctica] **28.** One of the most common names for dogs in the United States <u>is</u> Rover. **29.** Everybody in my family <u>enjoys</u> music and reading. **30.** Most of the mountain peaks in the Himalayan Range <u>are</u> covered with snow the year round.

EXERCISE 16, p. 96.

ANSWERS: **2.** are **3.** keeps **4.** makes **5.** is **6.** is **7.** Does **8.** Do **9.** is **10.** are **11.** are **12.** Are **13.** is **14.** beats **15.** provides **16.** oversimplifies **17.** is **18.** plan **19.** concerns **20.** is **21.** is **22.** appears **23.** are **24.** is **25.** speaks

Chapter 7: NOUNS

EXERCISE 1, p. 99.

ANSWERS: **3.** mice **4.** monkeys **5.** industries **6.** women **7.** foxes
8. geese **9.** sheep **10.** series **11.** beliefs **12.** leaves **13.** selves
14. echoes **15.** photos **16.** analyses **17.** hypotheses **18.** curricula [also
possible: *curriculums*] **19.** phenomena **20.** stimuli **21.** offspring **22.** bacteria

EXERCISE 2, p. 101.

ANSWERS: **3.** teeth **4.** boxes . . . oxen **5.** mice **6.** beaches . . . cliffs
7. leaves **8.** attorneys **9.** discoveries . . . laboratories **10.** fish **11.** wolves,
foxes, deer . . . sheep **12.** echoes **13.** pianos **14.** phenomena **15.** media

EXERCISE 3, p. 102.

ANSWERS: **(1)** Bacteria . . . things . . . organisms **(2)** Bacteria . . . bodies . . .
creatures **(3)** thousands . . . kinds . . . bacteria **(4)** Viruses . . . organisms . . .
viruses . . . cells . . . things . . . particles . . . hundreds . . . times **(5)** Viruses . . .
diseases . . . beings . . . illnesses **(6)** Viruses **(7)** officials . . . conditions
(8) officials . . . infections . . . bacteria . . . forms **(9)** infections . . . infections . . .
doctors

EXERCISE 4, p. 103.

ANSWERS: **2.** boy's **3.** boys' **4.** children's **5.** child's **6.** baby's **7.** babies'
8. wives' **9.** wife's **10.** Sally's **11.** Phyllis'/Phyllis's **12.** boss's **13.** bosses'
14. woman's **15.** women's **16.** sister's **17.** sisters' **18.** yesterday's
19. today's **18.** month's

EXERCISE 5, p. 104.

ANSWERS: **3.** father's **4.** I have four aunts. All of my aunts' homes . . . mother's
5. aunt's **6.** Five astronauts were . . . The astronauts' safe return **7.** children's
8. child's **9.** secretary's **10.** people's **11.** Bill's **12.** Bess's/Bess'
13. Quite a few diplomats are . . . Almost all of the diplomats' children **14.** diplomat's

EXERCISE 6, p. 104.

ANSWERS: **2.** bear's **3.** It's . . . world's **4.** individual's **5.** heroes' . . .
hero's **6.** Children's . . . they're . . . Adults' toys . . . children's toys

EXERCISE 7, p. 105.

ANSWERS: **2.** flowers . . . flower **3.** beans . . . bean **4.** babies . . . baby
5. children . . . child **6.** salads . . . salad **7.** faxes . . . fax **8.** cans . . .
can . . . potatoes . . . potato **9.** airplanes . . . Airplane **10.** mosquitoes . . .
mosquito **11.** two-hour . . . two hours **12.** ten years old . . . ten-year-old
13. ten . . . speeds . . . ten-speed **14.** six games . . . six-game **15.** three-letter
. . . three letters

EXERCISE 8, p. 107.

POSSIBLE RESPONSES: **1.** a cotton shirt, cotton balls, cotton wool [British English] **2.** a
grammar book, a grammar test **3.** a birthday card, a birthday present **4.** chicken
salad, chicken soup **5.** an airplane trip, an airplane ticket **6.** a telephone book, a
telephone call **7.** a mountain peak, a mountain climber **8.** a government official, a
government program **9.** a football game, a football uniform **10.** a bedroom table,

bedroom slippers   **11.** a silk scarf, silk pajamas   **12.** a morning newspaper, the morning news   **13.** a street sign, a street light   **14.** a newspaper headline, a newspaper article   **15.** a hotel lobby, a hotel room   **16.** a kitchen table, a kitchen sink   **17.** baby food, a baby bottle   **18.** vegetable soup, a vegetable brush   **19.** an office building, office furniture   **20.** a bicycle tire, a bicycle lane

EXERCISE 9, p. 107.

ANSWERS: **2.** jewelry (NC) . . . rings (C) . . . bracelets (C) . . . necklace (C)
3. mountains (C) . . . fields (C) . . . lakes (C) . . . scenery (NC)   **4.** Gold (NC) . . .
iron (NC)   **5.** iron (C)   **6.** baseball (NC) . . . baseball (C)

EXERCISE 10, p. 109.

ANSWERS: **3.** music   **4.** traffic   **5.** garbage   **6.** junk   **7.** stuff   **8.** thunder
9. screwdrivers   **10.** hardware   **11.** homework   **12.** luggage/baggage   **13.** this
information   **14.** advice   **15.** progress

EXERCISE 11, p. 110.

ANSWERS: **3.** trees, bushes, grass *(no change)*, dirt *(no change)*, and flowers   **4.** advice
(no change) . . . suggestions   **5.** words . . . vocabulary *(no change)*   **6.** two glasses
. . . water *(no change)*   **7.** Windows . . . glass *(no change)*   **8.** glasses . . . eyesight
(no change)   **9.** time *(no change)* . . . homework *(no change)*. . . . assignments
10. three times . . . a lot of time *(no change)*   **11.** typewriters, copiers, telephones, and
staplers . . . equipment *(no change)*   **12.** air *(no change)* . . . smoke, dust, and carbon
monoxide *(no changes)* . . . substances . . . air pollution *(no change)*   **13.** literature *(no
change)* . . . novels, poetry *(no change)*, and essays . . . poets . . . poems   **14.** seasons
. . . weather *(no change)*   **15.** happiness *(no change)* . . . patience *(no change)* . . .
rewards   **16.** machines . . . a modern factory *(no change)* . . . Modern factories . . .
machinery *(no change)*   **17.** travelers . . . luggage *(no change)* . . . suitcases . . . days
. . . months . . . traveler *(no change)* . . . stuff *(no change)* . . . day *(no change)*
18. garbage *(no change)* . . . magazines, envelopes . . . boxes . . . phone books . . . glass
bottles, jars . . . copper *(no change)* . . . brass *(no change)* . . . tin cans   **19.** stars . . .
grains . . . sand *(no change)*

EXERCISE 12, p. 113.

ANSWERS: **4.** A concert   **5.** An opera   **6.** Ø   **7.** A cup   **8.** Ø   **9.** An
island   **10.** Ø   **11.** A bridge   **12.** A valley   **13.** Ø   **14.** An adjective
15. Ø   **16.** Ø   **17.** A (tennis) player   **18.** A tree   **19.** Ø   **20.** Ø   **21.** Ø
22. A sentence   **23.** Ø   **24.** Ø   **25.** An orange   **26.** Ø   **27.** Ø   **28.** An
iron   **29.** A basketball   **30.** Ø

EXERCISE 13, p. 113.

ANSWERS: **5.** an accident   **6.** some homework   **7.** a table   **8.** some furniture
9. some chairs   **10.** some advice   **11.** a suitcase   **12.** some luggage
13. an earthquake   **14.** some letters   **15.** a letter   **16.** some mail   **17.** a machine
18. some new machinery   **19.** Some machines   **20.** some junk   **21.** an old
basket   **22.** some old boots

EXERCISE 15, p. 115.

ANSWERS: **3.** a good reason   **4.** the reason   **5.** the washing machine . . . a different
shirt   **6.** a washing machine   **7.** A: The radiator . . . a leak . . . the windshield
wipers B: the leak   **8.** A: The front wheel B: a parked car . . . a big pothole
A: the car B: a note . . . the owner . . . the car A: the note B: an apology   **9.** the
closet . . . the front hallway

EXERCISE 16, p. 116.

ANSWERS: **4.** Ø   **5.** A hat . . . an article   **6.** Ø . . . Ø   **7.** The brown hat
8. Ø . . . Ø   **9.** a long life   **10.** the life   **11.** an engineer   **12.** an engineer
13. the name . . . the engineer . . . an infection . . . the bridge   **14.** Ø . . . Ø
15. The jewelry

EXERCISE 17, p. 117.

ANSWERS: **1.** a new phone   **2.** the phone   **3.** Ø . . . Ø . . . Ø . . . Ø . . . Ø . . .
Ø . . . Ø   **4.** a sandy shore . . . Ø . . . the surface . . . Ø . . . Ø, Ø, Ø, Ø . . . Ø
. . . Ø   **5.** the sand . . . Ø . . . a crab . . . The crab . . . a good time . . . the beach
6. Ø, Ø . . . Ø . . . a person   **7.** Ø . . . Ø . . . the universe   **8.** Ø . . . Ø . . . a
thin layer . . . Ø . . . Ø   **9.** a recent newspaper article . . . an Australian swimmer
. . . a shark . . . a group . . . the shark . . . the swimmer . . . the dolphins . . . the
swimmer's life   **10.** Ø . . . Ø . . . Ø . . . an average . . . Ø   **11.** Ø . . . Ø
12. a fly . . . the ceiling . . . the fly . . . the ceiling

EXERCISE 18, p. 118.

1. i. ~~too much~~   **2.** a. ~~two~~   h. ~~too many~~
  k. ~~a little~~   b. ~~a couple of~~   j. ~~a few~~
  m. ~~a great deal of~~   c. ~~both~~   l. ~~a number of~~
               d. ~~several~~

EXERCISE 19, p. 119.

1. b. ~~several~~   g. ~~a few~~   **2.** e. ~~too much~~
  f. ~~too many~~   i. ~~a number of~~   h. ~~a little~~
                               j. ~~a great deal of~~

EXERCISE 20, p. 120.

ANSWERS: **3.** much mail   **4.** many letters   **5.** aren't many hotels   **6.** is too much
furniture   **7.** isn't much traffic   **8.** aren't many cars   **9.** much work   **10.** many
sides   **11.** much information   **12.** much homework   **13.** many people
14. much postage   **15.** is too much violence   **16.** much patience   **17.** many
patients   **18.** many teeth   **19.** isn't much international news   **20.** many fish are
21. many continents are   **22.** much progress

EXERCISE 21, p. 121.

4. Ø
  loaves of bread
  Ø
  jars of honey

5. novels
  Ø
  poems
  Ø

6. orange juice
  light bulbs
  hardware
  computer software

7. sleep
  information
  facts
  help

8. women
  movies
  scenes
  Ø

9. shirts
  Ø
  pens
  Ø

10. patience
  wealth
  Ø
  Ø

11. luck
  money
  advice
  Ø

12. ideas
  theories
  hypotheses
  Ø

EXERCISE 22, p. 122.

ANSWERS: 1. much furniture   2. many desks   3. many branches   4. much equipment   5. much machinery   6. many machines   7. many women   8. many pieces   9. many mice   10. much advice   11. many sheep   12. much homework   13. many prizes   14. many geese   15. much music   16. much progress   17. many races   18. much knowledge   19. many marriages   20. much information   21. much luck   22. many hypotheses   23. much mail   24. many offices   25. much slang   26. many roofs   27. many shelves   28. many teeth

EXERCISE 23, p. 123.

ANSWERS: 3. a little sunshine   4. very little sunshine   5. a few programs   6. very few television programs   7. a few drops   8. a little oil   9. very little jewelry

EXERCISE 24, p. 124.

ANSWERS: 3. a little salt   4. very little salt   5. a little music   6. very little traffic   7. very few friends   8. a few days . . . a few days   9. a few more minutes   10. a little more time   11. a few nuts   12. very few toys   13. a little rain   14. a little honey . . . a little milk   15. very little patience   16. very few problems

EXERCISE 25, p. 125.

ANSWERS: 3. Ø . . . Ø   4. of   5. Ø   6. of   7. Ø   8. of   9. Ø   10. of   11. Ø   12. of   13. of   14. of   15. Ø   16. of   17. Ø . . . of   18. Ø   19. of   20. Ø

EXERCISE 26, p. 126.

ANSWERS: 3. (of)   4. Ø   5. Ø   6. Ø . . . Ø . . . (of)   7. (of)   8. (of)   9. (of)   10. Ø . . . Ø

EXERCISE 27, p. 127.

ANSWERS: 4. Ø   5. of   6. of   7. Ø . . . Ø . . . Ø   8. of   9. Ø . . . Ø   10. of . . . of   11. Ø   12. Ø . . . of

EXERCISE 28, p. 128.

ANSWERS: 2. girls   3. children   4. child   5. member   6. members

EXERCISE 29, p. 129.

ANSWERS: 3. countries   4. each student / each of the students   5. (no change) 6. All (of) the furniture / Each piece of furniture   7. Some of the equipment / One piece of equipment / One of the pieces of equipment   8. each woman / each of the women / all of the women   9. places   10. (no change)   11. language   12. each of the errors / each error

Chapter 8: PRONOUNS

EXERCISE 1, p. 131.

ANSWERS: 1. Some North American food is very good, but I don't like most of it.   2. When we were schoolgirls, my sister and I used to play badminton after school every day.   3. If you want to pass your exams, you had better study very hard for them.   4. The work had to be finished by my boss and me after the store had closed for the night.   5. A hippopotamus spends most of <u>its</u> time in the water of rivers and lakes.   6. After work, Mr. Gray asked to speak to Tim and <u>me</u> about the company's new policies. He explained <u>them</u> to us and asked for <u>our</u> opinions.   7. <u>Children</u> should learn to respect other people. They need to learn how to treat other people politely, including their playmates.   8. My friends asked to borrow my car because <u>theirs</u> was in the garage for repairs.

EXERCISE 2, p. 132.

2. they . . . they = *pronouns;* monkeys = *antecedent*   **3.** She = *pronoun;* teacher = *antecedent;* them = *pronoun;* papers = *antecedent*   **4.** her . . . She = *pronouns;* Nancy = *antecedent;* it = *pronoun;* apple = *antecedent*   **5.** it = *pronoun;* dog = *antecedent*
6. She . . . She = *pronouns;* cat = *antecedent;* His . . . him = *pronouns;* Tom = *antecedent*
They = *pronoun;* dogs = *antecedent;* him = *pronoun;* Tom = *antecedent*

EXERCISE 3, p. 133.

ANSWERS: **2.** mine . . . yours   **3.** their books . . . hers . . . his   **4.** its   **5.** It's true . . . its way . . . its trip   **6.** Its name . . . It's a turtle . . . It's been [*It's been* = It has been]   **7.** Our house . . . Our neighbor's house . . . ours . . . theirs   **8.** It . . . its prey . . . its long, pointed bill . . . it . . . it . . . it . . . It's interesting . . . them

EXERCISE 4, p. 132.

ANSWERS: **3.** <u>Students</u> in Biology 101 <u>have</u> to spend three hours per week in the laboratory, where <u>they do</u> various experiments by following the directions in <u>their</u> lab <u>manuals</u>.   **4.** <u>Pharmacists fill</u> prescriptions, but <u>they are</u> not allowed to prescribe medicine.   **5.** *(no change)*   **6.** <u>Citizens have</u> two primary responsibilties. <u>They</u> should vote in every election, and <u>they</u> should serve willingly on a jury.   **7.** *(no change)*
8. <u>Lecturers need</u> to prepare <u>their</u> notes carefully so that <u>they do</u> not lose <u>their</u> place while <u>they are</u> delivering <u>their</u> speech(<u>es</u>).

EXERCISE 5, p. 135.

ANSWERS: **2.** s/he wants; he or she wants; they want   **3.** his/her; their   **4.** his/her; their   **5.** anyone; his/her; their   **6.** him/her; them   **7.** s/he . . . his/her; they . . . their   **8.** s/he pleases; they please

EXERCISE 6, p. 136.

ANSWERS: **2.** it consists   **3.** It   **4.** They   **5.** they   **6.** It doesn't   **7.** they
8. It was   **9.** They are . . . their . . . them   **10.** It is

EXERCISE 8, p. 137.

ANSWERS: **2.** himself   **3.** herself   **4.** themselves   **5.** ourselves   **6.** yourself
7. yourselves   **8.** oneself

EXERCISE 9, p. 138.

ANSWERS: **2.** herself   **3.** themselves   **4.** herself   **5.** yourself . . . himself . . . myself . . . ourselves . . . themselves   **6.** myself   **7.** himself   **8.** yourself
9. themselves   **10.** herself

EXERCISE 10, p. 139.

ANSWERS: **2.** enjoy himself   **3.** proud of yourselves   **4.** pat yourself   **5.** killed himself   **6.** entertained themselves   **7.** introduced myself   **8.** feeling sorry for yourself   **9.** talking to yourself   **10.** laugh at ourselves   **11.** promised herself   **12.** angry at himself

EXERCISE 11, p. 141.

ANSWERS: **3.** The pronouns refer to people in general. **4.** The pronouns refer to Alex. **5.** people in general **6.** Sonya **7.** people in general **8.** people in general **9.** people in the orchestra **10.** people in general

EXERCISE 12, p. 141.

ANSWERS: **2.** <u>Millions</u> of <u>years</u> ago, they had <u>wings</u>. <u>These</u> wings changed as the birds adapted to <u>their</u> environment. **3.** <u>Penguins'</u> principal food <u>was fish</u>. Penguins needed to be able to swim to find their food, so eventually their <u>wings</u> evolved into <u>flippers</u> that enabled <u>them</u> to swim through water with speed and ease. **4.** Penguins <u>spend</u> most of their lives in <u>water</u>. However, they lay their <u>eggs</u> on <u>land</u>. **5.** Emperor penguins have interesting egg-laying <u>habits</u>. **6.** The female <u>lays</u> one <u>egg</u> on the <u>ice</u> in Arctic regions, and then immediately <u>returns</u> to the ocean. **7.** After the female lays the egg, the male <u>takes</u> over. <u>He covers</u> the egg with <u>his</u> body until <u>it hatches</u>. **8.** <u>This</u> process <u>takes</u> seven to eight <u>weeks</u>. During <u>this</u> time, the male <u>doesn't</u> eat. **9.** After the egg <u>hatches</u>, the female returns to take care of the chick, and the male <u>goes</u> to the ocean to find food for <u>himself</u>, his mate, and their offspring. **10.** Although the <u>penguins'</u> natural habitat is in polar regions, we can see them in most major zoos in the world. <u>They seem</u> to adapt well to life in confinement, so we can enjoy watching <u>their</u> antics without feeling sorry about <u>their</u> loss of freedom.

EXERCISE 13, p. 143.

2. Another . . . Another . . . Another . . . the other **3.** The other **4.** The others **5.** The other **6.** others **7.** other **8.** another **9.** Others **10.** the other **11.** other **12.** others **13.** another **14.** another **15.** Another . . . Others **16.** others **17.** Another . . . Others . . . other **18.** the other **19.** the others **20.** another **21.** Another . . . The other

EXERCISE 15, p. 145.

ANSWERS: **2.** Another . . . other **3.** one another/each other **4.** the other **5.** other . . . other **6.** other **7.** others . . . others . . . other **8.** each other/one another . . . each other/one another . . . each other/one another . . . other **9.** other **10.** other **11.** another

EXERCISE 17, p. 147.

1. That book <u>contains</u> many different <u>kinds</u> of <u>stories</u> and <u>articles</u>. **2.** ~~The~~ English is one of the most important <u>languages</u> in the world. **3.** She is always willing to help her friends in every possible <u>way</u>. **4.** In the past, horses <u>were</u> the principal <u>means</u> of transportation. **5.** He succeeded in creating one of the best <u>armies</u> in the world. **6.** There <u>is a lot of equipment</u> in the research laboratory, but undergraduates are not allowed to use <u>it</u>. **7.** All of the <u>guests</u> enjoyed <u>themselves</u> at the reception. **8.** I have a <u>five-year-old</u> daughter and a <u>three-year-old</u> son. **9.** Each <u>state</u> in the country <u>has</u> a different language. **10.** Most of <u>the</u> people/ Most ~~of~~ people in my apartment building <u>are</u> friendly. **11.** A political leader should have the ability to adapt <u>himself/herself</u> to a changing world. **12.** In my opinion, ~~an~~ international <u>students</u> should live in a dormitory because they will meet many people and can practice their English every day. Also, if <u>they</u> live in a dormitory, <u>their</u> food is provided for <u>them</u>. **13.** When I lost my passport, I had to apply for ~~the~~ another one. **14.** When I got to class, all of the <u>other</u> students were already in their seats. **15.** Everyone <u>seeks</u> ~~the~~ happiness in their <u>lives</u>. OR Everyone <u>seeks</u> ~~the~~ happiness in <u>his/her</u> life. **16.** In my country, there <u>are</u> a <u>lot</u> of schools / ~~a lots of~~ schools. **17.** Writing compositions <u>is</u> very hard for me. **18.** It's difficult for me to

understand English when people <u>use</u> a lot of <u>slang</u>.   **19.** <s>A</s> <u>Students</u> at the university should attend class regularly and hand in their assignments on time.   OR   A student at the university should attend classes regularly and hand in <u>his/her</u> assignments on time.
20. In my opinion, <s>the</s> <u>English</u> is <u>an</u> easy language to learn.

EXERCISE 18, p. 148.

1. There <u>are</u> many different <u>kinds</u> of <u>animals</u> in the world.   **2.** My cousin and her husband want to move to <u>another</u> city because they don't like <s>a</s> cold weather.   **3.** I like to travel because I like to learn about other <u>countries</u> and <u>customs</u>.   **4.** Collecting stamps is one of my <u>hobbies</u>.   **5.** I came here three and a half <u>months</u> ago. I think I have made <s>a</s> good progress in English.   **6.** I was looking for my keys, but I couldn't find <u>them</u>.   **7.** When my mother was <u>a</u> child, she lived in a small town. Now this town is <u>a</u> big city with tall <u>buildings</u> and many <u>highways</u>.   **8.** English has borrowed quite a few of <u>words</u> from <u>other</u> languages.   **9.** There <u>are</u> many <u>students</u> from <u>different</u> countries in this class.   **10.** <u>Thousands</u> of <u>athletes</u> take part in the Olympics.   **11.** Education is one of the most important <u>aspects</u> of life. <u>Knowledge</u> about many different things <u>allows</u> us to live fuller lives.   **12.** All of the <u>students'</u> names were on the list.   **13.** I live in a <u>two-room</u> apartment.   **14.** Many <s>of</s> people prefer to live in small towns. Their attachment to their communities <u>prevents</u> them from moving from place to place in search of <u>work</u>.   **15.** <u>Today's</u> news is just as bad as <u>yesterday's</u> news.   **16.** Almost <u>all</u> of the students / Almost <u>all</u> <s>of</s> the students / <u>Most</u> (of the) students in our class <u>speak</u> English well. **17.** The teacher gave us <u>some</u> homework to hand in next Tuesday.   **18.** Today <u>women</u> work as <u>doctors</u>, <u>pilots</u>, <u>archeologists</u>, and many other <u>things</u>. Both my mother and father are <u>teachers</u>.   **19.** Every <u>employee</u> in our company <u>respects</u> Mr. Ward.   **20.** <u>Children</u> <u>need</u> to learn how to get along with <u>other</u> people, how to spend <u>their</u> time wisely, and how to depend on <u>themselves</u>. [Also possible, but more stylistically awkward in its use of pronouns: *A child needs to learn how to get along with <u>other</u> people, how to spend his or her time wisely, and how to depend on <u>himself or herself</u>.*]

Chapter 9: MODALS, PART 1

EXERCISE 1, p. 152.

ANSWERS: **1.** She can see it.   **2.** [no *-s* on modal auxiliary *can*]
3. [no *-s* on main verb *see*]   **4.** She can see it.   **5.** [no *to*]   **6.** Can you see it?
7. They can't go there.

EXERCISE 3, p. 154.

ANSWERS: **3.** mailing   **4.** if I stayed   **5.** opening/if I opened   **6.** if I asked
7. if I smoked   **8.** speaking   **9.** if I changed/changing   **10.** if I borrowed

EXERCISE 5, p. 155.

POSSIBLE COMPLETIONS: **2.** Could we have a few more minutes? / Could you give us a little more time?   **3.** Could I get a ride with you?   **4.** Would you mind meeting Wednesday instead?   **5.** Could you take a look at them?   **6.** May I help you? . . . Could I see what you have in silk scarves?   **7.** Would you mind changing seats / if we changed seats?   **8.** May I call you this evening?

EXERCISE 9, p. 158.

ANSWERS: **3.** don't have to   **4.** must not   **5.** doesn't have to   **6.** must not
7. don't have to   **8.** don't have to   **9.** must not   **10.** don't have to   **11.** must not   **12.** doesn't have to

EXERCISE 12, p. 161.

SAMPLE COMPLETIONS: **2.** hurt my feet . . . return them. **3.** finish your homework . . . forbid you to watch TV tonight. **4.** put antifreeze in the car **5.** be ready for the test . . . I don't feel confident. **6.** help us with dinner . . . We'd be happy to help. Shall I set the table? **7.** give up caffeine, but I love coffee . . . listen to your doctor. **8.** call your brother if you want him to pick you up at the airport next week . . . do that now. **9.** finished your report yet? . . . do it soon. **10.** swim . . . a lifeguard? . . . ask him to teach Mary how to swim. **11.** study or go to a movie? . . . study . . . you won't be prepared for class tomorrow. **12.** tired all the time . . . see a doctor . . . seeing an acupuncturist?

EXERCISE 13, p. 162.

[These are the stronger sentences in each pair.] **1.** b. **2.** b. **3.** a **4.** a. **5.** b. **6.** a.

EXERCISE 14, p. 162.

ANSWERS: **3.** must/have to **4.** have to/must [Note: *have to* is preferable because the situation is neither formal nor urgent.] **5.** should **6.** should [also possible: *have to/must*] **7.** should OR must/ have to [if it's a requirement of the school] **8.** must/has to **9.** should **10.** must

EXERCISE 15, p. 163.

ANSWERS: **1.** He/She shouldn't have left the door open. **2.** I should have gone to the meeting. **3.** (. . .) should have gone to see a doctor. **4.** (. . .) shouldn't have sold his/her car. **5.** (. . .) should have read the contract more carefully.

EXERCISE 16, p. 164.

EXPECTED RESPONSES: **1.** I should have worn a coat. **2.** I should have looked the word up in the dictionary. **3.** I should have written my friend a letter. **4.** I shouldn't have spent my money foolishly. **5.** I shouldn't have opened the window. **6.** I should have gone to the grocery store. **7.** I should have set my alarm clock. **8.** I should have gone to (New Orleans) with my friends. **9.** I should have had a cup of coffee. **10.** John should have married Mary. **11.** John shouldn't have married Mary. **12.** I should have stayed home yesterday. **13.** I should have gone outside and enjoyed the nice weather. **14.** I should have bought my girlfriend/boyfriend a different present. **15.** The little girl shouldn't have told a lie / should have told the truth. **16.** I should not have lent (. . .) my car.

EXERCISE 18, p. 166.

1. The building custodian <u>is</u> supposed to unlock the classrooms every morning.
2. We're not <u>supposed</u> to open that door. **3.** Where are we <u>supposed</u> to meet?
4. I have a meeting at seven tonight. I <u>am supposed</u> to be there a little early to discuss the agenda. **5.** When we go to the store, Annie, you <u>are</u> not <u>supposed</u> to handle the glassware. It might break, and then you'd have to pay for it out of your allowance.
6. I'm <u>supposed</u> to be at the meeting. I suppose I'd better go. **7.** Where have you been? You <u>were supposed</u> to be here an hour ago! **8.** A: I can't remember what the boss said. <u>Am</u> I supposed to work in the mail order room tomorrow morning and then the shipping department tomorrow afternoon? Or the other way around? B: How am I <u>supposed</u> to remember what you <u>are supposed</u> to do? I have enough trouble remembering what I <u>am</u> supposed <u>to do</u> / <u>am</u> supposed <u>to be doing</u>.

EXERCISE 20, p. 167.

[These are the stronger sentences in each pair.]   **1.** a.   **2.** a.   **3.** a.   **4.** a.
5. b.   **6.** b.   **7.** a

Chapter 10: MODALS, PART 2

EXERCISE 1, p. 174.

ANSWERS: **2.** B   **3.** A   **4.** B   **5.** C   **6.** B   **7.** A   **8.** B   **9.** C
10. A   **11.** B   **12.** B   **13.** B   **14.** C

EXERCISE 4, p. 177.

EXPECTED COMPLETIONS: **2.** must be rich.   **3.** must be crazy.   **4.** may/might/
could be at a meeting   **5.** must have the wrong number.   **6.** must be very proud.
7. must feel terrible.   **8.** may/might/could fit Jimmy.   **9.** must miss them very
much.   **10.** must be about ten.

EXERCISES 5–6, p. 179.

EX. 5 POSSIBLE RESPONSES: **2.** be at home   **3.** be thirsty   **4.** like nuts   **5.** have
many friends

EX. 6 POSSIBLE RESPONSES: **2.** Alex wasn't here today. / Alex never wears a hat.   **3.** I just
saw her yesterday. / She was in class with me last night.   **4.** There aren't any wolves
here.   **5.** She loves her job. / She needs her job.

EXERCISE 11, p. 183.

ANSWERS: **2.** must not like   **3.** must have been   **4.** must be   **5.** must have
forgotten   **6.** must not speak   **7.** must have left   **8.** must be   **9.** must have
hurt   **10.** must mean   **11.** must have been   **12.** must have misunderstood

EXERCISE 12, p. 185.

ANSWERS: **3.** must   **4.** should / ought to [also possible: *will*]   **5.** should   **6.** will
7. should / ought to   **8.** will   **9.** must   **10.** should / ought to / will   **11.** should /
ought to   **12.** should / ought to   **13.** should / ought to   **14.** must   **15.** should
have / ought to have   **16.** must have

EXERCISE 13, p. 186.

2. a. Jane   **3.** a. a rat   **4.** a. Mark   **5.** a. Janet
 b. Ron   b. a cat   b. my neighbor   b. Sally
 c. Sue   c. a mouse   c. Carol   c. Bob
 d. Ann   d. Andy

EXERCISE 15, p. 189.

ANSWERS: **3.** must be burning   **4.** may/might/could be talking . . . may/might/could be
talking   **5.** must be playing   **6.** may/might/could be staying . . . may/might/could be
staying   **7.** should be studying   **8.** must be kidding   **9.** may/might/could have
been kidding   **10.** must have been kidding

EXERCISE 17, p. 190.

ANSWERS: **2.** must be waiting   **3.** shouldn't have left   **4.** might have borrowed
5. must have been watching . . . must have forgotten   **6.** may have been attending [also

possible: *may have attended*]   **7.** might have been washing   **8.** must have left   **9.** might be traveling   **10.** must not have been expecting   **11.** must have been daydreaming . . . should have been paying . . . shouldn't have been staring   **12.** A: should have taken B: must be walking   A: might have decided . . . could be working . . . may have called

EXERCISE 24, p. 195.

ANSWERS: **2.** would give   **3.** used to be   **4.** used to be . . . would start   **5.** used to be . . . would get . . . would spend . . . would find . . . would gather   **6.** used to ask . . . would never let   **7.** would make . . . would put   **8.** would wake . . . would hike . . . would see   **9.** used to take   **10.** would be sitting . . . would always smile . . . would stand . . . (would) clear

EXERCISE 29, p. 202.

1. had better shut (should / ought to / have to / must shut)   **2.** could / would you hand (can / will you hand)   **3.** don't / won't have to go   **4.** can already say (is already able to say)   **5.** must / have to attend   **6.** had to wait   **7.** could / might go   **8.** would rather go   **9.** must not have seen   **10.** had better clean (should / ought to / must / have to clean)   **11.** can't / couldn't be (must not be) . . . may / might / could belong (must belong)   **12.** cannot go (must not / may not go)   **13.** should not have laughed   **14.** May / Can / Could I speak . . . can't come . . . May / Can I take   **15.** should / ought to take (could take) . . . can get   **16.** had to study . . . should have come   **17.** had better answer (should / ought to / have to answer) . . . might / could / may be   **18.** should have been / was supposed to be   **19.** could / might / may be   **20.** must have been daydreaming

EXERCISE 30, p. 204.

1. If you have a car, you can <u>travel</u> around the United <u>States</u>.   **2.** During class, the students must t̶o̶ sit <u>quietly</u>. When the <u>students</u> have questions, they must t̶o̶ raise their hands.   **3.** When you send for the brochure, you should <u>include</u> a self-addressed, stamped envelope.   **4.** A film director must <u>have</u> control over every aspect of a movie.   **5.** When I was a child, I c̶a̶n̶ <u>could</u> / <u>would</u> go to the roof of my house and <u>see</u> all the other houses and streets.   **6.** <u>When</u> I w̶a̶s̶ <u>worked</u> in the fields, my son would <u>bring</u> me oranges or candy.   **7.** I <u>broke</u> my leg in a soccer game three <u>months</u> ago.   **8.** <u>Will</u> / <u>Would</u> / <u>Could</u> you please help me with this?   **9.** Many <u>students</u> would rather t̶o̶ study on their own than <u>go</u> to <u>class</u>.   **10.** We <u>are</u> supposed to bring our books to class every day.   **11.** You can <u>have</u> a very good time as a tourist in my country. My country <u>has</u> many <u>different weather areas,</u> [also possible: *different climates,*] so you <u>had</u> better plan ahead before you <u>come</u>.   **12.** When you visit big <u>cities</u> in my country, you must t̶o̶ b̶e̶ <u>pay</u> attention to your wallet when you are in a <u>crowded</u> place because there <u>are</u> a lot of <u>thieves</u>.

EXERCISE 33, p. 206.

ANSWERS: **1.** had   **2.** happened   **3.** was driving   **4.** broke   **5.** did you do   **6.** pulled   **7.** got   **8.** started   **9.** should not have done   **10.** should have stayed   **11.** are probably   **12.** started   **13.** have been walking / had walked   **14.** went   **15.** discovered   **16.** didn't have   **17.** can think   **18.** could / might have gone   **19.** could / might have tried   **20.** could / might have asked   **21.** asked   **22.** told   **23.** was   **24.** allowed   **25.** drove   **26.** must have felt   **27.** took   **28.** took   **29.** might get / might have gotten   **30.** will know   **31.** must / have to / should leave   **32.** have to / must be   **33.** May / Could / Can I use   **34.** need   **35.** don't have   **36.** will / can take

Chapter 11: THE PASSIVE

EXERCISE 1, p. 209.

ANSWERS: **2.** is being opened **3.** has been opened **4.** was opened **5.** was being opened **6.** had been opened **7.** will be opened **8.** is going to be opened **9.** will have been opened **10.** Is . . . being opened **11.** Was . . . opened **12.** Has . . . been opened

EXERCISE 2, p. 209.

PART I ANSWERS: **2.** Customers <u>are served</u> by waitresses and waiters. **3.** The lesson <u>is going to be explained</u> by the teacher. **4.** A new idea <u>has been suggested</u> by Shirley. **5.** Ann <u>will be invited</u> to the party by Bill. **6.** That report <u>is being prepared</u> by Alex. **7.** The farmer's wagon <u>was being pulled</u> by two horses. **8.** The book <u>had been returned</u> (by Kathy) to the library (by Kathy). [Either position is acceptable.] **9.** By this time tomorrow, the announcement <u>will have been made</u> by the president. **10.** That note <u>wasn't written</u> by me. It <u>was written</u> by Jim. **11.** That pie <u>wasn't made</u> by Alice. <u>Was</u> it <u>made</u> by Mrs. French? **12.** <u>Is</u> that course <u>taught</u> by Prof. Jackson? I know that it <u>isn't taught</u> by Prof. Adams. **13.** Those papers <u>haven't been signed</u> (yet) by Mrs. Andrews (yet). [Either position is acceptable.] <u>Have</u> they <u>been signed</u> by Mr. Andrews? **14.** <u>Is</u> your house <u>being painted</u> by Mr. Brown? **15.** I <u>won't be fooled</u> by his tricks.

PART II ANSWERS: **16.** Omar <u>wrote</u> that sentence. **17.** The teacher <u>is going to collect</u> our papers. **18.** <u>Did</u> Thomas Edison <u>invent</u> the electric light bulb? **19.** Most drivers <u>don't obey</u> the speed limit on Highway 5. **20.** <u>Has</u> the building superintendent <u>informed</u> you of a proposed increase in our rent?

EXERCISE 3, p. 210.

ANSWERS: **3.** *(no change)* **4.** *(no change)* **5.** That theory was developed by Dr. Ikeda. **6.** The cup was dropped by Timmy. **7.** *(no change)* **8.** I was interviewed by the assistant manager. **9.** *(no change)* **10.** The small fishing village was destroyed by a hurricane. **11.** *(no change)* **12.** *(no change)* **13.** *(no change)* **14.** After class, the chalkboard is always erased by one of the students. **15.** *(no change)* **16.** *(no change)* **17.** *(no change)* **18.** The fire wasn't caused by lightning. **19.** The dispute is going to be settled by a special committee. **20.** Was the enemy surrounded by the army? **21.** *(no change)* **22.** Windmills were invented by the Persians around 1500 years ago.

EXERCISE 5, p. 212.

ANSWERS: **3.** This antique table was made in 1734. **4.** *(no change)* **5.** My purse was stolen. **6.** The coffee was being made when I walked into the kitchen. **7.** That book has been translated into many languages. **8.** That picture was drawn by Jim's daughter. This picture was drawn by my son. **9.** The applicants will be judged on the basis of their originality. **10.** *(no change)* **11.** Is that course being taught by Professor Rivers this semester? **12.** When was the radio invented? **13.** The mail had already been delivered by the time I left for school this morning. **14.** When are the results of the contest going to be announced? **15.** After the concert was over, the rock music star was mobbed by hundreds of fans outside the theater. **16.** Ever since I arrived here, I have been living in the dormitory because I was told that it was cheaper to live there than in an apartment. **17.** The new hospital is going to be built next year. The new elementary school has already been built. **18.** If a film is exposed to light while it is being developed, the negative will be ruined.

EXERCISE 6, p. 213.

2. Peggy = indirect object—Peggy has been awarded a scholarship by Indiana University.
3. Fred = indirect object—Fred was paid three hundred dollars in consulting fees.
4. Maria = indirect object—Maria has been given a promotion at her job as a computer programmer at Microsoft.
5. you = indirect object—You will be sent a bill.
6. people = indirect object—The starving people will be given a week's supply of rice.

EXERCISE 7, p. 213.

ANSWERS: **1.** You were invited to a party. **2.** Rice is grown in many countries. **3.** The game is being televised. **4.** Reading is taught in the first grade. **5.** You were told to be here at ten. **6.** That hat was made in Mexico. **7.** Dinner is going to be served at six. **8.** The news will be announced tomorrow. **9.** A mistake has been made. **10.** A test is being given (by the teacher) in the next room right now.

EXERCISE 9, p. 215.

ANSWERS: **2.** is surrounded **3.** is spelled [also possible, esp. in British English: *spelt*] **4.** will be built / is going to be built **5.** was divided / has been divided **6.** is worn **7.** was caused **8.** was ordered **9.** who was accidentally killed **10.** was reported **11.** was surprised **12.** was offered **13.** were frightened **14.** was confused **15.** is expected

EXERCISE 10, p. 216.

1. is produced **2.** is being treated **3.** will probably be won / is probably going to be won **4.** saw . . . was interviewed **5.** are controlled / are determined **6.** was caught . . . was being chased . . . jumped . . . kept **7.** appeared . . . have been named . . . described . . . are being discovered / are discovered **8.** was informed . . . was told **9.** is exposed . . . affects **10.** was discovered . . . called . . . was translated . . . had been built . . . do not exist **11.** was recognized . . . was asked . . . took . . . knew . . . multiplied . . . came **12.** brought . . . sent . . . were asked . . . was discovered . . . is still called

EXERCISE 11, p. 219.

ANSWERS: **4.** must be kept **5.** must keep **6.** couldn't be opened **7.** couldn't open **8.** may be offered **9.** may offer **10.** may already have been offered / may have already been offered **11.** may already have offered / may have already offered **12.** ought to be divided **13.** ought to have been divided **14.** have to be returned **15.** has to return . . . will have to pay **16.** had better be finished **17.** had better finish **18.** is supposed to be sent **19.** should have been sent **20.** must have been surprised

EXERCISE 12, p. 220.

EXPECTED COMPLETIONS: **2.** must be married **3.** must be written / have to be written **4.** must have been left **5.** should / ought to / has to be postponed **6.** should not be given **7.** should / ought to be encouraged **8.** may / could / might / will be misunderstood **9.** cannot be explained **10.** must have been embarrassed **11.** must / has to be pushed **12.** should / ought to have been built **13.** must / should be saved **14.** must / has to / should be done **15.** ought to / should be elected [advisability]; must/has to [necessity]; will be elected [prediction]; may/might/could be elected [possibility]

EXERCISE 14, p. 222.

ANSWERS: **1.** is usually delivered [also possible: *usually gets delivered*] **2.** were working . . . occurred . . . was hurt [also possible: *got hurt*] **3.** was not admitted . . . had already begun **4.** had already been offered **5.** is being organized **6.** will never be forgotten / is never going to be forgotten **7.** was . . . happened . . . flunked . . . dropped . . . was walking . . . fell . . . was stolen [also possible: *got stolen*] **8.** had (already) been rented (already) **9.** was being ignored **10.** did you buy . . . didn't buy . . . was given . . . Do you like **11.** is circled . . . are held . . . are circled **12.** worshipped **13.** have been destroyed **14.** were allowed . . . were not invited . . . were forbidden . . . were being held / were held **15.** was built . . . has often been described . . . was designed . . . took **16.** is being judged . . . will be announced / are going to be announced

EXERCISE 16, p. 224.

(1) <u>paper has been made</u> from various plants . . . In the past, <u>paper was made</u> by hand . . . <u>most of the work is done</u> by machines . . . Today <u>paper is made</u> from wood pulp
(2) In the mechanical process, <u>wood is ground</u> . . . During the grinding, <u>it is sprayed</u> . . . Then <u>the chips are soaked</u>
(3) First <u>the wood is washed</u>, and then <u>it is cut</u> into small pieces . . . Then <u>the chips are cooked</u> . . . After <u>the wood is cooked, it is washed</u>
(4) <u>The pulp is drained</u> to form . . . <u>(is) bleached</u> . . . and then <u>(is)</u> thoroughly <u>washed</u> again. Next <u>the pulp is put</u> . . . drier and a press, <u>they are wound</u>
(5) . . . how <u>it is made</u>.

EXERCISE 18, p. 226.

ANSWERS: **2.** is shut **3.** are turned **4.** is not crowded **5.** are bent . . . are folded **6.** is finished **7.** is closed **8.** was closed **9.** is stuck **10.** was stuck **11.** is/has been made . . . (is) swept . . . (are) washed **12.** is set . . . (are) done . . . (are) lighted / (are) lit **13.** is gone **14.** is torn **15.** is hidden

EXERCISE 19, p. 226.

ANSWERS: **2.** is . . . crowded **3.** is scheduled **4.** am exhausted **5.** am confused **6.** is stuck **7.** are turned off **8.** is insured **9.** are divorced **10.** is gone **11.** are . . . qualified **12.** am married **13.** is spoiled/spoilt **14.** is blocked **15.** is located **16.** was born **17.** Is . . . turned off **18.** are . . . done

EXERCISE 20, p. 228.

2. with **3.** for **4.** to **5.** to **6.** with **7.** in **8.** with **9.** to **10.** to **11.** with **12.** of **13.** to **14.** to . . . of **15.** with **16.** from **17.** with **18.** in **19.** to **20.** with **21.** to **22.** with **23.** for **24.** in/ with . . . to . . . with **25.** with . . . in . . . to

EXERCISE 22, p. 230.

2. is composed of **3.** am accustomed to **4.** is terrified of **5.** is finished with **6.** is addicted to **7.** is covered with **8.** am satisfied with **9.** is married to **10.** is divorced from **11.** am . . . acquainted with **12.** am tired of **13.** Are . . . related to **14.** is dedicated to **15.** is disappointed in/with **16.** is scared of **17.** is committed to **18.** are devoted to **19.** is dressed in **20.** are done with

EXERCISE 23, p. 232.

ANSWERS: **2.** am getting sleepy **3.** is getting late **4.** got wet **5.** is getting hot **6.** get nervous **7.** is getting dark **8.** got light **9.** am getting full **10.** is getting better **11.** Get busy **12.** Get well

EXERCISE 24, p. 233.

ANSWERS: **2.** got hurt **3.** got lost **4.** get dressed **5.** did . . . get married / are . . . getting / going to get married **6.** get accustomed **7.** am getting worried **8.** get upset **9.** got confused **10.** get done **11.** got depressed **12.** Did . . . get invited **13.** got bored **14.** get packed **15.** get paid **16.** got hired **17.** got fired **18.** didn't get finished **19.** got disgusted **20.** got engaged . . . got married . . . got divorced . . . got remarried

EXERCISE 26, p. 235.

ANSWERS: **3.** exciting **4.** excited **5.** surprising **6.** surprised **7.** frightened **8.** frightening **9.** exhausting **10.** exhausted

EXERCISE 27, p. 235.

ANSWERS: **1.** amazing (story) . . . amazed (person) **2.** depressing (story) . . . depressed (person) **3.** tired (person) . . . tiring (work) **4.** boring (movie) . . . bored (person) **5.** interested (person) . . . interesting (painting) **6.** embarrassing (situation) . . . embarrassed (person) **7.** disappointing (book) . . . disappointed (reader) **8.** A person who fascinates me is a fascinating person. I am fascinated by this person. **9.** frustrating (situation) . . . frustrated (person) **10.** annoying (noise) . . . annoyed (person) **11.** shocking (event) . . . shocked (person) **12.** thrilling (experience) . . . (thrilled) person

EXERCISE 28, p. 236.

ANSWERS: **2.** satisfying **3.** terrifying **4.** terrified **5.** embarrassing **6.** broken **7.** crowded **8.** locked **9.** injured **10.** annoying **11.** challenging **12.** expected **13.** growing . . . balanced **14.** spoiled / spoilt **15.** sleeping **16.** thrilling **17.** abandoned **18.** required **19.** Polluted **20.** furnished **21.** dividing **22.** elected **23.** printing **24.** Experienced **25.** amazing

EXERCISE 29, p. 237.

2. Two people got <u>hurt</u> in the accident and were <u>taken</u> to the hospital by an ambulance. **3.** The movie was so <u>boring</u> that we fell asleep after an hour. **4.** The students <u>were</u> helped by the clear explanation that the teacher gave. **5.** That alloy is <u>composed of</u> iron and tin. **6.** The winner of the race hasn't been <u>announced</u> yet. **7.** If you are <u>interested</u> in modern art, you should see the new exhibit at the museum. It is <u>fascinating.</u> **8.** Progress is <u>being</u> made every day. **9.** When and where <u>was</u> the automobile invented? **10.** My brother and I have always been <u>interested</u> in learning more about our family tree. **11.** I <u>don't</u> agree with you, and I don't think you'll ever ~~to~~ convince me. **12.** Each assembly kit is <u>accompanied</u> by detailed instructions. **13.** Arthur was <u>given</u> an award by the city for all of his efforts in crime prevention. **14.** It was late, and I was getting very <u>worried</u> about my mother. **15.** The problem was very <u>puzzling</u>. I couldn't figure it out. **16.** Many strange things ~~were~~ happened last night. **17.** How many <u>people</u> have you ~~been~~ invited to the party? OR How many <u>people</u> have ~~you~~ been invited to the party? **18.** When I returned home, everything <u>was quiet</u>. I <u>walked</u> to my room, <u>got undressed</u>, and <u>went</u> to bed. **19.** I didn't go to dinner with them because I had already ~~been~~ eaten.

20. In class yesterday, I was <u>confused</u>. I didn't understand the lesson.   21. I couldn't move. I was very <u>frightened</u>.   22. When we were children, we <u>were</u> very afraid of caterpillars. Whenever we saw one of these monsters, we <u>ran</u> / <u>would</u> run to our house before the caterpillars could attack us. I am still <u>scared</u> when I <u>see</u> a caterpillar close to me. 23. One day, while the old man was cutting down a big tree near the stream, his axe <u>fell</u> into the river. He sat down and <u>began</u> to cry because he <u>did</u> not have enough money to buy another axe.

Chapter 12: NOUN CLAUSES

EXERCISE 1, p. 240.

ANSWERS: [The noun clauses are <u>underlined</u>.]   **3.** Where did Tom go? **N**o one knows. **4.** No one knows <u>where Tom went</u>.   **5.** <u>Where Tom went</u> is a secret.   **6.** What does Anna want? **W**e need to know.   **7.** We need to know <u>what Anna wants</u>.   **8.** What does Alex need? **D**o you know?   **9.** Do you know <u>what Alex needs</u>?   **10.** <u>What Alex needs</u> is a new job.   **11.** We talked about <u>what Alex needs</u>.   **12.** What do you need? **D**id you talk to your parents about <u>what you need</u>?

EXERCISE 2, p. 241.

ANSWERS: **3.** where you live   **4.** What she said   **5.** when they are coming **6.** how much it costs   **7.** which one he wants   **8.** who is coming to the party **9.** who those people are   **10.** whose pen this is   **11.** Why they left the country **12.** What we are doing in class   **13.** Where she went   **14.** how many letters there are in the English alphabet   **15.** who the mayor of New York City is   **16.** how old a person has to be to get a driver's license   **17.** what happened   **18.** who opened the door

EXERCISE 3, p. 242.

I don't know . . . .
1. where (. . .) lives.   **2.** what country (. . .) is from.   **3.** how long (. . .) has been living here.   **4.** what (. . .)'s telephone number is.   **5.** where the post office is. **6.** how far it is to (Kansas City).   **7.** why (. . .) is absent.   **8.** where my book is. **9.** what kind of watch (. . .) has.   **10.** why (. . .) was absent yesterday. **11.** where (. . .) went yesterday.   **12.** what kind of government (Italy) has.   **13.** what (. . .)'s favorite color is.   **14.** how long (. . .) has been married.   **15.** why we are doing this exercise.   **16.** who turned off the lights.   **17.** where (. . .) is going to eat lunch/dinner. **18.** when (the semester) ends.   **19.** where (. . .) went after class yesterday.   **20.** why (. . .) is smiling.   **21.** how often (. . .) goes to the library.   **22.** whose book that is. **23.** how much that book cost.   **24.** who took my book.

EXERCISE 4, p. 242.

ANSWERS: **2.** Why is he coming? Please tell me why he is coming.   **3.** Which flight will he be on? Please tell me which flight he will be on.   **4.** Who is going to meet him at the airport? Please tell me who is going to meet him at the airport.   **5.** Who is Jim Hunter? Please tell me who Jim Hunter is.   **6.** What is Tom's address? Please tell me what Tom 's address is.   **7.** Where does he live? Please tell me where he lives.   **8.** Where was he last week? Please tell me where he was last week.   **9.** How long has he been working for IBM? Do you know how long he has been working for IBM?   **10.** What kind of computer does he have at home? Do you know what kind of computer he has at home?

EXERCISE 5, p. 243.

ANSWERS: **2.** is my eraser . . . it is   **3.** didn't Fred lock . . . he didn't lock   **4.** has he been . . . he has lived/has been living   **5.** you are taking . . . are you taking **6.** are we supposed . . . we are supposed

EXERCISE 7, p. 246.

I wonder . . . .
1. where my friend is. **2.** whether/if we should wait for him. **3.** whether/if I should call him. **4.** where my dictionary is. **5.** who took my dictionary. **6.** whether/if (. . .) borrowed my dictionary. **7.** who that woman is. **8.** whether/if she needs any help. **9.** why the sky is blue. **10.** how long a butterfly lives. **11.** what causes earthquakes. **12.** when the first book was written. **13.** who that man is. **14.** what he is doing. **15.** whether/if he is having trouble. **16.** whether/if I should offer to help him. **17.** how far it is to (Florida). **18.** whether/if we have enough time to go to (Florida) over vacation. **19.** whose book this is. **20.** whether/if it belongs to (. . .) / who(m) it belongs to. **21.** why dinosaurs became extinct. **22.** whether/if there is life on other planets. **23.** how life began. **24.** whether/if people will live on the moon someday.

EXERCISE 8, p. 246.

Could you please tell me . . . .
1. if this bus goes downtown? **2.** how much this book costs? **3.** when Flight 62 is expected to arrive? **4.** where the nearest phone is? **5.** whether/if this word is spelled correctly? **6.** what time it is? **7.** if this information is correct? **8.** how much it costs to fly from (Chicago) to (New York)? **9.** where the bus station is? **10.** whose pen this is?

EXERCISE 9, p. 247.

2. No one seems to know when <u>Maria will arrive</u>. **3.** I wonder why <u>Bob was late</u> for class. **4.** I don't know what ~~does~~ that word <u>means</u>. **5.** I wonder ~~does~~ <u>whether/if</u> the teacher <u>knows</u> the answer. **6.** What <u>they should</u> do about the hole in their roof is their most pressing problem. **7.** I'll ask her <u>whether/if she would like</u> some coffee or not. **8.** Be sure to tell the doctor where ~~does~~ it <u>hurts</u>. **9.** Why <u>I am</u> unhappy is something I can't explain. **10.** I wonder ~~does~~ <u>whether/if</u> Tom <u>knows</u> about the meeting or not. **11.** I need to know who <u>your teacher is</u>. **12.** I don't understand why <u>the car is not running</u> properly. **13.** My young son wants to know where ~~do~~ the stars go in the daytime.

EXERCISE 10, p. 247.

[The infinitives are <u>underlined</u>.] **2.** The plumber told me how <u>to fix</u> the leak in the sink. **3.** Please tell me where <u>to meet</u> you. **4.** . . . Sandy didn't know whether <u>to believe</u> him or not. **5.** . . . deciding which one <u>to buy</u>. **6.** . . . I don't know what else <u>to do</u>.

POSSIBLE COMPLETIONS: **7.** to say **8.** what to wear **9.** to live in a dormitory or an apartment **10.** to ski **11.** to give (. . .) **12.** to accept the job offer or (to) stay in graduate school **13.** to go . . . to get there

EXERCISE 11, p. 249.

POSSIBLE SENTENCES: **1.** It is a pity that Tim hasn't been able to make any friends. That Tim hasn't been able to make any friends is a pity. **2.** It is a well-known fact that drug abuse can ruin one's health. That drug abuse can ruin one's health is a well-known fact. **3.** It is unfair that some women do not earn equal pay for equal work. That some women do not earn equal pay for equal work is unfair. **4.** It is true that the earth revolves around the sun. That the earth revolves around the sun is true. **5.** It is surprising that Irene, who is an excellent student, failed her entrance examination. That Irene, who is an excellent student, failed her entrance examination is surprising. **6.** It is apparent that smoking can cause cancer. That smoking can cause cancer is apparent. **7.** It is a fact that English is the principal language of the business community throughout much of the world.   That English is the principal language of the business community throughout much of the world is a fact.

EXERCISE 12, p. 249.

SAMPLE RESPONSES: **1.** It is a fact that the world is round. That the world is round is a fact.   **2.** It is surprising that vegetation can survive in a desert. That vegetation can survive in a desert is surprising.   **3.** It is obvious that you need to wear warm clothing when it's cold. That you need to wear warm clothing when it's cold is obvious.   **4.** It is too bad that prejudice influences so many people. That prejudice influences so many people is too bad.   **5.** It is a well-known fact that women on the average live longer than men. That women on the average live longer than men is a well-known fact.   **6.** It is unfortunate that Ali had to miss class due to illness. That Ali had to miss class due to illness is unfortunate.   **7.** It is true that alcohol can cause birth defects. That alcohol can cause birth defects is true.   **8.** It is strange that we are destroying our own natural resources. That we are destroying our own natural resources is strange.   **9.** It is unlikely that you will live to be one hundred. That you will live to be one hundred is unlikely.   **10.** It is undeniable that the sun rises in the east. That the sun rises in the east is undeniable.

EXERCISE 13, p. 249.

SAMPLE COMPLETIONS: **2.** It seems to me that adequate health care is the right of every citizen.   **3.** It is my impression that time seems to go faster as I grow older.   **4.** It is my theory that excessively thin models encourage eating disorders in young women.   **5.** It is widely believed that herbs can heal.   **6.** It is thought that you can't teach an old dog new tricks.   **7.** It has been said that teenagers are more influenced by their peers than by their parents.   **8.** Given the number of cars on the road these days, it is a miracle that more people aren't killed in automobile accidents.

EXERCISE 14, p. 250.

SAMPLE COMPLETIONS: **2.** . . . we had this time together.   **3.** . . . I wasn't able to get a ticket to the soccer finals.   **4.** . . . you have been my teacher this year.   **5.** . . . Yoko quit school.   **6.** . . . you will like this restaurant as much as we do.   **7.** . . . the prices are so reasonable.   **8.** . . . it isn't raining today.   **9.** . . . my bus was late.   **10.** . . . I can't make it to your wedding.

EXERCISE 15, p. 250.

SAMPLE COMPLETIONS: **3.** One reason is that I want to study at an American university. Another reason is that I need to pass a written driver's test. A third reason is that I need to find a good part-time job.   **4.** One problem is that I'm homesick. Another problem is that I can't understand people when they speak fast. A third problem I have had is that I am having trouble finding an apartment for my family.   **5.** One advantage of owning your own car is that you don't need to rely on public transportation. Another advantage is that you can travel into the country on weekends. One disadvantage, however, of owning your own car is that it is expensive.

EXERCISE 16, p. 250.

ANSWERS: **2.** The fact that Rosa didn't come made me angry.   **3.** I feel fine except for the fact that I'm a little tired.   **4.** Natasha was not admitted to the university due to the fact that she didn't pass the entrance examination.   **5.** The fact that many people in the world live in intolerable poverty must concern all of us.   **6.** The fact that Surasuk is frequently absent from class indicates his lack of interest in school.   **7.** I was not aware

of the fact that I was supposed to bring my passport to the examination for identification.
8. Due to the fact that the people of the town were given no warning of the approaching tornado, there were many casualties.

EXERCISES 17 and 18, p. 252.

EX. 17:

1. Henry said, "There is a phone call for you."   **2.** "There is a phone call for you," he said.   **3.** "There is," said Henry, "a phone call for you."   **4.** "There is a phone call for you. It's your sister," said Henry.   **5.** "There is a phone call for you," he said. "It's your sister."   **6.** I asked him, "Where is the phone?"   **7.** "Where is the phone?" she asked.   **8.** "Stop the clock!" shouted the referee. "We have an injured player." **9.** "Who won the game?" asked the spectator.   **10.** "I'm going to rest for the next three hours," she said. "I don't want to be disturbed." "That's fine," I replied. "You get some rest. I'll make sure no one disturbs you."

EX. 18:

When the police officer came over to my car, he said, "Let me see your driver's license, please."

"What's wrong, Officer?" I asked. "Was I speeding?"

"No, you weren't speeding," he replied. "You went through a red light at the corner of Fifth Avenue and Main Street. You almost caused an accident."

"Did I really do that?" I said. "I didn't see a red light."

EXERCISE 21, p. 254.

ANSWERS: **4.** if I was hungry.   **5.** (that) she wanted a sandwich.   **6.** (that) he was going to move to Ohio.   **7.** whether/if I had enjoyed my trip.   **8.** what I was talking about.   **9.** whether/if I had seen her grammar book.   **10.** (that) she didn't want to go.   **11.** where Nadia was.   **12.** whether/if I could help him with his report. **13.** (that) he might be late.   **14.** (that) I should work harder. [also possible: *to work harder*]   **15.** (that) she had to go downtown.   **16.** why the sky is blue.   **17.** why I was tired.   **18.** (that) he would come to the meeting.   **19.** whether/if Ms. Chang would be in class tomorrow / would be in class the next day.   **20.** that the sun rises in the east.   **21.** (that) someday we would be in contact with beings from outer space. **22.** (that) he thought (that) he would go to the library to study.   **23.** whether/if Omar knew what he was doing.   **24.** whether/if what I had heard was true.   **25.** (that) sentences with noun clauses are a little complicated.

EXERCISE 24, p. 257.

3. was going . . . didn't know . . . worked   **4.** where the chess match would take . . . hadn't been decided   **5.** was . . . didn't think . . . would . . . speak . . . was getting . . . would be speaking   **6.** were . . . might be . . . could develop

EXERCISE 25, p. 258.

ANSWERS: **2.** she was excited about her new job and (that she) had found a nice apartment.   **3.** my Uncle Harry was in the hospital and that Aunt Sally was very worried about him.   **4.** that s/he expected us to be in class every day and that unexcused absences might affect our grades.   **5.** that Highway 66 would be closed for two months and that commuters should seek alternative routes.   **6.** that he was getting good grades but (that he) had difficulty understanding lectures.   **7.** that every obstacle was a steppingstone to success and that I should view problems in my life as opportunities to prove myself.   **8.** that she would come to the meeting but (that she) couldn't stay for more than an hour.

EXERCISE 28, p. 259.

POSSIBLE ANSWERS: **1.** Alex asked me what I was doing. I replied that I was drawing a picture. **2.** Ann asked Sue if she wanted to go to a movie Sunday night. Sue said that she would like to but that she had to study. **3.** The little boy asked Mrs. Robinson how old she was. She told him that it was not polite to ask people their age. **4.** My sister asked me if there was anything I especially wanted to watch on TV. I replied that there was a show at 8:00 that I had been waiting to see for a long time. She asked me what it was. When I told her that it was a documentary about green sea turtles, she wondered why I wanted to see that. I explained that I was doing a research paper on sea turtles and thought I might be able to get some good information from the documentary. I suggested that she watch it with me. She declined and said she wasn't especially interested in green sea turtles.

EXERCISE 30, p. 261.

1. Tell the taxi driver where ~~do~~ you want to go. **2.** My roommate came into the room and asked me why <u>I wasn't</u> in class. I <u>told him / said (that) I was</u> waiting for a telephone call from my family. OR My roommate came into the room and asked ~~me~~, "Why aren't you in class?" I said, "I am waiting for a telephone call from my family." **3.** It was my first day at the university, and I <u>was</u> on my way to my first class. I wondered who else <u>would</u> be in the class and what <u>the teacher would be like</u>. **4.** He asked me what ~~did~~ I <u>intended</u> to do after I <u>graduated</u>. **5.** Many of the people in the United States do not know much about geography. For example, people will ask you where <u>Japan is located</u>. **6.** What ~~does~~ a patient <u>tells</u> a doctor ~~it~~ is confidential. **7.** What my friend and I did ~~it~~ was our secret. We didn't even tell our parents <u>what we did</u>. **8.** The doctor asked <u>whether/if</u> I felt okay. I told him that I <u>didn't</u> feel well. **9.** <u>It is</u> clear that the ability to use a computer ~~it~~ is an important skill in the modern world. **10.** I asked him, "What kind of movies <u>do you like</u>?" He said ~~me~~, "I like romantic movies." OR I asked him what kind of movies <u>he liked</u>. He <u>told</u> me / said <u>(that) he liked</u> romantic movies. **11.** "<u>Is it</u> true you almost drowned?" my friend asked me. "Yes," I said. "I'm really glad to be alive. It was really frightening." **12.** <u>The fact that</u> I almost drowned makes me very careful about water safety whenever I go swimming. **13.** I didn't know where I <u>was</u> supposed to get off the bus, so I asked the driver where <u>the science museum was</u>. She <u>told</u> me the name of the street. She said she <u>would</u> tell me when <u>I should</u> get off the bus. **14.** My mother did not live with us. When other children asked me where ~~was~~ <u>my mother was</u>, I told them she <u>was</u> going to come to visit me very soon. **15.** When I asked the taxi driver to drive faster, he said, "I will drive faster if you pay me more." OR he said he would drive faster if I paid him more. At that time I didn't care how much <u>it would</u> cost, so I told him to go as fast as he <u>could</u>. **16.** We looked back to see where <u>we were</u> and how far <u>we were</u> from camp. We <u>didn't</u> know, so we decided to turn back. We <u>were</u> afraid that we <u>had wandered</u> too far. **17.** After the accident, I opened my eyes slowly and <u>realized</u> that I <u>was</u> still alive. **18.** My country is prospering due to ~~it is a~~ <u>the fact</u> that it has become a leading producer of oil. **19.** <u>It is</u> true that one must know <u>English</u> in order to study at an <u>American</u> university. **20.** My mother told me ~~what it was~~ the purpose of our visit. OR what ~~it~~ <u>the purpose of our visit was</u>.

EXERCISES 35 and 36, p. 264.

EX. 35 POSSIBLE ANSWERS: **2.** call **3.** tell **4.** speak **5.** write/send **6.** see **7.** contact **8.** be

EX. 36 ANSWERS: **1.** take **2.** be named **3.** stay **4.** be postponed **5.** be admitted **6.** be controlled . . . (be) eliminated **7.** have **8.** be **9.** know

10. be   **11.** be permitted   **12.** not be   **13.** return   **14.** be built   **15.** not tell . . . be told

EXERCISE 37, p. 265.

ANSWERS: **2.** whenever   **3.** whatever   **4.** whichever   **5.** whatever
6. Whoever   **7.** whatever   **8.** however   **9.** whoever   **10.** wherever
11. whomever/whoever . . . whomever/whoever   **12.** whatever
13. whichever   **14.** wherever   **15.** whatever . . . wherever . . . whenever . . .
whomever/whoever . . . however

Chapter 13: ADJECTIVE CLAUSES

EXERCISE 1, p. 268.

ANSWERS: **2.** The girl who/that won the race is happy.   **3.** The student who/that sits next to me is from China.   **4.** The students who/that sit in the front row are from China.   **5.** We are studying sentences which/that contain adjective clauses.   **6.** I am using a sentence which/that contains an adjective clause.   **7.** Algebra problems contain letters which/that stand for unknown numbers.   **8.** The taxi driver who/that took me to the airport was friendly.

EXERCISE 2, p. 269.

ANSWERS: **1.** The book which/that/Ø I read was good.   **2.** I liked the woman who(m)/that/Ø I met at the party last night.   **3.** I liked the composition which/that/Ø you wrote.   **4.** The people who(m)/that/Ø we visited yesterday were very nice.   **5.** The man who(m)/that/Ø I was telling you about is standing over there.   OR   . . . about whom I was telling you is standing over there.

EXERCISE 3, p. 269.

ANSWERS: **1.** The meeting which/that/Ø I went to was interesting.   OR   The meeting to which I went was interesting.   **2.** The man to whom I talked yesterday was very kind.   OR   The man who(m)/that/Ø I talked to yesterday was very kind.   **3.** I must thank the people from whom I got a present.   OR   I must thank the people who(m)/that/Ø I got a present from.   **4.** The picture which/that/Ø she was looking at was beautiful.   OR   The picture at which she was looking was beautiful.   **5.** The man about whom I was telling you is over there.   OR   The man who(m)/that/Ø I was telling you about is over there.
6. I ran into a woman with whom I had gone to elementary school.   OR   I ran into a woman who(m)/that/Ø I had gone to elementary school with.   **7.** The topic about which Omar talked was interesting.   OR   The topic which/that/Ø Omar talked about was interesting.   **8.** The people to whom I spoke were friendly.   OR   The people who(m)/that/Ø I spoke to were friendly.   **9.** Olga wrote on a topic about which she knew nothing.   OR   Olga wrote on a topic which/that/Ø she knew nothing about.   **10.** The candidate for whom I voted didn't win the election.   OR   The candidate who(m)/that/Ø I voted for didn't win the election.

EXERCISE 4, p. 270.

ANSWERS: **1.** I met last night—Did I tell you about the woman who(m)/that I met last night?   **2.** I was dancing with—The woman who(m)/that/Ø I was dancing with stepped on my toe.   OR   The woman with whom I was dancing stepped on my toe.   **3.** Joe is writing—The report which/that/Ø Joe is writing must be finished by Friday.   **4.** who examined the sick child—The doctor who/that examined the sick child was gentle.
5. I was waiting for—The people who(m)/that/Ø I was waiting for were late.   OR   The

people <u>for whom I was waiting</u> were late. **6.** <u>that occurred in California</u>—Did you hear about the earthquake <u>which occurred in California</u>?

EXERCISE 5, p. 270.

ANSWERS: **1.** She lectured on a topic <u>which/that/Ø I know very little about</u>. OR She lectured on a topic <u>about which I know very little</u>. [usual: *topic I know very little about*]
2. The students <u>who/that were absent from class</u> missed the assignment. [usual: *students who were absent from class*] **3.** Yesterday I ran into an old friend <u>who(m)/that/Ø I hadn't seen for years</u>. [usual: *friend I hadn't seen for years*] **4.** The young women <u>who(m)/that/Ø we met at the meeting last night</u> are all from Japan. [usual: *women we met at the meeting last night*]
5. I am reading a book <u>which/that was written by Jane Austen</u>. [usual: *book that was written by Jane Austen*] **6.** The man <u>who(m)/that/Ø I spoke to</u> gave me good advice. OR The man <u>to whom I spoke</u> gave me good advice. [usual: *man I spoke to*] **7.** I returned the money <u>which/that/Ø I had borrowed from my roommate</u>. [usual: *money I had borrowed from my roommate*] **8.** The dogcatcher caught the dog <u>which/that had bitten my neighbor's daughter</u>. [usual: *dog that had bitten my neighbor's daughter*] **9.** I read about a man <u>who/that keeps chickens in his apartment</u>. [usual: *man who keeps chickens in his apartment*]

EXERCISE 6, p. 271.

ANSWERS: **1.** In our village, there were many people <u>who</u> didn't have much money. OR In our village, many people didn't have much money. **2.** I enjoyed the book (that) you told me to read ~~it~~. **3.** I still remember the man who ~~he~~ taught me to play the violin when I was a boy. **4.** I showed my father a picture of the car I am going to buy ~~it~~ as soon as I save enough money. **5.** The woman ~~about~~ <u>whom</u> I was talking about suddenly walked into the room. OR The woman about <u>who(m)/that/Ø</u> I was talking ~~about~~ suddenly walked into the room. I hope she didn't hear me. **6.** Almost all of the people <u>who/that</u> appear on television wear makeup. **7.** I don't like to spend time with people <u>who/that lose</u> their temper easily. **8.** The boy drew pictures of people at an airport <u>who/that were</u> waiting for their planes. OR The boy drew pictures of people <u>who/that were</u> waiting for their planes at an airport. **9.** People who <u>work</u> in the hunger program ~~they~~ estimate that 3500 people in the world die from starvation every day of the year. **10.** In one corner of the marketplace, an old man ~~who~~ was playing a violin. OR In one corner of the marketplace, <u>there was</u> an old man who was playing a violin.

EXERCISE 8, p. 273.

POSSIBLE ANSWERS: **1.** Yes, the chair I am sitting in is comfortable. **2.** Yes, the man I saw was wearing a brown suit. **3.** Yes, the woman I talked to answered my questions.
4. Yes, the woman who stepped on my toe apologized. **5.** Yes, most of the students who took the test passed. **6.** Yes, the meat I had for dinner last night was good.
7. Yes, the woman who shouted at me was angry. **8.** Yes, I know the person who is sitting next to me. [Also possible: *the person sitting next to me*. **9.** Yes, I recognize the woman who came into the room. **10.** Yes, the coat I bought keeps me warm.
11. Yes, the TV program I watched last night was good. **12.** Yes, I finished the book I was reading. **13.** Yes, the hotel I stayed at was in the middle of the city. OR Yes, the hotel where I stayed was in the middle of the city. **14.** Yes, the exercise we are doing is easy. **15.** Yes, the waiter who served me at the restaurant was polite.
16. Yes, the student who stopped me in the hall asked me for the correct time. **17.** Yes, all the students who are sitting in this room can speak English. **18.** Yes, I found the book I was looking for. **19.** Yes, the boots/tennis shoes/loafers I am wearing are comfortable. **20.** Yes, I had a conversation with the taxi driver who took me to the bus station. **21.** Yes, I thanked the man who opened the door for me. **22.** Yes, the clerk who cashed my check asked for identification. **23.** Yes, the package I got in the mail was

from my parents.   **24.** Yes, the man who stopped me on the street asked me for directions.

EXERCISE 10, p. 275.

[The adjective clauses are <u>underlined</u>.]   **2.** I apologized to the woman <u>whose coffee I spilled</u>.   **3.** The man <u>whose wallet was stolen</u> called the police.   **4.** I met the woman <u>whose husband is the president of the corporation</u>.   **5.** The professor <u>whose course I am taking</u> is excellent.   **6.** Mr. North teaches a class for students <u>whose native language is not English</u>.   **7.** The people <u>whose house we visited</u> were nice.   **8.** I live in a dormitory <u>whose residents come from many countries</u>.   **9.** I have to call the man <u>whose umbrella I accidentally picked up after the meeting</u>.   **10.** The man <u>whose beard caught on fire</u> when he lit a cigarette poured a glass of water on his face. [Note: *when he lit a cigarette* is an adverb clause connected to an adjective clause.]

EXERCISE 11, p. 275.

ANSWERS: **1.** Maria is **a** student. I found her book. Maria is **the** student <u>whose book I found</u>.   **2.** Omar is **a** student. I borrowed his dictionary. Omar is **the** student <u>whose dictionary I borrowed</u>.   **3.** I used **a** woman's phone. I thanked her. I thanked **the** woman <u>whose phone I used</u>.   **4.** I broke **a** child's toy. He started to cry. **The** child <u>whose toy I broke</u> started to cry.   **5.** I stayed at **a** family's house. They were very kind. **The** family <u>at whose house I stayed</u> were very kind.   OR   **The** family <u>whose house I stayed at</u> were very kind.   **6.** **A** woman's purse was stolen. She called the police. **The** woman <u>whose purse was stolen</u> called the police.   **7.** (Placido Domingo) is **a** singer. I like his music best. (Placido Domingo) is **the** singer <u>whose music I like best</u>.   **8.** Everyone tried to help **a** family. Their house had burned down. Everyone tried to help **the** family <u>whose house had burned down</u>.

EXERCISE 12, p. 276.

ANSWERS: **3.** There is the boy <u>whose father is a doctor</u>.   **4.** There is the girl <u>whose mother is a dentist</u>.   **5.** There is the person <u>whose picture was in the newspaper</u>.   **6.** There is the woman <u>whose car was stolen</u>.   **7.** There is the man <u>whose daughter won a gold medal at the Olympic Games</u>.   **8.** There is the woman <u>whose keys I found</u>.   **9.** There is the teacher <u>whose class I'm in</u>.   **10.** There is the man <u>whose wife we met</u>.   **11.** There is the author <u>whose book I read</u>.   **12.** There is the student <u>whose lecture notes I borrowed</u>.

EXERCISE 13, p. 276.

ANSWERS: **3.** The students <u>whose names were called</u> raised their hands.   **4.** Jack knows a man <u>whose name is William Blueheart Duckbill, Jr.</u>   **5.** The police came to question the woman <u>whose purse was stolen outside the supermarket</u>.   **6.** The day care center was established to take care of children <u>whose parents work during the day</u>. [*day care center* = a place where very young children are cared for while their parents are at work]   **7.** We couldn't find the person <u>whose car was blocking the driveway</u>.   **8.** The professor told the three students <u>whose reports were turned in late</u> that he would accept the papers this time but never again.

EXERCISE 14, p. 277.

ANSWERS: **1.** The city <u>where we spent our vacation</u> was beautiful.   OR   The city <u>which/that/Ø we took our vacation in</u> was beautiful.   OR   The city <u>in which we spent our vacation</u> was beautiful.   **2.** That is the restaurant <u>where I will meet you</u>.   OR   That is the restaurant <u>which/that/Ø I will meet you at</u>.   OR   That is the restaurant <u>at which I will meet you</u>.   **3.** The town <u>where I grew up</u> is small.   OR   The town <u>which/that/Ø I grew</u>

up in is small.   OR   The town in which I grew up is small.   **4.** That is the drawer where I keep my jewelry.   OR   That is the drawer which/that/Ø I keep my jewelry in.   OR   That is the drawer in which I keep my jewelry.

EXERCISE 15, p. 277.

ANSWERS: **1.** Monday is the day when we will come.   OR   The day that/Ø we will come is Monday.   OR   The day on which we will come is Monday.   **2.** 7:05 is the time when my plane arrives.   OR   7:05 is the time that/Ø my plane arrives.   OR   7:05 is the time at which my plane arrives.   **3.** July is the month when the weather is usually the hottest.   OR   July is the month that/Ø the weather is usually the hottest.   OR   July is the month in which the weather is usually the hottest.   **4.** 1960 is the year when the revolution took place.   OR   1960 is the year that/Ø the revolution took place.   OR   1960 is the year in which the revolution took place.

EXERCISE 16, p. 278.

ANSWERS: **3.** A cafe is a small restaurant where people can get a light meal.   **4.** Every neighborhood in Brussels has small cafes where customers drink coffee and eat pastries.   **5.** There was a time when dinosaurs dominated the earth.   **6.** The house where I was born and grew up was destroyed in an earthquake ten years ago.   **7.** Summer is the time of year when the weather is the hottest.   **8.** The miser hid his money in a place where it was safe from robbers.   **9.** There came a time when the miser had to spend his money.   **10.** His new shirt didn't fit, so Dan took it back to the store where he'd bought it.

EXERCISE 19, p. 280.

POSSIBLE COMPLETIONS: **2.** I need to ask you.   **3.** he can trust.   **4.** I can do.   **5.** who can help you.   **6.** she meets.   **7.** she said.   **8.** the teacher says.   **9.** he says is true.   **10.** who is standing.   **11.** we took last week.   **12.** I took last term.   **13.** who came late   **14.** whose names began with letters in the first half of the alphabet . . . whose names started with letters in the last half of the alphabet . . .

EXERCISE 21, p. 282.

    3. *No commas—"who" can be changed to "that."*
    4. Matthew, who speaks Russian, applied for the job.—*"who" cannot be changed to "that."*
    5. *No commas—"which" can be changed to "that."*
    6. Rice, which is grown in many countries, is a staple food throughout much of the world.—*"which" cannot be changed to "that."*
    7. *No commas—"who" can be changed to "that."*
    8. Paul O'Grady, who died two years ago, was a kind and loving man.—*"who" cannot be changed to "that."*
    9. I have fond memories of my hometown, which is situated in a valley.—*"which" cannot be changed to "that."*
  10. *No commas—"which" can be changed to "that."*
  11. The Mississippi River, which flows south from Minnesota to the Gulf of Mexico, is the major commercial river in the United States.—*"which" cannot be changed to "that."*
  12. *No commas—"which" can be changed to "that."*
  13. Mr. Brown, whose son won the spelling contest, is very proud of his son's achievement.—*"whose" cannot be changed to "that."* [Second sentence = no commas.]
  14. Goats, which were first tamed more than 9,000 years ago in Asia, have provided people with milk, meat, and wool since prehistoric times.—*"which" cannot be changed to "that."*
  15. *No commas—"which" can be changed to "that."*

EXERCISE 22, p. 283.

ANSWERS: **3.** a. **4.** b. **5.** a. **6.** b. **7.** Only some apples were rotten. **8.** All the apples were rotten. **9.** Only some students were excused. **10.** All the students were excused. **11.** Cindy got one present. **12.** Cindy got several presents. **13.** There were other maps in the room, hanging on other walls. **14.** They were the only maps in the room.

EXERCISE 23, p. 283.

ANSWERS: **1.** *(no change)* **2.** We enjoyed Mexico City, where we spent our vacation. **3.** An elephant, which is the earth's largest land mammal, has few natural enemies other than human beings. **4.** *(no change)* **5.** At the botanical gardens, you can see a Venus's-flytrap, which is an insectivorous plant. **6.** *(no change)* **7.** One of the most useful materials in the world is glass, which is made chiefly from sand, soda, and lime. **8.** Glaciers, which are masses of ice that flow slowly over land, form in the cold polar regions and in high mountains. **9.** *(no change)* **10.** Petroleum, which some people refer to as black gold, is one of the most valuable resources in the world today. **11.** You don't have to take heavy clothes when you go to Bangkok, which has one of the highest average temperatures of any city in the world. **12.** *(no change)* **13.** Child labor was a social problem in late eighteenth-century England, where employment in factories became virtual slavery for children. **14.** *(no change)* **15.** The man, who was wearing a plaid shirt and blue jeans, was caught shortly after he had left the bank. **16.** The research scientist, who was well protected before she stepped into the special chamber holding the bees, was not stung.

EXERCISE 24, p. 285.

ANSWERS: **2.** Last night the orchestra played three symphonies, <u>one of which was Beethoven's Seventh</u>. **3.** I tried on six pairs of shoes, <u>none of which I liked</u>. **4.** The village has around 200 people, <u>the majority of whom are farmers</u>. **5.** That company currently has five employees, <u>all of whom are computer experts</u>. **6.** After the riot, over one hundred people were taken to the hospital, <u>many of whom had been innocent bystanders</u>.

EXERCISE 25, p. 285.

POSSIBLE COMPLETIONS: **2.** which is a Porsche. **3.** whom are in school at present. **4.** which is Conversational English. **5.** whom speaks my native language. **6.** which were expensive hardbacks. **7.** whom were newly graduated PhDs. **8.** which have three or more bedrooms.

EXERCISE 26, p. 286.

ANSWERS: **2.** They own an original Picasso painting, <u>the value of which is more than a million dollars</u>. **3.** I bought a magazine, <u>the title of which is *Contemporary Architectural Styles*</u>. **4.** My country is dependent upon its income from coffee, <u>the price of which varies according to fluctuations in the world market</u>. **5.** The genetic engineers are engaged in significant experiments, <u>the results of which will be published in the *Journal of Science*</u>. **6.** The professor has assigned the students a research paper, <u>the purpose of which is to acquaint them with methods of scholarly inquiry</u>.

EXERCISE 27, p. 286.

ANSWERS: **2.** My roommate never picks up after herself, <u>which irritates me</u>. **3.** Mrs. Anderson responded to my letter right away, <u>which I appreciated very much</u>. **4.** There's been an accident on Highway 5, <u>which means I'll be late to work this morning</u>. **5.** I shut the door on my necktie, <u>which was really stupid of me</u>. **6.** Sally lost her job,

which wasn't surprising.   **7.** She usually came to work late, <u>which upset her boss</u>.
8. So her boss fired her, <u>which made her angry</u>.   **9.** She hadn't saved any money, <u>which was unfortunate</u>.   **10.** So she had to borrow some money from me, <u>which I didn't like</u>.   **11.** She has found a new job, <u>which is lucky</u>.   **12.** So she has repaid the money she borrowed from me, <u>which I appreciate</u>.   **13.** She has promised herself to be on time to work every day, <u>which is a good idea</u>.

EXERCISE 28, p. 287.

SAMPLE SENTENCES: **2.** I didn't do well on the last test, which disappointed me.
3. The taxi driver was speeding, which made me nervous.   **4.** Sandra lied to her surpervisor, which shocked all of us.   **5.** David called from the police station, which means he's probably in trouble.   **6.** My best friend took me to dinner for my birthday, which was a pleasant surprise.   **7.** David didn't keep his date with Maria, which made her very unhappy.   **8.** A friend visited my ailing mother in her nursing home, which I appreciated very much.   **9.** The workmen outside my window were making a lot of noise, which made it difficult for me to concentrate.   **10.** My best friend said something unkind to me, which bothered me so much that I couldn't get to sleep.

EXERCISE 29, p. 288.

SAMPLE COMPLETIONS: [Words already provided in the text are in *italics*.]   **1.** My best friend has four *brothers, all of whom* are older than she is.   **2.** She mailed the package *early, which was fortunate* because she had written down the wrong due date.   **3.** I carpool to school with four *students, three of whom* live in my apartment building.   [*carpool* (noun or verb) = drive or ride together to save fuel]   **4.** The art director asked his staff for *ideas, none of which* he liked.   **5.** The women at the gala were wearing a lot of *jewelry, the value of which* was astronomical.   **6.** This school has many fine *teachers, some of whom* have taught here for more than 20 years.   **7.** I thought of home and my *mother, which made me* homesick.   **8.** The teenager delivered newspapers to earn *a little money, all of which* he spent on a new bicycle.   **9.** I have three *sisters, each of whom* is a college graduate.   **10.** We've just bought a *new car, the inside of which* smells like leather.
11. Anna bought a lot of new *clothes, some of which* she'll probably never wear.   **12.** My long-lost aunt arrived on our doorstep *two days ago, which surprised* everyone in the family.

EXERCISE 30, p. 288.

2. The blue whale, <u>which can grow to 100 feet and 150 tons,</u> is considered the largest animal that has ever lived.   **3.** The plane was met by a crowd of three hundred people, <u>some of whom had been waiting for more than four hours</u>.   **4.** In this paper, I will describe the basic process <u>by which raw cotton becomes cotton thread</u>.   **5.** The researchers are doing case studies of people <u>whose families have a history of high blood pressure and heart disease</u> to determine the importance of heredity in health and longevity.
6. At the end of this month, scientists at the institute will conclude their AIDS research, <u>the results of which will be published within six months</u>.   **7.** According to many education officials, "math phobia" (that is, fear of mathematics) is a widespread problem <u>to which a solution must and can be found</u>.   **8.** The art museum hopes to hire a new administrator <u>under whose direction it will be able to purchase significant pieces of art</u>.
9. The giant anteater, <u>whose tongue is longer than 30 centimeters (12 inches),</u> licks up ants for its dinner.   **10.** The anteater's tongue, <u>which can go in and out of its mouth 160 times a minute,</u> is sticky.

EXERCISE 33, p. 291.

[The adjective clauses are <u>underlined</u>.]   **2.** The people ~~who are~~ <u>waiting for the bus in the rain</u> are getting wet.   **3.** I come from a city ~~that is~~ <u>located in the southern part of the</u>

country.   **4.** The children ~~who~~ <u>attend**ing** that school</u> receive a good education.
5. The scientists ~~who are~~ <u>researching the causes of cancer</u> are making progress.   **6.** The fence ~~which~~ <u>surround**ing** our house</u> is made of wood.   **7.** They live in a house ~~that was~~ <u>built in 1890</u>.   **8.** We have an apartment ~~which~~ <u>overlook**ing** the park</u>.

EXERCISE 34, p. 291

2. Be sure to follow the instructions ~~that are~~ given at the top of the page.   **3.** The rules ~~that~~ <u>allowing</u> public access to wilderness areas need to be reconsidered.   **4.** The photographs ~~which were~~ published in the newspaper were extraordinary.   **5.** There is almost no end to the problems ~~that~~ <u>facing</u> a head of state.   **6.** The psychologists ~~who~~ <u>studying</u> the nature of sleep have made important discoveries.   **7.** The experiment ~~which was~~ conducted at the University of Chicago was successful.   **8.** Kuala Lumpur, ~~which is~~ the capital city of Malaysia, is a major trade center in Southeast Asia.   **9.** Antarctica is covered by a huge ice cap ~~that~~ <u>containing</u> 70 percent of the earth's fresh water.
10. When I went to Alex's house to drop off some paperwork, I met Jerry, ~~who is~~ his longtime partner.   **11.** Our solar system is in a galaxy ~~that is~~ called the Milky Way.
12. Two out of three people ~~who are~~ struck by lightning survive.   **13.** Simon Bolivar, ~~who was~~ a great South American general, led the fight for independence early in the 19th century.   **14.** Many of the students ~~who~~ <u>hoping</u> to enter the university will be disappointed because only one-tenth of those ~~who~~ <u>applying</u> for admission will be accepted.
15. There must exist in a modern community a sufficient number of persons ~~who~~ <u>possessing</u> the technical skill ~~that is~~ required to maintain the numerous devices upon which our physical comforts depend.   **16.** Many famous people did not enjoy immediate success in their early lives. Abraham Lincoln, ~~who was~~ one of the truly great presidents of the United States, ran for public office 26 times and lost 23 of the elections. Walt Disney, ~~who was~~ the creator of Mickey Mouse and the founder of his own movie production company, once was fired by a newspaper editor because he had no good ideas. Thomas Edison, ~~who was~~ the inventor of the light bulb and the phonograph, was believed by his teachers to be too stupid to learn. Albert Einstein, ~~who was~~ one of the greatest scientists of all time, performed badly in almost all of his high school courses and failed his first college entrance exam.

EXERCISE 35, p. 292.

[The adjective clauses are <u>underlined</u>.]   **2.** Corn was one of the agricultural products <u>which/that were introduced to the European settlers by the Indians</u>. Some of the other products <u>which/that were introduced by the Indians</u> were potatoes, peanuts, and tobacco.   **3.** He read *The Old Man and the Sea*, <u>which is a novel</u> <u>which/that was written by Ernest Hemingway</u>.   **4.** Mercury, <u>which is the nearest planet to the sun</u>, is also the smallest of the nine planets <u>which/that orbit the sun</u>.   **5.** The pyramids, <u>which are the monumental tombs of ancient Egyptian pharaohs</u>, were constructed more than 4,000 years ago.   **6.** The sloth, <u>which is a slow-moving animal</u> <u>which/that is found in the tropical forests of Central and South America</u>, feeds entirely on leaves and fruit.   **7.** Two-thirds of those <u>who are arrested for car theft</u> are under twenty years of age.   **8.** St. Louis, Missouri, <u>which is known as "The Gateway to the West,"</u> traces its history to 1763, when Pierre Laclède, <u>who was a French fur trader</u>, selected this site on the Mississippi River as a fur-trading post.   **9.** Any student <u>who does not want to go on the trip</u> should inform the office.   **10.** I just purchased a volume of poems <u>that/which were written by David Keller</u>, <u>who is a contemporary poet</u> <u>who is known for his sensitive interpretations of human relationships</u>.

EXERCISE 36, p. 292.

ANSWERS: **2.** Baghdad, the capital of Iraq.   **3.** seismographs, sensitive instruments that measure the shaking of the ground.   **4.** The Dead Sea, the lowest place on the earth's surface, ...   **5.** Buenos Aires, the capital of Argentina.   **6.** lasers, devices that produce a powerful beam of light.   **7.** Mexico, the northernmost country in Latin America, ...   **8.** Nigeria, the most populous country in Africa, ...   **9.** Both Mexico City, the largest city in the Western Hemisphere, and New York City, the largest city in the United States . . . .   **10.** The mole, a small animal that spends its entire life underground, . . . The aardvark, an African animal that eats ants and termites, ...

EXERCISE 37, p. 293.

2. Disney World, an amusement park located in Orlando, Florida, covers a large area of land that includes / land including lakes, golf courses, campsites, hotels, and a wildlife preserve.
3. Jamaica, the third largest island in the Caribbean Sea, is one of the world's leading producers of bauxite, an ore from which aluminum is made.
4. Robert Ballard, an oceanographer, [also possible: *Oceanographer Robert Ballard*] made headlines in 1985 when he discovered the remains of the *Titanic,* the "unsinkable" passenger ship that has rested on the floor of the Atlantic Ocean since 1912, when it struck an iceberg.
5. William Shakespeare's father, John Shakespeare, was a glove maker and town official who owned a shop in Stratford-upon-Avon, a town about 75 miles (120 kilometers) northwest of London.
6. The Republic of Yemen, located at the southwest tip of the Arabian Peninsula, is an ancient land that has been host to many prosperous civilizations, including the Kingdom of Sheba and various Islamic empires.

EXERCISE 38, p. 294.

1. One of the people who(m) I admire most/most admire is my uncle.   **2.** Baseball is the only sport in (which) I am interested in it.   OR   sport in which I am interested.
3. My favorite teacher, Mr. Chu, he was always willing to help me after class.
4. It is important to be polite to people who live in the same building.   **5.** She lives in a hotel which/that is restricted to senior citizens.   OR   hotel is restricted to . . .
6. My sister has two children, whose their names are Ali and Talal.   OR   My sister has two children. Their names are Ali and Talal.   **7.** He comes from Venezuela, (which is) a Spanish-speaking country.   **8.** There are some people in the government (who are) trying to improve the lives of poor people.   **9.** I have some good advice for anyone who he wants/anyone wanting to learn a second language.   **10.** My classroom is located on the second floor of Carver Hall, (which is) a large brick building in the center of the campus.   **11.** A myth is a story which/that expresses traditional beliefs.   OR   A myth is a story expressing traditional beliefs.   **12.** There is an old legend (which is) told among people in my country about a man living (OR man who lived) in the seventeenth century who saved a village from destruction.   **13.** An old man was fishing next to me on the pier was muttering to himself.   OR   An old man who was fishing next to me . . . .
14. When I was a child, I was always afraid of the beggars who they went from house to house in my neighborhood.   **15.** At the national park, there is a path which/that leads to a spectacular waterfall.   OR   At the national park there is a path leading to a spectacular waterfall.   **16.** The road (that) we took it through the forest it was narrow and steep.   **17.** There are ten universities in Thailand, seven of them which are located in Bangkok, (which is) the capital city.   **18.** I would like to write about several problems (which) I have faced them since I came/ since coming) to the United

States.   **19.** There is a small wooden screen <u>which/that</u> separates the bed from the rest of the room.   OR   There is a small wooden screen <u>separating</u> the bed . . . .   **20.** At the airport, I was waiting for some relatives <u>who(m)/that/Ø</u> I had never met ~~them~~ before.   OR   At the airport, I was waiting for some relatives. ~~which~~ I had never met them before.
21. It is almost impossible to find two persons <u>whose</u> ~~their~~ opinions are the same.
22. On the wall, there is a colorful poster which ~~it~~ consists of a group of young people (who <u>are</u>) dancing.   OR   On the wall, there is a colorful poster ~~which it~~ <u>consisting</u> of . . . .
23. The sixth member of our household is Alex, ~~that~~ (<u>who</u> is) my sister's son.   OR   The sixth member of our household is Alex, ~~that is~~ my sister's son.   **24.** Before I came here, I didn't have the opportunity to speak with people <u>whose native tongue is English</u>.   OR   people <u>for whom</u> English is their native tongue.

Chapter 14: GERUNDS AND INFINITIVES, PART 1

EXERCISE 1, p. 298.

ANSWERS: **2.** about leaving   **3.** of doing   **4.** for being   **5.** to having   **6.** from completing   **7.** about/of having   **8.** of studying   **9.** for helping   **10.** on knowing   **11.** in being   **12.** of living   **13.** for not going   **14.** in searching   **15.** for making   **16.** for not wanting   **17.** for washing . . . drying   **18.** to going   **19.** from running   **20.** to going   **21.** of clarifying   **22.** of stealing   **23.** of taking . . . (of) keeping   **24.** to wearing   **25.** to eating . . . (to) sleeping

EXERCISE 2, p. 300.

SAMPLE COMPLETIONS: **2.** for lending me his fishing rod.   **3.** about going to the opera tonight.   **4.** to living in an apartment.   **5.** about having a headache.   **6.** for not wanting to go to the dentist.   **7.** for being late to class.   **8.** about missing the bus.
9. in finding out about the landscape of Mars.   **10.** about/of going to Singapore next year.   **11.** for being late.   **12.** to driving on the left side of the road.   **13.** from going to the hockey game!   **14.** for taking care of ordering the paper for the copier?   **15.** to going to visit my grandparents.   **16.** of stealing a car.   **17.** to working in the school office, she types manuscripts for graduate students.   **18.** for not writing sooner.
19. of telling a lie.   **20.** from traveling   [BrE: *travelling*] long distances.

EXERCISE 3, p. 300.

SAMPLE COMPLETIONS: [The prepositions and their gerund objects are <u>underlined</u>.]
1. Yes, I had a good excuse   OR   No, I didn't have a good excuse <u>for being</u> late for class yesterday.   **2.** Yes, I am looking forward   OR   No, I'm not looking forward <u>to going</u> to Boston to visit my friends this weekend.   **3.** Yes, I thanked him/her   OR   No, I didn't thank him/her <u>for picking up</u> my pen.   **4.** Yes, I'm accustomed   OR   No, I'm not accustomed <u>to living</u> in a cold/warm climate.   **5.** Yes, I'm excited   OR   No, I'm not excited <u>about going</u> to Italy for a vacation.   **6.** Yes, I apologized   OR   No, I didn't apologize <u>for interrupting</u> Mehmet while he was speaking.   **7.** Yes, all of the students participated   OR   No, all of the students didn't participate <u>in doing</u> pantomimes.
8. Yes, I know who is responsible   OR   No, I don't know who is responsible <u>for breaking</u> the window.   **9.** Yes, I'm used to   OR   No, I'm not used <u>to having</u> my biggest meal in the evening.   **10.** The hot weather prevents me <u>from running</u> every morning.
11. Yes, Peter complains   OR   No, Peter doesn't complain <u>about/of having</u> a lot of homework to do.   **12.** Yes, I blame Susan   OR   No, I don't blame Susan <u>for staying</u> home sick in bed last week.   **13.** S/he went to a baseball game <u>instead of studying</u> grammar last night.   **14.** I wrote a few letters and read some news magazines <u>in addition to studying</u> last night.

EXERCISE 4, p. 301.

SAMPLE COMPLETIONS: **4.** by eating.   **5.** by drinking.   **6.** by looking it up in a dictionary.   **7.** by watching TV.   **8.** by waving to me.   **9.** by calling an exterminator.   **10.** by wagging her tail.   **11.** by sticking a knife in the toaster.   **12.** by coming home late at night.

EXERCISE 5, p. 302.

SAMPLE RESPONSES: [Words already provided in the text are in *italics.*]
1. Sam *enjoyed watching TV* last night.   **2.** Would you *mind opening the window?*
3. James *quit eating desserts.*   **4.** James *gave up eating desserts* for six months.   **5.** Bill *finished eating dinner* before he went out to play.   **6.** After Bill *got through eating dinner,* he ran out to play.   **7.** When it *stops raining,* we can go to the beach.   **8.** Why did you *avoid answering my question?*   **9.** I cannot *postpone doing my work* any longer.   **10.** I have *put off doing my work* as long as I can.   **11.** We *delayed leaving on vacation* because of the hurricane.   **12.** I must *keep working* or I won't get home until late tonight.
13. Ted *kept on working* through his lunch hour.   **14.** My sister must *consider getting a job* if she wants to redecorate her kitchen this year.   **15.** She really doesn't want to *think about getting a job.*   **16.** Let's *discuss going to a movie* this weekend.   **17.** We'll *talk about going to a movie* when we meet for dinner this evening.   **18.** David *mentioned going to a concert* instead of a movie.   **19.** Rita *suggested going on a picnic* if the weather is nice.   **20.** I *enjoy listening to music* in the evening.

EXERCISE 6, p. 303.

POSSIBLE COMPLETIONS: **2.** closing/opening   **3.** raining   **4.** running
5. taking/going on   **6.** studying   **7.** giving/having   **8.** laughing   **9.** hitting/running into/colliding with   **10.** going   **11.** doing/starting   **12.** making
13. going   **14.** taking   **15.** being

EXERCISE 9, p. 305.

POSSIBLE COMPLETIONS: **2.** understanding   **3.** doing   **4.** waiting   **5.** taking
6. listening   **7.** going   **8.** getting   **9.** making   **10.** watching   **11.** eating
12. traveling/going/driving   [BrE: *travelling*]   **13.** doing . . . talking on the phone.
14. going to museums and Broadway shows   **15.** understanding the lecturers when they speak too fast   **16.** going to class and studying English

EXERCISE 10, p. 306.

SAMPLE RESPONSES: [Words already provided in the text are in *italics.*]
1. I *have trouble remembering* phone numbers.   **2.** I have been *standing* at this counter for ten minutes *waiting* for a salesperson.   **3.** Anton *had a hard time learning* how to spell "Antarctica."   **4.** I enjoy *sitting* in the park and *thinking* about my girlfriend.   **5.** The children *have a good time playing* in the sandbox at the playground.   **6.** I was *lying* in the shade of a large tree *dreaming* about faraway places.   **7.** I *have difficulty pronouncing* Mr. Krzyzewski's name correctly.   **8.** The teenagers *had fun singing and dancing* at the local club.   **9.** I *found someone studying* at my usual desk in the library.   **10.** Jack *spent* 30 minutes *chatting* with Ellen instead of studying for his chemistry test.   **11.** Don't *waste* money *trying* to win the lottery.   **12.** I *caught* my brother *taking* my car without my permission.

EXERCISE 11, p. 307.

POSSIBLE COMPLETIONS: **3.** to get/look for   **4.** to complete/do/ finish   **5.** playing
6. to lend   **7.** to call/come   **8.** to finish/do   **9.** holding/opening   **10.** to be

... whispering/talking   **11.** getting . . . to wait   **12.** to use/consult   **13.** to write   **14.** not to touch   **15.** being/living   **16.** to be   **17.** to know   **18.** to write [also possible: *writing*]   **19.** to keep/have   **20.** to pass/take   **21.** to deliver/mail   **22.** to mail/accept   **23.** to find   **24.** to find   **25.** finding **26.** finding   **27.** to take   **28.** taking

EXERCISE 12, p. 309.

POSSIBLE COMPLETIONS: [The verbs and the infinitives which follow them are underlined.] **2.** The secretary asked me to give this note to Sue. I was asked to give this note to Sue.   **3.** My advisor advised me to take Biology 109. I was advised to take Biology 109.   **4.** When I went to traffic court, the judge ordered me to pay a fine. I was ordered to pay a fine.   **5.** The teacher warned Greg to keep his eyes on his own paper during the test. During the test, Greg was warned to keep his eyes on his own paper. **6.** During the test, the teacher warned Greg not to look at his neighbor's paper. Greg was warned not to look at his neighbor's paper during the test.   **7.** At the meeting, the head of the department reminded the faculty not to forget to turn in their grade reports by the 15th. The faculty was (also possible: *were*) reminded not to forget to turn in their grade reports by the 15th.   **8.** Mr. Lee told the children to be quiet. The children were told to be quiet.   **9.** The hijacker forced the pilot to land the plane. The pilot was forced to land the plane.   **10.** When I was growing up, my parents allowed me to stay up late on Saturday night. When I was growing up, I was allowed to stay up late on Saturday night.   **11.** The teacher encouraged the students to speak slowly and clearly. The students were encouraged to speak slowly and clearly.   **12.** The teacher expects the students to come to class on time. The students are expected to come to class on time.

EXERCISE 13, p. 310.

EXPECTED RESPONSES: [Verbs and infinitives are underlined.] **2.** The general ordered the soldiers to surround the enemy.   OR   The soldiers were ordered (by the general) to surround the enemy.   **3.** Nancy asked me to open the window.   OR   I was asked (by Nancy) to open the window.   **4.** Bob reminded me not to forget to take my book back to the library.   OR   I was reminded (by Bob) not to forget to take my book back to the library.   **5.** Paul encouraged me to take singing lessons.   OR   I was encouraged (by Paul) to take singing lessons.   **6.** Mrs. Anderson warned the children sternly not to play with matches.   OR   The children were warned sternly (by Mrs. Anderson) not to play with matches.   **7.** The Dean of Admissions permitted me to register for school late.   OR   I was permitted (by the Dean of Admissions) to register for school late.   **8.** The law requires every driver to have a valid driver's license.   OR   Every driver is required (by law) to have a valid driver's license.   **9.** My friend advised me to get some automobile insurance.   OR   I was advised (by my friend) to get some automobile insurance.   **10.** The robber forced me to give him all my money.   OR   I was forced (by the robber) to give him/the robber all my money.   **11.** Before the examination began, the teacher advised the students to work quickly.   OR   Before the examination began, the students were advised (by the teacher) to work quickly.   **12.** My boss told me to come to the meeting ten minutes early.   OR   I was told (by my boss) to come to the meeting ten minutes early.

EXERCISE 14, p. 310.

SAMPLE RESPONSES: [Words already provided in the text are in *italics*.] **1.** The teacher *reminded me to finish* my composition and hand it in. I *was reminded to finish* my composition and hand it in.   **2.** The teacher *asked me to go* to the front of the classroom. I *was asked to go* to the front of the classroom.   **3.** The ticket *permitted me to have* two free glasses of wine at the art show. I *was permitted to have* two free glasses of wine at the art show. **4.** My family *expected me to be* at the station when their train arrived. I *was expected to be* at the station when my family's train arrived. **5.** The park ranger *warned me not to go* into the national forest alone. *I was warned not to go* into the national forest alone. **6.** He also *advised me to take* a bottle of water and a compass. I *was* also *advised to take* a bottle of water and a compass. **7.** My employer *told me to open* the mail by 11:00 every morning. I *was told to open* the mail by 11:00 every morning. **8.** My doctor *encouraged me to visit* a warm, dry climate. I was *encouraged to visit* a warm, dry climate. **9.** Our teacher *requires us to take* a test every week. We *are required to take* a test every week.

EXERCISE 15, p. 312.

ANSWERS: **2.** to leave/leaving **3.** to lecture/lecturing **4.** to swim/swimming **5.** to see/seeing **6.** to move/moving . . . to race/racing . . . to move . . . to race **7.** driving . . . taking **8.** driving/to drive . . . taking/ (to) take **9.** to turn **10.** being **11.** to give **12.** playing **13.** doing **14.** to do **15.** to do **16.** carrying **17.** watching **18.** to do **19.** to inform **20.** not listening **21.** to explain **22.** holding . . . feeding . . . burping . . . changing [AmE = *diapers;* BrE = *nappies*]

EXERCISE 16, p. 314.

ANSWERS: **2.** cleaning **3.** to take **4.** to leave **5.** talking/to talk **6.** waiting . . . doing **7.** to stay . . . (to) paint **8.** quitting . . . opening **9.** to take **10.** looking . . . to answer **11.** postponing **12.** watching . . . listening **13.** to read/reading **14.** to go to camp/to go camping **15.** singing **16.** to take . . . to pay **17.** to stand **18.** not to wait

EXERCISE 17, p. 315.

SAMPLE RESPONSES: [Words already provided in the text are in *italics.*] **1.** Ms. Fisher *reminded* me *to finish* the marketing report before Friday. **2.** *We* always *had fun swimming* at the lake every summer. **3.** *Students are required to have* a laboratory notebook in Chemistry 101. **4.** *The counselor advised* Sharon *to take* an introductory math class. **5.** *I am trying to learn* French. **6.** Natasha *warned* me *not to open* my apartment door to strangers. **7.** *I like to go camping* in the Rocky Mountains. OR I *like going camping* . . . **8.** Roberto *was invited to go* to Surasuk's birthday party. **9.** Omar *promised not to tell* Mr. Stone that Toshi had cut class. **10.** *We aren't permitted to take* dogs into the student cafeteria. **11.** *My friend asked me not to tell* anyone about her illness. **12.** *When the wind began to blow/blowing,* we decided to return to our car. **13.** *I must remember to call* my dad tonight. **14.** Maria *told* me *not to worry about not being* dressed up for the dance. **15.** Sergio *was told to be* at the meeting at six. **16.** *I spent* five hours *writing* my last composition.

EXERCISE 19, p. 316.

ANSWERS: **1.** talking **2.** to play . . . not to make **3.** to look after **4.** paying **5.** chasing/to chase **6.** going . . . to go **7.** going skiing **8.** not to smoke **9.** not to know/not knowing **10.** whistling . . . to concentrate **11.** doing **12.** to quit . . . (to) look for **13.** to turn off **14.** to renew **15.** not to wait **16.** not to play **17.** to call **18.** convincing **19.** to throw away . . . (to) buy **20.** dropping out of . . . hitchhiking . . . trying to find **21.** to tell . . . to call . . . going swimming **22.** to ask . . . to tell . . . to remember to bring

EXERCISE 20, p. 320.

1. doing it.	**11.** to do it.	**21.** to do it?	**31.** doing it.	**41.** doing it.
2. to do it.	**12.** to do it.	**22.** doing it?	**32.** to do it.	**42.** to do it.
3. to do it.	**13.** to do it.	**23.** doing it?	**33.** to do it.	**43.** doing it.
4. to do it.	**14.** doing it.	**24.** to do it.	**34.** to do it.	**44.** to do it.
5. to do it.	**15.** to do it.	**25.** doing it.	**35.** doing it.	**45.** to do it.
6. doing it.	**16.** to do it.	**26.** doing it.	**36.** to do it.	**46.** doing it?
7. doing it.	**17.** to do it.	**27.** to do it.	**37.** to do it.	**47.** to do it.
8. to do it.	**18.** to do it.	**28.** doing it.	**38.** doing it.	**48.** doing it?
9. doing it.	**19.** doing it.	**29.** to do it.	**39.** doing it?	**49.** to do it?
10. doing it.	**20.** to do it.	**30.** doing it?	**40.** doing it.	**50.** to do it.

EXERCISE 21, p. 321.

ANSWERS: **1.** to bring   **2.** pronouncing   **3.** to eat   **4.** to hang up   **5.** to pull   **6.** to know   **7.** being   **8.** telling   **9.** to be   **10.** to do   **11.** to return . . . (to) finish   **12.** worrying   **13.** to play   **14.** telling   **15.** taking   **16.** to buy   **17.** to change   **18.** to have   **19.** being   **20.** hearing   **21.** promising to visit   **22.** to race   **23.** hoping . . . praying   **24.** to persuade . . . to stay . . . (to) finish

EXERCISE 24, p. 323.

SAMPLE SENTENCES: [The infinitives are <u>underlined</u>.]
2. It's important <u>to look</u> both ways before crossing a busy street.   **3.** It's not easy <u>to learn</u> a foreign language.   **4.** It's foolish <u>to dive</u> into water before checking its depth.
5. It must be interesting <u>to be</u> a foreign correspondent.   **6.** It's always a pleasure <u>to see</u> you.   **7.** It was clever of you <u>to buy</u> Microsoft stock when it was low.   **8.** It doesn't cost much money <u>to go</u> camping.   **9.** It's necessary <u>to have</u> a visa before you can travel to certain countries.   **10.** It takes time <u>to learn</u> how to play a musical instrument.

EXERCISE 25, p. 323.

SAMPLE SENTENCES: **2.** It's easy for Maria to speak Spanish because it's her native language.   OR   It's easy for someone to speak Spanish if s/he learns it as a child.   **3.** It's important for Toshi to learn English because he wants to attend an American university.   OR   It's important for someone to learn English if s/he plans to work at a foreign embassy.   **4.** It's essential for international students to get a visa if they plan to study here.   OR   It's essential for someone to get a visa if s/he wants to visit Russia.   **5.** It's important for engineering students to take advanced math courses.   OR   It's important for someone studying engineering to take advanced math courses.   **6.** It's difficult for me to communicate with Mr. Wang.   OR   It's difficult for someone who does not know sign language to communicate with a deaf person.   **7.** It is impossible for Abdul to come to class because he is in the hospital.   OR   It is impossible for someone to come to class if s/he is out of town.   **8.** It's a good idea for us to study gerunds and infinitives because we get to practice ways of connecting ideas.   OR   It's a good idea for someone who wants to speak English fluently to study gerunds and infinitives.

EXERCISE 26, p. 324.

SAMPLE COMPLETIONS: **2.** Skiing down a steep mountain slope is hard.   **3.** Meeting new people can be interesting.   **4.** Visiting Prague was a good experience.   **5.** Does climbing a mountain with a heavy pack on your back sound like fun to you?   **6.** Raising children demands patience and a sense of humor.   **7.** Rebuilding an engine is a complicated process.   **8.** Chewing gum in public is considered impolite in my country.

EXERCISE 27, p. 324.

SAMPLE RESPONSES: **1.** It's dangerous to climb a mountain. Mountain climbing is dangerous. **2.** It's easy to ride a bike. Riding a bike is easy. **3.** It's impolite to interrupt someone. Interrupting someone is impolite. **4.** It is important to keep the peace. Keeping the peace is important. **5.** It is wrong to drive through a stop sign. Driving through a stop sign is wrong. **6.** It takes a lot of time to do a job well. Doing a job well takes a lot of time. **7.** It's a good idea to park your car close to the curb. Parking your car close to the curb is a good idea. **8.** Is it difficult to learn a foreign language? Is learning a foreign language difficult?

Chapter 15: GERUNDS AND INFINITIVES, PART 2

EXERCISE 1, p. 326.

2. Helen borrowed my dictionary ~~for~~ to look up the spelling of "occurred." **3.** The teacher opened the window <u>to let</u> some fresh air in the room. **4.** I came to this school <u>to</u> learn English. **5.** I traveled to Osaka ~~for~~ to visit my sister.

EXERCISE 2, p. 327.

SAMPLE COMPLETIONS: **3.** (some) bread and coffee. **4.** buy (some) groceries. **5.** have my annual checkup. **6.** a checkup. **7.** stay in (good physical) shape. **8.** exercise and recreation. **9.** get (some) gas/petrol. **10.** (some) gas/petrol.

EXERCISE 3, p. 327.

ANSWERS: **3.** Ø **4.** in order **5.** in order **6.** in order **7.** Ø **8.** in order **9.** Ø **10.** in order **11.** in order **12.** in order **13.** Ø **14.** in order **15.** Ø

EXERCISE 4, p. 328.

POSSIBLE COMPLETIONS: **2.** careful to lock my doors. **3.** ready to go home. **4.** eager to see my relatives again. **5.** fortunate to have my family. **6.** ashamed to ask anyone for a loan. **7.** determined to succeed. **8.** hesitant to accept it without the support of his wife and children. **9.** delighted to accept the invitation. **10.** shocked to learn that he had actually gotten a job!

EXERCISE 5, p. 329.

POSSIBLE ANSWERS: **1.** Yes. (Maria) is fortunate to have a lot of good friends. **2.** Yes. I'm eager to go on vacation. **3.** Yes. I was delighted to meet Yoko's husband. **4.** Yes. I went to (Iceland) last summer. I was surprised to see Omar there too. **5.** Yes. I am prepared to take the test tomorrow. **6.** Yes. I am hesitant to ask (Yoko) a personal question. **7.** Yes. I was relieved to find out that (Kim) was okay. **8.** Yes. I was sorry to hear about (Jamal)'s accident.

EXERCISE 7, p. 330.

POSSIBLE COMPLETIONS: **3.** I don't want to watch a video. It's too late to start watching a video. **4.** I don't want to take a walk. It's too cold to take a walk. **5.** I don't understand nuclear physics. Nuclear physics is too difficult to understand. **6.** I can't meet my friend for lunch. I'm too busy to meet my friend for lunch. **7.** My son can't stay home alone. My son is too young to stay home alone. **8.** People can't climb the mountain. The mountain cliff is too steep to climb. **10.** I can finish my homework. I'm very tired, but I'm not too tired to finish my homework. **11.** I can carry my suitcase. My suitcase is very heavy, but it's not too heavy for me to carry.   **12.** I can talk to you for a few minutes. I'm very busy, but I'm not too busy to talk to you for a few minutes.

EXERCISE 8, p. 330.

POSSIBLE ANSWERS: **1.** She's very young.   **2.** A child is too young to read a novel, but an adult is old enough to appreciate good literature.   **3.** very   **4.** very   **5.** very **6.** very OR too   **8.** very   **9.** very   **11.** a. We need more envelopes. b. We need larger envelopes.   **12.** very   **13.** The sun is too bright to look at directly without special sunglasses.   **14.** You can't read if a room is too dark.   **15.** A cup is too full (to drink) if you can't lift it to your lips without spilling it.

EXERCISE 9, p. 332.

ANSWERS: **4.** to be invited   **5.** being understood   **6.** to be written   **7.** being hit   **8.** to be called   **9.** being elected   **10.** to have lost [also possible: *to be losing*] **11.** being told   **12.** to be loved . . . needed   **13.** not having written / not writing   **14.** having met / meeting   **15.** having been injured / being injured   **16.** to have escaped   **17.** having gone / going   **18.** to have been invited

EXERCISE 10, p. 333.

ANSWERS: **2.** to be changed/changing   **3.** to be cleaned/ cleaning . . . to clean **4.** to be ironed/ironing   **5.** to be repaired/repairing   **6.** to take . . . to be straightened/straightening   **7.** to be picked/picking   **8.** to be washed/washing

EXERCISE 12, p. 334.

ANSWERS: **3.** We greatly appreciate your/you taking the time to help us.   **4.** The boy resented our/us talking about him behind his back.   **5.** Their [<u>very</u> informal: *Them*] running away to get married shocked everyone.   **6.** I will no longer tolerate your/you being late to work every morning.   **7.** Sally complained about Ann's/Ann borrowing her clothes without asking her first.   **8.** We should take advantage of Helen's/Helen being here to answer our questions about the company's new insurance plan.

EXERCISE 13, p. 335.

ANSWERS: **1.** to be asked   **2.** drinking   **3.** washing   **4.** to relax   **5.** to answer   **6.** telling   **7.** beating   **8.** not being/not having been   **9.** to be awarded   **10.** to accept   **11.** getting . . . (in order) to help   **12.** to travel . . . (to) leave   **13.** Helping   **14.** to be liked . . . trusted   **15.** wondering **16.** to be chosen / to have been chosen   **17.** Living   **18.** doing . . . to interrupt **19.** to take/to have taken   **20.** (in order) to let   **21.** to cooperate   **22.** hanging **23.** to turn   **24.** hearing/having heard   **25.** leaving . . . going . . . (in order) to study **26.** asking/ having asked   **27.** driving . . . to drive   **28.** falling   **29.** (in order) to get   **30.** not being/not having been

EXERCISE 15, p. 337.

PART I POSSIBLE COMPLETIONS: **2.** sing/singing   **3.** walk/walking   **4.** shake/shaking **5.** knock/knocking   **6.** take off/taking off . . . land/landing

PART II EXPECTED COMPLETIONS: **2.** slam   **3.** snoring   **4.** playing   **5.** call **6.** walking   **7.** calling   **8.** play   **9.** singing . . . laughing   **10.** land **11.** burning   **12.** touch

EXERCISE 17, p. 338.

POSSIBLE COMPLETIONS: **2.** correct our own quizzes.   **3.** borrow your sweater?
4. tell you what to do.   **5.** (to) find her mother in the supermarket.   **6.** (to) locate
the registrar's office.   **7.** interrupt you.   **8.** (to) figure out how to operate this
computer?

EXERCISE 18, p. 340.

3. write   **4.** wash   **5.** to clean   **6.** cashed   **7.** to go   **8.** shortened
9. redo   **10.** filled   **11.** to lend   **12.** removed   **13.** cleaned   **14.** cry
15. to do   **16.** take

EXERCISE 19, p. 341.

POSSIBLE COMPLETIONS: **2.** go to bed when they don't want to.   **3.** bring us a
menu.   **4.** changed.   **5.** write on the chalkboard.   **6.** (to) move into a new
apartment.   **7.** print out two copies of my itinerary.   **8.** laugh.   **9.** go downtown
alone.   **10.** to replace our old refrigerator.

EXERCISE 21, p. 341.

1. Stop <u>telling</u> me what to do! Let me to make up my own mind.   **2.** My English is
pretty good, but sometimes I have trouble ~~to~~ <u>understanding</u> lectures at school.
3. When I entered the room, I found my wife ~~to~~ <u>crying</u> over the broken vase that had
belonged to her great-grandmother.   **4.** Sara is going to spend (the) next year ~~for~~
studying Chinese at a unversity in Taiwan.   **5.** I went to the pharmacy <u>to have</u> my
prescription ~~to be~~ filled.   **6.** You shouldn't let children <u>play</u> with matches.   **7.** When
I got home, Irene was lying in bed <u>thinking</u> about what a wonderful time she'd had.
8. When Shellcy needed a passport photo, she had her picture <u>taken</u> by a professional
photographer.   **9.** I've finally assembled enough information <u>to begin</u> writing my
thesis.   **10.** Omar is at the park right now. He is <u>sitting</u> on a park bench <u>watching</u>
the ducks swi<u>mm</u>ing in the pond. The sad expression on his face makes me ~~to~~ feel sorry
for him.

EXERCISES 22 and 23, pp. 342–343.

EX. 22 ANSWERS: **2.** trickling   **3.** to ignore   **4.** drink   **5.** move   **6.** play . . .
joining   **7.** being elected   **8.** to be told   **9.** have . . . join   **10.** drive
11. sipping . . . eating   **12.** (in order) to let . . . run   **13.** make   **14.** talking
15. being forced / to be forced to leave . . . (in order) to study . . . having
16. being   **17.** to have . . . to know . . . to handle   **18.** Looking . . . realize . . .
to be   **19.** staying . . . getting   **20.** having . . . adjusting

EX. 23 ANSWERS: **1.** being allowed   **2.** Observing . . . climbing/climb . . . realize (that)
3. (to) being surprised . . . planning   **4.** to have been performed   **5.** to be identified
6. to pick   **7.** having met/meeting . . . to be introduced   **8.** to have been
considered/to be considered   **9.** to sleep . . . thinking   **10.** to force . . . to use . . .
to feel . . . share   **11.** being accepted . . . concentrating   **12.** to persuade . . . to
give . . . to cut . . . working . . . to retire . . . take . . . being dedicated   **13.** to
commute . . . moving . . . to give . . . to live . . . (in order) to be . . . doing . . . doing
14. feel . . . to get . . . feeling . . . sneezing . . . coughing . . . to ask . . . to see . . .
go   **15.** chewing . . . grabbing . . . holding . . . tearing . . . swallow   **16.** to get
. . . running . . . having . . . sprayed   **17.** being treated . . . threatening to stop

working . . . to listen   **18.** being . . . being . . . to be understood . . . to bridge . . . teaching

EXERCISE 24, p. 345.

1. My parents made me ~~to~~ promise to write them once a week.   **2.** I don't mind ~~to~~ <u>having</u> a roommate.   **3.** Most students want <u>to</u> return home as soon as possible.
4. When I went ~~to~~ shopping last Saturday, I saw a man ~~to~~ drive his car onto the sidewalk.
OR . . . I saw a man <u>driving</u> his car <u>on</u> the sidewalk.   **5.** I asked my roommate to let me ~~to~~ use his shoe polish.   **6.** ~~To~~ <u>Learning</u> about another country ~~it~~ is very interesting.
OR   It is very interesting to learn about another country.   **7.** I don't enjoy ~~to~~ <u>playing</u> card games.   **8.** I heard a car door ~~to~~ open and <u>close</u>.   OR   I heard a car door ~~to~~ <u>opening</u> and closing.   **9.** I had my friend ~~to~~ lend me his car.   **10.** I tried very hard <u>not to</u> make any mistakes.   OR   I tried very hard to ~~don't~~ make <u>no</u> mistakes.   **11.** You should visit my country. It is <u>very</u> beautiful.   **12.** The music director tapped his baton <u>to begin</u> the rehearsal.   **13.** Some people prefer ~~to~~ <u>saving</u> their money to <u>spending</u> it.   OR Some people prefer to save their money <u>than</u> (to) spend it.   **14.** The task of <u>finding</u> a person who could help us wasn't difficult.   **15.** All of us needed to <u>go</u> to the cashier's window.   **16.** I am looking forward to <u>going</u> ~~to~~ <u>swimming</u> in the ocean.   **17.** When <u>you're</u> planting a garden, it's important to ~~be~~ <u>know</u> about soils.   **18.** My mother always <u>makes</u> me ~~to be~~ slow down if she <u>thinks</u> I am driving <u>too</u> fast.   **19.** One of our fights ended up with <u>my</u>/me having to <u>be</u> sent to the hospital <u>for</u>/to get stitches.   **20.** Please promise not <u>to tell</u> anybody my secret.   **21.** I would appreciate ~~having~~ <u>hearing</u> from you soon.   **22.** Maria has never complained about <u>having</u> a handicap.   **23.** Lillian deserves to be <u>told</u> the truth about what happened last night.   **24.** Barbara always makes me <u>laugh</u>. She has a great sense of humor.   **25.** Ali <u>doesn't</u> speak Spanish, and Juan <u>doesn't</u> know Arabic. But they communicate well by <u>speaking</u> English when they <u>are</u> together.   **26.** I enjoyed ~~to~~ <u>talking</u> to her on the phone. I look forward to <u>seeing</u> her next week.   **27.** During a fire drill, everyone is required <u>to leave</u> the building.   **28.** <u>Skiing</u> in the Alps was a big thrill for me.   **29.** Don't keep ~~to be~~ <u>asking</u> me the same questions over and over.   **30.** When I entered the room, I found my young son <u>standing</u> on the kitchen table.

Chapter 16: COORDINATING CONJUNCTIONS

EXERCISE 1, p. 348.

3. She spoke <u>angrily</u> and <u>bitterly</u> about the war. [adverb + adverb]   **4.** I <u>looked</u> for my book but <u>couldn't find</u> it. [verb + verb]   **5.** I hope <u>to go</u> to that university and <u>study</u> under Dr. Liu. [infinitive + infinitive]   **6.** In my spare time, I enjoy <u>reading</u> novels or <u>watching</u> television. [gerund + gerund]   **7.** He <u>will leave</u> at eight and <u>arrive</u> at nine. [verb + verb]   **8.** He <u>should have broken</u> his engagement to Beth and <u>married</u> Sue instead. [verb + verb]

EXERCISE 2, p. 349.

ANSWERS: **2.** Mary is opening the door and (is) greeting her guests.   **3.** Mary will open the door and (will) greet her guests.   **4.** Alice is kind, generous, and trustworthy.
5. Please try to speak more loudly and clearly.   **6.** He gave her flowers on Sunday, candy on Monday, and a ring on Tuesday.   **7.** While we were in New York, we attended an opera, ate at marvelous restaurants, and visited some old friends.   **8.** He decided to quit school, (to) go to California, and (to) find a job.   **9.** I am looking forward to going to Italy and eating wonderful pasta every day.   **10.** I should have finished my homework and (should have) cleaned up my room.   **11.** The boy was old enough to work and (to)

earn some money. **12.** He preferred to play baseball or (to) spend his time in the streets with other boys. **13.** I like coffee but not tea. **14.** I have met his mother (,) but not his father. **15.** Jake would like to live in Puerto Rico (,) but not (in) Iceland.

EXERCISE 3, p. 350.

POSSIBLE COMPLETIONS: **2.** the food—I like to become acquainted with the people, (the) customs, and (the) food of other countries. **3.** the noise—I dislike living in a city because of the air pollution, (the) crime, and (the) noise. **4.** economic—We discussed some of the social, political, and economic problems of the United States. **5.** a warm climate—Hawaii has a warm climate, many interesting tropical trees and flowers, and beautiful beaches. **6.** is a good leader—Mary Hart would make a good president because she is a good leader, works effectively with others, and has a reputation for integrity and independent thinking.

EXERCISE 4, p. 351.

POSSIBLE COMPLETIONS: **2.** competent **3.** said, "Good morning." **4.** reading the newspaper **5.** leave for work **6.** Swimming at the lake **7.** hiking on mountain trails **8.** supportive of those who are in trouble / generous to those in need / kind to people down on their luck

EXERCISE 5, p. 351.

1. By obeying the speed limit, we can save energy, lives, and <u>money</u>. **2.** My home offers me a feeling of security, <u>warmth</u>, and love. **3.** The pioneers labored to clear away the forest and <u>plant</u> crops. **4.** When I refused to help her, she became very angry and <u>shouted</u> at me. **5.** In my spare time, I enjoy taking care of my aquarium and <u>working</u> on my stamp collection. OR In my spare time, I enjoy taking care of my aquarium and ~~to~~ I work on my stamp collection. **6.** With their keen sight, fine hearing, and ~~they have a~~ refined sense of smell, wolves hunt elk, deer, moose, and caribou. **7.** All plants need light, ~~to have~~ a suitable climate, and an ample supply of water and minerals from the soil. **8.** Slowly and <u>cautiously</u>, the firefighter ascended the burned staircase. **9.** The Indian cobra snake and the king cobra use poison from their fangs in two ways: by injecting it directly into their prey or ~~they~~ <u>(by) spitting</u> it into the eyes of the victim. **10.** On my vacation, I lost a suitcase, broke my glasses, and ~~I~~ missed my flight home. **11.** When Anna moved, she had to rent an apartment, make new friends, and ~~to~~ find a job.

EXERCISE 6, p. 352.

What do people in your country think of bats? Are they mean and scary creatures, or are they symbols of happiness and <u>luck</u>?

In Western countries, many people have an unreasoned fear of bats. According to scientist Dr. Sharon Horowitz, bats are <u>beneficial and harmless mammals</u>. "When I was a child, I believed that a bat would attack me and <u>tangle</u> itself in my hair. Now I know better," said Dr. Horowitz.

Contrary to popular Western myths, bats do not attack humans and <u>are</u> not blind. Although a few bats may be infected, they are not major carriers of rabies or ~~carry~~ other dread diseases. Bats help natural plant life by pollinating plants, spreading seeds, and ~~they~~ <u>eating</u> insects. If you get rid of bats that eat overripe fruit, then fruit flies can flourish and <u>destroy</u> the fruit industry.

According to Dr. Horowitz, bats make loving, ~~pets, and they are~~ trainable, and ~~are~~ gentle pets. Not many people, however, are known to have bats as pets, and bats themselves prefer to avoid people.

EXERCISE 7, p. 353.

ANSWERS: **2.** is **3.** is **4.** are **5.** is **6.** are **7.** are **8.** are

EXERCISE 8, p. 353.

[The paired conjunctions are underlined.] **1.** John will call either Mary or Bob. OR Either John or Bob will call Mary. **2.** Sue saw not only the mouse but also the cat. OR Not only Sue but (also) the cat saw the mouse. **3.** Both my mother and (my) father talked to the teacher. OR My mother talked to both my teacher and my father. **4.** Either Mr. Anderson or Ms. Wiggins is going to teach our class today. **5.** I enjoy reading not only novels but also magazines. **6.** Oxygen is plentiful. Both air and water contain oxygen.

EXERCISE 9, p. 354.

PART I ANSWERS: **2.** Yes, both the driver and the passenger were injured in the accident. **3.** Yes, both wheat and corn are grown in Kansas. **4.** Yes, he both buys and sells used cars. **5.** Yes, I had both lunch and dinner with my friends. **6.** Yes, the city suffers from both air (pollution) and water pollution.

PART II ANSWERS: **8.** Yes, not only his cousin but also his mother-in-law is living with him. **9.** Yes, not only my country but also the United States has good universities. **10.** Yes, I lost not only my wallet but also my keys. **11.** Yes, she not only goes to school but also has a full-time job. **12.** Yes, he bought not only a coat but also a new pair of shoes.

PART III ANSWERS: **14.** Yes, I'm going to give my friend either a book or a pen for her birthday. **15.** Yes, either my sister or my brother will meet me at the airport. **16.** Yes, they can either go swimming or play tennis. **17.** Yes, I'm going to vote for either Mr. Smith or Mr. Jones. **18.** Yes, I'll go to either New Orleans or Miami for my vacation.

PART IV ANSWERS: **20.** No, neither her husband nor her children speak English. **21.** No, neither the students nor the teacher is wide awake today. **22.** No, they have neither a refrigerator nor a stove for their new apartment. **23.** No, she enjoys neither hunting nor fishing. **24.** No, the result was neither good nor bad.

EXERCISE 10, p. 355.

[The paired conjunctions are underlined.] **2.** Both Ron and Bob enjoy horseback riding. OR Not only Ron but also Bob enjoys horseback riding. **3.** You can have either tea or coffee. **4.** Neither Arthur nor Ricardo is in class today. **5.** Both Arthur and Ricardo are absent. OR Not only Arthur but also Ricardo is absent. **6.** We can either fix dinner for them here or take them to a restaurant. **7.** She wants to buy either a Chevrolet or a Toyota. **8.** Both the leopard and the tiger face extinction. **9.** Neither the library nor the bookstore has the book I need. **10.** We could either fly or take the train. **11.** The president's assistant will neither confirm nor deny the story. **12.** Both coal and oil are irreplaceable natural resources. OR Not only coal but also oil is an irreplaceable natural resource. **13.** Both smallpox and malaria are dangerous diseases. **14.** Neither her roommates nor her brother knows where she is. **15.** According to the news report, it will either snow or rain tonight.

EXERCISES 11 and 12, pp. 356–357.

EX. 11:   **2.** The teacher lectured. **T**he students took notes.   **3.** The teacher lectured, and the students took notes.   **4.** Elena came to the meeting, but Pedro stayed home. **5.** Elena came to the meeting. **H**er brother stayed home.   **6.** Her academic record was outstanding, yet she was not accepted by the university.   **7.** I have not finished writing my term paper yet. **I** will not be finished until sometime next week.   **8.** *(no change)* **9.** We had to go to the grocery store, for there was nothing in the house to fix for dinner. **10.** Kostas didn't have enough money to buy an airplane ticket, so he couldn't fly home for the holiday.

EX. 12:

1. A thermometer is used to measure temperature. **A** barometer measures air pressure. **2.** Daniel made many promises, but he had no intention of keeping them.   **3.** I always enjoyed mathematics in high school, so I decided to major in it in college.   **4.** Anna is in serious legal trouble, for she had no car insurance at the time of the accident.   **5.** Last night Martha had to study for a test, so she went to the library.   **6.** The ancient Egyptians had good dentists. **A**rchaeologists have found mummies that had gold fillings in their teeth.   **7.** Both John and I had many errands to do yesterday. **J**ohn had to go to the post office and the bookstore. **I** had to go to the post office, the travel agency, and the bank. **8.** I did not like the leading actor, yet the movie was quite good on the whole.   **9.** The team of researchers has not finished compiling the statistics yet. **T**heir work will not be made public until later.   **10.** We have nothing to fear, for our country is strong and united.   **11.** He slapped his desk in disgust. **H**e had failed another examination and had ruined his chances for a passing grade in the course.   **12.** I struggled to keep my head above water. **I** tried to yell for help, but no sound came from my mouth.   **13.** The earthquake was devastating. **T**all buildings crumbled and fell to the earth.   **14.** It was a wonderful picnic. **T**he children waded in the stream, collected rocks and insects, and flew kites. **T**he teenagers played an enthusiastic game of baseball. **T**he adults busied themselves preparing the food, supervising the children, and playing a game or two of volleyball. **15.** Some people collect butterflies for a hobby. **T**hese collectors capture them with a net and put them in a jar that has poison in it. **T**he dead butterflies are then mounted on a board.   **16.** Caterpillars eat plants and cause damage to some crops, but adult butterflies feed principally on nectar from flowers and do not cause any harm.   **17.** The butterfly is a marvel. **I**t begins as an ugly caterpillar and turns into a work of art.   **18.** The sight of a butterfly floating from flower to flower on a warm sunny day brightens anyone's heart. **A** butterfly is a charming and gentle creature.   **19.** When cold weather comes, some butterflies travel great distances to reach tropical climates.   **20.** Butterflies are admired throughout the world because they are beautiful. **T**hey can be found on every continent except Antarctica.

Chapter 17: ADVERB CLAUSES

EXERCISE 1, p. 360.

2. <u>When it began to rain,</u> he closed the windows.   **3.** He closed the windows <u>when it began to rain</u>.   **4.** <u>As soon as the rain began,</u> the children wanted to go outdoors. **T**hey love to play outside in the warm summer rain. **I** used to do the same thing <u>when I was a child</u>.   **5.** Jack got to the airport early. <u>After he checked in at the airline counter,</u> he went to the waiting area near his gate. **H**e sat and read <u>until his flight was announced</u>. **6.** Jack walked onto the plane, found his seat, and stowed his bag in an overhead compartment.   **7.** <u>Before the plane took off,</u> he fastened his seat belt and put his seat in an upright position.   **8.** Jack's wife doesn't like to fly <u>because she gets nervous on airplanes</u>.   **9.** <u>When Jack and his wife go on vacation</u>, they have to drive or take the train <u>because his wife is afraid of flying</u>.   **10.** I had a cup of tea <u>before I left for work this morning</u>, but I didn't have anything to eat. **I** rarely eat breakfast.   **11.** <u>After Ellen gets home from work</u>, she likes to read the newspaper. **S**he follows the same routine every day after work. <u>**A**s soon as she gets home</u>, she changes her clothes, gets a snack and a drink, and sits down in her favorite chair to read the newspaper in peace and quiet. **S**he usually has about half an hour to read the paper <u>before her husband arrives home from his job</u>.   **12.** <u>When you speak to someone</u> [*who is hard of hearing* = adjective clause], you do not have to shout. **I**t is important to face the person directly and speak clearly. **M**y elderly father is hard of hearing, but he can understand me <u>if I face him, speak slowly, and say each word clearly</u>. **13.** Greg Adams has been blind <u>since he was two years old</u>. **T**oday he is a key scientist in a computer company. **H**e is able to design complex electronic equipment <u>because he has a special computer</u> [*that reads, writes, and speaks out loud* = adjective clause]. **H**is blindness neither helps nor hinders him. **I**t is irrelevant to [*how well he does his job* = noun clause].

EXERCISE 2, p. 361.

SAMPLE COMPLETIONS: **1.** Since I came to this city, I've met a lot of nice people. **2.** Just as I was falling asleep last night, a mosquito buzzed in my ear and woke me up. **3.** I'll help you with your homework as soon as I finish washing the dishes.   **4.** I was late. By the time I got to the airport, my plane had already taken off.   **5.** One of my friends gets nervous every time she has to perform in public.   **6.** I will be here until I have completed my education.   **7.** I will remember my wedding day as long as I live. **8.** I heard the phone ring while I was in the shower.   **9.** Once summer comes, the traffic on the highway becomes heavier.   **10.** Shortly before I put supper on the table, the cat demanded to be fed.   **11.** I have been in this city for three years. By the time I leave, I will be able to speak English fluently.   **12.** The last time I was with my family, I was 24 years old.   **13.** The next time you see them, you'll be 28.   **14.** I will be with you just as soon as I finish checking this inventory.   **15.** Not long after I bought the car, I ran over a nail and got a flat tire.   **16.** I had already finished supper when you telephoned. **17.** Whenever I'm late for an important meeting, I get nervous.   **18.** Ever since I was a child, I've been afraid of snakes.

EXERCISE 3, p. 362.

[The adverb clauses are <u>underlined</u>.]   **3.** Cold air hovers near the earth <u>because it is heavier than hot air</u>.   **4.** <u>Since you paid for the theater tickets</u>, please let me pay for our dinner.   **5.** <u>Now that Larry is finally caught up on his work</u>, he can start his vacation tomorrow.   **6.** <u>Because our TV set was broken</u>, we listened to the news on the radio.   **7.** My brother got married last month. <u>Now that he's a married man</u>, he has more responsibilities.   **8.** <u>Since oil is an irreplaceable natural resource</u>, we must do whatever we can in order to conserve it.   **9.** Do you want to go for a walk <u>now that the rain has stopped</u>?   **10.** Many young people move to the cities in search of employment <u>since there are few jobs available in the rural areas</u>.   **11.** <u>Now that the civil war has ended</u>, a new government is being formed.   **12.** <u>Since ninety-two thousand people already have reservations with an airline company for a trip to the moon</u>, I doubt that I'll get the chance to go on one of the first tourist flights.

EXERCISE 4, p. 363.

SAMPLE COMPLETIONS: [The adverb clauses are <u>underlined</u>.]
1. <u>Now that I've finally finished cleaning my room</u>, I can watch TV.   **2.** The teacher didn't collect the papers <u>because the exercise is not going to be graded</u>.   **3.** <u>Since it's too</u>

expensive to fly across the country, we are going by bus.   **4.** Jack can't stay out all night with his friends <u>now that he is working the night shift</u>.   **5.** <u>Since we don't have class tomorrow</u>, we can stay up later tonight.

EXERCISE 5, p. 364.

ANSWERS: **3.** even though   **4.** because   **5.** Even though   **6.** Because   **7.** even though   **8.** because   **9.** even though   **10.** even though   **11.** because   **12.** Even though . . . because

EXERCISE 7, p. 365.

SAMPLE COMPLETIONS: **3.** Because it was a beautiful day, I went fishing.   **4.** Even though it was a work day, I went fishing.   **5.** Even though there were very few customers in the store, we decided to stay open until 9:00 P.M.   **6.** Because there were very few customers in the store, we closed early.   **7.** I wore heavy gloves because the temperature was below freezing.   **8.** Even though my feet were killing me and my head was pounding, I finished running the marathon.   **9.** Even though I was speeding, I didn't get a traffic ticket.
10. Even though I was tired, I finished my homework because my essay was due the next day.
11. Even though I didn't like baked beans when I was small, I always finished them because I wanted dessert.   **12.** Because we didn't have a television set while I was growing up, I watched TV at my neighbor's house even though my parents didn't approve.

EXERCISE 8, p. 366.

ANSWERS: **2.** D.   **3.** C.   **4.** C.   **5.** B.   **6.** B.

EXERCISE 11, p. 368.

　　2. Sam laughs at the jokes:
　　　　a. whether they're funny or not.   b. even if they're not funny.
　　3. You have to hand in your examination paper:
　　　　a. whether you're finished or not.   b. even if you're not finished.
　　4. We're going to go camping in the mountains:
　　　　a. whether it snows or not.   b. even if it snows.
　　5. Max can go to school:
　　　　a. whether or not he gets a scholarship.   b. even if he doesn't get a scholarship.
　　6. My grandfather wears his gray sweater:
　　　　a. whether or not the weather is cold.   b. even if the weather is hot.
　　7. I'm going to marry Harry:
　　　　a. whether you approve or not.   b. even if you don't approve.

EXERCISE 12, p. 369.

SAMPLE COMPLETIONS: **1.** We're not going to the park today even if the weather improves.
2. Even if she apologizes to her supervisor, Maria may lose her job.   **3.** Getting that job depends on whether or not you can speak English.   **4.** I'm going to help you whether you want me to or not.   **5.** I won't tell you even if you beg me.   **6.** I'm really angry! Maybe he'll apologize, and maybe he won't. It doesn't matter. Even if he tells me he's really sorry, I won't forgive him!   **7.** I'm exhausted. Please don't wake me up even if the house catches on fire.   **8.** I'm not going to go with him to the boxing match even if he begs me.   **9.** Even if it rains, I'm going to take my morning walk.   **10.** I'm going to quit school whether my parents like it or not.

EXERCISE 13, p. 369.

ANSWERS: **2.** In case / In the event that you need to see me, I'll be in my office tomorrow morning around ten.   **3.** In case / In the event that you need more information, you can call me.   **4.** In case / In the event that you have any more questions, ask Dr. Smith.   **5.** In case / In the event that Jack calls, please tell him that I'm at the library.   **6.** In case / In the event that you're not satisfied with your purchase, you can return it to the store.

SAMPLE COMPLETIONS: **7.** . . . you'll have to go to the library.   **8.** . . . you lose your credit cards.   **9.** . . . my parents decide to come for a visit.   **10.** . . . it rains. [*just* adds a bit of emphasis]   **11.** . . . the refugees can at last return to their homes.   **12.** . . . please start without me.   **13.** . . . it malfunctions.

EXERCISE 14, p. 370.

ANSWERS: **2.** You can't travel abroad unless you have a passport.   **3.** You can't get a driver's license unless you're at least sixteen years old.   **4.** Unless I get some film, I won't be able to take pictures when Ann and Rob get here.   **5.** You'll get hungry during class unless you eat breakfast.

EXERCISE 15, p. 371.

SAMPLE COMPLETIONS: **2.** I'm sorry, but you can't see the doctor unless you have an appointment.   **3.** I can't graduate from school unless I pass all my courses.   **4.** That food will spoil unless you put it in the refrigerator.   **5.** Unless it rains, we plan to have the birthday party in the backyard.   **6.** Certain species of animals will soon become extinct unless we stop destroying their habitats.   **7.** I will have to look for another job unless I get a raise [BrE: *rise*] in salary.   **8.** Tomorrow I'm going to call my sister unless I hear from her on e-mail today.   **9.** The political situation in (. . .) will continue to deteriorate unless the opposing sides commit to ending the hostilities and creating a lasting peace.   **10.** He doesn't say anything unless the teacher calls on him.   **11.** Unless you start learning how to use the Internet, the modern world will pass you by.

EXERCISE 16, p. 371.

ANSWERS: **2.** You can go to the party only if you have an invitation.   **3.** You can attend this school only if you have a student visa.   **4.** Jimmy chews gum only if he's sure his mother won't find out.   **5.** We will go to the movie only if you want to (go).   **6.** Water will freeze only if the temperature reaches 32°F / 0°C.   **7.** Only if you study hard **will you** pass the exam.   **8.** Only if you have a ticket **can you** get into the soccer stadium.   **9.** Only if Jake's homework is finished **can he** watch TV in the evening.   **10.** Only if I get a job **will I** have enough money to go to school.   **11.–13.** (*free response*)

EXERCISE 17, p. 372.

ANSWERS: **2.** I can't pay my bills unless I get a job. I can pay my bills only if I get a job.   **3.** Your clothes will get clean only if you use soap. Your clothes won't get clean unless you use soap.   **4.** I can't take any pictures unless I buy some film. I can take pictures only if I buy some film.   **5.** I don't wake up unless the alarm clock rings. I wake up only if the alarm clock rings.   **6.** Eggs won't hatch unless they're kept at the proper temperature. Eggs will hatch only if they're kept at the proper temperature.   **7.** Don't borrow money from friends unless you absolutely have to. Borrow money from friends only if you absolutely have to.   **8.** Anna doesn't talk in class unless the teacher asks her specific questions. Anna talks in class only if the teacher asks her specific questions.

Chapter 18: REDUCTION OF ADVERB CLAUSES TO MODIFYING ADVERBIAL PHRASES

EXERCISE 1, p. 375.

ANSWERS: **3.** Before I came to class, I had a cup of coffee. *Before coming to class*, I had a cup of coffee.   **4.** Before the student came to class, the teacher had already given a quiz. *(no change)*   **5.** Since I came here, I have learned a lot of English. *Since coming here*, I have learned a lot of English.   **6.** Since Bob opened his new business, he has been working 16 hours a day. *Since opening his new business*, Bob has been working 16 hours a day.   **7.** After Omar (had) finished breakfast, he left the house and went to his office. *After finishing / having finished breakfast*, Omar left the house and went to his office.   **8.** Alex hurt his back while he was chopping wood. Alex hurt his back *while chopping wood*.   **9.** You should always read a contract before you sign your name. You should always read a contract *before signing your name*.   **10.** Before the waiter came to the table, I had already made up my mind to order shrimp. *(no change)*   **11.** Before you ask the librarian for help, you should make every effort to find the materials yourself. *Before asking the librarian for help*, you should make every effort to find the materials yourself.   **12.** While Jack was trying to sleep last night, a mosquito kept buzzing in his ear. *(no change)*   **13.** While Susan was climbing the mountain, she lost her footing and fell onto a ledge several feet below. *While climbing the mountain*, Susan lost her footing and fell onto a ledge several feet below.   **14.** The Wilsons have experienced many changes in their lifestyle since they adopted twins. The Wilsons have experienced many changes in their lifestyle *since adopting twins*.   **15.** After I heard Mary describe how cold it gets in Minnesota in the winter, I decided not to go there for my vacation in January. *After hearing Mary describe how cold it gets in Minnesota in the winter*, I decided not to go there for my vacation in January.

EXERCISE 3, p. 377.

ANSWERS: **2.** *Believing that no one loved him,* **the little boy** ran away from home.
3. *Not paying attention to where she was going,* **Rosa** stepped into a hole and sprained her ankle.   **4.** *Having forgotten to bring a pencil to the examination,* I had to borrow one.
5. *Being a vegetarian,* **Chelsea** does not eat meat.   **6.** *Having (already) flunked out of school once,* **Mike** is determined to succeed this time.

EXERCISE 4, p. 377.

ANSWERS: **1.** *Before talking to you,* **I** had never understood that formula.   **2.** *Not wanting to spend any more money this month,* **Larry** decided against going to a restaurant for dinner.   **3.** *After reading the chapter four times,* **I** finally understood the author's theory.
4. *Remembering that everyone makes mistakes,* **I** softened my view of his seemingly inexcusable error.   **5.** *Since completing his Bachelor's degree,* **he** has had three jobs, each one better than the last.   **6.** *While traveling across the United States,* **I** could not help being impressed by the great differences in terrain.   **7.** *Before gaining national fame,* **the union leader** had been an electrician in a small town.   **8.** *Enjoying the cool evening breeze and listening to the sounds of nature,* **we** lost track of time.   **9.** *Having never flown in an airplane before,* **the little girl** was surprised and a little frightened when her ears popped.   **10.** *Before becoming vice-president of marketing and sales,* **Peter McKay** worked as a sales representative.

EXERCISE 5, p. 378.

ANSWERS: **2.** *Hearing that Nadia was in the hospital,* **I** called her family to find out what was wrong.   **3.** *(no change)*   **4.** *Living a long distance from my work,* **I** have to commute daily by train.   **5.** *Living a long distance from her work,* **Heidi** has to commute daily by train.   **6.** *(no change)*   **7.** *Not wanting to inconvenience my friend by asking her to drive me to the airport,* **I** decided to take a taxi.   **8.** *Sitting on a large rock at the edge of a mountain stream,* **I** felt at peace with the world.   **9.** *Being a married man,* **I** have many responsibilities.   **10.** *Trying his best not to cry,* **the little boy** swallowed hard and began to speak.   **11.** *Keeping one hand on the steering wheel,* **Anna** opened a can of soda pop with her free hand.   **12.** *(no change)*   **13.** *Recognizing his face but having forgotten his name,* **I** just smiled and said, "Hi."   **14.** *(no change)*   **15.** *(Being) Convinced that she could never learn to play the piano,* **Anna** stopped taking lessons.

EXERCISE 6, p. 378.

ANSWERS: **1.** [+ G] Having sticky pads on their feet, flies can easily walk on the ceiling.
2. [+ J] Having worked with computers for many years, Ed has an excellent understanding of their limitations as well as their potential.   **3.** [+ I] (Having been) Born two months prematurely, Mary needed special care for the first few days of her life.   **4.** [+ D] Having done everything he could for the patient, the doctor left to attend other people.   **5.** [+ A] Having never eaten / Never having eaten Thai food before, Sally didn't know what to expect when she went to the Thai restaurant for dinner.   **6.** [+ H] Having no one to turn to for help, Sam was forced to work out the problem by himself.   **7.** [+ C] Being an endangered species, rhinos are protected by law from poachers who kill them solely for their horns.   **8.** [+ B] (Being) Able to crawl into very small spaces, mice can hide in almost any part of a house.   **9.** [+ E] Having done very well in her studies, Nancy expects to be hired by a top company after graduation.   **10.** [+ F] (Being) Extremely hard and nearly indestructible, diamonds are used extensively in industry to cut other hard minerals.

EXERCISE 7, p. 379.

ANSWERS: **3.** *(no change)*   **4.** *Because* **I** *was too young to understand death,* **my mother** gave me a simple explanation of where my grandfather had gone.   **5.** *(no change)*
6. *While* **I** *was working in my office late last night,* **someone** suddenly knocked loudly at my door and nearly scared me to death!   **7.** *After* **we** *(had) hurried to get everything ready for the picnic,* **it** began to rain just as we were leaving.   **8.** *While* **I** *was walking across the street at a busy intersection,* **a truck** nearly ran over my foot.

EXERCISE 8, p. 380.

The answers may use either *upon* or *on.*
ANSWERS: **2.** *Upon crossing the marathon finish line,* Tina fell in exhaustion.   **3.** *Upon looking in my wallet,* I discovered I didn't have enough money to pay my restaurant bill.
4. I bowed my head *upon meeting the king.*   **5.** *Upon re-reading the figures,* Sam found that he had made a mistake.   **6.** . . . *Upon discovering it was hot,* the small child jerked his hand back, ...   **7.** Mrs. Alexander nearly fainted *upon learning that she had won the lottery.*   **8.** *Upon finishing the examination,* bring your paper to the front of the room.
9. . . . *Upon hearing my name,* I raised my hand to identify myself.   **10.** . . . *Upon hearing this,* Cook grabbed his telescope and searched the horizon.

EXERCISE 9, p. 381.

ANSWERS: **5.** *Before leaving on my trip,* I checked to see what shots I would need.
6. *(no change)*   **7.** *Not having understood the directions,* I got lost.   **8.** My father relunctantly agreed to let me attend the game *after talking/having talked it over with my mother.*   **9.** *Upon discovering / Discovering I had lost my key to the apartment,* I called the building superintendent.   **10.** *(no change)*   **11.** Garcia Lopez de Cardenas accidentally discovered the Grand Canyon *while looking for the legendary Lost City of Gold.*   **12.** *(no change)*   **13.** *After having to wait for more than half an hour,* we were finally seated at the restaurant.   **14.** *Before getting accepted on her country's Olympic*

running team, Maria had spent most of the two previous years in training.   **15.** *Not paying* attention to his driving, George didn't see the large truck until it was almost too late.

EXERCISE 10, p. 382.

1. . . . <u>When Watson heard words coming from the machine</u>, he immediately realized that their experiments had at last been successful.
→ Hearing words coming from the machine, = *adverb phrase*

. . . <u>After Bell had successfully tested the new apparatus again and again</u>, he confidently announced his invention to the world.
→ After having / Having successfully tested the new apparatus again and again, = *adverb phrase*

. . . <u>Because they believed the telephone was a toy with little practical application</u>, most people paid little attention to Bell's announcement.
→ Believing the telephone was a toy with little practical application, = *adverb phrase*

2. . . . <u>Because many people believe that wolves eagerly kill human beings</u>, they fear them.
→ Believing that wolves eagerly kill human beings, = *adverb phrase*
. . . <u>Because they are strictly carniverous</u>, wolves hunt large animals. . . .
→ Being strictly carnivorous, = *adverb phrase*

. . <u>Because it was relentlessly poisoned, trapped, and shot by ranchers and hunters</u>, the timber wolf, ...
→ Having been / Being relentlessly poisoned, trapped, and shot by ranchers and hunters, = *adverb phrase*

. . . In the 1970s, <u>after they realized a mistake had been made</u>, U.S. lawmakers passed laws to protect wolves.
→ In the 1970s, after realizing / after having realized / having realized that a mistake had been made, = *adverb phrase*

. . . Today, <u>after they have been unremittingly destroyed for centuries</u>, they are found in few places, ...
→ Today, after having been / after being / having been unremittingly destroyed for centuries, = *adverb phrase*

EXERCISE 11, p. 383.

POSSIBLE COMPLETIONS: **1.** After having finished my work, I decided to take a long walk.   **2.** Before going to Canada, I had never seen snow.   **3.** Since coming to this school, I have met a lot of interesting people.   **4.** Sitting in the park the other day, Mustafa saw a squirrel with a red tail.   **5.** Having heard a strange noise in the other room, the babysitter called a neighbor to help him investigate.   **6.** Being new on the job, I felt very unsure of myself.   **7.** Being the largest city in the United States, New York is a favorite tourist destination.   **8.** Upon reaching our destination, we leapt out of the car and ran toward the lake.   **9.** Receiving no answer when he knocked on the door, the mail carrier took the registered package back to the post office.   **10.** Exhausted by the long hours of work, the medical student was too tired to eat his dinner and went straight to bed.

EXERCISE 12, p. 384.

2. Because our leader could not attend the meeting, ~~so~~ it was canceled.   OR   ~~Because~~ **O**ur leader could not attend the meeting, so it was canceled.   **3.** <u>My wife and I like</u> to travel.
4. I always fasten my seat belt before ~~to~~ <u>starting</u> the engine.   OR   I always fasten my seat belt before ~~to~~ <u>I</u> start the engine.   **5.** I don't like our classroom **b**ecause it is hot and crowded. I hope we can change to a different room.   OR   I don't like our classroom. It is

hot and crowded. I hope we can change to a different room.   **6.** Since / Because the day was very warm and humid, ~~for that~~ I turned on the air conditioner.   **7.** Upon ~~I~~ <u>learning</u> that my car couldn't be repaired for three days, I <u>was</u> very distressed.   **8.** <u>Because</u> I missed the final examination ~~because~~, the teacher gave me a failing grade.   OR   Having missed the final examination, I received a failing grade.   **9.** Both my sister and (my) brother <u>are</u> going to be at the family reunion.   **10.** I hope my son will remain/remains in school until he <u>finishes</u> his degree.   **11.** My brother has succeeded in business because ~~of~~ he works hard.   **12.** Luis stood up, turned toward me, and <u>spoke</u> so softly that I couldn't hear what he said.   **13.** I was lost. I could ~~not~~ find <u>neither</u> my parents <u>nor</u> my brother. **14.** <u>Since</u> she <u>had</u> studied Greek for several years, Sarah's pronunciation was easy to understand.

Chapter 19: CONNECTIVES THAT EXPRESS CAUSE AND EFFECT, CONTRAST, AND CONDITION

EXERCISE 1, p. 385.

1. Because ~~of~~ Rosa's computer skills were poor, she was not considered for the job.
2. Rosa's computer skills were poor. **T**herefore, she was not considered for the job.   [OR . . .poor; therefore, she . . .]   **3.** Because Rosa's computer skills were poor, ~~therefore~~ she was not considered for the job.   OR   ~~Because~~ Rosa's computer skills were poor. **T**herefore, she was not considered for the job.   [OR . . .poor; therefore, she . . .]
4. Because Rosa's computer skills were poor, ~~so~~ she was not considered for the job.   OR ~~Because~~ Rosa's computer skills were poor, so she was not considered for the job.
5. Due to her poor computer skills, Rosa was not considered for the job ~~therefore~~.
6. ~~Consequently~~ Rosa's computer skills were poor. **C**onsequently, she was not considered for the job.   OR   <u>Because</u> Rosa's computer skills were poor, she was not considered for the job.

EXERCISE 2, p. 386.

3. because   **4.** because of   **5.** Because of   **6.** Because   **7.** because of
8. because of

EXERCISE 3, p. 386.

ANSWERS: **2.** the heavy traffic   **3.** his wife's illness   **4.** Dr. Robinson's excellent research on wolves   **5.** the noise in the next apartment   **6.** circumstances beyond my control

EXERCISE 4, p. 387.

1. A storm was approaching. Therefore, the children stayed home.
  A storm was approaching. The children, therefore, stayed home.
  A storm was approaching. The children stayed home, therefore.
2. I didn't have my umbrella. Consequently, I got wet.
  I didn't have my umbrella. I, consequently, got wet.
  I didn't have my umbrella. I got wet, consequently.

EXERCISES 5 and 6, p. 388.

EX. 5 ANSWERS: **1.** Because it was cold, she wore a coat.   **2.** *(no change)*   **3.** Because of the cold weather, she wore a coat.   **4.** *(no change)*   **5.** The weather was cold. **T**herefore, she wore a coat.   **6.** The weather was cold. **S**he, therefore, wore a coat.   **7.** The weather was cold. **S**he wore a coat, therefore.   **8.** The weather was cold, so she wore a coat.

EX. 6 ANSWERS: **1.** Pat always enjoyed studying sciences in high school. **T**herefore, she decided to major in biology in college.   **2.** Due to recent improvements in the economy, fewer people are unemployed.   **3.** Last night's storm damaged the power lines. **C**onsequently, the town was without electicity for several hours.   **4.** Because of the snowstorm, only five students came to class. **T**he teacher, therefore, canceled the class.   **5.** *(no change)*

EXERCISE 7, p. 389.

PART I:
2. The weather was bad. <u>T</u>herefore, we postponed our trip.   OR   We, <u>therefore</u>, postponed our trip.   OR   We postponed our trip, <u>therefore</u>.

3. <u>Since</u> the weather was bad, we postponed our trip.   OR   We postponed our trip <u>since</u> the weather was bad.

4. The weather was bad, <u>so</u> we postponed our trip.

5. <u>Because of</u> the bad weather, we postponed our trip.   OR   We postponed our trip <u>because of</u> the bad weather.

6. The weather was bad. <u>Consequently</u>, we postponed our trip.   OR   We, <u>consequently</u>, postponed our trip.   OR   We postponed our trip, <u>consequently</u>.

7. <u>Due to the fact that</u> the weather was bad, we postponed our trip.   OR   We postponed our trip <u>due to the fact that</u> the weather was bad.

PART II:
1. <u>Because of</u> her illness, she missed class.   OR   She missed class <u>because of</u> her illness.

2. <u>Because</u> she was ill, she missed class.   OR   She missed class <u>because</u> she was ill.

3. She was ill. <u>Consequently</u>, she missed class.   OR   She, <u>consequently</u>, missed class. OR   She missed class, <u>consequently</u>.

4. She was ill, <u>so</u> she missed class.

5. <u>Due to the fact that</u> she was ill, she missed class.   OR   She missed class <u>due to the fact that</u> she was ill.

6. She was ill. <u>Therefore</u>, she missed class.   OR   She, <u>therefore</u>, missed class. OR She missed class, <u>therefore</u>.

EXERCISE 8, p. 390.

2. Emily has never wanted to return to the Yukon to live <u>because of</u> the severe winters.   OR <u>Because of</u> the severe winters, Emily has never wanted to return to the Yukon to live.
3. It is important to wear a hat on cold days <u>since</u> we lose sixty percent of our body heat through our head.   OR   <u>Since</u> we lose sixty percent of our body heat through our head, it is important to wear a hat on cold days.   **4.** When I was in my teens and twenties, it was easy for me to get into an argument with my father, <u>for</u> both of us can be stubborn and opinionated.   **5.** <u>Due to the fact that</u> a camel can go completely without water for eight to ten days, it is an ideal animal for desert areas.   OR   A camel is an ideal animal for desert areas <u>due to the fact that</u> it can go completely without water for eight to ten days.
6. Bill's car wouldn't start. **T**herefore, he couldn't pick us up after the concert.   OR   **H**e, <u>therefore</u>, couldn't pick us up after the concert.   OR   **H**e couldn't pick us up after the concert, <u>therefore</u>.   **7.** Robert did not pay close attention to what the travel agent said when he went to see her at her office last week, <u>so</u> he had to ask many of the same questions again the next time he talked to her.   **8.** A tomato is classified as a fruit, but most people consider it a vegetable <u>since</u> it is often eaten in salads along with lettuce, onions, cucumbers, and other vegetables.   OR   <u>Since</u> it is often eaten in salads along with lettuce, onions, cucumbers, and other vegetables, a tomato is classified as a fruit.   **9.** <u>Due to</u> consumer demand for ivory, many African elephants are being slaughtered ruthlessly. <u>Consequently</u>, many people who care about saving these animals from extinction refuse to buy any item

made from ivory.   OR   Many people who care about saving these animals from extinction, <u>consequently</u>, refuse to buy any item made from ivory.   OR   Many people who care about saving these animals from extinction refuse to buy any item made from ivory, <u>consequently</u>.
10. <u>Because</u> most 15th-century Europeans believed the world was flat and that a ship could conceivably sail off the end of the earth, many sailors of the time refused to venture forth with explorers into unknown waters.   OR   Many sailors of the 15th century refused to venture forth with explorers into unknown waters <u>because</u> most Europeans of the time believed the world was flat and that a ship could conceivably sail off the end of the earth.

EXERCISE 9, p. 391.

ANSWERS: **3.** It was <u>such</u> an expensive car <u>that</u> we couldn't afford to buy it.   **4.** The car was <u>so</u> expensive <u>that</u> we couldn't afford to buy it.   **5.** The weather was <u>so</u> hot <u>that</u> you could fry an egg on the sidewalk.   **6.** During the summer, we had <u>such</u> hot and humid weather <u>that</u> it was uncomfortable just sitting in a chair doing nothing.   **7.** We're having <u>such</u> beautiful weather <u>that</u> I don't feel like going to work.   **8.** Ivan takes everything in life <u>so</u> seriously <u>that</u> he is unable to experience the small joys and pleasures of daily living.   **9.** I've met <u>so</u> many people in the last few days <u>that</u> I can't possibly remember all of their names.   **10.** Tommy ate <u>so</u> much candy <u>that</u> he got a stomachache.
11. There was <u>so</u> little traffic <u>that</u> it took us only ten minutes to get there.   **12.** In some countries, <u>so</u> few students are accepted by the universities <u>that</u> admission is virtually a guarantee of a good job upon graduation.

EXERCISE 10, p. 392.

ANSWERS: **2.** [H] Karen is <u>such</u> a good pianist <u>that</u> I'm surprised she didn't go into music professionally.   **3.** [G] The radio was <u>so</u> loud <u>that</u> I couldn't hear what Michael was saying.   **4.** [J] Small animals in the forest move about <u>so</u> quickly <u>that</u> one can barely catch a glimpse of them.   **5.** [B] Olga did <u>such</u> poor work <u>that</u> she was fired from her job.   **6.** [A] The food was <u>so</u> hot <u>that</u> it burned my tongue.   **7.** [E] There are <u>so</u> many leaves on a single tree <u>that</u> it is impossible to count them.   **8.** [F] The tornado struck with <u>such</u> great force <u>that</u> it lifted automobiles off the ground.   **9.** [K] Grandpa held me <u>so</u> tightly when he hugged me <u>that</u> I couldn't breathe for a moment.   **10.** [D] <u>So</u> few students showed up for class <u>that</u> the teacher postponed the test.   **11.** [I] Sally used <u>so</u> much paper when she was writing her report <u>that</u> the wastepaper basket overflowed.

EXERCISE 13, p. 393.

ANSWERS: **5.** Please be quiet <u>so (that)</u> I can hear what Sharon is saying.   **6.** I asked the children to be quiet <u>so (that)</u> I could hear what Sharon was saying.   **7.** I'm going to cash a check <u>so (that)</u> I have / will have enough money to go to the market.   [AmE = *check; BrE = cheque*]   **8.** I cashed a check yesterday <u>so (that)</u> I would have enough money to go to the market.   **9.** Tonight Ann and Larry are going to hire a babysitter for their six-year-old child <u>so (that)</u> they can go out with some friends.   **10.** Last week, Ann and Larry hired a babysitter <u>so (that)</u> they could go to a dinner party at the home of Larry's boss.   **11.** Be sure to put the meat in the oven at 5:00 <u>so (that)</u> it will be/is ready to eat by 6:30.
12. Yesterday, I put the meat in the oven at 5:00 <u>so (that)</u> it would be ready to eat by 6:30.
13. I'm going to leave the party early <u>so (that)</u> I will be able to get a good night's sleep tonight.   **14.** When it started to rain, Harry opened his umbrella <u>so (that)</u> he wouldn't get wet.   **15.** The little boy pretended to be sick <u>so (that)</u> he could stay home from school.   **16.** A lot of people were standing in front of me. I stood on tiptoes <u>so (that)</u> I could see the parade better.

EXERCISE 14, p. 394.

ANSWERS: **2.** [+ F] I turned on the radio <u>so that</u> I could listen to the news.   **3.** [+ A] I need to buy some detergent <u>so that</u> I can wash my clothes.   **4.** [+ C] Roberto fixed the leak in the boat <u>so that</u> it wouldn't sink.   **5.** [+ I] Mr. Kwan is studying the history and government of Canada <u>so that</u> he can become a Canadian citizen.   **6.** [+ B] Mrs. Gow put on her reading glasses <u>so that</u> she could read the fine print at the bottom of the contract.   **7.** [+ H] Jane is taking a course in auto mechanics <u>so that</u> she can fix her own car.   **8.** [+ J] Omar is working hard to impress his supervisor <u>so that</u> he will be considered for a promotion at his company.   **9.** [+ E] Po is saving his money <u>so that</u> he can travel in Europe next summer.   **10.** [+ G] During the parade, Toshi lifted his daughter to his shoulder <u>so that</u> she could see the dancers in the street.

EXERCISE 15, p. 394.

POSSIBLE COMPLETIONS: **1.** . . . I can make out this check.   **2.** He needs to study diligently . . . .   **3.** . . . I wouldn't miss the news.   **4.** . . . he wouldn't be hit by the speeding bus.   **5.** Samir set his alarm clock . . . .   **6.** . . . I can see more of the countryside.   **7.** I went over to his house . . . .   **8.** Spiro works at two jobs . . . .   **9.** . . . she can get a better job.   **10.** They prepared lots of delicious food . . . .   **11.** . . . he could make a downpayment on a car.   **12.** Finish your chores early . . . .

EXERCISE 17, p. 395.

PART I ANSWERS: **4.** but   **5.** Nevertheless   **6.** Even though   **7.** even though   **8.** but   **9.** Nevertheless

PART II ANSWERS: **10.** However   **11.** yet   **12.** Although   **13.** yet   **14.** Although   **15.** However

EXERCISE 18, p. 396.

2. Anna's father gave her some good advice, but she didn't follow it.   **3.** Even though Anna's father gave her some good advice, she didn't follow it.   **4.** Anna's father gave her some good advice. **S**he did not follow it, however.   **5.** Thomas was thirsty. **I** offered him some water. **H**e refused it.   **6.** *(no change)*   **7.** Thomas was thirsty. **Nevertheless,** he refused the glass of water I brought him.   **8.** Thomas was thirsty, yet he refused to drink the water that I offered him.

EXERCISE 19, p. 397.

SAMPLE ANSWERS: [Not every possible variation is included.]
   1. We went for a walk even though it was raining.
   It was raining, but we went for a walk anyway.
   It was raining. Nevertheless, we went for a walk.
   We went for a walk in spite of the rain.
   We didn't go for a walk because it was raining.
   2. Although his grades were low, he was admitted to the university.
   His grades were low, yet he was still admitted to the university.
   His grades were low. Nonetheless, he was admitted to the university.
   Despite his low grades, he was admitted to the university.
   Because of his low grades, he wasn't admitted to the university.

EXERCISE 20, p. 397.

POSSIBLE COMPLETIONS: **1.** I had a cold, but <u>I went to class</u> anyway.   **2.** Even though I had a cold, <u>I felt I had to finish my work</u>.   **3.** Although I didn't study, <u>I did well on the test</u>.   **4.** I didn't study, but <u>I did well on the test</u> anyway.   **5.** I got an "A" on the test even though <u>I hadn't done any extra studying</u>.　　**6.** Even though Howard is a careful driver, <u>he had an accident</u>.　　**7.** Even though the food they served for dinner tasted terrible, <u>I finished my plate because I didn't want to hurt my hosts' feelings</u>.　　**8.** My shirt still has coffee stains on it even though <u>I have washed it twice</u>.　　**9.** I still trust him even though <u>he lied to me</u>.　　**10.** Even though he was drowning, <u>no one tried to save him</u>. **11.** Although I tried to be very careful, <u>I spilled the coffee because my cup was too full</u>. **12.** Even though Ruth is one of my best friends, <u>I didn't tell her about my plans to elope with my boyfriend</u>.　　**13.** It's still hot in here <u>even though I opened a window</u>. **14.** Even though I had a big breakfast, <u>I was hungry by eleven o'clock</u>.

EXERCISE 21, p. 398.

SAMPLE SENTENCES:
2. I like living in a dorm in spite of / despite the noise.　OR　I like living in a dorm despite the fact that / in spite of the fact that it is noisy.　　**3.** In spite of / Despite the hard work, they enjoyed themselves.　OR　In spite of the fact that / Despite the fact that the work was hard, they enjoyed themselves.　　**4.** They wanted to climb the mountain in spite of / despite the danger.　OR　They wanted to climb the mountain in spite of the fact that / despite the fact that it was dangerous.　　**5.** In spite of / Despite the extremely hot weather, they went jogging in the park.　OR　In spite of the fact that / Despite the fact that the weather was extremely hot, they went jogging in the park.　　**6.** He is unhappy in spite of / despite his vast fortune.　OR　He is unhappy in spite of the fact that / despite the fact that he has a vast fortune.

EXERCISE 22, p. 398.

POSSIBLE COMPLETIONS:　**1.** I didn't particularly want to see that play, but I went anyway. **2.** He is very old, yet he still plays tennis at 6 o'clock every morning.　　**3.** The plane took off 20 minutes late. **N**evertheless, we arrived on schedule.　　**4.** Even though she wanted a new bike for her birthday, the little girl was happy to get a new doll.　　**5.** I wanted to go somewhere exotic for my vacation. **H**owever, I had to go back home because it was my mother's 60th birthday.　　**6.** The teacher dismissed the class when they had completed the test even though the hour wasn't over.　　**7.** Although my daughter is only three years old, she knows all the words to the "Alphabet Song."　　**8.** She never went to school. **H**owever, she has done very well in her job despite her lack of education.　　**9.** Despite the fact that my sister was visiting, I went to bed early.　　**10.** I have decided to go to Thailand even though I can't speak a word of Thai.

EXERCISE 23, p. 399.

1. Florida has a warm climate. *However,* Alaska has a cold climate.　OR　Florida has a warm climate. Alaska, *on the other hand,* has a cold climate.　　**2.** Fred is a good student. His brother, *however,* is lazy.　OR　Fred is a good student. His brother, *on the other hand,* is lazy.　　**3.** In the United States, gambling casinos are not legal in most places. *However,* in my country it is possible to gamble in any city or town.　OR　In the United States, gambling casinos are not legal in most places. In my country, *on the other hand,* it is possible to gamble in any city or town.　　**4.** Sue and Ron are expecting a child. Sue is hoping for a boy. *However,* Ron is hoping for a girl.　OR　Sue is hoping for a boy. Ron, *on the other hand,* is hoping for a girl.　　**5.** Old people in my country usually live with their children. *However,* the old in the United States often live by themselves.　OR　The old in the United States, *on the other hand,* often live by themselves.

EXERCISE 24, p. 399.

POSSIBLE COMPLETIONS:　**2.** the United Kingdom drive on the left-hand side.　　**3.** sister's apartment is always neat.　　**4.** makes friends easily and is very popular.　　**5.** know about only house pets. **6.** is easy to cut and shape. **7.** is very outgoing. **8.** some people are ambidextrous, which means that they can use either hand equally well.

EXERCISE 26, p. 400.

ANSWERS: **2.** because **3.** despite the fact that / even though / although **4.** because of **5.** now that **6.** , however, **7.** . However, OR , but **8.** . Therefore, **9.** , however, **10.** , but [also possible: *although/whereas*] **11.** although / even though / despite the fact that

EXERCISE 27, p. 401.

POSSIBLE SENTENCES: **2.** You should / had better / have to / must leave now. Otherwise, you'll be late for class. **3.** You should / had better / have to / must go to bed. Otherwise, your cold will get worse. **4.** You should / had better / have to / must have a ticket. Otherwise, you can't get into the theater. **5.** You should / had better/ have to / must have a passport. Otherwise, you can't enter that country. **6.** Tom should / had better / has to / must get a job soon. Otherwise, his family won't have enough money for food. **7.** You should / had better / have to / must speak both Japanese and Chinese fluently. Otherwise, you will not be considered for that job. **8.** Mary should / had better / has to / must get a scholarship. Otherwise, she cannot go to school. **9.** I am going to / should / had better / have to / must wash my clothes tonight. Otherwise, I won't have any clean clothes to wear tomorrow.

EXERCISE 28, p. 402.

POSSIBLE COMPLETIONS: **1.** I am going to finish this report even if it takes me all night. **2.** We have no choice. We have to go by train whether we want to or not. **3.** I will go to the concert with you only if you will come to the basketball game with me next week. **4.** Eric is very inconsiderate. He plays his CD player even if his roommate is trying to sleep. **5.** I can't hang this picture unless you tell me if it's level. **6.** Tomorrow I'd better get to the store. Otherwise, we will run out of food. **7.** You should take your umbrella in case it rains. **8.** I will help you move your piano only if no one else is available. **9.** I will be happy to attend your party unless you have also invited my ex-wife. **10.** You must take all your final exams. Otherwise, you can't graduate.

EXERCISES 29 and 30, pp. 402–403.

EX. 29 POSSIBLE COMPLETIONS:
2. I failed the exam because I did not study. **3.** Although I studied, I did not pass the exam. **4.** I did not study. Therefore, I failed the exam. **5.** I did not study. However, I passed the exam. **6.** I studied. Nevertheless, I failed the exam. **7.** Even though I did not study, I (still) passed the exam. **8.** I did not study, so I did not pass the exam. **9.** Since I did not study, I did not pass the exam. **10.** If I study for the test, I should pass it. **11.** Unless I study for the test, I am sure to fail it. **12.** I must study. Otherwise, I will surely fail the exam. **13.** Even if I study, I may still fail. **14.** I did not study. Consequently, I failed the exam. **15.** I did not study. Nonetheless, I passed the exam. **16.** I will probably fail the test whether I study or not. **17.** I failed the exam, for I did not study. **18.** I have to study so that I won't fail the exam. **19.** Only if I study will I pass the exam. **20.** I studied hard, yet I still failed the exam. **21.** You'd better study, or else you will fail the exam.

EX. 30 EXPECTED COMPLETIONS:
1. Because I was not hungry this morning, I did not eat breakfast. **2.** Because I ate breakfast this morning, I'm not hungry now. **3.** Because I was hungry this morning, I ate a large breakfast. **4.** I did not eat breakfast this morning even though I was hungry.

5. Although I was hungry this morning, I didn't have time to eat breakfast. **6.** I was hungry this morning. **T**herefore, I ate breakfast. **7.** I was hungry this morning. **N**evertheless, I didn't eat breakfast. **8.** I was so hungry this morning that I ate a large breakfast. **9.** I was not hungry this morning, but I ate breakfast anyway. **10.** I ate breakfast this morning even though I wasn't hungry. **11.** Since I did not eat breakfast this morning, I am hungry now. **12.** I ate breakfast this morning. **N**onetheless, I am hungry. **13.** I was not hungry, so I didn't eat breakfast. **14.** Even though I did not eat breakfast this morning, I'm not hungry now. **15.** I never eat breakfast unless I'm hungry. **16.** I always eat breakfast whether or not I'm hungry. **17.** I eat breakfast even if I'm not hungry. **18.** Now that I have eaten breakfast, I'm not hungry. **19.** I eat breakfast only if I'm hungry. **20.** I ate breakfast this morning, yet I'm hungry now. **21.** Even if I am hungry, I don't eat breakfast. **22.** I was not hungry. **H**owever, I ate breakfast this morning.

EXERCISE 32, p. 404.

POSSIBLE COMPLETIONS:

1. While some people are optimists, others are pessimists. **2.** Even though he drank a glass of water, he was still thirsty. **3.** Even if she invites me to her party, I will not go. **4.** I have never been to Hawaii. **M**y parents, however, have visited there twice. **5.** I couldn't open the car door, for my arms were full of packages. **6.** I need to borrow some money so that I can pay my rent on time. **7.** The airport was closed due to fog. **T**herefore, our plane's departure was postponed. **8.** The landing field was fogged in. **T**herefore, the airport was closed. **9.** As soon as the violinist played the last note at the concert, the audience burst into applause. **10.** Since neither my roommate nor I know how to cook, we took our visiting parents out to dinner. **11.** I am not a superstitious person. **N**evertheless, I don't walk under ladders. A paint can might fall on my head. **12.** The crops will fail unless we get some rain soon. **13.** Just as I was getting ready to eat dinner last night, the phone rang. **14.** We must work quickly. **O**therwise, we won't finish before dark. **15.** Some children are noisy and wild. **M**y brother's children, on the other hand, are very quiet and obedient. **16.** According to the newspaper, now that hurricane season has arrived, we can expect bad weather at any time. **17.** Ever since I can remember, my niece Melissa has been called "Missie" by her family. **18.** Although my grades were high, I didn't get the scholarship. **19.** The United States has no national health care, whereas Great Britain has socialized medicine. **20.** I was tired. **H**owever, I felt I had to stay awake because I was babysitting. OR I was tired; however, I felt I had to stay awake because I was babysitting. **21.** You must pay an income tax whether or not you agree with how the government spends it. **22.** I was listening hard. **N**evertheless, I could not understand what the person who was speaking was saying because she was standing too far from the microphone.

EXERCISE 33, p. 405.

1. Unless I study very hard, I will <u>not</u> pass all of my exams. **2.** My shoes and pants got <u>muddy even</u> though I walked carefully through the wet streets. **3.** My neighborhood is quiet and safe. **H**owever, I always lock my doors. **4.** Although I usually don't like Mexican food, ~~but~~ I liked the food I had at the Mexican restaurant last night. OR ~~Although~~ I usually don't like Mexican food, but I liked the food I had at the Mexican restaurant last night. **5.** Although my room in the dormitory is very small, ~~but~~ I like it **b**ecause it is a place where I can be by myself and <u>study</u> in peace and quiet. OR ~~Although~~ **M**y room in the dormitory is very small, but I like it **b**ecause it is a place where I can be by myself and <u>study</u> in peace and quiet. **6.** <u>Even though</u> I prefer to be a history teacher, I am studying in the Business School in order ~~for I can~~ <u>to</u> get a job in industry. OR Despite <u>the fact that I prefer</u> to be a history teacher, I am studying in the Business School in order for I can to get a job in industry.   7. A little girl approached the cage. **H**owever, when the tiger showed its teeth and growled, she ran to her mother **b**ecause she was frightened. **8.** Many of the people (who are) working to save our environment think that they are fighting a losing battle **b**ecause big business and the government have not joined together to eliminate pollution.   9. The weather was so cold that I didn't like to leave my apartment.   OR   The weather is so cold that I don't like to leave my apartment.   **10.** I have to study four hours every day because of my courses are difficult / because of my difficult courses are / because of the difficulty of my courses.   **11.** On the third day of our voyage, we sailed across a rough sea before to reaching the shore.   **12.** I can't understand the lectures in my psychology class. **T**herefore, my roommate lets me borrow her notes.   **13.** According to this legend, a man went in search of a hidden village. **H**e finally found it after walking two hundred miles.   **14.** Because my country it is located in a subtropical area, so the weather is hot.   OR   My country it is located in a subtropical area, so the weather is hot.   **15.** I will stay in the **U**nited **S**tates for two more years **b**ecause I want to finish my degree before going / I go home.

EXERCISE 35, p. 407.

2. Although a computer has tremendous power and speed, it cannot think for itself. **A** human operator is needed to give a computer instructions, for it cannot initially tell itself what to do.   **3.** Being a lawyer in private practice, I work hard, but I do not go into my office on either Saturday or Sunday. **I**f clients insist upon seeing me on those days, they have to come to my home.   **4.** Whenever the weather is nice, I walk to school, but when it is cold or wet, I either take the bus or get a ride with one of my friends. **E**ven though my brother has a car, I never ask him to take me to school because he is very busy. **H**e has a new job and has recently gotten married, so he doesn't have time to drive me to and from school anymore. **I** know he would give me a ride if I asked him to, but I don't want to bother him.   **5.** The common cold, which is the most widespread of all diseases, continues to plague humanity despite the efforts of scientists to find its prevention and cure. **E**ven though colds are minor illnesses, they are one of the principal causes of absence from school and work. **P**eople of all ages get colds, but children and adults who live with children get them the most. **C**olds can be dangerous for elderly people because they can lead to other infections. **I** have had three colds so far this year. **I** eat the right kinds of food, get enough rest, and exercise regularly. **N**evertheless, I still get at least one cold a year.   **6.** Whenever my father goes fishing, we know we will have fish to eat for dinner, for even if he doesn't catch any, he stops at the fish market on his way home and buys some.

EXERCISE 36, p. 408.

EXPECTED ANSWERS:
2. If you really mean what you say, I'll give you one more chance, but you have to give me your best effort. Otherwise, you'll lose your job.   **3.** Due to the bad weather, I'm going to stay home. Even if the weather changes, I don't want to go to the picnic.   **4.** Even though the children had eaten lunch, they got hungry in the middle of the afternoon. Therefore, I took them to the market so that they could get some fruit for a snack before we went home for dinner.   **5.** Whereas Robert is totally exhausted after playing tennis, Marge isn't even tired in spite of the fact that she ran around a lot more during the game. **6.** While many animals are most vulnerable to predators when they are grazing, giraffes are most vulnerable when they are drinking. **T**hey must spread their legs awkwardly in order to lower their long necks to the water in front of them. Consequently, it is difficult and time-consuming for them to stand up straight again to escape a predator. However, once they are up and running, they are faster than most of their predators.   **7.** Even though my boss promised me that I could have two full weeks, it seems that I can't take my vacation

after all <u>because</u> I have to train the new personnel this summer. <u>If</u> I do not get a vacation in the fall either, I will be angry.   **8.** <u>Since</u> education, business, and government are all dependent on computers, it is advisable for all students to have basic computer skills <u>before</u> they graduate from high school and enter the work force or college. <u>Therefore</u>, a course called "Computer Literacy" has recently become a requirement for graduation from Westside High School. <u>If</u> you want more information about this course, you can call the academic counselor at the high school.

EXERCISE 37, p. 409.

POSSIBLE COMPLETIONS:

1. I woke up this morning with a sore throat. Nevertheless, I went to work because I had to finish an important report.   **2.** I love cats. My sister, on the other hand, prefers dogs.
3. When a small, black insect landed on my arm, I screamed because it had startled me.
4. I don't eat desserts because I'm watching my weight. However, I had a piece of chocolate cake last night because it was my sister's birthday.   **5.** Even though I told my supervisor I would finish the report by tomorrow, I really need another day to do a good job.   **6.** According to the newspaper, now that the speed limit has been raised, there will be more traffic accidents. Therefore, people will have to drive more carefully than ever before.   **7.** Since neither the man who gave me the information nor the manager was in, I said I would call back another time.   **8.** When people who are critical find fault with others, they should try to be more patient because no one is perfect.   **9.** Since I didn't know whose sweater I had found, I took it to the "Lost and Found" department.
10. Even though the book which I was reading was overdue, I kept it until I had finished reading it. [*overdue* = past the deadline for returning it to a library]   **11.** What did the woman who came to the door say when you told her you weren't interested in her political views?
12. If what he said is true, we can expect more rain soon.   **13.** Because the man who donated his art collection to the museum wishes to remain anonymous, his name will not be mentioned in the museum guide.   **14.** Even though she didn't understand what the man who stopped her on the street wanted, she tried to be helpful.   **15.** Now that all of the students who plan to take the trip have signed up, we can reserve the hotel rooms.
16. Since the restaurant where we first met has burned down, we will have to celebrate our anniversary somewhere else.

EXERCISE 38, p. 410.

POSSIBLE ANSWERS:

1. We went shopping after <u>we</u> ate / after eating dinner, **b**ut the stores were closed.   OR
. . . **B**ut the stores were closed. We had to go back home even <u>though</u> we hadn't found what <u>we were</u> looking for.   **2.** I want <u>to</u> explain that I know <u>a lot</u> of gramm**ar**, but <u>my problem is that I don't know</u> enough <u>vocabulary</u>.   **3.** When I got lost in the bus station, a kind man helped me. **H**e explained how to read the huge bus schedule on the wall, **t**ook me to the window to buy a ticket, and showed me <u>where my bus was</u>. **I** will always appreciate his kindness.   **4.** I had never <u>understood</u> the <u>importance</u> of <u>knowing</u> English ~~language~~ **u**ntil I worked at a large, international company.   **5.** <u>When</u> I was young, my father found an American woman to teach <u>my brothers and me</u> English, but when we <u>moved</u> to <u>another</u> town, my father wasn't able to find <u>another</u> teacher for <u>another</u> five years.
6. I was surprised to see the room that I was given at/in the dormitory **b**ecause there <u>wasn't</u> any furniture and <u>it was</u> dirty.   **7.** When I <u>met</u> Mr. Lee for the first time, we played ping pong at the student center. **E**ven though we <u>couldn't</u> communicate very well, ~~but~~ we had a good time.   **8.** Because the United States is a large ~~and also big~~ country, ~~it means that they're various kinds live there and~~ it has a diverse population.   **9.** My grammar class ~~was~~ <u>started</u> at 10:35. When the teacher <u>came</u> to class, she returned the last

quiz to my classmates and <u>me</u>. After <u>that,</u> we ~~have~~ had another quiz.   **10.** If a wife has ~~a~~ <u>to</u> work, her husband should share the <u>housework</u> with her. If both of them help, the <u>housework</u> can be <u>finished</u> much faster.   **11.** The first time I went skiing**,** I was afraid to go down the hill**,** **b**ut somewhere ~~from~~ a little ~~corner~~ of voice in my head kept shouting, "Why not? Give it a try. You'll make it!" After <u>standing</u> around for ten minutes without moving**,** <u>I finally decided to</u> go down that hill.   **12.** *Possible revision:* This is a story about a man <u>who</u> had a big garden. One day he was sleeping in his garden. <u>When</u> he woke up**,** **h**e ate some fruit, ~~Then he~~ picked some apples**,** and ~~he~~ walked to a small river ~~and~~ <u>where</u> he saw a beautiful woman ~~was~~ on the other side. ~~And~~ **H**e gave her some apples, and ~~then~~ she gave him a loaf of bread. The two of them walked back to the garden. ~~Then~~ **S**ome children came and ~~were~~ <u>played</u> games with him. Everyone was laughing and smiling. <u>But when</u> one child destroyed a flower, ~~and~~ the man became angry and ~~he~~ said to them, "Get out of here**!**" <u>So</u> the children ~~left~~ and the beautiful woman left. Then the man built a wall around his garden and would not let anyone in. He stayed in his garden all alone for the rest of his life.

Chapter 20: CONDITIONAL SENTENCES AND WISHES

EXERCISE 1, p. 412.

ANSWERS: **2.** a. no b. yes c. no   **3.** a. yes b. no c. yes   **4.** a. no b. yes
5. a. yes b. no c. no   **6.** a. no b. yes   **7.** a. yes b. no   **8.** a. no b. no
c. yes

EXERCISE 2, p. 413.

ANSWERS: **2.** have . . . will write   **3.** had . . . would write   **4.** had . . . would
write   **5.** had had . . . would have written

EXERCISE 4, p. 415.

ANSWERS: **2.** would bake   **3.** have   **4.** had   **5.** is   **6.** were   **7.** would not
be . . . were   **8.** floats / will float   **9.** were . . . would not exist   **10.** does not
arrive   **11.** were . . . would not want   **12.** would human beings live . . . were
13. disappears / will disappear   **14.** had . . . would have to . . . would not be

EXERCISE 6, p. 417.

If there **were** only one village on earth and (if) it **had** exactly 100 people, 51 of them **would be** women and 49 of them **would be** men.

More than half of the people in the village (57 of them) **would be** from Asia, the Middle East, and the South Pacific. Twenty-one of them **would be** from Europe, 14 from the Western Hemisphere, and 8 from Africa.

Half the people in the village **would suffer** from malnutrition.

Thirty of the villagers **would be** illiterate. Of those 30, 18 **would be** women and 12 **would be** men.

Only one person in the village of 100 people **would have** a college education.

Six of the villagers **would own** half of the village's wealth. The other half of the wealth **would be shared** among the remaining 94 villagers.

Thirty-three of the people **would be** below 15 years of age, while 10 **would be** over 65.

EXERCISE 7, p. 418.

ANSWERS: **1.** have   **2.** had   **3.** had had   **4.** will go   **5.** would go   **6.** would
have gone   **7.** is   **8.** were . . . would visit   **9.** had been . . . would have visited

10. had realized . . . would not have made   11. had read . . . would not have washed
12. B: would/could have come . . . washed . . . had told   A: would have come . . . had called

EXERCISE 8, p. 419.

ANSWERS: **1.** But if I had known (that my friend was in the hospital), I would have visited her.   **2.** But if I had known (that you'd never met my friend), I would have introduced you.   **3.** But if I had known (that there was a meeting last night), I would have gone.
4. But if I had known (that my friend's parents were in town), I would have invited them to dinner.   **5.** But if I had known (that you wanted to go to the soccer game), I would have bought a ticket for you.   **6.** But if I had known (that you were at home last night), I would have visited you.   **7.** But if I had known (that my sister wanted a gold necklace for her birthday), I would have bought her one.   **8.** But if I had known (that you had a problem), I would have offered to help.

EXERCISE 9, p. 420.

ANSWERS: **2.** But if there were a screen on the window, there wouldn't be so many bugs in the room.   **3.** But if I had had enough money, I would have bought a bicycle.   **4.** But if I did have enough money, I would buy a bicycle.   **5.** But if you had listened to me, you wouldn't have gotten into so much trouble.   **6.** But if she had not received immediate medical attention, she would have died.   **7.** But if she had passed the entrance examination, she would have been admitted to the university.   **8.** But if we had stopped at the service station, we wouldn't have run out of gas.

EXERCISE 10, p. 420.

POSSIBLE COMPLETIONS: **1.** If I had been absent from class yesterday, I would have missed a quiz.   **2.** If I had enough energy today, I would go jogging in the park.   **3.** If ocean water weren't salty, we could drink it.   **4.** If our teacher didn't like his/her job, he/she would change professions.   **5.** If people had wings, we wouldn't have to rely on cars or airplanes for transportation.   **6.** If you had asked for my opinion, I would have given it to you.   **7.** If water weren't heavier than air, the earth as we know it couldn't exist.
8. If most nations didn't support world trade agreements, international trade would be impossible.

EXERCISE 11, p. 421.

ANSWERS: **1.** were . . . would tell   **2.** had had . . . would have taken   **3.** have . . . will give   **4.** had . . . wouldn't have to   **5.** had been . . . wouldn't have bitten
6. would we use . . . didn't have   **7.** doesn't rain . . . will die . . . die . . . will go
8. had not collided . . . would not have become . . . would be . . . still existed . . . would be

EXERCISE 13, p. 422.

ANSWERS: **4.** did   **5.** weren't   **6.** had   **7.** were   **8.** didn't   **9.** had
10. didn't   **11.** weren't   **12.** hadn't

EXERCISE 15, p. 423.

ANSWERS: **2.** But if she were here, the child wouldn't be crying.   **3.** But if you had been listening, you would have understood the directions.   **4.** But if he hadn't been driving too fast, he wouldn't have gotten a ticket.   **5.** But if I hadn't been listening to the radio, I wouldn't have heard the news bulletin.   **6.** But if it weren't broken, Grandpa would be wearing it.   **7.** But if you hadn't been sleeping, I would have told you the news as soon as I heard it.   **8.** But if I weren't enjoying myself, I would leave.

EXERCISE 16, p. 424.

ANSWERS: **2.** But if you hadn't left the door open, the room wouldn't be full of flies. **3.** But if you had gone to bed at a reasonable hour last night, you wouldn't be tired this morning. **4.** But if I had finished my report yesterday, I could begin a new project today. **5.** But if she had followed the doctor's orders, she wouldn't be sick today. **6.** But if I were you, I would have told him the truth. **7.** But if I knew something about plumbing, I could/would fix the leak in the sink myself. **8.** But if I hadn't received a good job offer from the oil company, I would seriously consider taking the job with the electronics firm.

EXERCISE 17, p. 425.

ANSWERS: **2.** Were I you, I wouldn't do that. **3.** Had they realized the danger, they would have done it differently. **4.** Were I your teacher, I would insist (that) you do better work. **5.** Should you change your mind, please let me know immediately. **6.** She would have gotten the job had she been better prepared. **7.** Were I you, I would look for another job. **8.** Should you need to reach me, I'll be at the Hilton Hotel in Seoul. **9.** Had they not dared to be different, the history of civilization would have to be rewritten. **10.** Should there be a global nuclear war, life on earth as we know it would end forever.

EXERCISE 18, p. 425.

ANSWERS: **3.** I would have answered the phone *if I had heard it ring.* **4.** I couldn't have finished the work *if you hadn't helped.* **5.** I would have gone to Nepal last summer *if I had had enough money.* **6.** *If I had not stepped on the brakes,* I would have hit the child on the bicycle. **7.** *If Olga had not turned down the volume on the tape player,* the neighbors probably would have called to complain about the noise. **8.** Tarek would have finished his education *if he had not had to quit school and find a job.*

EXERCISE 20, p. 426.

ANSWERS: **1.** would/could spend **2.** would/could have sent **3.** is completed **4.** weren't snowing **5.** would have gone **6.** would be **7.** were . . . would be **8.** had not been sleeping **9.** would forget . . . were not **10.** did not outnumber . . . could not eat **11.** A: were not B: would be sleeping **12.** were . . . would not be **13.** would not be . . . had **14.** would have been **15.** would not ride **16.** would not have come . . . had known **17.** will tell

EXERCISE 21, p. 427.

SAMPLE COMPLETIONS: **1.** If it hadn't rained yesterday, we would have had our barbecue outdoors. **2.** If it weren't raining, we would be going to the park today. **3.** You would have passed the test had you studied for it. **4.** Otherwise, we would have missed the turn. **5.** Without electricity, modern life would be very different. **6.** If you hadn't reminded me about the meeting tonight, I would have forgotten about it. **7.** Should you need any help, please ask me for assistance. **8.** If I could choose any profession I wanted, I would be a marine biologist. **9.** If I were at home right now, I would be taking a nap. **10.** Without your help yesterday, I could not have finished painting the kitchen. **11.** Were I you, I would finish my degree before returning home. **12.** What would you do if you had a chance to go to the moon? **13.** If I had the chance to live my childhood over again, I would keep a diary. **14.** Had I known the test would be so easy, I would not have stayed up late studying for it. **15.** Can you imagine what life would be like if humans had never invented the wheel?

EXERCISE 25, p. 430.

ANSWERS: **2.** as if/as though it were her native tongue. **3.** as if/as though you'd seen a ghost. **4.** as if/as though they were people. **5.** as if/as though he were a general in the army. **6.** as if/as though I had climbed Mt. Everest. **7.** as if/as though he didn't have a brain in his head. **8.** as if/as though we had known each other all of our lives. **9.** as if/as though a giant bulldozer had driven down Main Street. **10.** as if/as though I had wings and could fly. **11.** as if/as though he would burst. **12.** would . . . would . . . would . . . would

EXERCISE 26, p. 432.

ANSWERS: **2.** were shining **3.** had gone **4.** knew **5.** had told **6.** were wearing **7.** had **8.** had gone **9.** could **10.** would lend **11.** were coming **12.** weren't going to give **13.** could meet **14.** had come **15.** were lying

EXERCISE 28, p. 433.

6. had **7.** could **8.** did **9.** had **10.** could **11.** would **12.** were **13.** had **14.** did **15.** were

EXERCISE 29, p. 434.

ANSWERS: **1.** Rita wishes (that) it would stop raining. Yoko also wishes it would stop raining. **2.** Anna wishes Yoko would come to the concert. Anna wishes Yoko would change her mind. **3.** Bob's mother wishes he would shave off his beard. Bob probably wishes his mother wouldn't try to tell him what to do. **4.** Helen wishes Judy would pick up after herself, wash her dirty dishes, pick up her clothes and other stuff, and make her bed. Judy probably wishes Helen wouldn't nag her to pick up after herself.

EXERCISE 30, p. 435.

ANSWERS: **1.** were . . . were **2.** had come . . . had come . . . would have had **3.** weren't . . . were not . . . could/would go **4.** had paid **5.** had **6.** would turn **7.** A: were lying B: were **8.** A: didn't have B: were **9.** had **10.** had not gone **11.** would tell **12.** A: were wearing B: had known

Appendix: SUPPLEMENTARY GRAMMAR UNITS

EXERCISE 1, p. A2.

2. The <u>mechanic</u> (S) <u>repaired</u> (V) the <u>engine</u> (O). **3.** Those <u>boxes</u> (S) <u>contain</u> (V) old <u>photographs</u> (O). **4.** The <u>teacher</u> (S) <u>canceled</u> (V) the <u>test</u> (O). **5.** An <u>earthquake</u> (S) <u>destroyed</u> (V) the <u>village</u> (O). **6.** All <u>birds</u> (S) <u>have</u> (V) <u>feathers</u> (O).

List of nouns: *politician, taxes, mechanic, engine, boxes, photographs, teacher, test, earthquake, village, birds, feathers.*

EXERCISE 2, p. A2.

ANSWERS: **3.** divided = VT **4.** sneezed = VI **5.** happened = VI **6.** bought = VT **7.** won = VT **8.** won = VI **9.** disappeared = VI; shone = VI **10.** boiled = VT; made = VT; drank = VT

EXERCISE 3, p. A3.

                                       P   O of P

2. The waiter cleared the dirty dishes <u>from our table</u>.

               P   O of P

3. I parked the car <u>in the garage</u>.

               P   O of P

4. Trees fell <u>during the violent storm</u>.

                   P O of P   P   O of P

5. Cowboys depended <u>on horses</u>   <u>for transportation</u>.

              P   O of P   P   O of P

6. We walked <u>to the park</u>   <u>after class</u>.

EXERCISE 4, p. A3.

          S   VT   O   PP

3. <u>Sally</u> <u>wore</u> her blue <u>suit</u> <u>to the meeting</u>.

           S   VT   O

4. <u>Beethoven</u> <u>wrote</u> nine <u>symphonies</u>.

          S   VI   PP

5. <u>Bells</u> <u>originated</u> <u>in Asia</u>.

          S   VT   O   PP

6. <u>Plants</u> <u>need</u> a reliable <u>supply</u> <u>of water</u>.

          S   VT   O   PP   PP   PP

7. <u>We</u> <u>enjoyed</u> the <u>view</u> <u>of snowy mountains</u> <u>from the window</u> <u>of our hotel room</u>.

            S VT   PP   PP   PP   S

8. The <u>child</u> <u>sat</u> <u>between her parents</u> <u>on the sandy beach</u>. <u>Above her</u>, an <u>eagle</u>

   VI   PP

<u>flew</u> <u>across the cloudless sky</u>.

EXERCISE 5, p. A5.

       ADJ   ADV   ADJ

2. A <u>small</u> child cried <u>noisily</u> in the <u>third</u> row of the theater.

       ADJ   ADV

3. The <u>eager</u> player waited <u>impatiently</u> for the start of the game.

        ADV   ADJ

4. An <u>unusually</u> <u>large</u> crowd came to the concert.

        ADV   ADJ   ADJ

5. Arthur <u>carefully</u> repaired the <u>antique</u> vase with <u>special</u> glue.

        ADV   ADJ   ADJ   ADV

6. On <u>especially</u> <u>busy</u> days, the telephone in the <u>main</u> office rings <u>constantly</u>.

Nouns: *fire, house, child, row, theater, player, start, game, crowd, concert, Arthur, vase, glue, days, telephone, office.*

Total nouns = 16

Verbs: *spread, cried, waited, came, repaired, rings.*

Total verbs = 6

EXERCISE 6, p. A5.

ANSWERS: **1.** careless . . . carelessly **2.** easy . . . easily **3.** softly . . . soft

4. quietly **5.** well . . . good

EXERCISE 7, p. A5.

[Verbs and adverbs are <u>underlined</u>.]   **2.** Ted <u>often studies</u> at the library in the evening.
3. Ann <u>is often</u> at the library in the evening, too.   **4.** Fred <u>has already finished</u> studying for tomorrow's test.   **5.** Jack <u>is seldom</u> at home.   **6.** <u>Does he always stay</u> there?
7. He <u>often goes</u> into town to hang around with his buddies.   **8.** You <u>should always tell</u> the truth.

EXERCISE 8, p. A6.

ANSWERS: **1.** easy . . . easily   **2.** comfortable   **3.** carefully   **4.** sad
5. cheerfully . . . cheerful   **6.** carefully . . . good   **7.** quiet . . . quietly   **8.** dark

EXERCISE 9, p. A7.

2. Whales = *noun*
mammals = *noun*
breathe = *verb*
air = *noun*
3. dive = *verb*
deeply = *adverb*
beneath = *preposition*
surface = *noun*
under = *preposition*
water = *noun*
for = *preposition*
4. migrations = *noun*
among = *preposition*
swim = *verb*
from = *preposition*
to = *preposition*
icy = *adjective*

5. highly = *adverb*
trainable = *adjective*
intelligent = *adjective*
sensitive = *adjective*
refused = *verb*
Finally = *adverb*
immediately = *adverb*
took = *verb*
shared = *verb*
6. smell = *noun*
poor = *adjective*
eyesight = *noun*
extremely = *adverb*
wide = *adjective*
range = *noun*
of = *preposition*
sounds = *noun*
use = *verb*
sound = *noun*

7. with = preposition
clicks = *noun*
whistles = *noun*
songs = *noun*
gather = *verb*
around = *preposition*
communicate = *verb*
through = *preposition*

EXERCISE 10, p. A9.

1. Does she stay there? Where does she stay? Who stays there?   **2.** Is she staying there?
Where is she staying? Who is staying there?   **3.** Will she stay there? Where will she stay?
Who will stay there?   **4.** Is she going to stay there? Where is she going to stay? Who is
going to stay there?   **5.** Did they stay there? Where did they stay? Who stayed there?
6. Will they be staying there? Where will they be staying? Who will be staying there?
7. Should they stay there? Where should they stay? Who should stay there?   **8.** Has he
stayed there? Where has he stayed? Who has stayed there?   **9.** Has he been staying
there? Where has he been staying? Who has been staying there?   **10.** Is John there?
Where is John? Who is there?   **11.** Will John be there? Where will John be? Who will be
there?   **12.** Has John been there? Where has John been? Who has been there?
13. Will Judy have been there? Where will Judy have been? Who will have been there?
14. Were Ann and Tom married there? Where were Ann and Tom married? Who was
married there?   **15.** Should this package have been taken there? Where should this
package have been taken? What should have been taken there?

EXERCISE 11, p. A11.

ANSWERS: **1.** Who is that letter from?   **2.** Who wrote that letter?   **3.** Whose coat is
that?   **4.** When are Alice and John going to get married?   **5.** What color are her

eyes? **6.** What color is her hair? **7.** What kind of tea would you like? OR What would you like? **8.** What do you usually drink with your breakfast? **9.** What made her sneeze? **10.** How long does it usually take you to eat breakfast? **11.** How did you get to the airport? **12.** What does the boy have in his pocket? **13.** How many brothers and sisters do you have? **14.** Where did you grow up? **15.** How long does it take to get there by plane? **16.** What kind of novels do you like to read? OR What do you like to read? **17.** Which chapters will the test cover? OR What will the test cover? **18.** Why were you late? OR How come you were late? **19.** How long has she been sick? **20.** How many people are you going to invite to your party? **21.** Which camera should I buy? **22.** Who discovered radium? **23.** What are we doing? **24.** How's everything going?

EXERCISE 13, p. A12.

ANSWERS: [Subjects and auxiliary verbs which need to be added are <u>underlined</u>.] **2.** <u>Are you</u> expecting someone? **3.** <u>Did you</u> stay up late last night? **4.** <u>Have you</u> ever been there before? **5.** <u>Are you</u> nervous? **6.** <u>Do you</u> want a cup of coffee? **7.** <u>Have you</u> heard any news about your scholarship? **8.** A: <u>Are you</u> hungry? B: Yeah. <u>Are you?</u>

EXERCISE 14, p. A14.

1. No. **2.** A: Aren't you hungry? B: Yes. **3.** A: Didn't you sleep well? B: No. **4.** A: Doesn't it rise in the east? B: Yes, Annie. **5.** A: Don't you recognize him? B: No. **6.** A: Didn't he say he would be here by 4:00? B: Yes. **7.** A: Aren't you having a good time? B: No. **8.** B: Isn't the Mississippi the longest? A: No.

EXERCISE 15, p. A15.

ANSWERS: **2.** isn't she **3.** will they **4.** won't you **5.** are there **6.** isn't it **7.** isn't he **8.** hasn't he **9.** doesn't he [also possible: *hasn't he*] **10.** can they **11.** won't she **12.** wouldn't she **13.** are they **14.** have you **15.** isn't there **16.** can't they **17.** did they **18.** did it **19.** aren't I **20.** isn't it

EXERCISE 17, p. A17.

PART I ANSWERS: **1.** "friend's" **2.** "friends're" **3.** "Tom's" **4.** "students've" **5.** "Bob'd" **6.** "Bob'd" **7.** "Ron'll" **8.** "window's" **9.** "windows're" **10.** "Jane's" **11.** "boys've" **12.** "Sally'd" **13.** "Sally'd"

PART II ANSWERS: **14.** "Who's" **15.** "Who're" **16.** "Who's" **17.** "What've" **18.** "What'd" **19.** "What'd" **20.** "What'd" **21.** "Why'd" **22.** "When'll" **23.** "How long'll" **24.** "Where'm" **25.** "Where'd"

EXERCISE 18, p. A18.

ANSWERS: **2.** no . . . not . . . not **3.** No **4.** no **5.** not . . . not **6.** no **7.** not **8.** no **9.** no . . . no **10.** not **11.** no **12.** not

EXERCISE 19, p. A20.

2. I didn't see <u>anybody</u>. OR I <u>saw</u> nobody.
3. I <u>can</u> never understand him. OR I can't <u>ever</u> understand him.
4. He doesn't like <u>either</u> coffee <u>or</u> tea. OR He ~~doesn't~~ <u>likes</u> neither coffee nor tea.
5. I didn't do <u>anything</u>. OR I <u>did</u> nothing.
6. I <u>can</u> hardly hear the radio. OR I can't ~~hardly~~ hear the radio.
7. We couldn't see <u>anything</u> but sand. OR We <u>could</u> see nothing but sand.

8. Methods of horse training <u>have</u> barely changed at all in the last eight centuries.   OR
Methods of horse training haven't ~~barely~~ changed at all in the last eight centuries.

EXERCISE 20, p. A20.

ANSWERS: **2.** Seldom do I sleep past seven o'clock.   **3.** Hardly ever do I agree with her.   **4.** Never will I forget the wonderful people I have met here.   **5.** Never have I known Rosa to be dishonest.   **6.** Scarcely ever does the mail arrive before noon.

EXERCISES 21–24, pp. A22–A23.

EX. 21 ANSWERS: **2.** to   **3.** for   **4.** from   **5.** for   **6.** (up)on   **7.** from   **8.** in/at   **9.** to   **10.** in   **11.** of   **12.** from   **13.** for   **14.** about it   **15.** of

EX. 22 ANSWERS: **1.** for   **2.** to   **3.** (up)on   **4.** from   **5.** of   **6.** of   **7.** about   **8.** with   **9.** (up)on   **10.** for   **11.** from   **12.** to   **13.** for   **14.** of   **15.** for

EX. 23 ANSWERS: **1.** with   **2.** of   **3.** to   **4.** of   **5.** at   **6.** from   **7.** with   **8.** in   **9.** at   **10.** from   **11.** for   **12.** of   **13.** at/with   **14.** with   **15.** to

EX. 24 ANSWERS: **1.** to . . . for   **2.** from   **3.** with   **4.** to   **5.** (up)on   **6.** of   **7.** (up)on   **8.** for . . . to   **9.** about   **10.** of   **11.** of   **12.** to   **13.** of   **14.** with   **15.** to

EXERCISE 26, p. A25.

POSSIBLE COMPLETIONS: **2.** such as bread and butter.   **3.** such as a Honda or Volkswagen.   **4.** such as cancer and heart disease.   **5.** such as Iran and Venezuela   **6.** as tennis and soccer.   **7.** as the printing press and the computer chip . . . such as the atomic bomb and bacterial weapons   **8.** such as when I'm sick or when I'm trying to solve a difficult problem.   **9.** such as history and mathematics . . . such as languages and science are difficult.   **10.** such as when I'm at a theater or when I'm talking on the phone   **11.** such as three and eleven . . . such as six and ten   **12.** such as German and French . . . such as Chinese and Arabic

EXERCISE 27, p. A26.

POSSIBLE COMBINATIONS: **1.** <u>Furthermore</u>, it has interesting special features.   **2.** <u>In addition</u>, you should read as many magazines in English as you have time for. Watching television can <u>also</u> be helpful.   **3.** <u>Moreover</u>, a housing shortage has developed. <u>In addition</u>, there are so many automobiles . . . .   **4.** Physical exercise is <u>also</u> essential. <u>In addition</u>, sleep and rest should not be neglected.

EXERCISES 28–30, pp. A26–A28.

EX. 28:
1. had never spoken [also possible: *never spoke*]   **2.** hadn't come   **3.** be   **4.** wouldn't have come   **5.** was stamped   **6.** will probably continue / is probably going to continue . . . lives   **7.** will have been   **8.** going   **9.** Having heard   **10.** sitting / who is sitting   **11.** have been produced   **12.** would give / was going to give / is going to give   **13.** have known . . . met . . . was working [also possible: *worked*]   **14.** had been . . . would have met   **15.** were made   **16.** have been standing . . . are   **17.** would change . . . (would) decide   **18.** understood / could understand   **19.** Being . . . was respected / is respected   **20.** would not exist [also possible: *could not exist*]

EX. 29:

1. coming . . . has learned **2.** had already given **3.** apply / should apply
4. would have been / would be **5.** would be / was going to be **6.** Sitting . . .
watching **7.** had been informed **8.** was completely destroyed . . . had gone
9. embarrassing **10.** were **11.** invited **12.** puzzled . . . puzzling . . . give . . .
figure **13.** has been **14.** working . . . can/will be solved **15.** call

EX. 30 :

(1) finish / have finished taking
(2) will also finish / will also have finished
. . . have ever had
(3) have learned
(4) had anticipated / anticipated . . .
coming
(5) Living . . . going
(6) have given [also possible: *has given*]
(7) to encounter . . . (to) interact
(8) would like
(9) arrived . . . knew
(10) needed . . . (in order) to
communicate
(11) couldn't find . . . would use / used
(12) (in order) to communicate
(13) Knowing
(14) was
(15) to make
(16) became
(17) Hoping to improve
(18) (to) understand . . . appearing
(19) were saying / said
(20) bored
(21) think
(22) were experiencing / experienced
(23) was doing
(24) had wanted / had been wanting . . .
living
(25) studying

(26) began . . . had
(27) Not knowing
(28) to expect
(29) excited . . . finding
(30) chose . . . introduced
(31) sitting . . . talking
(32) were
(33) spoke / had to speak
(34) wouldn't / couldn't / didn't
understand . . . was saying
(35) was pleasantly surprised . . .
responded
(36) took . . . building
(37) progressed . . . found
(38) asked . . . spoke
(39) were
(40) hesitated to ask
(41) even interrupted . . . had never been
(42) not to be surprised
(43) sharing
(44) learning
(45) was
(46) am
(47) hadn't come . . . wouldn't have been
(48) could have / would have
(49) knew
(50) had . . . to make
(51) would be

INDEX

Able to, 198, 200 *(Look on pages 198 and 200.)*	The numbers following the words listed in the index refer to page numbers in the main text.
Be, A6 *(Look in the back part of this book on the sixth page of the Appendix.)*	The index numbers preceded by the letter "A" (e.g., A6) refer to pages in the Appendix, which is found in the last part of the text. The main text ends on page 437, and the appendix immediately follows. Page 438 is followed by page A1.
Continuous tenses, *3fn.* *(Look at the footnote on page 3.)*	Information given in the footnotes to charts and exercises is noted by the page number plus the abbreviation *fn.*

1

Phrases, defined, 239*fn.*
    prepositional, A3
    reduction of adjective clauses, 290
    reduction of adverb clauses, 374–376, 380
    reduction of noun clauses, 254
Place expressions with progressive verbs, 31
Plenty of, 119
Polite requests, 152–153
Possessive:
    in adjective clauses *(whose)*, 274, A10
    with gerunds, 334
    nouns (e.g., *John's book)*, 103
    pronouns/adjectives *(mine, my,* etc.), 132, 274
    in questions *(whose)*, A10
Prefer, 311*fn.*
Preposition(s):
    combinations with adjectives and verbs, A21
    combinations followed by gerunds, 299
    list, A3
    following stative passive verbs, 228
Prepositional phrases, A3
Present participle, 19
    as adjective (e.g., *amusing story)*, 235
    vs. gerund, 297*fn.*
    in reduction of adjective clauses, 290
    in reduction of adverb clauses, 375
    special expressions followed by (e.g., *have fun doing)*, 304
    spelling of *-ing* forms, 10
    with verbs of perception (e.g., *watch someone doing)*, 336
    in verb tenses, 3, 5
Present time (SEE Verb tenses)
Principle parts of verbs, 19
Progressive verbs, 3, 13, 31 (SEE ALSO Verb tenses)
    vs. stative, 15
Pronouns:
    impersonal, 140, 212*fn.*
    indefinite, 134, 280
    object, 132, 270
    personal, 132
        agreement with nouns, 134, 136
    possessive, 132, 274
    reflexive, 138
    relative (SEE Adjective clauses)
    subject, 31*fn.*, 132, 268
Pronunciation:
    -ed, 20
    -s/es, 84

Punctuation:
    adjective clauses, 281
    adjective phrases, 290
    adverb clauses, 70, 359, 389
    independent clauses, 355
    parallel structure, 287
    quoted speech, 251
    transitions, 387, 389
    (SEE ALSO Apostrophe; Commas; Hyphens; Periods; Quotation marks; Semicolon)

Q

Quantity (SEE Expressions of quantity)
Questions:
    information, A8–A10
    negative, A13
    tag, A15, A16*fn.*
    word order in, A8
    yes/no, A8, A12
Question words:
    with infinitives, 247
    in noun clauses, 240
    in questions, A9–A10
Quotation marks, 251
Quoted speech, 251

R

Reduction:
    of adjective clauses, 290
    of adverb clauses, 374–376, 380
    of noun clauses, 254
Reflexive pronouns, 138
Regular plural nouns, 100
Regular verbs, 19
Relative clauses, 267 (SEE ALSO Adjective clauses)
Relative pronouns, 267
Remember/forget, 311
Repeated action in the past *(would, used to)*, 195
Reported speech, 254
Restrictive/nonrestrictive, 281*fn.*
Raise/rise, 26
Run-on sentence, 355

S

-S/-es, 84, 88, 100, 103, 107
-Self/selves, 138